The Jury in America

AMERICAN POLITICAL THOUGHT

Wilson Carey McWilliams and Lance Banning
Founding Editors

The Jury in America

Triumph and Decline

Dennis Hale

University Press of Kansas

Published by the University Press of Kansas (Lawrence, Kansas 66045), which was organized by the Kansas Board of Regents and is operated and funded by Emporia State University, Fort Hays State University, Kansas State University, Pittsburg State University, the University of Kansas, and Wichita State University

Library of Congress Cataloging-in-Publication Data

Hale, Dennis (Dennis B.), author.
The jury in America : triumph and decline / Dennis Hale.
pages cm. — (American political thought)
Includes bibliographical references and index.
ISBN 978-0-7006-2200-9 (cloth : alk. paper)
ISBN 978-0-7006-2201-6 (ebook)
1. Jury—United States. I. Title.
KF8972.H261 2016
347.73'752—dc23

2015035633

British Library Cataloguing-in-Publication Data is available.

EU Authorised Representative Details: Easy Access System Europe
Mustamäe tee 50, 10621 Tallinn, Estonia | gpsr.requests@easproject.com

In memoriam
Wilson Carey McWilliams, 1933–2005
Scholar, teacher, friend

The Writer of the following Observations not being a lawyer by profession, some apology may seem necessary, for his attempting to write upon a subject, which may be thought more peculiarly the province of the professors of the law. But it is a subject, as he conceives, of great importance to the general interests of liberty, a subject in which every Englishman is concerned, and . . . which should be generally understood by men of all ranks, and especially by those who are liable to serve on juries.

—Joseph Towers, *An Inquiry on the Rights and Duty of Juries, in Trials for Libels; Together with Remarks on the Origin and Nature of the Law of Libels*

Ruler and ruled have different excellences; but the fact remains that the good citizen must possess the knowledge and the capacity requisite for ruling as well as for being ruled, and the excellence of a citizen may be defined as consisting in "a knowledge of rule over free men from both points of view."

—Aristotle, *Politics*

To love democracy well, it is necessary to love it moderately.

—Pierre Manent, *Tocqueville and the Nature of Democracy*

Contents

Preface and Acknowledgments

This is a book about the American jury system, both its criminal and its civil forms, and how that system has changed over time, especially during the past half century. I am a political scientist, not a lawyer, and my aim is to examine the jury as Tocqueville saw it: as a political institution, one of several components of a republican regime based on public participation in enforcing as well as making the laws.[1]

When I first began to think about writing a book on the jury system, it was in the context of a broader interest in the nature of American citizenship. As a political institution, the jury is an expression of the idea of direct participation in government—as contrasted with the more passive experience of voting—and it was this active dimension of jury service that first caught my interest. Jury service seemed different enough from the other political experiences of American citizens to warrant special investigation. My interest was piqued as well by a personal experience with jury duty: being called to the old Middlesex County Courthouse in Cambridge, Massachusetts, to await my turn for voir dire, only to be sent home without being called.

But no sooner had I begun my research than the jury system entered a period characterized by many observers as a crisis. One trial after another contributed to

1. For discussions of the jury system by attorneys, see (among many others) Jeffrey Abramson, *We, the Jury: The Jury System and the Ideal of Democracy* (New York: Basic Books, 1994); Randolph N. Jonakait, *The American Jury System* (New Haven, CT: Yale University Press, 2003); Neil Vidmar and Valerie P. Hans, *American Juries* (Amherst, NY: Prometheus Books, 2007); Robert P. Burns, *The Death of the American Trial* (Chicago: University of Chicago Press, 2009). For the first social science study of the jury system in the modern era, see Harry Kalven Jr. and Hans Zeisel, *The American Jury* (Chicago: University of Chicago Press, 1966).

increasing doubts, among laypeople and professionals alike, about whether juries were working the way they were meant to work. The examples are well known: the acquittal of O. J. Simpson for the murder of Nicole Brown Simpson and Ronald Goldman and his subsequent conviction for civil liability by a second and very different jury; the initial acquittal of Los Angeles police officers in the Rodney King brutality case; the hung jury in the trial of the Menendez brothers for the murder of their parents; the 1992 acquittal of Lemrick Nelson for the murder of Yankel Rosenbaum, a crime to which Nelson later confessed; enormous and allegedly unjustified damage awards in civil trials against "deep pocket" corporations. Reflecting on the lessons of the Simpson trial, legal scholar Albert W. Alschuler came to a grim conclusion: "Our jury system often appears to have grown preposterous."[2] These cases and others like them have revived a debate about whether juries are the best way to resolve civil and criminal cases—a debate that has been going on, as we will see, for a very long time.

Recent concerns about what the jury system has become only added to my curiosity about what the jury used to be. Where did juries come from? What were they meant to be? What were they supposed to accomplish? These questions led me back to the beginning of our country's history and beyond, into the ancient thickets of the common law. Trial by jury is an institution so old that no one is quite sure where it came from, and a rich mythology about jury trials has developed over the generations. But the historical record is clear enough to suggest that the jury has been controversial more than once during this time, and the first part of this book covers some of this history to lay the groundwork for an understanding of the emergence of the modern American jury system in the late nineteenth century.

But we cannot understand the jury without also going outside the legal system, to the larger political order of which the jury is a part. If the jury is a political institution, then its functioning cannot fail to shape and be shaped by changes in the regime: changes in prevailing ideas about justice, fairness, and equality; in the popular understanding of common words such as *reasonable* or *biased*; and in the definition of who is capable of exercising the most difficult duties of citizenship and what those duties are. Taking this broader view has two immediate advantages: first, it helps us understand more clearly the real significance of the jury system, and second, it helps us see that some of the apparent failures of the jury system are merely symptoms of failure in the polity. The tensions and contradictions of the modern jury are shared by, even produced by, modern democracy itself. In fact, because the jury is so old, so continuously present in the life of the American republic, it can act as a mirror, reflecting the changes taking place around it.

2. Albert W. Alschuler, "Our Faltering Jury," in *Postmortem: The O. J. Simpson Case*, ed. Jeffrey Abramson (New York: Basic Books, 1996), 135.

In that miniature version of the nation assembled to deliberate the fate of particular defendants and to judge particular facts, we might witness much larger things: an end to prosecution for seditious libel, new ideas about race relations, a new understanding of what it means to be *negligent*, new views about the importance of expertise, a new understanding of *judgment*. We might also witness the failure of citizenship: citizens' refusal to take their responsibilities seriously, their hostility toward disfavored groups, their fear of judgment itself. Criminal and civil trials and the jury decisions that result from them involve debates about the most fundamental questions of right; therefore, they go to the heart of what makes the nation what it is.

This study is composed, in more or less equal parts, of intellectual and political history, on the one hand, and institutional and policy analysis on the other. Chapter 1 focuses on juries in England and the colonies during the great constitutional struggles to limit the authority of the Crown and to protect the liberty of the citizen—a struggle in which changing ideas about jury trials played an important role. This discussion also introduces an element of colonial juries that received little attention from contemporaries but seems, in retrospect, to have been highly significant: the power of the jury to enforce the community's understanding of social order on its most recalcitrant members. Chapter 2 considers the jury system during the early decades of the republic, the American jury's most storied era. This chapter includes a discussion of Tocqueville's account of the jury system and its significance for American democracy. Chapter 3 looks at the jury during the critical but somewhat indefinite period in which the modern American legal system was being shaped—roughly the 1890s through the 1940s. During this half century American legal ideas and practices underwent significant changes, and these had a major impact on jury trials: the bar was professionalized and subjected to formal, bureaucratic supervision for the first time; judges struggled, with some success, to assert their authority over the plebeian juries created by the extension of the franchise in the previous generation; and the legal system was forced to confront the full complexity of an industrial civilization.

Chapter 4 covers the major changes influencing the postmodern jury, as jury laws were rewritten in response to the civil rights movement and to broad but subtle changes in how the jury's responsibilities were conceived. This chapter raises questions with direct relevance for contemporary controversies: What constitutes a constitutional jury? Under what conditions can citizens be excluded from a jury or from a jury pool? What does the law require of a juror? What is "bias" in the context of a jury deliberation? Is it ever appropriate to rank otherwise equal citizens with respect to their ability to deliberate and to judge?

Chapter 5 propels the story forward to more recent times and examines why the jury is said to be "vanishing." In part, this perception has been created by changes in criminal and civil procedure made in earlier decades. There are some in the scholarly, legal, and political communities who look with indifference on the prospect of a vanishing jury, and others who come to the jury's defense.

Chapter 5 ends with a consideration of four controversial modern trials to see how the previous pages might shed some light on the difficult decisions made by modern jurors.

In conducting the research for this book, I was ably assisted by several generations of students in the Political Science Graduate Program at Boston College, among them Kyle Dell, Kim Kosman, Devin Stauffer, David Trimmer, Charles Robinson, Maggie Lutz, Thomas Schneider, Robert Dealy, Tim Lehmann, and Jessica Goley. I am grateful to all of them for their diligent and skillful assistance. I would also like to thank Jerome Maryon, Esq.—a title to which he is entitled in the fullest sense—for helping me navigate the innards of the (late and unlamented) Middlesex County Courthouse to watch jury selection for a civil trial. What I learned there was invaluable.

I am also grateful to the Olin Foundation for financial assistance during an early stage of this research and to my excellent colleagues in the Boston College Political Science Department who gave me helpful advice and encouragement—Marc Landy, Shep Melnick, Robert Faulkner, and Christopher Bruell—as well as George Brown from the Boston College Law School. A special thanks is owed to Fred Woodward at the University Press of Kansas, who, after seeing a ten-page draft of the introduction, believed that a worthy manuscript would eventually grow, although neither he nor I could have predicted how long it would be. And I am grateful to my wife, Adele Travisano, who has been patient with my preoccupations for far longer than I could have wished.

Finally, no acknowledgment would be complete without a special mention of Wilson Carey McWilliams, to whose memory this book is dedicated. As a teacher at Oberlin College, Brooklyn College, and Rutgers University, Carey taught and inspired more students than perhaps even he could have remembered. One of the first lessons I learned from him, way back when, was to pay attention to the things that are most likely to be overlooked, which are often right in front of our noses. All of Carey's students sought to emulate his methods: look carefully, cherish the odd fact, dig deeper, find the universe in a grain of sand. He was a Democrat, but also a democrat, which means he was also a republican (although never a Republican) and had a great affection for the essential institutions of the American regime: the franchise, elections, political parties, the lively and eccentric politics of local places, the grand spectacle of citizens governing themselves. No one who studied with him ever saw the world the same way again, and without taking a survey, I can guarantee that none of us has ever regretted it. RIP.

Introduction
The Paradoxical Jury

> Our civilization has decided, and very justly decided, that determining the guilt or innocence of men is a thing too important to be trusted to trained men.
>
> —G. K. Chesterton

The fundamental democratic paradox is well known and easily stated. In a democracy, governing—a task requiring wisdom, the rarest of human gifts—is open, in principle, to all applicants and, in practice, to many who are not the least bit wise. The resolution of this paradox is written in the ongoing history of democratic governments and, in its broadest sense, is beyond the scope of this book.

This book focuses instead on one especially interesting and important example of the democratic paradox at work: the jury system, that peculiar Anglo-American legal institution in which some of the weightiest questions facing society are decided by (usually) twelve people plucked from the civic mass. The jury's verdict may send a defendant home, to prison, or to death row, or the jury may transfer money—sometimes lots of it—from one litigant to another. Jurors may do these things well or badly, but their decisions are usually final, and in criminal cases a jury's acquittal is always final. That such a system has lasted so long is often the subject of wonder (and sometimes scorn) among foreign observers of American law, but sometimes (and not only recently) among natives as well.[1]

As this quick summary suggests, understanding the jury is a way to understand democracy itself, with all its triumphs and failures. And yet, at its inception, the jury was not a democratic institution at all; it was simply a way for the English

1. Although *Anglo-American* might be a better term to use in the context of a historical discussion of juries, the jury is used much less often in Great Britain than it once was. The Canadian, Australian, and New Zealand experiences parallel the British, which leaves the United States as the last country where the jury trial is routinely available in both civil and criminal cases, both the serious and the trivial. The vast majority of jury trials worldwide, therefore, take place in the United States.

monarch to acquire vital information that only local subjects possessed. Its gradual evolution from a "tool of kings" to a "champion of the people's rights" is part of the long and tangled story of how republican ideas and institutions emerged in Great Britain and its colonies. In Britain's North American colonies, the jury was, in the beginning, a highly serviceable instrument of self-government, with many more functions than simply rendering verdicts. As colonial and then state governments became more differentiated, the jury's duties retreated steadily and became mostly judicial, and as state governments became more democratic, with easier suffrage and citizenship requirements, the American jury became what it was when Tocqueville saw it: "the majority vested with the right to pronounce decrees."[2]

It had also acquired by Tocqueville's time an additional purpose: educator of democratic citizens. Tocqueville's is the most famous argument along these lines, but, as demonstrated below, he was not alone in seeing both the need for such education and the possibility that jury service might be an important way to provide it. And here the jury comes very close to revealing the democratic paradox in crystalline form: only the wise are capable of judging rightly, but only those who have experience at judging can learn the wisdom that judging requires. Tocqueville was prepared to accept one of the logical conclusions of this paradox, at least in the case of civil trials: that although the jury system might not be good for litigants, it is very good for jurors, and therefore for society at large.[3]

The jury that Tocqueville envisioned was far more democratic in its composition than the juries of colonial or revolutionary America and, of course, far more democratic than the panels that struggled against the Stuart monarchy or served the Angevin kings. The jury would become even more democratic as the barriers to jury service set by property qualifications, gender, and (illegally after emancipation) race were reduced and then eliminated. In the aftermath of the Jacksonian era, the belief that jury service might educate citizens retreated before questions about the competence of democratic juries chosen from jury pools much less "gentrified" than those in England and the colonies. These questions were followed by even greater doubts about the competence of most Americans to perform the difficult duties imposed by modern citizenship. Lawyers and judges, once universally understood to be the teachers and senior partners of jurors, often came to be seen, and to see themselves, as the jury's adversaries. Bench, bar, and jury engaged in a three-cornered struggle for control of the courtroom and, increasingly, over the question of who could make decisions about the meaning and requirements of the law, an old problem dating back to the battle over seditious libel verdicts in England.

2. Alexis de Tocqueville, *Democracy in America*, trans. Harvey C. Mansfield and Delba Winthrop (Chicago: University of Chicago Press, 2000), 241.

3. Ibid., 285.

But the debate over whether juries could "find" or "determine" the law was gradually overtaken by one about whether juries could even understand the law, especially as the civil law became more complicated with the dawn of modern business. During the two generations between the Civil War and the Great Depression, doubts about the wisdom of jury trials in civil cases and in difficult or emotionally charged criminal trials grew apace. These doubts paralleled the broad Progressive enthusiasm for public administration, administrative centralization, and the power of professional expertise to resolve disputes "scientifically"—part of a larger movement to increase the weight of expertise in public decision making and to reduce the importance of popular participation. The result was a revolution in the federal courts, and especially in civil jurisprudence, that was accompanied by a gradual diminution in the importance of the jury system in both civil and criminal trials.

By the middle of the twentieth century, juries were still very much with us (thanks to their protected constitutional status), but they were far less important to the system of criminal and civil justice than in the previous century, and support for the jury was softer than ever before. To reformers of the post–World War II era, juries seemed hopelessly amateurish at best, and narrow-minded, bigoted, and ignorant at worst. The jury represented tyranny of the majority in its most virulent form, a view often echoed in popular fiction and in reports of sensational trials gone bad. In the popular stage play and film *Twelve Angry Men*, jurors are eager to vote for a conviction and get on with their lives, and they are stopped only by the heroic intervention of one brave man, "Juror No. 8." The most visible and grotesque miscarriages of justice took place in those southern courtrooms where justice was so often subordinated to the needs of white supremacy. This phenomenon too made its way into the popular culture—although in *To Kill a Mockingbird*, the heroic Atticus Finch fails in his bid to extract a just verdict from a jury of small-town southern bigots. The contemporary jury has had to bear the weight of these historic and popular suspicions, along with a variety of "postmodern" doubts about the possibility of "objective" deliberation or of a "truth" accessible to human judgment. Perhaps not coincidentally, the latest phase of the jury's long history evokes fear that the jury is "vanishing," especially in federal courts, as the number of both civil and criminal jury trials has dropped to levels below those of the 1960s. Jury trials are now a smaller percentage of case dispositions than at any time in our history.

Many fear for the jury, yet many others seek to extend and deepen the experience of citizenship in modern states. The paradoxical meeting of these two separate concerns brings us closer to the problem Tocqueville sought to understand: How can the amateurish and destructive instincts of a democratic regime be educated to a higher sense of responsibility? Is it really possible for ordinary citizens, untrained in the law and picked at random from the crowd, to exercise the wisdom required of rulers? If so, how? Under what conditions and circumstances does the jury system best serve the noblest ends of a republican regime? What are the obstacles to its proper functioning, and how can these obstacles be overcome?

These are some of the questions explored in the long discussion that follows. But first it is necessary to examine some of the earlier transformations of the jury system, to learn what it was at the beginning, what it became, and why. Following Aristotle's useful advice, let us begin at the beginning.

1

The Common-Law Jury in England and the Colonies

Our ancestors were careful, that all men of the like condition and quality, presumed to be sensible of each other's infirmity, should mutually be judges of each other's lives, and alternately taste of subjection and rule, every man being equally liable to be accused or indicted, and perhaps to be suddenly judged by the party, of whom he is at present judge, if he be found innocent.

—Lord Somers, *The Security of Englishmen's Lives, or the Trust, Power and Duty of the Grand Juries of England*

And hence it is that when a malefactor is asked at his arraignment, How will you be tried? He answers always according to law and custom, By God and my country; not by God and the King, or the King's deputy.

—John Milton, *Works*

THE PREMODERN JURY

The origin of the medieval English jury is the source of many disputes and not a few legends.[1] Was the jury brought to England by the Frankish kings, or did the

1. The literature on the early English jury is enormous. In this section I have drawn on the following: Ralph V. Turner, "The Origins of the Medieval English Jury: Frankish, English, or Scandinavian?" *Journal of British Studies* 7, 2 (May 1968): 1–10; Naomi D. Hurnard, "The Jury of Presentment and the Assize of Clarendon," *English Historical Review* 56, 223 (July 1941): 374–410; J. E. R. Stephens, "The Growth of Trial by Jury in England," *Harvard Law Review* 10, 3 (October 26, 1896): 150–160; Roger D. Groot, "The Jury of Presentment before 1215," *American Journal of Legal History* 26, 1 (January 1982): 1–24; Mike Macnair, "Vicinage and the Antecedents of the Jury," *Law and History Review* 17, 3 (Autumn 1999): 537–590; Thomas A. Green, "The Jury and the English Law of Homicide, 1200–1600," *Michigan Law Review* 74, 3 (January 1976): 413–499; and the essays collected in J. S. Cockburn and Thomas A. Green, eds., *Twelve Good Men and True: The Criminal Trial Jury in England, 1200–1800* (Princeton, NJ: Princeton University Press, 1988).

conquerors find it present already? If it was operating in 1066, was the jury an Anglo-Saxon invention, or was it imported by the Danes? Can we trace the jury's beginnings to those same German forests where historians once believed all free institutions were born? And how important were the thegns of the wapentake, or the Wantage Code of Ethelred? What did the barons mean when they demanded of King John that no freeman be imprisoned "except by the lawful judgment of his peers or by the law of the land"?[2] Were early juries mostly "self-informing" witnesses who testified to what they knew or had heard around the village? Who were these early jurors, and how far down into the social pile did authorities reach when choosing them?

For a long time, research on early English legal institutions was guided as much by contemporary political preoccupations as by a genuine curiosity about the past. The contest between the proponents of the Anglo-Saxon and the Norman origins of the jury is an obvious example, as is most eighteenth- and nineteenth-century commentary on the jury, which tended to see its history almost exclusively through the lens of the long struggle against the "wretched Stuarts." Blackstone's *Commentaries* falls into this category.

Contemporary historians are not without their own political obsessions, of course, especially concerning the "social" and "class" context of medieval legal institutions, which undoubtedly showed a more kindly face to the sober and industrious than to the rough and rowdy. But twentieth-century historiography has profited from the careful study of a surprisingly large collection of legal records stretching back to the twelfth century and earlier. A good example is the collection known as the Pipe Rolls, which recorded financial matters for the Exchequer. Since the administration of the courts involved the collection of fines for the Crown, the Pipe Rolls contain a wealth of information about trials and prosecutions. As English legal historian Naomi Hurnard put it, "there was money to be made by the Crown out of the punishment of crime," and royal revenues required good record keeping.[3] In addition, the various assizes (royal courts convened in the counties at more or less regular intervals) left their own records of cases and dispositions. From these records it is possible to learn much about the way legal institutions operated at the local level, generating accounts of the jury's origins that are in agreement on a number of elements. What emerges from these accounts is a picture of the jury that, like the portrait of an ancient ancestor, bears an uncanny resemblance to its contemporary descendant. Several features of this portrait stand out.

The sworn inquest, which used local witnesses to present information about local crimes, can be found as early as the late-tenth-century reign of Ethelred II.

2. Magna Carta, clause 39.

3. R. Stewart-Brown, "Serjeants of the Peace in Medieval England and Wales," quoted by Hurnard, "Jury of Presentment," 375.

These were the so-called presentment juries utilized in criminal cases, along with similar institutions summoned to give evidence about such matters as boundaries, feudal obligations, and debts.[4] Such panels were used, for example, to construct the Domesday Book under William I—which recorded for each shire in the kingdom both physical and legal details about the possession of land—and to settle disputes about the control of particular properties (the so-called possessory assizes, the medieval ancestor of the civil jury).[5] The underlying principle of these jury inquests was the same: local subjects had knowledge that, whatever its limitations, was treated as probative with respect to the matters under review, enabling the settlement of questions that might otherwise lead to festering conflicts and family feuds. It is not insignificant that such assizes also provided useful information to the Crown about who owned what, and under what terms. In criminal matters, however, the presentment juries were more like grand juries than petit juries, since their function was simply to bring cases to the attention of local justices. Guilt or innocence was determined either by compurgation (bringing witnesses to attest to the character of the accused) or by ordeal (the *judicium Dei*), which required the defendant to undergo a particularly nasty physical test, the passing of which indicated God's favor and, thus, acquittal.[6]

The Normans gradually introduced changes to the practices they encountered in England, but without altering the most important aspects of English legal traditions. The role of compurgators, for example, was eliminated from the trial phase, which was conducted entirely through ordeal or through the common Norman practice of wager of battle. But defendants, provided they were not "notorious," could still call on compurgators in the indictment phase, avoiding presentment altogether if "twelve good men and true" testified to the soundness of their character. This was the beginning of the separation of indictment from trial and, ultimately, of the grand jury from the petit jury, but it was not entirely intentional. To address local matters effectively, the king had no alternative but to deal with local people, and presentment juries were an efficient way to bring to the court's attention local crimes about which neither the king nor his agents could have independent information. In fact, local subjects were obligated, under penalty of fines, to report all crimes to the justices in a timely fashion. That they did not always do so is suggested by the need to fine them.

Although gentlemen and knights played an important role in these early presentment juries, subjects of the "middling sort"—yeoman farmers, tradesmen, and artisans—also served as jurors, often making up the majority of the panels. Based on their varied stations in life, jurors were expected to know something about the circumstances of the cases they were presenting, and this required sub-

4. Hurnard, "Jury of Presentment," 374–377.
5. Macnair, "Vicinage and the Antecedents of the Jury," 537–590.
6. Stephens, "Growth of Trial by Jury," 150–160.

jects who were close to the common folk, or even of them, provided they were "good men and true."

The monarchy sought to centralize this system, especially after the Conquest, but the Crown could not (or at any rate did not) dispense entirely with the decentralized nature of English public life, law enforcement included. As Hurnard put it, "The Angevins found the system of communal presentment in existence" in England and "appear also to have found in it an effective barrier" against the full centralization of the legal system in the hands of the Crown. "To this practice was opposed, not an institution which Henry himself had introduced, but the custom of the land."[7] That is, the institutions and practices that would eventually become the petit jury began in the counties, hundreds, and vills that had been part of the English government for centuries. It was partly this decentralization that guaranteed the participation of subjects of the middling sort on presentment juries. Decentralization also fixed the jury in the public's imagination as the "popular" element of the judiciary, enforcing the local understanding of such matters as criminal liability, even in the face of competing conceptions held by the royal justices, the Crown, and, in later generations, the Parliament. Locals had so much control over criminal prosecutions, in fact, that leniency toward criminals became something of a scandal at times, denounced from the pulpit, court, and throne alike. Especially with respect to homicide cases, trial jurors were often reluctant to convict defendants they believed "did not deserve to be hanged, even though they may actually have committed the crime for which they were being tried."[8]

All accounts recognize the importance of the events of the late twelfth and early thirteenth centuries to the subsequent development of the jury system. Three events were of special significance. In 1166 Henry II promulgated the Assize of Clarendon, which codified the traditional role of the presentment jury, even augmenting it in some respects. The assize also stipulated that all those accused of crimes would have to "seek their proof" through the "ordeal of water," unless the jury chose to offer the accused compurgation—apparently under the assumption that this would not be a common choice. From the perspective of the presented defendant, a successful compurgation would be tantamount to a not-guilty verdict, although it was much closer to what a modern grand jury does when it refuses to return an indictment.

The year 1215 saw two events of importance to the jury: the signing of the Magna Carta, in which the barons exacted a promise from King John to respect

7. Hurnard, "Jury of Presentment," 409–410.

8. The Statute of Westminster (1275) complains that "the peace is less kept, and the laws less used, and offenders less punished than they ought to be." Bernard William McLane, "Juror Attitudes toward Local Disorder: The Evidence of the 1328 Lincolnshire Trailbaston Proceedings," in Cockburn and Green, *Twelve Good Men*, 58.

"judgment by peers" (among many other demands, including the forgiveness of certain debts owed to Jews), and the decision by the Fourth Lateran Council, at the urging of Pope Innocent II, to ban clerical participation in the ordeals, which effectively meant their abolition.[9] The Magna Carta established that "the lawful judgment of his peers" would be, in effect, a constitutional privilege of English subjects—initially, of course, the "peers of the realm." But over time, the idea of judgment by one's peers came to represent a much broader claim that criminal defendants should be judged by their fellow subjects and not by magistrates acting alone in the name of the king. The effective abolition of trials by ordeal, meanwhile, created a hole that needed filling—a new way to reach credible judgments about criminal cases that would satisfy both the king and the local community. The presentment jury, already a customary institution of long standing, was ready to acquire a slightly different purpose.

With due allowance for local variations, then, the English legal system codified by the Assize of Clarendon, and subsequent decisions by Henry II and his successors, operated approximately as follows, until the abolition of the ordeal: A presenting jury—twelve subjects chosen from the vills, along with four knights chosen from the hundreds (subdivisions of the counties)—would bring to the attention of the justices accusations against members of the local community thought to have committed some offense. These accusations were often based on rumor, in which case the accused, if a person of good repute, would be offered compurgation. If successful, the defendant would be "quit" of the charges against him, amounting to acquittal via character reference. If, however, the accused were a "notorious" fellow known to be a habitual troublemaker, or if the presentment jury could produce facts in evidence against him (for example, that he had been captured in flight, that he had in his possession property belonging to the victim, or that there were witnesses to the crime), then the judge would either convict on the spot, if the evidence was conclusive, or require the accused to "seek his proof" through the ordeal.

The Assize of Clarendon formalized these arrangements, requiring that "anyone, who shall be found, on the oath of the aforesaid [the presentment jury], to be accused or notoriously suspect of having been a robber or murderer or thief, or a receiver of them be taken and put to the ordeal of water."[10] The assize thus confirmed the legitimacy of one particular form of the ordeal and clarified when it would be used; it also stipulated that the decision to put the accused to the risk of ordeal or conviction would be, in the first instance, the jury's to make, as a matter of fact if not of law. As a result, by the end of the twelfth century, ordeal

9. See Magna Carta, clauses 10 and 11.

10. D. C. Douglas, ed., *English Historical Documents*, vol. 2 (1042–1189) (New York: Oxford University Press, 1981), 441.

by water had become "the normal method of trial in crown pleas"—but only for those defendants to whom the presenting jury had failed to offer compurgation.[11]

Thus, although the Assize of Clarendon initiated the process of bringing law enforcement more effectively under royal control, it also codified what had long been local practice. Presenting juries were necessarily the first step in the process, for only local subjects had knowledge of what crimes had been committed in the county and who might be responsible for those crimes. Juries used this power to decide, in effect, which subjects would be "indicted" and which would be absolved: only those whom the jury would not absolve could be required, in the words of Glanvill's *Treatise on the Laws and Customs of the Realm of England* (1188), to "purge himself by the ordeal."[12]

Trusting jurors to distinguish between those defendants who should be allowed compurgation and those who would have to "prove" themselves followed logically, according to one historian, from their responsibility to report accusations in the first place.[13] That is, the presenting jury was not necessarily making an accusation on its own; it was merely reporting to the king's justices that certain accusations were circulating in the county. Jurors could be expected to know something about the relative credibility of these accusations. A certain man might be said, for example, to have committed a rape. Another might be said to have cows in his possession that he could not account for. A spouse might have died under mysterious circumstances, suggesting poisoning. The jury would record its response to such rumors, and one of the frequent responses was that although the defendant had been accused, the jury itself did not suspect him. The records are filled with the formulaic court Latin used to render such "verdicts": *rettati/non malecreduntur* (accused/not suspected), *dicitur/non malecreditur* (it is said/not suspected), and *capti/non malecreduntur* (captured/not suspected). Or, if the jury recorded that the accusations were believed (*rettatus/malecredunt*), the accused would face the full harshness of the ordeal, unless he were too notorious to "purge himself." In such cases, the jury's decision would amount to a conviction, and the court would immediately impose a sentence.[14]

The Assize of Clarendon thus strengthened the jury—unintentionally, in Hurnard's view—by giving more weight to the jury's verdict, even if it were based only on circumstantial evidence. As compensation, perhaps, for this additional authority, the assize required verdicts from two sets of jurors, including one taken from the neighborhood of the crime. This second jury can be considered the an-

11. Margaret H. Kerr, Richard D. Forsyth, and Michael J. Plyey, "Cold Water and Hot Iron: Trial by Ordeal in England," *Journal of Interdisciplinary History* 22, 4 (Spring 1992): 575.

12. Ibid., 576.

13. Groot, "Jury of Presentment before 1215."

14. Ibid., 12.

cient origin of the petit jury, as distinguished from the presentment jury, which we now call the grand jury.[15]

As evidence of its authority, a jury could, even at this early date, make judgments about intent. In a case from Stafford in 1199, a man was accused of killing a child with an arrow; his plea was that it had been an accident, and the jurors attested that this was a true account. In a similar case from Yorkshire in 1212, a defendant who killed a man with a stone claimed that the death was accidental. The jurors agreed, and as in the first case, the accused did not have to seek proof through the ordeal. In cases of this sort, the usual next step would be to seek a pardon from the king.[16]

The juries of the vills and hundreds were operating in effect as gatekeepers, sorting the accused (not defendants, as it was not yet the jury's function to judge them) into two paths—one leading to compurgation and acquittal, and the other leading to the ordeal and possibly execution. What separated the paths was not what the judge believed, and even less what the king desired, but what the jurors were prepared to attest to—namely, that the accused was or was not credible. Only in the latter case would the ordeal be prepared.[17]

Medieval ordeals varied by time and place. Some were harder to survive than others and left festering wounds, forcing priests to declare God's disfavor. Such a verdict normally led to execution by hanging if the crime were a homicide, or branding, mutilation, and banishment in the case of thievery. Surviving the ordeal was a sign of God's favor, resulting in a verdict of not guilty pronounced by a priest—a practice that the clergy increasingly regarded as "an impious absurdity," although it may have satisfied the local community that God's judgment had been clarified, despite some members' dislike of the result.[18]

The ordeal stipulated by the Assize of Clarendon, the "ordeal of water," was one method of revealing God's will. It involved lowering the defendant, suspended by a rope and clothed only in a loincloth, into a pond at least twelve feet deep, with his hands tied behind his knees. If, in this helpless position, the defendant sank, he was judged to be innocent and pulled from the water—hopefully before drowning. Sometimes the survivor was required to "abjure [leave] the kingdom" or forfeit property to the king but was otherwise unmolested. If, however, the defendant floated, he would be judged guilty, taken from the water, and punished appropriately, usually within hours. In homicide cases the

15. Hurnard, "Jury of Presentment," 408.

16. Groot, "Jury of Presentment before 1215," 10–11.

17. Ibid., 5.

18. This argument has been advanced by Paul R. Hyams, "Trial by Ordeal: The Key to Proof in the Early Common Law," in *On the Laws and Customs of England: Essays in Honor of Samuel Thorne*, ed. Morris S. Arnold et al. (Chapel Hill: University of North Carolina Press, 1981), 98, 100; see also Kerr et al., "Cold Water and Hot Iron," 573–595.

defendant would be executed by hanging; otherwise, he would be punished by mutilation, usually branding, but sometimes by more drastic measures such as the loss of a hand or a foot.[19]

Aside from its brutality, the obvious flaw in this procedure was its arbitrary quality. This became a source of concern to, among others, the clergy (although apparently not to the king). This may be one reason why the records indicate that the vast majority of those sent to the ordeal "passed." According to the study by Margaret Kerr and her colleagues, in one list of 275 presentments "between 1194 and 1208, an accused was put to death or maimed in only eight recorded cases."[20] Another flaw in the ordeal of water was that it discriminated against women. Even at that time, it was apparently understood that women, having a larger percentage of body fat than men, would almost never sink and would therefore almost never be acquitted. As a result, women were rarely put to the ordeal of water; they were "awarded" the ordeal of hot iron instead.[21] For the same reason, rotund, middle-aged men fared worse than fit young men fresh from working the fields (precisely the type who might get into drunken scrapes and accidentally kill someone). This difficulty suggests an important early advantage of the jury: its judgment, its "gatekeeping," was a comparatively rational method of getting as close to the truth as the community was likely to get. An additional advantage was that the judgment of the jury was seen as the judgment of the community, and for that reason it carried greater weight in practice, however small it might appear in contrast to the judgment of God.

Judgment by a jury chosen from among the familiar faces in a village would have satisfied the locals without inconveniencing the king. The king's interest was in suppressing violent crime and collecting fines and confiscated property from malefactors. After the Conquest, the most common violent crime in need of suppressing was that committed by Saxons against Normans. But as memories of the Conquest faded, the problem of violence per se would have troubled the king's subjects as much as it troubled the king himself. In fact, the king's most important service to his people was often keeping the "king's peace" on the highways and in the forests. Historian Thomas A. Green reports that "homicide was a daily fact of life in medieval England," and many other historians report levels of criminality

19. Kerr et al., "Cold Water and Hot Iron," 578.

20. Ibid.

21. Ibid. Looking at the "eyre rolls" (court records) from 1194 to 1208, Kerr et al. found that eighty-four men were ordered to the ordeal, and seventy-nine were sent to the ordeal of cold water. During the same period, only seven women were sent to trial on presentment, and they were all ordered to the ordeal of hot iron; none were sent to the ordeal of water (578–582). The ordeal of hot iron required the defendant to hold a red-hot poker for a stated length of time; the wounds were then bound in cloth, and the defendant was locked up. A priest checked to see if the wounds had been healed by God's favor. Healing meant acquittal; festering meant conviction.

that contemporaries judged to be scandalous—an implicit rebuke to the king. Under these circumstances, it is not difficult to imagine how a meeting of the minds could emerge between local law-abiding subjects and the king's justices sent to suppress crime.[22]

The Lateran Council's ban on trial by ordeal (followed by a ban on trial by combat, which was already limited to certain classes of the population) applied throughout Europe. What replaced the ordeal depended on local circumstances. On the Continent, the method that filled the void was "the confession as proof," which led to "torture to obtain it." In England, however, what emerged was the jury verdict, more or less as it is understood in modern times. One historian concludes: "Eventually, the difference in proofs helps explain how the continental systems became inquisitorial while the English-based systems became accusatorial."[23]

Because it depended on local knowledge, the jury anchored the English legal system in the shires, townships, and counties, rather than in the royal court. Even the Crown's efforts to centralize the administration of justice—such as having circuit judges hold "eyres" in the counties at stated times—tethered the Crown's justice to the judgment of local subjects. "The trial jury's power to implement that role," Green writes, "derived mainly from the fact that the bench was dependent upon the jury for information regarding the circumstances of presented offenses and the credibility of persons presented."[24] But the same arrangement also compelled the participation of local subjects because it required men of the hundreds and the knights who served with them to present information about all crimes, especially homicides, under penalty of fines.[25] (They eventually used this author-

22. Green, "Jury and the English Law of Homicide," 416.

23. Groot, "Jury of Presentment before 1215," 1. Edward L. Glaeser and Andrei Shleifer argue that "the historical evolution of legal systems in France and England starting in the twelfth and thirteenth centuries has shaped how these systems operate. . . . Specifically, [the two kingdoms] opted for different levels of control that the sovereign exercised over judges. France went in the direction of adjudication by royally controlled professional judges, while England moved toward adjudication by relatively independent juries." Edward L. Glaeser and Andrei Shleifer, "Legal Origins," *Quarterly Journal of Economics* 117, 4 (November 2002): 1194.

24. Thomas A. Green, "A Retrospective on the Criminal Trial Jury, 1200–1800," in Cockburn and Green, *Twelve Good Men*, 359.

25. This was true not only in courts of law. Lay participation was essential to the administration of England's first "property tax"—the "aid on moveables," which dated to 1194. This tax, which assessed moveable property such as livestock, household goods, and luxury items, was administered by "juries of assessment" made up of local subjects who could be trusted to know who owned what. See Dennis Hale, "The Evolution of the Property Tax: A Study of the Relation between Public Finance and Political Theory," *Journal of Politics* 47, 2 (June 1985): 387–388.

ity to bring charges against royal officials for various kinds of misconduct.[26]) This system also depended on local subjects because they were the only ones who knew anything about crimes committed in the court's jurisdiction. Even when trials were held at the royal court in Westminster, the jurors were brought from the crime's location to testify as to what they had heard or seen.

With the abolition of the ordeals, the Crown, "in search of a new method of proof, turned once again to lay cooperation." This involved the defendant "putting himself on the country." That is, a jury of twelve would return a verdict of guilty or not guilty, usually by reciting the details of the case and announcing the verdict. But this practice would not have seemed to be a radical departure from custom; rather, it was a "continuation and enhancement of traditional practices."[27] The criminal jury, or something very much like it, was therefore already an "ancient" institution by the middle of the thirteenth century.

After the abolition of the ordeal, the process worked roughly as follows in the case of a homicide: The coroner assembled an inquest jury made up of men from the vill where the killing took place. The coroner noted the cause of death, as well as the names of any suspects supplied by the inquest jury. The sheriff was then directed to arrest the suspect, who would be held for trial by a circuit judge at the next meeting of the court.[28] At "gaol delivery," the suspect was taken from the jail and presented by the sheriff, the charges were read, and the defendant entered a plea, usually not guilty.[29] A jury was then sworn, its members having been called from the hundred where the killing took place. After the Assize of Clarendon, jurors were taken from among the presentment jurors, and by the fourteenth century, they came from a separate group of eighteen jurors chosen in the hundreds. Excluded from the jury were relatives of the defendant or the deceased, as well as anyone known to have a grudge against either; however, "with these two excep-

26. "Based on the evidence of the 1328 proceedings, local inhabitants had legitimate grounds to complain about such officials as those of Somerton Castle in Kesteven, who often did not pay for supplies taken from neighboring villages, or Ralph Cressy, coroner of Kesteven, who, if over a hundred presentments are accurate, routinely demanded and collected fees before providing services that were supposed to be free." McLane, "Juror Attitudes toward Local Disorder," 45.

27. Green, "Retrospective," 363.

28. These circuit courts were supposed to be convened at regular intervals, although this rule was not always followed, which meant that suspects might be bound over for many months. Beginning in the early fourteenth century, the courts were scheduled to meet twice a year in each county, and that eventually became the norm.

29. The contemporary records (*Placita Corone*, or "Pleas of the Crown") show that "very few defendants ever confessed." Green, "Jury and the English Law of Homicide," 424, n. 44. Before the era of the "correctional institution," conviction meant corporal punishment, including mutilation and branding for noncapital crimes. With the exception of pleading for the mercy of the court, there was no such thing as plea bargaining.

tions, familiarity with the facts of the case was a desideratum rather than a bar to jury service."[30]

Evidence on the background of jurors is spotty and comes mostly from periods later than the twelfth and thirteenth centuries, but they were usually taken from social ranks higher (but not much higher) than that of the accused. An early-fourteenth-century assize roll lists jurors in Lincolnshire, for example, and of the 248 individuals who served, 42 had "gentry or equivalent status," and another 54 had experience in public office either at the local level or in the service of the Crown.[31] These "notables" constituted just about 38 percent of those who served, and we must assume that the others were men of lower ranks: tradesmen, artisans, yeoman farmers, and the like. Similar records from early-fifteenth-century Derbyshire show that the gentry made up 58 percent of jurors.[32] Hertfordshire rolls from the late sixteenth and early seventeenth centuries suggest that individuals of the "middling sort" made up the bulk of jurors, supplemented by varying percentages of men from the gentry. "It was . . . Hertfordshire's yeomanry that formed the social backbone of the county's jury system"—that is, property owners, although at the lower end of the scale, holdings would have been small.[33]

Once assembled, the jury would hear the evidence and deliver a verdict. The gaol delivery rolls do not reveal how the jury reached a verdict; jurors would, of course, hear the defendant's story, and they would have to make up their minds about his alibi or perhaps his explanation, such as claiming he had acted in self-defense. Their general knowledge of the defendant's character and past behavior, as well as what they had "just learned in the rumor mill of the gaol delivery session," almost certainly factored into their decision. The judge would also question the defendant in the presence of the jury. The jury's duty was to "render a verdict on the basis of their knowledge of the facts, whether that knowledge was first-hand or gleaned from those whom they chose to believe. They were gatherers as well as weighers of evidence, and their sworn verdict regarding the facts was determinative." Juries worked fast, bringing in several verdicts in a single day's session of court.[34]

The practical importance of the jury can be seen most clearly in homicide cases, especially in the way that juries, over three centuries, "interpreted" the English homicide laws. Those laws, beginning with the Assize of Clarendon, were notoriously harsh, stipulating death by hanging for all forms of "felonious ho-

30. Ibid., 423.

31. McLane, "Juror Attitudes toward Social Disorder," 42.

32. Edward Powell, "Jury Trial at Gaol Delivery in the Late Middle Ages: The Midland Circuit, 1400–1429," in Cockburn and Green, *Twelve Good Men*, 96, table 4.6.

33. P. G. Lawson, "Lawless Juries? The Composition and Behavior of Hertfordshire Juries, 1573–1624," in Cockburn and Green, *Twelve Good Men*, 133.

34. Green, "Jury and the English Law of Homicide," 423–424.

micide." Only two categories of "nonfelonious homicide" were recognized by the law: "justifiable" and "excusable." For example, if a thief were killed while running off with his booty, or if an outlaw were killed while trying to avoid capture, his death would be labeled "justifiable" homicide, and once the facts were accepted by the justice of the peace, acquittal of the killer would be automatic. "Excusable" homicide included killing by accident or killing in self-defense. Perpetrators of excusable homicides were not eligible for acquittal, but they were commonly granted pardons by the king, although they sometimes had to wait several months (in jail) before being pardoned.[35]

The more difficult cases—and there were a great many of them—were the deaths that resulted from common brawling or sudden fits of passion, as well as killing under circumstances that did not meet the narrow Angevin understanding of "self-defense." By the thirteenth century, self-defense had come to mean "slaying out of literally vital necessity: the slayer, under mortal attack, had acted as a last resort to save his own life." These homicide statutes, however, were often in direct conflict with local ideas about "just deserts" or "justified self-defense." Thomas A. Green observes that "in an age when fighting was common and death could result from even a superficial wound," community sentiment would have defined as noncapital crimes many killings that would have resulted in hanging had the law been strictly enforced. In earlier times, such killings would have been settled between families, through the payment of compensation by kinfolk. These were no longer matters for private bargaining; they were violations of the king's peace, and the king's justices presided over their resolution.[36]

The jury's rendering of a verdict, even if it were subsequently questioned by the judge, "ended the matter": *quietus est*, for acquittal; *suspendatus est* ("he is hanged"); or *remittitur ad gratiam domine regis* ("remitted to the grace of the king," or authorized to seek the king's pardon). This was the case even if the jury's verdict did not quite square with the letter of the law. Judges had no means of second-guessing the jury because they had no independent access to the facts, and in most cases, the coroner's report was too brief to support an alternative explanation of events.[37]

The finality of jury verdicts is all the more surprising, given the evidence of the assize rolls: a very high percentage of verdicts was for acquittal, and acquittal rates were highest in homicide cases. The reason is almost certainly that jurors, appalled by the harshness of the homicide statutes, were determined to enforce a different understanding of homicide, dividing the universe of killings into categories that were not recognized by the law. On the one hand were the truly egregious killings that deserved capital punishment—killing for gain, killing by stealth, and

35. Ibid., 420–421.
36. Ibid.
37. Ibid., 424–425, 425, n. 47.

killing with "malice aforethought" (the original definition of murder), whether by stealth or not. On the other hand were the most common forms of killing, which did not fall into these categories: killing to avenge an insult; accidental killing during reckless brawling, sometimes under the influence of alcohol; killing in the heat of passion; and killing in self-defense, even if the defendant could have escaped his assailant rather than confront him. Whatever the law might say, juries apparently believed that "a violent attack could be met with a violent response. A man whose life was threatened did not have to seek some means of escape; indeed, he need not do so though he was not in danger of losing his life."[38]

In such cases jurors would simply return a verdict of "not guilty," just as in earlier decades they had refused to "present" such cases for trial (finding that the defendant was "accused but not suspected"). In the post-ordeal era, verdicts were more precise but not less inscrutable. In case after case, juries released defendants that the king gladly would have hanged, and these freed defendants often engaged quietly in the kin bargaining the law aimed to supplant. In cases of self-defense, for example, the accused would often be found to have met the exacting standards of the statute, even when the evidence suggested otherwise. A jury might find that the defendant had "attempted to flee" from his assailant, only to be "overtaken," giving him no choice but to pull his dagger and stab his attacker in the chest. Or, while attempting to flee, the defendant may have been chased to a place from which he had no egress: a hedgerow, a ditch, or, even more suspiciously, a wall. Defendants who had killed during a brawl were excused by saying they had been attacked while trying to "break up" the fight. And so forth. When the court had no independent access to evidence, these justifications, even when they sounded fishy, had to be taken at face value. Eventually, many judges came to accept that such explanations reflected community sentiment and, for that reason, should be respected. Green reports the following judge's remarks for the record in 1454:

> If a man assaults you in order to beat you it is not lawful for you to say you want to kill him and to endanger his life and limb: but if the case is such that he has you at such advantage that he intends to kill you as you seek to flee . . . or if you are on the ground under him; . . . then it is lawful for you to say that if he won't desist, you want to slay him to save your own life, and thus you may menace him for such special cause.[39]

38. Thomas A. Green, *Verdict According to Conscience: Perspectives on the English Criminal Trial Jury, 1200–1800* (Chicago: University of Chicago Press, 1985), quoted in McLane, "Juror Attitudes toward Local Disorder," 59.

39. Green, "Jury and the English Law of Homicide," 428, n. 57.

THE PALLADIUM OF OUR LIBERTIES

As early as the fourteenth century, then, the job of the juror had evolved into something that a modern lawyer, and a modern juror, would recognize without much difficulty. Jurors listened to evidence "and use[d] their common sense to figure out what really happened and whether the law had been violated."[40] Sometimes they followed their own understanding of the law rather than the court's, and they were frequently more lenient toward lawbreakers than the statutes required. But for good or ill, the jury system meant that the English judiciary had its roots in a popular institution in which men of several ranks shared the task of judging, giving the English jury the reputation it carried into the seventeenth century as the "palladium" of English liberties.[41]

But to know whether the law has been violated, one must first know what the law is. Even a juror determined to "shade" or to "fudge" the law needs to understand the law, if only to be able to get around it effectively. So in addition to using common sense about the facts of a case, and whatever knowledge they might possess about the character of the litigants or defendants, jurors were sometimes required to determine "what the meaning of the law was and whether it applied to the specific circumstances at hand"—although, as will become apparent, there were narrower and broader interpretations of this deceptively simple idea.[42]

To say what the law is and whether it applies to a particular set of circumstances is a great power, and under the English legal system, it was clear where this power resided: with judges. The steadily accumulating body of common law represented the collective wisdom of generations of English jurists ruling in cases touching on every aspect of the law and every detail of daily life. But there was almost always some room for jurors to make judgments about what the law required and what it meant. This was the case with respect to the homicide laws, and it is clear that jurors used their discretion to return "merciful" or partial verdicts (guilty on some charges but not on others) that spared the defendant from the gallows. Juries exercised their discretion even more aggressively after the Crown began to use magistrates to present to local juries, in the king's name, both the

40. James Levine, *Juries and Politics* (Pacific Grove, CA: Brooks/Cole, 1992), 23.

41. The phrase is Blackstone's, from *Commentaries on the Laws of England*: "So that the liberties of England cannot but subsist, so long as this palladium remains sacred and inviolate; not only from all open attacks, (which none will be so hardy as to make) but also from all secret machinations, which may sap and undermine it; by introducing new and arbitrary methods of trial, by justices of the peace, commissioners of the revenue, and courts of conscience." William Blackstone, *The Commentaries of Sir William Blackstone, Knight, on the Laws and Constitution of England* (New York: American Bar Association, 2009), 459–460.

42. Levine, *Juries and Politics*, 23.

accusation and the evidence against local defendants. This form of centralization had long been sought by the monarch and resisted by local subjects, in all three estates.[43] The consequence was an increase in partial verdicts, some of them skirting the boundary of outright resistance.

A jury's refusal to convict when the facts clearly indicate guilt is known in modern times as "jury nullification"—effectively repealing a law by refusing to convict anyone accused of violating it, however obvious his guilt. Green refers to the rendering of merciful and partial verdicts as "quasi-nullification" and notes that it was rarely punished. (Briefly, in the seventeenth century, uncooperative jurors were sometimes bound over for Star Chamber proceedings, or they were fined on the spot by the judge.[44]) What is now referred to as true nullification—the absolute refusal of a jury to convict a clearly guilty defendant on the grounds that either the law in question or its particular application is illegitimate—would not have found many supporters up to the sixteenth and seventeenth centuries. And those who supported the jury's right to reach a "contrary" verdict did not call it nullification—they referred to it as "judging the law" or "finding the law," a point taken up in more detail in the next chapter. But the conflicts between king and Parliament from the Civil War through the Restoration transformed the local jury's inevitable discretion over partial and merciful verdicts into something with a sharper political edge: the "ancient right" of jurors to defend subjects' liberty by applying the relevant law in a way that differed from the judge's instructions, effectively blocking prosecutions that jurors thought unjust.

The power to render such "general verdicts" put the jury on a collision course with royal authority, but it was the very possibility of such power, and its use in cases with political significance (unlike ordinary homicide cases), that led to the popular link between trial by jury and the defense of liberty. A good example is Joseph Towers's pamphlet *An Enquiry and Observations on the Rights and Duties of Juries*, published in London in 1764 and reprinted in 1785. Towers asserts what was then a common view: that the purpose of jury trial is to serve as a check on royal power, thus making it central to English freedom, especially in cases of "seditious libel." This requires that the jury have the authority to determine the law as well as the facts: "But if juries should ever be tame and senseless enough to give up the right of determining the law, as well as the fact, in libel causes, the liberty of the press is then wholly at the discretion of the judges."[45] *An Enquiry*

43. Thomas A. Green, "The Jury, Seditious Libel, and the Criminal Law," in *Juries, Libel, & Justice: The Role of English Juries in Seventeenth- and Eighteenth-Century Trials for Libel and Slander*, ed. R. H. Helmholtz and Thomas A. Green (Los Angeles: University of California, 1984), 37–91.

44. Ibid., 45.

45. Joseph Towers, *Observations on the Rights and Duty of Juries in Trials for Libels* (Dublin: Moncrieffe, Jenkin, White, 1785), 143–144.

assumes that this "ancient" right of juries has been curtailed by the king in modern times and that the rights of Englishmen are threatened as a result. Consequently, Towers's pamphlet is directed to jurors themselves—a plea to take their responsibilities more seriously, to stop doing the bidding of the Crown by convicting defendants of seditious libel.

Jurors render these suspect verdicts, Towers argues, because they fail to appreciate their power to determine law as well as fact. By limiting the jury to the consideration of only "fact"—that is, did the defendant publish the offending pamphlet?—the Crown can expect to win every case, since the defendant would not be in court in the first place if he had not published the pamphlet. The real question is whether the content of the pamphlet constitutes a violation of the law, and according to Towers, that is not a matter that has traditionally been left exclusively to judges to decide. Towers argues that juries have customarily considered questions of law, citing the fact that English juries have always had the power to decide whether a killing was murder, manslaughter, or self-defense. Finally, Towers argues that a statement must be false in order to be libelous; indeed, indictments for seditious libel frequently charged the defendant with making a "false, scandalous, malicious" statement against the king or his ministers. It follows, therefore, that a jury is fully entitled to consider the truthfulness of the statement claimed to be libelous, and if the jury finds that the charges against the government are true, the defendant cannot be guilty of libel—that is, of making a "false" statement. How this claim worked out in practice—and its legacy for the English and colonial understanding of the jury—can be seen from a consideration of the great cases in which the right to speak the truth was proclaimed most triumphantly: Bushell's Case in 1670,[46] the Case of the Seven Bishops in 1688,[47] and the trial of printer John Peter Zenger in colonial New York in 1735.[48]

Bushell's Case was the result of the prosecution of William Penn and William Mead for "unlawful assembly and disturbing the peace," the disturbance in question being a public Quaker meeting.[49] Since there was no question that Penn and Meade were Quakers and that they had held a public meeting as charged, the Crown expected a quick conviction. The jury, however, acquitted the two men, and the judge took that decision as an act of defiance. He told the jurors that they must continue their deliberations until they reached "a verdict the Court will accept." When they still refused to convict, the judge fined them and sent them back to deliberate some more. Once again, the jury refused to convict, forcing the judge

46. "Case of the Imprisonment of Edward Bushell for Alleged Misconduct as a Juryman," 22 Charles II A. D. 1670 [Vaughan's Reports, 135], http://www.constitution.org/trials/bushell/bushell.htm (accessed April 30, 2015).

47. "Trial of the Seven Bishops for Publishing a Libel," 12 How. St. Tr. 183 (1688).

48. "The Trial of Mr. John Peter Zenger," 17 How. St. Tr. 675 (1735).

49. Alan W. Scheflin, "Jury Nullification: The Right to Say No," *Southern California Law Review* 45 (1972): 172.

to relent, but he continued the jurors' fines.[50] The jury foreman, Edward Bushell, refused to pay his fine and was jailed. He took his case to the Court of Common Pleas, where Chief Justice Vaughan issued the famous verdict that ended the practice of "attaint," that is, the punishment of jurors for reaching verdicts that displeased the court.[51]

The Case of the Seven Bishops followed James II's Declaration of Indulgence in 1687, which removed many of the obstacles to Catholic worship and Catholic participation in the public life of the kingdom, to the great dismay of the nation's Protestants.[52] The king, acting as head of the Church of England, had ordered that the declaration be read from the pulpits of all Anglican churches; seven bishops of the Church of England refused, on the grounds that the king's declaration repealed an act of Parliament, a power that, under the laws of England, the king did not possess (said the bishops).[53] When they sent James a petition setting forth this argument, he responded by charging them with seditious libel and locking them in the Tower of London. A jury in the Court of King's Bench found the bishops not guilty, going against the instructions of several members of the panel of judges presiding at the trial. Soon thereafter James was deposed, and the English Bill of Rights of 1689 specifically protected the "right to petition" without fear of punishment.[54] The jurors in the Case of the Seven Bishops, it was said, thus helped pave the way for the Glorious Revolution.

John Peter Zenger, publisher of the *New York Weekly Journal*, was indicted in 1735 for publishing seditious libel against colonial officials in New York.[55] As

50. See ibid., citing "Penn & Mead's Case," 6 Howell's 951 (1670): "Gentlemen," said the judge, "you shall not be dismissed till we have a verdict that the court will accept; and you shall be locked up, without meat, drink, fire, and tobacco; you shall not think thus to abuse the court; we will have a verdict by the help of God, or you shall starve for it."

51. "Case of the Imprisonment of Edward Bushell."

52. See Declaration of Indulgence of King James II, April 4, 1687: "We do . . . declare, that it is our royal will and pleasure, that from henceforth the execution of all and all manner of penal laws in matters ecclesiastical, for not coming to church, or not receiving the Sacrament, or for any other nonconformity to the religion established, or for or by reason of the exercise of religion in any manner whatsoever, be immediately suspended; and the further execution of the said penal laws and every of them is hereby suspended." Andrew Browning, *English Historical Documents 1660–1714* (New York: Oxford University Press, 1953), 395.

53. Green, "Jury, Seditious Libel and Criminal Law," 37.

54. See An Act Declaring the Rights and Liberties of the Subject and Settling the Succession of the Crown (English Bill of Rights, 1689): "That it is the right of the subjects to petition the king, and all commitments and prosecutions for such petitioning are illegal." http://www.avalon.law.yale.edu/17th_century/england.asp (accessed January 9, 2014).

55. On the Zenger case, see Simon Stern, "Note: Between Local Knowledge and National Politics: Debating Rationales for Jury Nullification after Bushell's Case," *Yale Law Journal* 111 (2002): 1815–1859.

in England, the law did not consider truth to be a defense to criminal libel. However, Zenger's attorney, Andrew Hamilton, argued that since the things Zenger had published about the officials were true, they could not be libelous. The jury acquitted, against the instructions of the judge.[56] From then on, colonial officials were reluctant to bring seditious libel charges against the colony's newspapers, and the Zenger trial (and his bold rescue by a "jury of his peers") became a famous milestone in the history of freedom of the press. In this understanding, the jurors in these cases were not defying the law or reaching a verdict contrary to the evidence. They were simply finding that the defendants in question had not "in fact" committed libel and therefore could not be guilty of seditious libel.

In practice, jurors and judges did not locate the line between "fact" and "law" in precisely the same place—a difficulty that would be carried forward into the nineteenth and twentieth centuries. That a particular subject had written a particular pamphlet was no doubt a fact, but the pamphlet's tendency to incite sedition (or not) was no less of a fact. Since, by its very nature, the crime of sedition must touch the sentiments of ordinary Englishmen, or else it could have no effect, it followed (according to many pamphleteers) that ordinary Englishmen were the best judges of what is and is not seditious. So argued, among many others, Robert Morris in his 1770 letter to Sir Richard Ashton: "Who [is] more interested than juries (for juries are composed of the people) to preserve the peace and order of the state? . . . Juries are a tribunal ever changing as the times; they judge of men's writings and actions by what they see and feel."[57]

As time went on, the English libel cases acquired a mythic importance in political debate, and the myth obscured some important details. For example, Vaughan's ruling in Bushell's Case did not declare or discover an unambiguous or unlimited right of jurors to ignore a court's instructions on the law.[58] But because all these cases concerned manifestly political charges—unlawful assembly and seditious libel—the "ancient jury right" to reach an independent judgment about the law became synonymous with the jury's role as the defender of English liberty.

What Vaughan's decision unquestionably established is that a juror cannot be punished for reaching a verdict that seems to reject the court's instructions on the law. The practical effect of this ruling was clear: with nothing to fear from an attaint, jurors could return any verdict they pleased. If they returned a general

56. Steven E. Barkan, "Jury Nullification in Political Trials," *Social Problems* 31 (1983): 32.

57. Robert Morris, *A Letter to Sir Richard Aston . . . Containing a Reply to His Scandalous Abuse; and Some Thoughts on the Modern Doctrine of Libels* (1770), quoted in Green, "Jury, Seditious Libel, and Criminal Law," 61.

58. See, for example, David Pepper's discussion of this point in "Nullifying History: Modern-Day Misuse of the Right to Decide the Law," *Case Western Reserve Law Review* 50 (Spring 2000): 599–643.

verdict—a single finding of guilty or not guilty—it would be impossible to know whether their verdict (if it seemed to depart from the court's instructions on the law) was based on a judgment about the facts or a disagreement about the law. In a general verdict, Vaughan reasoned, jurors "resolve both law and fact complicately, and not the fact by itself."[59] If a jury could not come to its own conclusion about what the law required, it could return a "special verdict," finding the facts and asking the judge to apply the relevant law to generate a verdict. An English court could also require the jury to return a special verdict, but such orders were rare in England.[60]

This mixing of law and fact reveals a larger difficulty: even when a jury listens attentively and respectfully to what the judge has to say about the meaning of the law, applying the judge's instructions to the facts of the case requires the jury to exercise a certain amount of discretion. The law uses words that need to be defined, and there may be disagreements about the meaning of what the judge has said. If trials are presided over by more than one judge (as was fairly common in the seventeenth and eighteenth centuries), there may be disagreements from the bench as well, requiring the jury to make up its own mind.

This is perhaps most clearly true in libel cases. A charge of libel is, in part, simply a matter of fact and therefore easily settled by the jury: did defendant X publish article Y, and did the statements made therein clearly indicate particular persons in authority (known as "establishing the innuendo")? This was the law as explained to the jurors in the Zenger case and in all libel cases in England prior to the passage of Fox's Libel Act in 1792.[61] But under the old law, if the jury answered "yes" to the standard questions posed by the judge, it would have to find the defendant guilty as charged.

But according to another view, the matter is more complicated. In the Zenger trial, in addition to arguing that the jury should have a hand in interpreting the law, the defense pointed out that in a libel prosecution, the jury "should find that statements must be false before they can be deemed libelous."[62] This was not, however, how the law defined libel. Under the controlling English statute of the day, the definition of libel was almost comically broad: "written censure upon

59. "Case of the Imprisonment of Edward Bushell."

60. Leon Green, *Judge and Jury* (Kansas City, MO: Vernon Law Book Co., 1930), 379.

61. 32 Geo. 3, c. 60 (1792). The legislative title of this act was An Act to Remove Doubts Respecting the Functions of Juries in Cases of Libel, and it confirmed a jury's right to return a general verdict in a libel case without being "required or directed by the court . . . to find the defendant . . . guilty merely on the proof of the publication." In effect, it gave the jury the right to decide whether a particular publication was, in fact, libelous.

62. Pepper, "Nullifying History," 615, n. 16, citing James Alexander, *A Brief Narrative of the Case and Trial of John Peter Zenger* (1735).

any public man whatever for any conduct whatever or upon any law or institution whatever."[63] In this view, truth was not a defense in a libel case; in fact, it was a liability: "the truer the statement the greater the libel" was a rule based on the (not entirely fanciful) notion that if the terrible things said about the government turned out to be true, they would be all the more damaging to public order and tranquility.[64]

Zenger's attorney appealed to what he claimed was the traditional English common-law view (as opposed to the parliamentary statute), in which a statement's falsehood had been a requirement in libel prosecutions. The judge and prosecution, Hamilton claimed, had simply misstated the higher, common law of libel, and it was the jury's obligation to correct them. Simply put, a true statement could not be libelous.[65] Hamilton's example was the Case of the Seven Bishops. In that case, he explained, the jurors had recognized that "the petition of the bishops [was] no libel, that is [it contained] no falsehood [or] sedition, and therefore found them not guilty."[66] The bishops' petition expressed no more than the settled law of England.[67] Likewise, if the jury in New York could not determine that Zenger had deliberately published a falsehood, it could not find him guilty of libel. Hamilton was, in essence, calling on the jury to perform the role that the judge had failed to carry out (in Hamilton's view). "Rather than a call to reject the law," one historian concluded, "this was a call to apply it in good faith."[68]

In the prosecution of Penn and Meade for unlawful assembly and disturbing the peace, the jury was presented with a similar difficulty. At one level, the facts of the case were not in dispute. Penn and Meade had held a public gathering of Quakers at a time when such meetings (indeed, all services outside the Church of England) had been banned by the Conventicle Act of 1664—thus the charge of

63. Paul G. Willis, "Juries and Judicial Review," *Western Political Quarterly* 3 (1950): 66, 68.

64. See Harold L. Nelson, "Seditious Libel in Colonial America," *American Journal of Legal History* 3, 2 (April 1959): 160. During the republican era in the United States, the claim that truth is no defense to a libel charge was often attributed to the judges of the Star Chamber. The defense in *People v. Croswell* made this claim: "The opposite doctrine, which mentions that a writing is equally libelous, whether true or false, originated in a polluted source, the despotic tribunal of the Star Chamber." People v. Croswell, 3 Johns. Cas. 337 (1804), 12. The *Croswell* case is discussed in chapter 2.

65. Pepper, "Nullifying History," 603, n. 16.

66. Ibid.

67. Their petition was so far from sedition, in fact, that five of the seven bishops refused to swear allegiance to William in 1689, for which defiance they were dismissed from their bishoprics. See Thomas Babbington Macaulay, *The History of England from the Accession of James II*, vol. 3 (New York: Cambridge University Press, 2008).

68. Pepper, "Nullifying History," 617, n. 16.

"unlawful assembly."[69] As in a libel trial, the defendants' guilt seemed to be only a matter of establishing whether they had in fact committed the acts named in the indictment—acts the defendants themselves did not deny. But the defendants urged the jury to look beyond the indictment to the common-law understanding of "unlawful assembly and disturbance of the peace," an understanding that did not include (according to the defendants) the peaceable behavior named in the charge. What, after all, could be less "disorderly" or "riotous" than a Quaker meeting? The jury's responsibility was therefore to "judge the law"—that is, to understand and then apply the law correctly, not in the incorrect manner urged by the court. Because the traditional understanding of "disturbing the peace" did not include the events named in the indictment, the court's instructions on the law were simply wrong and, for that reason, should be ignored.[70] In this way, by coming to a conclusion about a fact (a true statement is not libelous, and a peaceful meeting is not a public disturbance), the jurors would also be reaching a conclusion about a law (the law cannot mean truth-telling when it says "sedition," and it cannot mean a Quaker meeting when it says "disturbance").

This was not, it should be stressed again, the view of Chief Justice Vaughan in the decision that freed Bushell in 1670 and ended the threat of attaint. Vaughan's argument was both more subtle and less congenial to popular sensibilities. First, the division of responsibilities in court is clear and logical, according to Vaughan: the jury is responsible for judging the facts, and the judge is responsible for explaining the law. Second, this arrangement is natural because it is based on the respective capacities of both parties. The presumption that a jury can render a judgment about the law is "not intelligible," Vaughan insisted, for "no jury can be charged with the trial of matter in law . . . no evidence ever was or can be given to a jury of what is law or not; nor no such oath can be given to, or taken by, a jury to try matter in law."[71]

Likewise, the judge cannot tell the jury what the evidence is or what that evidence signifies. The judge "can never know what evidence the jury have, and consequently he cannot know the matter of fact, nor punish the jury for going against their evidence, when he cannot know what their evidence is." That evidence is "much other than" the evidence heard in court, because the law supposes that the jurors know the vicinage and its affairs and are therefore in possession of "personal knowledge, by which they may be assured, and sometimes are, that what is deposed in court is absolutely false; but to this the judge is a stranger."[72]

69. 16 Car. 2, c. 4 (1664). The act forbade assemblies of more than five persons worshipping outside the Church of England.

70. Pepper, "Nullifying History," 611–612, n. 16.

71. "Case of the Imprisonment of Edward Bushell."

72. Ibid.

In other words, the jury can know what is going on in town; it can know the cast of characters and their various quirks and habits, and thus it can judge their credibility—just as juries had done in the twelfth century, when they offered some of the accused compurgation rather than sending them to the ordeal. This was perhaps the distinctive characteristic of the ancient "witnessing jury," in which "twelve good men and true" from the village testified as to what they knew about the parties to a dispute, the character of the defendant, the events leading up to an altercation, or who had made promises to whom. But in this view, although the jurors could know the facts, they could not possibly understand the law itself, anymore than the judge could have any real knowledge of the rustic surroundings in which the trial took place.

This view of the jury's role took shape in a world of vills, shires, hundreds, and market towns, where any civil dispute or criminal act would involve persons and events known to everyone in town, including the jurors, but not the judge, who occupied an entirely different social rank and commonly rode the circuit from county to county, never acquiring a close association with any particular town. However, even in 1670, this would not have been an accurate description of most English courtrooms, and certainly not those in London: judges still rode circuits, but towns and even villages had grown larger than the rural communities served by the twelfth-century jury.[73] Nonetheless, the role of the jury as "fact finder" has rested, for much of our history, on the claim that juries can know, or understand, what judges cannot. Chief Justice Vaughan did not dispute this view. "It is absurd a jury should be fined by the judge for going against their evidence," he concluded, "when he who fineth knows not what it is."[74]

But by the same reasoning, judges know what jurors cannot know: the law itself. For this reason, jurors are required to defer to the opinion of the court on matters of law—indeed, in Vaughan's formulation, it would be impossible for jurors, given their loutish ignorance, to have any opinions on the law whatsoever. If they returned a verdict the court disagreed with, it would have to be because of

73. See John Langbein, "The Criminal Trial before the Lawyers," *University of Chicago Law Review* 45 (1978): 263–298. Langbein points out that because the vicinage requirement had been abandoned in favor of countywide jury lists long before the Bushell case, Vaughan's decision made no sense, relying as it did on an obsolete understanding of the jury (that jurors know the local facts; that they know who is lying and who is telling the truth). But Vaughan may have been playing the statesman in this case, trying to draw a line between the rights of the jury and the authority of the court so that, although the court was in control, something was left (or so it seemed) for the jury. Vaughan's decision seems determined to preserve a significant purpose for jury trials. We should not be surprised to see this political result from such a political trial. See also Stern, "Note: Between Local Knowledge and National Politics."

74. "Case of the Imprisonment of Edward Bushell."

their judgment about the facts.[75] No other explanation could possibly make sense. And disagreements between judge and jury about such factual matters are to be expected, Vaughan declared: "I would know whether anything be more common than for two men, students, barristers or judges, to deduce contrary and opposite conclusions out of the same case in law. And is there any difference that two men should infer distinct conclusions from the same testimony? . . . And this often is the case of the judge and jury."[76]

Such artful Tory subtlety about dimwitted jurors and learned judges would become increasingly unpopular, especially in colonial America. The colonial jury was already a more important and more powerful institution than the common-law juries in England, and the grand jury, in particular, had evolved into an important institution of local government in the New World.[77] By the time of the American Revolution, this kind of jury was as familiar to Americans as the legislative assembly, the town meeting, and the sanctity of contract, and its importance extended far beyond its role in the trials involving seditious libel. Few Americans would have quarreled with John Adams's conclusion that if a judge's view of the law violated a fundamental political principle, then "it is not only . . . [the juror's] right, but his duty, in that case, to find the verdict according to his own best understanding, judgment, and conscience, though in direct opposition to the direction of the court."[78] By the late eighteenth century, the right to find a "verdict according to . . . conscience" had achieved the status of conventional wisdom. Thus, the British cabinet's decision to remove customs violations from the purview of the jury was seen by the colonists as virtually a declaration of war against the colonies.[79]

75. See also Green, *Verdict According to Conscience*, 256–264; Langbein, "Criminal Trial before Lawyers." This is further evidence of Vaughan's political art: what is left on the court's side is what is most important—namely, to say what the law means.

76. "Case of the Imprisonment of Edward Bushell."

77. James Nendza, "The Jury and Republican Government: The Early American Understanding" (unpublished manuscript, 1999). For the use of juries as "quasi-administrative bodies," see F. Thornton Miller, *Juries and Judges versus the Law: Virginia's Provincial Legal Perspective, 1783–1828* (Charlottesville: University of Virginia Press, 1994), 99–102. See also Robert P. Burns, *The Death of the American Trial* (Chicago: University of Chicago Press, 2009), 50–51.

78. John Adams, *Diaries of John Adams*, entry for February 12, 1771, Adams Family Papers, Massachusetts Historical Society, Boston.

79. "Comment: The Changing Role of the Jury in the Nineteenth Century," *Yale Law Journal* 74 (1964): 170–192.

THE JURY IN COLONIAL AMERICA

Trial by jury was a feature of the earliest constitutional arrangements in every British North American colony save one, and it was understood to be an "English right" with both prudence and custom on its side—although the "right" meant slightly different things in different places. As John M. Murrin notes, "New England's first recorded statute involved juries." This was the declaration by the Plymouth Colony in December 1623 that "all Criminall facts, and also all [matters] of trespasses and debts betweene man & man should [be tried] by the verdict of twelve Honest men to be Impanelled by Authority in forme of a Jury upon their oaths."[80] Only New Haven declined to adopt jury trials; there, the intense religious devotion of the colony's leaders led them to reject judgment by lay citizens, reserving such weighty matters for magistrates in both civil and criminal matters.[81] But in every other colony, including the equally pious Massachusetts, the right to a jury of one's peers—a "jury of the vicinage," as the old documents phrased it—was a fundamental part of the legal system.

Some general caveats are in order before we look at some specific cases. First, the jury received consistent rhetorical support from virtually all commentators on the law and on politics. Public support increased over time and became especially insistent toward the end of the colonial period, when conflict with English officials was most intense. One sign of the jury's importance to colonial Americans was the power colonial governments placed in the hands of jurors. Jurors in the law courts of the early colonies, especially in New England, "were permitted to decide questions that in England were reserved for Chancellors or common law judges."[82] Although colonial judges were operating inside a thoroughly English legal system, they did not normally have the powers enjoyed by judges in England. They could not, for example, comment on the evidence or force juries to deliberate again if they returned a verdict the judge disliked.[83] In addition to being a sacred right of English subjects everywhere, the jury had the very practical advantage of allowing citizens to control the power of judges and

80. John M. Murrin, "Magistrates, Sinners, and a Precarious Liberty: Trial by Jury in Seventeenth-Century New England," in *Saints and Revolutionaries: Essays in Early American History*, ed. David Hall, John M. Murrin, and Thad W. Tate (New York: Norton, 1984), 157 (brackets in original).

81. Ibid., 170–182. The ban on juries ended when the Crown transferred authority over New Haven to the colony of Connecticut.

82. Stephen N. Subrin, "How Equity Conquered Common Law: The Federal Rules of Civil Procedure in Historical Perspective," *University of Pennsylvania Law Review* 135, 4 (April 1987): 927.

83. Burns, *Death of the American Trial*, 51. Burns notes that the "American suspicion of government found a natural expression in the jury trial" (51).

magistrates. This was more important in some colonies than in others. For example, political conflict between settlers and colonial officials was more pronounced in the southern colonies than in New England, where for much of the seventeenth century, church members and magistrates held similar views on the importance of public order. But even in New England, the gap between citizens and magistrates began to widen, and the jury became a way to defend subjects from officialdom. This gap would never entirely disappear, even after independence.[84]

Second, the jury was usually much more important in civil cases than in criminal cases. By the seventeenth century, in both England and British North America, most subjects accused of felonies were tried before magistrates and justices of the peace; only in the most serious cases, where the punishment was either death or banishment, were juries impaneled. Defendants often confessed in felony cases, because a penitent felon could usually expect some mercy from the court. This was especially true in Puritan New England, where magistrates placed a high value on sincere repentance. Civil jury trials, in contrast, were frequent. Civil juries were commonly used whenever large sums of money were at stake, although there was considerable variation in the definition of "large." In Massachusetts, at least, juries were used even when small sums were involved.[85] But as time passed, juries also became agencies of local government, especially grand juries, which were used not only to present criminal defendants but also to investigate the conduct of public officials and public agencies, to supervise public construction projects, and to make determinations about just compensation in eminent domain proceedings. Grand juries issued reports and made recommendations, and they sometimes shared the legislative prerogatives of assemblies, governors, and magistrates.[86] Along with its role in major criminal and civil cases, the jury was a constant presence in the most important matters dealt with by colonial governments. This made American juries substantively different from English juries, and the contrast became sharper as time and experience drew America farther from the aristocratic model of English government.

English legal practice is the starting point for an understanding of the early American jury, but it is important to keep in mind the society in which the colonial jury operated. All the colonies adopted English legal forms—county magistrates, petit and grand juries, courts of sessions, the hue and cry, and common-law writs, among many others. But these legal arrangements were superimposed on communities that were significantly different from the villages and counties where

84. John M. Murrin has reconstructed the pattern of jury use in the New England colonies and finds clear evidence of a greater demand for the jury as more and more New England settlers came from outside the community of devout Puritans. Murrin, "Magistrates, Sinners, and a Precarious Liberty," 206.

85. Ibid., 155–157, 163–174, 183.

86. Nendza, "Jury and Republican Government," 5–7.

English laws were enforced. In the beginning, especially, many North American settlements were necessarily primitive, given the difficult circumstances under which they were established. In some places (Plymouth during its first winters, for example), these conditions amounted to a civil emergency, justifying extraordinary measures. Colonial governments were also responsible for relatively small populations. After twenty years of settlement, the Massachusetts Bay Colony had just over 20,000 inhabitants living in roughly thirty towns. Government on such a scale would naturally be conducted differently from government in a nation as large as England.[87]

Most important, these early communities differed politically from those at "home" (as the records consistently refer to England), since the putative head of each colony was a very distant monarch who was preoccupied for most of the seventeenth century with religious wars and threats to the royal authority, leaving local governance by default in the hands of governors, assemblies, town meetings, and judges. And this de facto independence of the American colonies worked a subtle change in the argument for the right to a jury trial.

In England, the jury was the "palladium of our liberties" because each criminal defendant had the king as his accuser. To insist that the king persuade twelve of the defendant's neighbors of his guilt, beyond a reasonable doubt, seemed an essential guarantee of the subject's liberty. Furthermore, the king was the head of the government, "His Most Dread Majesty," the "fountain of justice," and the mainspring of political activity throughout the kingdom. But where the royal authority was distant and preoccupied—missing, in fact, for the eleven years of the Commonwealth, roughly corresponding to the third decade of settlement in America—the defendant's accuser was more likely to be one of his own neighbors. This was likelier still in small towns and villages, where every man knew every other man's business, where crime was hard to conceal, and where the respectable folks kept a close watch on the miscreants.

In New England especially, but to some degree in all the colonies, the natural authority of the small-town gentry was buttressed by a powerful religious code. In Massachusetts and Plymouth, for example, no one could be a member of the town meeting who was not also a member of the church—therefore, only church members could serve on juries.[88] That authority was manifested, in varying degrees, through the related institutions of the town meeting, the congregation, and the court. Juries were a normal part of this authority structure and were as democratic as the town meeting. They gave the decisions of the judicial branch the important element of popular legitimacy—whether the case involved a capital crime or a simple civil dispute between neighbors. When defendants or litigants

87. David Hackett Fischer, *Albion's Seed: Four British Folkways in America* (New York: Oxford University Press, 1989), 16–17.

88. Murrin, "Magistrates, Sinners, and a Precarious Liberty," 197.

chose not to use the jury, it remained in the background as a sign of the community's self-governing character. Even in New York, well outside the orbit of the Puritan theocracy (and even in the seventeenth century a more cosmopolitan and rowdy place than New England), it is possible to observe in the mundane details of law enforcement and civil procedure the emergence of a social and political democracy that would eventually transform the jury from a defender of the subject's liberty into an agency of self-government. The defense of liberty would never disappear as an important element of juries; indeed, it would make a comeback in the decades before the Revolution, as discussed below. But the argument that the jury protects the subject from the king necessarily lost some of its force when the source of prosecution became not the monarch but a magistrate who took his oath before town selectmen after being appointed by the governor on the advice of councils and elected assemblies.

As the jury lost some of its importance as the subject's defense against a distant king, a second and more important purpose took its place. Just as the jury can bring the community's understanding of justice to the courtroom, enforcing "the shared morality of ordinary citizens," it can also draw members of the public directly into the administration of government.[89] Contemporary observers saw this exposure to public responsibility as a source of political education, which was immensely important because the colonies were, in fact if not in theory, almost completely self-governing. The educational role of the jury was an American contribution to what had heretofore been an English theory of the jury. English commentators, preoccupied with limiting royal absolutism or with the efficient delivery of the king's justice, saw the jury as "palladium" or "tool," respectively. The idea of the jury as a "school for citizens" could emerge only gradually, and only under the political conditions prevailing in the North American colonies.

Tocqueville has given us the most thorough analysis of these conditions. In the great "still-empty cradle" of North America, a "democracy such as antiquity had not dared to dream of sprang full-grown and fully armed from the midst of the old feudal society."[90] But in the seventeenth and eighteenth centuries, Americans were not yet self-conscious about what they were creating in the New World. Their innovations in the jury system were part of a much broader effort to adapt familiar English institutions to unfamiliar, difficult, and sometimes urgent circumstances. Very gradually, however, American commentators on legal and political matters were coming face-to-face with the democratic paradox: good government requires citizens with the skill and character to decide wisely, but neither skill nor character can be developed without experience in the actual practice of government. Service on juries soon came to be seen as one way for citizens to acquire

89. Burns, *Death of the American Trial*, 50.

90. Alexis de Tocqueville, *Democracy in America*, trans. Harvey C. Mansfield and Delba Winthrop (Chicago: University of Chicago Press, 2000), 27, 35.

such experience, in a setting where the consequences of poor judgment would not be socially catastrophic.

James Nendza describes the view of the jury that became solidified by the middle of the eighteenth century: "While the jury's role of fact-finder was widely acknowledged, the jury was primarily understood as a political institution, which, on the one hand, would achieve results different from those to be expected from a trial conducted by a judge alone, and, on the other, would have an educating effect on the jurors themselves."[91] The jury would both check governmental power and allow the people to participate in government; in this way, the people would be able to learn the principles of a republican political order. But in the process, juries and judges would soon discover that even in a republican political order, there would be plenty of occasions when juries and judges found themselves on opposite sides of the argument about justice.

Three colonies—Virginia, New York, and Massachusetts—are examined here to illustrate common patterns, important local variations, and how the jury gradually assumed its fully republican shape.

Virginia

The First Charter of Virginia (1606) is typical of early colonial documents. It declares that the colony's subjects "shall have and enjoy all liberties, franchises and immunities within any of our other dominions to all intents and purposes as if they had been abiding and born within this our realm of England."[92] This language was understood in the seventeenth century to mean the liberties and immunities of the common law, including the right to a trial by a jury of the vicinage, as in England,[93] although there is no specific mention of a jury right in either the First Charter or the Second Charter, granted in 1609.[94] The Third Charter, issued in

91. Nendza, "Jury and Republican Government," 2–3.

92. The First Virginia Charter (April 10, 1606), http://www.let.rug.nl/usa/documents/1600-1650/the-first-virginia-charter-1606.php (accessed January 6, 2014).

93. William Stoebuck argues that when English subjects in North America appealed to the "common law," they were referring "almost exclusively [to] the public aspects they felt guaranteed political freedom, i.e., constitutional principles, such as trial by jury." William B. Stoebuck, "Reception of English Common Law in the American Colonies," *William and Mary Law Review* 10, 2 (1968): 410.

94. The Second Virginia Charter (May 23, 1609), http://www.let.rug.nl/usa/documents/1600-1650/the-second-virginia-charter-1609.php (accessed January 6, 2014). Oliver Perry Chitwood's *Justice in Colonial Virginia* (Baltimore: Johns Hopkins Press, 1905), cites two civil cases from 1607 that were tried by juries, both of them suits for slander brought against the first president of the Governing Council by John Smith (66). The use of juries in Virginia was apparently based on custom and not on the language of the royal charters.

1612, grants Virginia the right to "hold and keep a court and assembly for the better [ordering] and government of the said plantation," but there is no mention of how the courts would operate or whether the traditional "rights of Englishmen" include a jury trial. In fact, the Third Charter, noting the great increase in "insolences, misdemeanors and abuses, not to be tolerated in any civil government," gives the Governing Council the authority to proceed summarily against all who "offend or misbehave themselves."[95]

It was not until 1642, well after the adoption of the colony's first real constitution in 1621 (Ordinance and Constitution of the Virginia Company), that petit juries were mentioned in the records of the county courts.[96] This makes Virginia unusual among the American colonies, and the reason is undoubtedly the troubled circumstances of its first decades. The early Virginia colony combined features of a company town with the discipline of a military outpost. In addition, its early years were marked by violent factional conflicts in which the law became a weapon, especially the laws regarding mutiny, sedition, and libel.[97] Under the Second Charter, for example, the new president of the Governing Council, Sir Thomas Gates, was given the authority to proceed according to "natural right and equity [rather] than upon the niceness . . . of the law." As a result, the colony's subjects lived under what amounted to martial law.

The colony had three governors and experienced numerous legal and political upheavals in its first several years of existence. By 1619, however, conflict had moderated, and the Crown was persuaded to give Virginia a limited right of self-government. The first Assembly (later known as the House of Burgesses) was called to session in August of that year. Two years later these arrangements were formalized in the Ordinance and Constitution, after which Virginia's government took the form it maintained, with relatively few changes, until 1776. That form, however, was unofficial; because of various last-minute disagreements, the new charter proposed for the colony never received the king's final approval. Thus, by default and by custom, the fundamental constitutional requirement remained that Virginia's laws were to be as near as possible to English laws.[98]

In the case of law enforcement, this meant the English system of county mag-

---

This pattern appears in other colonies as well, which supports the notion that the jury right had become part of the familiar legal landscape and was known to all English subjects. Therefore, they would expect it wherever they were governed by English law, even if it were not specifically mentioned.

95. The Third Virginia Charter (March 12, 1612), http://www.let.rug.nl/usa/documents/1600–1650/the-third-virginia-charter-1612.php (accessed January 6, 2014).

96. Chitwood, *Justice in Colonial Virginia*, 86, n. 54.

97. Arthur Scott, *Criminal Law in Colonial Virginia* (Chicago: University of Chicago Press, 1930), 6–8.

98. Ibid., 12–15.

istrates. For each county, eight to twenty justices of the peace (or county commissioners) were appointed by the governor to administer the law and try minor cases. Judgments from the counties could be appealed to the General Court. The most serious criminal cases—those punishable by banishment or the loss of "life or member"—and civil cases involving in excess of £10 were under the original jurisdiction of the General Court.[99] The General Court heard all its cases at the capital, not in the vicinage, presumably based on the belief that such serious matters should not be left to jurors in the backwoods counties, who might err on the side of harshness in order to suppress crime in their own communities. "We conceive it no ease or benefit to the people," the Assembly declared in 1655, "to have their lives taken away with too much ease . . . 'tis a maxim that no deliberation can be too much pondered that concerns the life of the meanest man."[100] For that reason, the General Court called its jurors from among the bystanders doing business at the court (the so-called talesmen); they did not come from the vicinity of the crime.

In addition to their concern that felons not be treated too harshly in the counties, members of the Governing Council (who were appointed by the governor and were among the most prominent and wealthy men in the colony) did not wish jurors from the hinterland to dominate the grand juries, which, as in other colonies, had more than law enforcement functions. Among other powers (deciding on the routes of new roads, for example), grand juries had the authority to investigate political offenses, such as alleged malfeasance by governors and members of the General Court. Holding grand jury deliberations in the capital gave the authorities greater control over who would be chosen to sit on the jury, thereby sparing themselves the risk of being investigated by strangers.[101]

But because trials in the vicinage were an essential element of the "liberties of Englishmen," the practice of holding major trials in the capital and using bystanders as jurors was a frequent source of complaint. In 1662 the Assembly changed the law to require that half the jurors in capital trials be called from the vicinage. In 1734 this compromise was abandoned, and all jurors were drawn from the neighborhood of the crime and housed in the capital for the duration of the trial—an obvious hardship on the jurors, which might lead a defendant to risk the mercy of the court rather than incur the wrath of neighbors forced to abandon their farms and their families for a lengthy and expensive stay in the capital.[102]

Trial procedures also followed familiar English models. In an inquiry into

99. Ibid., 45–46. See also Hugh F. Rankin, "The General Court of Colonial Virginia: Its Jurisdiction and Personnel," *Virginia Magazine of History and Biography* 70, 2 (April 1962): 142–153.

100. Scott, *Criminal Law in Colonial Virginia*, 47–48.

101. Ibid., 71.

102. Ibid., 86–88. It is easy to see the connection between this experience in Virginia and the language of the Sixth Amendment: "In all criminal prosecutions, the accused shall enjoy the right to a speedy and public trial, by an impartial jury of the State *and district*

a death, for example, a coroner's inquest would be held, and the jury would attempt to determine the cause and nature of the death (accident, suicide, homicide, or natural causes) and identify the person responsible, using local witnesses as the principal sources of information. Witnesses were also encouraged to report crimes to the magistrates, sometimes earning the right to share in any fines.[103] When a suspect was finally identified, the sheriff would be directed to take him into custody to await "gaol delivery" at the next meeting of the General Court. If the suspect fled, the hue and cry was raised, the suspect was declared an outlaw, and his goods were forfeited to the Crown.[104] The origins of these practices date to thirteenth-century England.

Once in custody, the defendant would be brought before a magistrate and questioned; witnesses would be called and sworn. At this point, as in England, the judges (of the General Court or the county courts) could acquit the defendant if they were satisfied with his answers; if not, the prisoner would be held until he could be formally indicted by a grand jury of twenty-four "of the most capable persons" taken from the list of freeholders in the county.[105] Defendants were allowed to have counsel even at the indictment stage, but it was rare for this right to be exercised. Professional attorneys were in short supply, and their fees had to be paid by the defendant, who was seldom wealthy.

After the 1640s, if the case proceeded to trial, the defendant had a right to a jury.[106] Jurors were to be chosen from the "most able men" available, in the judgment of the local sheriff, whose duty it was to summon them—the same procedure used in England, and ultimately a source of complaints about secret jury manipulation.[107] The laws governing jury selection did not originally include a property

---

wherein the crime shall have been committed, which district shall have been previously ascertained by law" (emphasis added). Article III, by contrast, requires only that the trial be held "in the State where the said Crimes shall have been committed." The addition of the phrase "and district" barred the practice of holding all trials at a central location chosen by the government, such as in the capital city.

103. Ibid., 52. This is an intriguing difference between the political life of the colonies and the political life of England, where only the Crown collected fines owed by miscreants. In England the incentive to report crimes was to avoid a fine for not reporting crimes.

104. Hugh F. Rankin, "Criminal Trial Proceedings in the General Court of Colonial Virginia," *Virginia Magazine of History and Biography* 72, 1 (January 1964): 50–52.

105. Ibid., 54–56.

106. Ibid., 60.

107. Those who failed to respond could be fined 400 pounds of tobacco or its cash equivalent. Shortages in the venire were made up by impaneling those bystanders at the court who were also "good and lawful freeholders" (ibid., 91). Under the Constitution, federal jurors were to be summoned by officers of the federal court, and suspicions of jury rigging almost immediately attached to the practice, as a consequence of the Sedition Act trials in 1798–1799 (discussed in chapter 2).

qualification, but stricter requirements were demanded by the Virginia Company in London. In 1699 the Assembly passed a law setting a £100 freehold requirement for jury service in General Court trials and a £50 freehold requirement in the county courts.[108] These requirements excluded a substantial portion of the free white male population of the colony. Perhaps to compensate for the limited (and gentrified) jury pool, defendants had a right of challenge that was nearly identical to modern rules: any number of potential jurors could be challenged for cause, and up to twenty could be challenged peremptorily. "Cause" was generously defined to include not only the traditional categories (relation by blood or marriage, or known partiality) but also social standing: a prospective juror could be challenged for cause on the grounds that he did not possess an estate of sufficient value. The limit of twenty peremptory challenges, however, was *rigidly* enforced, and any defendant who demanded more than the maximum would immediately be declared guilty and sentenced to be hanged.[109]

Vacant spots on the jury were filled from among the bystanders at the court, so excessive challenges would effectively deprive a defendant of his right to a jury of his neighbors, once the vicinage requirement had been established. For some defendants, this was no doubt the result they sought, which may be the reason for the draconian limit on peremptory challenges. The contemporary records make it clear that colonial Virginians were aware that excessive use of challenges could be used strategically to "pack" a jury. The so-called Parson's cause, in which Patrick Henry made a name for himself as a trial attorney, was tried before a jury widely regarded by contemporaries to have been packed.[110]

At the lowest level of the judicial system, the justices of the peace in the county courts disposed of all petty criminal matters, often without a jury, through "summary" procedures very similar to the ones then prevailing in England. Contempt of court was also dealt with summarily. This practice was formally authorized by a 1728 act of the Assembly that exempted from jury trials those cases in the county courts in which the penalty was less than £5.[111] For more serious but noncapital crimes, defendants were entitled to jury trials, but they often waived that right in favor of either pleading guilty or choosing a bench trial.

That this marginalization of the jury right caused no discernible protest is a matter of some wonder. Virginians frequently referred to the jury as the "Englishman's birthright," and an eighteenth-century legal manual was typical in its praise of the jury as "that happy way of Trial which . . . hath continued beyond all memory to this present Day."[112] But in colonial Virginia, juries were not a constant

108. Ibid., 89.

109. Ibid.

110. Scott, *Criminal Law in Colonial Virginia*, 91.

111. Ibid., 50.

112. Richard Starke, *The Office and Authority of a Justice of the Peace, Explained*

presence in the enforcement of the criminal law and in the administration of the courts. Summary judgment and bench trials made the justice of the peace, not the jury, the central element in the law enforcement process at the local level. Magistrates, however, were often assisted by grand juries, which made their first appearance in Virginia in 1641; by a 1645 act of the Assembly, grand juries were to be impaneled twice a year in the counties to collect information about all noncapital offenses, and this practice continued throughout the colonial period—although the law was apparently not consistently obeyed.[113]

New York

The earliest laws governing the colony of New Amsterdam–New York were a mixture of Dutch and English legal practices, combined with measures meant to solidify the control of a series of proprietors. Occasional demands for greater participation in the colony's government were met with resistance. The consequence of this history was political uncertainty, conflict between Dutch and English settlers, and a largely unsuccessful effort to establish self-government. Once English rule was solidified, English legal practices became the norm, but this did not lead to the establishment of anything resembling a representative government.

It did not help matters that after 1665 (save for a brief restoration of Dutch rule in the 1670s), the colony's proprietor was the Duke of York (soon to become James II), from whom the colony took its English name. The body of regulations written for the government of his new possession became known as the Duke's Laws, and they were the de facto constitution of the colony until the ascension of William and Mary in 1689 brought another series of changes. Although these laws contained provisions for calling and impaneling jurors—as well as details about how much they would be paid, how many there must be (no more than seven and no fewer than six), and how they would be housed if trials lasted longer than a day—they did not stipulate when or even if juries were required, despite mandating unanimous verdicts in capital cases.[114] This silence encouraged the assumption that the duke intended for New York to adopt the familiar practices of "home," a notion buttressed by language stating that whatever was done in New

---

and Digested under Proper Titles (Williamsburg, 1774), cited by Scott, *Criminal Law in Colonial Virginia*, 86.

113. Scott, *Criminal Law in Colonial Virginia*, 66–68.

114. "LAWES. Established by the Authority of His Majesties Letters Patents . . . ," under "Jurors and Juryes," nycourts.gov/history/legal-history-new-york/documents/charters-duke-transcript.pdf (accessed January 3, 2014). See also Julius Goebel Jr. and T. Raymond Naughton, *Law Enforcement in Colonial New York: A Study in Criminal Procedure: 1664–1776* (New York: Commonwealth Fund, 1944).

York "shall be not contrary to the laws and statutes of this our Realm of England but as near as may be agreeable thereunto."[115]

Since English criminal practice by the seventeenth century had come to mean summary procedure by justices of the peace, the use of juries in criminal cases had become rare and was confined, for the most part, to capital offenses. English court records of the time show, for example, that the ratio of trials to presentments at the assizes was very low, and this pattern was repeated in New York. As in England, "the court did not trouble to impanel a jury but upon examination of 'proofs upon oath' or 'testimoneys' permitted the defendant to make his defense and then proceeded to sentence." But the ambiguity of the jury provisions of the Duke's Laws became a source of complaint, so the laws were changed. The first change came rather quickly, in 1666: an amendment "to require a jury of twelve at Assizes," rejecting the heretical requirement for a jury of seven. However, this change seems to have been directed mostly at civil trials rather than criminal complaints. Trial practice was tightened up again in 1669, and defendants were given an opportunity to challenge jurors, clearly suggesting that juries were now expected to be utilized in at least some criminal cases.[116]

As in England, justices sat in and out of "sessions"—that is, together, at regular intervals at a central location; and singly, at irregular intervals in remote locales.[117] Justices of the peace were drawn from the small class of local notables who were untrained in the law but considered deserving of the proprietor's recognition, although technically, their commissions were held by royal favor (by the favor of the proprietor's brother, Charles II). The office of justice of the peace combined in one place powers that were judicial, legislative, and executive; in New York, as in England, the justices were the true "rulers of the county" (as Maitland called them), unfettered by any notion that powers should (or even could) be separated for liberty's sake.[118] The justices tried criminal offenders and presided over civil litigation, only occasionally with the assistance of juries. They also exercised broad responsibility for issuing and enforcing the extensive economic and social regulations typical of a seventeenth-century colony, such as the sale of essentials (flour, bread, and wine), the construction and upkeep of public roads and fences, and the licensing of peddlers and river pilots. They provided for public safety by regulating building materials and issuing fire codes, and they were responsible for quelling public disturbances, riots, and unruly gatherings. They had broad authority for the colony's moral well-being as well, providing for

115. Goebel and Naughton, *Law Enforcement in Colonial New York*, 3.

116. Ibid., 3, 559, 560–561.

117. Martin L. Budd, "The Legal System of 1691," *Harvard Law Review* 80 (1967): 1752–1772, in *Courts and Law in Early New York: Selected Essays*, ed. Leo Hershkowitz and Milton M. Klein (Port Washington, NY: Kennikat Press, 1978), 12–13.

118. Goebel and Naughton, *Law Enforcement in Colonial New York*, 110.

the care of out-of-wedlock children and punishing drunkenness, profanity, and lewd behavior. (They could also investigate accusations of witchcraft, but unlike authorities in New England, those in New York apparently paid little attention to the "dark arts.") The justices maintained the jails and the poorhouses and supervised the overseers of the poor.[119] Above them were the higher courts—whose jurisdiction encompassed appeals, serious felonies and misdemeanors, and capital cases—and the (appointed) governor's office, serving as the court of last resort.

In 1683 the duke was persuaded to grant a modest degree of self-government: "such a form of Government . . . as shall have all the advantages and privileges . . . which his Majesty's other plantations in America . . . enjoy, particularly in the choosing of an Assembly."[120] These same instructions included the injunction that "no man's life, member, freehold, or goods be taken away or harmed . . . but by established and known laws not repugnant to but as nigh as may be agreeable to the laws of the kingdom of England."[121] Two years later, having ascended to the throne upon the death of his brother, James II rescinded his promise and sent Edmund Andros to be the new governor of the (now) royal province of New York.

New York responded by adopting a Charter of Liberties in 1683 (rejected by the king), which included the standard rights that were now on the tip of every English tongue, including the right to be tried by a jury of the vicinage. The charter stipulated that all trials should be decided by twelve men "as neer as may be peers or Equals" of the neighborhood, in the county "where the same should arise and grow." The Judicature Acts of 1691 and 1692, passed by the New York Assembly in the wake of the Glorious Revolution and the English Bill of Rights, protected the right to a jury trial and specifically protected the jury's right to determine the law as well as the facts.[122]

Yet in New York, as in Virginia, the proclamation of the jury right, even in the midst of the Glorious Revolution, did not lead to a sudden increase in jury trials. New Yorkers were far more concerned about establishing self-government, which at the time meant a representative assembly and courts responsive to the public rather than to the king. One reason for this otherwise odd reluctance to use juries is that, in the English mind, trial by jury was so linked with protection against persecution by the Crown that the familiar face of the local magistrate, operating so far from London and beyond the effective reach of royal authority, did not inspire the same kind of dread. As a result, New York law continued to ignore juries for a wide range of petty misdemeanors that were under the control

119. Budd, "Legal System of 1691," 12–13; Goebel and Naughton, *Law Enforcement in Colonial New York*, 108–110.

120. Goebel and Naughton, *Law Enforcement in Colonial New York*, 7, n. 21.

121. Ibid.

122. William E. Nelson, "The Law Finding Power of Colonial American Juries," *Ohio State Law Journal* 71, 5 (2010): 1015.

of the local magistrates. "There was no question," according to one history of the period, "of raising constitutional issues and no talk of the liberty of Englishmen, because the trial of these causes, being committed to local authorities, involved no collision with the agencies of prerogative and presented no threat of a kind which caused political uneasiness to the groups sharing in the government of the Province."[123]

New Yorkers actually added to the summary jurisdiction of local magistrates from time to time, most notably in 1732, when the Assembly exempted from the right to a jury trial all offenses less serious than grand larceny. In response, the Crown's own attorney general was put in the odd position of having to warn the colonists not to trample on "that Grand Bulwark of our Freedom & Safety, the tryal by Jury," by giving magistrates the power to "punish the subject criminally without the judgment of their peers and thereby throw down that barrier against the arbitrary power of the Crown which it is the peculiar happiness of our constitution to have established."[124]

The role of the jury in criminal proceedings, then, was confined to the most serious crimes: grand larceny, rape, homicide in its various gradations, and sedition. But even in such serious cases, a jury was not a foregone conclusion. Defendants could simply confess, of course, and hope for mercy, or they could waive the jury and submit to a bench trial. They often did so (as they do in modern times). The records of the quarter sessions for New York City for the years 1691 to 1776 contain 248 confessions, 17 judgments entered for want of a plea, and only 94 cases (or 26 percent) in which defendants pleaded not guilty and went to trial. There is nothing in the record to suggest how many of those trials involved juries or how the cases were decided.

There were clear incentives for defendants to opt for the strategy of submitting, confessing, or choosing a bench trial. Remorseful confessions were often rewarded with lighter sentences. Another incentive was to avoid the expense of a long jury trial, since defendants were charged for their own room and board while incarcerated, and sometimes for the expenses of the jurors if they had to be brought from a distant place. (It was to avoid this difficulty, while preserving the jury of the vicinage, that circuit courts were created.[125]) Assizes and Supreme Court proceedings were held in New York and Albany, so even if defendants were out on bail, they would still have to bear the expense of a lengthy out-of-town stay if they chose a jury trial over a quick decision by a single judge. And if a defendant wished to avail himself of the services of an attorney, he would have to bear the cost; there was no such thing as a public defender, even in the higher courts, and even when defendants were prosecuted by the Crown's attorney general. (The

123. Goebel and Naughton, *Law Enforcement in Colonial New York*, 382–383.
124. Ibid., 607.
125. Ibid., 604.

use of lawyers in criminal cases was quite rare, even in the eighteenth century, in part because attorneys were quite rare.[126])

But the greatest incentive for avoiding jury trials in ordinary criminal cases was probably the patrician makeup of the jury pool and the lack of sympathy for miscreants. Under the Duke's Laws, the first jurors called were the overseers of the town where the case originated—akin to town selectmen. Since cases had usually been examined by the town before being preferred at sessions, the jury would include many who had already reached a conclusion on the merits of the case.[127] After reforms to the judicial system in 1683, jurors were chosen from the full complement of propertied citizens, but the jury pool still contained only the most successful and prosperous citizens. As in England, freeholding was the basic requirement for jury service, with higher standards for grand jurors than for petit jurors. In 1699 New York enacted a statutory minimum for petit jury service of a house with ten acres freehold in the country or a house in town (Albany or New York City) combined with a personal estate of £50 (raised to £60 in 1741).[128] This standard established the gentry as the dominant jury class—prosperous farmers in the country, and artisans and professionals in town.[129] This jury pool represented only a small portion of the white male population of the colony. In Westchester County, the List of Freeholders for 1763 contains only 801 names out of a total white male population (aged sixteen years and older) of 3,947—an eligibility rate of only 20 percent of the class entitled, in theory, to the full rights and privileges of citizenship.[130]

But as conditions in the colony became more settled, New Yorkers began to demand more formal and explicit guarantees of due process. First came the expansion of the jury pool, in 1683, beyond the overseers of the towns. In the years following, procedures were tightened and made more formal. Under Thomas Dongan's governorship (1683–1688), efforts were made to bring trial procedures more in line with the common-law procedures in England:

> If a charge was brought to the stage of indictment, the magistrates no longer followed the former method upon presentment of examining the evidence until the prisoner saw fit to confess or they were satisfied to convict or discharge. Now the defendant was arraigned, the indictment was read and he was required to plead. If the defendant elected to put himself on the country,

126. "Between 1691 and 1778 only four of the eleven Chief Justices of New York had any degree of legal training." Anton-Herman Chroust, "The Legal Profession in Colonial America," *Notre Dame Lawyer* 34, 1 (1957–1958): 58.

127. Goebel and Naughton, *Law Enforcement in Colonial New York*, 567–568.

128. Ibid., 467. Compare this to the £100 requirement enacted the same year in Virginia.

129. Ibid., 567.

130. Ibid., 467.

the formal joinder of issue took place, the petit jury was summoned and the trial then proceeded.[131]

Similarly, the charter adopted by the Assembly in 1691 (ultimately rejected by the Crown) included demands for specific procedural safeguards: grand jury presentment in all capital and criminal cases, petit juries for the trial of indictments, regular procedures for bail, and the defendant's right to challenge jurors. These were not, of course, "new rights" but the familiar common-law protections known to all English subjects. These rights were becoming more important to New Yorkers not because of fear of Crown prosecutions but because of more local concerns. New York, like Virginia, was the scene of considerable political conflict surrounding the governor's office. Such conflict raised the specter of politically motivated prosecutions and heightened people's awareness of the importance of the old common-law guarantees. Another cause, suggested by one study of the criminal law in colonial New York, was the conflict between rich and poor that influenced the treatment of criminals. New York's criminal code, though not nearly as harsh as England's, was harsh enough to suggest the importance of "softening" the rule of law by reaffirming the promise of a jury trial whenever a defendant risked "life or member."[132]

Procedural safeguards also included the right to challenge jurors on the grounds that they were not "indifferent." It is not clear what limit the law placed on the challenging of jurors or whether the practice was as liberal in New York as it was in Virginia. But the use of "struck" juries in special cases suggests that the problem of finding unbiased jurors was understood at a very early date. In this procedure, first used in civil cases, both plaintiff and defendant were given a chance to "strike," or remove, names from a list of jurors until a total of twenty-four remained, from which twelve were chosen at random. In criminal trials, when a juror was challenged for bias, the jurors already chosen were responsible for deciding whether the challenged juror was capable of being an "indifferent man."[133]

One aspect of English practice that drew increasing support from New Yorkers was the use of the grand jury. Colonial practice regarding presentment, information, and indictment varied considerably and was often more informal than the letter of the law suggests. Although there was a provision for grand jury indictments, there is no record of a grand jury meeting in New York before 1681; it seems to have been the practice throughout the colony to prosecute many crimes based on complaints made directly to the constables or magistrates, without passing through a grand jury first. Forms of accusation displayed no clear pattern and

131. Ibid., 571.
132. Ibid., 326–327.
133. Ibid., 618–619.

were not carefully prescribed by statute. The justices of the peace, who lacked formal (or even informal) legal training, would not have been in a position to insist on proper forms, in any case. "Informations" and "complaints" were often referred to in the records as "indictments," even when there is no evidence of grand jury involvement.[134] Gradually, however, the grand jury became the common method of initiating prosecution in capital and other serious felonies, although the use of presentment by officials did not disappear entirely. For lesser crimes, however, "complaints would [continue] to be brought by sheriffs, constables, and other minor officials."[135]

Once it was established, the grand jury became something more than a vehicle for bringing indictments prepared in advance by prosecutors. Grand juries (whose members were chosen from the most prosperous freeholders) often insisted on conducting their own investigations and maintaining maximum control over prosecutions.[136] But the grand jurors were not content to influence only the criminal law. As in other colonies, New York's grand juries frequently investigated such matters as the conduct of public officials or the state of public services and institutions, and they came to act as the "voice of the county" in areas far beyond the criminal statutes—often trespassing on the legislative and executive functions of the justices of the peace. Eventually, New York's justices succeeded in confining the grand jury to the single role of presentment, a more limited role than the grand jury played in Virginia, Massachusetts, and other colonies. But the grand jury's willingness to go beyond the issuing of criminal indictments suggests that colonial subjects were already beginning to accept the expansion of juries into the political space left vacant by the Crown's separation from its North American subjects.

The significance of this expansion would become clear in the decades immediately preceding the American Revolution, when New York juries (like their counterparts in Massachusetts) began to reject Crown prosecutions for violation of the Navigation Acts and other tools of British "oppression." As already noted, one famous form of oppression blocked by the jury was prosecution for seditious libel to shut down criticism of the government. The trial of John Peter Zenger in 1735 demonstrated how important the jury's "law-finding" power was, in a case involving citizens' right to criticize their own government. Now the colony that had once been so willing to expand the summary jurisdiction of local magistrates discovered anew the importance of jury trials to the liberty of English subjects—just as the Crown's prosecutor himself had once been forced to remind them.

Such cases also produced an early version of the science of "jury manage-

134. Ibid., 329–332. This informality was consistent with the practice in English courts at the time.

135. Ibid., 336–337.

136. Ibid., 356.

ment," since Crown prosecutors had to take special care in the way they presented evidence and prepared witnesses to appear before skeptical jurors. One official recorded a now familiar complaint: "Lengthening a cause by a multiplicity of evidence not necessary, puts those things necessary out of the remembrance of the jury, and brings things into darkness and obscurity."[137]

In colonial New York, the age of the modern jury had dawned.

Massachusetts

It was in Massachusetts, and in New England more generally, that devotion to the English jury system was most intense. As already noted, every New England colony except for New Haven adopted jury trials for civil cases and capital crimes as part of a broader commitment to the common law. In fact, the Massachusetts Bay Company imported almost the entire English legal system, including sheriffs, constables, justices of the peace, magistrates, the hue and cry, and the full panoply of common-law forms and pleadings. In part, this is what the company was required to do by the terms of the charter it received from Charles I in 1629. That charter explicitly authorized the company to establish a government in New England ("one Body corporate and politique"), declaring the governor, deputy governor, and their assistants to be "a full and sufficient Court or Assemblie . . . for the handling, ordering, and despatching of all such Buysinesses and Occurents as shall from tyme to tyme happen." The charter put them on notice, however, that nothing they did in their new home was to be "contrairie to the Lawes of this our Realme of England."[138]

The governor and the Court of Assistants were named in the charter, but their replacements were to be chosen "from tyme to tyme" by the freemen of the company, with whom the governor and the assistants were instructed to "consult and advise of the Businesses and Affaires of said Company."[139] There were no particular stipulations about what the laws should be (there is, for example, no mention of juries), beyond the general admonition that they not be contrary to existing English practices. But even without this requirement, it is doubtful that the settlers would have acted otherwise, for what is most striking in the old records is the extraordinary formality of the Puritan leaders and their determination to avoid, as much as possible, innovations in the familiar English legal order—even while they were making radical changes in religious practice and ultimately, though sometimes unwillingly, in political arrangements.

137. *Memoir of the Life of William Livingston*, cited by ibid., 631–632.

138. The Charter of Massachusetts Bay (1629), http://www.avalon.law.yale.edu/17th_century/mass03.asp (accessed January 10, 2014).

139. Ibid.

The Court of Assistants met for the first time on August 23, 1630, just three months after the first ships of the Winthrop Fleet had reached New England. The colony had not yet grown beyond the 700 or so who had arrived with the first convoy in June (another 1,000 would join them in the coming months, as more ships straggled into the harbor), and they were undoubtedly busy constructing permanent homes in anticipation of winter, storing provisions, looking for new sources of fresh water, and bartering for food with the local tribes.[140] Despite the presence of so much urgent business, the court—the governor, deputy governor, and seven assistants—convened and solemnly declared that they would be "justices of the peace for the present time, in all things to have like power the Justices of peace hath in England for reformation of abuses and punishing of offenders." They then turned their attention to other urgent business: arranging for the construction of homes for members of the clergy and for the maintenance of clergy households.[141]

At its second meeting, which took place in early September, the court turned to more conventional business, dealing with commercial and administrative matters, setting wages for various trades, and establishing the prices to be charged for essential materials, such as cut lumber. It also acted as the public prosecutor, ordering the arrest of "renegade" Englishman Thomas Morton, who had been running a very un-Puritan encampment down in Quincy, and it dealt with a case of fraudulent trading in cloth, ordering the offender, Mr. Clearke, to pay costs and a fine. By its third meeting, held on September 28, the court had a suspicious death to deal with: Mr. Austen Bratcher had been found beaten at "Mr. Cradocks planation"—the first such case in the official records. Following English practice from medieval times, the assistants impaneled a coroner's jury to inquire into the matter, and this jury returned a verdict that "the strokes given by Walter Palmer were . . . the means of the death of Austen Bratcher and so to be manslaughter." At its November meeting the court impaneled a petit jury, which heard the case against Mr. Palmer and found him not guilty of manslaughter, "so the Court acquits him." The other order of business at this November meeting concerned the troublesome Mr. Clearke, who was "prohibited cohabitation & frequent keeping company with Mrs. Freeman, under paine of such punishment as the Court shall think meet to inflict."[142]

This combination of responsibilities—mixing the purely judicial with the political, the administrative, and even the moral—would not survive the passing of the emergency conditions that prevailed at the colony's inception. By 1634, the

140. On the size of the first convoy to Massachusetts, see Fischer, *Albion's Seed*, 13–17. This was the beginning of a migration that would eventually bring about 20,000 people to the Massachusetts Bay Colony in roughly a decade.

141. *Records of the Court of Assistants of the Colony of the Massachusetts Bay, 1630–1692*, vol. 2 (Boston: County of Suffolk, 1904), 1–3.

142. Ibid., 4, 7, 8.

freemen in the colony who were not assistants, and whose social status barred them from holding the high office of magistrate or justice of the peace, objected to decision making by such a small committee, however eminent its members. They prevailed upon the Court of Assistants to fulfill the promise of the charter (whose contents Governor Winthrop had apparently kept from them for as long as he could) by establishing that the members of the General Court would be chosen by all the colony's freemen, who would select two deputies from each town. Among other things, this arrangement ensured that the "popular" part of the Massachusetts government dramatically outnumbered the "assistants," who in 1642 were formally separated into the upper house of what was now a bicameral legislature. (These events also signaled the arrival of a vigorous spirit of township independence that would shape New England for generations to come.) All laws were now to be voted on by the General Court in joint session. The Body of Liberties, adopted by the General Court the previous year, codified the language in the charter, stipulating that the governor, deputy governor, and assistants would "be from tyme to tyme constituted, elected and chosen out of the Freemen of the saide Company." "From tyme to tyme" was defined as yearly.[143]

This form of bicameralism could be considered a feature of English government, in which the (relatively) popular House of Commons shared lawmaking authority with the House of Lords. But under the circumstances prevailing in New England, this was in fact a very different arrangement. First of all, the House of Commons was far less "common" than the town meetings in places such as Newtowne (Cambridge), Watertown, Medford, Charlestown, and Boston, where the free male citizens—yeoman farmers, artisans, and shopkeepers—elected the deputies to the General Court. Nor were the members of the Court of Assistants titled nobility, despite their greater wealth and social prominence. (Although the assistants were wealthy, only one, Sir Richard Saltonstall, bore a title: Lord of the Manor of Ledsham, in Yorkshire.) Furthermore, despite the Puritan respect for learned elders, New England towns displayed a spirit of independence that often verged on the cantankerous, insisting on the recognition of their rights and prerogatives as firmly as any lord. Note, for example, how quickly the townsmen pushed Governor Winthrop to reveal the charter and agree to its terms.[144] This spirit would pull the government of the colony in a more popular direction, ultimately leading to the fateful confrontation with an increasingly unpopular English colonial administration a century and a half later. Juries would play an important role in this drama.

143. The Charter of Massachusetts Bay (1629).

144. Winthrop's annoyance at being pushed undoubtedly had something to do with his near impeachment in 1645, an experience he reflects on in his famous "Little Speech on Liberty." See Scott J. Hammond, Kevin R. Hardwick, and Howard L. Lubert, eds., *Classics of American Political and Constitutional Thought*, vol. 1 (Indianapolis: Hackett, 2007), 18–19.

In the early years, before the growing population required a more complex system of quarter courts (later called county courts), most of the serious criminal cases and civil cases involving large sums were heard by the Court of Assistants, which also heard appeals of cases from the lower courts. (Even small judgments were sometimes appealed.) The Court of Assistants almost always referred matters to a jury, even cases on appeal, and some of these appeals were against jury verdicts in the lower courts. For example, in October 1692 plaintiff John Sands brought an action against Captain Edward Hutchinson, appealing a jury verdict in favor of Hutchinson in the county court. "The reasons of Appeale and evidences in the Case produced were read Comitted to the Jury [and] . . . the Jury brought in their verdict they found for the plaintiff Reversion of the former Judgment and forty-two shillings damage & costs of courts."[145] Juries in the Court of Assistants handled many such civil cases (Puritans were notably litigious, and they became increasingly so as conditions became more settled), but they also handled more serious cases as well: murder, piracy, rape, and witchcraft (in the early years). In cases involving Indians, mixed juries were impaneled. In April 1674 the trial of "Tom Indian" for the rape of "Sarah the wife of John Jempson an Indian" was held before "a jury of twelve men six English & six Indians against none of which he Objected." The defendant was found guilty and sentenced to death.[146]

But the juries did not act as rubber stamps, as the case of Mr. Palmer, cited above, suggests; they did not automatically convict those brought to trial by the authorities. In May 1675 an action was brought against one Mary Parsons for "several acts of witchcraft," and "putting hirself on hir trial, the Jury brought in their verdict they found hir not Guilty—& so she was discharged."[147] One "Jack Negro," a household slave accused of "Beastiality with a Cow," was tried by a jury and acquitted.[148]

In fact, there were enough instances of disagreement between juries and assistants, and in later years between juries and judges in the quarter courts, that the question of what to do in such cases led to a major political controversy. Jury-magistrate conflicts had always been referred to the General Court, but by the 1660s, the propriety of allowing the legislature to overturn jury verdicts had come into question. A proposal was made to end this practice, and the governor formed a committee of clergymen to mediate the issue. Their recommendation empowered the jury: judges would be directed to accept jury verdicts, even when they disagreed with them, unless the verdicts were "evidently contrary to law and evidence," in which case an "attaint jury" of twenty-four freemen would be

145. *Records of the Court of Assistants of the Colony of the Massachusetts Bay, 1630–1692*, vol. 1, ed. John F. Cronin (Boston: County of Suffolk, 1901), 16.

146. Ibid., 22.

147. Ibid., 32.

148. Ibid., 74.

formed to consider anew the original jury's verdict. The General Court enacted this proposal in 1672. Perhaps as the clergy suspected, the attaint juries nearly always sided with the petit juries, and from this time on, it became a matter of constitutional principle that jury verdicts (in criminal cases) were final. But according to legal historian William E. Nelson, on the whole, "juries acted with self-restraint and cooperated with judges." Massachusetts Bay was, after all, a fairly close-knit community, and its governing class was not rigidly separated from the "hinterland," as was often the case in colonies like Virginia. It was not until the era of the Navigation Acts and similar British policies that this cooperation came (temporarily) to an end.[149]

From the beginning, juries in New England were more commonly used in civil cases than in criminal cases, unless the case was a capital one. And at various times, civil cases were eligible for jury trial only if they involved large sums (more than forty shillings), but this restriction gradually disappeared. The Plymouth Colony, as already noted, protected jury trials very broadly in its first laws: "all criminal facts, and also all [matters] of trespass and debts between man and man should [be tried] by the verdict of twelve honest men."[150] But by 1636, Plymouth had changed the law so that criminal juries were guaranteed only in capital cases. Apparently, many of Plymouth's leading citizens shared New Haven's enthusiasm for judgment by magistrates, but they were unable to carry the day completely or for long. By 1661, juries were once again available for misdemeanors (defined as crimes involving fines of less than £10), which, along with civil cases, made up the majority of the colony's judicial business.[151]

Even when defendants were entitled to jury trials, however, they sometimes surrendered that right, both in civil cases and in noncapital criminal trials. In Massachusetts, surrendering that right was itself a right specified in the Body of Liberties, written largely by Puritan minister Nathaniel Ward and ratified by the Great and General Court in 1641. Liberty No. 29 states that in civil cases, both plaintiff and defendant may, by mutual consent, choose a trial by bench or by jury, "unless it be where the law upon just reason hath otherwise determined. The like libertie shall be granted to all persons in criminal cases."[152] It is not clear from the documentary records why the choice of bench or jury trial was considered a right, but it is probably safe to assume that most defendants could expect to be convicted as readily by a jury of their peers as by a magistrate. In the small-town context in which these trials took place, it would have been difficult for anyone to hide his actions from the neighbors, and a magistrate might be more lenient than twelve local "saints."

149. Nelson, "Law Finding Power of Colonial American Juries," 1006.

150. Murrin, "Magistrates, Sinners, and a Precarious Liberty," 157.

151. Ibid., 159.

152. The Liberties of the Massachusets Collonie in New England (1641), http://history.hanover.edu/texts/masslib.html (accessed January 7, 2014).

For most of the seventeenth century, the judicial system of the Massachusetts Bay Colony continued to operate within the framework established in the 1630s. The local magistrates in the towns made up the broad base of the judicial and administrative pyramid. A law dating back to 1638 gave these magistrates general jurisdiction to "hear and determine," without a jury, all civil cases involving debt or damage under twenty shillings (raised to forty shillings in 1648). The criminal jurisdiction of the magistrates was limited to specified small offenses, which apparently made up in frequency what they lacked in gravity: disorderly conduct (drunkenness being the most common), social impropriety (such as "abusing" ministers of the gospel, profane swearing, absence from church, lewd conduct, and "railing" and "scolding"—offenses similar to slander), uncooperative behavior (refusing the assignment of "watch and ward" or failing to come to the assistance of the constables), and minor cases of assault.[153] On the same level as the magistrates were the "commissioners for ending small causes"—the ancestor of the small-claims court—who heard civil cases in towns without regular magistrates.

The quarter courts (later called county courts)—the middle tier of the system—handled slightly larger civil cases (involving amounts less than £10) and noncapital criminal cases; criminal cases were almost always heard by judges sitting alone. The Court of Assistants—the upper house of the legislature—was the venue for the most serious cases; it had original jurisdiction over capital cases, criminal cases involving loss of limb or banishment, civil cases involving large sums, and all cases of divorce. As already noted, most of these cases were committed to juries.[154]

Finally, each town had limited judicial powers exercised through its selectmen, who received the magistrates' oaths and prepared the lists of eligible jurors.[155] The magistrate thus took his place alongside the town meeting and the selectmen as the judicial branch of the local government. However, unlike the selectmen, the magistrate was ultimately responsible to the county courts rather than the local freemen. Still, the vicinage's attitude toward the criminal justice system was normally one of the magistrate's chief concerns.

In addition to their strictly judicial functions, the quarter courts and the local magistrates had important political and administrative responsibilities. Together,

153. Joseph H. Smith, ed., *Colonial Justice in Western Massachusetts (1639–1702): The Pynchon Court Record* (Cambridge, MA: Harvard University Press, 1961), 70–73. In 1640 twenty shillings would have purchased roughly three bushels of wheat in Massachusetts. See Estelle May Stewart and Jessie Chester Bowen, *History of Wages in the United States from Colonial Times to 1928* (Washington, DC: Bureau of Labor Statistics, 1934), table 1, 19.

154. Smith, *Colonial Justice*, 68.

155. Ibid., 65–66.

they saw to the construction and upkeep of roads, bridges, and jails, as well as the licensing of taverns and inns. The magistrates also shared important political and administrative duties with the town meeting and selectmen: keeping accurate records of births and deaths; maintaining the commons, highways, and other public amenities; licensing "ordinaries" (inns); regulating weights and measures (and sometimes wages); caring for the poor; keeping track of Indians, Frenchmen, and Quakers, all of whom lived in the colony only with town permission; supporting the clergy and maintaining church property; suppressing heresy; and ensuring military preparedness (magistrates could levy fines on town officials for failing to keep adequate stores of arms and ammunition, for example).[156] Throughout the seventeenth and eighteenth centuries, county courts and magistrates often fulfilled these administrative and political duties with the assistance of juries, both grand and petit. Thus, the jury was involved in the smallest as well as the greatest matters of the colony's governance, on both the judicial and the administrative sides.

The tone of these early court proceedings, and some sense of the true significance of the jury in early Massachusetts, can be gathered from the contemporary records. In addition to the records of the Court of Assistants cited earlier, a few more examples suggest how the court, working alone and in partnership with the jury, shaped the political, commercial, and moral world of colonial Massachusetts.

As already noted, the third meeting of the Court of Assistants dealt with a suspicious death, which the court evidently believed to be a case of manslaughter, although the jury refused to convict. The records also include many indictments for murder. For example, in July 1637, John Williams "being indicted about the death of John Hobbe confessed that he killed the said Hobbe, so the Jury found him guilty of murder." The records do not indicate the sentence, but murder was a hanging offense (one of many). A year later, "Dorothy the wife of John Talbie being by her own confession guilty of the unnatural and untimely death of her daughter Difficult Talbie was by the Jury found guilty, & so was condemned to be hanged."[157] Note that in each of these cases, despite the defendant's confession in open court, the verdict was pronounced by the "Jury of Life and Death" (the name given to a jury convened for capital cases). This was generally the case in murder convictions. Clearly, the intention was for the community's voice to be heard when the most terrible punishment was imposed.[158]

The Court of Assistants, being responsible for commercial regulations, was eager to prevent commercial fraud and false advertising. Therefore, it punished Nicholas Knopp for "taking upon him to cure the scurvy by a water of no worth

156. Ibid., 72–86.

157. *Records of the Court of Assistants*, 2:69, 78.

158. John Murrin summarizes the contemporary view as follows: "because death is final, the larger community ought to be involved in any judicial decision that terminated a life." Murrin, "Magistrates, Sinners, and a Precarious Liberty," 189.

nor value"; he was ordered to pay a fine to the colony and repay his customers, or be whipped.[159] The court was also responsible (as were authorities in the towns) for enforcing the observance of the Sabbath; accordingly, there are many cases like this one: "John Baker shall be whipped for shooting at fowl on the Sabbath day." Likewise, there are many efforts to enforce sobriety, such as fining George Frost ten shillings "for beeing distempered with wine."[160] The enforcement of sexual morals was a more serious matter. Adultery, fornication, bestiality, and "lying with mankind in the manner of a woman" were all capital crimes, set out as such in the Body of Liberties in 1641. Two examples are typical. In 1637 "John Bickerstaffe was censured to be severely whipped for committing fornication with Ales Burwood," who in turn was censured and sentenced to whipping "for yielding to Bickerstaff without crying out, & concealing it 9 or 10 days." In 1638 John Davies was sentenced to be "severely whipped . . . & to wear the letter V" on his clothing for "gross offenses in attempting lewdness with diverse women."[161]

Citizens were frequently punished for failure to perform their civic duties, such as showing up for jury service or taking their turn at the night watch. But it was also common for towns themselves to be fined for neglecting their collective duties: the town of Weymouth was assessed a fine for "defect in their highways," the town of Concord "for want of a pair of stocks," and the town of Cambridge "for want of a watch house, pound, & stocks."[162]

Another useful collection of colonial judicial records comes from the county court in Springfield. This collection, known as the Pynchon Court Record, is a set of diaries kept by the magistrates of the local court in Springfield between the years 1639 and 1702, and it takes its name from the first magistrate of the Springfield court, William Pynchon.[163] Springfield, situated on the Connecticut River about thirty miles north of Hartford, was originally part of Connecticut, but it broke away in 1641 after political disagreements between the leaders of the two communities. The Springfield court was created by a vote of the local citizens, until such time as the General Court, sitting in Boston, could direct otherwise; the legislature eventually chose to confirm what the local citizens had set up. It also confirmed the town's choice of William Pynchon as its commissioner, a post clearly modeled after the justice of the peace in England.[164] Yet because of the way the court was created and its first magistrate was chosen, the commissioner was a far more democratic office than the English justice of the peace.

William Pynchon was born in England in 1590 and was one of the found-

159. *Records of the Court of Assistants,* 2:67.
160. Ibid., 1:66, 2:81.
161. Ibid., 2:79, 81.
162. Ibid., 79, 80.
163. See Smith, *Colonial Justice.*
164. Ibid., 31.

ers of Springfield, named after the English town from which Pynchon hailed. Pynchon was a gentleman on the fringes of the landed gentry, a man of learning (though he lacked legal training) and a devout Puritan. It was this latter characteristic that drove him back to England in 1651, after he published a theological tract that the colony's leaders judged to be heretical. He was replaced as magistrate by Elizur Holyoke; John Pynchon, William's son, was appointed in 1652, along with Samuel Chapin. Holyoke, Pynchon, and Chapin kept the court records until 1702.[165]

The Pynchon Court Record reveals a mix of petty crimes and civil disputes typical of an agricultural community in any age, with some characteristic seventeenth-century New England flourishes thrown in, such as a civil action for slander resulting from a witchcraft rumor. It also records various bits of municipal business: the names of citizens who had qualified to take the freeman's oath, votes for town offices, decisions about financial business, announcements of marriage intentions, publication of wills. The most common cases heard by juries in the Springfield court were ordinary civil suits involving small sums—unlike the rest of Massachusetts Bay, where most small claims were handled by magistrates without juries. Despite the small stakes, the civil juries took their responsibilities very seriously. An entry for February 8, 1644, begins with the simple announcement that "Thomas Mericke complaines against Robert Ashly in an action of Revew about a pigg." The jury of six is then named (six was a common jury size in the seventeenth century, apparently because of the shortage of citizens qualified for jury duty). But determining the ownership of the pig was no simple matter, for the record notes that "the Jury haveinge bin held most . . . till nere midnight desyred liberty not to bring in this verdict" until the next day, a request that was granted. The next day the jury returned a verdict for the defendant and assessed court costs against the plaintiff.[166]

On March 2, 1654, the diary records a complaint by the widow Margaret Bliss against Thomas Mirack, charging that Mirack had ignored a financial settlement reached between them as a result of arbitration (the dispute involved the setting of a hedge). The record lists the members of the jury (George Colton, Rowland Thomas, Miles Morgan, Griffith Jones, Robert Ashley, and Anthony Dorchester), which found for the plaintiff and ordered Mirack to pay a fine of over £4.[167]

At the same session, Anthony Dorchester (named as a juror in the Bliss-Mirack case) and Jonathan Taylor were "presented for not wardinge on the Lecture day being February 9th 1653 (1654)." Taylor pleaded the excuse of illness and was freed. "And Anthony Dorchester acknowledginge his offence and with all his pleas beinge considered was judged to pay 2s 6d: which the Constable is to Levy for the use of the watch or ward." (Failure to perform his watch and ward

165. Ibid., 32–64.
166. Ibid., 214.
167. Ibid., 230.

duties apparently did not exclude Mr. Dorchester from jury duty.)[168] Dorchester was not finished yet, for he was next charged by the Widow Bliss with letting his pigs damage her Indian corn. Since Dorchester chose to contest this charge, a new jury had to be named: the above-mentioned Ashley, Thomas, Jones, and Morgan, joined by Benjamin Cooley and Thomas Cooper. Dorchester's fellow jurors may have had some sympathy for his plight (or perhaps they were getting tired of the litigious Widow Bliss), as they found for the defendant and charged the court costs to the widow.[169] This practice of "rotating" jurors in and out of cases during the same session of the court was a common one.

Paternity cases were a frequent source of civil complaints. On January 24, 1655, the diary records a charge against Samuel Wright Jr. by Mary Burt for fathering her illegitimate child. "The said Samuel desired to be tried by a Jury of 12 men." If he hoped for leniency from his fellow male citizens, he was sorely disappointed, for the jury found him guilty "of committinge wickedness with Mary Burt in havinge the use of her body 3 severall tymes, whereby wee fynd him to be the father of the said child." He was ordered to be whipped with twelve stripes "well layd on" and to pay child support for a period of seven years. Mary Burt was also sentenced to be whipped with twelve lashes well laid on (postponed because of her pregnancy) and to the care of her child.[170]

The entry for April 9, 1655, lists a defamation complaint brought by John Stiles of Windsor "against John Bennet . . . for defaminge his wife, in saying shee was a light woman and that he could have a leape on her when he pleased." Ruling without a jury, the magistrate found for the plaintiff and ordered Bennet to be whipped and fined forty shillings.[171] Massachusetts treated defamation and slander as criminal matters, following the English view that slander tended to breach the peace. But since the fines did not exceed the forty-shilling limit, magistrates could hear these cases without juries. This was true even of the most serious kinds of slander—those involving witchcraft accusations. Slander and defamation cases occupied a considerable portion of the court's time.

Another minor criminal complaint handled by the local magistrates was the offense of "abusing authority." On November 30, 1659, John Matthews was "presented for refusinge to obey a summons sent from Authority and Served on him before witness by Francis Hacklinton in August last and for his contemptuous and high carriage towards him that was sent with the Summons: commanding him off his ground and holding up his sickle at him and usinge other high words and unfitting carriage." The uncooperative Mr. Matthews was fined five shillings by the magistrate.[172]

168. Ibid.
169. Ibid.
170. Ibid., 230–231.
171. Ibid., 236.
172. Ibid., 243.

The final type of case handled locally was "misbehavior," which included disturbing the peace, drunk and disorderly conduct, and general mischief. On July 31, 1690, John Crowfoote and John Buck, detribalized Indians who were living in town, were brought before the magistrate "for being last Wednesday Night the 30th of July past In Drink, If not Drunk and that at a very unseasonable time being 10 a clock at Night If not past as the Testymonys speake: I Doe Sentence each of them forthwith to pay 5s a piece."[173] Crowfoote and Buck appear more than once in the record.

Because the great majority of the cases listed in the Pynchon Court Record were decided by magistrates without help from jurors, it is difficult to determine the precise role played by juries in the local legal system. However, when jury verdicts did occur, they were no different from the verdicts rendered by magistrates in similar cases. Magistrates and jurors were partners, rather than opponents, in a social order that required respectable citizens to help administer justice. The freeman's oath made this expectation explicit: it required newly admitted freemen to swear in public "by the great and dreadfull Name of the Ever-living God" to be "true and faithful" to the Commonwealth and to "yield assistance thereunto, with my person and estate . . . and . . . truly endeavor to maintain and preserve all the Liberties & Priviledges thereof, submitting myself unto the Laws made and established by the same."[174]

Thus, while the rhetoric surrounding the ancient right of Englishmen to jury trials emphasized the protection of the subject's liberty, the actual practice of juries in Springfield and in Boston was more complicated. The jurors helped govern their fellow citizens; the jury was, in effect, part of the sovereign power, not the final barrier between the subject and the Crown. Tocqueville, observing this history from the vantage point of 1830, argues that "the man who punishes the *criminal* is really the master of society."[175] In fact, the worst offenders against the public peace might have preferred judgment by a distant monarch: drunken revels, after all, would mean far less to the king than to the neighbors across the road.

Nelson has framed the "jury question" this way: "We care about jury power because it serves as a proxy for a more important issue—the issue of how much power local communities enjoy to live by their own law rather than the law of some central authority."[176] This was clearly the issue in England under the Angevin kings, but with respect to colonial America, this formulation is true but imprecise. There are times—New England in the seventeenth century and most of the eighteenth as well—when the jury is *part* of the "central authority," or at

173. Ibid., 323–324.

174. Ibid., 218. Even as early as 1648, the freeman's oath made no mention of the king.

175. Tocqueville, *Democracy in America*, 260.

176. Nelson, "Law Finding Power of Colonial American Juries," 1028.

least the authority that matters, the one responsible for a particular criminal prosecution or the resolution of a civil dispute. The defendant being tried, turning his gaze from the sober and upright judge to the equally sober and upright citizens impaneled to judge him, might be forgiven for not noticing much of a difference.

In the towns and villages where the freemen ruled, citizens high and low struggled against the steady hand of social authority and their own unruly desires, and the freemen tried to bring miscreants to "due submission" to authority, with sometimes disappointing results. The drunken rowdies Crowfoote and Buck might stand for hundreds of reprobates throughout the colony who failed to live up to Puritan standards and who gloried in their failure to repent. Such chronic offenders against the public peace got little sympathy from the magistrates, but they probably would have gotten no more sympathy from their neighbors.

When juries were called on, the jurors were expected to be disinterested—that is, not partial—without being uninformed or uninvolved. Their value as expert witnesses was precisely their intimate knowledge of the plaintiff and the defendant—though not necessarily of the details of the dispute itself. In any case, it is difficult to see how, in small communities like those of colonial New England, disinterested panels could be found for so many civil and criminal cases, if by "disinterested" we mean "uninformed." (The same names show up continually in the records, sometimes as jurors, sometimes as plaintiffs or defendants in civil suits, sometimes, as in the case of Mr. Dorchester, serving in both capacities on the same day.) A suggestive example from the Pynchon Court Record is George Moxon's January 2, 1640, complaint against John Woodcoke for slander, alleging that Woodcoke had taken a "false oath against him at Hartford and demand[ing] of John Woodcoke for the said slander 9£ 19s." The jury that was hearing cases during this session of the court included three men called by Moxon as witnesses—a lack of indifference that drew no comment from the bench or even from the defendant Woodcoke. Perhaps predictably, the jury ruled in Moxon's favor (although it awarded him only £6 13s).[177]

Although there were many variations on this model, the simple pattern of summary justice under the supervision of judge-magistrates was common enough to justify a generalization: *the jury was less important to the legal system than it was to the political system as a whole*. Before the Stamp Act troubles, colonists did not see jury trials through the prism of conflict with the Crown, as a way to protect subjects from royal tyranny. In their view, the jury was just another element of local government that was ultimately responsible to higher authorities. But even those authorities—the Court of Assistants and the General Court—were relatively immune from royal meddling. If a citizen needed to be protected from an unjust conviction, he probably needed to be protected from the *town* rather than from the king.

177. Smith, *Colonial Justice*, 205.

The colonial jury therefore anchored the most important decisions—life-and-death criminal matters as well as minor civil cases—in the community, not in officialdom. Even when juries were not impaneled and magistrates administered summary judgment, the magistrates still needed to be attentive to local sentiments. Magistrates were not elected, of course; nor were the county judges from whom the magistrates held their commissions. But working in such close proximity to town meetings and town selectmen—relying on the latter, for example, to provide jury lists—magistrates were almost certainly seen as *local* officials rather than agents of the colony's leaders, and still less as agents of the Crown. Although the colonists would soon praise the English jury for protecting the king's enemies from prosecution for seditious libel, such matters were as far from the ordinary life of the colonies as the king himself, at least before the 1760s. In the years leading up to the Revolution, to be sure, Americans began to see the jury as English subjects saw it—as the palladium of their liberties. This was especially the case when prosecutions for seditious libel multiplied and the Crown tried to circumvent juries to enforce the Navigation Acts and the Stamp Act. Then, at last, there *was* a central power, distant and unfriendly to the liberties of the colonists, against which the jury could act as a shield. But until that time, the jury had a different, though no less political, role to play in the life of the American colonies.

If juries played a relatively small role in criminal trials, why were they important at all? First, they were essential elements of the most *serious* criminal trials, those that might end in the loss of "life or member or banishment."[178] The use of juries in capital cases ensured that the community's sense of justice would be invoked before the most awful sentences were imposed—and, as in England, jurors could use their verdicts to circumvent the death penalty. Juries effectively abolished the death penalty for adultery in Massachusetts, to cite one example.[179] Juries were also essential to civil cases, which increased in number and complexity as the colonial economy developed and as the colonists became even more litigious than they had been in the beginning. And in Massachusetts, as in other colonies, juries filled the place occupied in later generations by councils, committees, and executives, performing many of the administrative duties of local government. Massachusetts juries supervised the construction of roads, buildings, and other public works, and they determined "just compensation" for private property taken for public improvements; they inquired into the expenditure of public money; they "remonstrated" with public officials thought to be derelict in their duty; and they collected information for the use of magistrates. As in the case of summary justice, the practice of using juries to perform some of the duties of

178. It is telling that the law in colonial Massachusetts treated banishment from the colony as nearly the equivalent of a death sentence or the loss of a hand or foot.

179. After 1644, "no Massachusetts jury would convict for adultery." See Murrin, "Magistrates, Sinners, and a Precarious Liberty," 192.

local government makes sense in the context of small-town and rural life, where a small population must spread the burdens of governance as broadly as possible. A seventeenth-century jury would be, in this sense, not unlike the governing body of any modern association with a small membership, whose leading members share the various burdens of running the association.

To be chosen for such a role requires, quite naturally, a certain standing in the community. A credible jury requires credible jurors: from the earliest days of settlement, jury service was restricted to freemen—that is, those who had qualified for and taken the freeman's oath—but not just any freeman, automatically.[180] Towns were authorized to choose for the venire those citizens judged most fit for office. This process began with the magistrate sending a warrant to the town constable, directing him to notify the freemen of the town (i.e., the town meeting) to choose as many "able and discreet" men as would be needed for jury duty. Those chosen were subject to a fine if they did not appear. In the early days, when the town meeting and the magistrate's court took place simultaneously, jurors would probably be chosen from among the bystanders, without the use of a warrant.[181]

Upon appearing in court, the jurors were sworn, which took the following form in the seventeenth century: "You Swear by the Living God, that in the Cause or Causes now legally to be committed to you by this Court; You will true Tryal make, and just Verdict give therein, according to the Evidence given you, and the Laws of this Jurisdiction: so help you God, etc."[182] Either the plaintiff or the defendant could challenge a juror; it was the challenger's choice whether to leave the decision regarding the challenge to the bench or to the rest of the jury. If the challenge were upheld—that is, if the challenged juror were judged incapable of being indifferent—a substitute was found from among the bystanders.

The law specified that the jury's charge in civil cases was to "find the matter of fact with the damages and the costs," as the evidence directed. The judge's role was then to declare the judgment or to direct the jury to "find according to law"—but there is no case of a directed verdict in the Pynchon Court Record. There are several, however, in the Court of Assistants records. Because its cases were more serious, they may have sparked more judge-jury disagreement. Nor is there any evidence in the Pynchon Court Record of the jury exercising its right, under the colony's laws, to seek advice in open court on any matter of law that troubled the jurors, and there is no case in which the judge and jury openly disagreed about a verdict. Drawing jurors from the homogeneous body of freemen, and making them full partners with the magistrate, helped ensure that verdicts were based on a common sense of what justice required.

All this began to change when the British government reasserted its authority over its North American colonies, a process that began after the Restoration and

180. Smith, *Colonial Justice*, 205.
181. Ibid., 180–181.

gathered force after the Glorious Revolution. By then, however, magistrates, jurors, assemblies, and town meetings had been working together in New England for four generations, without serious conflict. It was only then—after the government of the original charter had been replaced by governors and judges appointed by the Crown and often sent directly from England—that disputes between judges and juries became more frequent and more serious. This conflict revived an old question that had greatly agitated England but had been mostly mooted in the colonies' formative decades: do juries have the right to judge the law?

2
The Republican Jury

It seems . . . anomalous, at first view, that men coming from the ordinary pursuits of life, and with no previous training, should be called upon to decide questions of law. But reflection relieves, if it does not remove the difficulty. In the first place, it is conceded that the jury must take the law and apply it to the facts. To do this intelligently and justly, they must, to some extent, understand it.

—J. Thomas, dissent in *Commonwealth v. Philip Anthes* (1855)

The jury is before everything a political institution; one ought to consider it as a mode of the sovereignty of the people, or place it in relation to the other laws that establish this sovereignty. The jury forms the part of the nation charged with assuring the execution of the laws, as the houses [of the legislature] are the part of the nation charged with making the laws.

—Alexis de Tocqueville, *Democracy in America*

THE HERITAGE OF THE COMMON-LAW JURY

By the time His Majesty's North American subjects had begun to imagine themselves citizens of an independent nation, the common-law jury had been firmly planted for generations and was as familiar as the English language itself. The right to an impartial jury of the vicinage was one of the most important "rights of Englishmen" that Americans believed were no longer safe under an English government.

It is difficult to overstate the support for the jury system, both criminal and civil, among eighteenth-century Americans. Along with the principle of representation in the legislature, juries were understood to be an essential part of any free government.[1] As the conflict with Great Britain became more serious, Americans

1. See Jack N. Rakove, *Original Meaning: Politics and Ideas in the Making of the Constitution* (New York: Vintage Books, 1997), 290–295; Robert P. Burns, *The Death of*

focused on one element of the jury's history in particular: English juries' dramatic resistance to Crown prosecutions for seditious libel. The most famous cases from the time of the Stuarts—Bushell, the Seven Bishops—were legendary in America, and to this list had been added a case closer to home: the unsuccessful prosecution for seditious libel of New York printer John Peter Zenger. In all these cases, and others like them, citizens who had published or written claims about the government that greatly displeased the king and his official family had been acquitted of sedition by juries, even though the facts of publication were undisputed.

Because the jury had acquitted Zenger with a general verdict of not guilty, his case seemed to illustrate, like the English cases from the previous generation, that the jury system was a powerful obstacle to tyranny. Here was an institution in which ordinary citizens could stand against judges, prosecutors, and even the monarch himself, refusing to convict a subject either unfairly charged or charged with behavior (criticizing officials, for example) that jurors believed should not be considered a crime among free men. The jury could perform this service because of its right to bring in a "general verdict," conflating judgment on the evidence and judgment on the law into one complex result, the separate parts of which could not be isolated for inspection.

The jury's role was strengthened by the frequency with which juries were used in civil trials. As in the seventeenth century, noncapital criminal cases were more often decided by magistrates than by juries in the eighteenth century—if, that is, the defendant did not simply plead guilty. But civil cases involving even modest sums often went to juries. A typical example comes from the records of the Superior Court of the Province of Massachusetts Bay: *Baker v. Frobisher*, decided during the August term of 1762. The plaintiff, Frobisher, charged the defendant, Baker, with selling "unmerchantable soap." Citing authorities, the court ruled that "every man is bound to see his goods are merchantable at the time of sale," but because there was evidence that "the plaintiff's wife, who was the contractor, saw a sample of the soap," the court directed the jury to find for the defendant. And so the jury found.[2] In another action from the same term involving a dispute between a tenant and a landlord over an unpaid debt, the court directed the jury to award court costs to the landlord, "which they did," despite a disagreement among the judges over how the case should be settled.[3] But juries were not

the American Trial (Chicago: University of Chicago Press, 2009), 40–42. Burns notes that "it was a matter of national identity that American trials were fairer and more democratic than were their English forebears" (40–41).

2. Baker v. Frobisher, August Term 2 Geo. 3 (1765), in *Reports of Cases Argued and Adjudged in the Superior Court of Judicature of the Province of Massachusetts Bay, between 1761 and 1772*, ed. Josiah Quincy Jr. (Boston: Little, Brown, 1865), 4.

3. Jackson v. Foye, August Term 2 Geo. 3 (1765), ibid., 26.

always so obliging, and their right to return a verdict "contrary to the mind of the court" became the subject of a growing debate.

The everyday experiences of juries, combined with a growing revolutionary spirit, encouraged Americans to embrace a proposition about the common-law jury that would preoccupy jurists for much of the coming century and has never entirely disappeared from the debate: the idea that juries have a right, inseparable from the jury system itself, to reach an independent judgment about the law, even if that judgment is contrary to the explicit instructions of the court. As we saw in the previous chapter, juries did this under the Angevins when they refused to treat manslaughter or killing in self-defense as hanging offenses. A version of this claim appears in the modern idea of jury nullification. But in colonial and republican America, as in thirteenth-century England, juries were not understood to have "nullified" a law but rather to have "interpreted," "applied," or "judged" it.[4] And this idea drew continued inspiration in the colonies from conflicts with British authorities over the enforcement of the Navigation and Revenue Acts.

It was in the context of this conflict that John Adams expressed a view about the "jury right" that few Americans would have doubted: if a judge's view of the law violates a fundamental political principle, then "it is not only . . . [the juror's] right, but his duty, in that case, to find the verdict according to his own best understanding, judgment, and conscience, though in direct opposition to the direction of the court."[5] By the late eighteenth century, the right to find a "verdict according to conscience" had achieved the status of conventional wisdom.[6]

4. A search of several digital archives turned up no use of the phrase "jury nullification" and no use of the word "nullification" or "nullify" in the context of jury trials until 1911, when it was used in its contemporary sense to describe a jury's refusal to enforce an unpopular law. "A flagrant example of the 'lawlessness' of jurors in Illinois and of the impotency of judges under such a system to prevent outright nullification of the law was recently afforded in Chicago where thirteen different juries in the face of incontrovertible evidence refused to convict saloon keepers for violating the Sunday closing law, thus presenting an example of a complete breakdown in the machinery of law enforcement." See J. W. G., "Juries as Judges of the Law," *Journal of the American Institute of Criminal Law and Criminology* 2, 2 (July 1911): 183–185. Even when "nullification" was a word in common use—such as during the controversies over the Virginia and Kentucky Resolutions against the Sedition Act, or in the later campaigns against the tariff and the Fugitive Slave Act—the word was not used in the context of jury decisions. States might "nullify" a federal law, or at least threaten to do so, but juries "found" or "judged" the law. The contemporary jury nullification debate is discussed in chapter 5. I am grateful to Nina Bogdanovsky, senior digital reference librarian at Boston College, for her help in conducting this search.

5. John Adams, *Diaries of John Adams*, entry for February 12, 1771, Adams Family Papers, Massachusetts Historical Society, Boston.

6. "Comment: The Changing Role of the Jury in the Nineteenth Century," *Yale Law Journal* 74 (1964): 170.

This right was not absolute, however. It required the juror to be loyal to the "fundamental principles" of the law or the constitution in the face of a judicial ruling that seemed to violate those principles: only in such extreme cases would a jury be justified in ignoring a judge's instructions on the law. Juries could do this because it is precisely these fundamental principles that ordinary citizens understand best. Technical questions, of lesser importance than principles, might be left to those who had studied the endless complexities of common-law pleadings. The jury was to judge only the important things, and its power was to be exercised as a last resort. This, too, Adams stated very forcefully, in the same diary entry quoted above: "The general Rules of Law and common Regulations of Society, under which ordinary Transactions arrange themselves, are well enough known to ordinary Jurors. The great Principles of the Constitution, are intimately known, they are sensibly felt by every Briton—it is scarcely extravagant to say, they are drawn in and imbibed with the Nurses Milk and first Air."[7]

This view, it should be stressed, was also held by judges—even by Tory judges. Judge Robert Auchmuty, a Loyalist during the Revolution, noted in a 1763 case (in which a superior court jury had returned a verdict "contrary to the mind of the Court"): "I confess I wish for a power in the court to set aside verdicts, but not for an unlimited one. . . . The Court is not to be judge of the law and fact too absolutely; if it should be, it takes away all verdicts but such as are agreeable to the mind of the Court. It would be opening a door to great inconveniences to the subject."[8]

Jurors may have been encouraged to engage in such assertiveness by three facts about the legal order in colonial and early republican America: (1) many judges were not lawyers, (2) the supply of trained attorneys varied from state to state but was not large anywhere, and (3) some courts continued the English practice of sitting with multiple judges. (The Superior Court of Judicature in Boston used four, and sometimes five, judges in the 1760s.) That lawyers were relatively scarce on either side of the bench is generally acknowledged, although, given the uneven preservation of records, caution is necessary when making this assumption. According to Roscoe Pound, writing in 1938, most high court justices in the colonies were nonlawyers in the century prior to independence, and this circumstance changed only gradually.[9] A study of law enforcement in the colony

7. Adams, *Diaries*, February 12, 1771. The "constitution" referenced here is, of course, the British Constitution. How much truer Adams's statement would have been about the American Constitution or the Massachusetts Constitution. This is certainly how Adams would have seen it, and indeed, this is how the founding generation understood matters: a constitution written by a special assembly elected for that purpose would bring home to every citizen the principles of the law.

8. Quincy, *Reports of Cases Argued and Adjudged in Superior Court*, 83–85.

9. Roscoe Pound, *The Formative Era in American Law* (Boston: Little, Brown, 1938),

of New York concluded that "judges in colonial New York were, on the whole, an ignorant lot, ill-suited to hold office." Of 328 justices of the peace in the province in 1763 (outside of New York City), 194 "had no legal training or knowledge at all."[10] A study of the Massachusetts courts in the decades prior to the Revolution paints a slightly different picture. While there were only fifteen practicing lawyers in the colony in 1740, that number had risen to seventy-one by 1775.[11] The record of the Superior Court of Judicature of the Province of Massachusetts Bay lists the lawyers who were authorized to appear at various terms, and these lists were sometimes long. For example, the court called twenty-six individuals to be "barristers at law" for its August term in 1762 (among them John Adams and Robert Treat Paine).[12] Meanwhile, the number of judges in Massachusetts with formal legal training (all at Harvard College) grew dramatically after the middle of the eighteenth century. From 1642 to 1745, there were nineteen judges on the Massachusetts Superior Court, and only nine of them had formal legal training (other professions included minister, "gentleman," physician, merchant, soldier, and tavern keeper). Between 1745 and 1775, however, only one of the fourteen judges on the Superior Court lacked legal training.[13]

This evidence suggests that the early American legal system existed for a century and a half as a partnership among literate citizens whose knowledge of the law was based on familiar common-law principles relevant to ordinary questions posed by the circumstances of colonial life. What duties does a physician owe to his patients? What is a trespass? What is a common-law right-of-way? What does "breach of promise" mean? What rights does a creditor have against a defaulting debtor? How should estates be handled if there is no written will?

But it was also a central theme of the republican enthusiasm of the age that citizens can and should know the law and defend the fundamental principles underlying it. As James Wilson said, "every citizen, in a government such as ours, should endeavor to acquire a reasonable knowledge of its principles and rules, for the direction of his conduct, when he is called to obey, when he is called to

---

cited in "Comment: Changing Role of the Jury," 171, n. 6. Pound found that of ten chief justices and twenty-three associate justices of the colonial courts between 1692 and 1776, only one chief justice and two associates were lawyers.

10. See Douglas Greenberg, "The Effectiveness of Law Enforcement in Eighteenth-Century New York," *American Journal of Legal History* 19, 3 (1975): 184.

11. Daniel H. Flaherty, "Criminal Practice in Provincial Massachusetts," in *Law in Colonial Massachusetts, 1630–1800*, ed. Daniel R. Coquillette (Boston: Colonial Society of Massachusetts, 1984), 193.

12. Quincy, *Reports of Cases Argued and Adjudged in Superior Court*, 35.

13. Charles R. McKirdy, "Massachusetts Lawyers on the Eve of the American Revolution: The State of the Profession," in Coquillette, *Law in Colonial Massachusetts*, 329–332.

answer, and when he is called to judge."[14] Jurors were partners of the court as well as members of the sovereign people. Juries in the republican era, Robert P. Burns concludes, "were understood to have the ultimate authority on the normative as well as the factual side, to be 'judges of the law.'"[15] They were not the passive recipients of judicial instruction, even if the judge's knowledge of the law was acknowledged to be superior to their own. In the matter of law, jurors were not rustic simpletons but gifted amateurs.

This was the view in colonial America, and it continued to be the view in republican America. It was proclaimed by judges, orators, editors, and jurors themselves, and it was a view that united Republicans and Federalists. Chief Justice John Jay, in *Georgia v. Brailsford*[16]—one of only four Supreme Court cases tried with a jury—sent the case to the jurors after four days of testimony, making the following observation:

> It may not be amiss, here, Gentlemen, to remind you of the good old rule that on questions of fact, it is the province of the jury; on questions of law it is the province of the court to decide. But it must be observed that by the same law which recognizes this reasonable distribution of jurisdiction, you have nevertheless a right to take upon yourselves to judge of both, and to determine the law as well as the fact in controversy. On this and on every other occasion, however, we have no doubt you will pay that respect which is due to the opinion of the court: for, as on the one hand, it is presumed, that juries are the best judges of facts, it is, on the other hand, presumable that the court is the best judge of law. But still both objects are lawfully, within your power of decision.[17]

As Wilson argued, when law and fact are "inseparably blended" in a general verdict, then "the jury must do their duty, and their whole duty; they must decide the law as well as the fact." Nonetheless, he concluded, the jurors "must determine [legal] questions, as judges must determine them, according to law."[18]

14. James Wilson, *Lectures on Law* [1791], vol. 2, pt. 2, chap. 6 ("Of Juries"), http://oll.libertyfund.org/?option=com_staticxt&staticfile=show.php%3Ftitle=2074&chapter=166640&layout=html&Itemid=27 (accessed January 24, 2014).

15. Burns, *Death of the American Trial*, 140, n. 28.

16. Georgia v. Brailsford, 3 U.S. 1 (1794). Because it was a suit "between a State, or the Citizens thereof, and foreign States, Citizens, or Subjects" (US Constitution, Article III, section 2), this action came under the original jurisdiction of the Supreme Court. The Eleventh Amendment, removing such cases from the Court's jurisdiction, would not be ratified until the following year.

17. Ibid.

18. Cited by David Pepper, "Nullifying History: Modern-Day Misuse of the Right to Decide the Law," *Case Western Reserve Law Review* 50 (Spring 2000): 617.

In courts with multiple judges, jurors could hardly avoid judging the law, since the judges themselves might disagree in their charges to the jury.[19] This had been true in England as well. The Case of the Seven Bishops had been heard by four judges, each of whom gave a slightly different answer to the central question in the case: did the law define the bishops' petition as seditious? At a minimum, it would have been necessary for jurors to prefer one judge's "law" to another's.

In light of this long experience, the British decision in 1767 to extend the jurisdiction of the admiralty courts, beginning in Massachusetts, came as a shock. An even greater shock was the threat to try some offenders in England. The admiralty courts had always heard civil cases without juries, and this was a noncontroversial practice. Most of these cases involved maritime and insurance claims, and they were heard without juries because of the general view that these issues were too technical and specialized for ordinary citizens; they were especially foreign to the farmers and shopkeepers who made up the typical eighteenth-century colonial jury. The most interested parties—the insurers and the shippers—were generally satisfied with the performance of the admiralty courts, so trying such cases without juries was not seen as a threat to the "rights of Englishmen."

Using the admiralty courts for criminal prosecutions under the Revenue Acts was a different matter. British authorities had been slow to adopt this tactic—perhaps sensing how much antagonism it would generate—and they did so only after repeated attempts to prosecute colonists for smuggling had come to naught before colonial juries. Massachusetts governor William Shirley claimed as early as the 1750s that "trial by jury here [in Boston] is only trying one illicit trader by his fellows, or at least by his well-wishers." One of his successors, Governor Francis Bernard, complained in 1761 that "a Custom house officer has no chance with a jury" in Massachusetts.[20]

These practices brought colonists, legislatures, and officials into conflict with British authorities in North America and in England. The conflict was especially intense in Massachusetts, where many of the issues that would ultimately drive the American Revolution were first argued before grand juries. This was partly a consequence of the fact that Governor Thomas Hutchinson, appointed by the Crown in 1769, presided over sessions of the Superior Court, where customs violators had been tried prior to the decision to transfer such cases to the admiralty courts. Among his other duties, the governor, as chief justice, periodically addressed the grand jury about its responsibilities, the importance of law to a civilized society, and its duty to take instructions in the law from judges. In his charge to the grand jury during the March 1767 term, for example, the chief justice noted that there "has been a failure of law amongst us" recently "which has been very detrimental.

19. "Comment: Changing Role of the Jury," 174, n. 27.

20. Albert W. Alschuler and Andrew G. Deiss, "A Brief History of the Criminal Jury in the United States," *University of Chicago Law Review* 61 (1994): 867.

Doubts and differences in opinion have been, which has caused a great deal of confusion. . . . I wish for the laws to be put in due execution for the public good, and am as much for the liberties of the people, as any man, so far as is consistent with the welfare of the community."[21]

But during the August term of the same year, Hutchinson was forced to return to this theme. His comments had produced a public outcry, and he was being portrayed (unfairly, in his view) as an enemy of liberty. This injustice inspired him to reflect publicly on the subject of seditious libel: "Pretty high notions of the liberty of the press, I am sensible, have prevailed of late among us; but it is very dangerous to meddle with, and strike at this Court. . . . To carry this absurd notion of the liberty of the press to the length some would have it—to print every thing that is libelous and slanderous—is truly astonishing, and of the most dangerous tendency."[22] (To "strike at this Court" meant to libel it.) Newspapers, Hutchinson conceded, could not be forbidden in advance to publish a particular charge, but they could be held responsible for the consequences after publication. He then warned Boston that seditious libel cases did not have to proceed like other criminal matters, from a grand jury indictment to a trial before a petit jury: "This Court may proceed in a far more summary manner, to bring the offender to justice—This Court will ever take proper care to secure their honor by keeping up their authority."[23] In other words, because juries would acquit editors tried for seditious libel in the law courts (just as they acquitted those who violated the Navigation Acts), the colony will not try them before juries, even if that policy offends the British Constitution.

A more direct challenge to the traditional understanding of the jury could not be imagined. To preserve the honor and authority of officials, juries would have to be avoided. The jury had once again become, as it had been under the Stuarts, the palladium of the subjects' liberty and one of the essential prizes in the war for independence.

THE JURY IN THE STATES

In 1776, contemplating the possibility of dissolving the connection to Great Britain, delegates to the Continental Congress adopted a resolution urging the colonies to write new constitutions, clarifying the governing arrangements that would be in force in the event of independence. By 1778, ten of the thirteen colonies had done so. Massachusetts (whose first effort had been rejected by the voters) adopted a new constitution on its second try, in 1780. Only Rhode Island and Connecticut failed to comply.

21. Quincy, *Reports of Cases Argued and Adjudged in Superior Court*, 234.
22. Ibid., 244–245.
23. Ibid., 246.

Of the eleven newly adopted constitutions, only three (Delaware, New Hampshire, and South Carolina) failed to include a specific protection for jury trials. Delaware did so indirectly, however, with its reference to "the common law of England, as well as so much of the statute law as has been heretofore adopted in practice in this State, [remaining] in force."[24] New Hampshire's new constitution was a very brief framework of government offices established to secure "peace and good order" during the "unhappy" conflict with the "parent State"—almost as if its authors expected that the conflict would be resolved quickly and life would return to normal. South Carolina's new constitution, although it did not guarantee jury trials, assumed their existence, since Article XVIII gave the courts the responsibility to "cause jury-lists to be made, and juries to be summoned."[25]

Most of the new constitutions included specific guarantees of jury trials in criminal cases, although some made more general guarantees. Georgia guaranteed jury trials in "all causes, of what nature soever." Maryland declared that the inhabitants are entitled to "the trial by jury according to the course of that law . . . as existed at the time of their first emigration."[26] Only Georgia specifically protected juries' right to "be judges of law, as well as of fact," and it also forbade special verdicts. But "if all or any of the jury have any doubts concerning points of law, they shall apply to the bench, who shall each of them in rotation give their opinions."[27]

So widespread was this view of the jury that many conventions may have thought it unnecessary to debate or even provide special provisions for juries in their new constitutions. In his notes to the *Reports of Cases Argued in the Superior Court of Judicature of the Province of Massachusetts Bay*, Samuel L. Quincy, writing in 1865, states that in "the Colony of Massachusetts, the right of the jury to determine the laws was never denied in criminal cases," and it was "alternately recognized and disallowed" in civil cases. There was, he added, only one American judge "between the Revolution and the year 1800, who is known to have denied the right of the jury to decide the law in a criminal case"—a Court of Common Pleas judge in Pennsylvania, who was "afterward impeached" and removed from office.[28] Most of the new constitutions referenced "the common law of England" as the template for judicial proceedings or in their explanations

24. Constitution of Delaware, 1776, http://www.constitution.org/cons/early_state_cons.htm (accessed January 22, 2014).

25. Constitution of South Carolina, 1778, Article XVIII, http://www.constitution.org/cons/early_state_cons.htm (accessed January 22, 2014).

26. Constitution of Georgia, 1777, Article XL; Constitution of Maryland, 1776, Article III, http://www.constitution.org/cons/early_state_cons.htm (accessed January 22, 2014).

27. Constitution of Georgia, 1777, Article XLI. In Georgia, as in England (and many of the colonies), trials were often conducted before panels of judges.

28. Quincy, *Report of Cases Argued and Adjudged in Superior Court*, appendix II, 558, 569.

of rights more generally, and this reference was widely understood to mean the common-law jury with its usual features: judgment by twelve good men and true from the vicinage, who could judge the law as well as the facts, and whose decisions would have to be unanimous, at least in criminal trials.[29]

Ironically, considering the controversies that followed, only six of the new state constitutions specifically protected the right to a jury trial in civil cases: Georgia, Massachusetts, North Carolina, Pennsylvania, Virginia, and Maryland.

THE CONSTITUTIONAL DEBATE ON THE JURY SYSTEM

Given the enthusiasm for jury trials, protection of the criminal jury in the proposed federal Constitution of 1787 was to be expected. But the failure to provide a similar protection for civil juries, and the alleged failure to provide adequately for criminal juries, was seen by many as an ominous sign that the new Constitution would not adequately protect the rights of American citizens. This became one of the most effective arguments of the Anti-Federalists.

The failure to even mention civil juries was especially alarming. Colonial records make it clear that Americans were a notably litigious bunch, even when they were still His Majesty's subjects, and there is no reason to think that independence had made them less so.[30] Civil litigation was a common method of resolving commercial disputes, protecting property rights, collecting debts, and defending reputations. And while the right to pursue private justice in the courts was not as old as the Magna Carta or as sacred as the criminal jury, the use of juries in civil cases was a common practice of long standing in the colonies.

Although the British effort to evade jury trials in revenue cases had figured in the "long train of abuses" cited in the Declaration of Independence, the silence of

29. In fact, the right to live under English common law was one of the earliest demands of the Continental Congress: "That the respective colonies are entitled to the common law of England, and more especially to the great and inestimable privilege of being tried by their peers of the vicinage, according to the course of that law." Resolution No. 5, *Declarations and Resolves of the First Continental Congress*, October 14, 1774, http://www.avalon.law.yale.edu/18th_century/resolves.asp (accessed April 30, 2014).

30. Reference has already been made to two collections of Massachusetts cases from the seventeenth and eighteenth centuries—the Pynchon Court Record and *Reports of Cases Argued and Adjudged in the Superior Court*. The Pynchon Court Record covers the years 1639–1702 and is 426 pages long; *Reports of Cases* covers the years 1761–1772 and is 606 pages long. In both records the vast majority of the cases are civil. Although some of them are unusual (defamation charges resulting from a witchcraft accusation, for example), most are the kinds of cases that any modern lawyer would recognize: disputes about wills, property transfers, torts (gardens trampled by cows), defective products (green wood sold for dry), trespasses, debts, and divorces.

both the Virginia Plan and the rival New Jersey Plan on the subject of juries drew no comment.[31] Jury trials were not mentioned at all until the draft constitution compiled by the Committee of Detail in August. Article XI, section 4, states simply: "The trial of all criminal offenses (except in cases of impeachment) shall be in the State where they shall be committed; and shall be by jury."[32] On August 28 this language was amended to provide for jury trials for crimes committed outside of any state, "at such place or places as the legislature may direct." This language became Article III, section 2, paragraph 3: the only provision in the original Constitution on the subject of the jury.

Very near the end of the convention, on September 12, Hugh Williamson of North Carolina noted the Constitution's failure to make "provision . . . for juries in civil cases and suggested the necessity of it."[33] Nathaniel Gorham of Massachusetts replied with an objection that produced little comment at the time but raised an important difficulty: "It is not possible to discriminate equity cases from those in which juries are proper."[34] Gorham suggested that, for this reason, the legislature should be allowed to make such distinctions, rather than placing possibly inappropriate instructions into the Constitution itself. But Elbridge Gerry of Massachusetts "urged the necessity of juries to guard against corrupt Judges"—reflecting the experience (especially in Boston) with British admiralty courts and with judges appointed by royal governors.[35]

Gorham's question about how to discriminate between jury cases and equity cases prompted a significant response from George Mason of Virginia, who "perceived the difficulty mentioned. . . . The jury cases cannot be specified. A general principle laid down on this and some other points would be sufficient. He wished the plan had been prefaced with a Bill of Rights. . . . It would give great quiet to the people."[36] This was the first mention of a bill of rights at the convention (according to Madison's notes), but Gerry's motion to appoint a committee to prepare such a bill was defeated unanimously. This decision may simply have reflected the delegates' exhaustion (it was mid-September); the prospect of opening a subject as complex as a bill of rights, so late in the game, must have been a

31. Hoffman notes, "There was surprisingly little discussion of the right to a jury trial in the records of the constitutional debates." Morris B. Hoffman, "The Case for Jury Sentencing," *Duke Law Journal* 51 (2002–2003): 968. Because the criminal jury was such a familiar part of the judicial order, it may not have occurred to anyone at the convention that it needed to be defended or even debated.

32. James Madison, *Notes of Debates in the Federal Constitution of 1787* (New York: W. W. Norton, 1987), 393.

33. Ibid., 630.

34. Ibid.

35. Ibid. Mason and Gerry were among the delegates who refused to sign the proposed Constitution, citing the lack of a guarantee of civil juries as one of their reasons.

36. Ibid.

discouraging one. Whatever the reason, the failure to include a bill of rights would become a major objection to the Constitution; that it should begin as a disagreement over civil juries is proof of the high regard Americans had for the jury in both its civil and criminal forms. This devotion would produce three of the first ten amendments to the Constitution.

THE JURY DEBATE IN THE RATIFYING CONVENTIONS

As in the pamphlet literature and the newspaper debates, deliberations in the state ratifying conventions often focused on the Philadelphia convention's failure to protect the civil jury. This omission seemed to be a deliberate downgrading of a customary right. There were many other complaints about the Constitution, however, and some of them were of greater moment than the failure to protect civil juries. Every state that proposed amendments, for example, included a prohibition against direct taxation by the federal government. Six states ratified the Constitution without proposing amendments of any kind, in part because (as in Maryland) there were so many amendments on the table that the delegates could not agree which ones to propose. Of the seven states that did propose amendments, however, six included protection of the civil jury, and three of these also included guarantees for the grand jury and the vicinage requirement for criminal trials.[37]

A frequent complaint was that the Constitution had "abolished" civil juries. And while Publius might describe this argument as "disingenuous,"[38] the opponents of the Constitution correctly discerned in the convention's "silence" on the matter a doubt about the wisdom of civil juries, or at least a notable lack of enthusiasm for their use in certain cases. At the Pennsylvania ratifying convention, James Wilson defended his colleagues' silence with two arguments. First, because the people choose the legislature, "the interest of government cannot be separate from that of the people." Therefore, the legislature can be entrusted with the task of making regulations "with respect to the mode of trial."[39] Second, because the

37. The ratification documents can be found at the Yale Law School's online Avalon Project: http://www.avalon.law.yale.edu/subject_menus/18th.asp (accessed January 25, 2014). See also Bernard Schwartz, *The Bill of Rights: A Documentary History* (New York: Chelsea House, 1971), vol. 2; Pauline Meier, *Ratification: The People Debate the Constitution: 1787–1788* (New York: Simon & Schuster, 2010); Akhil Reed Amar, *The Bill of Rights: Creation and Reconstruction* (New Haven, CT: Yale University Press, 1998).

38. Alexander Hamilton, John Jay, and James Madison, *The Federalist*, ed. Robert Scigliano (New York: Modern Library, 2000), 530.

39. Jonathan Elliot, *The Debates in the Several State Conventions on the Adoption of the Federal Constitution*, vol. 2 (New York: B. Franklin, 1968), 488. Wilson's argument might apply to any of the guarantees in the Constitution, an inference he almost certainly

states have different provisions for civil juries, "no particular mode of trial by jury could be found that would suit them all." To adopt one "general regulation" would be to impose unpopular innovations on states with different methods of summoning and qualifying jurors and different rules for distinguishing between equity and common-law jurisdictions, among other distinctions. In Wilson's view, it was better to let "time, reflection, and experience" generate "the proper regulations on this subject."[40]

The critics countered, why not simply guarantee that the civil jury would be protected, as the criminal jury was (despite some differences among the states), and then let Congress figure out the details? Or why not state that each federal court would be obliged to follow the civil procedures in the state where it was meeting, the solution eventually settled on by the Judiciary Act of 1789?[41] Despite their differences, the critics claimed, the states were not so different that some kind of general guarantee was impossible.

Wilson's first argument, however—that under a popular government there is no need for the elaborate protections appropriate under a king—points to the central fault line dividing politically active Americans of the time. Put simply, the question was this: had the achievement of popular government solved the political problem, or had it only changed its terms? In the flush of independence, many Americans were no doubt sympathetic to the first perspective, believing that a free and virtuous people could never act in a tyrannical or unjust manner. But the failure of the state governments and the rudimentary national government under the Articles of Confederation had tempered this enthusiasm. Even popular governments could act unjustly, a view ultimately shared by members of both the Federalist and Anti-Federalist factions. James Madison's arguments in Federalist Nos. 10 and 51 make a very strong case for the view that no government can be trusted, not even a republican government, given the facts of human nature. Under certain circumstances, and notwithstanding the views of staunch Federalists like James Wilson, the interests of the people and the government could sometimes be very different indeed, even when the government had been freely elected.

Among the Anti-Federalists were many who were convinced that the new Constitution did not fully come to terms with this problem. No government could

---

did not intend. John Jay, however, made explicit what Wilson only implied, pointing out in the New York Convention that a bill of rights is necessary under a king, but not where the people rule. See Meier, *Ratification*, 337.

40. Elliot, *Debates*, 2:488.

41. "And be it further enacted, That the laws of the several states, except where the constitution, treaties or statutes of the United States shall otherwise require or provide, shall be regarded as rules of decision in trials at common law in the courts of the United States in cases where they apply." Judiciary Act of 1789, section 34, http://www.constitution.org/uslaw/judiciary_1789.htm (accessed January 25, 2014).

be trusted, to be sure. But some governments might be less trustworthy than others, and a Congress so far removed from the people because of the great size of the country would be especially dangerous. Surely it could never be trusted to protect a right as fundamental as that of the civil jury. And the civil jury was not just an ordinary right; it was, in the language of the ratification amendments, an essential right that was almost always described in language similar to that used by the New York convention: "one of the greatest securities to the rights of a free people" that should, for that reason, "remain inviolate."[42]

Furthermore, behind the silence on civil juries, critics sensed (as they did with regard to other provisions of the Constitution) a secret agenda—in this case, a long-term plan to impose the civil-law system and suppress the common law. This charge was made explicitly by at least one delegate to the Pennsylvania convention, who argued that "the trial by jury was intended to be given up [under the Constitution] and the civil law was intended to be introduced into its place, in civil cases."[43] In his reply to this argument, Wilson acknowledged, with alarming honesty, the "limitations" of the civil jury. The jury, Wilson conceded, has "excellences that entitle it to superiority over any other mode," but he added a significant qualifier: "in uses to which it is applicable."[44] Its great value is the jurors' ability to "be acquainted with the characters of the parties and the witnesses,—where the whole cause can be brought within their knowledge and their view."[45] To Wilson, the jury was still a body of citizens whose job was to exercise judgment on matters about which they had knowledge that others (including judges) might not possess—the clear implication being that in other cases the jury might be ignorant of matters that others were in a better position to judge.

According to this view, the jurors themselves had to possess certain qualities to perform their duties properly. They must be sober and reliable, of course, and they must not have any animus against the parties (even though they might know their characters and reputations). But they must also be capable of understanding the issues involved in the case. As Wilson put it, the jury, when operating within its proper sphere, can "hear every thing that is alleged"—and more. The jurors "not only hear the words, but they see and mark the features of the countenance; they can judge of weight due to such testimony."[46] They cannot do these things properly, however, in two particular circumstances: when they are asked to judge what their experience prevents them from understanding, and when they are nat-

42. "Ratification of the Constitution by the State of New York, July 26, 1788," http://www.avalon.law.yale.edu/18th_century/ratny.asp#b1 (accessed January 25, 2014).

43. Or at least this is how Wilson characterized the remarks of Mr. Smilie, the member from Fayette. Elliot, *Debates*, 2:515.

44. Ibid., 516.

45. Ibid., 488–489.

46. Ibid.

urally and inevitably partial to one of the parties. The first circumstance occurs when jurors are expected to know (for example) "the law of nations, or the marine law, that is, the general law of mercantile countries."[47] International trade and its complexities—which would include matters involving marine insurance—are not within the ken of most citizens who serve on juries.

The second circumstance—lack of impartiality—is a constant danger to be guarded against. But of course, that danger is magnified by one of the common-law juror's supposed virtues: familiarity with the parties. Familiarity might breed partiality or even contempt. When we know our neighbors well, we are likely to have an opinion about them, whether good or ill. It is possible for a juror's opinion of his neighbor to cross the line into partiality. This is what justified the practice of "striking": giving each side a chance to remove a certain number of jurors suspected of being biased. In some of the colonies (Virginia, for example), that right was very generous (unlimited challenges for cause, and up to twenty peremptory challenges). However, a special kind of partiality is inevitable when one party to a suit is from another state, for then it becomes a matter of patriotism to root for one's neighbor, whatever one's private view of him might be. In such a case, as Wilson pointed out, the "plaintiff comes . . . a stranger, unknown as to his character or mode of life, while the other party is in the midst of his friends, or perhaps his dependents."[48] No matter how many jurors the out-of-state party strikes, everyone left will still be a local. Would such a jury trial produce justice? Could a requisite number of jurors be found who were not partial to citizens of their own state? The Constitutional Convention was therefore wise, Wilson concluded, to leave Congress with the task of arranging for jury trials in civil cases—a matter requiring lengthy debate and difficult compromises among the competing arrangements in the states.[49] And perhaps it also produced some sober second thoughts by Americans about the value of civil juries in all private controversies.

The Pennsylvania Minority—whose members refused to endorse the Constitution and published the influential "Address and Reasons of Dissent" in December 1787—claimed that the judicial power under the Constitution would be based on the "civil law," as one Mr. Smilie had claimed. But this group had an additional fear: because, under the civil law, "the judge determines both on law

47. Ibid.

48. Ibid. For a good example of the kind of partiality Wilson was afraid of, consider Eli Whitney's ultimately futile effort to defend his cotton gin patent before southern juries. Whitney's device was so simple that it was easy to copy, and planters could process their cotton on homemade gins without paying fees to Whitney's company. Local jurors generally refused to enforce an outsider's patent against their own neighbors. Whitney eventually gave up and returned north to pursue other business interests. Jeanette Mirsky and Allan Nevins, *The World of Eli Whitney* (New York: Macmillan, 1952).

49. Elliot, *Debates*, 2:488–489.

and fact . . . facts as well as law, would be re-examined [on appeal], and even new facts brought forward in the court of appeals."[50] The claim that jurors had a common-law right to judge the law as well as the facts was a widespread but not universally held belief; however, no one doubted (at least publicly) the claim that only jurors could find the facts. The jury's right to determine the facts was the very essence of the jury right; without that power, juries would be useless, since every judgment that displeased the court could be overturned as contrary to either the law or the evidence. Thus, the Pennsylvania Minority's objection had enough force to produce the language of the Seventh Amendment: "and no fact tried by a jury, shall be otherwise re-examined in any court of the United States, than according to the rules of the common law."[51]

The language of the Seventh Amendment was a victory for the Anti-Federalist effort to preserve something old to counter the schemes of the innovators—a strategy aimed at more than just the Constitution's jury provisions, as Herbert Storing has demonstrated.[52] The preservation of the common-law jury meant a defense of all the traditional elements of that jury—elements easily identified because of the ubiquity of the jury in England and the colonies, and because of the great body of commentary on jury practices in court decisions. Englishmen had certain rights that Americans had "inherited" (that is, "birthrights"): to be tried by twelve impartial men of the vicinage, to challenge jurors suspected of bias, and to have the facts in their case judged by the jury alone. There could be no appeal of a jury's verdict of acquittal in a criminal case, and no higher court could reexamine the facts of a case once a jury had determined those facts to its own satisfaction. Jurors could not be punished for reaching verdicts to which judges took exception, and the jury was not bound by the judge's instructions about the law.

The fact-finding role of the jury required an additional protection—of the "vicinage." This requirement was associated with the traditional common-law jury and was thought to be especially important in criminal trials. As the word suggests, this requirement was redolent of ancient times and long-ago circumstances; the word was quaint even in 1789. But the vicinage requirement was important both

50. Herbert J. Storing, *The Complete Anti-Federalist* (Chicago: University of Chicago Press, 1981), 3:38–41.

51. The so-called reexamination clause of the Seventh Amendment effectively guarantees the jury's right to have the final word about the facts of a case, confining appellate review to matters of law only. It was understood by nineteenth-century courts to mean that appellate courts can never retry issues of fact already settled by the jury. See Parsons v. Bedford, 28 U.S. 433 (1830). In the twentieth century this principle has been undermined, in the view of some critics, by the Federal Rules of Civil Procedure, a matter taken up in chapters 4 and 5.

52. Herbert J. Storing, *What the Anti-Federalists Were For: The Political Thought of the Opponents of the Constitution* (Chicago: University of Chicago Press, 1981).

to the traditional authority of the jury and to the rights of defendants and litigants. First, jurors who were from the vicinage of the crime knew where to look for the facts, unlike judges. This was true of the English criminal juries, which could be expected to know which witnesses were trustworthy and which were habitual liars. The job of the common-law jury was, in principle, a simple one: "to say what the fact was. . . . Is a person legitimate, or a nativus, or an idiot, or insane?"[53] The judge, usually traveling the circuit from town to town, could not possess such local knowledge. Also, being a person of exalted status, his knowledge would be inhibited by an unbridgeable status gap, even in his own hometown.

Second, defendants were entitled to be tried by men who knew their character, and this would be impossible if they stood trial in a strange place.[54] Suspicious Anti-Federalists pointed out that the government could seriously cripple a defendant's ability to defend himself by arranging for a distant trial, far from the scene of the crime and (probably) far from the defendant's home. This was the view of Agrippa, an Anti-Federalist commentator, who wrote that a man would be "forced to take his trial among strangers, friendless and unsupported, without it's being known whether he is habitually a good or a bad man."[55] Article III of the Constitution, however, required only that a trial "shall be held in the state where the said crimes shall have been committed." So theoretically, a defendant from New York City might be tried in Albany for a crime committed near his home. Federalists scoffed at the likelihood of such skullduggery; they did not believe that even Anti-Federalists could impute such foolhardy wickedness to government officials who had been chosen through broad popular suffrage and would have to stand for reelection. John Marshall was incredulous: "Will a man on the Eastern Shore," he asked at the Virginia Ratifying Convention, "be sent to be tried in Kentucky [then still part of Virginia]? A Government by doing this would destroy itself." No, he continued; the criminal jury is adequately protected, and the defendant is to be tried by a jury of his own countrymen "and probably of his vicinage."[56]

Writing of the civil jury specifically, Federal Farmer had a less conspiratorial objection but one that spoke more directly to Anti-Federalist concerns:

53. James B. Thayer, "'Law and Fact' in Jury Trials," *Harvard Law Review* 4, 4 (1890–1891): 148.

54. This argument assumes what was usually taken for granted: that all the elements of a crime—the location, the victim, the defendant, and the jury—would be local. In an increasingly mobile society, this assumption would become unreliable. Interestingly, the same assumption was not always made about civil cases, where it was acknowledged that a party in one state might bring a case against a party in another state. Business was becoming national, but everyone apparently expected crime to remain local.

55. Storing, *What the Anti-Federalists Were For*, 237.

56. Virginia Ratifying Convention, in *John Marshall Papers*, vol. 1, ed. Herbert Alan Johnson (Chapel Hill: University of North Carolina Press, 1974), 227–285.

> When I speak of the jury trial of the vicinage or the trial of the fact in the neighborhood,—I do not lay so much stress upon the circumstance of our being tried by our neighbors: in this enlightened country men may be probably impartially tried by those who do not live very near them: but the trial of facts in the neighborhood is of great importance in other respects. Nothing can be more essential than the cross examining witnesses, and generally before the triers of the facts in question. The common people can establish facts with much more ease with oral than written evidence; when trials of facts are removed to a distance from the homes of the parties and witnesses, oral evidence becomes intolerably expensive, and the parties must depend on written evidence, which to the common people is expensive and almost useless; it must be frequently taken ex parte, and but very seldom leads to the proper discovery of truth.[57]

The jury was how the common people participated in government, making it a political institution and not exclusively a judicial one. Federalist concerns over whether civil juries could handle complex cases, or problems of distinguishing cases at law from cases at equity, were somewhat beside the point, from this perspective; there were more important matters at stake than simply getting cases decided properly.

James Madison took such complaints seriously enough that his first submission of a bill of rights included a stipulation that "the trial of all crimes [save impeachment and military trials] shall be by an impartial jury of the freeholders of the vicinage, with the requisite of unanimity for conviction, of the right of challenge, and other accustomed requisites."[58] The same proposal included a guarantee of jury trials in civil cases, a guarantee of "speedy and public trials," a compulsory process for obtaining witnesses, and the assistance of counsel. This proposal hit all the right notes: whatever the precise boundaries of a vicinage might be, the area defined by those boundaries would be small enough to allay the defendant's fear of being tried among strangers. The term "freeholders" set a property standard for jury service that most farmers and artisans could meet, and the inclusion of such traditional elements as "challenge" and "unanimity" signaled Madison's full acceptance of the "ancient right" in its most gloriously

57. Federal Farmer, "Letter IV," in Storing, *Complete Anti-Federalist*, 2:53. This is a gentle reminder that many citizens eligible for jury service would be illiterate, or nearly so. They could therefore not be expected to rely on "documents" but would need to hear oral testimony in open court. The need to "see and hear" witnesses testifying would become, in the twentieth century, an argument against privileging documents over live testimony in civil cases.

58. House of Representatives, *Annals of Congress*, 1st Cong., 1st sess. (1789), 424.

ancient form. The wording "other accustomed requisites" filled in whatever gaps might appear in the future.

But while Anti-Federalists were lobbying Madison for concessions on the jury, the ratification debates were bringing up some of the same doubts about the civil jury that had surfaced briefly at the Constitutional Convention. Some of these doubts would anticipate later controversies and concerns. In Massachusetts Mr. Gore objected to one of the most respectable arguments for the "jury of the vicinage"—that local jurors would possess local knowledge helpful to the resolution of a case. He stated: "The idea that the jury coming from the neighborhood, and knowing the character and circumstances of the party in trial, is promotive of justice, on reflection will appear not founded in truth. . . . The great object is to determine on the real merits of the cause, uninfluenced by any personal considerations; if therefore, the jury could be perfectly ignorant of the person in trial, a just decision would be more probable."[59] Thus began a long argument, which continues today, over the precise degree of "ignorance" required of a juror, who might not know any of the parties personally but might "know" them from the publicity generated by their case. Although this seems like a very modern problem,[60] it was raised as early as the treason trial of Aaron Burr in 1807, when there were objections to the selection of jurors who knew of Burr's notorious reputation, even though they did not know him personally.[61] Chief Justice Marshall settled the question by conceding that "were it possible to obtain a jury without any prepossessions whatever . . . it would be extremely desirable . . . ; but this is perhaps impossible, and therefore will not be required."[62]

In South Carolina Mr. Barnwell objected to the view that jury trials are always the best alternative in private suits: "particular circumstances may arise, which would induce even the greatest advocates for this right to yield it for a time." He also spotted what we would now identify as a "federalism problem."

59. Elliot, *Debates*, 2:109–114.

60. It came up in the spring of 2015 in the trial of Dzhokar Tsarnaev for his role in the terrorist attack on the Boston Marathon in 2013. Given the amount of publicly available surveillance footage and the extensive coverage in the media, it was unlikely that any citizen called to jury service could have avoided concluding that Tsarnaev was guilty. That would have been true even if his attorneys' efforts to have the case moved to a different city had been successful.

61. "Many in heavily Republican Virginia were inclined to believe Burr had acted traitorously, and this popular belief made jury selection more difficult and time consuming." Charles F. Hobson, "The Aaron Burr Treason Trial," in *Federal Trials and Great Debates in United States History*, http://www.fjc.gov/history/docs/burrtrial.pdf (accessed January 15, 2014). See also Robert K. Faulkner, "John Marshall and the Burr Trial," *Journal of American History* 53, 2 (September 1966): 247–258.

62. United States v. Burr, 25 F. Cas. 49, no. 14,692g (C.C.D. Va. [1807]).

Would a citizen of Carolina, he asked, in a suit against Georgia, want to be tried by a jury in Georgia?[63] Charles Pinckney raised the same objection: in a suit between citizens of different states, from which state would jurors be chosen? If from both, it would be a hardship on the party from the distant state. Pinckney then raised an even more fundamental objection that got closer to an issue lurking in the background of the quarrel over civil juries: that the democratic impulse to submit to "the people" questions that should be decided by more capable authorities was not an entirely healthy impulse. In explaining why it might be unwise to include particular jury provisions in the Constitution, Pinckney reminded delegates that, under the Articles of Confederation, Congress had once voted to give capture cases to juries, "contrary to the practice of all nations."[64] Realizing its mistake—an American jury was unlikely to favor a foreign ship owner over an American claimant, leading to potentially grave diplomatic consequences, as well as injustice—Congress repealed the law. That mistake could not have been so easily corrected, Pinckney pointed out, if it had been a constitutional provision rather than a mere statute.[65]

PUBLIUS ON THE JURY

After the convention ended, it fell to Alexander Hamilton to defend the decision not to include a protection for civil juries, the subject of Federalist No. 83.[66] Hamilton began by denying that this decision constituted a "failure," referring instead to the convention's "mere silence . . . in regard to civil causes." This was not the same as abolishing civil juries, he argued. "Every man of discernment must at once perceive the wide difference between silence and abolition."[67] It followed, therefore, that whereas the convention had chosen to constrain Congress with respect to criminal juries, it had decided to give Congress the discretion to provide for civil juries when it was proper to do so. These initial observations introduced

63. "Debates in the South Carolina Ratifying Convention, 1788," in Schwartz, *Bill of Rights*, 2:741–742.

64. Ibid.

65. Ibid., 742–743.

66. Hamilton et al., *Federalist*, 530–545. At just over 5,800 words, Federalist No. 83 is the longest of the Federalist Papers (nearly twice the length of No. 10, and three times the length of No. 51); it appeared in three installments between July 5 and July 12, 1788.

67. The civil jury, of course, is not the only subject on which the Constitution is "silent." If Hamilton had slavery in mind when he wrote this passage, a logical inference is that if the framers did not intend to abolish the civil jury, they may have hoped to give Congress the authority to limit its use in federal courts, even "placing it on the path to ultimate extinction," to borrow Lincoln's famous formula regarding slavery.

the real theme of No. 83, which is the impropriety of jury trials in certain kinds of civil cases.

Hamilton first conceded what all Americans would have conceded—that the trial by jury in criminal cases is essential to the preservation of liberty. It might be "curious," he ventured, to discuss whether the criminal jury is as useful in a popular government as it is under a hereditary monarch.[68] Like Wilson in Pennsylvania and Jay in New York, Publius is suggesting that the achievement of popular government may have rendered some of the traditional suspicions of authority obsolete—an idea clearly rejected in other contexts (most famously in Federalist Nos. 10 and 51).[69] But, Publius quickly concedes, such discussion would produce little benefit in a country where "all are satisfied of the utility of the institution, and of its friendly aspect to liberty. . . . But I must acknowledge that I cannot readily discern the inseparable connection between the existence of liberty and the trial by jury in civil cases."[70] The great landmarks in the history of jury trials involved the power of governments to harass opponents in the criminal courts through "arbitrary impeachments, arbitrary methods of prosecuting pretended offenses, and arbitrary punishments upon arbitrary convictions." Against such "engines of judicial despotism," the criminal jury and habeas corpus—both amply protected in the Constitution—are the great remedies. As for the use of civil juries to protect citizens from "aggressive exercise of the power of taxation," a cause célèbre in colonial America, the circumstances are now very different. Under a republican government, "willful abuses of a public authority . . . are offenses against the government for which the persons who commit them may be indicted and punished." That is, revenue officers now serve the sovereign people, not the Crown; they are well within the reach of the people's vengeance—and they know it. So, of course, are the officials who employ them, since they must face the judgment of the voters.[71]

Thus, if there is any virtue to civil juries, it must "depend on circumstances foreign to the preservation of liberty"—as direct a challenge to the traditional view of the civil jury as one can find in the literature of the founding era. One such virtue is protection against corruption of the judicial process, which would require the suborning of both a judge and a temporary body of jurors. Because the corruption of both simultaneously would be difficult—the identity of the jurors being unknown until the last moment—it would not succeed as a tactic. The civil

68. Hamilton et al., *Federalist,* 534.

69. James Madison's famous question appears in Federalist No. 51: "But what is government itself, but the greatest of all reflections on human nature? If men were angels, no government would be necessary. If angels were to govern men, neither external nor internal controls on government would be necessary." Hamilton et al., *Federalist*, 53.

70. Ibid., 534.

71. Ibid., 534–535.

jury's ability to retard corruption, added to its excellence in settling most property questions, would warrant its protection in the Constitution, "if it were possible to fix the limits within which it ought to be comprehended." Hamilton's reference to "limits" was an allusion to the differing civil jury provisions in the states, which variety, "we are authoritatively informed," kept the convention from protecting civil juries in the first place. Chancery, probate, equity, and admiralty jurisdictions were variously available or appropriate for different types of disputes in many states. Georgia used only common-law courts, Hamilton reported, and even allowed appeals from one jury to another. Some states had chancery courts, while others did not. Some states even used juries in their admiralty courts.[72]

The extent to which this diversity posed a true obstacle to the constitutional protection of civil juries would become a matter of dispute in the ratifying conventions and in the congressional debate over framing the Bill of Rights. The convention's reluctance, critics concluded, could not be explained by the "inconvenience" of diverse procedures; it must have proceeded from other motives entirely. They did not consider that the explanation might have been the delegates' exhaustion or the need to start the ratification process, since they did not know how late in the convention the issue had come up. If they had known that the issue of the civil jury, or the larger issue of a bill of rights, had not even been mentioned until mid-September, they might have been even more alarmed.

In fact, there is not much evidence in Madison's notes to suggest that the diversity of practices prevented a constitutional guarantee for the civil jury. Gorham's objection had been that "it is not possible to discriminate equity cases from those in which juries are proper."[73] (Some in the founding generation—Thomas Jefferson, for example—argued that juries should be used even "in the Chancery courts, which have already engulfed and continue to engulf, so great a proportion of the jurisdiction over our property."[74]) Hamilton's "greatest objection" was more pointed and went beyond the difficulty of sorting out equity matters and common-law jurisdiction; he questioned the suitability of the use of the civil jury in many situations: "I feel a deep and deliberate conviction that there are many cases in which the trial by jury is an ineligible one."[75] In particular, property disputes involving foreign nations—prize cases—commonly turned on the interpretation of the laws of nations, with which jurors had no familiarity at all. Nor would jurors

72. Ibid., 536–537.

73. Madison, *Notes of Debates*, 630.

74. *The Works of Thomas Jefferson*, ed. Paul Leicester Ford (New York: G. P. Putnam's Sons, 1904), 3:78. I owe this citation to Stephen N. Subrin, "How Equity Conquered Common Law: The Federal Rules of Civil Procedure in Historical Perspective," *University of Pennsylvania Law Review* 135, 4 (April 1987): 928, n. 106.

75. Hamilton et al., *Federalist*, 539. On Hamilton's doubts and Federalist doubts more generally, see James Nendza, "The Jury and Republican Government: The Early American Understanding" (unpublished manuscript, 1999), 13–19.

have much regard for the important foreign policy considerations generated by such cases. Ipswich fishermen would have little concern for America's relations with Great Britain or with other nations having an interest in North Atlantic fishing grounds. And although jurors were supposed to consider only matters of fact, "in most cases legal consequences are complicated with fact in such a manner as to render separation impracticable." Noting that in Britain prize cases were heard in privy council, Hamilton raised the possibility that weighty matters of foreign affairs might be decided, in the United States, by local juries.[76]

Yet Hamilton did agree that equity jurisdiction presented a special problem for the civil jury. "The great and primary use of a court of equity is to give relief in extraordinary cases, which are exceptions to general rules." To give such cases to juries would merely "unsettle the general rules." Ordinary citizens might understand ordinary business well enough, but the exceptions could puzzle them:

> The circumstances that constitute cases proper for courts of equity are in many instances so nice and intricate that they are incompatible with the genius of trials by jury. They require often such long, deliberate, and critical investigation as would be impracticable to men called from their occupations, and obliged to decide before they were permitted to return to them. The simplicity and expedition which form the distinguishing characters of this mode of trial require that the matter to be decided should be reduced to some single and obvious point; while the litigations usual in chancery frequently comprehend a long train of minute and independent particulars.[77]

This is an elegant and diplomatic way of expressing an uncomfortable truth: some things are just too hard for average citizens to understand, given their limited experience, and are better left to the experts. The "peculiar genius" of the jury system is that common-law jurors know what is common and can judge it accordingly. But these same jurors lack the experience, the patience, the time, and the learning to understand the uncommon disputes among merchants and men of substantial business, to parse the terms of complicated commercial agreements, or to weigh the foreign policy interests of the government against the claims of parties. It is the old problem of maritime insurance writ large.

Hamilton anticipated another modern argument: that efforts to extend the jury to matters properly handled in equity courts "will tend gradually to change the nature of the courts of law, and to undermine the trial by jury by introducing questions too complicated for a decision in that mode."[78] Frequent bad decisions would bring the entire institution of the jury into disrepute, even in those forums where its use was entirely appropriate or even (as in criminal trials) absolutely

76. Hamilton et al., *Federalist*, 539.

77. Ibid., 540. A recent example of the kind of "nice and intricate" case Hamilton had in mind might be *Apple v. Samsung*, discussed in chapter 5.

78. Ibid., 540–541.

necessary. And because "the changes which are continually happening in society" will inevitably challenge the understanding of common-law jurors, new methods of resolving questions of property should be allowed to emerge, outside the shadow of the jury.[79]

But it was the Anti-Federalist position that prevailed in the end: the Seventh Amendment provided for jury trials in "suits at common law," and the Sixth Amendment restated, in stronger terms, Article III's guarantee of jury trials in all criminal prosecutions. As James Nendza reminds us, the Anti-Federalist "attack on the Constitution for its failure to include a provision guaranteeing the right to trial by a jury in civil cases struck a powerful chord among the people."[80] The Anti-Federalists were concerned not only about the particular failure to provide for civil juries but also about what that failure augured for the protection of individual citizens and for the republican character of the Constitution and the new American political order. The greatest fear was the fear of oligarchy, and the absence of civil juries seemed to confirm the oligarchic intentions of the convention's leaders or, at a minimum, their failure to appreciate the danger that oligarchy presented. For their part, the convention's leaders seemed to be taken aback by the complaints about civil juries. They had anticipated objections regarding limits on the states, the powers of the executive, and the tenure of federal judges, but they had not expected such fears about the jury system, and some were perplexed by the demand for a bill of rights more generally.

Some Anti-Federalists, such as Luther Martin, stressed the value of the civil jury as a defense against arbitrary power. Martin (influenced by a common American reading of Blackstone) described the civil jury as the "only sure palladium of the rights, the liberties, and the property of society."[81] Other Anti-Federalists noted that the government itself would frequently be a party to civil suits—not all civil cases involve disputes between private citizens—and that in such cases, a jury trial would be an essential guarantee of civil liberty.[82]

Civil juries would also provide a democratic balance to the "aristocratic" temper of the judiciary. The Anti-Federalist writer known as Federal Farmer described the jury as "the lower house of the judiciary."[83] Anti-Federalists often cited Blackstone's comment that when judges alone decide cases, "their decisions . . . would have a bias towards those of their own rank and dignity, for it is not to be expected, that the few should be attentive to the rights of the many."[84] On a

79. Ibid., 544.

80. Nendza, "Jury and Republican Government," 20.

81. Ibid., 22, n. 66.

82. Ibid., 24–26.

83. "Letters from the Federal Farmer, XV," in Storing, *Complete Anti-Federalist*, 2:320.

84. Nendza, "Jury and Republican Government," 27. It should be noted that Black-

related note, Maryland Farmer observed that the jury has no equal in "the task of deterring and curbing the insolence of office."[85] Part of this "balance" involved the introduction of "plain common sense" into a forum that would otherwise be filled with "petty-fogging" legal talk. As Storing has summarized the Anti-Federalist view, the question "was not fundamentally whether the lack of adequate provision for jury trial would weaken a traditional bulwark of individual rights (although that was also involved) but whether it would fatally weaken the role of the people in the administration of the government."[86]

Finally, the Anti-Federalists defended the jury, both civil and criminal forms, as a way of educating republican citizens—an argument that is conspicuously missing from Hamilton's cautious defense of the civil jury.[87] In the Anti-Federalist view, jury service exposes the citizen to the law and to the judge's experience of the law, thereby elevating the citizen's knowledge—a nice twist on Hamilton's fear that civil cases would prove too "nice and intricate" for non-specialists. Jury trials also force an "open and public discussion of all causes."[88] Jurors would be forced to take responsibility for their decisions and for the actions of others, "to come forward, in turn, as the sentinels and guardians of each other."[89] By judging others, jurors would learn how to distinguish between justice and vengeance, and the common people would understand how to rule responsibly—an argument that would be restated by Tocqueville forty years later. Maryland Farmer wrote: "Should every opportunity be taken away [from them] of exercising their reason, you will reduce them to that state of mental baseness, in which they appear in nine-tenths of this globe—distinguished from brutes, only by form and the articulation of sound—Give them power and they will find understanding to use it."[90]

---

stone's remark made more sense in the British context than it did in republican America, where judges were sometimes not even educated in the law. The professionalization of the bench and the bar was still a long way off.

85. Cited by ibid., 25, n. 72.

86. Storing, *What the Anti-Federalists Were For*, 19.

87. The problem of educating republican citizens was the greatest unattended issue in the otherwise splendid work of the convention, and this applies to *The Federalist* as well. For a discussion of this problem, see Wilson Carey McWilliams and Dennis Hale, "The Constitutional Convention and the Founding Principles," in *Principles of Constitutional Order: The Ratification Debates*, ed. Robert L. Utley Jr. and Patricia B. Gray (Lanham, MD: University Press of America, 1989), 11–32; and Wilson Carey McWilliams, "Democracy and Mystery: On Civic Education in America," in *Redeeming Democracy in America*, ed. Patrick J. Deneen and Susan J. McWilliams (Lawrence: University Press of Kansas, 2011), 211–220.

88. "Aristocrotis" cited in Nendza, "Jury and Republican Government," 29.

89. Ibid., 30.

90. Ibid., 31.

THE CONGRESSIONAL DEBATE ON CIVIL JURIES

In total, the state ratifying conventions proposed 210 amendments—amounting to nearly 100 different amendments when duplicates are omitted.[91] There was, however, a general consensus on a much smaller number of rights considered to be fundamental and therefore deserving of protection. Madison drew on this consensus to propose eight "articles of amendment," including fourteen separate rights, which he submitted to Congress on June 8, 1789. (The right to hunt and fish, proposed by the Pennsylvania Minority, was one of the fundamental rights that did not make the cut. Another was the right to be free of direct taxes levied by the federal government, which had been demanded by each of the seven states that proposed amendments.)

Madison had reason to feel a sense of urgency. Although all but two states (Rhode Island and North Carolina) had ratified the Constitution, many state ratifications had been successfully concluded only because of an explicit expectation that a bill of rights would be passed or at least considered by Congress at its first opportunity. Conventions in Rhode Island and North Carolina had voted to remain out of the Union until amendments had been added to guarantee rights not protected in the original. Madison's own campaign for a seat in Congress had nearly been scuttled because of this issue: James Monroe, his opponent, had tried to brand Madison as an opponent of a bill of rights. More ominously, Virginia and New York had proposed in May that a second constitutional convention be held to consider amendments. Madison's quick action took the wind out of such proposals.[92]

Of the eight articles Madison introduced in June, four contained changes to the judicial system. These amendments protected against excessive fines and bail, as well as cruel and unusual punishment; protected citizens against "unreasonable searches and seizures"; guaranteed all accused persons "a speedy and public trial," as well as compulsory process and the assistance of counsel; forbade any state from violating the right to a jury trial in criminal cases; established a minimum dollar amount (to be determined later) before civil judgments could be appealed; and provided that the "trial of all crimes" (except impeachment and military trials) "shall be by an impartial jury of freeholders of the vicinage," and then only after presentment or indictment by a grand jury. Finally, the last of the amendments concerned with the judicial system stated that, "in suits at common law, between man and man, the trial by jury, as one of the best securities to the rights of the people, ought to remain inviolate."[93]

91. Schwartz, *Bill of Rights*, 2:983.
92. Ibid., 1006.
93. *Annals of Congress*, 424–450.

There was much opposition to suspending the House's considerable unfinished business during this hectic first session of Congress—tax laws had not been passed, nor had the courts been established—to take up the amendments "at this time." Mr. Smith observed, "it must appear extremely impolitic to go into the consideration of amending the Government, before it is organized, before it has begun to operate."[94] There was also some opposition to any amendments at all, both from Federalists, who did not like the idea of a bill of rights, and from Anti-Federalists, who feared that the addition of a bill of rights would sink the chances for a new convention.[95] But the threat of a second convention ("How dangerous such an expedient would be I need not mention," said Mr. Page) and the force of Madison's argument eventually won the day.[96] "It appears to me," Madison said, "that this House is bound by every motive of prudence, not to let the first session pass over without proposing to the State Legislatures some things to be incorporated into the constitution, that will render it as acceptable to the whole people of the United States, as it has been found acceptable to a majority of them. . . . We have in this way something to gain, and, if we proceed with caution, nothing to lose."[97]

The House postponed debate on the amendments until Madison pushed for decisive action in July, nearly six weeks after making his proposal. The members decided on a Committee of Eleven (North Carolina and Rhode Island were still not represented in Congress), which reported a draft of the amendments on July 28. At that point the debate began in earnest, as the House voted to consider the amendments as a Committee of the Whole. The discussion of the jury amendments took place near the end of the committee debate, beginning on August 17 and ending the next day, when the entire list of amendments was reported to the House.

If the official report of the congressional debate is accurate, the jury provisions occasioned very little controversy.[98] There was some objection to the amendment forbidding state interference with freedom of religion, press, speech, and jury trials, but it passed handily in both chambers. (The amendment failed to be ratified by the states, however, almost certainly because of a desire to protect state sovereignty over the "police power," which included religion.) There was disagreement over forbidding appeals to the Supreme Court of civil judgments less than $1,000—an amendment answering the Anti-Federalist fear that (in Madison's words) "persons of opulence would carry a cause from the extremities of

94. Schwartz, *Bill of Rights*, 2:1017.

95. Leonard Levy, "The Bill of Rights," in *Constitutional Opinions: Aspects of the Bill of Rights* (New York: Oxford University Press, 1986), 119.

96. Schwartz, *Bill of Rights*, 2:1022.

97. Ibid., 1024, 1025.

98. *History of the Congress Exhibiting a Classification of the Proceedings of the Senate and House of Representatives from March 4, 1789 to March, 1793* (1843), 152–155, in Schwartz, *Bill of Rights*, 2:1054–1120.

the Union to the Supreme Court, and thereby prevent the due administration of justice." Although Madison expressed skepticism about the likelihood of such an evil, he agreed it "ought to be guarded against." The proposal was adopted by the House but rejected by the Senate.[99] The second part of the proposal, limiting the reexamination of facts already tried to a jury, passed without comment.

The next day the House passed the amendment guaranteeing "a speedy and public trial," along with other familiar protections: the right to confront accusers and to call witnesses, the right to compulsory process, and the right to the assistance of counsel. There was a brief discussion of the use of the word "vicinage" in the jury amendment, and Mr. Burke of South Carolina moved to substitute the phrase "district or county in which the offense has been committed," noting that this was the practice in his home state. This phrase would bring the amendment more into line, he thought, with the language used in the other states, while calming the fear that defendants might be "dragged from one extremity of the State to the other for trial, at the distance of three or four hundred miles." The members, however, voted to retain Madison's original language, which Mr. Lee observed was "well understood by every gentleman of legal knowledge." The only mention of civil juries was the terse notation that "the 3d clause of the 7th proposition, as follows, 'In suits at common law, the right of trial by jury shall be preserved,' was considered and adopted."[100]

On August 19 the entire House began consideration of the amendments. Although there was significant debate over where to put the amendments (into the text or at the end), as well as several attempts to add other amendments, there was no discussion of the jury provisions. The entire list was approved on August 24 and sent to the Senate. Deliberations in the Senate produced at least one important amendment to the House language: "On Monday, the 7th, the subject being again before the Senate, the twelfth article was agreed to, after the addition of these words: 'where the consideration exceeds twenty dollars.'"[101]

The debate about the Bill of Rights took place simultaneously with the consideration of various acts to get the government up and running, including the Judiciary Act of 1789. Much of the debate on the judiciary concerned objections to the establishment of federal district courts, which were seen as an unnecessary duplication of the functions of state courts and a dangerous intrusion on the states. The discussion of federal district courts, however, became enmeshed with the

99. Ibid., 1113.

100. Ibid., 1117.

101. Ibid., 1138, 1150. Twenty dollars was, of course, a more impressive sum in 1790 than it is today—the equivalent (according to one recent estimate) of twenty acres of land in some states. 28 U.S.C. § 1332 establishes a $75,000 threshold for diversity of citizenship cases brought to the federal courts. Most state legislatures have also raised the bar to civil actions to amounts higher than $20. On the constitutional status of the clause, see "The Twenty Dollars Clause," *Harvard Law Review* 118, 5 (March 2005): 1665–1686.

language of the jury amendment. What is a district? What exceptions does the amendment that protects criminal juries (originally the Eighth Amendment) make to the "jury of the vicinage"? Will those exceptions prove to be a hardship or allow the despotic treatment of citizens who are unpopular with the government?

Discussions of the Judiciary Act focused on two elements of the jury system: use of the now obsolete term "vicinage," and the method of constructing the venire—the prospective jurors summoned to court—from the list of all those qualified for jury service.[102] One fear was that defendants could be dragged to the other end of the state and "tried among strangers" if the ancient word for "locality" was abandoned. The other fear was that officials who were biased against the defendant would be able to choose equally biased jurors—the old problem of the "stacked" jury.

The Judiciary Act was crafted to avoid these problems, but they did not go away. Section 29 required that in all capital cases the "trial shall be held in the county where the offense was committed." At the time, counties were small enough that no defendant had to worry about being tried among strangers or having to pay the expenses of witnesses forced to travel to wherever authorities chose to conduct the trial (a more realistic concern). The Judiciary Act also required each federal district court to observe the jury qualifications in force in the state where the court was sitting. As a result, different federal districts might be imposing different jury qualifications, a form of diversity that would become increasingly controversial in the twentieth century. In addition, the act mandated that jurors be "designated by lot or otherwise in each State . . . according to the mode of forming juries therein now practiced." That is, based on the list of state-qualified jurors, federal officials would construct a jury list using the same method followed in the state courts. But in a decision whose implications would become clear during the two years of the Sedition Act, section 29 gave to the clerk of the federal court and the US marshal for the district the responsibility for issuing writs of venire facias and serving them on prospective jurors. Whereas the states would be responsible for qualifying citizens for jury service and compiling lists of qualified jurors, federal officials would preside over the process of summoning jurors to court, where the final act of impaneling the jury would take place.[103]

102. There is an ambiguity here that was not discussed in Congress: "vicinage" had always referred to the area from which jurors were summoned—that is, the neighborhood of the crime—with the unstated assumption that this would also be the neighborhood where the defendant resided. Here again, there is evidence of the impact on contemporary debates of a much older social world where the victims of crime and those charged with crimes were usually neighbors. See Drew Kershen, "Vicinage," *Oklahoma Law Review* 29, 4 (Fall 1976): 801–860.

103. The Judiciary Act of 1789, 1 Stat. 73, chap. XX, An Act to Establish the Judicial Courts of the United States.

Perhaps as a direct result of the debate over the Judiciary Act, Mr. Burke of South Carolina objected to the provision for choosing juries in cases of insurrection or invasion. In such cases, the government would be allowed to choose jurors from anywhere in the state, rather than from the vicinity of the alleged crime. Burke outlined his concerns:

> If a man be charged with treason, or other offense against the Government, committed as far back as Lake Ontario, instead of being brought to trial in the county, or district, where he is said to have committed the offense, as the State law directs at present, he is to be dragged down to the city of New York, to take his trial there; not by a jury taken from the country at large, as at present, but this section is so subtly framed, that a jury may be picked, not merely within the city, but within any particular ward of it.[104]

Clearly, for those who were worried about the Constitution's jury provisions, the criminal jury was still a means of protecting citizens from a despotic government: all the quarrels (though there were not many) concerning the jury amendments and the jury provisions of the Judiciary Act were about bolstering the power of the individual who was up against the entire weight of the government. The romantic vision of the stolid English juror standing up to the Crown was not far from the minds of Americans—even after the Crown was long gone and the government had been chosen by the defendant's own neighbors.

On September 23 the House considered the Conference Committee's report on the differences between the two houses and proposed to "recede from their disagreements to all the amendments," with two exceptions. The House insisted on restoring the original language of what we now know as the First and Sixth Amendments. The Senate's version of the Bill of Rights had deleted almost the entire criminal jury amendment, leaving in place only the language requiring grand jury indictments for "capital or otherwise infamous crimes." One reason for the Senate's decision was the Federalist view that the Constitution already provided sufficient protection for criminal juries in Article III, section 2, paragraph 3. But another reason was that the "vicinage" requirement in the House language seemed either too strict or too vague.[105] The unamended Constitution required jury trials "in the State where the said crimes shall have been committed." The term "State" had the advantage of describing a definite jurisdiction, whereas "vicinage" could mean either the "general vicinity" or the "immediate neighborhood."

104. *Annals of Congress*, 865–866.

105. This was Madison's explanation, at any rate. In his letter to Pendleton dated September 14, 1789, Madison noted that the Senate had struck at some of the most "salutary" amendments—in this case, because of the states' varying practices with respect to the size of the territory from which jurors were summoned. Cited in Schwartz, *Bill of Rights*, 2:1157. See also Kershen, "Vicinage," 824–826.

In the end, the House and Senate agreed to a compromise narrowing the size of the jurisdiction, giving us the final language of the Sixth Amendment: "In all criminal prosecutions, the accused shall enjoy the right to a speedy and public trial, by an impartial jury of the State and district wherein the crime shall have been committed, which district shall have been previously ascertained by law; and to be informed of the nature and cause of the accusation—to be confronted with the witnesses against him—to have compulsory process for obtaining witnesses in his favor, and to have the assistance of counsel for his defense."[106] The motion passed by a vote of thirty-seven to fourteen. Madison voted yes, but Burke voted no—even though the House had agreed to drop the word "vicinage" and replace it with "State and district." "State" was definite enough to please the Federalists, and "district" was small enough to satisfy the Anti-Federalists.

With that final compromise, Congress sent the amendments to the president for transmittal to the states. On the same day, the president signed the Judiciary Act. The republican jury was constitutionally and legislatively secure at last.

THE JURY AS A POLITICAL INSTITUTION

It was this republican jury that Tocqueville encountered roughly a generation after the founding. It is appropriate to discuss Tocqueville's argument here, because it introduces some themes and difficulties that would preoccupy American observers of the jury system in the near and distant future.

Tocqueville's account of the jury in *Democracy in America* ("On the Jury in the United States Considered as a Political Institution") occurs in volume 1, part 2, chapter 8 ("On What Tempers the Tyranny of the Majority in the United States").[107] Chapter 7 is titled "Omnipotence of the Majority in the United States and Its Effects," and chapter 9 is "Principal Causes Tending to Maintain a Democratic Republic in the United States." The discussion of the jury system, therefore, occupies a central position in Tocqueville's broader analysis of the strengths, weaknesses, limits, and possibilities of American democracy.

Trial by jury is the third of three causes that mitigate tyranny of the majority: the first is the "absence of administrative centralization," and the second is the "spirit of the lawyer." All three mitigate tyranny by limiting, counterbalancing, or disciplining democracy—a proposition that is more easily grasped in the first two cases than in the third. The lack of centralized administration means that "the majority, which often has the tastes and instincts of a despot, still lacks the most perfected instruments of tyranny."[108] The legal profession is naturally conserva-

106. Schwartz, *Bill of Rights*, 2:948.

107. Alexis de Tocqueville, *Democracy in America*, trans. Harvey C. Mansfield and Delba Winthrop (Chicago: University of Chicago Press, 2000), 250–264.

108. Ibid., 250.

tive but also reliably republican, bringing to public life "habits of order, a certain taste for forms, [and] a sort of instinctive love for the regular sequence of ideas." These characteristics lead the legal profession to oppose "the revolutionary spirit and unreflective passions of democracy."[109] The jury, however, seems to augment the power of the majority by placing into a sample of its membership the power to judge guilt and innocence ("the majority vested with the right to pronounce decrees").[110] How, then, does the jury take its place among the institutions and practices that mitigate democratic tyranny?

Tocqueville begins this section by noting that the jury can be considered in two ways: as a judicial institution and as a political institution. As a judicial institution, he comments, "its utility could be contested," especially in civil cases. "The institution of the jury had its birth in a society barely advanced, in which one scarcely submitted any but simple questions of fact to the courts; and it is not an easy task to adapt it to the needs of a very civilized people, when the relations of men among themselves have singularly multiplied and have taken on a learned and intellectual character."[111]

This was, as noted earlier, a prominent source of Federalist doubts about the utility of civil juries in all cases. But Tocqueville's concern in this section is not how well juries decide private disputes and criminal indictments; instead, it is the political consequence of their doing so on a regular basis, "for, if it exerts a great influence on the fate of cases, it exerts a much greater one still on the very destinies of society." The jury may be aristocratic or democratic, depending on the class from which jurors are chosen, but "it always preserves a republican character, in that it places the real direction of society in the hands of the governed or in a portion of them, and not in those that govern." The jury is republican because the "genuine sanction of political laws is . . . found in the penal laws, and if the sanction is lacking, the law sooner or later loses its force. Therefore, the man who judges the criminal is really the master of society. Now, the institution of the jury places the people themselves, or at least one class of citizens, on the judge's bench. The institution of the jury, therefore, really puts the direction of society into the hands of the people or of this class."[112] England is an aristocratic republic because, among other reasons, jurors are chosen only from those with significant land or income; in America, by contrast, every citizen who is entitled to vote is also entitled to serve on a jury—even though "the exercise of this right is not

109. Ibid., 252.

110. Ibid., 241.

111. Ibid., 258. On the other hand, as we saw in chapter 1, medieval juries did not always confine themselves to the facts of the homicide cases presented to them; they also decided which of the king's laws would be enforced in their full severity, and which would be mitigated.

112. Ibid., 260.

put indiscriminately in all hands."[113] Nevertheless, the jury is "as direct and as extreme a consequence of the dogma of the sovereignty of the people as universal suffrage." Jury service and voting are "equally powerful" ways of ensuring that the majority rules. "The jury forms the part of the nation charged with assuring the execution of the laws, as the houses [of the legislature] are the part of the nation charged with making the laws; and in order that society be governed in a fixed and uniform manner, it is necessary that the list of jurors extend or contract with that of electors."[114]

But if the jury augments the authority of the majority, how does it mitigate majority tyranny at the same time? The answer to that question begins with Tocqueville's discussion of the civil jury, which he found to be as significant as the criminal jury—perhaps more so—despite his view that its "utility could be contested" from a strictly judicial perspective. Criminal trials, after all, are scarcer than civil trials; if the jury were confined to criminal cases, it would be far less visible. When the jury is introduced into civil cases, therefore, "its application falls before one's eyes at each instant . . . it touches all interests; each comes to cooperate in its action; it thus penetrates into the usages of life; it bends the human mind to its forms, and is so to speak intermingled with the very idea of justice." Civil trials touch on the ordinary and inevitable conflicts that occur among a busy and commercial people—in contrast to the rarer cases of violent criminality that occupy the criminal courts. ("There is almost no one who fears being the object of a criminal prosecution one day; but everyone can have a lawsuit.") It is mostly on civil juries, therefore, that democratic citizens have the opportunity to be educated:

> [The jury] serves to give to the minds of all citizens a part of the habits of mind of the judge; and these habits are precisely those that best prepare the people to be free. It spreads to all classes respect for the thing judged and the

113. Ibid., appendix XVII, 697–698. Tocqueville looked at the jury laws of New York, Ohio, Louisiana, and the New England states and found that officials with various titles (e.g., selectmen in New England towns, trustees in Ohio) "choose for each district a certain number of citizens having the right to be jurors, and in whom they suppose the capacity to be such." Such officials had powers that were "very extensive and quite arbitrary . . . and they often use them, it is said, to turn away unworthy or incapable jurors, above all in New England." Ibid. In the seventeenth century, New England juries were composed of "freeholders of good report" whose names were chosen at the town meeting, suggesting that some "freeholders" might not be "of good report." Public officials or citizens at the town meeting were required to make a "supposition" as to a citizen's capacity to serve; the right to serve was qualified by reputation—a practice that survived in most jurisdictions in the United States until the 1960s, in the form of the key-man system for compiling lists of qualified jurors. The abandonment of the key-man system is discussed in chapter 4.

114. Ibid., 261.

> idea of right. . . . It teaches men the practice of equity. . . . The jury teaches each man not to recoil before responsibility for his own acts—a virile disposition without which there is no political virtue. It vests each citizen with a sort of magistracy . . . [and] serves incredibly to form the judgment and to augment the natural enlightenment of the people.[115]

The jury, therefore, ought to be considered a "school, free of charge and always open, where each juror comes to be instructed in his rights, where he enters into daily communication with the most instructed and the most enlightened members of the elevated classes. . . . I think that the practical intelligence and good political sense of the Americans must principally be attributed to the long use that they have made of the jury in civil matters."[116]

Quite simply, the jury mitigates the tyranny of the majority by improving citizens' understanding of both their duties and their rights, teaching them civic responsibility and curbing the natural human temptation toward tyranny. And while Tocqueville is not sure that trial by jury is always useful "to those who have lawsuits," he is certain that the institution is very good for jurors. "I regard it as one of the most efficacious means society can make use of for the education of the people."[117]

Some of those opposed to constitutional protection of the civil jury argued that its use was inappropriate in complex commercial cases. Tocqueville does not deny this problem. But he confesses that he is "little moved by arguments from the incapacity of jurors in civil matters," and his reasoning may be surprising to modern readers: in such complex cases, the jury "has only the appearance of a judicial body." The jury only sanctions the decision of the judge; to that decision they "lend the authority of the society that they represent, and he, that of reason and the law."[118] Because civil causes turn on more than "simple facts that good sense easily comes to appreciate" (the situation in most criminal cases),[119] jurors are willing to look to the judge for guidance—especially because a civil case pits two citizens against each other, rather than one lonely citizen against the great power of the state. In the latter case, the jury is likely to mistrust the judge, who may be seen as a person representing the authority of the government; in the former case, the jury is likely to see the judge as a "disinterested arbiter between the passions of the parties," which makes jurors more likely to look to the judge for guidance on complicated matters of law they might otherwise fail to grasp.

This habit, in turn, carries over to criminal cases and actually increases the authority of judges. Because citizens look to judges to help them decide civil

115. Ibid., 261–262.
116. Ibid.
117. Ibid.
118. Ibid., 263.
119. Ibid.

cases, they are more willing to trust judges in criminal cases. The influence of the judge, therefore, "extends well beyond the precincts of the courts," and the jury, which "seems to diminish the rights of the magistracy, therefore really founds its empire, and there is no country where judges are as powerful as those where the people come into a share of their privileges. . . . Thus the jury, which is the most energetic means of making the people reign, is also the most efficacious means of teaching them to reign."[120]

If the jury is a school and the jurors are students, then the legal profession—judges and lawyers both—are the faculty. In this understanding there is a partnership between the jury and the court, and the lawyers—drawn in an aristocratic direction by their tastes and in a democratic direction by their interests—provide the link. It is in this complex dynamic that we can see the tension between democracy and aristocracy that Tocqueville observed in modern democracy. Crucial to this tension, at least in America, is the nature of the legal profession: the "spirit of the lawyer," as Tocqueville observes, is an aristocratic one, conservative in temperament but at the same time open to the people. Lawyers, because of what they have learned, "form a sort of privileged class among [persons of intelligence]," a compact body whose "unity of methods" binds their minds as no mere interest could. "Hidden at the bottom of the souls of lawyers one therefore finds a part of the tastes and habits of aristocracy." The jury and the judge (promoted from the pool of lawyers) are therefore not adversaries, although they could become so, should the judge exercise his power in an arbitrary or despotic manner. But under normal circumstances, the jury is the place where the law can exercise a salutary influence over the demos, an "aristocratic element . . . mixed without effort into the natural elements of democracy."[121]

REPUBLICAN SCHOOLMASTERS AND REPUBLICAN CITIZENS

As the federal judiciary under the new Constitution was getting under way, the judge-jury partnership was in full flower. But this partnership was part of a larger relationship in which judges and citizens were engaged in the common enterprise of establishing and enforcing the law. To further this common purpose, Congress devised a plan to require Supreme Court justices to serve on circuit courts—to "ride circuit"—so that the nation's highest judicial authorities would have contact with citizens on a regular basis. In this way judges would have an opportunity to impress on citizens the importance of their responsibilities to the law and to the Constitution. This arrangement persisted even though it placed great physical burdens on the justices, who had to spend considerable time traveling by coach or

120. Ibid., 263–264.
121. Ibid., 252, 256.

schooner from city to city, far from their families and from the civilized comforts of New York and Philadelphia.[122]

Commonly, the judge assigned to a particular district would begin the term by addressing the grand jury on important legal questions that might come before it. These addresses were often published, customarily "at the request of the grand jurors," gaining a much wider currency and giving citizens a chance to read and think about the highest legal matters. The teaching function of these addresses is apparent from the way they were written. In June 1795, for example, Associate Justice William Paterson addressed the Delaware grand jury on the importance of the regular enforcement of the Neutrality Act of 1794, which pro-French partisans in Delaware disliked intensely. This lecture touched on the law of nations, the meaning of the treaty power, the wisdom of the framers in placing that power where they did, and the dreadful consequences if Americans let their sympathy for one party to an international conflict drag the nation into war.[123] These addresses were given even when there were no significant legal matters pending in the district—a sure sign that they had purposes beyond law enforcement.

Among the more difficult questions engaging the thoughtful attention of grand juries during these early years were the disturbances in western Pennsylvania during the summer of 1794, known as the Whiskey Rebellion. Farmers who objected to the new federal excise tax on distilled spirits took up arms against tax collectors, the courts, and federal marshals. The rebellion was put down by an army of 13,000, called up by President Washington from the militias of several states and commanded by General Harry Lee. The troops were accompanied by

122. The letters the justices wrote to their wives and friends cite the difficulties imposed by the practice of riding circuit. They complained of bad roads, swamps, illness, rustic lodgings in roadside inns, shortages of cash, terrible food, and homesickness. Congress included a provision in the Judiciary Act of 1801 ("An Act to Provide for the More Convenient Organization of the Courts of the United States," 2 Stat. 89) to eliminate circuit riding; however, shortly after assuming office, the Jefferson administration persuaded Congress to restore the old practice, which persisted until the Judiciary Act of 1869. See Maeva Marcus and James R. Perry, eds., *Documentary History of the Supreme Court of the United States, 1789–1800*, 8 vols. (New York: Columbia University Press, 1985–2007), 3:94, 419, n. 1.

123. "William Paterson's Charge to the Grand Jury of the Circuit Court for the District of Delaware (June 8, 1795)," ibid., 57–61. Here is the grand jury's response: "Sir. / The Grand Inquest for the district of Delaware, impressed with the importance of your address . . . to them yesterday; presume the publication thereof, will tend to disseminate and inculcate Ideas, that may be useful to our fellow Citizens: We therefore . . . take the liberty of Soliciting your Honor for a Copy . . . thereof." On the importance of the judges as "schoolmasters," see Ralph Lerner, "The Supreme Court as Republican Schoolmasters," *Supreme Court Review* (1967): 127–180.

President Washington himself and by Treasury Secretary Alexander Hamilton, who had proposed the tax in the first place.[124]

This event confirmed the worst fears of both Anti-Federalists (that the national government is a tyranny enforced by bayonets) and Federalists (that democracy's secret tendency is toward anarchy). To those charged with enforcing the law, it must have seemed a moment of supreme danger. In 1795, while the trials of the insurgents were still in progress, many grand juries heard admonitions of the sort delivered by Justice Paterson on April 2 to the grand jury in New Jersey. Paterson first reminded the jurors (as these charges always did) of the importance of the "office, into which you have been sworn," to the "good order, peace, and prosperity of the government under which we live." He then praised the "citizens of this state" for their outstanding record of lawfulness and for their great assistance in suppressing "that dangerous insurrection" of the year before. He told the jurors it would not be necessary to explain to them the nature of indictable offenses, since the "penal code is plain and concise, and reduced, in the most important points to written exactitude and precision." Another happy circumstance rendered this "unpleasing task" unnecessary: the "improbability of any crimes having been committed in [New Jersey] against the United States." Rather than instruct the grand jury on the law, Paterson chose to instruct them on the importance of education to the survival of "good government" and "republican principles." "The mind, without literature or science, is in a rude and dark state, and incapable of high or useful exertions; even genius, uncultivated, loses half his force. . . . Ignorance may be called the mother of slavery as well as of superstition."[125]

Meanwhile, Paterson's colleague James Iredell was in Connecticut discussing the vital importance to a free society of obedience to the law. "In vain have the people chosen their own constitutions of government (as well general as particular) if the governments established under them are not submitted to" peaceably. "Common sense . . . and the lowest notions of republican government, revolt against the absurd idea that when once a majority constitutionally authorized has passed a law, which all are bound to obey, any may disobey with impunity." Nevertheless, in a country like the United States—a "land of liberty"—prosecutions must be conducted not "rashly" but with "deliberation and solemnity," and above all they must be conducted "impartially." The law is "no respecter of persons." No institution is better suited to the achievement of these important ends than the grand jury, Iredell remarked, "composed, as it usually is (and always ought to

124. On the Whiskey Rebellion, see Stanley Elkins and Eric McKitrick, *The Age of Federalism: The Early American Republic, 1788–1800* (New York: Oxford University Press, 1993), 478–485.

125. "William Paterson's Charge to the Grand Jury of the Circuit Court for the District of New Jersey (April 2, 1795)," in Marcus and Perry, *Documentary History*, 3:11.

be) of a select number of respectable and disinterested members of the community, selected for a single time only, and who may justly be presumed to have no views but to promote the interest and happiness of their common country." In the rest of his address, Iredell explored the difference between offenses committed against the United States, which are the particular business of the grand jury in a circuit court, and offenses committed against the state of Connecticut, which are not the court's business. He then defined offenses against the United States more precisely ("violations of the law of nations, or violations of some duty to the United States in particular") and made brief reference to the wise checks on the legislative power itself, so that obedience can be enforced "without hardship or oppression."[126]

The relationship between judge and jury was not one-sided, as shown by the "Presentment of the Grand Jury of the Circuit Court for the District of Georgia" delivered on April 29, 1795. Not a presentment of any indictable offense, this document presents, rather, a "grievance": namely, that the "Courts of Admiralty in the United States have a power too unlimited—We therefore recommend to the next Congress seriously to consider on the propriety of restoring to the people of the United States a privilege the most sacred—that of trial by Jury in those Courts."[127] The use of juries in admiralty courts had been a common practice after the Revolution, and the denial of juries in customs trials had been part of the "long train of abuses" that justified the Declaration of Independence. But the practice proved to be a disappointment, ironically, and the Judiciary Act of 1789 provided that such trials would be conducted in federal courts without juries, as part of the court's responsibility for "all Cases of admiralty and maritime Jurisdiction."[128] Not surprisingly, this return to the British practice struck many Americans as a loss that Congress should rectify as soon as possible. Congress declined to do so, however, leaving maritime cases in the hands of judges exclusively.[129]

The deliberate attacks on officials charged with enforcing the hated whiskey tax brought American citizens into armed conflict with one another for the first time since Shays' Rebellion in Massachusetts in 1786. The trials of the persons responsible would now require citizens to sit in judgment of fellow citizens who were charged not with ordinary felonies (murder, assault, robbery, fraud) but with

126. "James Iredell's Charge to the Grand Jury of the Circuit Court for the District of Connecticut (April 25, 1795)," ibid., 28–30.

127. "Presentment of the Grand Jury of the Circuit Court for the District of Georgia (April 29, 1795)," ibid., 39.

128. United States Constitution, Article III, section 2, clause 1.

129. This controversy is still alive, and some states have recently returned maritime cases to juries. See Douglas Truxillo, "Maritime Defendants Now Have a Right to Jury Trial in Louisiana State Court," http://www.corporate.findlaw.com/law-library/maritime-defendants-now-have-right-to-jury-trial-in-louisiana.html (accessed January 30, 2014).

the extraordinary (and capital) crime of treason.[130] The Constitution had defined treason prudently, requiring "overt acts" and leaving opinion out of it: treason "shall consist only in levying War against [the United States], or in adhering to their Enemies, giving them Aid and Comfort." Further, no such charge could be sustained without the testimony of two witnesses "to the same overt Act, or on Confession in open Court."[131] The trials of the Whiskey Rebellion leaders for treason must have seemed a terrible responsibility in a country so new, especially in Pennsylvania, where the rebellion had taken place.[132]

Consequently, in charging the grand jury in the Pennsylvania circuit on May 4, 1795 (the trials continued until late summer), Justice Paterson turned his attention to the important task of distinguishing rebellion against a tyrannical government from acts of violence against a government chosen by the people themselves. The government of the United States, Paterson noted, "is a government of laws, and not of men; a government, which has freedom for its basis, and the happiness of the people for its object. Crimes perpetrated against such a government ought to be considered as pointed against the peace, the well-being, the political existence, and, if I may so phrase it, the majesty of the people themselves." Although there were a few other offenses worthy of the jury's "particular notice" (including forgery of bank notes and violations of the Neutrality Act), treason was the real subject of Paterson's address. "Alas! Gentlemen, that any circumstances should have arisen to render it necessary for courts to take cognizance of this crime." And while we "regret and deplore" its existence, we must "be mindful of our duty, and be faithful to our country and its laws." All persons who "take up arms against the government," who "resist and prevent the regular administration of justice" by using force, all these "come within the description of levying war." All who "make insurrections under the pretense of redressing national or public grievances, whether they be real or imaginary," or who use force to effect "the repeal of a law" are also guilty of treason.[133]

It was especially important that the jury understand the kind of problem the Whiskey Rebellion presented, Paterson implied, because it was precisely this problem that was most fatal to republics. "The constitution and laws contain the

130. The death penalty for treason was provided for in the Crimes Act of 1790, chap. 9, 1 Stat. 112.

131. United States Constitution, Article III, section 3, clause 1.

132. The jury that convicted Philip Vigol of treason asked Albert Gallatin to compose a petition to President Washington, seeking a pardon; all members of the jury signed it. Albert Gallatin to Hannah Gallatin, June 1, 1795, in Marcus and Perry, *Documentary History*, 3:53. Washington pardoned both of the men who had been sentenced to death for leading the rebellion.

133. "William Paterson's Charge to the Grand Jury of the Circuit Court for the District of Pennsylvania (May 4, 1795)," in Marcus and Perry, *Documentary History*, 3:40–41.

articles of our political faith; they point the path we are to go, and the rule by which we are to walk. They are the work of the people, declarative of their will, and as such ought to be reverenced and obeyed."[134]

The major controversies troubling the nation during this period regularly came before the grand juries in the federal circuits, not simply as matters requiring investigation or presentment but as subjects for these floating seminars on the nature of republican government. Thus, during the spring and fall circuits in 1796, Justice Iredell explained to the grand juries in New Jersey and Pennsylvania the importance of the Jay Treaty and of President Washington's Proclamation of Neutrality, and the jurors in both places responded with lengthy disquisitions of their own.[135] No doubt these charges and replies served a partisan purpose in, or were at least relevant to, the struggle between the Federalists and the Jeffersonians, but this does not lessen their value as instruction or the significance of the fact that they were unnecessary from a strictly judicial perspective, there being no crimes under consideration that had anything to do with the Jay Treaty or the Proclamation of Neutrality.

THE SEDITION ACT TRIALS

The events that put the greatest strain on the judge-jury partnership, however, were the prosecutions arising out of the Sedition Act of 1798. During the Washington and Adams administrations, the political divide between the pro- and anti-Constitution factions degenerated into a disorganized brawl between the supporters of Washington, Hamilton, and Adams, on one side, and those of Jefferson and Madison, on the other. The most extreme forms of partisanship found expression in the newspapers of the day, which published angry and hysterical denunciations of their opponents. Those coming from the Republican side were not notably worse than those coming from the Federalist side, except that the Republicans were directing their venom at the government—at Washington and Adams in particular—and this opened them to the charge of sedition.

The attacks that led to the sedition trials were clearly meant to achieve precisely what the law sought to punish: to bring Congress and the president "into contempt or disrepute" and to "excite against them . . . the hatred of the good people of the United States."[136] Although the Sedition Act permitted the "truth

134. Ibid., 42.

135. See "Justice Iredell's Charge to the Grand Jury of the Circuit Court for the District of Pennsylvania, and Their Reply," ibid., 106–114; and "The Reply of the Grand Jury of the Circuit Court for the District of New Jersey," ibid., 102–104.

136. "An Act in Addition to the Act Entitled, 'An Act for the Punishment of Certain Crimes against the United States,'" July 14, 1798, section 2.

of the matter contained in the statement" to be cited as a defense, the comments made about Adams, to cite just one example, were either obviously false or not provable, and it is difficult to believe that the individuals who made such claims actually believed them. James Callender wrote that Washington and Adams were "poltroons" and "venal" and that Adams was a "libeler" and "incendiary" whose hands reeked "with the blood of the poor . . . sailor."[137] Hamilton was "the Judas Iscariot of our country" and an obvious monarchist as well. Adams was a "poor old man" in his "dotage."[138] Surely Thomas Jefferson, who supported Callender financially throughout this period, did not believe that Adams was "venal" or an "incendiary."[139] Yet on both sides of the debate, extravagant claims were the norm, and they dominated in the popular press. It is difficult to find anything in the newspapers of the day that contemporary Americans (subject to their own ludicrous partisan fits) would consider normal political discussion. There is almost nothing, for example, that could be considered a sober assessment of an alliance with England, the treaty ending the Revolutionary War, the appropriate policy toward France, or any other questions that were the subject of contemporary debate. Walter Berns writes that "America probably has not known a time when its politics were conducted with such vehemence and hatred."[140]

Although there was considerable eloquence and intelligence among the leaders on both sides of the divide, such qualities were found almost exclusively in private letters or official state documents. What partisans had to say for publication was another matter entirely.[141] Both sides blasted away at the personal character (and even the physical appearance) of their opponents, with no regard for the truth of their accusations, trafficking in the wildest conspiracy theories. Adams, in addition to enduring ridicule for his personal foibles (his insistence on pomp in the presidential office, for example, or his prose style) and his mild corpulence, was accused of crimes that could only be described as treasonous. It was said that he was in league with the British Crown, which was paying him handsomely to

137. See Walter Berns, "Freedom of the Press and the Alien and Sedition Laws: A Reappraisal," *Supreme Court Review* (1970): 109–159. The British Navy was impressing American seamen who were alleged to be British citizens. Adams's "crime" was that he had not retaliated by seeking a declaration of war against Great Britain.

138. John Ferling, *Adams v. Jefferson: The Tumultuous Election of 1800* (New York: Oxford University Press, 2004), 136–137.

139. On Jefferson's relationship with Callender, see ibid. and John Chester Miller, *The Wolf by the Ears: Thomas Jefferson and Slavery* (New York: Free Press, 1977).

140. Berns, "Freedom of the Press," 109.

141. One notable exception was *The Pacificus-Helvidius Letters*, in which former allies Hamilton and Madison argued the merits of the president's authority in foreign affairs, among other subjects. But even these *Letters* are notably less temperate than *The Federalist*.

subvert the liberties of the American people. He was also accused of falsifying Talleyrand's diplomatic letters to justify going to war with France. John Marshall, not yet on the Supreme Court, worried that "government cannot be . . . secured, if by falsehood and malicious slander, it is to be deprived of the confidence and affection of the people."[142]

Between 1798 and 1800, fourteen suspects were indicted by federal grand juries under the Sedition Act (including James Callender), and three more were indicted by state governments under their own sedition laws. With one exception, every defendant who went before a jury was convicted.[143] For the crime of insulting Presidents Washington and Adams, defendants suffered a fate that the seven bishops, William Penn, and John Peter Zenger, among others, had managed to escape.

What had gone wrong? From the perspective of the Federalists, of course, nothing had gone wrong. Seditious Republican editorialists and agitators had been tried and found guilty by their fellow citizens. Unlike the bishops, Penn, and Zenger, the Sedition Act defendants were guilty of saying things that were not true. The jury had performed its traditional function of finding the facts and applying the law as expounded by the judge. The very language of the Sedition Act made it clear that this was what jurors were expected to do—"to determine the law and the fact, under the direction of the court, as in other cases."[144] Republicans, of course, were horrified. How could the palladium of our liberties fail so spectacularly just a decade after the successful battle to adopt the Bill of Rights? It was particularly galling that this failure concerned the very crime—seditious libel—on which the jury's reputation had been forged during the campaign against the "wretched Stuarts."

In some ways, however, the Sedition Act clarified and even strengthened the authority of the jury, because it made explicit what the English common law of libel had left uncertain—namely, that there must be evidence of intent to defame in order to prove the existence of a criminal libel.[145] It would no longer be enough to say bad things about government officials; those things would have to be provably false, and their falsehood would have to be known to the author at the time of publication. Thus, one of the "facts" left for the jury to determine was the one that defined the crime in the first place, and this was tantamount to deciding what

142. John Marshall, "Report of the Minority on the Virginia Resolutions," January 22, 1799, in *Classics of American Political and Constitutional Thought*, vol. 1, ed. Scott J. Hammond, Kevin R. Hardwick, and Howard L. Lubert (Indianapolis: Hackett, 2007), 669.

143. Elkins and McKitrick, *Age of Federalism*, 703. See also Amar, *Bill of Rights*, 87–88.

144. Sedition Act, section 3.

145. Section 2 of the Sedition Act prohibits the publication of "false, scandalous and malicious writing . . . with the intent to defame the said government."

the law means. Coming just six years after Fox's Libel Act in Great Britain,[146] the Sedition Act was actually a more "liberal" understanding of criminal libel than Fox's famous reform, which did not include any consideration of intent but made it clear that truth would be a defense against a libel charge. But the inclusion of "intention" shows how the "facts" and the "law" could be mixed in a complicated way, leaving the jury to decide whether the elements of libel were present in any particular case. Jurors would need to understand the meaning of "intent to defame" and then decide whether the statements made about public officials were plausibly true or so obviously false that no well-intentioned person could have believed them at the time they were published. It was the job of the judges to teach the jury about the law and its requirements, but the jurors made the final decision.

The sedition controversy was also another opportunity for federal judges to exercise their schoolmaster function because public opinion was unsettled and in need of guidance on both sides of the partisan divide. Although the stakes for these defendants were much less than for those prosecuted after the Whiskey Rebellion—a Sedition Act violation was a misdemeanor punishable by no more than two years in prison and a fine not to exceed $2,000—the general agitation was much more widespread. The rebellion of the whiskey distillers was localized and was not popular in other states, since any taxes not paid by the Pennsylvania distillers would have to be made up by the citizens of other states. By contrast, the conflict sparked by the Sedition Act was nationwide; it involved the nation's leading political figures, it implicated fundamental political principles, and it helped generate the country's first party system and its first partisan contest for the presidency.[147]

In October 1798 Justice Paterson addressed the grand jury of the Circuit Court for the District of Vermont. A Republican member of the House of Representatives from Vermont, Mathew Lyons, would soon be indicted for violating the Sedition Act, and the charges and countercharges associated with the XYZ Affair, the Jay Treaty, and the possibility of a war with revolutionary France provided the dramatic backdrop for Paterson's seminar on free speech and its limits in a republic. Paterson began, as usual, by stressing the importance of the "office, into which you have been sworn," as well as the value of the jury's republican character, which gives it an "authority [that] descends to the lowest, and reaches to the highest character of social life." Paterson then repeated a favorite analogy that was likely to catch the attention of citizens from all levels of society: that between the circulation of fraudulent currency notes and the circulation of "false, scandalous, and malicious writings, publications, and libels against the government

146. 32 Geo. 3, c. 60, 1792.

147. On the general alarm prompted by the Sedition Act trials, see Elkins and McKitrick, *Age of Federalism*, 703–711; on the foreboding sparked by the election of 1800, see Ferling, *Adams v. Jefferson*.

of the United States." Over and over Paterson repeated such words as "false," "defamatory," "malicious," "lies," and "calumny." These were the elements that distinguished seditious publications from ordinary and even vigorous criticism of the government. Furthermore, because such publications were directed against an elected government, they were "leveled against the people themselves."[148] This was perhaps the most important lesson for citizens to learn—namely, that they were no longer struggling against a foreign oppressor; they were now called on to support a government of their own creation, and this would require firm resolve. "For the constitution, government, and constituted authorities of the United States are emphatically the creation and work of the people, emanating from their authority, and declarative of their will. To support them is our primary duty—to attempt their destruction is an offense of deep malignity."[149]

Likewise, Justice Chase, in his April 1800 charge to the grand jury of the Circuit for Pennsylvania, explained the intricate connection between the duties of judges and the duties of petit jurors in both criminal and civil cases. Turning to the vexing question of the proper relation between judge and jury on the matter of determining the law, Chase made a subtle but traditional set of distinctions between criminal and civil cases, on the one hand, and between the jury's responsibility and the judge's, on the other. In criminal cases, judges have an obligation "to assist and advise the petit jury on all questions of law," and it would show "improper suspicion" on the part of jurors if they did not "pay a proper respect" to the judge's opinion on such an important matter. Such respect is a "solemn" obligation mandated both by religion and by self-respect. If a jury were to convict a defendant in a criminal trial against the weight of the evidence, the "peculiar mildness" of the law provided the remedy of a new trial; in civil cases, should a jury ignore the judge's direction as to the law, it risked having its judgment set aside.

But then Justice Chase reaffirmed in the clearest terms the traditional view of the power of the jury in criminal cases: although juries in civil cases must simply follow the judge's direction regarding the law, in criminal cases, "I am fully convinced, that the petit jury have the right to decide the law, as well as the fact . . . and consequently . . . give a general verdict of guilt or acquittal; and that the court have no right to refuse or control such a verdict; and that their duty only requires them to assist and advise the jury, on all questions of law, that may occur on the trial of criminal cases."[150] Given Chase's notoriety as the most irascible of the Federalist judges, this exploration of the rights and duties of juries suggests the nature of the partnership that both Federalists and Republicans understood to exist between judge and jury in the republican era.

148. Elkins and McKitrick, *Age of Federalism*, 293, 294.

149. Ibid.

150. "Samuel Chase's Charge to the Grand Jury of the Circuit Court for the District of Pennsylvania (April 12, 1800)," in Marcus and Perry, *Documentary History*, 3:408–417.

Chase's comments and rulings in the sedition trial of James Callender—probably the most famous of these trials—demonstrate even more clearly what was meant by the statement that juries could "find the law and the facts" when they were mixed, as they were understood to be in libel cases. That the views expressed on this occasion were those of a Federalist judge is notable; the extent to which the new circumstances of a republican government operating under a written constitution complicated the question of the jury's authority is even more so.

Callender was charged with twelve counts of sedition for publishing a collection of "false, malicious, and defamatory" materials about President Adams and former president Washington in a paper entitled "The Prospect before Us," with the intention of "excit[ing] the hatred of the good people of the United States" toward the president in particular and the government in general. The statements printed under Callender's name were sensational and vitriolic, like so much of the rhetoric of the day. They accused the Federalist presidents of a series of odious crimes committed from the basest of motives, putting the liberties of the new republic in imminent peril.[151]

Under the Sedition Act's second section, falsehood and intention to defame were equally necessary to convict. A false statement might be made unknowingly, but a false statement made with the intention to defame could not be excused on the grounds of ignorance. Section 2 stated that if any person "shall write, print, utter or publish" material that is "false, scandalous and malicious" against the government or its officials, "with intent to defame the said government" or its officials, "or to bring them . . . into contempt," such person is guilty of a crime. However, section 3 stated that the defendant may present as evidence of his innocence "the truth of the matter contained in the publication charged as a libel. And the jury who shall try the cause, shall have a right to determine the law and the fact, under the direction of the court, as in other cases."[152]

These requirements suggested an interesting problem to one of Callender's attorneys, Mr. Hay. If the truth of the statements could be offered as a defense against the charge of libel—and this meant every statement, not just a few—didn't this impose an impossible burden on the defendant? After all, how could a statement such as "President Adams is an avowed aristocrat" be proved either true or false? Similarly, how could one prove or disprove Callender's claim that President Adams had "changed his principles"? This would require the defense to establish what Adams's principles had once been and then compare them to what Adams believed at the moment. Didn't such an enterprise involve an inquiry into opinions rather than facts?

151. See the trial summary in United States v. Callender, 25 F. Cas. 239, no. 14,709 (C.C.D. Va. [1800]).

152. Sedition Act, section 3.

> Mr. H. said that the object of the law was to punish a man, not for . . . erroneous deductions or opinions, but for "fact falsely and maliciously asserted." If this idea was correct, it became a matter of consequence to do what had never been done perhaps before, to draw a line of discrimination between fact and opinion; because if the indictment contained against the traverser charges [him] of being guilty of error in opinion as well as falsehood in fact, it was so far defective.[153]

Justice Chase would have none of it, appealing to the "commonsense" understanding of the jurors over the tortured and misleading arguments of attorneys:

> Must there be a departure from common sense [Chase inquired] to find out a construction favorable to the traverser? This construction admits the publication, but denies its criminality. If the traverser certainly published that defamatory paper, read it and consider it. Can any of you say, that the president is a detestable and criminal man? The traverser charges him with being a murderer and a thief, a despot and a tyrant! Will you call a man a murderer and a thief, and excuse yourself by saying it is but mere opinion—or that you heard so? Any falsehood . . . may be justified by this species of argument.[154]

No, Chase insisted; the only question here is "with what intent the traverser published these charges? Are they false, scandalous, and malicious, and published with intent to defame? It is for the jury to say, what was the intent of such imputations, and this is sufficiently obvious."[155]

Voir dire in this case consisted of Justice Chase asking prospective jurors just one question: "Have you ever formed and delivered an opinion upon this charge?" After answering satisfactorily, the jurors were sworn. Once jury selection was completed, the judge explained the issue in these terms, stressing, as did the law itself, the necessity of both falsehood and malicious intent: "it must be proved that the traverser wrote or published the book—that the charges were false, scandalous and malicious, and that he wrote them with intent to defame, and that if he could prove the charges he must be acquitted."[156]

In presenting the case for the government, the district attorney, Mr. Nelson, explained to the jurors the particular questions they would have to answer. First, did the defendant publish the material in question (i.e., "The Prospect before Us")? Second, "with what view, and for what purpose [was] a paper like this . . . composed and published?" That is, was it intended to be "a candid and fair dis-

153. *Callender*, 242.
154. Ibid., 244.
155. Ibid.
156. Ibid., 245.

cussion of constitutional subjects, or real grievances, or of political opinions and principles generally?" If that were the case, then the paper would not constitute libel within the meaning of the law. Alternatively, if the jury concluded that the allegations in the paper were true, then the defendant would have successfully defended himself against a libel charge. But if the jury concluded that the publication "does not contain the truth in all parts, you must find the traverser guilty." This speech suggested a tougher standard for the defense against libel—that is, the defendant must prove that every one of his statements is true, or else the statement as a whole would be false. In his summing up, Nelson reaffirmed this standard: "For the questions you are to try, gentlemen of the jury, are: Was this paper published by the traverser? Was the intention criminal? that is, is the matter false, scandalous and malicious? The evidence which you have heard ascertains the first question, and an examination of the paper, or such parts of it as are laid in the indictment, will decide the second question."[157]

But it is clear that deciding whether the writings were "scandalous and malicious," as well as "false," was the jury's responsibility. And in deciding, the jurors would have to somehow determine the author's intentions. That is, they would have to decide, as a matter of fact, whether the author's intentions were those required by the law. Did the defendant intend to speak falsely of the president, or were his views mere expressions of "erroneous" opinion, honestly offered?

After some fruitless motions intended to demonstrate the truth of the claims in Callender's writings, the defense came to the heart of its argument, raising an issue that would increasingly trouble the judge-jury relationship in republican America. Defense counsel Mr. Wirt told the jury that, because it was the practice in Virginia to recognize the common-law jury's power to determine the law and the facts, it was not only the jury's right but also its obligation to acquit the defendant if, in its view, the Sedition Act violated the Constitution of the United States. Wirt was told to take his seat, and Justice Chase read a lengthy opinion denying that the petit jury had or could have any such right "to decide on the constitutionality of a law, and that such a power would be extremely dangerous" (he had learned beforehand that the defense would make this claim and was suitably prepared). The following colloquy ensued:

> Mr. Wirt.—I shall state to the court, in a few words, the reasons which have induced me to ascribe this right to the jury. They are sworn to give their verdict according to the evidence, and the law is evidence; if the jury have no right to consider the law, how is it possible for them to render a general verdict? Suppose, for example, an indictment for murder—how can the jury pronounce a verdict of guilty, or not guilty, if they have not the right as well of ascertaining whether the facts have been committed, as whether they

157. Ibid.

amount to a breach of law? This doctrine is too clearly established to require the aid of authorities.

Chase, Circuit Justice.—No man will deny your law—we all know that juries have the right to decide the law, as well as the fact—and the constitution is the supreme law of the land, which controls all laws which are repugnant to it.

Mr. Wirt.—Since, then, the jury have a right to consider the law, and since the constitution is law, the conclusion is certainly syllogistic, that the jury have a right to consider the constitution.

Chase, Circuit Justice.—A non sequitur, sir.[158]

Here, Mr. Wirt sat down.

In his charge to the jury, Justice Chase emphasized the necessity of proving intent in order to convict. Did the defendant make statements he knew to be false, intending to harm the reputation of the person he named? However, Chase would not allow the jury to hear an argument about its right to rule on the constitutionality of congressional acts, which he distinguished sharply from the right to determine the law and the facts:

> The statute, on which the traverser is indicted, enacts "that the jury who shall try the cause shall have a right to determine the law and the fact, under the direction of the court, as in other cases." By this provision, I understand that a right is given to the jury to determine what the law is in the case before them; and not to decide whether a statute of the United States produced to them, is a law or not, or whether it is void, under an opinion that it is unconstitutional, that is, contrary to the constitution of the United States.[159]

The jury, Chase continued, is to "compare the statute with the facts proved, and then . . . decide whether the acts done are prohibited by the law. . . . This power the jury necessarily possesses." However, it is "a very different thing, to determine that the statute produced is no law." That function cannot belong to the jury, for it has already been given, by the Constitution itself, to the judiciary.[160]

Moreover, the consequence of giving this function to the jury would be that laws passed by Congress would be in force in some jurisdictions but not in others. This would introduce great inconsistency and uncertainty into the law, a theme to which judges would return often in the following decades. "The doing [of] certain acts will be held criminal, and punished in one state, and similar acts may be held innocent, and even approved and applauded in another." In concluding, Chase

158. Ibid., 253.
159. Ibid., 255.
160. Ibid., 256.

took care to reaffirm the older understanding while rejecting the newer, improper (in his opinion) claim: "I have uniformly delivered the opinion, 'that the petit jury have a right to decide the law as well as the fact, in criminal cases;' but it never entered into my mind that they, therefore, had a right to determine the constitutionality of any statute of the United States."[161]

After deliberating for two hours, the jury returned a verdict of guilty, and the court fined Callender $200 and sentenced him to a nine-month prison term.[162]

The sedition trials exposed two difficulties with the jury system in a republican government, and the debate over these difficulties has continued in one form or another ever since. The first difficulty concerns the composition of the jury and, more precisely, the establishment of qualifications for jury service and the process of impaneling a jury for a particular trial. The second difficulty concerns the relationship between the jury and the judge. Are they adversaries or partners? Or is the relationship more like that between an experienced teacher and a group of intelligent seminar students, as Tocqueville implied?

I use the term "difficulties" because it was rare for critics of the sedition trials to blame the jury system itself, and only slightly less rare to blame the actual jurors. Having achieved its mythical status as the palladium of our liberties, the jury system could not now be scorned, however disappointed republicans might be with its performance. But they could point out that the jury system would work better if certain questionable practices were remedied. And thus began the battle to reform the jury system—a battle the republicans eventually lost. Each of these difficulties is discussed in turn below.

JURY SELECTION

Jury laws varied in the colonies, and in the states after independence, but the differences were relatively minor. The basic pattern was that voters and jurors were essentially the same group: male freeholders (or, in some states, taxpayers) who also met the locality's residency requirements constituted the jury pool—that is, the list of citizens from which the venire (those summoned to court for a particular session) was chosen. The amount of property that qualified as a "freehold" varied from state to state, but property ownership was so widespread in America that one-half to three-quarters of the population of adult white males likely met the voting requirements of their states—at least for the lower house of the legislature,

161. Ibid., 256, 258.

162. Ibid. Chase's comments in the Callender trial were cited during his impeachment in 1804, along with remarks he made in the sedition trial of John Fries and his public complaints about the dissolution of lower courts presided over by Federalist judges. The Senate (with a substantial Republican majority) acquitted Justice Chase in March 1805.

and therefore for the US House of Representatives.[163] In a few states there were higher property qualifications for jury service than for voting; in no state was the opposite the case. The only religious test for jury service that survived into the republican era was one that barred atheists, and this persisted in only a few states.[164]

Although meeting the property and residency requirements automatically made a citizen a voter, there was another hurdle to overcome to become a juror: one had to be on the list from which the venire was chosen, a decision made by local officials. State jury laws made it clear that jury service required certain qualities that did not figure in voting requirements and went beyond the property qualification. In fact, whereas voting was understood to be a right, and there was universal agreement on a citizen's right to be tried by a jury, jury service was understood to be a duty rather than a right. In fact, it was closer to an office than a right; the jury was often likened to the "lower house" of the judiciary, balancing judges in the same way the democratic House balanced the slightly aristocratic Senate.

For this reason, jury statutes often used words such as "reputation," "judgment," "integrity," and "intelligence" to describe the special characteristics required for the successful performance of this office, words that were never used in the context of the voting laws. The Delaware statute of 1811 was not untypical in commanding the county sheriff to summon "sober, discreet, and judicious freeholders, lawful men and of fair characters."[165] North Carolina declared the citizen's right to be tried by a jury made up of "good and lawful men."[166] In Connecticut juries were to be composed of "able, judicious and lawful freeholders of the town."[167] The expectation that a jury be something more than a purely random selection had always been a feature of the common-law jury, and words like "sober" and "discrete" appeared in seventeenth-century colonial documents. Since these qualities could not be measured objectively, in the way property, taxpaying,

163. Alshculer and Deiss, "Brief History of the Criminal Jury," 877, n. 54, citing research in Willi Paul Adams, *The First American Constitutions: Republican Ideology and the Making of the State Constitutions in the Revolutionary Era* (Raleigh: University of North Carolina Press, 1980), and Chilton Williamson, *American Suffrage from Property to Democracy, 1760–1860* (Princeton, NJ: Princeton University Press, 1960).

164. Alschuler and Deiss, "Brief History of the Criminal Jury," 877–878. Free blacks were either not eligible for jury service or not called. "It is believed that 1860 was the first year in which African-Americans served on juries, in either the North or the South." James Forman Jr., "Juries and Race in the Nineteenth Century," *Yale Law Journal* 113 (2004): 910.

165. Alschuler and Deiss, "Brief History of the Criminal Jury," 878, n. 57.

166. Henry D. Potter, *Laws of the State of North Carolina, Including the Titles of Such Statutes and Parts of Statutes of Great Britain as Are in Force in Said State*, vol. 1 (Raleigh, NC, 1821), 42.

167. Zephaniah Swift, *The Public Statute Laws of the State of Connecticut, as Revised and Enacted by the General Assembly, in May 1821* (Hartford, CT, 1821), 45.

and residence could be measured, their discovery required the exercise of discretion by the officials responsible for choosing prospective jurors. And as we have seen, Tocqueville observed that whereas the right to serve on a jury "extends to everyone. . . . the exercise of this right is not put indiscriminately in all hands." Those chosen were "supposed" by the magistrates (whose powers, Tocqueville claimed, were "very extensive and quite arbitrary") to have the requisite qualities for service.[168]

The Judiciary Act of 1789 gave states the authority to qualify jurors for both state and federal courts, requiring each federal court to use the jury lists prepared by the state where the court sat.[169] Thus, state legislators held the keys to federal jury service, a concession to federalism that was not formally abolished until the Civil Rights Act of 1957.[170] State legislatures first defined the threshold qualifications for jury service (age, tax status, and so on). Officials with a variety of titles—selectmen, supervisors, trustees, sheriffs—then combed through the list of names meeting these objective qualifications, choosing those who possessed, in their judgment, whatever additional qualities of "intelligence," "judgment," or "integrity" the statutes imposed.[171] These names were then placed on the jury list, or into the "jury wheel" (literally a wheel that could be spun, mixing the name cards randomly), from which venires were chosen as needed by the various courts served by the list. The Judiciary Act gave federal officials the authority to take the next step, known as "summoning the venire," or calling jurors from the state jury lists to serve in federal court.[172]

Whoever controlled the summoning of the venire exercised considerable influence over the ultimate composition of the jury. It was inevitable, therefore, that as partisan feelings intensified in the United States during the 1790s, the partisan-

168. Tocqueville, *Democracy in America*, 697–698, n. XVII.

169. An Act to Establish the Judicial Courts of the United States, section 29, 1 Stat. 73, 88 (1789).

170. Pub. L. No. 85-315, September 9, 1957, 71 Stat. 634–638, section 152, established the qualifications for jury service in federal court, independent of state qualifications. At the time of its passage, an important part of this reform was its omission of gender from the list of qualities to be considered by jury commissioners, making women eligible for jury service in all federal courts for the first time. Exclusion based on race was already illegal, but the 1957 act gave federal jury commissioners the opportunity to evade racially discriminatory jury lists in the South. See chapters 3 and 4 for further discussion.

171. It should be stressed that while the law gave officials a discretionary authority over jury selection, not all officials in all places took the trouble to exercise that discretion, being content to choose jurors randomly from the list of those who were qualified. After Reconstruction, officials in the southern states used this discretion to keep blacks who were otherwise eligible for jury service from being chosen. See chapters 3 and 4 for further discussion of segregated jury lists.

172. Alschuler and Deiss, "Brief History of the Criminal Jury," 880.

ship of those who selected jurors would become a matter of some importance. In 1798 this meant that a Federalist secretary of state (Timothy Pickering), appointed by a Federalist president (John Adams) and confirmed by a Federalist Senate, appointed Federalist marshals to work under the supervision of federal judges, all of them appointed under Federalist presidents and confirmed by Federalist Senates. Not surprisingly, the marshals tended to summon Federalist jurors, following the age-old practice of "packing" juries. They did this simply by choosing jurors from towns known to be reliably Federalist and avoiding jurors from Republican towns. Given the intense partisanship of the time, it is likely that there were Federalist and Republican towns in most states.

Republican complaints about packing therefore had some credibility—certainly a lot more credibility than Republican charges that President Adams was secretly allied with the British Crown. Every member of the jury that had convicted James Callender in Virginia was a Federalist, according to local reports at the time. They had convicted Callender in less than two hours.[173] Thomas Jefferson confided in private letters his belief that the jury that convicted Thomas Cooper (after a "brief" deliberation) had also been "packed" with Federalists.[174] Republican congressman Matthew Lyon, convicted in the middle of his reelection campaign, pointed out that the jurors in his trial came from the same towns as the members of the grand jury that had indicted him.[175]

The packing controversy generated a new round of Republican versus Federalist invective in the press, and it led to an attempt to change the method of choosing jurors in federal court. A bill introduced by Charles Pinckney of South Carolina would have mandated the selection of jurors by lot, from the list of "all taxable male inhabitants" supplied by state authorities where the federal court sat. The bill's preamble noted that "the drawing of juries by lot appears to be the most safe and impartial mode for securing the due and upright administration of justice."[176] The lottery would be administered by the federal supervisor of the revenue in each state, taking the task away from marshals or other officers who served the court directly. The bill died in committee.

The failure to reform jury selection left the system as it was: with states defining eligibility for both state and federal trials, while federal marshals or federal court clerks supervised the summoning of jurors, who were sometimes chosen by lot and sometimes by "other means," depending on the laws of the state. Once

173. James Morton Smith, *Freedom's Fetters: The Alien and Sedition Laws and American Civil Liberties* (Ithaca, NY: Cornell University Press, 1956), 348.

174. Jefferson to Edmund Pendleton, April 19, 1800, cited by ibid., 319, n. 27.

175. Ibid., 232–235.

176. "A Bill to Establish an Uniform Mode of Drawing Jurors by Lot, in All the Courts of the United States," in *Debates and Proceedings of the United States Congress*, 8th Cong., 1st sess. (1803–1804).

partisan rancor died down, this arrangement was only occasionally controversial. In 1810 critics of the embargo laws complained that marshals "used their discretionary power so as to place on the juror lists only the names of persons sympathetic to the position of the federal government."[177] After the Civil War, the selection of jurors for federal trials in the South underwent a minor alteration, requiring bipartisan participation in the management of jury selection procedures. The act (passed by the Fortieth Congress, the first postwar Congress with a Democratic majority in both chambers) abolished the loyalty oath that had barred former Confederate officers and officials from jury service, and it required that juries in the federal court be selected by the clerk of the court and a citizen from "the other major political party" in the district.[178]

Republicans were certain that random selection would be enough to solve the problem of partisan packing and put the jury system back on its pedestal. Writing in the *City Gazette and Daily Advertiser* (Philadelphia), an anonymous editorialist identified the impartiality of the jury as the key to its fairness. "No man can be said to be truly and completely free, where juries are not chosen impartially by lot, and where they cannot be packed by a sheriff or marshal."[179] Included in this issue of the *City Gazette* was a copy of Senator Pinckney's speech on behalf of his proposal to establish a "uniform mode of drawing juries by lot in the courts of the United States," which would put the United States well ahead of England "in the purity and impartiality of our judicials."[180] The great defect in the current jury system, Pinckney argued, was the inconsistency of the process, especially the fact that in some states jurors were picked by federal marshals, who were political appointees. To the marshal was "left the monstrous and dangerous power of summoning proper or improper, dishonest or upright men—men who may be the friends or enemies to the parties who are on their trial, or who on political questions may be known to be opposed to them, and to hold opinions diametrically contrary to those which are perhaps in the course of the trial to be submitted to them for their decision." The power to select, he concluded, was the power to govern the opinion of juries—a position shared by generations of attorneys from the republican era to the present.

And yet Pinckney's defense of jury selection by lot conceded (without marking the inconsistency) that impaneling an impartial jury might require a subjective judgment—something a genuinely random process was incapable of making. That is, the jurors summoned must be, according to Pinckney, "proper" and "upright"—which was no doubt precisely how the Federalist marshals viewed the

177. Drew L. Kershen, "The Jury Selection Act of 1879: Theory and Practice of Citizen Participation in the Judicial System," *Law Forum* 1980, 3 (1980): 727.

178. Ibid., 728–729.

179. *City Gazette and Daily Advertiser*, June 28, 1800, 2.

180. Ibid.

jurors they chose from the Federalist towns in their districts. After all, what honest and upright man would hesitate to send a seditious Republican to prison for a few months?

The old meaning of impartial was tolerably clear: no man on the jury was the defendant's enemy, and no man was so close to the defendant as to render him incapable of voting guilty. Achieving this measure of impartiality, under the old English and colonial jury system, was fairly simple. Each side in a civil case, and the defendant in a criminal case, was allowed to strike a fixed number of names from the list of jurors. In this way, no defendant or litigant could complain about a packed jury. The only way around such a procedure would be for the official summoning the venire to ensure that there were enough jurors left to convict even after the defendant's friends had been struck. In English criminal trials, this meant, essentially, impaneling a jury of solid citizens willing to uphold the law.

But the new problem—revealed by the existence of Federalist towns and Republican towns and jurors' willingness to convict under the Sedition Act—was itself a consequence of a more democratic jury than the one known in England. A large percentage of the citizenry was eligible for jury service and for the suffrage—property qualifications in America were much lower than they were in Britain—and politics was seen almost exclusively through a partisan lens. It was thus inevitable that politics would intrude into court proceedings. A juror might have no personal feelings, one way or another, about the defendant, but he might despise (or endorse) the defendant's politics. Would such a juror be capable of making an "impartial" judgment based solely on the facts at issue? Or would he be rendering a political verdict?

Despite these concerns, republicans never achieved their goal of a truly random process for jury selection, and throughout the nineteenth century and well into the twentieth, jurors in state and federal courts were chosen by methods that gave court officials a considerable degree of discretion, as Tocqueville noted in the 1830s. This method—sometimes referred to by its old common-law name, venire facias ("cause to appear")—was found in the colonies and the states after the Revolution. Under this arrangement, the court directed the county sheriff (or the US marshal in federal court) to summon a specified number of "good and lawful men" for service as jurors. The common-law understanding of "good" was someone with the appropriate moral character, and this presumed that the sheriff or marshal knew something about the prospective jurors on the list. A "lawful" man was one who met the legal qualifications for jury service, one of which was the absence of any criminal record.[181]

Besides the danger of juries being packed by the officials choosing them, there was another difficulty with the venire facias that, over time, became as serious as the first. Nonrandom selection of jurors was more time-consuming than

181. Kershen, "Jury Selection Act of 1879," 728, n. 76.

random selection. Some states therefore abandoned the strictly common-law version of the venire facias in favor of something simpler: compiling a large list of names (sometimes simply all male taxpayers in the district) at regular intervals, and then choosing names at random as jurors were needed. Sometimes court officials interviewed those on the list to determine if they were suitable. Only then were their names placed into the jury wheel. These methods did not violate the Judiciary Act of 1789, which required federal jurors to be chosen "by lot or otherwise," giving states the discretion to use whatever method they deemed most suitable. Therefore, throughout the republican era and far into the modern era, jury selection in state and federal courts was characterized by diverse arrangements—random selection of names on various lists; the deliberate selection of citizens thought to be most worthy of consideration, based on whatever local officials knew about their character, intelligence, and integrity; or some combination of random and nonrandom procedures.[182] Population growth would present an obvious challenge to such methods, but as the next chapter shows, the practice of "culling" source lists for the most suitable candidates occurred even in major cities well into the twentieth century. And, as discussed in chapter 4, the practice of culling may have survived into the twenty-first century, through the careful use of the peremptory challenge.

BENCH, BAR, AND JURY: THE MASSACHUSETTS RECORD

In the early nineteenth century the combination of a broadly democratic suffrage and a long tradition of robust juries created a situation unique in Anglo-American law. Grand and petit juries were firmly established not only as judicial institutions but also as important elements of local government. Grand juries routinely investigated public institutions and officials, making recommendations and issuing criticisms, in addition to performing the traditional task of returning indictments in criminal matters.[183] Petit juries returned verdicts in criminal cases and settled civil disputes, and in both instances they considered themselves partners in the task of judging—if not quite the equal of judges, at least their junior partners. And judges usually agreed with this assessment.[184] This partnership between judge and jury was the result of many factors: the historical memory of the English sedition

182. Ibid., 730–731.

183. Amar, *Bill of Rights*, 85–87; Nendza, "Jury and Republican Government." See also F. Thornton Miller, *Juries and Judges versus the Law: Virginia's Provincial Legal Perspective, 1783–1828* (Charlottesville: University Press of Virginia, 1994), 99–102, on the use of juries as "quasi-administrative bodies."

184. Nendza, "Jury and Republican Government."

trials; the frequent lack of professionalism on the bench; the practice of trying cases before multiple judges; the general assertiveness of republican citizens; and the understanding of the jury as the lower house of the judiciary, where ordinary citizens could, however briefly, practice the art of ruling.

Yet none of these elements of the jury system was set in stone, and some were controversial in certain quarters. There were arguments over the jury's powers or rights, especially in light of the new political circumstances following independence. The bench grew increasingly professional, and there were signs of an emerging professional bar, which would soon add a powerful third member to the courtroom partnership. Fewer cases were heard before multiple judges, lending a greater aura of finality to judicial decisions and advice. And as the suffrage broadened and deepened, more and more doubts were expressed about the competence of jurors. Could every voter be a good juror? Most state laws continued to insist on nonobjective qualifications for jury service that were not required of mere voters, such as "reputation" or "judgment" or "integrity"; however, not all state courts took these requirements seriously. And critics of the jury system wondered about a conflict between the jury as a political institution and the jury as a means of delivering justice in private suits or in criminal cases, especially those of a highly emotional nature or with sensitive political overtones (such as those cases tried under the Sedition Act).

Steadily, over the course of the nineteenth century, these pressures and doubts led to changes in the understanding of the jury system and in the way it functioned. It would be too much to say that the system was "transformed"—the changes were not as dramatic or as final as that, and some elements of the modern jury system would be instantly recognizable to a citizen transported from the 1830s.[185] But the system did change, in part because of a new view, especially among judges, about the jury's ancient right to decide for itself the most important questions of law.

The defense of the jury's role in a republican government rested, to a large extent, on the claim that jurors could judge the law. The jury was an obstacle to oppressive government because of its ability to reach a separate conclusion about the meaning of the law and therefore about the disposition of the case. When they did this, jurors were said to be "finding" the law, "judging" the law, or sometimes "determining" the law. Jurors, in other words, did essentially the same thing that judges did. And while it might look as if the jury were ignoring the judge, it would be more accurate to say that the jury had simply conceived an opinion of the law that was at odds with the opinion of the judge. And why should they not disagree from time to time? The jury, said John Taylor of Caroline, is merely the "lower

185. For example, it was known that voir dire could be used to "strike" jurors likely to be unsympathetic. In addition, many of the community's most educated and professional citizens sought to avoid the burden of jury service (as they still do). See Greenberg, "Effectiveness of Law Enforcement," on the evasion of jury service in New York.

judicial branch," more democratic and rambunctious than the "upper house." It could be expected to disagree with its colleagues on the bench, just as members of the House disagreed with their colleagues in the Senate.[186]

It was the essence of the republican idea that citizens who ruled themselves by choosing legislators and voting in town meetings were fully capable of understanding the law. They were, after all, the source of all laws—including the original and supreme law of the Constitution—a claim that could not have been made by or on behalf of English jurors, however heroic their service under the Stuarts or the Angevins. And if ordinary citizens were not capable of understanding the law, republican government would make very little sense.

Furthermore, if the law presented unusually complex questions—more likely in civil than in criminal cases, but not unheard of in the latter—then it was the job of the judge to explain the law in terms accessible to laymen. This was fully consistent with the idea that the judge and jury were partners rather than adversaries. It was a common practice in the republican era for judges "to talk more freely to the jury," summarizing and commenting on the trial and explaining the law "in simple, non-technical language. Instructions were clear, informative summaries of the state of the law." Chief Justice Richard Bassett of Delaware, for example, explained the law of adverse possession to a jury in 1794 as follows: "If you are in possession of a corner of my land for twenty years by adverse possession, you may snap your fingers at me."[187] Thus informed as to the law's meaning, the jury could make up its own mind about what the law required it to do.[188]

Yet there were many cases, especially criminal ones, in which the jury's right to judge the law as well as the facts put it at odds not with the Crown but with the legislature. In many states, for example, it was hard to obtain a conviction in certain murder cases because of jurors' reluctance to send men to the gallows unless the killing had been willful, premeditated, or especially vicious. This reluctance, in fact, led to various reforms in the criminal law—a good example of the jury acting as a political institution. Two states (Michigan and Wisconsin) abolished the death penalty, and other states gave formal recognition to the modern idea,

186. John Taylor of Caroline, "An Inquiry into the Principles and Policy of the Government of the United States" (1814), cited in Amar, *Bill of Rights*, 95. Amar notes that juries were likened to "militias" by some writers of the time.

187. Lawrence M. Friedman, *A History of American Law* (New York: Simon & Schuster, 1973), 137.

188. The importance of explaining the law—especially constitutional law—to an audience of intelligent lay citizens was on Chief Justice Marshall's mind and explains some of his literary strategy. In some ways, Marshall's opinion in *Marbury v. Madison* (1801) is like a graduate seminar, which accounts for its careful explication and the sober, even tedious way he reveals each element of the problem, one at a time. See Robert K. Faulkner, *The Jurisprudence of John Marshall* (Princeton, NJ: Princeton University Press, 1968).

implicit in numerous rulings going back to the Middle Ages, that there are "degrees" of homicide that deserve different degrees of punishment.[189] As noted in chapter 1, English jurors had been refusing to send men to the gallows for noncapital killings since the Assize of Clarendon in 1187, but English legislators did not respond to these "promptings" until the early nineteenth century. In the more democratic circumstances of America, the jury's influence was more direct and more immediate.[190]

Thus, the jury's ability to return a general verdict in criminal cases meant that it could enforce an informal code of justice, recognizing the legitimacy of the law in general but rejecting its strict enforcement when jurors felt that a narrow or literal interpretation would result in an injustice. But the claim that jurors could make up their own minds about what the law meant soon bumped up against the claims of republicanism itself. After all, it is one thing for jurors to "bend" the law to protect a drunken rowdy from being hanged by the king. It is quite another thing to ignore a law passed by a democratic legislature elected by one's fellow citizens, and even more unusual for a jury to presume the right to declare an act of that legislature unenforceable. But even the more modest and traditional "maxim"—that jurors were to judge law and fact together—seemed (to some critics) to make a uniform legal code impossible and might therefore be incompatible with a "government of laws."[191] Was it possible that the ancient right of the jury to find the law had been rendered obsolete by the successes of republican government? Such questions were debated all over the country; a sampling of the debate in Massachusetts suggests how the debate proceeded.[192]

When the Massachusetts legislature passed a law in 1808 specifically authorizing the jury "to decide at their discretion, by a general verdict, both the fact and the law, involved in the issue," it was stating what had already become the common rule. And when Massachusetts debated a new constitution in 1820, a proposal that "the jury may determine both the law and the fact" was rejected because this principle was already the "law of the land." One delegate remarked that "the right of deciding on the law as well as the fact, is a part of the common law of the country."[193]

189. Friedman, *History of American Law*, 248–251.

190. Parliament was slow to act, despite pleas from judges that the criminal law be reformed, partly so that criminals could be punished more regularly, even if by lesser penalties. This phenomenon is discussed in Jerome Hall, *Theft, Law and Society* (Indianapolis: Bobbs-Merrill, 1952); Frank McLynn, *Crime and Punishment in Eighteenth Century England* (New York: Routledge, 1989); and Thomas A. Green, "The Jury and the English Law of Homicide, 1200–1600," *Michigan Law Review* 74, 3 (January 1976): 413–499.

191. Friedman, *History of American Law*, 251.

192. In what follows, I rely heavily on "Comment: Changing Role of the Jury."

193. Ibid., 174–175.

But the ambiguous nature of the jury's right to judge the law, and judges' growing impatience with this assertion, is apparent in a trial presided over by Supreme Court justice Joseph Story, who was riding circuit in the Massachusetts federal district in 1835.[194] John Battiste was charged with violating a federal law under which the trafficking of slaves was a capital offense.[195] Battiste was defended by the most illustrious attorney of the day, Daniel Webster, who argued that the jury had the right to determine the meaning of the statute under which Battiste had been charged.

Justice Story made an equally forceful argument against that claim, beginning his charge to the jury by insisting that for his "whole professional life" he had opposed the view espoused by "learned counsel for the prisoner": that "in criminal cases, and especially in capital cases, the jury are the judges of the law, as well as of the fact."[196] They are not so, Story reasoned, although he made the traditional concession that, in a general verdict, law and fact are decided by the jury together. And when jurors decide law and fact together, he stated, they "have the physical power to disregard the law, as laid down to them by the court. But I deny, that, in any case, civil or criminal, they have the moral right to decide the law according to their own notions, or pleasure."[197]

Battiste was the mate on the brig *America*, whose captain had accepted a fee to transport captured Africans "in shackles" from one Portuguese settlement to another on the Angolan coast. The passengers had been enslaved before boarding the ship, none of the crew had any financial interest in the slave "property" they were transporting, and the ship's journey (as Story informed the jury) was lawful in every other way. So the question for the jury was this: Did the antitrafficking law make the transporting of slaves from one place to another, far across the ocean, a capital offense? Were Battiste's actions on the *America* consistent with what Congress intended to be punishable by death?

The case was complicated in two other ways. First, while Justice Story rejected Webster's claim that the jury could judge the law, he explained the law to the jury in a way that virtually guaranteed an acquittal for Webster's client. Second, in the process of denying that the jury had a right to judge the law, Story laid out the elements of the law just as a good teacher would lay out the elements of a seminar problem, conforming to the traditional view that jury and judge were partners in the common enterprise of understanding the law. What teacher, after all, would take such care to explain a problem unless he believed his audience had both the responsibility to understand it and the ability to do so? To under-

194. United States v. Battiste, 24 F. Cas. 1042 (1835).
195. Act of 1820, chap. 113, section 4 (3 Stat. 600).
196. *Battiste*, 1043.
197. Ibid.

stand their duty, it was obvious that the jurors had to understand what Congress intended when writing the law. Did the law mean to make the mere transportation of slaves from one place to another a capital crime? Or did "trafficking" mean something more sinister, and if so, what?

Webster insisted that for an individual to engage in the slave trade, the victim had to be free when he came into contact with the defendant and had to be enslaved as a result (even if only partly) of the defendant's actions. How could Battiste enslave men who were already slaves before he met them?[198] In his charge to the jury, Story pointed out the flaw in this argument, which was that if the defendant had stolen slaves from one owner and then sold them to another, pocketing the profits from the transaction (which was not part of the charges against Battiste), then by Webster's argument, the defendant could not be accused of "trafficking" because his victims were already slaves when he kidnapped them. Such sophistry would make the law "but an empty sound, and a mere nullity, in a practical sense."[199] This construction could not stand, and Story so informed the jury.

Although there was no evidence that the crew had helped capture the Africans or had profited from their enslavement, there was no question that Battiste's ship had carried the slaves from one port to another. Therefore, "the question for the jury to decide," Story declared in his charge, "is whether such a transportation of these negroes is a capital offense, within the true intent of the act." That Battiste was obviously guilty of something was irrelevant, Story cautioned. "I have no doubt that he is guilty of a misdemeanor . . . but that is unimportant . . . on the present occasion." What mattered was how the congressional act should be construed, and Story offered his own interpretation for the jury to consider: The act "intended to punish, as a capital offense, the decoying or forcibly bringing or carrying or receiving on board any negro . . . with intent on the part of the party . . . to make such negro . . . a slave in future, without any reference whatsoever to his antecedent state . . . whether slave or free." Given this intention, it was easy (Story reasoned) to separate trafficking from mere transportation. If Congress had had the latter in mind, "then it would be equally a capital offense under the same act for an American ship to transport a Spanish merchant with his domestic slaves, merely as passengers for hire, from one port of the Island of Cuba to another." Yet, according to Story, Congress could not have intended this unreasonable result. "It would confound all moral distinctions in regard to crimes." It would confound an entirely innocent act with the most "hardened atrocity."[200] Thus instructed, the jury acquitted Battiste, who was later indicted for violating a different section of the act, pleaded no contest to the charge (a misdemeanor), and was sentenced.

198. Or so Story's summary of Webster's argument suggests. See ibid., 1044.

199. Ibid.

200. Ibid., 1044–1045.

But what if Story had explained the law differently? What if he had said that Battiste's actions were precisely the ones Congress had meant to criminalize in order to discourage the slave trade? This interpretation of the law was by no means a fanciful one. If Battiste and his captain knew their passengers had been enslaved (and since the men were shackled, this was obvious), and if they willingly passed the slaves from one set of owners to another, how could a reasonable man not conclude that they were "engaged" in the trading of slaves, rather than simply giving passage to a slave owner traveling with his household? And it would certainly be possible to earn steady profits from the slave trade by offering one's ship in this manner, allowing the trafficking to proceed more smoothly. It is not hard to imagine a staunchly abolitionist jury embracing this construction. The same problem could occur with many laws whose interpretation left room for doubt.

One year later, in 1836, in a sign that Story's rejection of the jury's right was becoming more popular among state lawmakers, the Massachusetts legislature repealed the old state law affirming the jury's power. Case law in the 1840s continued to recognize the jury's law-finding authority, at least in criminal cases. But in 1845 this right was attacked very forcefully from the state bench by Chief Justice Lemuel Shaw in *Commonwealth v. Porter*.[201]

The Porter case concerned an innkeeper charged with selling liquor without a license. His attorney tried to argue that, under a correct reading of the law, Porter's innkeeper's license allowed him to sell liquor. But the judge stopped the defense counsel, on the grounds that "the proposition stated . . . was purely a question of law, and as such was to be decided by the court, and not by the jury." Porter's attorney tried several times to convince the jury that his own interpretation of the licensing laws was correct, but each time the judge told him such matters were for the court, not the jury, to decide. The final admonition came during defense counsel's closing argument, when he tried to tell the jurors that they were not bound by the court's instructions on the law, which were wrong in several particulars. "He was then interrupted and stopped by the court, and the court ruled that it was the duty of the jury, for the purposes of the present trial, to adopt and follow the said several rulings and decisions of the court, as the settled law applicable to this case," and if there were any questions about the accuracy of the court's interpretation of the law, these must be taken up in the appeals process.[202]

The judge nevertheless instructed the jurors that although it was their duty to follow the rulings of the court, "they occupied an independent position, and, being required to return only a general verdict, they possessed the power of rendering a verdict in opposition to the said rulings and decisions, whereby [said rulings] would in fact be overruled and reversed; and that, if the jury should do so, in violation of what the court had thus prescribed as the rule of their duty, they would

201. 51 Mass. 263 (1845).
202. Ibid., 2, 4–5.

in no way be amenable to punishment by the law." That is, they had the power to substitute their own judgment of the law for the court's, even though they had no moral right to do so. Porter was convicted on one count of the indictment, and he appealed to the Supreme Judicial Court on the grounds that he had been denied his right to argue the law before the jury and had therefore been denied his right to a jury trial.[203]

To many in Massachusetts (where the licensing laws were unpopular in some parts of the state), denying a defendant's right to argue the law before a jury and rejecting the jury's authority to determine the law for itself must have seemed like a blow to the commonwealth's ancient liberties. In the past, the understanding had been that the judge's responsibility was to explain the law in layman's terms, not simply to "decide" the law or "give the law" to a passive jury, which would then be required to apply that law mechanically to a set of facts. In arguing the case on appeal, Porter's counsel stressed the long pedigree of this right, citing Vaughan's decision in Bushell's Case, Jay's instructions in *Georgia v. Brailsford*, and numerous Massachusetts cases. If a court cannot "compel a jury to find a special verdict," counsel asked, "how then can a jury be compelled to find a verdict according to the court's view of the law?"[204]

Furthermore, if all sides admit that the jury has the *power* to decide the law—because of its right to return a general verdict without fear of attaint—then does it not also have the *right* to do so? Citing Alexander Hamilton's argument in *People v. Croswell*[205]—a case brought under New York State's common law of libel in 1804—Porter's counsel argued that if the jury has the power it must also have the right, since the law would not concede the power without conferring the right as well. This had been Hamilton's argument in 1804: that "power and right are con-

203. Ibid., 5–6.

204. Ibid., 6.

205. 3 Johns. Cas. 337 N.Y. (1804). This case had a particular significance in the history of seditious libel cases—it was the only time a Federalist was charged with sedition—and in many ways it was the final scene of the Sedition Act drama. Croswell had been charged, under the state's common law, of libeling then-president Thomas Jefferson by writing, in the *Wasp*, that Jefferson had paid James Callender to publish false statements defaming the character of John Adams, George Washington, and other leading Federalists. Croswell had asked that the trial be delayed so that Callender (who had turned against Jefferson) could come from Virginia to testify to the truth of the accusation; the judge ruled the truth to be irrelevant, and Croswell was convicted. He appealed, and Alexander Hamilton volunteered his services as defense counsel, in what would be his last case. The New York Supreme Court returned a split decision, with two judges (Kent and Thompson) ruling for and one judge (Lewis) ruling against Croswell's claim that he had been denied his right to a jury trial. In the wake of this widely publicized trial, the state legislature rewrote the libel law, making the truth of a statement a defense against a libel accusation, which had been the core of Hamilton's defense.

vertible terms when the law authorizes the doing of an act which shall be final, and for the doing of which the agent is not responsible."[206] Porter's counsel continued:

> To admit that the jury have the power, unrestrained by law, but have not the right to use the power which the law gives them, is to assume that the jury, in the exercise of a lawful power, will do wrong, or that the law is wrong in giving them the power. The law will not permit a wrong to be done, and therefore, if it empowers the jury to pass upon the law in the exercise of their judgment, it is no more to be assumed that they will do wrong, than that the judge will do wrong in the use of his judgment and discretion, where he is unrestrained.[207]

The commonwealth's attorneys denied there had ever been such a thing as the jury's right to determine the law in opposition to the clear instructions of the court: "The nature of our institutions, our whole legislation, and the practice of our courts, disprove the right of a jury to decide questions of law."[208] Because the Massachusetts Constitution guaranteed to all citizens the right to "a government of laws, not men," and the "impartial interpretation of the laws" by judges, it would be absurd to claim that each jury could decide what the law meant. The commonwealth cited Justice Story in *United States v. Battiste*:

> It is the duty of the jury to follow the law, as it is laid down by the court. If the jury were at liberty to settle the law for themselves, the effect would be, not only that the law itself would be most uncertain, from the different views which different juries might take of it, but in case of error, there would be no remedy or redress by the injured party; for the court would not have any right to review the law, as it had been settled by the jury.[209]

But in addition to claiming that Porter's argument would lead to inconsistency and even incoherence in the law, the commonwealth reached back in time for a distinctly nonrepublican precedent: the famous (or infamous) argument of Lord Mansfield in the libel trial of the Reverend William Shipley, dean of St. Asaph, in 1783. Shipley had been charged with seditious libel for the publication of a mildly satiric publication, *A Dialogue between a Gentleman and a Farmer*, the gist of which was that many government officials were incompetent, corrupt, or both. It was not difficult for such a publication to fall afoul of the all-inclusive definition of libel cited in chapter 1: "written censure upon any public man whatever for any conduct whatever or upon any law or institution whatever."[210] Ship-

206. Commonwealth v. Porter, 51 Mass. 263 (1845), 12, citing *People v. Croswell.*

207. Ibid.

208. Ibid., 8.

209. 2 Sumner 243, cited by ibid., 9–12.

210. Paul G. Willis, "Juries and Judicial Review," *Western Political Quarterly* 3 (1950): 68.

ley's counsel argued that the jury has a right to decide the question of whether, as a matter of law or as a matter of fact (the distinction being blurred), a publication is the result of seditious intent. Lord Mansfield had no patience with such arguments, insisting that the reluctance to let judges decide the law was "puerile rant and declamation."[211] Mansfield then anticipated a problem that would soon preoccupy American jurists and that Chief Justice Shaw explored in the Porter case: the legal uncertainty that would follow if juries decided the law for themselves:

> In opposition to this [argument that juries must follow the judge] what is contended for?—that the law shall be, in every particular cause, what any twelve men, who shall happen to be the jury, shall be inclined to think; liable to no review, and subject to no control, under all the prejudices of the popular cry of the day. . . . Under such an administration of law, no man could tell, no counsel could advise, whether a paper was or was not punishable.[212]

But then Mansfield (echoing Justice Vaughan in the Bushell decision) made the kind of High Tory argument that could be made in America only at great peril:

> [The jury] do not know, and are not presumed to know the law; they are not sworn to decide the law; they are not required to do it. Upon the reason of the thing, and the eternal principles of justice, the jury ought not to assume the jurisdiction of the law. They do not know, and are not presumed to know anything of the matter. It is the duty of the judge, in all cases upon general issues, to tell the jury how to do right, though they have the power to do wrong, which is a matter between God and their own conscience. To be free, is to live under a government by law. Miserable is the condition of individuals, dangerous is the condition of the State, if there is no certain law, or (which is the same thing) no certain administration of law, to protect individuals, or to guard the State.[213]

Yet the republican view was quite simply that the jury could know the law and could arrive at a proper understanding of it—albeit with the assistance of the court.[214] And as Porter's attorney pointed out, the fact that the law concedes the

211. Robert Walker, "Security, Freedom of Speech and Criminal Justice in the Age of Pitt, Burke, and Fox," Bentham Club Address at UCL Faculty of Laws, March 2008, http://www.ucl.ac.uk/laws/alumni/presidents/docs/walker_08.pdf (accessed February 2, 2014).

212. Rex v. Shipley, 4 Dougl. 73, 99 E. R. 774 (1784).

213. Rex v. Dean of St. Asaph, 21 St Tr 847 (1784), cited in *Porter*, 10–11.

214. This was true of the criminal law only. "It was conceded that the law in civil cases was likely to be more complex than the law in criminal cases. This distinction was used to explain the fact that the jury's right to decide the law was claimed only in criminal cases." In fact, the criminal law should be simple, so that citizens could more readily understand their obligations. "Comment: Changing Role of the Jury," 180.

court's duty to "assist" the jury in understanding the law presumes that the jury can and, of course, should understand the law. Why would it be necessary for jurors to understand the law if they are not supposed to make up their own minds about what the law requires?[215]

Chief Justice Shaw's previous opinions had been cited by both sides in the Porter case, but his current opinion sought to dispose of the claim that jurors have a right to determine the law against the instructions of the court:

> We consider it a well settled principle and rule . . . that it is the proper province and duty of judges to consider and decide all questions of law which arise, and that . . . it is the proper province and duty of the jury, to weigh and consider evidence, and decide all questions of fact. . . . It would be alike a usurpation of authority and violation of duty, for a court . . . to decide authoritatively on the questions of fact, and for the jury to decide ultimately and authoritatively upon the questions of law.[216]

Shaw's rejection of the "ancient right" provoked a major controversy that was still alive eight years later, in 1853, when Massachusetts held another constitutional convention that adopted a provision meant to overrule Porter: "In all trials for criminal offenses, the jury, after having received the instruction of the court shall have the right, in their verdict of guilty or not guilty, to determine the law and the facts of the case."[217] This was no more than what countless writers, in and out of the judicial system, had stated for generations in republican America, in the colonies, and in England. But the growing chorus of doubts from the bench on this score was a troubling sign. Just how troubling became clear with passage of the Fugitive Slave Act in 1850.[218]

The Fugitive Slave Act authorized the federal circuit courts to appoint special commissioners to supervise the process of returning "persons held to service or labor" to their former owners in the South. The commissioners were authorized to issue warrants for the apprehension, without due process, of all such fugitives, who were to be brought before the commissioners and, upon the presentation of "satisfactory" proof of ownership, returned to their former owners. No testimony was to be taken from the fugitive, nor did the fugitive have the right to a trial, since being a fugitive slave was not technically a crime. The word "jury" does not appear in the language of the act. However, section 7 makes it clear that hindering, obstructing, or in any way interfering with the enforcement of the act was a federal crime that would be tried in district court. As the authors of the act anticipated, abolitionists

215. *Porter*, 13–14.
216. Ibid., 23–24.
217. "Comment: Changing Role of the Jury," 177.
218. Acts of 1850, chap. 60, 9 Stat. 462, http://www.avalon.law.yale.edu/19th_century/fugitive.asp (accessed February 3, 2014).

blocked its enforcement throughout the North. They hid fugitive slaves, sometimes seizing them from federal marshals and breaking into jails or even courtrooms to do so. When the rescuers were put on trial (the usual charge being "interference with federal process"), they were often acquitted by sympathetic jurors. As a result, between 1850 and the secession crisis, prosecution under the Fugitive Slave Act was effectively ended almost everywhere in the North. In Syracuse, New York, for example, twenty-four slave rescuers were tried in four separate trials; when the first three groups of defendants were acquitted, the government decided not to press charges against the fourth.[219] Defense attorneys normally tried to inform jurors that they had a right to reach their own conclusions about the meaning of the law as well as the facts, and that they could refuse to convict on the grounds that the federal law in question was unconstitutional. Judges refused to allow such appeals to continue, at least in front of the jury—yet juries acquitted nonetheless. So common were these acquittals that "the federal judiciary regularly admonished jurors in such cases not to vote their consciences."[220]

In Boston abolitionists broke into a courtroom to rescue a fugitive slave named Shadrach and helped him escape to Montreal. Eight defendants were indicted for this rescue, and the trial of the first three defendants began in May 1851; they included Shadrach's attorney, Robert H. Morris. As expected, the defense put the Fugitive Slave Act on trial in a state where the law was notably unpopular. Prosecutors fought back, asking prospective jurors during voir dire if they had any views on the law that would "induce [them] to refuse to convict a person indicted under it, if the facts set forth in the indictment . . . are proved against him, and the court direct you that the law is constitutional."[221] But the trial was barely under way when the judge removed one of the jurors after receiving information that he had lied about his views on the law and intended to acquit anyone charged with blocking its enforcement.[222]

Morris's trial was then remitted to the federal circuit court under a rule that allowed such remittals whenever, "in the opinion of the [district] court, difficult and important questions of law are involved in the case."[223] The Morris case involved more than one such question: What is the constitutional status of slavery, and how should jurors understand their responsibilities to the Constitution? What

219. Ibid.

220. See Clay S. Conrad, *Jury Nullification: The Evolution of a Doctrine* (Washington, DC: Cato Institute, 1998), 80.

221. Lysander Spooner, *An Essay on the Trial by Jury* (Boston: B. Marsh, 1852), 8. It should be noted that the term "jury nullification" does not appear in Spooner's book, and he does not write of a jury's right to "nullify" a law.

222. Conrad, *Jury Nullification*, 81–82. See also Jeffrey Abramson, *We the Jury: The Jury System and the Ideal of Democracy* (New York: Basic Books, 1994), 80–85.

223. United States v. Morris, 1 Curt. 23 (1851), 1324.

power does the jury have to judge the law? What evidence is necessary to prove that an escaped "slave" is really a slave and not a free Negro?

Among the arguments offered in Morris's defense was one that focused on the jury's fact-finding role. For the defendant to be convicted of interfering with a federal process, wouldn't the government have to prove that the person alleged to be an escaped slave actually is a slave? This line of argument was popular among abolitionists. Even Abraham Lincoln, who advised citizens to obey the Fugitive Slave Act until it could be repealed, added a significant proviso: so long as "a free man be not in any case surrendered as a slave."[224] Lincoln's qualification arose because not all Negroes in America were slaves; therefore, the identification of any particular Negro as an "escaped slave" normally required proof. It followed that if the person whose liberty had been secured was not a slave, then no crime had been committed. It could be argued that a defendant accused of helping a slave run away had really been helping a kidnapping victim escape. And it was up to the jury to decide such questions—questions of fact that, after all, were no different from disputes about the ownership of a piece of land or a cow or a cord of firewood.[225] If a slave is "property," abolitionists asked, where is the deed or the bill of sale? What kind of evidence would a court (or, in the slave's case, the federal commissioners appointed to enforce the law) demand or accept before handing someone over to the purported master?[226] Manumission was a legally complex process that differed from one slave state to another, and southern states were increasingly hostile to the process; by 1860, most slave states had banned most forms of manumission. But even where manumission was legal, it could be challenged by the widows, children, and creditors of slave owners, so "freed" slaves might suddenly find their status challenged. Public records, even those predating the Fugitive Slave Act, suggest that identifying evidence such as birthmarks, scars from old injuries, and general height and weight were often enough to justify a runaway slave's loss of freedom, and abolitionists emphasized the often arbitrary nature of such practices.[227] This standard of evidence could accurately identify a

224. First Inaugural Address, 1861, in Abraham Lincoln, *Speeches and Writings 1859–1865* (New York: Literary Classics of the United States/Viking Press, 1989), 216.

225. The authors of the Fugitive Slave Act apparently anticipated this difficulty, requiring only that the proof offered be "satisfactory" to the commissioners themselves (section 4). No challenge to the slave owner's evidence was provided for (specifically, no testimony could be taken from the alleged slave), and since these were summary proceedings before a federal magistrate, no jury was asked to "find" the fact in question. On the legal complications arising from the Fugitive Slave Act prosecutions, see Jenni Parrish, "The Booth Cases: Final Step to the Civil War," *Willamette Law Review* 29 (1993): 237–278.

226. See Thomas D. Morris, *Southern Slavery and the Law: 1619–1860* (Chapel Hill: University of North Carolina Press, 1996), 371–399.

227. See, for example, Sandra Boyd Williams, "The Indiana Supreme Court and the

particular person without accurately identifying his or her status as a free citizen: thus the concern that a free man might be mistaken for a slave.

These questions received a perverse but logical answer involving the application of an old common-law principle to human "property." Abolitionists dared the federal courts to talk about slaves as if they were really no different from inanimate property, and Justice Benjamin Curtis rose to the challenge.[228] "This is . . . a question of property," he argued, "and, by the common law, possession is evidence of property, unless the circumstances accompanying the possession rebut the inference of property." Just as the common law teaches that in the case of inheritance, "it is competent and sufficient evidence, that B treated A as his son," someone who is commonly considered to be a slave can be identified as such in a court of law. It would not be necessary to produce documents or testimony tracing a particular Negro's ancestry to the eighteenth century—this would normally be impossible and therefore could not be required by the law. Justice Curtis felt compelled by an abundance of authorities "to come to the conclusion that, though the fact of slavery . . . is to be proved, it may . . . be proved by such evidence as, upon the principles of the common law, is competent and sufficient."[229]

But even if the jury were compelled to accept that the man Morris rescued was held to bondage in Virginia, might it acquit the defendant because the law he broke violated the Constitution—if not the letter of the Constitution, then its guiding spirit? In that case, the jurors would, in effect, be exercising the power of judicial review—a power not usually conceded to the jury, even by those (like Justice Chase) who conceded the jury's power to find the law. The report of the Morris case notes:

> [While] one of the counsel for the defendant was addressing the jury, he stated the proposition that, this being a criminal case, the jury were rightfully the judges of the law, as well as the fact; and if any of them conscientiously believed the [Fugitive Slave Act] to be unconstitutional, they were bound by their oaths to disregard any direction to the contrary which the court might give them; and he was about to address the jury in support of this assertion, when he was stopped by the court, and informed that he could not be permitted to argue this proposition to the jury; that the court would hear him, and if

Struggle against Slavery," *Indiana Law Review* 30 (1997): 305–318, which describes the investigation of one "Freeman" who was said to be an escaped slave from St. Louis named "Sam." He was identified only after the US marshal forced him to remove his clothing to reveal the whipping marks on his body.

228. Curtis was known for his antislavery views (he would write one of the two dissents in the Dred Scott case), and defendants undoubtedly expected him to be sympathetic to their cause.

229. *Morris*, 1330–1331.

> they should be of the opinion that the proposition was true, the jury would be so informed by the court; and the counsel then addressed the court in support of the position.[230]

Justice Curtis delivered a long response in which he explored the argument about the jury right, going back to Bushell's Case and examining some of the landmarks used by proponents of the right, such as Justice Jay's remarks in *Georgia v. Brailsford*. Curtis frankly doubted that Jay's remarks could have been properly reported, because the chief justice's statements were in conflict: first he said that questions of law are the province of the judge and questions of fact are the province of the jury; then, in the next breath, he supposedly said that juries can be judges of both. "I cannot help feeling much doubt respecting the accuracy of this report; not only because the different parts of the charge are in conflict with each other, but because I can scarcely believe that the chief justice held the opinion that, in civil cases . . . the jury had the right to decide the law. Indeed the whole case is an anomaly."[231] And yet, this complicated formula was a very common one, its complexity coming from the fact that the jury was obliged to listen carefully to the judge, as the senior partner, and then come to its own conclusion about how to apply the law to the facts. That this required the jury to understand the law was taken for granted by republican-era judges and commentators. How could a jury apply the law without understanding it, whether the law in question was civil or criminal? And if jurors must understand the law, it was inevitable that their understanding might differ, even if only slightly, from that of the judge.

Curtis acknowledged that this controversy went well beyond the Fugitive Slave Act. "That it has been a familiar saying among the profession in this country, and an opinion entertained by highly respectable judges, that the jury are judges of the law as well as of the facts, I have no doubt."[232] And then, as if to partially take back his earlier statement, Curtis conceded:

> I believe it to be true [in some cases], for they [jurors] are the sole judges of the application of the law to the particular case. In this sense, theirs is the duty to pass on the law—a most important, and often difficult duty, which, when discharged, makes the difference between a general and a special verdict, which, although they may return, they are not bound to return. They are a coordinate branch of the tribunal, having their appropriate powers and

230. Ibid.

231. Ibid., 1334. *Brailsford* was a civil case—a dispute about a debt—and in fact, many of those who argued the jury's right to find the law confined their arguments to criminal cases.

232. Ibid., 1335–1336.

> rights and duties, with the proper discharge and exercise of which no court can, without usurpation, interfere.[233]

But Curtis would go no further than this. If a jury were to "intentionally fail to apply to the case the law given to them by the court, it would be, in my opinion, as much a violation of duty as if they were knowingly to return a verdict contrary to the evidence." Curtis was unconvinced by counsel's "strong appeal" to the importance of the jury right to the protection of civil liberties. As long as judges "are obliged to express their opinions publicly, to give reasons for them . . . and to stand responsible for them . . . I can apprehend very little danger of the laws being wrested to purposes of injustice." And should juries take it upon themselves to judge the laws made by their own legislatures, then justice, which requires enforcement of the law "uniformly and impartially, without respect of persons or times, or the opinions of men," would be subverted. Thus, Curtis concluded, it is "my firm conviction . . . that under the constitution of the United States, juries, in criminal trials, have not the right to decide any question of law . . . and that . . . their duty and their oath require them to apply to the facts, as they may find them, the law given to them by the court."[234]

Nevertheless, the jury acquitted Morris and his two codefendants. As in the Syracuse case, the failure of the first trial persuaded the government to drop the charges against the remaining defendants.[235] Since the jurors in the Morris case were not allowed to hear an argument about their right to find an act of Congress unconstitutional, or even a defense of the "good old rule" that juries can judge the law, it is impossible to say what their acquittal of Morris meant. But the evidence that Morris had helped rescue Shadrach from the federal marshals was quite clear; therefore, the jury's verdict almost certainly meant that, at a minimum, it refused to send someone to jail for rescuing a slave.

And this possibility brings us closer to the real heart of the claim about the jury's right to "find"—that is, to understand and apply—the law. Did the Fugitive Slave Act violate the Constitution? Possibly not, given the straightforward language of the "fugitive slave clause" (Article IV, section 3).[236] But even if the Fugitive Slave Act fit narrowly within the limits of the Constitution, that did not exonerate the institution of slavery. If slavery itself was unconstitutional, there could be no such person as an escaped slave, and the fugitive slave law would be a nullity. Slavery

233. Ibid., 1336.

234. Ibid.

235. Abramson, *We the Jury*, 82.

236. "No person held to service or labor in one state, under the laws thereof, escaping into another, shall, in consequence of any law or regulation therein, be discharged from such service or labor, but shall be delivered up on claim of the party to whom such service or labor may be due."

clearly violated the spirit and the tendency of the Constitution; even more clearly, slavery was incompatible with the Declaration of Independence. The institution was an assault on the higher principles of natural justice and natural rights that were recognized by all decent citizens and that gave the Constitution its greatest significance. And if these things were true, then no juror in good conscience could find anyone guilty of violating such a brazenly unjust law. Lysander Spooner spoke for many abolitionists, as well as many defenders of the "ancient jury right," when he wrote that there is a "universal principle of moral obligation, that arises out of the nature of men and their relations to each other, and to other things—and [which] is consequently as unalterable as the nature of men. . . . [T]his natural law is no other than the rule of natural justice."[237] Or, as the Anti-Federalists might have put it, sometimes the lower house of the judiciary should simply vote no.

Although defenders of the principle sought the moral high ground, juries' obstruction of the Fugitive Slave Act seemed like something other than a noble stand, even to the many Americans who opposed slavery (like Justice Curtis himself). It seemed more like a dangerous and arbitrary form of law enforcement that was not always motivated by the highest principles of human freedom. After all, when jurors were not resisting slavery, they were resisting enforcement of the liquor laws by refusing to convict tavern owners who sold liquor without a license. And nobody claimed that the liquor laws were unconstitutional or that they violated the higher law.

Opponents of the proposed jury provision in the new Massachusetts Constitution therefore tried to shift the ground of the debate from the jury's ancient right to the new problem presented by the jury's power in a popular government of laws: arbitrary rule by the people. Defenders of the jury were focusing on the judge, as they had been trained to do by their ancestral memory, and on the sovereign, whose bidding (so republicans believed) guided the judge's decisions (although even Lord Mansfield prided himself on the independence of the English judge, on whom subjects could rely for impartial justice). Opponents urged delegates to think about the problem of public opinion. If juries could "determine" the law, different juries would find different laws in similar circumstances. This was the republican version of arbitrary rule; as in the worst tyranny, no man could know with certainty what behavior would keep him out of prison. Under a government of laws, the citizen should be able to count on the knowable principles of positive law—"a coherent set of principles by which men could order their lives and predict the consequences of their actions."[238]

In the Massachusetts Constitutional Convention of 1853, the crucial vote to order the jury resolution to a second reading passed by a vote of 192 to 146, suggesting significant opposition to what had once been a "universal maxim"

237. Lysander Spooner, *The Unconstitutionality of Slavery* (Boston: B. Marsh, 1860), 5–6.
238. "Comment: Changing Role of the Jury," 179.

accepted by Federalists and Republicans alike.[239] The voters ultimately rejected the new constitution, but not because of the jury provisions, which were quickly enacted into law in the 1855 session of the legislature.[240] At his first opportunity, Chief Justice Shaw ruled that the new law must be interpreted to mean only a general affirmation of the jury's right to bring in a general verdict. To interpret it in any other way, Shaw argued, would violate the Constitution's guarantee of a trial before an impartial judge and jury under standing laws.[241]

The 1855 jury statute was probably the high-water mark for jury independence in Massachusetts. In the decades that followed, courts began to make greater use of directed verdicts and—after 1860—the practice of questioning jurors. If a judge felt that the jurors' answers were inconsistent with the general verdict they had just delivered, he could order a new trial. However, this stopped short of the special-verdict statutes in other states, which permitted the judge to enter a judgment on the jury's "fact-findings."[242]

In an effort to restore some of the jury's independence, the Massachusetts legislature passed a law forbidding the judge to comment on the evidence—betraying a certain lack of faith in jurors' ability to resist being influenced by the judge's comments, but attempting to bolster the jury's last redoubt. But courts simply reasserted their right to "guide the jury in reaching its conclusions of fact." This had been a common-law power at the time of independence, and it had been further established in Massachusetts by *Commonwealth v. Child* in 1829. In that case, the defendant claimed the trial judge had influenced the jury against him by stating his opinion about the evidence. The Supreme Judicial Court found nothing wrong with this practice. Chief Justice Parker argued in *Child*, "We know of no rule requiring the judge to conceal his opinion [about the evidence]. . . . [I]f the evidence on one side is strong, compared with that on the other side, I think it is my duty to make the jury comprehend that it is so."[243]

239. *Journal of the Constitutional Convention of the Commonwealth of Massachusetts, Begun and Held in Boston, on the Fourth Day of May, 1853* (Boston: White & Potter, 1853), 311.

240. "In all trials for criminal offenses, it shall be the duty of the jury to try, according to established forms and principles of law, all causes which shall be committed to them, and, after having received the instructions of the court, to decide at their discretion, by a general verdict, both the fact and the law involved in the issue, or to find a special verdict, at their election; but it shall be the duty of the court to superintend the course of the trials, to decide upon the admission and rejection of evidence, and upon all questions of law raised during the trials, and upon collateral and incidental proceedings, and also to charge the jury, and to allow bills of exception; and the court may grant a new trial in cases of conviction." St. 1855, c. 152, cited in Commonwealth v. Anthes, 71 Mass. (5 Gray), 185 (1855).

241. *Commonwealth v. Anthes*; "Comment: Changing Role of the Jury," 183.

242. "Comment: Changing Role of the Jury," 185.

243. Ibid., 184–186.

A legislative commission recommended, among other changes, that the rule based on *Child* be overturned: "The courts shall not charge juries with respect to matters of fact, but they may state the testimony and the law." These developments signaled "an acceptance of the concept that the issues in a lawsuit could be clearly divided into questions of law and fact, with a corresponding division of function between judge and jury, coupled with growing doubt about the jury's independence."[244] But of course, the inevitable mixing of law and fact had been the source of the jury's right to judge the law in the first place. As Justice Vaughan had said in Bushell's Case, the law and facts are "mixed complicately." No judicial ruling or legislative act could change that primal fact. To assert a clear distinction between law and fact, to claim that a judge's commentary on the law would have no bearing on the jury's understanding of the facts, was simply to avoid the ancient problem altogether. The knot would simply not come untied.

THE LAW AND THE FACTS

These developments came to a head, at least in terms of constitutional law, in the 1895 decision by the US Supreme Court in *Sparf and Hansen v. United States*.[245] Sparf and Hansen were accused of murdering their shipmate, Fitzgerald, while aboard a merchant ship at sea (thus the federal jurisdiction) and disposing of the body by tossing it overboard, meaning there was no physical evidence to establish the nature of the crime and no witnesses other than the defendants. (A third defendant was tried separately.) Hansen confessed to the ship's captain, in the presence of Sparf, that they were both guilty of the crime.

At their trial (in the Circuit Court for the Northern District of California), the defendants requested that the judge instruct the jury that it could convict on the lesser included charge of manslaughter rather than murder, which would mean imprisonment rather than a death sentence. But the judge refused, on the grounds that the facts of the case did not, in his opinion, warrant a lesser charge: if the evidence proved that a "felonious homicide" had taken place, the judge reasoned, "there is nothing in this case to reduce it below the grade of murder."[246]

After deliberating for a time, according to the Supreme Court trial summary, the jury requested additional instructions from the court. It was clear from the jurors' request that they wished to find the defendants guilty of manslaughter rather than murder, which prompted the following poignant but somewhat obscure exchange between judge and jury:

244. Ibid., 187.
245. Sparf and Hansen v. United States, 156 U.S. 51 (1895).
246. Ibid., 61. See also the discussion of this case by Abramson, *We the Jury*, 85–88.

Court: In a proper case, it may be murder or it may be manslaughter, but in this case it cannot be properly manslaughter. As I have said, if a felonious homicide has been committed, the facts of the case do not reduce it below murder. Do not understand me to say that manslaughter or murder has been committed. That is for you gentlemen to determine from the testimony and the instructions I have given you. . . .

Juror: We have got to bring a verdict for either manslaughter or murder?

Court: Do not misunderstand me. I have not said so.

Juror: I know you have not.

Court: I cannot direct you what conclusion to come to from the facts. I direct you only as to the law. A judgment on the facts is your province . . . but as one of the tribunals of the country, a jury is expected to be governed by the law, and the law it should receive from the court.[247]

The jury then brought in a verdict of guilty, and the defendants appealed on the grounds that their constitutional right to a jury trial had been compromised by the judge's refusal to permit an argument about the jury's historic right to judge both the facts and the law. The Supreme Court agreed to hear the appeal.

Justice Harlan began his decision for the Court by agreeing with the trial judge, observing that a verdict less than murder "would have been in flagrant disregard of all the proof, and in violation by the jury of their obligation to render a true verdict." A lesser verdict "would have been the exercise by the jury of the power to commute the punishment for an offense actually committed, and thus impose a punishment different from that prescribed by law."[248]

Harlan then proceeded to the heart of the matter, which was the widely held view that a jury could "determine" the law. Note, however, that Harlan's presentation of the problem obscured a significant difficulty. The jury in this case was not so much determined to "commute the punishment for an offense actually committed" as it was determined to decide correctly what the offense had been. The facts of the case gave the jury reason to believe (or perhaps only to hope—there is no way to know for certain) that the offense was manslaughter rather than murder. It is possible that the jurors were simply reluctant to send two young men to the gallows for what might have been the result of a drunken brawl. The jury was not, in other words, absolving the defendants of responsibility. It merely disagreed with the judge about the nature of that responsibility. The jury was reaching a different conclusion about the meaning and requirements of the law, as juries had done in the English sedition cases and in the homicide trials under the Angevins, yet the jury's conclusion was, as always, a complex mixture of law and fact.

But given the long history of the jury's alleged "right to judge the law and the

247. *Sparf and Hansen*, 62.
248. Ibid., 64.

facts," Harlan felt compelled to lay this ghost to rest once and for all. He began at the beginning (or at least the American beginning), with Chief Justice Jay's argument in *Georgia v. Brailsford* that the jury can, in fact, judge the law as well as the facts (the "good old rule"), even though jurors ought to let the judge guide them on the law.[249] Harlan, like Justice Curtis in 1851, simply doubted that Jay had said the words attributed to him. Jay could not have said this, Harlan reasoned, because the two parts of his charge "conflict with each other," one part saying the judge should decide the law, and the other saying the jury could decide the law if it chose to do so. "If the Chief Justice said that it was the province of the court to decide questions of law, and the province of the jury to decide questions of fact, he could not have said that the jury had the right . . . to judge of and determine both law and fact."[250] And yet this complicated argument—"we do the law, you do the facts, but of course you can do both"—had been the standard view among citizens and judges alike throughout the colonial and republican periods. Even Justice Chase had said so.

Harlan then examined more than a dozen decisions during the nineteenth century in which, he believed, courts had rejected the idea that juries can decide as they please about matters of law. Commenting, for example, on Henfield's Case,[251] Harlan noted that Justice Wilson had "stated that the jury, in a general verdict, must decide both law and fact, but that 'this did not authorize them to decide it as they pleased,' and that 'the questions of law coming into joint consideration with the fact, it is the duty of the court to explain the law to the jury, and give it to them in direction.'"[252] Yet it had never been the republican claim that juries could determine the law "as they please." Rather, jurors must be able to understand the law before they can "apply it to the facts," which meant that the process was by no means a simple matter of "taking the law" from the judge. As one federal judge put it in 1806, "the jury is not . . . above the law" simply because it has the right to "determine" the law. "In exercising this right, [the jurors] attach to themselves the character of judges, and as such are as much bound by the rule of legal decision as those who preside upon the bench."[253] But once the jury is acknowledged to have an obligation to understand the law, it is almost automatically involved in the process of "finding" what the law actually means.

After discussing the views of several English and American jurists, Harlan concluded that there can be no warrant in either English or American law for the view that juries have a right to judge the law or to reach determinations about the

249. *Georgia v. Brailsford*, 22.
250. *Sparf and Hansen*, 25–26.
251. 11 F. Cas. 1099 (C.C.D. Pa. [1793]).
252. *Sparf and Hansen*, citing Hensfield's Case, 32.
253. Justice Tallmadge, in United States v. Smith, 27 F. Cas. 1233 (1806), 42, cited by Justice Gray, ibid., 209.

law in opposition to the court's instructions. As Justice Curtis had argued in the Morris case, giving juries this right would mean that each jury could decide what the law was, and the goal of a "government of uniform laws," where every man knew what his rights and duties were, would be permanently frustrated. Jurors must therefore take the law as given and apply it to the facts:

> We must hold firmly to the doctrine that in the courts of the United States it is the duty of juries in criminal cases to take the law from the court and apply that law to the facts as they find them to be from the evidence. Upon the court rests the responsibility of declaring the law; upon the jury, the responsibility of applying the law so declared to the facts as they, upon their conscience, believe them to be. Under any other system, the courts, although established in order to declare the law, would for every practical purpose be eliminated from our system of government as instrumentalities devised for the protection equally of society and of individuals in their essential rights. When that occurs our government will cease to be a government of laws, and become a government of men. Liberty regulated by law is the underlying principle of our institutions.[254]

This decision settled the question, at least from the perspective of constitutional law, whether judges are obligated to let juries hear arguments about the law from defense counsel.

Three judges wrote dissenting opinions in the Sparf case, although only one of the dissents, by Justice Gray (with Justice Shiras concurring), objected to the majority's views on the powers of the jury.[255] On the very cusp of the modern era in jury trials, Justice Gray tried to recover and articulate the grounds on which the jury had functioned in England, the colonies, and the early republic, and to defend the "good old rule" that the essence of the jury is the jurors' right to judge both the law and the facts. Gray's dissent is very long (112 pages in the original pagination, longer than the majority decision itself), apparently in an effort to crush the majority's conclusion under an overwhelming weight of precedent, and it summarizes a wealth of cases, statutes, and observations by Milton, Bacon, Littleton, Coke, and others—all to establish the English jury's right to return a general verdict mixing law and fact together. The idea that an English subject had the right to be tried by "God and my country" rather than by "God and my King" was an idea "as old as Bracton," Gray observed.[256] About the particular trial under review, Gray argued that "by instructing the jury that they were bound to accept the law as given to them

254. *Sparf and Hansen*, 97–98.

255. The other issue in the case, not relevant to this discussion, concerned the admissibility of a confession made by one defendant in the presence of another defendant, implicating the latter in the crime.

256. *Sparf and Hansen*, 122–125.

by the court, [the judge] denied their right to decide the law. . . . It is our deep and settled conviction . . . that the jury, upon the general issue of guilty or not guilty in a criminal case, have the right, as well as the power, to decide, according to their own judgment and consciences, all questions, whether of law or of fact, involved in that issue." Gray acknowledged that this right had been the subject of "earnest and repeated controversy in England and America, and eminent jurists have differed in their conclusions upon the questions." But the historical evidence, Gray argued, compelled the conclusion that the right of the jury to determine both the law and the fact was at least as old as the Magna Carta. Juries might indeed refer the question of law to the court by reciting the facts and asking for a special verdict, "but they were not bound and could not be compelled to do so, even in a civil action." And even when jurors were still subject to the peril of an attaint for mistaking the law, their error could be corrected only by another jury, not by the judge alone.[257]

Gray spent much time summarizing Vaughan's observation about law and fact being "mixed complicately." As Vaughan pointed out, the jurors "answer not singly to the question what is the law, yet they determine the law in all matters, where issue is joined and tried in the principal."[258] And it must be so, Vaughan explained, for if the judge can tell the jury what its verdict must be, then "what either necessary or convenient use can be fancied of juries, or to continue trials by them at all?" That is, as Gray summarized Vaughan's conclusion, "if a jury, especially in criminal trials, were obliged to follow the directions of the court in matter of law," the institution would no longer serve any useful purpose and might as well be dispensed with.[259]

This argument raises a central question: why are juries a good thing if (as all admit) judges know more about the law than jurors do (which was especially true by the end of the nineteenth century) and if juries, when they take it upon themselves to decide the law in opposition to the court, run the clear risk of committing a gross error? Gray's answer to this question placed the jury in its historical context as a barrier against tyranny. Remarking on the Case of the Seven Bishops—in which each of the four judges gave a slightly different charge to the jury regarding whether the bishops' petition constituted libel—Gray noted that the judges "concurred in submitting that question, as a question of law, to the decision of the jury." And the judges did this not so the jurors could act simply as "umpires between those judges who thought the paper was a libel and those judges who thought it was not, but as the tribunal vested by the law of England with the power and the right of ultimately determining . . . all matters of law, as well as of fact, involved in the general issue of guilty or not guilty."[260]

257. Ibid., 117–118, 119, 120, 123.
258. Ibid., 134 (citing Vaughan's decision in Bushell's Case).
259. Ibid., 132 (citing Vaughan), 135.
260. Ibid., 141.

Although there was no doubting the extraordinary significance of the Case of the Seven Bishops, the view of the jury's power revealed by that verdict was, according to Gray, part of a consistent theme stretching from the Magna Carta to the colonies to the government under the Constitution. There "can be no doubt," he wrote, that the English authorities who defended the jury as the rightful decider of law and fact "were of the very highest authority, and were so considered by the founders of the Republic." Gray cited here John Adams's reference to recent claims to the contrary by some English jurists, Lord Mansfield among them. Those views, Adams said, would have made of juries "mere ostentation and pageantry, and the court absolute judge of law and fact." Gray then cited Theophilus Parsons, chief justice of the Massachusetts Superior Court, as he charged the jury in a civil action for slander:

> Both parties have submitted the trial of this issue to a jury. The issue involved both law and fact, and the jury must decide the law and the fact. To enable them to settle the fact, they were to weigh the testimony; that they might truly decide the law, they were entitled to the assistance of the judge. If the judge had declined his aid in a matter of law, yet the jury must have formed their conclusion of law as correctly as they were able.[261]

This view of the jury, Gray concluded, could be found in all the New England states, with the possible exception of Rhode Island, as well as in New York.

Gray here stressed the argument of Alexander Hamilton as he defended Harry Croswell in the New York Supreme Court against the charge of libeling President Jefferson.[262] In the lower court, the judge had told the jury that the question of libel was an inference for the court to derive from the evidence, and that the understanding of the jury's role in New York was that of Lord Mansfield in the case of the dean of St. Asaph[263]—namely, that juries cannot possibly express an opinion on the law and must confine their deliberations to the facts. Hamilton had responded with a defense of the jury's right that emphasized its importance to the protection of public liberty—a view that more and more judges came to doubt as the spread of democracy seemed to make tyranny unlikely and as judges and lawyers alike developed a greater concern for the accuracy, and consistency, of verdicts. Hamilton argued several propositions in his defense of Croswell, as summed up in his trial notes:

> In the general distribution of powers in our system of jurisprudence, the cognizance of law belongs to the court, of fact to the jury; that often as they are

261. Ibid., 172, 173, 176, 178–179.

262. See note 205 above for a description of the peculiar political circumstances of this case.

263. *Rex v. Dean of St. Asaph*.

> not blended, the power of the court is absolute and exclusive. . . . [But] that in criminal cases, the law and fact being always blended, the jury, for reasons of a political and peculiar nature, for the security of life and liberty, is entrusted with the power of deciding both law and fact. . . . That in criminal cases, nevertheless, the court are the constitutional advisors of the jury in matter of law.[264]

Here is the old partnership—so important to the traditional understanding of the jury—between a learned judge and an intelligent jury, in which each side brings to the administration of justice its particular strengths. Yet in the end, the English and therefore the American law was clear, according to Gray: since no man may be punished in a criminal case except by the judgment of his peers, the jurors must have the final word, unless they themselves choose to separate their consideration of the law and the facts by requesting a special verdict.

To the objection that juries will make mistakes about the law, the traditional argument had an answer, summarized by Justice Kent's opinion in *Croswell*:[265]

> I am aware of the objection to the fitness and competency of a jury to decide upon questions of law, and, especially, with a power to overrule the directions of the judge. . . . But in human institutions, the question is not, whether every evil . . . can be avoided, but what arrangement will be productive of the least inconvenience. And it appears to be most consistent with the permanent security of the subject, that in criminal cases the jury should, after receiving the advice and assistance of the judge as to the law, take into their consideration all the circumstances of the case, and the intention with which the act was done, and to determine upon the whole, whether the act done be, or be not, within the meaning of the law.[266]

264. Cited in *Sparf and Hansen*, 181–182.

265. The New York Supreme Court ruled two to one in favor of Croswell's claim that he had been denied his right to a jury trial.

266. *Sparf and Hansen*, 185. John Adams made a similar point about juries' willingness to seek guidance from the court. In his law diary he recorded the following observation: "Every intelligent man will confess that cases frequently occur, in which it would be very difficult for a jury to determine the question of law. Long chains of intricate conveyances; obscure, perplexed and embarrassed clauses in writings: researches into remote antiquity . . . would confound a common jury and a decision by them would be no better than a decision by lott. And indeed juries are so sensible of [this] and of the great advantages the judges have [to] determine such questions, that, as the law has given them the liberty of finding the facts specially and . . . praying the advice of the court in the matter of law, they very seldom neglect to do it when recommended to them, or when in any doubt of the law." John Adams, *Diaries of John Adams*, vol. 16, January 10, 1771–November 28, 1772, 6–7, Adams Family Papers, Massachusetts Historical Society, Boston, masshist.org /digitaladams/archive/diary (accessed February 9, 2014).

In any case, Kent argued, the amateurishness of the jury compensates for the judge's tendency to develop views of a case that "may often be (with the most upright motives) too speculative and refined, and not altogether just in their application to every case." The rules favored by judges might be too "severe and oppressive," and judging human motivations does not always require "a master's skill in the science of the law," but rather knowledge "of the passions, and of the springs of human action," which knowledge is often "the lot of ordinary experience and sagacity."[267]

Justice Gray concluded from these earlier cases (and the many others he summarized or quoted from extensively) that "until nearly forty years after the adoption of the Constitution . . . not a single decision of the highest court of any State, or of any judge of a court in the United States, has been found, denying the right of the jury upon general issue in a criminal case to decide . . . the law in that issue." And many of those who defended this right were among "the most eminent and steadfast supporters of the Constitution," including John Marshall, John Adams, Alexander Hamilton, Samuel Chase, and James Wilson.[268] Although the right had certainly been questioned in the middle decades of the century, Gray pointed out that the best guidance for understanding the Constitution comes from the earlier generation rather than the later.[269] In any case, the proper question is not whether this understanding of the jury creates "the wisest and best system to be established by the people or by the legislature" but whether this is what, "in the light of previous law, and of contemporaneous or early construction of the Constitution, the people did affirm and establish by that instrument." Doubts about the jury, in other words, must confront the immoveable obstacle of constitutional law and tradition. But those doubts must also confront the republican objection to placing too much trust in officials. It is true, Gray conceded, that there may be "less danger of . . . oppression from judges appointed by the President elected by the people, than from judges appointed by a hereditary monarch." But "it cannot be assumed that judges will always be just and impartial," and "there is surely no reason why the chief security of the liberty of the citizen, the judgment of his peers, should be held less sacred in a republic than in a monarchy."[270]

Justice Gray's lengthy summary of the case law makes it abundantly clear that the authority of jurors to judge the law as well as the facts was considered, well into the nineteenth century, an essential element of the right to a jury trial—at least (or especially) in criminal cases, and generally in civil cases as well. In case

267. *Sparf and Hansen*, 186.

268. Ibid., 219. These "upholders of the Constitution" were, of course, all Federalists, and this may be Justice Gray's attempt to equate what was now being presented as a "radical" doctrine with the most "conservative" of the nation's founders.

269. Ibid., 221.

270. Ibid., 235.

after case, judges explained the law to the jury, often using words nearly identical to Justice Baldwin's charge to the jury in the case of George Wilson, tried in 1830 for robbing the mail: "We have thus stated to you the law of this case . . . but you will distinctly understand that you are the judges both of the law and fact in a criminal case, and are not bound by the opinion of the court; you may judge for yourselves."[271]

271. Ibid., 211.

3
The Modern Jury

All that can be expected of any system of judicial administration among men is that it makes the nearest approach that man can make to the unerring judgment of an infallible mind.

—Report of the Special Committee, American Bar Association, 1885

On the inquest it was shown that Buck Fanshaw, in the delirium of a wasting typhoid fever, had taken arsenic, shot himself through the body, cut his throat, and jumped out of a four-story window and broken his neck—and after due deliberation, the jury, sad and tearful, but with intelligence unblinded by its sorrow, brought in a verdict of death "by the visitation of God." What could the world do without juries?

—Mark Twain, *Roughing It*, 1899

THE CHANGING NINETEENTH-CENTURY JURY

The Supreme Court's insistence that juries have no right to judge the law is a convenient way to date the end of one era and the beginning of another, but the modern jury was the product of several developments over many decades. I introduce these developments here and then consider them in greater detail in the discussion that follows.

Democratization of the Franchise

The republican jury was based on a view of jury service that was quietly at odds with the boisterous, "democratical," and equalitarian spirit of the Jacksonian era. In the traditional view, jurors—the famous "twelve good men and true"—were a cut above the average citizen, marked by the special qualities thought to be necessary for judgment. These qualities were variously described as "integrity," "reputation," "intelligence," and "character." A simple but by no means foolproof way to ensure such qualities, early in the nineteenth century, was to impose a property qualification for jury service equal to or greater than the property qualifications for the suffrage. But to guarantee that the proper citizens were chosen—for even among the male property owners of a town, there might be those whose lack of sense would corrupt the verdict—jury officials were given powers of selection that Tocqueville described as "extensive" and even "arbitrary."[1] As a result, there were typically more voters than jurors.

Property qualifications for voting disappeared almost completely during the Jacksonian era, but many states continued to impose some form of property requirement for jury service.[2] It is sometimes said, therefore, that the extension of jury rights "lagged behind" the extension of voting rights, and such lagging is usually portrayed as an anomaly. But the understanding in the republican era was that jury service called for qualities of character and judgment that exceeded those required for voting. Voting was a right, whereas jury service was a duty, even an office. But as late as 1854, long after the franchise had been decoupled from property ownership, Lysander Spooner, the most famous of the American defenders of the "ancient jury right," complained that jurors in Arkansas, Missouri, Indiana, Alabama, Florida, and Virginia had to own a significant amount of property, and in other states, local officials such as sheriffs and commissioners had the power to "disenfranchise" potential jurors—that is, decline to choose them.[3]

But over time, the number of states that enforced property requirements declined, and the inflation of property values eroded the significance of those requirements that were still on the books. In addition, the courts' increasing business necessitated ever greater numbers of jurors, and this growing demand often overwhelmed the desire for "refined" qualities in jurymen. By the end of the nineteenth century, complaints about the quality of jurors were becoming commonplace. Juries, it was said, no longer reflected the substantial, propertied, successful, and intelligent elements of the community, raising questions about their effectiveness or (as it was now frequently called) their "efficiency." If jurors could

1. Alexis de Tocqueville, *Democracy in America*, trans. Harvey C. Mansfield and Delba Winthrop (Chicago: University of Chicago Press, 2000), 697.

2. Rosemarie Zagarri, "Suffrage and Representation," in *A Companion to the American Revolution*, ed. Jack Greene and J. R. Pole (Malden, MA: Blackwell, 2000), 662–667. Zagarri concludes that "by 1824 the right to vote had become independent of property ownership and taxpaying," with the exception of Rhode Island, Virginia, and Louisiana (665). State property qualifications for jury service survived in some states well into the twentieth century; see the discussion below. For the view that the survival of the property qualification was puzzling, given the extension of voting rights, see Albert W. Alschuler and Andrew G. Deiss, "A Brief History of the Criminal Jury in the United States," *University of Chicago Law Review* 61 (1994): 867–928.

3. Lysander Spooner, *An Essay on the Trial by Jury* (Boston: B. Marsh, 1852), 154–155.

not be relied on to deliver intelligible verdicts, then perhaps the jury system was no longer worth preserving.

Democratization also raised questions about how the jury could be used as a means of civic education. To profit from the education in the law that the jury was thought to provide, jurors would have to be minimally educated to begin with. Was it likely that men with little education, or little experience of "business" (a word used much more often in the modern than in the republican period), would be able to give attentive consideration to a judge's instructions? And could judicial guidance tame the most tempestuous and least educated elements of the community, whose lack of property and learning no longer formed a barrier to service?

In a democratic society, of course, such challenges are not confined to the jury system. One might say that here, the problem of the jury reveals the larger problem of democracy itself: how can the many be made wise, or at least wiser than they used to be, or wise enough to render judgment in court? Beginning in the late nineteenth century, observers of the courts, persuaded that many citizens were incapable of the wisdom required for judgment, argued more or less openly for greater restrictions on the power of juries and greater authority for judges. The Supreme Court's decision in *Sparf and Hansen* appeared to establish, finally, the judge's authority over the jury in matters of law. And while that "finality" was a bit deceptive—the jury's responsibility to follow the judge's guidance on the law has been questioned repeatedly since then, and these questions have even spawned a movement—*Sparf and Hansen* had the effect of moving the discussion of the jury in a new direction.[4] Having established that the judge was supposed to explain the law to the jury, the new question to be pondered was whether the typical juror could grasp what the judge was saying—especially in the more complicated environment of civil litigation.

Emergence of a Professional Bar

For most of its history, trial by jury was a machine with only two working parts: the judge and the jury. By the turn of the twentieth century, a third part had been added: the professional bar. As the legal profession became more conscious of its status, lawyers became more willing to challenge judges for influence over trials. This was not a sudden change; it was a trend that grew more important as the business of the courts increased. The most common way that lawyers sought to control the courtroom was by gaining control of juries, from the time they were impaneled to the final instructions they received before retiring to consider their

4. The movement in question promotes the right of "jury nullification" and is linked with the Fully Formed Jury Association. Jury nullification is discussed in chapter 5.

verdicts. In the process, the legal profession worked a change in the understanding of how the jury system functions, bringing into the courtroom some of the same disturbing questions about mass psychology that were troubling observers of public opinion and elections.[5]

New View of the Judge-Jury Relationship

The relationship between judges and jurors had once been seen as a partnership in which the judge, as the senior partner, advised jurors about the meaning and requirements of the law, while the jurors found the facts and applied the law as they understood it. The vehemence with which the Supreme Court majority in *Sparf and Hansen* assaulted this arrangement suggests a sea change.

The Supreme Court confirmed the new relationship twenty-five years after *Sparf and Hansen* in *Horning v. District of Columbia*.[6] Horning was a pawnbroker who had tried to evade DC's usury laws by taking his pledges just outside the district's boundary, while doing the rest of his business inside it. The facts in the case were not disputed, and Horning's only defense was that he believed his acts were legal because, technically, they had not been committed inside the district. The trial judge's charge to the jury evoked the language of the judge in the trial of Penn and Meade—minus the threat of attaint:

> In conclusion, I will say to you that a failure by you to bring in a verdict in this case can arise only from a willful and flagrant disregard of the evidence and the law as I have given it to you, and a violation of your obligation as jurors. . . . Of course, gentlemen of the jury, I cannot tell you, in so many words, to find defendant guilty, but what I say amounts to that.[7]

5. One of the earliest, and certainly the most famous, speculation was Walter Lippmann's *Public Opinion* (New York: Harcourt, Brace, 1922). However, doubts about the public's ability to understand public affairs were a feature of democratic self-reflection throughout the republican era as well. They were a central concern, for example, of Horace Mann and a principal reason for his efforts to reform public education. Mann wrote, "Every native-born child amongst us imbibes notions, either false or true," on a wide range of political and economic questions. If these notions turn out to be false, and if those possessing such false notions are "invested with the political rights of citizenship, with power to give an authoritative voice and vote upon the affairs of his country, he will look upon all existing things as rubbish which it is his duty to sweep away, that he may have room for the erection of other structures planned after the model of his own false ideas." Horace Mann, "The Necessity of Education in a Republican Government (1839)," in *Lectures on Education* (Boston: Ide & Dutton, 1855), 117–164.

6. 254 U.S. 135 (1920).

7. Ibid., 140. The quotation from the trial judge is taken from Justice Brandeis's dissent.

This forthright command generated an appeal, on the grounds that the judge had, in effect, directed a verdict of guilty. In his opinion for the majority affirming the conviction, Justice Oliver Wendell Holmes argued that the judge had only done his duty, however "peremptory" his tone might have been. Holmes then summarized the jury's role as follows:

> The facts were not in dispute, and what [the judge] did was to say so and to lay down the law applicable to them. In such a case . . . the function of the jury if they do their duty is little more than formal. The judge cannot direct a verdict . . . [b]ut the judge always has the right and duty to tell them what the law is upon this or that state of facts . . . but the jury were allowed the technical right . . . to decide against the law and the facts—and that is all there was left for them after the defendant . . . took the stand.[8]

Had the jury managed to work up some sympathy for pawnbrokers, it might have refused to convict Horning. But that was merely a "technical right," according to Holmes: "The judge cannot direct a verdict it is true, and the jury has the power to bring in a verdict in the teeth of both law and facts. But the judge always has the right and duty to tell them what the law is upon this or that state of facts that may be found, and he can do the same none the less when the facts are agreed."[9]

In the twentieth century judges would craft a new, more directive relationship with jurors, often in competition with attorneys and, increasingly, with appellate courts. Jurors would be firmly instructed about what the law meant, up to and sometimes across the invisible boundary between "instructing the jury" and "directing a verdict." Judges, meanwhile, found their own supervision of the trial process increasingly challenged by appellate courts as well as by lawyers in both state and federal courts, as the highest levels of the judiciary sought to bring a highly decentralized system under greater central control.

Increase in Complex Commercial Disputes

Highly complex commercial disputes occupied an increasing share of the courts' time and attention, just as doubts about the average juror's ability to understand his responsibilities were reaching their peak.[10] The civil jury had always been a

8. Ibid.

9. Ibid., 187.

10. At both the state and federal levels, courts became much busier in the late nineteenth century. Civil and criminal cases grew in number, but the number of courts, and the staff and other resources needed to run them, remained fixed or grew at a much slower pace. Lawrence M. Friedman, *A History of American Law* (New York: Simon & Schuster, 1973), 335.

central part of the judicial system, for several reasons, as we have seen. There had always been more civil than criminal jury trials. In the past, Americans sued one another over everything from defective soap and trampled gardens to allegations of witchcraft and sexual misconduct (see chapter 1). Now they sued one another over unfulfilled commercial contracts, defective products, and industrial accidents. In contrast, criminal defendants often chose to plead guilty rather than face a jury trial, and those criminal cases that made it to court involved few complex questions of either law or evidence. Civil cases were therefore a significant proportion of all the trials settled by juries, which is why the Anti-Federalists had been so intent on preserving them: take away civil disputes, and trial by jury might shrink to nothing.

Yet even in the early republic, there had been some sympathy for Alexander Hamilton's observation that certain kinds of civil cases presented "nice and intricate" problems that might better be left to judges. This was a minority view, to be sure, and even the normally forceful Hamilton never pressed it. But the emergence of a modern industrial and commercial economy, with its "intricate" contract and liability cases, brought the issue of jury competence in civil litigation squarely to the front of the debate. By the end of the nineteenth century, the idea that amateurs could fairly judge complex civil cases had lost much of its support among the business community and the legal profession. And this was true of conservative as well as progressive jurists, who could agree on this much: the Age of the Expert had arrived.

Emergence and Triumph of Progressive Legal Doctrines

Progressives were deeply suspicious of the jury system, in part because they shared the growing doubts about the competence of lay judgment in civil cases, although some progressives appreciated the jury as a blunt instrument for beating up on corporations. But behind these doubts lay something bigger: the progressive view of juries was the product of a distinctively progressive view of the law itself. The jury system made little sense to progressives because, in their view, the traditional understanding of the law made little sense. The law was not a disembodied search for truth; still less was it a path to justice. The law, as Holmes famously argued, was not a "mystery" but a "profession." "We are studying what we shall want in order to appear before judges, or to advise people in such a way as to keep them out of court."[11] In a complex society, "obeying the law" is neither a simple task nor a self-evident moral obligation. Judging the law is therefore no simple task either, and ordinary citizens cannot be expected to do it most of the time,

11. Oliver Wendell Holmes Jr., "The Path of the Law," *Harvard Law Review* 10 (1897): 457–478.

especially in civil cases that involve such a tangle of law and evidence that they baffle even the attorneys. The clear import of progressive efforts was therefore to subordinate lay judgment to the disciplines of the professional bar and (even better) the professional administrative tribunal, where complex judgments could be made by those who knew what they were doing.

Decline in the Popular Image of the Jury System

Increasingly, the "palladium of our liberties" was subjected not just to criticism but to something approaching derision. Jurors were said to be ignorant, biased, careless about their duties, and more concerned with mercy or a quick escape to the local tavern than with the dispassionate enforcement of the law. The most educated and experienced citizens were eager to escape the burden of their jury obligations (and compliant state legislatures were willing to help them do so), and their absence made the jury more "plebeian" than it otherwise would have been. The jury system could also reveal the ugly side of democracy, such as in cases pitting unpopular minorities against unsympathetic majorities. Doubts about the jury were therefore consistent with growing doubts about democracy itself, which were more openly expressed in the years after the Civil War than they had been in the early republic. All too often, it was claimed, jurors took the side of the majority against the dictates of justice, siding with the popular litigant against the unpopular one. This problem was especially acute when race was involved, but even in the absence of racial differences, unpopular defendants (or unpopular victims) found scant justice from juries of their peers—or so it was said in the press. This was a marked contrast to the almost universal public praise of the jury system in the republican era—praise that even the Sedition Act trials, with their shocking conviction rates, had not dented.

Meanwhile, black citizens continued to be excluded from jury service, especially in the South, despite consistent Supreme Court rulings declaring that such exclusion was unconstitutional. This introduced into the jury debate a new theme: the jury cannot be considered a useful part of the justice system unless it is "broadly representative" of the communities from which jurors are drawn. This argument would eventually be applied to women, day laborers, and members of ethnic minorities excluded by either statute or custom. There is a potential conflict between a jury that is "above average" and a jury that is a "cross section" of the community, and this conflict came to a head, beginning in the 1940s, with the long campaign to reform jury selection, first in the federal courts and then in the states.

THE "CRISIS" OF THE MODERN JURY

By the late nineteenth century, the "palladium of our liberties" was an institution in crisis, at least according to its critics, including those who supported the jury system and hoped to see it improved. A discussion from 1879—*A Practical Treatise on Juries* by Hugo Hirsch, a member of the New York bar—is used here to introduce some of the themes that would shape the jury debate for much of the modern period. It also provides a rough sketch of how the jury system actually worked at the turn of the twentieth century.[12]

In form, Hirsch's work looks much like a textbook on jury law. Its chapters lay out the law regarding such matters as challenging jurors, the penalties for non-attendance, juror qualifications, and so forth. But Hirsch informs us in the preface that the work was "originally intended for the instruction of the citizen alone, as to his duties as juror, and his rights and privileges as such." It eventually grew because there was no comparable work explaining these matters systematically to lawyers. The resulting work, then, was meant to serve the needs of laymen and professionals alike, an acknowledgment that a level of sophistication might be attained through a discussion of the law that was neither too simple for attorneys nor too complicated for typical citizens with a decent education and the proper civic disposition.[13]

Immediately, however, we come to what must have inspired Hirsch to conceive such a work in the first place: "The complaint is constantly made that the jury system is bad, and that it is time we had a change, etc. This complaint is ill-founded and misapplied."[14] It is ill-founded because the long history of the jury shows that it has led to the "improvement of the laws and institutions of the countries which have adopted it." So while it can certainly be improved, it must not be "changed or abolished. . . . The complaint, if any, should be made against the juror, not the system."[15]

Ordinary citizens needed a treatise on the jury, then, because so many of them did not understand their responsibilities or did not perform them adequately.

12. Hugo Hirsch, *A Practical Treatise on Juries, Their Powers, Duties, and Uses, in All Actions and Proceedings, Both Civil and Criminal, under the Common Law, and under the Statutes of the United States and of the State of New York* (New York: George S. Diossy, 1879).

13. Hirsch's concern for educating citizens offers a contrast to contemporary jury textbooks, which are aimed exclusively at practitioners. A useful example is Nancy Gertner and Judith H. Mizner, *The Law of Juries*, 5th ed. (St. Paul, MN: Thompson/West, 2011). There is no explicit concern for civic education in *The Law of Juries*, whereas Hirsch's *Practical Treatise* aims to improve the understanding of prospective jurors and attorneys simultaneously.

14. Hirsch, *Practical Treatise*, v.

15. Ibid., vi.

During the republican era, it was much more common to hear complaints about judges than about jurors, although complaints about the latter were not unheard of. That situation was essentially reversed in the modern period, when debates over the suitability of the jury system were frequently focused on citizens' ability to meet the responsibilities imposed by jury service. "We believe," Hirsch concludes in his preface, "that our jury system is not in need of any improvement, but that the juror is." And the organizing assumption of everything that follows is "that this improvement should consist of the education of those who will hereafter become jurors, in their duties, rights, etc."[16]

Hirsch's discussion of New York law shows that the official understanding was, as in the republican period, that jurors ought to be above average in terms of intelligence, understanding, and character. As in times past, the first way to achieve that goal was to restrict jury service to property owners: the New York State requirement, even as late as 1879, was $250 of assessable personal property or $150 of "freehold estate in real property."[17] (This law did not apply in New York City, which used its home-rule privilege to abolish property qualifications for jury service in 1847.)[18] The prospective juror could have no criminal record and had to be of "fair character," "approved integrity," "sound judgment," and "well-informed."[19] The jury law's property qualifications were not high, but they would have excluded many men who were entitled to vote, a circumstance common in many other states in the nineteenth century.[20] Even with these restrictions, however, the New York jury pool of Hirsch's day would have been much more inclusive than those of the early nineteenth century, when property qualifications for both jury service and voting were much higher in real terms.

16. Ibid., viii.

17. New York State's "freehold" requirement of $250 in property remained on the books until it was repealed in 1967, by which time inflation had made it irrelevant. The law survived a constitutional challenge, however, as late as 1949. See Alschuler and Deiss, "Brief History of the Criminal Jury," 879.

18. William Mack, *Cyclopedia of Law and Procedure*, vol. 24 (New York: American Law Book Company, 1907), 201.

19. Hirsch, *Practical Treatise*, 20.

20. See C. La Rue Munson, "Selecting the Jury," *Yale Law Journal* 4 (1894–1895): 173–189. Munson points out that it was "almost universally" the case that citizens qualified for jury service by state law must be over twenty-one and a resident and voter in the county where the court met. "Every juror must be an elector." But it was not necessarily the case that every elector could be a juror; Munson reports that there were property qualifications for jury service in several states in the 1890s, including New York, Virginia, North Carolina, Texas, Mississippi, and Indiana (175, n. 7). John Proffatt concludes from a study of state laws that "about a third of our States require a property qualification for a juror." John Proffatt, *A Treatise on Trial by Jury: Including Questions of Law and Fact* (San Francisco: Sumner, Whitney, 1880), 162.

However, as the statutes make clear, the desire for a capable jury was at war with a not very secret desire among citizens to avoid jury service—a constant refrain throughout the modern period. The result was a long list of automatic exemptions granted by state legislatures, and as the years passed, these exemptions became more numerous and more scandalous. In New York, executive officials from the governor to the superintendent of the insurance department, members of the legislature, court officers, and sheriffs and undersheriffs were all automatically excused from jury service. A separate section of the law provided a long list of private professions and occupations that were entitled to exemptions, if requested: clergymen, employees of the state asylum, prison wardens, doctors and surgeons, attorneys, professors, and employees in the textile and iron industries. Also entitled to exemptions were the officers of steamboats, superintendents and conductors of railways, telegraph operators, officers in and veterans of the state militia, and firemen.[21] Although the formal justification for these exemptions was the essential nature of such employees (firemen, most obviously), it is difficult to see how that argument could plausibly apply to professors and clergymen, much less to telegraph operators and veterans of the state militia.

Complaints about disqualifications and exemptions would figure prominently in efforts to reform the jury system in the twentieth century—in particular, efforts to decouple federal jury selection from state jury qualification laws. These efforts also reveal how most commentators understood the jury. The problem with exemptions was that they degraded the quality of the jury pool, eliminating many members of the community whose education, reputation, and experience could prove invaluable in court. Given the expanding universe of voters and the relatively low property qualifications for jury service, those left in the jury pool were average, at best, in terms of their education and accomplishments—and often well below average. At the beginning of the era of the modern jury, therefore, arguments for more "inclusive" juries were actually pleas to recover the participation of the wealthy, the professional, and the educated.

It is difficult to know how much discretion was left in the hands of jury commissioners and others charged with administering jury selection in the states. Administration of the jury system has been thoroughly decentralized for most of our history (and compared with many other elements of American government, it remains so). Although it is relatively easy to discover what state laws required, it

21. Hirsch, *Practical Treatise*, 20–25. New York's exemptions and disqualifications were not unusual. Surveying the situation in the 1940s, William J. Hickey found exemptions for accountants, actuaries, chiropodists, Christian Scientists, funeral directors, linotype operators, millers, pharmacists, doctors, dentists, attorneys, newspaper editors, schoolteachers, school bus drivers, school janitors and boiler tenders, telegraph operators, railroad employees, and members of organized fire companies. William J. Hickey, "Improvement of the Jury System in Federal Courts," *Georgetown Law Journal* 35 (1946–1947): 507.

is harder to know how those laws were actually enforced. The New York statute, which was fairly typical, put the initial steps of the process in the hands of the most local of local officials: town supervisors, clerks, and assessors—just where Tocqueville had found it. In New York these officers were charged, once a year, with "making a list of persons to serve as trial jurors for the then ensuing three years." That is, those on the list could be called at any time during the three-year period, possibly more than once—perhaps explaining the constant lobbying of the legislature for exemptions.[22] Names were to be taken from the property assessment rolls, however, not the voter rolls, making the property qualification, not the franchise, the gateway standard for jury service, at least outside of Manhattan.

To prevent manipulation of jury selection, three duplicate lists were kept under lock and key—the obvious inference being that local officials had been caught "packing" the jury box with persons likely to rule in a way favorable to themselves or their political allies, friends, or relatives. One of these lists was transferred to the county clerk, who composed "ballots" with one name per ballot; these were deposited in a special jury box, after destroying the unused ballots from the previous term. Then, on a designated day prior to the start of the new court term, the county clerk drew from the box the names of at least thirty-six persons (the maximum to be determined by the court's workload) to serve as jurors for the term. The law required the drawing to be witnessed by the sheriff or an appointed deputy. The names were then given to the sheriff, whose duty was to "serve upon each person named," in person, at least six days before the beginning of the term, a "written notice to attend the term."[23] Anyone who was served and did not attend could be fined $10 to $25 for "each day that he so neglects to attend." The absent juror could be jailed until the fine was paid.[24]

22. Hirsch, *Practical Treatise*, 37.

23. Ibid., 38–40, 41. This rather short notice was perhaps another reason why so many people sought to be excused or exempted. A common complaint about the jury system in the modern period was the lack of attention paid to the convenience or comfort of those called to serve, and this problem was addressed by nearly all the formal proposals for improving the jury system. These complaints have not ceased, although contemporary citizens are usually given much more time to plan for jury duty. See chapter 5 for a discussion of contemporary proposals for improving the administration of the jury system.

24. Ibid., 44–45. The average daily wage for federal employees in 1892 was $3.02. A fine that was three to eight times the average federal civil service salary should have been a significant deterrent to scofflaws, even those at the higher end of the salary scale. The data do not indicate whether the fines were consistently enforced, however. And of course, highly paid professionals would be less likely to worry about the fines, and many would be automatically exempted anyway because of their occupations. Bureau of the Census, *Historical Statistics of the United States: Colonial Times to 1957*, series D603–617 (Washington, DC: Bureau of the Census, 1960), 91–92.

The jury box thus contained the names of property owners compiled from the assessors' lists, presumably at random (the law seems to anticipate various attempts at cheating), minus the long list of worthy gentlemen the legislature had been persuaded to excuse: legislators, clerics, firemen, telegraph operators, undertakers, and others. Thus, the attorneys were left with a group of citizens frequently described as below average in terms of their education, experience, and standing in the community (even though they could meet the modest property requirements), or at least well below the standard thought to be necessary to perform the duties of a juror. The attorneys' challenge was to sift through the panel, looking for those jurors who might be sympathetic to their client's case or those jurors most amenable to persuasion, after removing those who might be troublesome or whose sympathy was in doubt. The tool available for this purpose was the challenge: the challenge for cause, and the peremptory challenge.

The practice of challenging or "striking" jurors was of such long standing that it was said to be one of the rights attached to the jury trial, brought over from England and planted successfully in the New World.[25] The challenge for cause was a request to remove a juror, either because the juror favored one of the parties ("challenge for favor") or because the juror had expressed an opinion on the case ("challenge for principal cause"). It was the practice in New York and many other states, when such a challenge for favor was raised, for the judge to appoint two of the prospective jurors present in court to be "triers" of the challenge. (Once two jurors had been seated, they became the triers.) The triers' responsibility was to examine the juror and determine whether he was "indifferent" and capable of giving a "true verdict . . . according to the evidence." One of the duties of a juror, in other words, was to participate in jury selection. Challenges for favor were more common when juries were chosen in small towns, where jurors were likely to know some of those involved in a case, if only by reputation. Challenges for principal cause, in the modern era, were often the result of newspaper publicity and the mysterious process by which members of the public were induced to share an "opinion" about a highly publicized criminal or civil case.

Hirsch notes that, "to be a sufficient ground for disqualifying a juror from sitting in the trial of a criminal prosecution, the opinion formed by him must be

25. The Anti-Federalists had demanded that the Constitution's provision for jury trials acknowledge the "whole" of the jury right—that is, all the practices associated with the common-law jury, such as trial in the vicinage, the requirement of unanimity, the twelve-man jury, and others. Their only success in this regard was the reference to the common law in the Seventh Amendment concerning the jury's control over questions of fact. Nevertheless, the Supreme Court has ruled that the constitutional jury is the common-law jury as it was in 1789, the year the first Judiciary Act was passed. See Parsons v. Bedford, 28 U.S. 433 (1830), and the more limited twentieth-century ruling, Baltimore & Carolina Line v. Redman, 295 U.S. 694 (1935).

fixed and unconditional" or "of such a nature as to require affirmative evidence to remove it."[26] The case law also held that "mere opinions thrown out as a jest, or to avoid being impaneled, will not . . . operate as a disqualification."[27] These standards were not new; they were entirely consistent with the standard defined by Chief Justice John Marshall in the treason trial of Aaron Burr in 1807:

> The opinion which has been avowed by the court is, that light impressions which may fairly be supposed to yield to the testimony that may be offered, which may leave the mind open to a fair consideration of that testimony, constitute no sufficient objection to a juror; but that those strong and deep impressions which will close the mind against the testimony that may be offered in opposition to them, which will combat that testimony, and resist its force, do constitute a sufficient objection to him. Those who try the impartiality of a juror ought to test him by this rule.[28]

Jurors were thus expected to be rational, open-minded, and fair—not oblivious to events going on in their community, and not so indifferent to the public world that they had formed no opinion at all, especially about matters as serious as murder or (in Burr's case) treason. If jurors could not meet this exacting standard, that failure might be described as a moral failure with important civic consequences. The impartial juror was not a blank slate but an intelligent student. Nor was he a "myth," as some contemporary observers of the jury would have it.[29] He was simply a good citizen called to perform a difficult task.

To learn whether prospective jurors harbored "immutable" prejudice or whether they had some other disqualification cognizable by the court (e.g., an inability to speak or understand English), jurors could be questioned. The court posed the questions—sometimes to the entire panel, sometimes to jurors individually—and it is likely that some of the questions originated with the attorneys. Once challenges for favor and cause had been exhausted and a full twelve-man jury had been seated but not yet sworn, plaintiffs, defendants, and prosecutors had

26. Hirsch, *Practical Treatise*, 111.

27. Ibid., 112.

28. United States v. Burr, 25 F. Cas. 49, no. 14,692g (C.C.D. Va. [1807]). See also Robert K. Faulkner, "John Marshall and the Burr Trial," *Journal of American History* 53, 2 (September 1966): 247–258.

29. See, for example, Roy Grutman and Bill Thomas, "The Myth of the Impartial Jury," in *Lawyers and Thieves* (New York: Simon & Schuster, 1990), 117–132. "Jurors are not selected at random. They are made to order for each case, and how they're put together, the ingredients purposely added and left out, has more to do with who wins or loses than anything else that happens in court" (120). I have more to say about this perspective in chapter 4.

one more opportunity to shape a jury that was more to their liking, through the use of peremptory challenges.[30] To challenge peremptorily means to exercise a challenge without having to state a reason. The number of such challenges was controlled by statute; it varied from state to state, between civil and criminal cases, and by the severity of the offense. Because the "conformity principle" required federal courts to observe the civil and criminal procedures of the states where they met, the number of peremptory challenges in federal trials varied by district.[31] In New York, according to Hirsch, in a trial for any offense punishable by death or a prison term of more than ten years, the defendant was entitled to challenge twenty jurors peremptorily; the people could challenge no more than five. For lesser crimes, the defendant could challenge five and the people could challenge three. In civil cases, each side was entitled to only two peremptory challenges.[32]

Having established how the jury is impaneled, Hirsch turns to the general duties of jurors, including the kind of advice Hirsch believes modern citizens should heed. In the section "Duties before Trial," for example, in discussing the circumstances that might justify being excused, Hirsch urges businessmen to pay greater attention to their public responsibilities:

> Many persons who, on being drawn for the first time as jurors, think that the only thing necessary for them to say to the judge is, that their business will not allow them to attend, and upon this statement they suppose they have the right to be excused as jurors. It is time that business men should have a more reasonable and enlightened view on this subject, and that they should consider jury duty not an onerous, but an honorable one.[33]

30. "Man" is the appropriate word here, as only one state (Wyoming) had extended the jury right to women at the time of the publication of Hirsch's textbook.

31. The Judiciary Act of 1789 required federal district courts to adhere to the practices of the states where the court sat, with respect to jury qualifications and jury selection (section 29) as well as trial procedures (section 34). Conformity in jury selection was reauthorized by the Act of July 20, 1840, chap. 47, 5 Stat. 394, which clarified and extended the principle enunciated in the Judiciary Act of 1789, and by the Conformity Act of 1872, 28 U.S.C. § 724.

32. Hirsch, *Practical Treatise*, 137–139. These rules were somewhat more generous to defendants in capital cases than are the current Federal Rules of Criminal Procedure, which allow twenty challenges each to the defendant and the prosecution. The contemporary law and the practice of peremptory challenges are discussed later. See also Neil J. Kressel and Dorit F. Kressel, *Stack and Sway: The New Science of Jury Consulting* (Boulder, CO: Westview Press, 2002).

33. Hirsch, *Practical Treatise*, 150. For evidence that citizens still seek to avoid jury service because they have "more important business to attend to," see my report on jury selection in a contemporary civil trial in a Massachusetts state court: Dennis Hale, "All Rise," *Boston College Magazine* (Summer 2005): 26–33.

Other helpful advice follows: do not discuss pending cases with other jurors; report any attempts to influence your opinion of a case; inform the court of any conflicts not brought out by the questions; and pay particular attention to the oath, "and especially to that part which speaks of 'trying the issues according to the evidence.'"[34] That is, jurors must ignore the impressions attorneys will try to plant—the legal profession having already developed, apparently, into a combination of learning and showmanship. Pay no attention, Hirsch advises the juror-to-be, to the superficial tricks, to the "good-looking woman" or the "one dressed in mourning, or one who sheds tears," or to the "evidence as adduced on the part of a lodge-brother or a person engaged in the same business or profession as the juror." Listen carefully; pay attention to the evidence; ask questions if you need to; do not be swayed by appeals to emotion, and note particularly when counsel promises evidence but does not produce it; do not be fooled by appearances, either by elegance or plainness of dress. And anticipating by nearly fifteen years the decision in *Sparf and Hansen*, Hirsch comes down firmly on the court's side of the argument regarding who may determine the law: "Particular attention should be paid to the charge of the judge, as it is from him the jury must receive the law, and instructions as to the application of the law on the points in question. And they are bound to act in accordance with his charge, regardless of the consequences."[35]

After the end of testimony, and after the charge, Hirsch notes, it is time for jurors to retire to the jury room, where they should spend no more than a few minutes electing their foreman and taking a preliminary vote. "An honest juror," he explains, "should always be willing to state his reasons in the jury-room for his vote, and should always be willing to listen to the reasons and arguments of the others; and if he does this, and is conscientious in his voting, and if the case is one in which the evidence would uphold his opinion and vote, he has a right to adhere to his opinion, even if opposed by the remaining eleven jurors." If there is uncertainty, however, about the evidence or about the judge's instructions, then the jury has an obligation to return to the court to ask for clarification.[36]

Hirsch notes that in a criminal case, the jury's job is over when it reaches a verdict. But in a civil case, there is still the matter of damages—a comparatively simple matter when the question is "goods sold and delivered, money loaned or advanced," and so forth. In such cases the amount of damages is "actually determinable by the evidence adduced" (e.g., what the goods cost or what payment was promised), and the final judgment is merely one of "fair calculation and adjustment." But there is another category of action in which "the amount of damages is not actually determinable by the evidence given on the trial," and Hirsch

34. Hirsch, *Practical Treatise*, 152.
35. Ibid., 152–153, 156.
36. Ibid., 158.

spends some time explaining how jurors ought to handle these difficult cases. Such cases—for example, product liability cases—were frequently implicated in complaints about the jury system at the time, because juries returned allegedly irrational verdicts, particularly in cases involving railroads, steamboats, and automobiles. Once again, Hirsch admonishes jurors to pay close attention to the judge's charge to the jury, for the judge "has exclusively the power and right to instruct the jury on whether the case on trial is one in which they may find nominal damages only, or actual damages, or actual and exemplary or punitive damages, and they must find in accordance with these instructions."[37]

That jurors were not following judges' instructions is clearly implied by the criticism leveled at the jury system during this period, especially in cases involving "contributory negligence"—a concept about which jurors were notably skeptical when the defendant was a "deep-pockets corporation." The doctrine of contributory negligence, as it developed in the late nineteenth century, asserted that if the victim had contributed at all to his own accident, this relieved the defendant of any responsibility for the ensuing damages. A famous example comes from Oliver Wendell Holmes's ruling in a Supreme Court case involving a man killed at a rail crossing, whose estate had won a jury verdict against the railroad:

> It appears to us plain that nothing is suggested by the evidence to relieve [the decedent] Goodman from responsibility for his own death. When a man goes upon a railroad track, he knows that he goes to a place where he will be killed if a train comes upon him before he is clear of the track. . . . In such circumstances, it seems to us that, if a driver cannot be sure otherwise whether a train is dangerously near, he must stop and get out of his vehicle, although obviously he will not often be required to do more than to stop and look. . . . It is true . . . that the question of due care very generally is left to the jury. But we are dealing with a standard of conduct, and when the standard is clear, it should be laid down once for all by the Courts.[38]

The doctrine of contributory negligence was denounced from the pulpit, in the press, and, most important, in state legislatures, many of which moved to restrain the doctrine's use in state courts. Yet the doctrine's most determined opponents were jurors, who frequently ignored the judge's instructions and voted merciful verdicts designed to help the victims of industrial accidents, even when the victims were at least partly to blame for their own misfortunes.[39] They did this so often that they "essentially created a regime of comparative negligence

37. Ibid., 159.
38. Baltimore & Ohio Railroad Co. v. Goodman, 275 U.S. 66 (1927), 70.
39. Note, however, that in the *Goodman* case, the jury's verdict for the plaintiff survived at the appellate level, suggesting at least some sympathy, even from the bench.

long before the legislature and judges had eliminated contributory negligence as a defense."[40]

But even when liability was undisputed, there was rarely a simple answer to the question of an appropriate financial award for damages suffered. How much money will justly compensate a man who can no longer work or who has endured suffering at the hands of an allegedly careless defendant? How much will compensate a decedent's estate? Jurors apparently had their own rough methods for answering such questions, in the absence of clear guidelines either in the law or in judges' instructions. Hirsch was particularly scornful of the following approach to determining punitive damages: each juror would write an amount on a piece of paper, the amounts would then be added and divided by twelve, and the resulting average was announced as the award. "This manner of reaching a conclusion is illegal and unjust, and cannot be reconciled with their oath as jurors."[41]

Hirsch's recommendation, however, reaffirms the understanding that jurors are engaged in a deliberative process. In his view, the jurors ought to begin by clarifying among themselves what kind of damages the plaintiff deserves: nominal, actual, or punitive. The first two are easily given a monetary value by virtue of the statute or the evidence presented by the plaintiff (medical costs, for example). The third category of damages, because it lacks any statutory or evidentiary ground, is discretionary and therefore subject to fanciful decisions, so Hirsch suggests a procedure to anchor the deliberation in reality: one of the jurors begins with a motion naming a particular amount, and that amount is discussed and voted up or down. The emphasis here is on discussion and its contribution to a just outcome. In the process of debating this motion, jurors "may, perhaps, be reminded of evidence they may have forgotten, or may see the case in a different light . . . thus, by argument, reason and vote, they may come to a conclusion that will be proper and legal." The jury must not hurry this conclusion, a principle that invites another piece of advice by Hirsch and a glimpse, if Hirsch is a reliable guide, into the reality of jury deliberations in 1879. Hirsch notes the "reprehensible course" that is "often" taken by weary jurors eager to finish and go home, "namely, the unconscientious desire or willingness to agree to anything for the purpose of getting away."[42]

Nor must jurors succumb to the temptation to "couple their verdict in a criminal case with a recommendation to mercy, unless the circumstances of the case admit of such recommendation." So-called merciful verdicts in criminal cases, Hirsch claims, are often merely tactics designed to get reluctant jurors to vote for

40. Robert P. Burns, *The Death of the American Trial* (Chicago: University of Chicago Press, 2009), citing Nancy Marder, "The Myth of the Nullifying Jury," *Northwestern University Law Review* 93 (Spring 1999): 910.

41. Hirsch, *Practical Treatise*, 160.

42. Ibid., 160–162.

conviction; therefore, they are not genuinely unanimous verdicts but "a manner of compromise" that should be discouraged. "The moral responsibility of juries in criminal cases is very great" and should be exercised with the utmost care and gravitas.[43] The jurors' responsibility is not simply to render a correct decision; "their duty is to arrive at a just decision." Men may be in doubt as to what constitutes a just decision, especially in civil cases, where each side can make a reasonable case, but jurors should have the courage to put such doubts aside. "All that is required and can be expected" in such cases is that "they should be satisfied . . . that the preponderance of proof justifies the decision; and when so satisfied, they should not suffer a doubt to prevent the decision from being made." Ruling is about making choices, and absolute certainty can rarely be achieved through the evidence: if it could, there would be no question of choice in the first place.[44] The difficulties confronted by juries are the difficulties confronted by all who share in ruling.

At one time, Hirsch's defense of the jury system would have been common and uncontroversial. By the 1880s, however, such old-fashioned views were losing their hold on the legal profession, and complaints about the jury, once confined to private grumbling, were becoming more open and more frequent. Still, at the beginning of the modern era, most lawyers were prepared to say, along with Hirsch, that the jury system was fundamentally sound, provided three reforms could be achieved: (1) if jurors could be persuaded, or taught, to perform their duties responsibly, avoiding irrational or merciful verdicts; (2) if the exemptions that excluded so many successful men from jury service could be eliminated; and (3) if judges could be given adequate authority to guide the jury during the trial by commenting on the evidence, where appropriate, and instructing jurors more clearly about the law in terms that laymen could understand.

Writing in 1887, Supreme Court justice Samuel Miller confessed that during his career as an attorney in private practice, he had thought little of juries. He had considered them necessary in criminal cases but of "doubtful utility" in civil cases, where litigants would be better served by letting a panel of three judges decide all questions of law and fact together.[45] But after twenty-five years on the bench, he had acquired a new appreciation for the jury, on both the civil and the

43. Ibid., 163.

44. Hirsch reports that New York State law specifically forbade the use of lots or any other procedure based on chance to arrive at a verdict. Evidence of such a procedure would warrant a new trial. And "where great levity was exhibited by the jury in their deliberations, and where the result . . . was reached by a course of frivolous experiments having but an imperfect bearing on the issue, the verdict was set aside." Jurors were supposed to take their job seriously, not simply bring the proceedings to an end. Ibid., 195, 196.

45. Samuel F. Miller, "The System of Trial by Jury," *American Law Review* (November–December 1887): 861.

criminal side. His earlier view had been a consequence of judges' failure to exercise proper control over juries—not properly "instructing the jury upon the law . . . which is essential to a right result in a jury trial." A case "submitted to the unregulated discretion of a jury, without that careful discrimination between matters of fact and matters of law which it is the duty of the court to lay before them, is but little better than a popular trial before a town meeting."[46]

Justice Miller expressed what was becoming a more common view among judges (and a view that would soon be given authoritative expression by the Supreme Court): that there is a natural division of labor in the courtroom, with juries judging the facts and judges determining the law. To preserve this division, judges should be careful in the way they explain the law to juries because, in the absence of this arrangement, "a jury trial is but a farce."[47] Like many others at the time, Miller worried that the jury system was falling into disrepute because of the low quality of the jurors themselves. The system would inspire more confidence if those chosen to serve were intelligent, familiar with "habits of business," and morally pure. Given that this was not currently the case, it would be sensible to abandon the requirement of unanimity, so that one or two "undisciplined minds" could not render useless the labors expended during a long trial or deny a worthy plaintiff the just recognition of his rights. We should also, Miller argued, abandon the effort to find jurors whose "impartiality" was nothing more than blank ignorance of the world around them. Jury selection at the present time meant looking for individuals with the following qualifications:

> [Someone] who knows nothing of the facts, who is not related to the defendant, and whose mind is totally unaffected by information he may have derived from any source. . . . This has resulted, as common observation shows, in excluding the intelligent man and accepting the ignorant one. . . . [T]he man really best qualified to try a prisoner and render a fair verdict is excluded from the jury box, while the ignorant and stupid, those who take no interest in the world around them . . . are the remnant who remain.[48]

46. Ibid., 861–862.

47. Ibid., 863.

48. Ibid., 867. Justice Miller's complaint implies that jury selection had already acquired some of the qualities associated with contemporary jury trials. That is, if jurors were being challenged because they had the kind of general knowledge of a case that came from reading the newspaper every day, then the attorneys were deliberately using the voir dire to find jurors who were entirely ignorant, and not just about the case in question. This is also a fair inference from Hirsch's warning that prospective jurors not be "fooled" by the weeping widows and congenial lodge brothers on the witness list. That jury selection and trial strategy are linked comes as no surprise to contemporary litigators; that the practice has such a long pedigree is less well known. The problem of peremptory challenges is discussed in chapter 4.

One of the nation's most esteemed law professors, former Iowa Supreme Court justice John F. Dillon, in a series of lectures at Yale in 1894, echoed Justice Miller's complaints about the jury system and shared his change of heart from the bench. "I have tried literally thousands of cases with juries," Dillon said, "and the instances are few where I had reason to be dissatisfied with their verdicts."[49] Yet there was clearly a problem with the jury, Dillon believed, especially in civil cases. "Many of our best lawyers . . . in their lighter moods, openly ridicule it, and in their more serious moods openly denounce it." Like Miller, Dillon believed that part of the problem was judges who were not doing their duty, especially with regard to instructing juries. "If the courts will clearly instruct juries, and will exercise when they ought to do so the power to set aside verdicts and grant new trials, there will be less complaints about trial by jury, and less agitation for a change in the law [of unanimity]"—a change that Justice Dillon, parting company with Justice Miller, believed would be "wholly unwise."[50]

But another reason for unsatisfactory jury verdicts was that jurors were not always taken from "the better class of citizens in respect of intelligence, moral character, and business experience." And in a footnote Dillon explained that "character and intelligence in jurymen were from the first considered indispensable. . . . [T]here never was a time and never a country where it was so important, as now and here, to require juries to be composed of substantial citizens, men of intelligence, moral character, and varied experience in the affairs of life. . . . [R]eform must begin here." Dillon also noted the conflict over judicial control of the courtroom. He recommended that state legislators (some of whom had undoubtedly been "blocked by a judge from misleading [a] jury") cease their efforts to "degrade" judges to the status of mere "moderators" in the courtroom, without any power to charge jurors, comment on the evidence, or give instructions that went beyond "barren and unintelligible" statements of the law. If the proper division of labor between judge and jury were followed, Dillon concluded, there would be fewer misunderstandings, more reasonable verdicts from juries, and more public respect for and confidence in the jury system. The system would then be allowed to perform its important educational function outside the courtroom, by teaching citizens what they could not otherwise learn, "acquir[ing] and disseminat[ing] a knowledge of the laws among the local communities from which they come, and to which they return."[51]

Dillon's lectures were published one year before the *Sparf and Hansen* decision, but his portrayal of the ideal courtroom relationship—with judges in charge of the law and juries in charge of the facts—was fully in line with the vision of the

49. John F. Dillon, *The Laws and Jurisprudence of England and America: Being a Series of Lectures Delivered before Yale University* (Boston: Little, Brown, 1894), 121–122.
50. Ibid., 131–132.
51. Ibid., 125, 125 n. 1, 125–126, 167–168.

majority in that case. This vision of the ideal judge-jury relationship was different from that which prevailed in the republican era, even though the difference was subtle. The republican understanding of the jury conceded the judge's superior knowledge of the law but insisted that jurors could understand the law—in fact, they must understand it to "apply the law to the facts," as the official formula required. Dillon's understanding of this relationship presumed that the judge's account of the law would always prevail, which had the clear tendency to turn every jury verdict into a special verdict. The jury would find the facts and apply them to the law in precisely the way the judge had instructed, almost as if the judge were returning the verdict, rather than the jury. In the face of this presumption, state legislators became increasingly suspicious of judges, and judicial efforts to control the conduct of trials inspired resistance, a trend that had been going on for much of the nineteenth century. The most common manifestation of this resistance was state legislatures' efforts to limit what judges could say to jurors about the facts, and it became increasingly difficult for judges to comment on evidence in any way that might suggest "fact-finding" or to charge juries in a way that seemed to "direct" a verdict.[52]

Judge Dillon was quite frank about the effect of these changes: they made it harder for judges to control juries, since the judge was forced to be only a "moderator," required by law to "confine his charge or instructions to a barren, and to the jury often unintelligible, statement of the law of the case."[53] In Wisconsin, for example, state law held that if any judge shall "make any comments upon the law or facts to the jury on the trial of any cause, without the same being reduced to writing before it is given, any judgment which shall be rendered upon the verdict shall be reversed." In North Carolina, "no judge, in giving a charge, shall give an opinion whether a fact is fully or sufficiently proven, such matter being the true office and province of a jury; but he shall state, in a plain and direct manner, the evidence in the case, and declare and explain the law arising therefrom." All such laws denied the judge the opportunity to exercise the supervisory function that juries so badly needed—resulting in the jury's low reputation in many quarters, especially with respect to civil trials.[54]

But if the civil jury's reputation was so bad, why should Americans continue to support civil juries? Why not simply abolish them? Calls to do so were rare, in part because the Constitution placed both the civil jury and the criminal jury

52. The effort to control how judges commented on the evidence was part of a more general pattern: states' "tighter definition" of the roles of judge and jury during the nineteenth century. "Statutes took away the judge's right to comment on evidence. . . . This made the jury less liable to domination by the judge." But it also led to more formal, and even formulaic, jury instructions, which jurors often found incomprehensible. See Friedman, *History of American Law*, 136–137.

53. Dillon, *Laws and Jurisprudence of England and America*, 125–126.

54. Ibid., 126–127.

beyond the reach of ordinary majorities. Still, such demands were not unheard of: legal reformers in general, and progressives in particular, were increasingly willing to broach in public what many were thinking in private. But so were many stalwart Republicans in the legal profession. William Howard Taft, to name one illustrious example, was frank in his insistence that the civil jury should be abolished and the criminal jury reformed. In a speech at Yale Law School in 1905, Taft called for the elimination of civil juries: "We cannot escape a re-examination . . . of constitutional limitations" when so much is at stake. But in the United States, "constitutional limitations adopted centuries ago . . . have to some extent outlived their usefulness." Attorneys are allowed to mislead jurors, and this increases the chances of there being a miscarriage of justice. The law "throws the reins on the back of the jury, and the verdict becomes rather the vote of a town meeting than the sharp, clear distinction of the tribunal of justice." According to Taft, the jurors themselves might not be so bad, but they encourage bad behavior in others—that is, in lawyers, who see an opportunity and cannot resist it.[55]

All who defended the jury at the turn of the twentieth century were quick to acknowledge that there were many on the other side, both in and out of the courts. Rising to the defense of the jury, US District Court judge Oliver P. Shiras, writing in the *Yale Law Journal* in 1891, noted the "not unfrequent" demands for the abolition of the jury, on the grounds that it has proved to be a failure—and conceded immediately that there was much truth in these objections.[56] Two objections were especially noteworthy to Shiras. First, under the current methods for selecting jurors, those who might be best suited for service were excused—a common complaint. Second, because of the increasing complexity of modern business, "the questions of fact involved in the litigation of the day have become so intricate and complex, that a jury, as usually constituted, is not competent to consider and decide" such disputes. Is it reasonable to expect that juries composed of "farmers and artisans" are "fitted to sift out evidence, to reason clearly and logically . . . and apply to the facts the rules of law given them by the court . . . ?" Little wonder, then, that "verdicts are largely the results of chance or prejudice."[57]

Yet these problems could be relieved by improving the methods for selecting jurors "and by awakening public sentiment" to the need for all "good citizens" to share the burden of jury service—a gentle reminder that the "men of good character and average education and ability" who have been exempted by state legis-

55. William Howard Taft, "The Administration of the Criminal Law," *Yale Law Journal* 15, 1 (1905–1906): 4. For another example, see William L. Scott, "Should Trial by Jury in Civil Cases Be Abolished?" *American Law Review* 20 (1886): 661–679. Taft had harsh words for the way criminal trials were conducted, calling them a "disgrace to civilization" in most of the states.

56. Oliver P. Shiras, "The Jury System," *Yale Law Journal* 1, 2 (December 1891): 45–51.

57. Ibid., 46.

latures should stop complaining about the jury system and do their duty instead. It made much more sense to reform jury selection than to abolish the jury, for the disappearance of the jury system would be a serious loss, Shiras believed.[58] Even though getting to the correct verdict was the most important goal of the courts, "of almost equal importance" was ensuring that justice was done in a way that was fair and that satisfied the defeated parties and the community as a whole, especially in cases that divided the community's sentiments. "If a case is determined by a verdict of a jury . . . it is a much more difficult matter for the defeated litigant" to convince his neighbors that an injustice has been committed. The public will forgive the errors of twelve local men quicker than they will forgive the rich and powerful. When judges make these decisions by themselves, they have to accept the burden of the public's hostility: the jury system shields the judge from the public's anger.[59] Jury service also educates the citizen, an important part of the republican defense of the jury system. "Under our form of government," Shiras writes, "it is of the utmost importance that . . . the mass of the people should . . . actively participate" in the machinery of government. Citizens who serve on juries have an opportunity to hear evidence and weigh arguments, gaining valuable insight into "the practical working of the laws, as they touch the manifold business interests of the community."[60]

In any case, having watched juries from the bench, Shiras notes that jurors are actually better than judges at resolving certain kinds of disputes. Jurors are asked to "determine the facts pertaining to past transactions [which] . . . occur among men of average knowledge and ability." Jurors, in other words, are often asked to understand the actions of men very much like themselves. "The knowledge possessed by a jury of twelve men of fair average ability and judgment, in matters of this kind is greater than that possessed by a judge."[61] When jurors fail to understand, it is usually because they have been misled by attorneys or confused by poorly crafted instructions from the judge.[62]

THE INEFFICIENT JURY IN AN AGE OF REFORM

Confused and ignorant jurors, hamstrung judges, arcane procedures, wasted time and wasted money, and the best citizens excused from duty—these were the problems of the jury system at the dawn of the modern era. In a word, the jury system

58. Ibid.

59. Ibid., 49. This was also Tocqueville's view: "The jurors pronounce the ruling that the judge has rendered. To this ruling, they lend the authority of the society that they represent, and he, that of reason and the law." Tocqueville, *Democracy in America*, 263.

60. Shiras, "Jury System," 50.

61. Ibid., 47.

62. Ibid., 48.

had become inefficient—an argument made in 1914 in an influential article by Edson Sunderland, a professor at the University of Michigan Law School and future historian of the American Bar Association.[63] By 1914, the word "inefficient" carried a great deal of weight. It had acquired a wealth of meanings in the language of reform generally and of progressivism in particular; no institution that carried the label could be expected to find favor with any reform-minded citizen, whatever his other political views might be. Sunderland was certain that the civil jury, especially, had become entangled with practices completely unsuitable to modern times. Although he would not call for the abolition of civil juries, Sunderland was instrumental in mounting and guiding a movement for procedural reform that would have a profound impact on the jury, especially in the federal courts.

The "distinguishing feature" of the common-law jury, Sunderland wrote, had been its restricted jurisdiction. Unlike juries on the Continent, and unlike English juries in pre-Norman times, the jurisdiction of the common-law jury had always been confined to questions of fact. This restriction saved the English jury from the fate of juries on the Continent, where jurors had lost the long contest with judges over the interpretation of statutes. They had lost this contest, Sunderland concluded, for an obvious reason: "Men temporarily called from the ordinary affairs of life, untrained in the law, are incapable of performing the functions of judges in any but the most primitive communities."[64] No one reading this passage could fail to make the connection to the long debate about juries and the law during the republican era. They would have concluded, along with Sunderland, that if the jury were not confined to functions that its members could actually perform, sooner or later, juries would be superseded, no matter how well protected by the Constitution, just as juries had been rendered obsolete in Europe. To save the jury (from its friends as well as its enemies), it would have to be brought up to date, like so many other elements of American government. And the place to begin, Sunderland reasoned, was with a reconsideration of what the jury is for.

Once upon a time, the "cumbersome common law jury" had operated as a barrier to tyranny. For this reason, it had not yet been discarded in favor of some "expert and well trained agency for sifting evidence and finding facts."[65] As Jeremy Bentham had observed, one of the virtues of the jury was its tendency to "infuse weakness into the body of the law." The jury system made the law less efficient, and therefore less terrible, by applying (in Bentham's words) "a bridle to arbitrary power in the hands of a judge."[66] But Sunderland argued that this old view of the jury as a "palladium of popular liberties" made little sense now that the people ruled. "The need for the jury as a political weapon of defense has been

63. Edson R. Sunderland, "The Inefficiency of the American Jury," *Michigan Law Review* 13 (1914): 302–316.

64. Ibid., 303.

65. Ibid., 304.

66. Jeremy Bentham, *Principles of Judicial Procedure* (1837), chap. 23, quoted at ibid.

steadily diminishing for a hundred years, until now the jury must find some other justification for its continuance."[67] The argument for keeping the jury must now turn on its utility as a fact finder. But how could the jury survive the reality that the "fact finders" themselves were "untrained and irresponsible" amateurs?[68] Here, Sunderland claimed, was precisely the place to recall the virtue of the judge-jury relationship under the common law:

> [Judges] undertook to give the jury the benefit of their experience and skill by advising them in difficult cases respecting the weight and effect of the evidence . . . the judges did not hesitate to tell the jury what they believed the evidence had shown, and the jury did not resent it, for it was advice, not a command, and the jury were always expressly informed that if it did not appear to them as sound they were at liberty to disregard it.[69]

Furthermore, even the judge's expression of a strong opinion about evidence had never been considered improper in England, and it did not form the basis for successful appeals in English courts.

But these "sensible" views were rejected in America after the Revolution, according to Sunderland, when Americans were determined to rein in the power of judges by restricting what they could say about the evidence (and by insisting, although Sunderland does not mention this, that juries could also judge the law, even if this meant contradicting a judge's instructions). Throughout the republican era, states adopted statutory or constitutional provisions that prohibited judges from "finding the facts of the case" or even commenting on the evidence, sometimes at a very early date. The Tennessee Constitution of 1796 provided a typical formula: "The judges . . . shall not charge juries with respect to matters of fact." Sunderland found similar prohibitions in twenty-one of the forty-eight states (at the time), and in many states without legislative or constitutional language, the courts themselves had adopted the rule. In two-thirds of the jurisdictions in the United States, judges were theoretically powerless to instruct the jury on the relative merits of the evidence accepted at trial.[70] And, of course, the Seventh Amendment prohibited any court's reconsideration of a fact found by a jury.

Sunderland's description of the common-law jury in England matches very closely the jury in the American colonies and in the states in the republican period, when the ideal judge-jury relationship was understood to be a collegial one. In fact, much of the reform suggested by Sunderland appears to be aimed at restoring the old judge-jury relationship from the era of Chase and Marshall. But neither Sunderland nor his colleagues in the legal profession were prepared to draw the

67. Ibid., 305.
68. Ibid.
69. Ibid.
70. Ibid., 307–309.

likely inference: restoring the old judge-jury collegiality might require letting jurors come to their own conclusions about what the law required them to do—not surreptitiously, but openly, as one of the most important functions conceded to them by Federalist and Republican judges alike.

Most important, Sunderland refused to acknowledge what Americans of the constitutional era had learned from their own experience and from their reading in political history: just because a government is popular does not mean it can be trusted. Kings are not alone in ruling unjustly or unwisely, and an American citizen might need protection from officialdom (or from the majority), just as a subject under the Angevins might need protection from the king. The republican-era defenders of the jury saw it not simply as a way to settle cases but as a barrier to the people's exclusion from the administration of the law—as the "lower house of the judiciary"—as well as a rich source of the kind of civic education essential to the health of a republican political order.

Sunderland's proposals, despite their undercurrent of yearning for the old judge-jury partnership, were characteristic of the age's emphasis on restoring the "efficiency" of jury trials. First of all, much would be gained by reducing the "time, strain and scandal in impanelling juries. . . . Why should a judge sit helpless for days and weeks while lawyers wrangle and struggle over the selection of a jury?"[71] This waste of time occurred, Sutherland claimed, because lawyers were looking for jurors who could be easily manipulated—since they knew the judge would be powerless to stop them. "In the face of a clear, dispassionate and candid analysis of the merits of the case by an impartial judge . . . the tricks and artifices [of attorneys] would fail; the worse would not appear the better reason; the jury, taken into the confidence of the court and treated like reasonable and self-respecting men, would feel the dignity and responsibility of their position."[72]

Second, giving the judge more latitude with respect to his comments on the evidence would facilitate a clearer presentation of that evidence. The rules of evidence, Sunderland noted, were so complicated that neither lawyers nor judges could explain them—a complexity founded on the principle that jurors were so weak-minded and fickle that they must not be allowed to hear or see evidence that might mislead them. Quoting an observer of English trials, Sunderland suggested the ideal: "both sides [in the English courtroom] rely on the judge to eliminate from the minds of the jury the effect of evidence wrongly introduced."[73]

Third, judges who were free to comment on the evidence would be free to exercise effective control over trials. Not being able to comment openly, but be-

71. Ibid., 310. Here is evidence of how important lawyers considered jury selection to be, of their deep interest in preserving and expanding peremptory challenges, and of their increasing conflict with judges for control of the courtroom.

72. Ibid., 311.

73. Ibid., 312.

ing forced to do so covertly ("In every sound he utters there lurks the possibility of reversible error"), the judge became "aloof from the contest . . . an umpire or moderator rather than . . . a participant," letting the trial proceed as it would and throwing "responsibility for a proper decision . . . upon the parties." By contrast, judges in England, and to some extent judges in federal court, were freer to restrain counsel and exert a "personal influence . . . to guide the jury and cause them to avoid absurdities and extremes."[74]

The problems Sunderland outlined were most notable in the state courts, where there was great diversity in rules and procedures, and where many legislatures kept a tight leash on judges. In many states, judges were elected; in all states, judges were required to be mindful of legislative sensibilities to a much greater degree than was the case in federal courts. But the federal system was yoked to the state system by the "conformity principle"—the requirement that proceedings in federal district court conform as nearly as possible to the rules of the state in which the district court met. This arrangement had been reaffirmed by Congress as recently as 1872. No significant reform in the federal courts could take place until either the conformity principle was repealed—and, as one of the bedrocks of American federalism, its repeal was nearly unthinkable—or the states could be inspired, simultaneously, to reform their own procedures, all in a common direction. This seemed even more unlikely.

Yet the law journals were filled with suggestions, and then demands, for the radical improvement of the administration of the American judicial system: that judges take greater control of trials, that forms of civil and criminal proceedings be modernized, that jury selection be reformed. When suitably instructed, properly guided, and not befuddled by unnecessarily complex procedures, the argument went, an intelligent jury would come to the right decision in nearly every case—provided an intelligent jury could be found.

The reform of the American legal system therefore required action on three fronts, each presenting significant challenges: (1) judges would have to be given more authority to guide trials; (2) the federal courts would have to be liberated from the conformity principle, and better procedures would have to be designed and approved by Congress; and (3) jury selection procedures would have to be changed to ensure that the right kind of citizens served on juries. To these goals the newly formed American Bar Association quickly turned its attention.

JURY REFORM AND THE AMERICAN BAR ASSOCIATION

The American Bar Association (ABA) was founded in 1878, and its first constitution included the goals of improving both the "science of jurisprudence" and the

74. Ibid., 313.

"administration of justice." It was not long before the ABA took up Hirsch's plea that lawyers take the lead in jury reform, a project that would occupy a considerable amount of the association's attention for much of the next century.

The ABA's interest in jury reform mixed self-interest (lawyers wanted more than anything else to win cases) with patriotism (the jury was an important American institution that had to be saved from itself). A minority of members despised the jury as a relic. But the consensus—at least among those chosen to run the association—was supportive of a reformed jury system. An example was ABA president Joseph H. Choate's annual address to the group in 1898.[75] Choate, a prominent member of the New York bar and scourge of the Tweed Ring, was one of the nation's most illustrious attorneys. He described arguing before a jury as "the proudest and most delightful privilege of our whole professional life. It atones for all the drudgery and painful labor of the rest of our professional work." The current system was not without its problems, and some of these might be inseparable from the institution itself, but Choate was convinced that most of the jury's shortcomings could be remedied "not by any material alteration, but by a better administration of the system as it now exists," paying special attention to improvement of the judge-jury relationship. Taking as his model the "great judges" of the past, such as Lemuel Shaw, chief justice of the Massachusetts Superior Court, Choate described the ideal judge as one who could masterfully instruct the jury on all the elements of the case—the evidence, the legal issues, and the relevance of the testimony presented in court—weaving everything together in a way that dispelled all doubts and confusion:

> And the result was that when the judge's charge was finished, the jury understood the case as they had never realized it till then, they understood what questions they had to decide, and what material they had for making up their decision. How they should decide those questions was their own business, and those great judges never presumed to suggest or interfere; and there is no doubt that that was jury trial, according to the uniform course of the common law both in England and America.[76]

This portrait of the ideal judge-jury relationship, emphasizing the judge rather than the jury, had an obvious appeal to judges. But it also appealed to anyone who wished to bring greater order to the courts. Nothing seemed more likely to achieve this than increasing judges' authority over the conduct of trials—for example, by allowing judicial commentary on the evidence as well as on the law. But other reforms would be needed, according to Choate: getting better jurors; relieving the trial judge of the burden of giving jury instructions with the appellate courts

75. Joseph H. Choate, "Trial by Jury," annual address to the American Bar Association, Philadelphia, 1898.

76. Ibid., 24.

breathing down his neck; and, above all, simplifying the procedures, which were, Choate believed, the true cause of "delay" in the courts.[77]

By the time Choate gave this talk, his view of the "jury problem" was widely accepted in the profession and had already formed the core of the ABA's first study of the judicial system, published in 1885. Written under the direction of David Dudley Field and Judge John F. Dillon, the report bore an unwieldy title: *The Report of the Special Committee Appointed to Consider and Report Whether the Present Delay and Uncertainty in Judicial Administration Can Be Lessened, and if so, by What Means*.[78] The report's explanation of "delay and uncertainty" and its recommendations for reform were fully in line with Choate's analysis thirteen years later.

The central focus of the 1885 report was not the jury system per se but the many causes of the "dilatory and uncertain administration of justice" found in courts everywhere, in federal and state courts and in civil and criminal proceedings alike. This situation was the inevitable product of "complex procedure, inadequate judiciary, procrastination, retrials, unreasonable appeals, [and] uncertain law." In this account, the jury system was just one of many reasons for the poor performance of the courts—the main reason being the common law itself, with its complex forms of action that "[expose] the suitor to unnecessary entanglement in a maze of forms, over and above the hazard of the law and the evidence; the hazard of doubtful law conjectured out of irreconcilable precedents, and of disputed facts extracted from contradictory evidence." The condition of the legal order in 1885 was "chaos," and the report stated very simply: "It is idle to think of going on as we are going. The confusion grows worse all the time. Chaos deepens and thickens daily." A typical trial started late, spent far too much time choosing a jury, and then bogged down as soon as the first witness was questioned, as one objection after another was debated for hours, with the whole dreary process repeated the next day and the next. Meanwhile, the jury sat befuddled, its members' time utterly wasted. Then, as soon as the trial ended, the appeals began, and the case was all too often tried anew, wasting the time of yet another jury.[79]

The report recommended that this process be simplified: state the facts, judge the facts, apply the law, reach a verdict, or enforce a judgment. "These several steps may be shorter or longer. . . . The problem is how to expedite them all, preserving at the same time every right of the parties, and to cut off, with an unsparing hand, whatever is not necessary to this design." And this must be done, the report conceded, against the wishes of at least one of the parties to a lawsuit, since

77. Ibid., 20–21.

78. *The Report of the Special Committee Appointed to Consider and Report Whether the Present Delay and Uncertainty in Judicial Administration Can Be Lessened, and if so, by What Means* (Philadelphia: Dando Printing & Publishing Co., 1885), 320–368.

79. Ibid., 324, 332, 350–351, 354.

there would always be one party (and, although the report was discreetly silent on this point, one lawyer) who wanted a delay. For this reason, the 1885 report urged the adoption of simpler forms of proceeding and more extensive codification of precedents into laws, basing trials on the "one hundred and twenty-five" volumes of statutes rather than the "ten to fifty thousand volumes" of cases and precedents—that is, "judge-made law."[80]

All this, however, would have to take place under the trying conditions of American federalism, which celebrated each state's right to construct its own judicial system, within the very wide latitude permitted by the Constitution. The conformity principle seemed an insurmountable obstacle to a reformation of the federal and state judicial systems simultaneously. But the ABA was convinced that the inefficiency and irrationality of the judicial system was due to the lack of uniformity across state jurisdictions in such matters as jury selection standards, trial procedures, and general administration of the courts. The Conformity Act of 1872 "had introduced intolerable confusion into the federal practice and had become a serious burden to the Bar and the public," Sunderland told the association.[81] Almost from the moment of its founding, therefore, the ABA established as one of its goals the homogenization of judicial procedure under the guidance of a central authority, a project that came to be known as "uniformity." It was ultimately successful, but not for a half century or more.

In 1912 the ABA established a Committee on Uniform Judicial Procedure, resolving that a "complete uniform system of law pleading should prevail in the federal and state courts" and that the Supreme Court should prepare and put into effect "a system for use in the federal courts."[82] But the concept of uniformity, along with the bills the ABA drew up, was deeply opposed in Congress, and especially in the Senate, despite the support of ABA luminaries such as William Howard Taft, Elihu Root, and Alton Parker; forty-six state bar associations; and several former attorneys general of the United States.[83] It was not until the 1930s that prospects for the uniformity movement brightened—reflecting, perhaps, the general reconsideration of federalism that took place during the Depression. Whatever the reason, centralizing the administration of justice had become a major plank in the platform of American legal reform, with important supporters among both legal progressives and traditional conservatives. The jury system,

80. Ibid., 333, 334, 349.

81. Edson R. Sunderland, *History of the American Bar Association and Its Work* (Ann Arbor: University of Michigan Press, 1953), 164. The 1872 act, however, did not "introduce" diverse procedures; it merely reaffirmed a principle established with the adoption of the Constitution.

82. "Report of the Committee on Uniform Judicial Procedure," in *36th Annual Report of the American Bar Association* (Baltimore: Lord Baltimore Press, 1913), 541.

83. Sunderland, *History of the American Bar Association.*

perhaps the most decentralized element in American government, would soon be a prime target.

In addition to a uniform system of procedures at the state and federal levels, the ABA pursued another line of reform concerning which procedures should be adopted throughout the federal and state courts. Here, the report's reference to the "ten to fifty thousand volumes" of cases and precedents is significant, because it marks the ABA's first foray into the controversial terrain of "codification," with strong hints of something even more radical: the importation of some of the procedures and practices of the equity courts into the common-law courts.

In the republican period, the reform of common-law procedure—sometimes referred to as the "simplification" and "codification" of the common law—had been supported by reformers both inside and outside the legal profession. For lawyers, codification meant a straighter path from the beginning to the end of a lawsuit, with fewer opportunities for procedural slips that could generate reversible errors. For reformers outside the profession, codification promised to restore the citizen's role in the judiciary by ridding the legal system, to the extent possible, of the arcane, technical, "pettifogging," and inscrutable elements of common-law pleading. All such mysteries privileged the priests of the profession—the lawyers and judges—over the congregants. Thomas Paine, for example, had denounced the "chicanery of law and lawyers" as early as 1805, speaking for all those who suspected that the common law had become little more than a bag of tricks by which judges (and clever lawyers) could trump legislators.[84] Even many lawyers agreed that the law should be accessible to the citizens who had to live under it—and who had to understand it when exercising the office of juror. Codification—converting the library of judicial precedents into clearly organized statutes—was one way to achieve this; simplifying courtroom procedures was another.[85]

The codification movement achieved its most important victory with a code of procedure written by New York attorney David Dudley Field and adopted (in part) by the New York State legislature in 1850.[86] The Field Code was inspired by the view that the common law had become encrusted with such procedural rigidity that it was more an obstacle than an aid to justice. Meanwhile, legal reformers were looking to the equity courts—once the bête noir of republicans because of

84. Friedman, *History of American Law*, 94–95.

85. On republican-era legal reform, including the codification movement, see Robert W. Gordon, "The American Codification Movement," *Vanderbilt Law Review* 36 (1983): 435. For a discussion of the codification movement more generally and its significance for antebellum legal reform, see Friedman, *History of American Law*, and Perry Miller, *The Life of the Mind in America, from the Revolution to the Civil War* (Cambridge, MA: Harvard University Press, 1965), 239–265.

86. The law enacting the Field Code was entitled "An Act to Simplify and Abridge the Practice and Pleadings and Proceedings of the Courts of the State." See Gordon, "American Codification Movement," 431.

their association with the hated Navigation Acts—as a model of (relative) procedural simplicity. In former times, the equity courts in England had been referred to as the "courts of conscience" because they heard cases in which the strict application of the law would work an injustice. (The earliest such courts were presided over by bishops.) Such cases called for an "equitable"—that is, fair—remedy rather than a merely "legal" remedy.[87] Judges at equity usually did not hear oral testimony in open court; they based their decisions on written documents, whose production they were authorized to compel, and which they could study in the solitude of their chambers. In contrast, in a trial at law a jury was essential to find the facts, and oral testimony was essential because jurors need to see and hear witnesses on the stand in order to judge their honesty and credibility. (Also, many jurors were illiterate and could judge based only on what they could see and hear.) Equity courts operated without juries because their task was less the establishment of facts than the construction of remedies. Gradually, the equity courts became the favored venue for disputes involving complicated or technical questions that ordinary jurors would be unlikely to understand—maritime insurance cases, for example, which became more frequent as England developed a greater seagoing trade.

By the time of the American Revolution, equitable jurisdiction had come to stand for a set of arrangements that had definite appeal to lawyers and litigants seeking a neutral arbiter to resolve knotty commercial disputes. The judge could keep all the elements of the case in his own hands, out of public view and away from the control of amateurs. For that reason, equity courts were anathema to republicans—all the more so when the British government began to transfer cases under the Navigation Acts to the equity courts, where no jury could interfere. After the Revolution, it was not uncommon for republican writers to demand that juries be used in equity courts as well as in common-law courts, and this was a position fervently held by Field himself.[88]

Field, however, was convinced that the common-law courts would be greatly improved if they borrowed some of the techniques of equity, giving judges more leeway to control the conduct of trials. The equity courts and the common-law courts would remain separate, but the latter would operate with fewer and simpler forms of action, and the same procedures would apply to "all types of cases, regardless of substantive law, the number of issues and parties, or the stakes."[89] But Field was a conservative New York Democrat who believed

87. "The bill in equity became the procedural vehicle for the exceptional case." Stephen N. Subrin, "How Equity Conquered Common Law: The Federal Rules of Civil Procedure in Historical Perspective," *University of Pennsylvania Law Review* 135, 4 (April 1987): 919.

88. It is significant that although several states adopted the Field Code, none exported the jury system to the equity courts.

89. Subrin, "How Equity Conquered Common Law," 934.

in states' rights, property rights, and free markets. He was committed to the idea of the jury as a central element of the judiciary, and he had no intention of making the judge the sole arbiter of what went on in court. Procedures might be loosened up, and judges might be given somewhat more authority to guide trials, but "flexible" or "elastic" procedures would mean "no law at all," and judges' discretion had to be kept to a minimum. "The law is our only sovereign," he wrote. "We have enthroned it."[90]

Under the Field Code—which was adopted in enough states to apply to a majority of the population—pleadings were designed to reveal each side's position clearly and to narrow the controversy as much as possible without doing violence to the rights of the parties. The rules for verifying factual claims were strict enough to discourage frivolous lawsuits. Plaintiffs and causes of action could be joined more easily than under the common-law rules, but not as easily as in the equity courts. Testimony in open court was preferred to written documents, and there were restrictions on interrogatories, admission of new evidence, and oral depositions.[91]

By the late nineteenth century, however, "procedural reform" had acquired a different set of political meanings, and a different coalition had emerged to achieve it—even though David Dudley Field, aged eighty-one and in the last decade of his life, was among those who participated in the production of the ABA's 1885 report. This time, however, it was not Jacksonian Democrats who were pushing for reform but practicing attorneys and their corporate clients, who agreed that the civil courts needed some "plain common sense" to dispel the mysteries of civil procedure that caused so many expensive and frustrating delays and reversals. In the absence of such reform, the 1885 report noted, the law is "chaos" and "every law-suit . . . an adventure, more or less."[92]

Yet in 1885 the ABA was certain that the jury itself was also a cause of delay and inefficiency, in addition to the outmoded forms of pleading. "Whatever may be said in other respects of the institution of the jury for civil cases," the 1885 report declares, "it cannot be denied that it is the cause of great delays."[93] The first delay stemmed from the need for unanimity: when a jury was "discharged, by reason of disagreement," the entire case had to be tried all over again before another jury. A second "and much more considerable cause of delay in the final result" was the ordering of new trials because of some procedural violation, such as "misdirection of the court or an erroneous admission or rejection of evidence." A solution to this problem would be to increase the number of special verdicts, in

90. Ibid., 934, 935.

91. Ibid., 937.

92. *Report of the Special Committee on Delay and Uncertainty*, 350.

93. Ibid., 340. This view was not shared by all attorneys. It was rejected, as noted above, by Joseph Choate, a future president of the association.

which the jury was asked, by the judge, to answer questions about the facts in the case, leaving the law, and the final verdict, to thc court.[94]

But codification and procedural reform remained an elusive goal—indeed, the full ABA rejected the codification proposal at its next convention. A proposal to allow less-than-unanimous verdicts in civil and criminal trials inspired considerable opposition, as did the call for more special verdicts.[95] Unanimity was understood, at the time, to be one of the characteristics of the English common-law jury as it existed when the Constitution was ratified.[96] It therefore enjoyed constitutional protection, at least in the federal courts, but it also enjoyed support among attorneys defending criminal clients, who hoped a single holdout juror would refuse to convict. Increasing the use of special verdicts would require action by Congress and by state legislatures, which were generally unsympathetic to this departure from the good old republican standard. Yet the ABA's leadership, if not its membership, was willing to trade a significant portion of the "ancient jury right" for more efficient results.[97]

94. Ibid.

95. The American Bar Association has gone back and forth on unanimous verdicts in criminal trials. Although the full membership rejected the idea of nonunanimous verdicts in 1885, by the 1950s, the members had changed their minds. With the support of ABA recommendations from 1968, the Supreme Court ruled in 1972 that the Sixth Amendment right to a jury trial does *not* require unanimous verdicts in state criminal trials (Apadoca v. Oregon, 406 U.S. 404). Then, in 1976, ABA members reversed their position again, insisting on the centrality of the unanimity requirement. By then, the Supreme Court had ruled in cases from Oregon and Louisiana that the common-law jury guaranteed by the Constitution does not require unanimous verdicts in state criminal trials, however customary the principle might have been. The ABA's current understanding of the jury system is discussed in chapter 4.

96. Justice Story had argued this in his *Commentaries on the Constitution of the United States*, section 1779. In 1897 the Supreme Court ruled that "unanimity was one of the peculiar and essential features of trial by jury at the common law. No authorities are needed to sustain this proposition." American Publishing Co. v. Fisher, 166 U.S. 465 (1897), at 468. In 1930 the Court observed that, under the Constitution, a criminal jury trial "means a trial by jury as understood and applied at common law, and includes all the essential elements as they were recognized in this country and England when the Constitution was adopted." This "is not open to question. Those elements were—(1) that the jury should consist of twelve men, neither more nor less; (2) that the trial should be in the presence and under the superintendence of a judge having power to instruct them as to the law and advise them in respect of the facts; and (3) that the verdict should be unanimous." Patton v. United States, 281 U.S. 276 (1930), at 288. See also "Comment: A Constitutional Renvoir: Unanimous Verdicts in State Criminal Trials," *Fordham Law Review* 41 (1972): 115.

97. *Report of the Special Committee on Delay and Uncertainty*, 350.

PROCEDURAL REFORM AND THE JURY SYSTEM

During the republican era, the dominant question had been whether juries had the right to judge the law. Toward the end of the nineteenth century, however, the issue of juries and the law took on a new dimension. Jurors, critics claimed, were simply ignoring the law, especially in civil cases in which the defendant was a large corporation, and especially when that large corporation happened to be a railroad. By the 1870s, the most notorious product liability cases involved railroad accidents, and the most common complaint brought against jurors was that they simply would not treat the railroads fairly.[98]

Since there are no empirical studies of jury decisions in the nineteenth century, it is impossible to know how much truth there was to complaints about "rogue juries" in accident cases, but it is probably safe to assume that the phenomenon was real enough. Typically, a wage-earning plaintiff or his estate would bring suit against a railroad for negligence that had allegedly caused the plaintiff's injury or death. Such cases presented juries with difficult choices. With no public safety net for wage earners to fall back on, the plaintiff's family or survivors would be left destitute if the plaintiff lost, whereas the railroad's loss from even a very generous settlement would be trivial. The defense offered by railroads and other corporate defendants—the doctrine of contributory negligence—did not prove popular with jurors.[99]

Juries bending the law to show mercy is an old story. Medieval English juries did this in response to the Angevin homicide laws. Criminal juries were suspected of "rule bending" even in Puritan Massachusetts, refusing to convict on the capital offense of fornication but finding defendants guilty of "lewd and lascivious conduct," for which the penalty was whipping. For most of our history, juries have agreed with the poets (and the Gospels) that justice is best served with mercy. But when juries bend the law consistently, they reshape it by establishing how the law is understood and applied in the real world of the courtroom. Juries can also bring about formal changes in the statutes, as in England, where Parliament finally caught up with jurors and established "grades" of killing (first-degree murder, manslaughter, negligent homicide, and so forth).[100]

98. "It is hardly an exaggeration to say that railroads revolutionized the law of jury control." Renee Lettow Lerner, "The Rise of Directed Verdict: Jury Power in Civil Cases before the Federal Rules of 1938," *George Washington Law Review* 81 (2013): 453.

99. Stephan Landsman argues that one of the functions of the jury in the late nineteenth century was to "ameliorate the consequences of harsh tort doctrines. Judges permitted jurors to whittle away at the contributory negligence doctrine." Stephan Landsman, "The History and Objectives of the Civil Jury System," in *Verdict: Judging the Civil Jury System*, ed. Robert Litan (Washington, DC: Brookings Institution, 1993), 47. See also Burns, *Death of the American Trial*, 60–61.

100. See Thomas A. Green, "The Jury and the English Law of Homicide, 1200–1600," *Michigan Law Review* 74, 3 (January 1976): 497 ff.

Most discussions of the "juror problem" in the early decades of the twentieth century focused on the civil jury, with its reams of evidence and complex proceedings that were often beyond the comprehension of lawyers, let alone ordinary citizens. Disappointment with the conduct of civil trials moved most reformers; criminal trials were occasionally notorious (as Mark Twain's remark in the epigraph of this chapter suggests), but most criminal defendants pleaded guilty. And those criminal cases that did make it to the jury stage did not open the door to the procedural and evidentiary difficulties common to civil litigation. Judges were said to be another part of the problem: their failure to explain the law clearly was one reason jurors did not understand the law and therefore delivered the "wrong" verdict. Yet getting better jurors was not the central focus of the legal profession's reform efforts. That focus continued to be outdated forms of common-law pleading, the politicization of state judiciaries, the increasing costs in time and money of civil litigation, and the frustrating tendency for lower court judgments to be overturned on technical or procedural grounds. These varied themes had one important element in common: they all looked to increase trial judges' authority over what went on in court.

At the twenty-ninth annual meeting of the American Bar Association, held in St. Paul, Minnesota, in the summer of 1906, Roscoe Pound summarized a generation's worth of frustration with the legal system in what would become one of the most famous legal talks of the era. Entitled "The Causes of Popular Dissatisfaction with the Administration of Justice," the speech was widely praised and circulated in legal and political circles.[101] It led to the creation of one of the ABA's most influential committees, whose efforts to make the federal courts more efficient would result in a dramatic transformation of judicial procedure roughly three decades later.[102]

Although Pound had little to say about juries specifically, his analysis of the public's dissatisfaction with the administration of justice had important implications for the jury system. One sign of public dissatisfaction, Pound argued, was the growing tendency to replace courts with administrative commissions, "freed, as far as constitutions will permit, from judicial review." That is, courts were unpopular because they could not act with the kind of efficiency displayed by administrative commissions—a clear indication of the direction reform ought to take. The inefficiency of the civil courts was especially troublesome, because those courts administered the rules that made it possible for each individual to "act without conflict with the activities of his fellows in a busy and crowded world."

101. Roscoe Pound, "The Causes of Popular Dissatisfaction with the Administration of Justice," 29th Conference, pt. 1, in *Annual Report of the American Bar Association* (1906): 395–417.

102. This was the Special Committee to Suggest Remedies and Formulate Proposed Laws to Prevent Delay and Unnecessary Cost in Litigation, whose work is described below. The ultimate result of these efforts was the promulgation by the Supreme Court of the Federal Rules of Civil Procedure in 1938.

The popular dissatisfaction with justice was therefore primarily a dissatisfaction with civil justice.[103]

There were many reasons for this dissatisfaction, and Pound was quick to assert that this was not a new or even an exclusively American story. "Even the wonderful mechanism of modern German judicial administration is said to be distrusted by the people," he observed. The problem, in other words, was often with the people, rather than with the law. Among other faults, the people were impatient with the law, and some of this impatience was inevitable: the law was always seen as too mechanical; the law always progressed more rapidly than public opinion; the public always assumed that the administration of the law was an easy task that even amateurs could manage; and the public was impatient with any form of restraint. But other causes were intrinsic to America, and they stemmed from the fact that, unlike England, America was yoked to outmoded legal and political ideas: individualism; the separation of powers (which led to "jealousy"); the "sporting" theory of justice, which made litigation into a game (i.e., the adversarial system); and the heavy reliance on case law (i.e., law rather than equity).

The first of these complaints—individualism—was a favorite target of progressive reformers.[104] Individualism, Pound asserted, teaches that "the individual is supposed at common law to be able to look out for himself and to need no administrative protection." But in "our modern industrial society," Pound argued, "this whole scheme of individual initiative is breaking down. . . . The courts have not been able to do the work which the common law doctrine of supremacy of law imposed on them," and this has led to the widespread view that the courts are "inefficient."

Meanwhile, the courts, which are powerless to "give relief," seem "to obstruct public efforts to get relief by legislation." That is, they continually meddle in the work of the legislature with their outmoded defense of limited government and the separation of powers. For instance, according to Pound, the income tax amendment would not have been necessary otherwise, nor would the public be treated to the "spectacle" of administration being "paralyzed" by the law (by legislators jealous of the power of bureaucrats). "The chief concern of the common law is to secure and protect individual rights," but the pressing need of the day is for legislative and administrative action to confront modern problems and, in particular, for "protection against individuals, natural or artificial." In England,

103. The criminal courts, by contrast, dealt with "revenge and its modern outgrowth, punishment," both of which "belong to the past of legal history." Pound is not clear on this point, but it is unlikely that he believed violent crime to be a thing of the past. Crime would continue, but in an ideal world, criminal trials apparently would not.

104. See, for example, Herbert D. Croly, *The Promise of American Life* (New York: Macmillan, 1914). On the Progressives and their impact on American political practice, see Sidney M. Milkis and Jerome M. Mileur, eds., *Progressivism and the New Democracy* (Amherst: University of Massachusetts Press, 1999).

such old-fashioned common-law notions were easily swept away by the supremacy of the House of Commons; in America, however, old-fashioned ideas enjoyed the protection of the federal and state constitutions, as a result of which the "law restrains, not individuals alone, but a whole people."[105]

But even beyond the difficulties imposed by the Constitution, "our system of courts is archaic and our procedure behind the times." There were too many judicial systems (counting the states and their municipalities), too many different types of courts with overlapping jurisdictions, and an "obsolete Chinese Wall between law and equity in procedure." All state procedural systems were behind the times, and there had been no significant procedural reform, Pound claimed, since the Field Code in 1848. "We still try the record, not the case." Procedural chaos led to the profligate granting of new trials, decisions overturned on technicalities, and jurisdictional conflicts—problems that had been largely eliminated in England but grew worse in America by the day. No wonder the public had lost its interest in justice; no wonder that "jury service [was] a bore and the vindication of right and law secondary."[106]

It is hard to believe that an audience of turn-of-the-century lawyers could have digested this whole indictment without some discomfort, yet the speech's reception indicated how much had changed in the legal profession in the generation since the Civil War. And although Pound had little to say about juries, what he did say was notably uncomplimentary, if somewhat circumspect: "Modern experience with juries, especially in commercial causes, does not warrant us in hoping much from any form of judicial referendum. Public opinion must affect the administration of justice through the rules by which justice is administered rather than through the direct administration. All interference with the uniform and automatic application of these rules, when actual controversies arise, introduces an anti-legal element which becomes intolerable."[107] Coupled with the reference to "commercial causes," it is clear what Pound is referring to here: jurors who return verdicts against corporate defendants that are not plainly justified by the prevailing doctrines of negligence.

The most important practical significance of Pound's speech was his reference to the "obsolete Chinese Wall between law and equity." In other words, for every disadvantage of common-law pleading, a remedy could be found in equity practice. At equity, judges could join issues and parties at will, compel discovery, and rule on matters of evidence, without having to worry about "misdirecting" the jury. With no jury to instruct, there were fewer opportunities for reversible error on the judge's part or for errant jury verdicts that had to be set aside or overturned on appeal. Given the "chaos" of the law courts, it was easy to understand the appeal of the equity courts as a model.

105. Pound, "Causes of Popular Dissatisfaction."
106. Ibid.
107. Ibid.

Pound's speech led to a second major effort by the American Bar Association to study the judicial system and make recommendations for its reform. The Special Committee to Suggest Remedies and Formulate Proposed Laws to Prevent Delay and Unnecessary Cost in Litigation (Pound was one of its members) issued a series of annual reports. Its first report, published in 1908, left the jury system untouched.[108] Yet the jury was silently implicated in some of the report's conclusions (as it was by Pound): delay and uncertainty might not be caused by jurors, but jurors were the instruments by which such delay was achieved by those who knew how to "play the game" skillfully."[109] Skillful attorneys misled juries, leaving judgments open to appeal, and they blocked judges from adequately charging juries before they retired to consider their verdict. Yet it is hard not to avoid the conclusion, reading between the lines, that smarter or more experienced jurors would not be so easily fooled.

The Special Committee soon turned its attention more directly to the jury, however. The implications of procedural reform for the jury system were especially evident in the committee's eighth annual report, published in 1915. This report recorded one victory and one defeat in the ABA's campaign for procedural reform. The victory was congressional enactment of a "Law and Equity Bill," making it easier to move cases from the equity to the law side of the court, and vice versa, and to amend pleas without having to begin trials all over again.[110] "We feel," the committee members wrote, "that the country is to be congratulated" on the passage of this bill, "which has already been availed of to simplify and expedite procedure."[111] This early experiment in merging law and equity was a forerunner of the more significant merger achieved in 1938 with the adoption of the Federal Rules of Civil Procedure.

The defeat was the Senate's rejection of a "Reformed Procedure Bill" that would have made special verdicts more common in federal court, a more direct assault on the jury system than the law and equity bill—which was why the Senate refused to pass it. The report acknowledged an "objection" by one senator (only one is mentioned, but it is hard to believe there were no others) to the "merits" of the bill—namely, that the practice of putting specific fact questions to the jury "perplexed and confused" the jurors. Other objections, and apparently the decisive ones, concerned the bill's erosion of the conformity principle by "creating such a practice in states where the local sentiment was against it." This objection

108. "Report of the Special Committee to Suggest Remedies and Formulate Proposed Laws to Prevent Delay and Unnecessary Cost in Litigation," 31st Conference, *Annual Report of the American Bar Association* (1908): 542.

109. Ibid., 543.

110. The Law and Equity Act of 1915 (38 Stat. 956).

111. "Eighth Annual Report of the Special Committee to Suggest Remedies and Formulate Proposed Laws to Prevent Delay and Unnecessary Cost in Litigation," *American Bar Association Journal* 1 (1915): 376.

was so strong that the committee concluded, "there was no probability" of passing any bill that included such a provision at any time in the foreseeable future.[112] However, the committee declared its opinion that the campaign for special verdicts "should not be given up."[113]

A separate concern of the ABA was the growing workload of the federal courts and the resulting backlog of cases. Beginning in 1913, when he left the White House, President Taft began a campaign to create at-large judges who would operate as a "flying squadron," moving from court to court as needed. This idea soon led Taft to a more ambitious administrative solution: a "conference of judges" that would determine which courts required additional judges and then assign judges to them on an as-needed basis. Beyond these immediate workload concerns, those who supported the "judicial conference" idea hoped it would lead to broader administrative reforms in the federal judiciary in keeping with the general spirit of "streamlining" the conduct of government, an idea closely related to the new enthusiasm for the "science of administration."[114]

But Congress insisted on keeping reforms as close to the traditional understanding of the judiciary as possible—rejecting the "flying squadron" idea and requiring permanent district assignments, although there was support for the creation of more judgeships. But much of what Taft and others wanted was achieved by a 1922 statute establishing the Conference of Senior Circuit Judges, whose members were charged with analyzing the administrative needs of the federal courts and making recommendations to meet those needs, subject to the approval of Congress.[115]

From the perspective of the procedural reformers inside the ABA, the creation of the Conference of Senior Circuit Judges was a major victory. Writing in

112. Ibid.

113. Ibid., 377.

114. The phrase was first associated with Woodrow Wilson: "The science of administration is the latest fruit of that study of the science of politics which was begun some twenty-two hundred years ago." Woodrow Wilson, "The Study of Administration," *Political Science Quarterly* 2, 2 (June 1887): 198.

115. The Conference of Senior Circuit Judges was the brainchild of Taft (appointed chief justice in 1921) and Attorney General Harry M. Daugherty, who hoped to blunt congressional dissatisfaction with the federal courts by making them more efficient through such methods as reorganizing the workload, shifting resources to the busiest courts, and increasing the number of judges. The name was changed to the Judicial Conference of the United States in 1948. The conference quickly took on a broader mandate than Taft had anticipated, developing into a full-fledged administrative organ, complete with an Administrative Office of the United States Courts. For a fuller discussion of the Judicial Conference, see Peter Graham Fish, *The Politics of Federal Judicial Administration* (Princeton, NJ: Princeton University Press, 1973). The act that created the Conference of Senior Circuit Judges is 42 Stat. 837, September 14, 1922.

the *Harvard Law Review*, Felix Frankfurter and James Landis summarized the hopes progressives placed in this new quasi-administrative body:

> It is the first recognition by Congressional legislation that effective and economic adjudication is to no small measure dependent upon the ways in which the federal courts transact business. . . . The judiciary, like other political institutions, must be directed. . . . An executive committee of the judges, with the Chief Justice of the United States at its head, is a fit and potent instrument for the task.[116]

The Conference of Senior Circuit Judges would eventually turn its attention to the jury system in federal courts, but its first target, in keeping with the spirit of the ABA in the 1910s and 1920s, was reform of civil and criminal procedure, achieved in 1938 (Federal Rules of Civil Procedure) and 1946 (Federal Rules of Criminal Procedure). These reforms (especially the former) were clearly inspired by the ABA's criticisms from almost the moment of its founding: bring the business of the courts up to date, streamline procedures, increase efficiency, reduce time and costs, bring greater predictability to the outcome of private litigation, give judges more flexibility in charging juries, and, ultimately, merge equity and law into a single set of procedures to be used throughout the federal courts, not only eliminating outmoded procedures but also establishing uniform procedures by ending the conformity principle.

The common thread linking these disparate reforms is that they all gave judges greater control over the conduct of trials. In 1885 this aim had revealed a division within the ABA, since many trial lawyers had their own ideas about the distribution of power in the courtroom. This was one reason for the membership's rejection of proposals to increase special verdicts and abolish the unanimity requirement for jury verdicts. But by 1915, the membership had apparently changed its mind, and the association stood fully behind the work of the Special Committee inspired by Pound. This evolution was consistent with the general direction of progressive thinking, which aimed (in Woodrow Wilson's famous words) to "straighten the paths of government, to make its business less unbusiness-like, to strengthen and purify its organization, and to crown its duties with dutifulness."[117]

It would be hard to find any part of the American legal order less businesslike than the jury system. Yet support for the jury among the general public, members of Congress, and even much of the legal profession was high enough that concerns about the inefficiency of the civil jury were almost always expressed cautiously and mixed with statements of praise for a reformed jury system. Yet it

116. Felix Frankfurter and James Landis, "The Business of the Supreme Court of the United States—A Study in the Federal Judicial System—VI: The Conference of Senior Circuit Judges," *Harvard Law Review* 40 (1926–1927): 456.

117. Wilson, "Study of Administration," 219.

is also clear that a more robust criticism—calling for the abolition of civil juries, for example—was rarer than it might have been, had there been any realistic expectation that the Seventh Amendment could be repealed. Taft's call for the civil jury to be abolished (made when he was a member of Teddy Roosevelt's cabinet) made him a rare exception to this rule. In the absence of such protection, however, the progress of judicial reform in America surely would have taken a different path, and the civil jury would have vanished, as it has to a large extent in Canada, the United Kingdom, and other common-law jurisdictions in the Anglosphere.

But there was no mistaking the general drift of the reform agenda: to make trials more efficient, it would be necessary to increase the power of judges and decrease the power of juries. Procedural reform would be the means of accomplishing both these aims at a single stroke. Civil reform would henceforth have a common theme: make the common-law courts more like the equity courts, let judges be judges, and let procedures further the goal of efficiency instead of subverting that goal at every turn.

THE MERGER OF LAW AND EQUITY

The movement to import equitable procedures into the law courts, energized by Roscoe Pound, had limited success at first. Persuading Congress to endorse a radical change in civil procedures, or to abandon the conformity principle, was an uphill struggle, and not even the prestige of luminaries such as Taft (who became chief justice in 1921) made it simpler. But beginning in 1911 the ABA, under the direction of Thomas Shelton, began to push for an "enabling act" authorizing the Supreme Court to write a new set of uniform rules for the federal courts that would automatically become law unless vetoed by Congress.[118] Reform would concentrate on two linked goals: overcoming the conformity principle, and importing into the law courts the practices and procedures of the equity courts, aiming (in the most comprehensive version of the proposal) at the complete merger of law and equity into a single system. The need for such a change was increasingly acknowledged in the legal profession, if not (yet) in Congress. Pound's speech had achieved such notoriety in part because he had articulated what many in the profession were already thinking: that common-law rules and practices were so

118. The Rules Enabling Act of 1934 (28 U.S.C. § 2072) gave the Supreme Court the authority to create procedural rules, subject to amendment by Congress, for the entire federal court system. Working with the Judicial Conference, the Court enacted the Federal Rules of Civil Procedure in 1938 and the Federal Rules of Criminal Procedure in 1946, thus effectively ending the conformity principle with respect to *trial procedures*. Ending the conformity to state *jury selection procedures* would not be achieved until the Jury Selection and Service Act of 1968, discussed in chapter 4.

hopelessly tangled that procedure had become the enemy of substance and, therefore, the enemy of justice.

It is also true, however, that Pound ventured into territory where more conservative reformers were reluctant to follow. For example, his objection to the contemporary legal order went well beyond the problem of rigid procedures; the entire adversary system had become an outmoded means of dealing with social problems. In fact, it was the common law's fixation on individual and private rights that was the primordial source of the law's disorder, placing an undue concentration (in the words of one historian) on "individual and private rights, thus neglecting the importance of the community and the need for government protection of the individual."[119] Furthermore, the "private lawsuit"—based on the assertion of a "merely" private claim—was no longer useful for handling the "broader social questions" raised by the development of modern commerce and industry. Legal decisions should serve the purpose of social reform, according to Pound, and should result not from a mechanical application of rules but from the weighing of alternative social policies. Judges, in other words, should govern, not just settle cases.[120]

This was a familiar progressive tune: times have changed, and the old assumptions no longer hold; we need a twentieth-century legal system to deal with twentieth-century problems, yet we are still stuck in the age of William Blackstone, John Marshall, and Federalist No. 51.[121] Instead of letting experts handle our problems, we let lawyers compete in court for the right to throw pixie dust into the eyes of poorly educated jurors called from their factories, shops, and farms. The result is the inefficiency seen throughout the legal order—and for progressives, especially, the concept of efficiency had by now acquired an almost spiritual importance. "In the present scientific and industrial world, increased efficiency is the keynote of an advancing civilization," wrote Charles Boston in 1912.[122] Efficiency comes from the regular application of expertise to social and economic problems, and there was no reason that this principle, so evidently successful in science and industry, should not be applied to the courts. It was a "good sign," Boston thought, that the public was coming around to this point of view.[123]

119. Subrin, "How Equity Conquered Common Law," 945.

120. Ibid., 947.

121. Progressive writers such as Woodrow Wilson had been making this argument, on an even broader scale, about the fundamental unsuitability of the Constitution to the challenges of the modern age. See Woodrow Wilson, *Congressional Government* (Boston: Houghton, Mifflin, 1885); Croly, *Promise of American Life*.

122. Charles Boston, "Some Practical Remedies for Existing Defects in the Administration of Justice," *University of Pennsylvania Law Review* 61 (1912): 1.

123. In the absence of public opinion surveys, it is impossible to say whether this assertion was more of a wish than a fact. If state legislatures could be considered a measure of public opinion, however, Boston was wrong about the relative popularity of "experts" over "amateurs," a category that included legislators as well as jurors.

And among those elements of the court that were most in need of improvement, the civil jury stood high on the list. "The economic waste is great; the panel is always larger than the need; in order to get a jury of twelve men, twenty-four or so are kept in attendance and in idleness; such of them that have remunerative employment, at a loss to themselves and the community."[124] What had once been a fundamental element of a republican regime was now simply a distraction from the task of wage earning.

Boston was eager, however, to lavish praise on judges and to urge that they be freed from the shackles placed on them by democratic legislatures. "Give the judges an intelligent and fair law, a simple and flexible procedure, an opportunity to administer actual justice upon the facts and merits of a controversy, relieve them from the necessity of observing unconscionable technicalities which are not of their making."[125] Make the judge an administrator, in effect.

Pound had pointed the way out of these difficulties: return to the courts the traditional powers of the equity judge, along with the judge's traditional prestige.[126] Pound concluded that "the equitable principle of complete disposition of the entire controversy between the parties should be extended to its full extent and applied to every type of proceeding."[127] This was the mission that would now guide the advocates of reform, and it was a mission that joined otherwise antagonistic political forces: conservatives like Thomas Shelton and Charles Clark, progressive Republicans like William Howard Taft, and more radical progressives like Roscoe Pound and Jerome Frank.[128] The idea of procedural reform was beginning to command support from a broad and powerful coalition of Republicans, Democrats, and Progressives: the nation's first and last experience, perhaps, of "tripartisanship."[129]

124. Boston, "Some Practical Remedies," 13.

125. Ibid., 32.

126. Subrin, "How Equity Conquered Common Law," 945–946. Subrin points out that early in his career, Pound published a law review essay urging that judicial robes not be abandoned in favor of business attire, in order to preserve the judge's magisterial image.

127. Ibid., 947.

128. Jerome Frank would become one of the best-known critics of the jury system; his *Law and the Modern Mind* (New York: Brentano's, 1930) was uncommonly blunt in its rejection of the idea of lay juries: "Is it likely that twelve men, summoned from all sorts of occupations, unaccustomed to the machinery of the law, unacquainted with their own mental workings and not known to one another, can, in the scant time allowed them for deliberation, do as good a job in weighing conflicting testimony as an experienced judge? . . . It is hard to conceive that any astute person can take seriously the stereotyped praise of the jury, uttered daily by sophisticated lawyers" (193).

129. Subrin believes that liberals and conservatives "shared the same ideology" with regard to court reform. Subrin, "How Equity Conquered Common Law," 949. Among reform-minded Republicans, only Joseph Choate was notable for a robust defense of the jury system. But Choate was from another, more republican era, having joined the Republican Party upon its founding in 1856.

What explains this convergence? For reformers like Pound, the judge was the closest thing to an expert inside the American courtroom: to empower such expertise was to privilege substance over procedure and the community over the individual. It would be even better if the knottiest social problems could be settled by administrative tribunals and kept out of the courtroom altogether, but until that happy day, giving judges more control over trials would have to do. For conservatives like Thomas Shelton, the judge was the only thing standing between the rights of litigants and the utter chaos unleashed by unscrupulous attorneys with unrealistic clients arguing their cases before gullible juries. Judges should therefore have more discretion, and the rules by which trials were conducted should be more flexible. Procedure should not be a "fetish," and American judges should take as their model the English judge, who could dismiss procedural technicalities almost at will.[130]

Clearly, one thing did not belong in this newly painted picture of the judge-run courtroom: the jury, that apotheosis of amateurism, the most ancient of all the "relics" of common-law practice and procedure, the oldest "fetish" of them all. Progressives were especially dismissive of the jury system, which they associated with the old-fashioned suspicion of government that characterized the age of revolution and constitution making in the long-ago eighteenth century.[131] With the establishment of popular democracy, such fussiness about the authority of the people's government no longer made sense. Progressive historian James Allen Smith believed that even the criminal jury had been rendered irrelevant by "the ascendancy of corporate wealth and influence," the instrument by which the "oppression of the ruling classes" made itself felt throughout the court system.[132] Progressives were especially contemptuous of those elements of government that protected so-called negative liberty (such as the jury system) and were eager to promote "positive liberty" through government action, even if that meant government by unelected administrators. Smith believed that the entire "elaborate system of Constitutional restraints" from the eighteenth century was "passive" and outdated, and this view became increasingly common throughout the universe of legal reform, even among those who were far less radical than Smith.[133]

130. Ibid., 951.

131. I am grateful for the work by Kim Kosman Hendrickson, who was my graduate assistant in the political science doctoral program at Boston College. Kim Kosman Hendrickson, "Progressives Try the Jury" (unpublished manuscript, 2005).

132. J. Allen Smith, *The Spirit of American Government* (New York: Macmillan, 1907), 117.

133. Ibid., 291–295. See also W. F. Willoughby, *Principles of Judicial Administration* (Washington, DC: Brookings Institution, 1929), for a progressive attack on the jury system from within political science. Willoughby was an economist, a student of public adminis-

Most important, this was the view of Charles Clark and Edson Sunderlund, the principal architects of the 1938 Federal Rules of Civil Procedure. Both of them believed that the civil jury was a wasteful and anachronistic relic.[134] "Juries," Sunderland wrote in 1913, "cannot be permitted to exercise blind and unreasoning power to oppress litigants. They must conduct themselves as sensible and reasonable men. They cannot be suffered to base verdicts on caprice, conjecture, passion or prejudice."[135] Clark, dean of the Yale Law School, was the coauthor of a study of civil jury trials in Connecticut in 1934, which concluded that "whatever the political, psychological or jurisprudential values of the jury as an institution may be, its use in the civil litigation covered by this study is certainly not impressive. The picture seems to be that of an expensive, cumbersome and comparatively inefficient trial device."[136]

But without launching a frontal attack on the jury system, Clark, Sunderland, and their colleagues managed to craft a set of rules that avoided rather than abolished the civil jury, by the simple expedient of making it easier for judges to resolve cases before the trial even began.[137] The tools that made this possible were borrowed from the equity courts: extensive pretrial discovery and expanded summary judgment. Both tools gave judges the opportunity to resolve cases in the absence of a jury—or, indeed, without even convening a trial. Perhaps because these reforms did not openly challenge the Seventh Amendment, they did not arouse much opposition in Congress, which could have blocked the reforms, or among the members of the Supreme Court, whose approval was required before the reforms could become law. Nonetheless, the Federal Rules of Civil Procedure, which have been amended at least once in each decade since the 1930s, are largely responsible for the phenomenon of the "vanishing civil jury," as jury trials have been reduced to a fraction of 1 percent of all civil case dispositions, from levels as high as 30 percent in the generation before the reforms (see chapter 5).

---

tration, and the first director of the Brookings Institution; he was president of the American Political Science Association in 1930.

134. Lerner, "Rise of the Directed Verdict," 518.

135. Edson Sunderland, "Directing a Verdict for the Party Having the Burden of Proof," *Michigan Law Review* 11 (1913): 198, cited by ibid., 520.

136. Charles E. Clark and Harry Shulman, "Jury Trial in Civil Cases—A Study in Judicial Administration," *Yale Law Review* 43 (1934): 867, cited in Kristin Knudsen Latta, "The Role of Non-Lawyers on Administrative Tribunals," *Alaska Law Review* 31 (2014): 38, n. 2.

137. This project inspired quiet doubts among some members of the committee that was composing the new rules. They were especially "disquieted by the proposal to expand summary judgment, and insisted that there should be no threat to the jury system; we should be clear, one said, 'that we are not trying to introduce a rule which will substitute trial by affidavit for trial by jury.'" Burns, *Death of the American Trial*, 65–66.

FEDERALISM AND THE CAMPAIGN FOR UNIFORMITY

As in so many areas of American policy, achieving the jury reforms recommended by the ABA and the Conference of Senior Circuit Judges was complicated by federalism. State laws regulated everything from jury selection to judicial commentary on evidence, which meant that state legislatures determined who could serve on a federal jury and how federal trials would be conducted, leaving room for considerable diversity from one district to another. In the age of centralization, this diversity seemed increasingly illogical.

The steady stream of guilty verdicts in the Alien and Sedition Act trials had inspired a brief but abortive effort to federalize jury selection by requiring that federal jurors be chosen only by lot, rather than "by lot or otherwise, in each State respectively according to the mode of forming juries therein now practiced."[138] That this effort came to nothing says much about the assumptions underlying the jury system in the republican era and about the commitment to a decentralized judiciary. But in the late nineteenth century, views about federalism had been transformed. What the republican era had celebrated as "the rights of the states" the Progressive Era regarded with skepticism, at best. The varied procedures for choosing jurors and conducting trials now seemed to be major causes of inefficiency in the courts, wholly unjustified by any of the concerns about popular government that had inspired these provisions in the first place.

These stirrings of dissatisfaction did not produce immediate results. When Hirsch published his textbook in 1879, it was still the case—and would remain so formally until 1957—that eligibility for jury service in federal court was the same as that for service in the highest court of the state in which the federal court conducted its business.[139] When federal court officials selected names for jury service, they were using lists compiled under state law and managed by state officials. State legislatures had considerable discretion when forming their own jury laws, both in principle and in practice. They were prohibited by the Fourteenth Amendment, federal statutes, and judicial rulings from excluding citizens from jury service "on account of race, color, or previous condition of servitude"[140]—a

138. Judiciary Act of 1789, section 29.

139. Rev. Stat., title XIII, chap. 15, para. 800, as amended in 1879. Jury selection was not fully federalized until the Jury Selection and Service Act of 1968. The conformity principle was first breached with the adoption of the Federal Rules of Civil Procedure in 1938 and the Federal Rules of Criminal Procedure in 1946; they did not, however, touch the issue of jury selection. The Civil Rights Act of 1957 established separate qualifications for service on federal juries, but the states were free to adopt their own jury selection rules, subject to the constraints imposed by judicial rulings, most notably with respect to racial discrimination.

140. Act of March 1, 1875, chap. 114, para. 4. The Supreme Court ruled in 1880 that the equal protection clause of the Fourteenth Amendment and section 4 of the Civil Rights

prohibition honored mostly in the breach, especially in the South. Otherwise, states were free to exempt or to openly exclude nearly anyone they wished, and they used this authority to disqualify or routinely excuse, among others, women, wage laborers, those without property, the very young and the very old, the illiterate and semiliterate, former convicts, Chinese Americans, Mexican Americans, habitual drunkards, and keepers of bawdy houses. In many states, in other words, among those who were eligible to vote (including women after 1919), a great many were disqualified from jury service—on top of a large number whose professions and occupations entitled them to automatic exemptions.

The process of choosing names for federal jury service from among all those who met state eligibility requirements was in the hands of a court clerk and a jury commissioner. Both were appointed by the presiding judge in the federal court, with the stipulation (since 1879) that the clerk and commissioner be of opposite political parties.[141] It was further stipulated that the selection of names for the jury wheel (names supplied by state officials) be done without reference to political party affiliation. Both these requirements were reactions to accusations of Republican Party control of courts in the former Confederacy during the Reconstruction years and to Democratic Party control of jury selection in many northern cities, making it difficult to prosecute political corruption cases.

An "impartial" jury, therefore, was one whose selection betrayed no evidence of partisanship—not a surprising view, considering the importance of political parties to all kinds of political decisions, both high and low, in the nineteenth century. It would be a rare case that did not present at least the possibility of partisan implications, even if these were no more than personal feuds left over from past election campaigns. But while attempting to control for partisan meddling, the modern jury regime preserved the republican-era reality of decentralized and discretionary jury selection. In addition to the statutory categories, republican-era jury officials often had (as Tocqueville noted) "arbitrary" power when selecting names from among those who were formally eligible. They could exclude citizens

---

Act of 1875 prohibited the exclusion of citizens from jury service based on race (Strauder v. West Virginia, 100 U.S. 303 [1880]). The same year, the Court ruled that the right to be considered did not mean the right to serve on any particular jury (Virginia v. Rives, 100 U.S. 313 [1880]).

141. This requirement was included in section 2 of H.R. Res. 2381, "An Act for Making Appropriations for Certain Judicial Expenses," signed by President Hayes on June 30, 1879. It was one of the compromises the Democrats insisted on when they attained their first congressional majority since the end of the Civil War. The same act abolished the loyalty oath required to reestablish the voting rights of former Confederates, and it was passed on a strict party-line vote. See Drew L. Kershen, "The Jury Selection Act of 1879: Theory and Practice of Citizen Participation in the Judicial System," *Law Forum* 1980, 3 (1980): 707–767.

who did not meet, in their view, the nonobjective criteria for jury service, such as "intelligence," "character," "judgment," or "integrity." And, of course, they could exclude citizens for other, less defendable reasons as well, given the extent of their discretion. During the era of the modern jury, that power was perhaps less arbitrary than in Tocqueville's time, but it was certainly considerable. The formal qualifications for jury service were merely the first in a series of filters.

In New York, for example, jurors were to be of "fair character," "approved integrity," "sound judgment," and "well-informed."[142] Such qualifications gave state jury officials a certain degree of discretion when making up the jury lists, and this discretion shaped the lists used by federal courts as well. Sometimes commissioners also turned to prominent members of the local community, and to the leaders of local service and philanthropic organizations, for advice about jurors. These leaders—the so-called key men in the community—often supplied names for the commissioners to consider.[143] Beginning in the 1940s this discretionary power of state and local jury officials would become a major target of jury reform and a major battleground for the defenders of the traditional jury system.

Almost simultaneously with the adoption of the new Federal Rules of Civil Procedure in 1938, the American Bar Association was completing another study of the legal system, under the auspices of its new Section on Judicial Administration. This section produced an ambitious and comprehensive plan for "improving the administration of justice" in the state courts. Part of that effort was a set of recommendations for reform of the jury system in the states. "It was thought," according to the ABA's 1938 report, "that there would probably never be a better time to undertake a comprehensive reform of the procedure of the [state] courts, long regarded as one of the outstanding duties of the legal profession."[144] The Section on Judicial Administration appointed separate committees to report recommendations in seven areas (including judicial administration, pretrial proce-

142. Hirsch, *Practical Treatise*, 20, citing New Code, para. 1027. Jury qualification rules still disqualify many who are eligible to vote, such as those who cannot read or speak English, have a criminal record, or have a disability that would make it difficult to provide "satisfactory" service as a juror. See, for example, Maryland's jury qualifications rules, at courts.state.med.us/juryservice/faqs (accessed March 1, 2014).

143. The key-man system is discussed in more detail below and in Jeffrey Abramson, *We the Jury: The Jury System and the Ideal of Democracy* (New York: Basic Books, 1994), 115–117; Randolph N. Jonakait, *The American Jury System* (New Haven, CT: Yale University Press, 2003), 121–123; and Jon Van Dyke, *Jury Selection Procedures: Our Uncertain Commitment to Representative Panels* (Cambridge, MA: Ballinger, 1977), 86–90. Like the nonobjective qualifications for jury service, the key-man system has never been found unconstitutional by the Supreme Court, but it was eliminated by the Jury Selection and Service Act of 1968, discussed in chapter 4.

144. "Report of the Section of Judicial Administration," *Annual Report of the American Bar Association* 63 (1938): 522.

dure, and trial practice). One committee was devoted to "trial by jury including selection of jurors,"[145] and it reported two recommendations. First, jurors serving in state court should be selected by commissioners appointed by the court, an effort to spread the federal model of judges, clerks, and jury commissions to the states. The use of jury commissions in federal court had been authorized (but not required) by the Jury Selection Act of 1879.[146] The commissioners were appointed by, and worked under the supervision of, the district court judge (as did the clerk, who was also appointed by the judge). The commissioners received only a per diem stipend for their part-time efforts. States varied considerably in their administrative arrangements for jury selection. Some states followed the federal model of jury commissions appointed by judges; in others, jurors were chosen by judges themselves, by municipal officials, or sometimes by party officials. This riot of diverse procedures would have to be brought under control by the promotion of a single, rational model of jury administration that the states would be encouraged to adopt. And the ABA would lobby state legislatures to do so.

Second, big cities should adopt the so-called Cleveland system for selecting jurors.[147] Briefly (it is described more fully below), Cleveland's jury selection system was designed to achieve two goals: to create a jury pool whose members were drawn from all walks of life, and to impanel jurors who were average or above in terms of their ability to understand cases and come to reasonable conclusions based on evidence. To achieve the first goal, officials worked with the list of registered voters; the second goal required a time-consuming process of interviewing prospective jurors once they had replied to the jury summons.

Before making its recommendations, the committee summarized the current criticisms of the jury system, giving us a detailed look at what the legal profession understood to be the system's weaknesses in the 1930s. Little of what the committee had to say was new. Acknowledging the criticism of the jury system in many quarters, the committee insisted that most of this criticism "could be eliminated by proper selection of jurors in the first instance, by courageous refusal on the part of the Bench to accept inadequate excuses for not serving as jurors, and, by proper conduct of jury trials by the Bar and Bench." The committee also acknowledged the importance of the jury system as "the chief remaining governmental function in which lay citizens take a direct and active part . . . the best means within our knowledge of keeping the administration of justice in tune with the community."[148] It was therefore very important that the system be rescued from its shortcomings and restored to its previous vigor.

145. "Report of the Committee on Trial by Jury Including Methods of Selection of Jurors," *Annual Report of the American Bar Association* 63 (1938): 559; hereafter cited as *1938 ABA Report on Jury Trials*.

146. See Kershen, "Jury Selection Act of 1879."

147. *1938 ABA Report on Jury Trials*, 562.

148. Ibid., 559.

Among these shortcomings was wasteful administration. Jurors were kept idle in the court while officers tried to determine how many were needed; others were kept idle after being challenged. Last-minute decisions to waive the jury in civil cases, or plea bargains in criminal cases, added to the inefficiency. Some states, the committee noted, had attempted to reduce these inefficiencies by allowing smaller juries in civil trials, if the parties expressly agreed. The committee therefore made a number of suggestions designed to expedite trials and make better use of jurors' time: acquainting jurors with the nature of their responsibilities before they are permitted to sit on cases (this is the origin of the current practice of judges or other officials addressing jurors before the voir dire), keeping jurors safe from any attempt to influence them while they are waiting to be called, and urging judges to give instructions to the jury in "language which the jurors will understand and appreciate, and not with a view of dictating a legal masterpiece."[149]

But the first task was to increase the caliber of jurors, which "hinges largely upon the method of selection." The goal was to remove jury selection "as far as possible from political influence" and put it "in the hands of competent and independent commissioners who will weed out those least qualified."[150] The committee noted that "of course" the jurors chosen "should represent a cross-section of the community"—one of the earliest appearances of the term "cross section" in the jury debate. It would not do, the committee pointed out, "to have juries composed entirely of working men or entirely of business or professional men," or for the jurors to be chosen entirely from one city in a large county.[151] To make its point clearer, the committee included a lengthy quote from a report of the Boston Bar Association on methods of selecting jurors, published in 1935. Note that at this point in the debate, the problem of jury selection was considered to have two parts: drawing jurors from an adequate cross section of the community (defined largely in terms of class and occupation), and finding jurors who were competent. The committee asked:

> What kind of jury do we want? Should it be strictly a cross-section of the community, or should it be selected solely on the basis of ability to understand and decide cases. This is a large and important subject. The advantages of intelligence and ability . . . are obvious. . . . On the other hand, if ability . . . is all that is sought it would probably be best to leave the matter to the judges. . . . The jury is more than the mere decider of cases. It is a balance wheel in the administration of justice. . . . It . . . is an educational institution. . . . [T]he

149. Ibid., 560.

150. Ibid., 560–561.

151. In these passages, the word "men" sometimes means males and sometimes means citizens generally, since by 1938, several states had qualified women to serve on juries. Jury service by women is discussed separately below.

> jury is "called upon to pass upon matters involving every class in the community, on disputes between rich and poor . . . employers and employees . . . corporations and individuals . . . property owners and wage earners, between those of different races and creeds." In such disputes a jury fairly representative of all classes and creeds will be more intelligent. The problem is to find honest jurors with sufficient intelligence to understand the issues presented and yet representative of the community.[152]

It was to approximate this composition more closely that the committee recommended the Cleveland system of jury selection, especially for big cities. Under that system, judges appointed two jury commissioners; neither could be an attorney, and, echoing the rule in the federal courts, they were to be from different parties. The commissioners then estimated the number of jurors the court would have to call for the coming term to fill the predicted number of juries. This number was then divided into the total number of registered voters on the lists maintained by the election board; the resulting quotient was called the "key number." If the key number were seven, for example, then every seventh name on the voting list would be chosen and given a consecutive number. Persons chosen in this way would be notified to report for examination by the jury commissioners, to determine their fitness to serve.

The Cleveland Jury Commission explained in one of its annual reports what it meant by "fitness": "physically and mentally healthy," a "good reputation for honesty and morality," literate in English, and "of sufficient intelligence and experience in life to be able to understand the various problems presented in both civil and criminal litigation." To determine a juror's fitness, the commissioners used a simple index-card system, listing each prospective juror's answers to demographic questions (age, address, marital status, employment, education, and so forth). Each card also contained a final judgment about the candidate's fitness to serve. There is no indication in the description of the Cleveland system that jurors were required to complete a written examination or to answer a common set of questions. The final judgment about a candidate's fitness apparently resulted from the informal interview with the jury commissioners—a practice that gave the commissioners a good deal of discretion but was also time-consuming. The names of those found to be suitable after these interviews were then written on another set of index cards, the cards were placed in the jury wheel, and "each week a sufficient number of names are drawn for service for two weeks." Jurors were excused at the end of the two-week period unless their trial continued past that time. This process appears to have been genuinely selective: out of 13,063 letters mailed during the 1937 term, just over 1,700 prospective jurors were legally exempt, deceased, or no longer living in Cleveland, leaving 11,266 to be examined. Of that number, 7,659 were

152. *1938 ABA Report on Jury Trials*, 561.

found to be acceptable, or just under 68 percent; roughly one-third of the registered voters examined for jury duty were found to be unqualified.[153]

The committee described similar jury selection procedures in Detroit and California. In California the complaint had been that the same "housewives" (women were qualified for jury service in California in 1937) and "elderly men" showed up on the jury lists year after year because the lists were composed in a "hit-and-miss fashion, by taking names from the rosters of various organizations, names suggested by judges and others for jury service, and names of persons who presented themselves as prospective trial jurors."[154] This was a variation of the key-man system of jury selection, briefly described above.[155] Under this arrangement, jury commissioners solicited the names of likely jurors from key men (and sometimes women, after passage of the Nineteenth Amendment) in the community: civic leaders, clergymen, businessmen, schoolteachers, newspaper editors, officers of social service clubs, trade union officials, and so on. The sources varied from state to state, as did the care with which the process was conducted. The key-man system was replaced in Los Angeles County by a variation on the Cleveland key-number system, in which names were chosen randomly from voter lists and randomly from the various precincts in the county (e.g., every twelfth name from every fifth precinct), so that no part of the sprawling Los Angeles area dominated the jury pool. Those individuals chosen were then required to appear before the jury commission for examination. Any person who was "manifestly unfit"—because of ill health, old age, poor English skills, or poor hearing or eyesight—was immediately dismissed by an assistant. Those remaining were given a written examination that began with a simple vocabulary test, followed by a test of the juror's ability to understand written instructions of the sort "ordinarily given in both criminal and civil cases." Those who passed this test were considered fit for service, at which point the jury commissioner would respond to requests for exemption. If there were "little question that the juror would be excused by the Court," the commissioner dismissed the juror; if the commissioner believed the request might not be approved, the juror's name was added to the list.[156]

In commenting on the test administered to prospective jurors, the judges who prepared the report for the ABA committee noted that "the English jury system, as adopted in this country, calls for an average jury of average American citizens and no attempt has been made to raise the mental standard too high." However, as we have already seen, the jury system adopted during both the colonial and the republican eras did not look for "average" citizens; it sought those who were in some

153. Ibid., 564. The cohort approved for service was almost exactly divided between men and women (3,643 and 3,523, respectively).

154. Ibid., 565.

155. Not to be confused with the key-number system, as used in Cleveland.

156. *1938 ABA Report on Jury Trials*, 566.

sense "exemplary"—noted for their integrity, intelligence, honesty, or character. Whatever it was looking for, the Los Angeles system apparently had some difficulty finding it, because the Los Angeles commissioners were even more selective than those in Cleveland. Of 10,398 citizens who responded to jury notices in 1937 (out of 13,231 letters sent), only 3,306 were approved for service, a mere 31.7 percent of those examined.[157] During the second session in 1937, the approval rate dropped to 21.8 percent. Thus, in Los Angeles County in the late 1930s, two-thirds to four-fifths of the potential jurors who took the trouble to respond when summoned were found, on examination, to be unqualified to serve.

RACE, CLASS, GENDER: INVENTING THE REPRESENTATIVE JURY

The American Bar Association's consideration of jury selection came at a time when the Supreme Court was turning its attention to the questions looming behind all discussions of the jury. How much does selectivity undermine the common-law conception of an "impartial jury" and become something more like the ancient practice of "packing"? Racial discrimination in jury selection had consistently been found to violate the equal protection clause of the Fourteenth Amendment, beginning in 1880 in *Strauder v. West Virginia*.[158] Subsequent decisions applied the same principle to Asian Americans and Mexican Americans, but until the 1940s the case law was silent about whether other forms of "exclusion" (sometimes in the form of exemptions) might be constitutionally suspect.[159]

The *Strauder* Court argued that the state law in question, which limited jury service in West Virginia to "white male persons," had the effect of stigmatizing citizens because of their race:

> The very fact that colored people are singled out and expressly denied by a statute all right to participate in the administration of the law, as jurors, because of their color, though they are citizens, and may be in other respects fully qualified, is practically a brand upon them, affixed by the law, an assertion of their inferiority, and a stimulant to that race prejudice which is an impediment to securing to individuals of the race that equal justice which the law aims to secure to all others.[160]

157. Ibid., 567.

158. Strauder v. West Virginia, 100 U.S. 303 (1880).

159. The leading discrimination cases against Mexican Americans are Hernandez v. Texas, 347 U.S. 475 (1954), and Castaneda v. Partida, 430 U.S. 482 (1977); for Asian Americans, the leading case is United States v. Cannady, 54 F.3d 544 (9th Circuit, 1995).

160. *Strauder*, 308.

The *Strauder* principles were reaffirmed in several similar cases in the following decades, and in 1940, in *Smith v. Texas*, the Court tried once more to strike a blow against the administrative practices of the southern states. But in the process, it introduced a new element into jury law, one that would provoke a controversy far beyond the issue of race.[161]

The *Smith* case was depressingly familiar. After being convicted of rape by an all-white jury, Smith challenged his conviction by asserting that he had been indicted by a grand jury chosen from a jury panel from which blacks had been almost entirely excluded. Because this exclusion was intentional and systematic, his indictment violated the Fourteenth Amendment right to equal protection of the laws. It had long been recognized that an indictment by a jury chosen in such a discriminatory manner was unconstitutional, and this part of Smith's claim was not challenged by the state of Texas. Rather, the state denied that the absence of black jurors was the result of a concerted scheme of racial discrimination. One jury official testified that he had chosen as grand jurors the names of men he recognized from the tax assessor's list, and he "was not personally acquainted with Negroes."[162] Not surprisingly, the Court did not find this argument persuasive. Writing for a unanimous Court, Justice Hugo Black pointed out that since the question presented involved a "basic right protected by the Federal Constitution," it was the Court's responsibility to "appraise the evidence as it relates to this constitutional right."[163] Then Justice Black said something surprising: "It is part of the *established* tradition in the use of juries as instruments of public justice that the jury be a body truly *representative* of the community."[164] This remark was surprising because representativeness was not an established feature of the common-law juries defined by Article III and by the Sixth and Seventh Amendments; nor had the Court articulated such a standard in its pre–Civil War decisions or its post–Fourteenth Amendment decisions. Under the traditional understanding, defendants were entitled to an impartial jury chosen in the district where the crime "shall have been committed." The case law had, over the years, clarified what "impartial" meant (e.g., it did not necessarily mean "being unaware" of the case being tried), and Congress had identified deliberate racial exclusion as contrary to public policy.

None of these traditional views of the jury involved a claim that different parts of the community should be "represented" on the jury. Nor had twenti-

161. Smith v. Texas, 311 U.S. 128 (1940).

162. Ibid., 132. Although southern states were very good at keeping black citizens from voting, they were not as eager to keep blacks from paying their property taxes. States that used the tax rolls as the first cut for jury service (like Texas) were therefore unusually vulnerable to Fourteenth Amendment challenges, since it was easy to compare the tax rolls with the voting registration and jury lists.

163. Ibid., 130.

164. Ibid., emphasis added.

eth-century legal reformers identified a lack of representativeness as one of the problems with the jury system. At most, the legal profession's campaign to reform the jury system had urged that jurors be drawn from various walks of life (especially from the educated and successful parts of the community, whose members were often exempt) and that they show evidence of competence. Representation, in contrast, was a feature of a legislature, not a jury. Most important was that a jury be impartial and capable of reaching a sensible judgment. If anything, the jury should not represent the least capable citizens, the illiterates, the mentally lazy, or the scofflaws looking to reach a quick verdict so they could get home to their suppers or their ale.

None of these concerns about the jury had anything to do with race; nor was the idea of "representation" necessary to reassert the authoritative argument of *Strauder v. West Virginia* that the systematic exclusion of blacks from the jury pool was a plain violation of the Fourteenth Amendment and unconstitutional on its face. *Strauder* said nothing about "representative juries" or the "cross-section" principle, harking back instead to the oldest common-law understanding of the jury as "a body of men composed of the peers or equals of the person whose rights it is selected or summoned to determine; that is, of his neighbors, fellows, associates, persons having the same legal status in society as that which he holds." Justice William Strong, for the majority, cited Blackstone's *Commentaries* for the claim that the jury is a "bulwark of the [subject's] liberties," and he cited Bentham on the problem of "jury packing," a practice that, in the context of the postwar South, took on a new and even more sinister form:

> It is well known (Justice Strong wrote) that prejudices often exist against particular classes in the community, which sway the judgment of jurors, and which, therefore, operate in some cases to deny to persons of those classes the full enjoyment of that protection which others enjoy. Prejudice in a local community is held to be a reason for a change of venue. The framers of the constitutional amendment must have known full well the existence of such prejudice and its likelihood to continue against the manumitted slaves and their race, and that knowledge was doubtless a motive that led to the amendment.[165]

Nor was the question one of diverse membership on the petit jury itself, but only whether, "in the composition or selection of jurors by whom he is to be indicted or tried, all persons of his race or color may be excluded by law, solely because of their race or color, so that by no possibility can any colored man sit upon the jury." Such exclusion of blacks from the venire, on account of their race, was a plain violation of both the Fourteenth Amendment's equal protection clause and the Civil Rights Act of 1875.[166]

165. *Strauder*, 309.
166. Ibid., 305.

In *Neal v. Delaware*, decided one year later, Justice John Marshall Harlan reaffirmed the *Strauder* decision, writing for the Court that "to compel a colored man to submit to a trial before a jury drawn from a panel from which was excluded, because of their color, every man of his race, however well qualified by education and character to discharge the functions of jurors, was a denial of the equal protection of the laws," even though a state may legally "confine the selection of jurors" to men, property owners, adults, and those with certain educational qualifications.[167] In *Martin v. Texas*, decided in 1906, the Court once again insisted that a defendant has the right to be tried by a jury whose members are chosen by criteria that are not racially discriminatory, without defining a requirement that juries be "representative" or that jurors be taken from a "cross section" of the community.[168] And in a 1935 decision growing out of the infamous Scottsboro case, the Court found that the habitual exclusion of blacks from the jury pool for both grand and petit juries—supported by "illusory" state arguments about the "lack of qualified negroes"—required that the defendant's conviction be reversed and the case remanded.[169]

In his *Smith* ruling, Justice Black made no further reference to "representation," devoting the rest of his short opinion to demonstrating the emptiness of the state's claim that no racial discrimination was involved in the astonishing scarcity of black jurors in Harris County, Texas, in the 1930s. "If there has been discrimination, whether accomplished ingeniously or ingenuously, the conviction cannot stand."[170]

Perhaps because the outcome of the *Smith* case was unremarkable—just another southern conviction set aside because of racial discrimination, a distressingly regular occurrence—Justice Black's apparent expansion of jury theory provoked little immediate comment. But the new standard appeared again just two years later in *Glasser v. United States*,[171] a case that had nothing to do with race. Glasser was a lawyer working in the US attorney's office in Chicago; he was convicted, along with two colleagues, of taking bribes to fix liquor law cases in the city—a fraud against the United States. Among the numerous procedural violations alleged by the various defendants during their trial was a complaint about the manner in which their jury had been chosen. There were six women on the jury, and all, according to Glasser, had been chosen from a list of names supplied

167. Neal v. Delaware, 103 U.S. 370 (1881), 386.

168. Martin v. Texas, 100 U.S. 316 (1906).

169. Norris v. Alabama, 294 U.S. 587 (1935). For an account of the Scottsboro incidents and their aftermath, see Dan T. Carter, *Scottsboro: A Tragedy of the American South* (Baton Rouge: Louisiana State University Press, 2007), and James Goodman, *Stories of Scottsboro* (New York: Pantheon, 1994).

170. *Smith,* 132.

171. Glasser v. United States, 315 U.S. 60 (1942).

by the Illinois League of Women Voters. Furthermore, all had attended a class on the jury system, where they had acquired a "good government" perspective and therefore a bias in favor of the prosecution.

The facts recounted in the *Glasser* record tell a story worthy of Damon Runyon: crooked lawyers, bootleggers, thugs, double-crossing partners, and dishonest politicians, all set against the rich mosaic of Chicago in the 1930s, where no ethnic group was so small that it could not generate its own crime syndicate. It is easy to see why these particular defendants would not welcome members of the League of Women Voters on their jury. But would such a jury constitute an impermissible departure from the Sixth Amendment's standard of impartiality?

This question did not, strictly speaking, present itself. Glasser's claim about the jury selection process was based on a single article his lawyers had discovered, "Woman and the Law," which had appeared in the *American Bar Association Journal* in April 1940. The article recounted the experience of one woman, "L. T. S.," called for jury duty in federal court for the northern district of Illinois. "When I arrived in the jury room at the appointed hour," she wrote, "I found about seventy-five other people had responded to the same summons. With one exception, the women were all members of the League of Women Voters, who had been recommended by that organization at the invitation of the court. . . . The men had apparently been chosen at random." The author described being examined for the jury in a case that was obviously Glasser's, but she was rejected by the district attorney and ended up serving on a different trial a few days later.[172]

In his opinion for the majority,[173] Justice Frank Murphy conceded that no further action on Glasser's complaint about the League of Women Voters had been taken in the trial court, by either the defense or the prosecution. "The Government did not controvert the affidavits by counter-affidavits or formal denial, and it does not appear from the record that any argument was heard on them. . . . Glasser, in his affidavit, offered to prove the allegations contained therein, but the record is barren of any actual tender of proof on his part." There was therefore, Murphy concluded, no cause for ruling that an error had been committed in constituting the jury.[174]

Nevertheless, before reaching the conclusion that the defendant's claim had no legal substance, Murphy expounded at some length on the history of the jury and the "development" of the concept of "what a proper jury is." We began our history as a nation, Murphy wrote, with the common-law jury imported from England, but we then transformed it from a "privilege" (as Blackstone had labeled it) into a "right" through Article III of the Constitution and the Sixth Amendment. In

172. "Woman and the Law," *American Bar Association Journal* 26 (1940): 354.

173. Justice Felix Frankfurter dissented on a matter having nothing to do with the jury question.

174. *Glasser*, 87.

the same way, we transformed "whatever limitations were inherent in the historical common law concept of the jury as a body of one's peers."[175] The old-fashioned common-law notion had been replaced by a new view that was more "in harmony with our basic concepts of a democratic society and a representative government." Murphy's only source for this new view, however, was the Court's own decision, just two years earlier, in *Smith v. Texas*, with its intriguing reference to the jury as a "body truly representative of the community."

The question immediately arises: which part of the community was not represented on the *Glasser* jury or in the pool from which it was chosen? There were six women on the jury, but this by itself would not make it more representative, Murphy argued, if it could be proved that these jurors had been chosen in a way that turned the jury into the "organ of any special group or class." But since no demographic information had been offered about the social or economic backgrounds of the women on the jury, it was not clear which "class" or "group" they were representing—unless it might be the class of law-abiding and dutiful citizens, or, as L.T. S. referred to them (perhaps immodestly), "women of education and intelligence who . . . had become greatly interested in the problems of government" (as distinguished, presumably, from the "men chosen at random"). Nevertheless, Murphy concluded that if it were true, as Glasser charged, that the names of the women on the jury had been proposed by the League of Women Voters and that other women had been "systematically excluded," the defendant would have grounds for challenging the panel.

It is important to note, however, that no evidence was presented, and no claim made, that the League of Women Voters had proposed names for this particular jury. It had only suggested names for the list of qualified jurors or, possibly, the venire chosen for that particular session of the federal court. Nor was there any evidence that women who were not members of the league were barred from the venire or removed from it prior to the trial. The solicitation of names from "key men" in the community—a phrase that covered organizations as well as persons—had been standard practice since the nineteenth century and had never raised judicial eyebrows in the past (with the exception of those cases from the South in which jury commissioners offered the lame excuse that they were not personally acquainted with any "colored people"). Yet now, Justice Murphy was suggesting, the American understanding of the jury had evolved beyond such crude methods—in fact, it had evolved beyond the era of the common law altogether.

Murphy also stressed the significance of another claim made by Glasser, even though this one was as moot as the other: that members of the League of Women Voters had attended "jury classes whose lecturers presented the views of the prosecution."[176] Since the views presented could not have concerned Glasser and his

175. Ibid., 85.
176. Ibid., 84.

codefendants directly (the class had taken place prior to their indictments), the women had been exposed only to general remarks on the importance of the law in a free society and the central role played by jurors in the legal system. A Supreme Court justice could hardly find such views controversial or inappropriate: an indictment presupposes, after all, that the conduct alleged is a danger to society and ought to be discouraged. And it was unlikely that the women heard anything substantially different from what prospective jurors might be told by a court official prior to being selected. Such civics lectures, recommended by the ABA in its 1938 report, are now a regular feature of the jurors' orientation session when they arrive at court.[177]

Justice Murphy's concern apparently involved what had once been considered not only normal but also desirable: that the twelve citizens chosen for any given jury be "good and true," of "fair character" and "sound judgment," exemplary rather than typical. In his decision, Murphy paid homage to this old (and apparently obsolete) standard, conceding that those charged with selecting jurors "may exercise some discretion to the end that competent jurors may be called. But they must not allow their desire for competent jurors to lead them into selections which do not comport with the concept of the jury as a cross-section of the community." Even though officials might be operating from the highest motives, they must ensure an impartial jury:

> Deliberate selection of jurors from the membership of particular private organizations does not conform to the traditional requirements of jury trial. . . . [T]he dangers inherent in such a method of selection are the more real when the members of those organizations, from training or otherwise, acquire a bias in favor of the prosecution. The jury selected from the membership of such an organization is then not only the organ of a special class, but, in addition, it is also openly partisan.[178]

Here, one suspects, is the true target of Murphy's digression: the key-man system of soliciting names for the jury wheel, which relied, to varying degrees, on private organizations (although not on "particular" ones, but on many of them), as well as on civic leaders, ministers, teachers, and others likely to know enough about the characters of individuals to recommend them for jury duty. There is no question that such a system might be "biased" in the direction of sober, industrious, and literate citizens, who were once considered the ideal jurors.[179] Therefore,

177. This recommendation appears in the *1938 ABA Report on Jury Trials*, 560. Contemporary jurors are subjected to videotaped lectures on the importance of the jury system and the duties of the juror; the format is different, but the substance is much the same.

178. *Glasser*, 86.

179. Why such jurors would be *partisan*, however, is harder to understand. The word could refer, in this context, to party organizations; although the League of Women Voters

there is no way to avoid the conclusion that the *Smith* and *Glasser* decisions, and those that followed in their broadening wake, introduced not only a more insistent supervision of state jury systems by the federal courts but also a new principle of jury selection: the representative, or cross-section, jury. Justice Murphy's opinion contained just a hint of something new: that jury selection should no longer focus on competence; rather, it should be based on the social and demographic characteristics of prospective jurors, and even their philosophical orientations (if we take literally his warning about "bias in favor of the prosecution"). Although this new principle was introduced in the context of racial discrimination, it had, in theory and in practice, a much wider application. In fact, it was superfluous to the long effort to break down racial segregation in the jury system, whose landmark cases were entirely focused on fulfilling the promise of the Civil War Amendments: that slavery would not be replaced by some new form of racial oppression.

The old complaints about the jury system, from before the turn of the century and continuing through the 1930s, were not about "unrepresentative" juries but about the venire's lack of educated and professional men, owing to their exemption from jury service. Their absence meant that juries would be below average with respect to the qualities of judgment required of jurors. These complaints looked forward to reforms that would open the venire to the entire community, leaving the court with the task of sorting the qualified from the unqualified. Juries needed more doctors, lawyers, ministers, teachers, businessmen, skilled workers, farmers (outside of the harvest season), policemen, and factory managers. These arguments for a more inclusive venire rested on the claim that competent jurors would be easier to find if a wider net were cast, particularly among the educated and successful—precisely those most likely to secure exemptions. Still, these were not arguments for a venire that was a "cross section" of society and still less for one that was "representative." Always, the goal was competence, not representation. There were, after all, many groups that should not be represented in the venire: felons, illiterates, "repeat jurors," and those lacking the intelligence to follow the proceedings.

The *Smith* and *Glasser* decisions were unanimous on the jury standard (Justice Frankfurter dissented in the *Glasser* case on other grounds). But Justice Murphy prompted a significant dissent from off the bench when he defended the "representative" standard in a speech to the ABA shortly after *Glasser* was handed

---

was a critic of the Democratic Party organization then in control of Chicago, it was not affiliated with the Republican Party and counted many progressive Democrats among its members. "From the beginning," says a contemporary account, "no pains were spared to avoid the League's identification with parties. . . . To set out to be political, without being partisan . . . was a delicate undertaking." Marguerite M. Wells, *A Portrait of the League of Women Voters at the Age of Eighteen* (Washington, DC: National League of Women Voters, 1938), 16.

down. One of those present that evening was federal district court judge Merrill Otis, chairman of the ABA's Section on Judicial Administration. Otis replied to Murphy in an article published in the *American Bar Association Journal* in January 1943.[180] Noting that the "time-tried and time-tested method . . . of selecting jurors in federal courts has been challenged," Otis observed that this challenge came from the highest quarters. He was "concerned" (as were others, he claimed) by the "dictum" handed down by "a Supreme Court Justice" that "the desire for competent jurors was of secondary consequence. . . . Is there," Otis asked, "something inconsistent between the concepts historically involved in the institution of the jury and the desire that jurors shall be competent?"[181] Otis believed that those who spoke of cross sections really had in mind social and economic class, and since they knew that upper-class citizens were frequently excused because of their professions, what they really wanted, Otis insisted, was the increased participation of lower-class citizens. "Since they full well know that the middle brackets now adequately are represented, it is the lowest stratum for whose representation they are most concerned. These gentlemen need juries of the weak and ignorant."[182]

But Otis was convinced that a different understanding of "cross section" was possible, one that operated "horizontally" rather than "vertically." This interpretation of "cross section" recognized "that the community is made up of many segments. White and black. Catholics and Protestants. Men who work mostly with their brains and men who work mostly with their hands. A hundred segments. *In every segment there are men of outstanding intelligence and integrity.* . . . Let juries be selected from the intelligent and upright in each segment, with no segment systematically excluded."[183] No other understanding of the phrase "representative of the community" could be justified, Otis claimed, because of what jurors must do. "The jury's job is not a simple job. It requires unusual mental qualities. But the juror must also have the moral qualities of a judge [including] integrity and moral courage in a high degree." Otis then cited Blackstone's rule that juries must be composed of "sensible and upright jurymen." "I am not willing," he said, "to concede that our conception of what a jury ought to be is something inferior to the jury of the common law." In fact, he pointed out, state statutes confirmed the common-law conception that jurors must be "good men and true"—"sober, discreet, judicious; intelligent, well-informed, experienced; esteemed in the communities in which they live for character, integrity and sound judgment."[184]

180. Hon. Merrill E. Otis, "Selecting Federal Court Jurors," address delivered before the Section of Judicial Administration, American Bar Association, *American Bar Association Journal* 29 (January 1943): 19–21.

181. Ibid., 19.

182. Ibid., 20.

183. Ibid., emphasis in original.

184. Ibid.

So how would such juries be chosen? Otis compared the "every man is fit" system with the "selective" system. Under the former, everyone who was not obviously unfit would be thrown into the jury pool, and names would be picked at random. Under the latter system, "the jury commissioner and the clerk, whom the judges have named . . . ascertain, by inquiry of citizens who are most outstanding for intelligence and character, what citizens in the several communities are reputed to be men of intelligence and character. So they gather perhaps a thousand names. . . . No other system possibly can secure jurors of the highest quality."[185] Why would some people oppose this system and wish for another? Some claimed that such juries were easily packed, but Otis denied that this had been a problem in the federal courts. Others, "for selfish reasons, do not wish jurors of intelligence and integrity." Here, Otis cited the prosecution of the Pendergast machine in Missouri, which had been successful, he claimed, only because a challenge to this more selective way of choosing jurors had been rejected by the Court of Appeals.[186]

Perhaps the circumstances of the *Glasser* case threw these issues into sharper relief: there was something almost Brechtian in the defendants' insistence on being tried by a jury purged of those committed to law enforcement or tutored in the requirements of jury service.[187] Perhaps Otis heard in Glasser's plea the echoes of defendants past or the lawyerly tricks that had helped keep them out of prison. Whatever the reason, Otis's lament was prophetic: there is no clearer portrayal of the difference between the old and the new understanding of the jury system than the contrast between the "every man is fit" and the "selective" methods for filling the jury wheel. The former—the guiding principle of the Jury Selection and Service Act of 1968—has become so much a part of the conventional wisdom that many are surprised at how new it is. The latter has been firmly (but unfairly) associated with various disreputable practices (such as racial discrimination) and antiquated notions (male-only juries) for which it bears no responsibility.

Four years later, the issue of "class bias" in jury selection came up again. This time, it involved a question vital to the traditional discretion exercised by state officials over jury selection, prompting a spirited defense of the traditional arrangement from the bench. *Thiel v. Southern Pacific Railway*[188] concerned an apparently deranged (or perhaps larcenous) passenger who had jumped out the window of a moving railway car and then filed a civil suit to recover damages—a "slip and fall" case taken to the extreme. Thiel's argument was that the railroad should have known that he was "out of his normal mind" and taken appropriate measures to

185. Ibid.

186. Ibid., 21.

187. Glasser's argument about the "pro-prosecution" point of view almost anticipates the complaints of critical legal theory that the law is merely (and necessarily) the agent of the powerful.

188. Thiel v. Southern Pacific Railway Co., 328 U.S. 217 (1946).

guard or restrain him. But before the trial could get under way, Thiel challenged the method by which the jury lists had been compiled, contending that his jury had been chosen from a list that consisted "mostly" of "business executives or those having the employer's viewpoint. . . . thus giving a majority representation to one class or occupation and discriminating against other occupations and classes . . . particularly the employees and those in the poorer classes." The trial court denied this motion, and a jury was chosen; Thiel then challenged the jury itself, on the same grounds of "class bias." The court again denied his motion, the trial was held, and the jury found in favor of the railway. In rejecting Thiel's motion for a new trial, the court pointed out that five of the twelve jurors had been members of the "employee class" and might be expected to show sympathy for "people who belong to the working or employee class." The Ninth Circuit affirmed the lower court's decision, but the Supreme Court agreed to consider the question "whether petitioner's motion to strike the jury panel was properly denied."[189]

In introducing his opinion, Justice Murphy reiterated what had become the conventional wisdom: that the "American tradition of trial by jury . . . necessarily contemplates an impartial jury drawn from a cross-section of the community," citing as authority for this tradition the *Glasser* and *Smith* rulings from four and six years earlier, respectively. This did not mean, Murphy conceded, that every jury must contain "representatives" from all "economic, social, religious, racial, political and geographical groups" in the district—an apparent response to Otis's observation that no single jury could possibly represent the great diversity of American society or even a single judicial district. Such demographic precision would "frequently" be impossible, Murphy agreed, but there must not be "systematic and intentional" exclusion of any group.[190] "Jury competence is an individual rather than a group or class matter." To ignore this truth would be to risk "class distinctions and discriminations that are abhorrent to the democratic ideals of trial by jury."[191]

Murphy acknowledged that although a state law creating an illegal classification could not be used to select a federal jury, "for the most part," jury qualifications and exemptions were state responsibilities. What, then, had been the error in the selection of the *Thiel* jury? The "undisputed evidence" showed, Murphy wrote, that the clerk of the court and the jury commissioner admitted that in making up the jury lists, they had deliberately excluded all those whose records indicated they worked for a daily wage.[192]

Property qualifications for jury service were common in the states well into the twentieth century and were one way of determining competence. California

189. Ibid., 220.
190. Ibid.
191. Ibid.
192. Ibid., 222.

did not use them, however, so they did not figure into *Thiel*. In that case, jury officials did not use an argument about competence to explain their exclusion of day laborers; instead, they used an argument based on their own convenience and the convenience of the laborers themselves. Jury officials had to get the right number of citizens in the right place and at the right time for jury duty; anything that obstructed this process (such as hearing individual appeals for exemption) slowed it down. Because the pay for jury service was just $4 per day, and day laborers could earn $10 a day, they always asked to be excused from jury duty, and judges always said yes—one case at a time. "And so," the jury commissioner testified, "in order to avoid putting names of people in who I know won't become jurors . . . I do leave them out."[193] The evidence showed, however, that laborers who were paid by the week or by the month, and even the wives of day laborers, were included on the jury lists.[194] Given this evidence, it was hard to justify the claim that the district's jury list had been purged of citizens sympathetic to the "workers' perspective."[195]

In his rejection of the local practice, Justice Murphy refused to acknowledge the administrative motives that encouraged it, insisting on what the jury commissioners had never denied: "one who is paid $3 a day may be as fully competent as one who is paid $30 a week, or $300 a month." The commissioners' concern was not the competence of the laborers but their desire to be excused. To this concern, Murphy had two responses. First, although a judge would be fully justified in "excusing a daily wage earner for whom jury service would entail an undue financial hardship," there could be no justification for a blanket exclusion of daily wage earners in the absence of any "effort [by the commissioners] to determine in advance which individual members of [this] class would suffer."[196] But that was precisely what the commissioners were trying to avoid—the effort of calling and processing jurors who were likely to suffer the exact same hardship, be excused by the judge, and have to be replaced, one at a time. Second, and of equal importance to the assertion of the new "cross-section" standard for the jury, Justice Murphy announced that since the trial court had failed to act properly when refusing to strike the jury panel, the Supreme Court was now forced to reverse the judgment "in the exercise of our power of supervision over the administration of justice in the federal courts." Not even the presence of five members of the laboring class on the jury could wipe away the original sin of excluding the day laborers.[197]

193. Ibid.

194. Ibid.

195. Justice Murphy claimed that the excluded category "constitute[d] a very substantial portion of the community," but his own footnote cites Census Bureau data showing that wage earners in manufacturing were only 5.5 percent of the population of the San Francisco County–Oakland industrial area in 1939. Ibid., 223, n. 3.

196. Ibid., 224.

197. Ibid., 225, citing McNabb v. United States, 318 U.S. 332 (1943). The Supreme Court

Justice Frankfurter's dissent (with Justice Stanley Reed concurring) began with this anomaly: that the jury was suspected of class or "property prejudice," despite the presence of five members of the "laboring class." Neither the district court nor the Ninth Circuit Court of Appeals had found anything amiss with the jury's verdict or with the way the jury had been constituted. No claim that the jury's selection had been manipulated in favor of a particular class or person had been made, and none, Frankfurter concluded, could have been sustained. "What is challenged is a long-standing practice adopted in order to deal with the special hardship which jury service entails for workers paid by the day."[198] In Frankfurter's view, what was being overturned was a humane practice, not a scheme to give control over trials to the rich and powerful. And he saw something else at work: involved in the background of the *Thiel* case was not a "constitutional issue" but a problem of "judicial administration." The issue on which the Court had divided was simply whether a long-established practice designed to "relieve the economically least secure" was reason enough to throw out a judgment "which is inherently without flaw."[199]

Frankfurter readily agreed that the jury must be drawn "from a pool broadly representative of the community as well as impartial in a specific case." No one could be excluded for reasons "unrelated to his fitness"—for example, because of the color of his skin. But groups could be excused, and frequently were, for reasons of public policy, such as "doctors, ministers, lawyers, and the like," without raising constitutional questions. The majority opinion conceded that "the choice of means by which unlawful distinctions and discriminations are to be avoided rests largely in the sound discretion of the trial courts and their officers." In other words, in a decentralized system, courts ought to be parsimonious in intruding into local administrative arrangements.

So the only proper question—"freed from all atmospheric innuendoes"—was this: did the district judge in this case abuse the discretion that is necessarily his in excusing, in advance, laborers for whom jury service would be a severe hardship, such that they would certainly be excused later? To conclude, as the majority did, that jury officials had done so and that their actions raised the specter of class

---

was unwilling, at the time, to follow Justice Murphy's argument about the "cross-sectional" ideal as far as he would have liked. In two decisions handed down in 1947 and 1948, the Court upheld the use of so-called blue-ribbon juries, deliberately chosen to include jurors with special professional or educational qualifications. In Fay v. New York (322 U.S. 261 [1947]) and Moore v. New York (333 U.S. 565 [1948]), the Court found that the use of special juries did not violate the equal protection clause of the Fourteenth Amendment. The dissents in both cases stressed the incompatibility of the blue-ribbon jury with the idea of a "representative jury."

198. *Thiel*, 226–227.

199. Ibid., 227.

bias was "unfair to the administration of justice," Frankfurter continued, "and no less unfair to a group of judges of long experience and tested fidelity." Had these workers appeared one by one, and had they been excused one by one, this judgment would not have been reversed. The exclusion of the day laborers did not remove a group that was likely to view the case differently from those weekly and monthly workers who had been chosen to serve. "And American society is happily not so fragmentized that those who get paid by the day adopt a different social outlook, have a different sense of justice, and a different conception of a juror's responsibility than their fellow workers paid by the week."[200]

No doubt, Frankfurter concluded, many changes in American society will require a "reexamination" of the jury system in the federal courts. But he recommended the Conference of Senior Circuit Judges and the House and Senate Judiciary Committees as the appropriate forums for the discussion of such reforms—a route much preferable to reform by "adjudication," which can deal with only one phase of an "organic problem," and only by reversing a judgment that is "free from intrinsic infirmity," jeopardizing other cases in which similar jury procedures were used. As Frankfurter stated, this "reminds too much of burning the barn in order to roast the pig."[201]

CENTRALIZING JURY SELECTION

The *Smith*, *Glasser*, and *Thiel* decisions came against the backdrop of not only the ABA study and recommendations from 1938 but also an investigation of the federal jury system by a special committee of the Conference of Senior Circuit Judges. This probe began in 1941 as part of the conference's broad investigation of the administration of the federal courts.[202] The jury committee was chaired by Judge John C. Knox, senior justice of the Southern District of New York, and Knox was closely identified with its recommendations and their public defense. The *Report to the Judicial Conference of Senior Circuit Judges of the Committee on Selection of Jurors* was completed in 1943, and its findings and recommendations would inform congressional action on the jury system for the next twenty-five years.[203]

200. Ibid., 227–230.

201. Ibid.

202. Another major part of this effort produced the Federal Rules of Criminal Procedure, adopted by Congress in 1946, after considerable debate.

203. Judicial Conference of the United States, Committee on Selection of Jurors, *Report to the Judicial Conference of Senior Circuit Judges of the Committee on Selection of Jurors* (1943); also known as the Knox Committee Report. This report is also discussed in Hickey, "Improvement of Jury System," 500–516, and William Wirt Blume, "Jury Selection Analyzed: Proposed Revision of Federal System," *Michigan Law Review* 42

The Knox Committee's proposals were directed at the two major complaints: that the quality of jurors in both state and federal courts was below average, and that jury selection standards varied chaotically from state to state and therefore (because of the conformity principle) from district to district in the federal courts. In fact, the conformity principle was implicated in both problems: since federal commissioners were forced to conform to state law, whatever corruption had worked its way into the state system corrupted the federal system as well. There was hope that the process might work in reverse: just as some states had reformed their civil procedures in response to the Federal Rules of Civil Procedure adopted in 1938, perhaps they might imitate federal jury reforms as well.[204] As we will see, this hope went largely unfulfilled.

Accordingly, the Knox Committee proposed to repeal the conformity principle, first by establishing a separate set of qualifications for jury service in federal courts, and then by creating an orderly method for choosing jurors in federal courts that would not be controlled by state jury officials. For the first time since the Judiciary Act of 1789, there would be exclusive federal control over federal juries, and the conformity principle would be formally abandoned. Legislation reflecting these principles was introduced in the Senate in the second session of the Seventy-Eighth Congress, but the Senate failed to act. The same legislation was introduced in the House during the first session of the Seventy-Ninth Congress, and hearings began in June 1945.

It immediately became clear that the main obstacle to the jury plan was the lingering devotion to federalism on the part of many members of Congress, who saw separate federal rules for jury qualification as a threat to states' rights. Some of this resistance came from political conservatives in the South and West, such as Hatton W. Sumners, a Mississippi Democrat who chaired the House Judiciary Committee, and Patrick McCarran, the Nevada Democrat who chaired the Senate Judiciary Committee until 1953. Some members were opposed to the inclusion of women on federal juries in states where women were barred from jury service

---

(1943–1944): 831. Judge Knox explained and defended the committee's recommendations in "Selection of Federal Jurors," *Journal of the American Judicial Society* 31 (1947): 9.

204. In his testimony before Congress on the Judicial Conference recommendations, Judge Knox made an explicit comparison to the success of the Federal Rules of Civil Procedure, which many states had adopted because they were "an improvement." He believed they might do the same thing with jury selection rules. "It seems to me that sooner or later we have got to establish a complete system of Federal courts run as the Congress thinks they should be run, and I think thereby the procedure in many of the States will sooner or later be definitely improved." *Improvement of the Jury System in Federal Courts. Hearings before the Committee on the Judiciary, House of Representatives, 79th Congress, 1st Session, on H.R. 3379, H.R. 3380, H.R. 3381, June 12 and 13, 1945* (Washington, DC: Government Printing Office, 1945), 6.

under state law. Farm-state legislators feared that farmers would be summoned at harvest time. Other members felt duty-bound to defend the independence of their states' judicial systems, however antiquated they might be. Many no doubt dreaded the deluge of complaints from outraged morticians, schoolteachers, actuaries, chiropodists, telegraph operators, and others with long-standing exemptions from jury duty. And always in the background was the unspoken but well-known obstacle of racial discrimination, mostly but not exclusively in the southern states. It would be far more difficult to preserve a whites-only jury system if there were a new standard for jury selection in federal courts. In fact, as the civil rights movement picked up steam in the late 1950s, it campaigned to remove all administrative discretion from the process of jury selection, a goal completely at odds with both the letter and the spirit of the Knox Committee reforms.

The specific reforms proposed by the Knox Committee, contained in three separate bills, were relatively straightforward. The first bill would establish simple and uniform qualifications for jurors in all federal courts. All citizens aged twenty-one or older would be eligible for service, with the following exceptions:

- Anyone who had been convicted of a felony or a misdemeanor involving moral turpitude.
- Anyone who could not read, write, speak, and understand the English language.
- Anyone who suffered from a mental or physical infirmity "rendering efficient jury service" impossible—a fact to be established by the jury commission or the court.
- Anyone who had served on a jury in the past year.
- Active-duty members of the armed forces.
- Public officials "actively engaged in the discharge of their official duties."

In addition to these disqualifications, persons or groups might be temporarily exempted if, in the court's opinion, service would impose "undue hardship" (a concession to farmers). There was, however, no mention of gender in these disqualifications, and no concession (except for the "undue hardship" provision) to the legion of "special" and "essential" professions and occupations whose lobbyists had secured exemptions under state law. Morticians and bridge tenders might escape service on a state jury, but they would no longer be excused from service on a federal jury.[205]

The second bill established a process for appointing part-time and, if justified by the volume of business, full-time jury commissioners to administer the jury selection system. The commissioners would be appointed by, and accountable to, the senior district judge; they and the court clerk (also appointed by the judge) would constitute the jury commission. The third bill raised the fees paid to jurors to $4

205. Ibid., 1–2.

per day, and up to $10 per day for trials lasting more than a month. Jurors would also be compensated for travel and lodging expenses.[206] The substance of these two bills had been on the reform agenda for decades. The 1879 Jury Selection Act had authorized, without requiring, the appointment of jury commissioners in federal districts, and both the ABA and the Conference of Senior Circuit Judges believed that a professionally administered jury system would be much more efficient, and this would require full-time staff serving under the direction of the court. The obsolete fees paid to jurors had also been a source of complaint for decades.[207]

In his testimony before the House Judiciary Committee in 1945, Judge Knox summarized the broad purpose of these reforms. To ensure that jurors were "truly representative of the community, the sources from which they are selected should include all economic and social groups. From whatever sources drawn, those chosen should possess as high a degree of intelligence, morality, integrity, and common sense as can be found by those who make the selection."[208] Here, Knox came down firmly on the side of Judge Otis in his quarrel with Justice Murphy: a sound selection process takes the best people available from the many "segments" of society and from the many walks of life in the district. For this reason, nearly all adults should be qualified, except for illiterates, felons, and the severely disabled: the net should be cast as widely as possible before the culling begins.

But after automatically qualifying nearly everyone, the Conference of Senior Circuit Judges recommended the establishment of an administrative mechanism that gave a certain degree of discretion (how much would soon be in dispute) when choosing the names to be placed in the jury wheel. Jury selection, in the conference's opinion, was a matter of selecting from the widest possible field those citizens who displayed the qualities necessary for jury service. This was the reason for establishing a professional jury commission. The brunt of the criticisms since the turn of the century had been that jury selection was haphazard, that it was left to part-time and overworked court clerks, and that the jury pool had been severely depleted by unnecessary exemptions. To find better jurors, it would be necessary to broaden the search and then professionalize the sorting process to make it truly and effectively selective.

Choosing the sources from which names were taken, Knox argued, should be "entrusted to the good faith of the clerk and jury commissioner, acting under

206. Ibid., 2–3.

207. Congress did not raise jury fees in federal court until 1949, when they were increased from $4 to $7 per day. 63 Stat. 411, Act of July 14, 1949, chap. 333. The $4 fee had been established in 1937, after being reduced in 1932 in response to the collapse of federal revenues during the Depression. See *The Jury System in the Federal Courts: Report of the Judicial Conference Committee on the Operation of the Jury System*, ed. Shackelford Miller Jr. (St. Paul, MN: West Publishing Co., 1960), 81. Jurors are currently paid $40 per day in federal courts; the fee increases to $50 a day if the trial lasts for more than a week.

208. *Improvement of the Jury System*, 15.

the direction of the district judge." Nevertheless, the conference proposed a set of guidelines for the court to follow in the exercise of its good-faith discretion. The sources should "include all groups in the community"; race, social standing, and economic status should be considered "only to the extent necessary" to prevent discrimination. And quite clearly, women would be called to jury service in federal courts, even if they were not qualified, or were automatically exempted, under state law.[209]

Before Knox got very far into his testimony, he was interrupted by Chairman Sumners, who observed, "What we are up against, Judge Knox, is that we represent people of the various States" who will object to a federal jury procedure "different from that which the people of the States are accustomed to." His particular concern was that the bill, "if enacted, would make women . . . eligible for jury service" in states where they were currently disqualified.[210] Conceding that this was so, Knox encouraged Sumners to take the long view: "That is quite true, and of course it is inevitable that that is going to be the fact throughout the country." (It was not yet a fact, however, in Sumner's home state of Mississippi; nor was it a fact in Massachusetts, where women served for the first time in 1951.) The judge urged the chairman, and others opposed to the inclusion of women, not only to accept the inevitable but also to acknowledge that women had proved themselves to be capable jurors in the states where they were already qualified and that their inclusion was especially important, given the wartime shortage of men.[211]

What Knox was most insistent upon was the need for better jurors. The jury system, he testified, was "one of the really great achievements of English and American jurisprudence," and it should not be "impaired and frittered away." But this would be its fate if the quality of jurors could not be improved. First, this would mean bringing back those who were now exempted: "But where, I inquire, are high intelligence, sound judgment, and wide experience to be found when persons with these qualifications are either exempt from service or flee from it as though it were the wrath of God!" The result of all these exemptions was that "millions of persons, possessing the best and most intelligent brains in all the land, are relieved by law of the duty of aiding the courts in their search for justice."[212]

Here, Judge Knox was perhaps being deliberately provocative. The comment about "best brains" may have been an oblique reference to the "everyone is fit" theory of jury selection criticized by Judge Otis. "I am told, from time to time," Knox said, "that the selection of jurors should be a democratic process and that

209. The exclusion of women was not limited to the South. In 1945 women were also excluded from jury service in Massachusetts, New Hampshire, New Mexico, Oklahoma, South Dakota, and Wyoming. Ibid., 39.

210. Ibid., 6.

211. Ibid., 7.

212. Ibid., 8, 11.

persons who serve [in my court] are hand-picked. . . . I cannot do otherwise than admit my guilt." Explaining his meaning, the judge observed that in the Southern District of New York, "We [judges] select [the jurors]. We interview them and find out whether we feel that they are qualified for intelligent, worth-while jury service."[213]

Emmanuel Celler (D-NY) asked whether the judge thought the phrase "hand-picked" might be a little "improvident," to which Knox made the following reply, which deserves to be quoted at length because of the way it frames a conflict that would prove to be more durable than the conflicts over states' rights, female jurors, and racial discrimination:

> Let me tell you why [judges select jurors]. If, in making up our jury lists, my court were to follow suggestions that have been made to me, our panels would be filled not only with the halt, the lame, and the blind, but also with the venal and corrupt. For example, men whom I respect have said that the jurors should not be selected but should be taken willy-nilly from the voting registers. That suggestion was given a trial, and with this result: in some sections of [New York City] more than 20 percent of the persons so summoned were found to be nonresidents of the buildings from which they were registered. A further large percentage was found to be made up of persons who only with difficulty could speak and understand the English language.[214]

Furthermore, many of those who were, in the judge's estimation, fully qualified were the sole owners of small businesses "to whom jury service would mean ruination." The voter register experiment was therefore abandoned. "I had the thought that in the district court the public was entitled to jurors who were something more than election-day floaters, the habitués of district clubhouses, and the illiterate and ignorant."[215]

When asked how the lists of prospective jurors were compiled in his court, Knox described a modified version of the key-man system. The jury commissioners "interview people, get lists of names from business houses, consult directories of various kinds, telephone books, club directories, trade journals. . . . They send out for these persons and ask them to come down to be interviewed . . . and [we] form an estimate as they are examined as to whether or not they appear to be fair-minded persons." The names of those who passed this examination were then placed on the jury list. Based on the ABA's research into the operation of the jury system in federal courts, some variation of this process was used "to a greater or lesser extent" throughout the federal system in the 1940s, as it had been

213. Ibid., 11. That is, the judge and the clerks qualified jurors for the jury list; they did not choose them for particular trials.

214. Ibid.

215. Ibid.

in decades past. Later in his testimony, Judge Knox asserted that there were, at the time, between 12,000 and 14,000 names on the list in his district, which he conceded was "quite an accumulation."[216]

Representative Raymond Springer (R-IN) wanted to know about "working people and farmers," and he received Knox's assurance that "we try to get them as best we can, and we have a great many of them" (by "them," he undoubtedly meant "working people," there being no farmers in New York City). And there would have been more working people on the jury lists were it not for the exemptions for employees of the war industries. "What we have in mind is that every economic and social group in the community shall be represented upon the jury list."[217]

When the Knox Committee Report was taken up in the Senate, the debate focused less on the makeup of jury panels and more on the threat to states' rights posed by the end of the conformity principle. The spoken objections concerned the impaneling of women in states where they could not serve and the elimination of the "hardship" exemptions doled out by state legislatures to special-interest groups. But as in the House, the unspoken problem of racial discrimination loomed in the background.[218]

The Senate debate, however, also reaffirmed the two requirements for federal jury selection that were now becoming part of a consensus: to draw jurors from all walks of life and all segments of the community, *and* to find better jurors than the current system was delivering. In fact, the second goal—better jurors—was explicitly connected to the first goal—a broader collection of names from which to choose. Under the current system, one senator observed, the large number of state exemptions meant that the rules "often limit jury duty to those who are least qualified to serve."[219] It all depended on how the original set of names was winnowed to remove those who, though formally qualified, were found to be unsuitable. In his House testimony, Judge Knox had insisted on this point, observing that "jurors should not be chosen haphazardly" and that "the intelligent selection of jurors . . . is not only eminently desirable, but necessary." It is important to note that Knox made this comment in the context of a discussion of racial discrimination: the "careful" selection of jurors, rather than the "haphazard" methods now in force, would reduce rather than protect discrimination related to "social, political, and racial differences." But whether this sorting could be done properly—indeed, whether sorting of any kind should be done—would soon become the chief bone of contention in the debate over improving the jury system.[220]

216. Ibid., 12–13.

217. Ibid., 13–14.

218. See "The Legislative History of the 1948 Judicial Code as It Relates to the Process of Selection of Federal Jurors," appendix A in Rabinowitz v. United States, 366 F.2d 34 (1966), 60–67.

219. Ibid.

220. *Improvement of the Jury System*, 15.

Both the Seventy-Ninth and Eightieth Congresses rejected the Judicial Conference's proposal to abandon the conformity principle.[221] What became the Judicial Code of 1948 continued the federal practice of disqualifying any juror not qualified for jury service in the highest state court—a defeat of the Knox report's most ambitious reform.[222] Other Judicial Conference recommendations were more successful. The appointment of full-time jury commissioners was authorized, and juror pay was increased. By default, however, Congress made no changes to the existing arrangements for collecting the names of prospective jurors or for vetting those names before they were placed in the jury wheel. Whatever practices were being followed in the 1940s therefore continued into the 1950s—including the various manifestations of the key-man system, as well as the illicit practices that kept black citizens off state and federal juries in the South.

To ascertain what those practices actually were at the end of the 1940s, Arthur Vanderbilt, chief justice of the New Jersey Supreme Court, conducted a study of judicial administration in the nation's courts and published the results in 1949.[223] Judge Vanderbilt was interested in determining to what extent the ABA's 1938 recommendations on jury reform had been acted on in the states. A secondary interest was the impact of the Judicial Conference (Knox Committee) Report on jury selection in the federal courts, even though the Judicial Code of 1948 was not yet a year old. The ABA and Knox reports were in agreement about the major failings of the jury system, and both suggested that the system might wither away if it were not quickly reformed. Both cited the poor quality of jurors as one of the system's major failings, and they agreed about the reason: the "haphazard" administration of the jury system in the states, and the wholesale exemptions handed out to the most intelligent and experienced citizens. Both urged the elimination of most exemptions and recommended full-time jury commissioners, along with questionnaires and interviews of prospective jurors to weed out those who were genuinely not fit for "efficient service."[224] Both reports insisted that the selection of jurors from a "cross section" of the community was not inconsistent with the selection of those "most fit" for service.[225] The main difference between the two reports was that the Judicial Conference went a step farther than the ABA by calling for the formal abolition of the conformity principle.

221. The Conference of Senior Circuit Judges was renamed the Judicial Conference of the United States in 1946, during the Seventy-Ninth Congress.

222. While Congress was debating the Judicial Conference's recommendations, the Supreme Court handed down its decision in Ballard v. United States (329 U.S. 187 [1946]), which held that the exclusion of women from a federal jury in a state where women were qualified for jury service would be grounds for reversal.

223. Arthur Vanderbilt, *Minimum Standards of Judicial Administration* (New York: Law Center of New York University, 1949).

224. Ibid., 146 ff.

225. See *1938 ABA Report on Jury Trials*, 561.

Vanderbilt found that since the release of the Judicial Conference report in 1943, a number of states had moved in the direction of a less haphazard and more deliberate process of jury selection. In twenty states, some form of investigation was now taking place before names were placed in the jury wheel, the goal being to determine "whether the juror is the type of person who . . . has qualities of intelligence, experience, education, etc. that would make him a satisfactory juror." In ten states, jurors were qualified based on officials' personal knowledge of the candidates; in five states, information supplied by others was the only information relied on. Two states used a combination of interviews, questionnaires, personal knowledge, knowledge of others, and even (in California) IQ tests. In only eleven states did the investigation focus exclusively on formal, objective requirements. Vanderbilt concluded from this survey that in only "a few states" had the courts responded by establishing a truly "scientific or businesslike" method of judging the competence of prospective jurors. Nevertheless, in at least twenty states, some kind of investigation, however unscientific, was conducted before jurors' names were added to the wheel. The ABA's recommendation that state courts establish jury commissions to administer the selection process apparently fell on fertile ground, as jury commissioners chose the names for the jury wheel in thirty-four out of forty-eight states. Yet in all or part of twenty-four states, names for the jury wheel were still being chosen by elected officials at the county or municipal level, and in some cities, names for the jury wheel in municipal court were still being chosen by mayors.[226]

THE CIVIL RIGHTS ACT OF 1957

While jury reforms made their way, fitfully, through Congress and the states, the civil rights movement intensified its campaign to secure voting rights in southern states, and this battle necessarily involved a parallel campaign against segregated juries. As the Eisenhower administration's civil rights bill was moving through Congress in 1956 and 1957, the jury selection practices of the southern states became a natural target. The bill that became the Civil Rights Act of 1957—the first such act since Reconstruction—was mostly a voting rights bill. But to enforce voting rights in the South, it would be necessary to discipline state officials who were either actively engaged in obstructing the registration of black voters or ignoring such obstruction. Those officials who ignored a federal court order could be tried for contempt of court, but their cases would almost certainly be tried before all-white juries. The source of this problem was the conformity principle, forcing federal courts to use jury lists provided by state officials, even when those lists were known to be corrupt or incomplete. In fact, even some *federal* jury com-

226. Vanderbilt, *Minimum Standards*, 183–188.

missioners in the South used their discretion in ways that would avoid offending "local customs."

The administration's bill accordingly proposed something drastic: to withdraw the right to a jury trial in federal contempt cases involving voting rights.[227] This unprecedented assault on the "ancient jury right" split the bill's liberal supporters in Congress and inspired a debate in the Senate over the question of fixing rather than circumventing the jury system. Senator Joseph O'Mahoney, a liberal Democrat from Wyoming, proposed an amendment, cosponsored by Senator Estes Kefauver of Tennessee, restoring jury trials in contempt cases—a move denounced by the administration as an effort to "gut" the civil rights bill. In response to this concern, Senator Frank Church of Idaho, also a liberal Democrat, introduced amended language aimed at preventing the discriminatory administration of jury selection in federal courts by, in effect, abolishing the conformity principle. "There is no reason," Church argued, "why Congress should not modify Federal law so as to safeguard against discrimination on the basis of race, color, or creed, in the selection of jurors who are to serve in Federal courts."[228]

Church described three objectives of the new language he proposed for the O'Mahoney amendment. First, it would establish "reasonable and uniform qualifications" for jurors in federal court—an aim "in complete accord with the generally accepted principle that Federal rules should govern Federal practice."[229] In other words, federal courts would manage their own jury selection procedures and leave state practices alone, a compromise aimed at securing the maximum number of Democratic votes in Congress. Second, the amendment would place federal jury selection "entirely in the hands of the Federal courts, thus avoiding practices under State law that, in effect, may systematically exclude citizens from jury duty in Federal courts on account of race or color." The effective abolition of the conformity principle would thus disentangle the federal courts from racially discriminatory state practices.[230]

These objectives were fully consistent with the letter and spirit of the Knox Committee Report, and in that sense, they continued the tradition of jury reform stretching back to the turn of the century—with two exceptions. First, missing from Church's defense was any reference to what had always been the other side of the coin of "inclusiveness"—namely, the need to select for "intelligence" or "competence" or some other nonobjective criteria essential to an "efficient" jury deliberation. Second, Church's third objective added something new: the proclamation of "another civil right—the right to serve as a juror," which would now

227. See *Rabinowitz*, appendix B, 48 ff., for a summary of the legislative history of the Civil Rights Act of 1957.

228. Ibid., 48–49.

229. Ibid., 49.

230. Ibid.

be conferred on "a large segment" of black Americans who had long been denied that right.[231] The proclamation of a "right to serve as a juror" was as surprising as the Eisenhower administration's plan to end jury trials in federal voting rights cases. The latter certainly would have raised constitutional questions, had it been enacted, and it might not have survived scrutiny by the Warren Court. The former, though it was included in the bill as adopted, has been ignored by the Supreme Court, except to dismiss it as moot. The Court has repeatedly confirmed that the jury right protected by the Constitution belongs to defendants in criminal trials and to parties in civil cases, not to prospective jurors. Only those with cases before the courts may challenge the exclusion of any person or class of persons.[232]

Of lasting importance in the Church-O'Mahoney amendment, therefore, was not what it added but what it subtracted. By failing to affirm the need for intelligent jurors, the Civil Rights Act of 1957 planted in the legislative history "evidence" that Congress no longer wanted jury commissioners to select for qualities that had long been considered essential to the efficient functioning of the jury. And a decade later, a federal appeals court handed down a decision that used this evidence to craft a new view of the common-law jury and how its members should be selected.

231. Ibid.

232. The Supreme Court has never identified a constitutional right to serve on a jury—only a right not to be excluded from the jury list or the venire on the grounds of race, color, ethnicity, or gender. Gertner and Mizner's textbook states that the Court's ruling in Powers v. Ohio (499 U.S. 400 [1991])—that a defendant not of a juror's race may challenge that juror's exclusion from the jury—"elaborated further on the evolving right of the public to serve on juries" (*Law of Juries*, 144–145). There has been no evolution in that direction since 1991.

4

The Postmodern Jury

> Integrity, intelligence, sound judgment, a sense of responsibility—in short, all those qualities of a first-class citizen which cause a man to be esteemed by his fellows—are to be found among the unheralded just as often as among the prominent.
>
> —Form letter to "suggesters" from the Jury Commission, US District Court, District of Connecticut, 1960, soliciting names of prospective jurors

> It is not feasible for the courts to conduct a general inquiry into the fitness of the jurors in the court room and in practice they do not do so.
>
> —Clarence N. Callender, *The Selection of Jurors: A Comparative Study of the Methods of Selection and the Personnel of Juries in Philadelphia and Other Cities*

> I don't like the idea of lawyers selecting jurors.
>
> —William Marbury, Esq., testimony before Senate Judiciary Committee, 1967

WHO IS QUALIFIED?

The Civil Rights Act of 1957 finally established uniform qualifications for federal jurors, but it left standing the right of state legislatures to establish jury qualifications for their own courts—within the latitude permitted by the federal Constitution. This meant that the long-standing tradition of highly diverse state jury practices would continue. Some of these state variations were relics (the exclusion or exemption of women), some were merely quaint (farmers exempted at harvest time), and some were illegal (the de facto exclusion of blacks). This hodgepodge of practices had been one of the main reasons for seeking to abolish the conformity principle in the first place, a goal that the Conference of Senior Circuit Judges (renamed the Judicial Conference in 1948) had been seeking since at least 1941.[1] Congress, however, had refused to go along, rejecting Judicial Conference proposals in each session from 1941 to 1957.[2]

1. 1 Stat. 73, sec. 29, para. 1789. See the discussion in chapter 3 and Hon. Arthur J. Stanley Jr., "Federal Jury Selection and Service before and after 1968," *F.R.D.* 66 (1975): 375.

2. The legislative history is summarized in Rabinowitz v. United States, 366 F.2d 34 (1966), appendix A, 64.

One ostensible reason for this refusal was the reluctance to qualify women for federal jury service in those states where they were disqualified or exempted under state law.[3] But by 1957, these restrictions had been abandoned by all but three states, and the traditional objection to female jurors had lost much of its earlier support in Congress.[4] What remained, however, was southern legislators' fear that federal control of jury selection would end the de facto exclusion of African Americans from jury lists, not just for federal trials but for state trials as well. Thus the congressional compromise: new rules for the federal courts, while leaving state jury laws untouched.[5]

The achievement of uniformity in federal jury selection meant that the federal courts would now be free to manage their own jury selection procedures, without having to honor the quaint, inefficient, and sometimes illegal practices of the states—although it was hoped that the federal standards would inspire emulation at the state level. In federal courts, therefore, statutory exemptions would be kept to a minimum, and the broad qualifications first proposed in 1948 would now apply throughout the federal system. Federal jury law would bar only a few categories from jury service: noncitizens, illiterates, convicted felons, and the physically or mentally unfit.[6] A separate statute authorized exemptions for active-duty military personnel, members of police and fire departments, and public officials "actively engaged" in their duties.[7] Everyone else would be *qualified*. Whether they would also be *suitable* was another matter, and this would be determined, as in the past, by the jury commissioners operating in each federal district, under the supervision of the district judge. Federal jury selection would continue to be selective after 1957, and it would continue to involve discretion.

This was entirely consistent with the view of the Judicial Conference. Judge John C. Knox of the Southern District of New York, the principal author of the conference's 1943 report, had achieved brief notoriety in the 1940s by claiming that in his New York City court, the names being placed in the jury wheel had been "hand-picked" after the careful examination of all prospective jurors by the jury commission. He insisted that the alternative method being urged by critics—

3. Ibid.

4. Several states qualified women but either provided blanket exemptions (in which case a woman would have to volunteer to serve) or automatically granted hardship exemptions to women who asked for them. As a result, women were underrepresented on the jury lists in many states.

5. The main focus of the law was not juries but voting. The main provisions of the Civil Rights Act created a US Commission on Civil Rights (section 101) and established federal civil penalties for interfering with the right to vote, even "under color of law" (section 131). Pub. L. No. 85-315, 71 Stat. 634 (1957).

6. 28 U.S.C. § 1861.

7. Ibid., 1862, 1863.

random selection from voter lists—would fill the jury wheel with the names of "thugs," "illiterates," and "club house floaters."[8]

Federal jury selection would still be selective, but there would now be a greatly expanded pool of candidates, in keeping with the emerging consensus that jury selection should be a process of choosing the "best" from each identifiable "segment" of the population. In all its reports issued between 1943 and passage of the Jury Selection and Service Act of 1968,[9] the Judicial Conference stressed the same combination of factors required for an effective jury system: that jurors be "drawn from every economic and social group in the community" and that "those chosen to serve as jurors should possess as high a degree of intelligence, morality, integrity, and common sense, as can be found."[10] The 1960 report hailed passage of the Civil Rights Act of 1957, celebrating its jury provisions and noting that, at last, "large groups of intelligent, qualified citizens, including women and professional people, previously unavailable [to the federal courts] . . . under State law have been rendered eligible for federal jury service."[11]

8. *Improvement of the Jury System in Federal Courts. Hearings before the Committee on the Judiciary, House of Representatives, 79th Congress, 1st Session, on H.R. 3379, H.R. 3380, H.R. 3381, June 12 and 13, 1945* (Washington, DC: Government Printing Office, 1945), 11. In 1949, during the trial of Communist Party leaders accused of violating the Smith Act, critics of the prosecution drew 3,000 protesters to Madison Square Garden to denounce the grand jury and to demand "a truly democratic system of jury selection." "Attack U.S. Jury System," *New York Times*, March 4, 1949, 22; see also "Challenge to Jury in Red Trial Ended," *New York Times*, March 2, 1949, 17. Lawyers for the defendants had demanded an investigation of Judge Knox's insistence on "hand-picking" the jurors (i.e., examining them for fitness rather than selecting them at random from the voting lists). One of the young lawyers who worked on the Smith Act prosecutions was Communist Party member Victor Rabinowitz. Nearly twenty years later, he would defend his daughter, Joni Rabinowitz, in the case that inspired the Jury Selection and Service Act of 1968, which ended the use of nonobjective jury selection standards. The Rabinowitz family triumphed over Judge Knox, although it took another generation to do so. Victor Rabinowitz discusses his daughter's case in *Unrepentant Leftist: A Lawyer's Memoir* (Urbana: University of Illinois Press, 1996), 255–276. The Rabinowitz case is discussed below.

9. 28 U.S.C. § 1861, discussed in detail below.

10. This language from the Knox Committee Report is quoted in *The Jury System in the Federal Courts: Report of the Judicial Conference Committee on the Operation of the Jury System*, ed. Shackelford Miller Jr. (St. Paul, MN: West Publishing Co., 1960), 17. The official title of the Knox Committee Report is *Report to the Judicial Conference of Senior Circuit Judges of the Committee on Selection of Jurors* (Washington, DC: Judicial Conference of the United States, 1943).

11. *Jury System in the Federal Courts*, 17. See the Judicial Conference's full-length reports on the jury system in the federal courts (1958 and 1960) and its annual reports (1953–1960) on the judicial system as a whole, which paid more limited attention to jury selection. Judicial Conference of the United States, *Operation of the Jury System in the*

However, before any selection could begin, a list would have to be constructed. How the jury list was put together would play a decisive role in what followed—another argument for abandoning the conformity principle. For at least a generation, there had been growing dissatisfaction among judges and attorneys with how the states were performing this task. In addition to giving away too many statutory exemptions—which could now be ignored in federal court—state jury officials were accused of being either careless or discriminatory, using out-of-date lists, or, especially in the South, deliberately omitting the names of black citizens, regardless of their qualifications. For this reason, the Knox Committee Report had urged federal jury commissioners not to rely on the lists supplied by the states.[12] The main argument for the employment of full-time jury commissioners at competitive salaries was that they would be able to supplement or even supersede the sloppy or illegal lists provided by the states. Therefore, jury selection in federal court often started with state lists (usually voter registration lists) but did not rely on them exclusively. Voter lists were sometimes supplemented with state and local census records, tax assessors' lists, city directories, or even membership lists of private organizations such as the Rotary Club.

Another method of finding names for federal jury wheels was to ask so-called key men in the community to recommend suitable citizens, a practice found in both state and federal courts. The Knox Committee did not condemn the key-man system but warned that in some states, this practice did not produce reliable lists—this may have been an oblique reference to the South. Instead, the committee made several suggestions to improve the management of the key-man system without abandoning it. First, those persons suggested by key men should be asked to complete a questionnaire to determine whether they were truly fit for service. Second, the key men should be "those citizens of the district who are mostly likely to be impartial and who are known to have a high sense of civil responsibility." And third, the same key men should not be asked repeatedly to suggest names. In its 1960 report the Judicial Conference noted its "general agreement" with this statement, showing that the conference did not believe the 1957 Civil Rights Act had abolished the key-man system or that its provisions would forbid the application of qualitative measures to the most comprehensive list of names.[13]

The key-man system had an important practical advantage for jury commissioners pressed to locate capable jurors: those making the recommendations presumably knew something about the persons they suggested, giving their rec-

---

Federal Courts (St. Paul, MN: West Publishing Co., 1958); *Jury System in the Federal Courts* (1960); Judicial Conference of the United States, Committee on the Operation of the Jury System, *Annual Reports*, 1953–1960.

12. Knox Committee Report, 24, cited in *Jury System in the Federal Courts*, 20.

13. Ibid., 20–21.

ommendations added credibility. The key men might be clergymen, businessmen, teachers, officers of service clubs, or officers of political parties or labor unions. They might know their nominees personally or only by reputation, but at least they knew something about these individuals that made them stand out from the crowd. In time, jury commissioners might come to rely on some key men more than others, based on the commissioners' perception of how well certain nominees performed as jurors. For these reasons, some version of the key-man system was used, along with other methods, to collect names for jury lists in most state and federal courts for most of the nineteenth century and well into the twentieth. In preparation for its 1960 report, the Judicial Conference conducted a survey of federal judges and found that the key-man system was "the most widely used" method of collecting names for federal jury lists. The same survey found that two-thirds of the federal districts administered questionnaires to prospective jurors "to eliminate jurors not having the statutory qualifications and to allow an exercise of discretion in selection."[14]

The long reliance on the key-man system suggests the importance of "subjective" qualities to the traditional theory of the jury system—qualities that could not be determined simply by looking at lists of names and addresses of voters or taxpayers or drawing jurors from among the bystanders at court. The qualities most sought, such as intelligence, integrity, morality, and common sense, could be found only by consulting those who knew, or at least knew of, the persons concerned. The alternative—personal examinations—was time-consuming and expensive, making it difficult for courts that used part-time jury commissioners who were paid (as late as 1960) no more than $5 per day.

Yet determining such information was critical, according to the Judicial Conference. It observed in its 1960 report that "greater care in the compilation of the list of jurors" was essential to the larger goal of jury reform, and it made a number of recommendations designed to achieve this end: the law should clarify the district judge's responsibility to supervise the work of the jury commission; questionnaires should be used "to supply information as to the qualifications of jurors," and, when feasible, such questionnaires should be supplemented by personal interviews; and the position of jury commissioner should be made full time where needed (e.g., in large cities). These reforms were essential "if the jury system is to be retained as a vital part of the administration of justice in the modern world."[15] Jury commissions operating with full-time clerks and commissioners, under the direct supervision of the district judge, would be able to conduct the kind of investigations needed to find jurors with the appropriate qualifications. "The . . . time and attention given to the process of jury selection and to per-

14. Ibid., 62–63.
15. Ibid., 11–12.

sonal interviews of prospective jurors will result in better selection."[16] Although it was imperative that the source lists "include all economic and social groups," the Judicial Conference argued that it was equally important that "there should be a weeding out of unqualified persons." A "perceptive jury commissioner can do this," but he would have to exercise some discretion, selecting the names of qualified persons "who . . . are intelligent, honest, fair-minded, of good reputation and capable of rendering satisfactory service"—a task that required "more information than is contained in a telephone book or a city directory."[17]

The 1960 report noted that there were many differences in the "mechanics of the jury system" in the federal districts, and for this reason, the Judicial Conference did not recommend "uniformity in these methods as the conditions in the districts also vary greatly." But the report commended the "efficiency with which the whole process is conducted in some places" and offered, as exhibit 3, an example "worthy of consideration." That example came from the District of Connecticut, and a summary of the procedure was prepared by the clerk of the district court, Gilbert C. Earl.[18] The Connecticut report is worth considering in some detail, for it highlights the very different jury selection regime instituted by the Jury Selection and Service Act just eight years later.

In Connecticut, Earl reported, the jury commission began the process of jury selection by first compiling a list of suggesters—a "number of citizens from a wide variety of backgrounds" who were thought to "have a wide acquaintance in their respective communities and [were] esteemed therein as persons of good character, approved integrity, sound judgment and fair education." The entire jury commission examined this list to "minimize the possibility" that any geographic area or any racial, religious, or occupational group had been "inadvertently discriminated against" when compiling the names. When all the commissioners agreed on the list of suggesters, the initial phase of the jury selection process was complete. The jury commission then wrote to the suggesters, asking them to "furnish to the Jury Commission the names of residents of their communities who, in their considered opinions, are qualified for jury service."[19] The commission's letter outlined what the suggesters should look for, first identifying the threshold qualifications for jury service (age, residence, literacy, and so forth—all required by the current federal law), but adding the following request:

> In addition to the statutory qualifications, please bear in mind that a prospective juror should be esteemed in his community as a person of good

16. Ibid., 40.

17. Ibid. Here, the word "qualified" sheds its technical meaning—"meeting the formal requirements of the statute"—and acquires its more common meaning of "competent or knowledgeable."

18. "Exhibit 3: Selection of Jurors by Jury Commission," ibid., 103–107.

19. Ibid., 103.

> character, approved integrity, sound judgment and fair education. In determining "esteem," please keep in mind that this does not require wide public recognition or high place. Integrity, intelligence, sound judgment, a sense of responsibility—in short, all those qualities of a first-class citizen which cause a man to be esteemed by his fellows—are to be found among the unheralded just as often as among the prominent.[20]

Once the suggesters returned their lists of names, the jury commission sent a letter to each person named, along with a questionnaire soliciting information to determine whether the person was eligible for service (e.g., whether he or she had served within the year or had a disability that might prevent effective service). As the questionnaires were returned, the commissioners examined them, and if further information was required, another letter was sent. Finally, the commissioners met to consider all the available information and to determine, for each name suggested, "whether or not such prospective juror meets all of the statutory standards for inclusion in the jury array." The names of those accepted and those rejected were then placed in separate files. The last step in the process was for the two jury commissioners, in the presence of witnesses and with the court reporter recording the proceedings, to take turns placing the index cards with the accepted names into the jury box, one at a time, until all the cards had been used or the quota had been reached for that session of the court.[21]

It is important to emphasize the general approval of the key-man system, even by the highest administrative tribunal in the federal judiciary, because the system was being pressured by a powerful trend in Supreme Court decisions.[22] These decisions were increasingly suspicious of the exercise of any discretion by jury officials in the process of selecting jurors, and not just in cases involving race. The 1946 decision in *Thiel v. Southern Pacific*[23] had rejected the wholesale exemptions traditionally given to day laborers, along with the commissioners' justification for those exemptions—namely, the administrative inconvenience of having to call men who were certain to ask for and be granted hardship exemptions, one at a time. The Court rejected this argument, featuring in its rejection one of the earliest proclamations of the "historic" standard of the "representative" jury.[24]

But the exclusion of blacks from jury lists in southern states was clearly the most dangerous and illegal exercise of administrative discretion, and from the late 1950s on, the problem of racial discrimination in jury selection increasingly

20. Ibid., 106.

21. Ibid., 104–105.

22. The key-man system was also generally supported in Congress, as the debate over the 1957 Civil Rights Act made clear.

23. Thiel v. Southern Pacific Railway Co., 328 U.S. 217 (1946).

24. See chapter 3 for a discussion of the *Thiel* decision and Frankfurter's dissent.

dominated Court rulings, law review articles, the legal strategy of the civil rights movement, and the reform agenda in Congress. As in so many other areas of American political and legal practice, the claims of equality and the assertion of administrative discretion were headed for a collision. And not surprisingly, the element of the jury system that came under the most intense scrutiny and criticism—at least outside the Judicial Conference, where it continued to receive some deference—was the key-man system of compiling jury lists.

THE CAMPAIGN AGAINST THE KEY-MAN SYSTEM

That the key-man system had its roots in a world very different from our own hardly needs mentioning, and like all systems involving discretion, it was subject to some fairly predictable abuses. By the time the system was abolished by the Jury Selection and Service Act of 1968, it had already been abandoned in about half the federal districts, replaced by random selection from various lists without any screening for subjective qualities of intelligence, morality, or common sense, following the lead not of the Judicial Conference but of a series of federal court decisions that continued the line of argument enunciated in *Smith*, *Glasser*, and *Thiel*.[25] Given the Judicial Conference's finding that the key-man system was the "most widely used" method of collecting names for federal juries in 1960, its rapid decline in the ensuing decade is notable.

By the mid-1960s, the most important failing of the key-man system—and of discretionary jury selection more generally—was its alleged complicity in the exclusion of black Americans from jury service, especially in state and federal courts in the South. In 1966 the Court of Appeals seemed to condemn the key-man system directly in *Rabinowitz v. United States*, insisting that the jury qualifications established by the Civil Rights Act of 1957 (citizenship, age, and residence) should be considered the *maximum* qualifications rather than the minimum.[26] The key-man system had survived the new jury selection rules established by the 1957 act because it was still possible for jury commissioners, having compiled lists of all those who met the minimum requirements, to select those who, in their opinion, also met the stricter standards imposed by the traditional view of jury service. But now, the Fifth Circuit argued, this ancient practice of imposing standards such as intelligence and moral character should be considered a violation of the law. The key-man system was thus rendered suspect in the federal courts, at least at the appellate level. By the time of its effective repeal by Congress, however, it had never been ruled unconstitutional by the Supreme Court.

The *Rabinowitz* case grew out of the civil rights movement's efforts to chal-

25. For a discussion of these cases, see chapter 3.
26. These qualifications are listed in section V of the 1957 act.

lenge the convictions of civil rights activists by all-white juries. A group of black demonstrators had been convicted by one such jury, and the Student Nonviolent Coordinating Committee organized sidewalk protests against one of the jurors, who owned a store in Macon, Georgia. When this group was charged, in federal court, with conspiracy to harass a federal juror (by picketing his store), they all denied being present at the demonstration; they were all subsequently indicted for perjury and convicted in district court. The defendants appealed on the grounds that the process for selecting the grand and petit jurors had unconstitutionally permitted jury commissioners to use their discretion in choosing names for the venire. Joni Rabinowitz was tried separately from her five codefendants, but because the legal questions were identical, the appeals court decided both cases at the same time.[27]

The *Rabinowitz* case was unlike the typical jury discrimination cases that characterized the sorry history of racial segregation in the southern legal system. For one thing, the grand jury that handed down the indictments included five black members out of twelve—a somewhat unusual circumstance in the South, even in federal courts. The charges did not carry long prison terms or the death penalty, and the trial was not conducted in the shadow of a lynch mob. But the *Rabinowitz* case shared with those more serious and more notorious cases the practice of choosing jurors from a venire that included a minuscule number of black citizens. As witnesses would testify, blacks simply did not serve on juries in Georgia—a complaint common to the South in general. And it was this pattern that the defendants' attorneys (including Joni Rabinowitz's father, Victor, a veteran of the jury selection battle in Judge Knox's court in 1949) intended to attack.

The juries in both cases had been chosen by the clerk of the court, his deputy, and the jury commissioner appointed by the district judge, in conformance with the federal statute governing jury selection (28 U.S.C. § 1864). This statute preserved much of the jury commissioners' traditional discretion, including their use of key men and suggesters to provide names for the jury wheel. But while the key-man system used in Connecticut in 1960 had earned the praise of the Judicial Conference, it was clear that the practice in Georgia was fatally infected by the racial segregation that defined public life in the South in the days before the civil rights revolution.

The court record shows that while blacks were roughly 35 percent of the population of the Macon Division of the Middle Georgia District in 1960, Negroes constituted less than 6 percent of the names in the jury wheel.[28] The jury commissioners testified that the first jury list for the Macon Division (with eighteen counties) had been compiled in 1926, and this list had been updated eight times

27. The paired case was Jackson et al. v. United States, 366 F.2d 34 (1966).
28. *Rabinowitz*, 83.

since then.[29] The jury list used in 1966 had last been updated in 1959, using the 1953 list as a starting point. The 1953 list had been reduced by eliminating the names of those who had died, moved, or become too old to serve, and new names, collected by the clerk and the commissioner, had been added. All those on the new list were then sent questionnaires, and one of the questions asked about the prospective juror's race. The jury commissioner recalled that about 4,000 of these questionnaires had been mailed, and the records show that 2,338 of the questionnaires were returned. Out of these responses, 1,985 names were selected for the jury wheel, and only 117, or 5.9 percent, were Negroes—all but 4 of them holdovers from 1953.[30] Based on this pattern, the defendants challenged both their indictment and their conviction on the grounds that the methods used to compile the jury list led to the illegal exclusion of blacks (despite the integrated grand jury).

Under questioning by the Fifth Circuit, the clerk of the district court, Mr. Cowart, presented a picture of the jury commission's activities that will not surprise anyone familiar with the old racial regime in the South. Cowart asserted that he did not choose the names of many black Georgians because he "naturally" did not "know many Negroes," having most of his dealings with "the white race." When asked whether he had sought the names of Negro doctors, teachers, ministers, and other professionals in the counties under his jurisdiction, he replied that, "unfortunate as it may be . . . I don't know too many Negroes." He did recall writing to one Negro funeral home director.[31]

Mr. Simmons, the jury commissioner, testified that he had chosen many people with whom he was personally acquainted or took the suggestions of "friends whose opinions and integrity I valued." Some of these individuals were active in civic life; others were business owners, professionals, or members of local churches. "I carried around in my pockets for the several months we were at work a little book and a pad of paper on which I could record people's names as they happened to occur to me."[32] And in response to the court's question—"You don't know any Negroes in places like Twiggs County, Bleckley or Decatur or any of those?"—Simmons responded, as Cowart had, that his "acquaintance is generally, predominantly, of course, with the White race."[33] The appeals court decision observes that although Simmons traveled extensively throughout the counties of the Middle District, he "could not recall having made any inquiries of Negroes, whether businessmen, school teachers, ministers, doctors, or civil service employees, though he had asked a number of whites to suggest the names of competent Negro jurors." Noting that the rate of illiteracy among black residents of

29. Ibid., 40.
30. Ibid., 38.
31. Ibid., 42.
32. Ibid., 40.
33. Ibid., 43.

the Middle District was higher than that among whites, Cowart could not recall ever approaching black schoolteachers, doctors, ministers, nurses, lawyers, "or anybody else in that class which we assume has more than average education. . . . I don't know too many Negroes."[34]

Mr. Doyle, the chief deputy clerk, testified that in his efforts to keep the jury list current, he stopped at the county courthouse and "talked to the various officials in the county, asked them first of all, from their knowledge of the people in their community, to help me mark off of our list those who had deceased or moved away, and then give me the names of additional jurors to whom we might send questionnaires." Of course, none of the courthouse officials were African American.[35]

In response, the government argued that, as deficient as the jury selection process appeared to be in the Middle District, these deficiencies could not touch the indictments themselves, since there had been five blacks on the grand jury. For that reason, the indictments should stand, even if the jury verdicts were overturned. This would allow the "court's supervisory function [to be] adequately discharged," while preserving the possibility of another jury trial with a reformed selection process. But the appeals court rejected this argument, ruling that the jury selection process in Georgia involved two violations of federal law. First, the method the clerk and commissioner used to compile the jury list "violated the federal statutory scheme by applying statutorily incorrect standards to prospective jurors." Second, the method for "obtaining names of prospective jurors"—that is, the key-man system—"violated the statutory scheme. Either violation would require that we reverse the convictions and direct that the indictments be dismissed."[36]

In explaining these findings, Justice Rives, writing for the court, relied on the increasingly authoritative rulings from the previous two decades, giving little attention to the much longer tradition from which those decisions had departed. In his summary of jury history, for example, Rives skipped quickly from the medieval English jury to the post–Civil War *Strauder* decision to the 1940 ruling in *Smith v. Texas*, which had held that the "established tradition" of jury trial in America required that the jury "be a body truly representative of the community." Justice Rives then cited the affirmation of this principle in the *Glasser* case, which, he argued, had a particular relevance to the question at hand. In *Glasser*, Justice Murphy had observed that if the requirement of representativeness is met,

34. Ibid., 40.

35. Ibid.

36. Ibid., 44. The ruling simply assumed that the key-man system could not be administered in a racially neutral way, so it is not clear whether the ruling applied to the key-man system generally or only to the particular version of it practiced in Georgia. As a practical matter, this question was rendered moot by passage of the Jury Selection and Service Act of 1968, discussed below.

"the officials charged with choosing federal jurors may exercise some discretion to the end that competent jurors may be called. But they must not allow the desire for competent jurors to lead them into selections which do not comport with the concept of the jury as a cross-section of the community." Any tendency in a different direction, no matter the motives, would lead "to the irretrievable impairment of substantial liberties."[37]

According to Justice Rives, the drafters of the Civil Rights Act of 1957, moved by these arguments, had established separate juror qualifications for service in federal courts, eliminating everything but the age and residency requirements and excluding only ex-convicts; those who could not read, write, speak, or understand English; and those who were unable, "by reason of mental or physical infirmities, to render efficient jury service."[38] Thus, the circuit court was on solid ground in ruling that any attempt to impose a "qualitative" filter to the names going into the jury wheel would contradict the statute, unless the ban on those with mental infirmities might be applicable to those so "lacking in judgment and common sense" as to be unqualified to sit in judgment of others.

Although the racially discriminatory nature of jury selection in Georgia was obvious from the court record, there is nothing to suggest that a racially neutral key-man system would have been hard to devise. The questioning of the jury commissioners and the court clerk make it clear what they might have done, had they wished to (or had they dared to). They could have solicited names of likely jurors from black ministers, doctors, professionals, teachers—even funeral home directors—and from men and women in the community known for their character, intelligence, and judgment, just as commissioners had been doing for generations. What stood in the way of a racially impartial jury in Georgia in 1966, in other words, was not the key-man system but the persistence of the regime of white supremacy.

When Congress took up the administration's civil rights proposals in 1967, however, it was apparently difficult to imagine how to defeat racism without also eliminating the discretionary authority to seek those citizens "most suitable" for jury service. What helped propel the antidiscretion agenda was that Supreme Court rulings dating from the late 1930s had described as "traditional" what was in fact a new standard for jury selection: the "representative" or "cross-section" jury. The exclusion of black citizens in Georgia thus might appear to be just a variant of the same practice that exempted day laborers in San Francisco or that sought, in colonial times, to eliminate "pudding heads" from the jury lists. All such uses of discretion, however different their motives or their consequences, could be dismissed with equal contempt.

37. Ibid. In *Glasser*, the threat to the "representative" principle was the use of female jurors recommended by the League of Women Voters.

38. Civil Rights Act of 1957, part V, section 152.

The Judicial Conference reports had consistently taken a different approach, endorsing some level of discretion by jury officials and recommending the use of questionnaires and even personal interviews to choose those citizens who seemed to have the "ability" to serve effectively. No one had defended the idea of "selecting" jurors more forcefully than Judge Knox himself, who always linked the need for "representative" source lists with the need to find the best citizens from each of the recognizable groups in the community.

In his decision for the Fifth Circuit, however, Justice Rives made much of the fact that when Judge Knox had referred to the qualifications for federal jury service as "minimum" qualifications in his 1945 House testimony, he had done so only in the context of hardship exemptions—which the 1948 jury statute allowed federal judges to give, at their discretion, whenever the "public interest" required it. Knox had been responding to complaints from, among others, farm-state congressmen who wanted to protect the custom of exempting farmers during harvest time. Other legislators in the 1940s continued to demand protection for the practice of excusing mothers, volunteer firefighters, or other persons or classes of persons who might require (or demand) special exemption from jury service at particular times.[39] Specifically, Knox had testified: "A uniform standard of minimum qualifications should be adopted for all Federal jurors. It should provide for wide qualifications and few exceptions, leaving to the district judges a degree of discretion in determining whether or not certain individuals or classes of persons should, at particular times, be subject to jury service. For example, there is the case of farmers at harvest time. You could leave them . . . out of the wheel." He said essentially the same thing to the Senate when the bill was being debated in the next Congress, referring to "a uniform standard of . . . wide qualifications, and few exemptions," but leaving judges "a degree of discretion" in exempting certain "individuals or classes" at particular times.[40]

The legislative history of the jury statute, included as an appendix to the decision, noted that the original legislation proposed in 1948 by the Judicial Conference would have directed the jury commissions in each district to "choose from the eligible citizenry, 'without reference to party affiliation' those qualified persons 'who in their opinion are intelligent, honest, fair minded, of good reputation and capable of rendering satisfactory service.'"[41] But this language was not included in the final version of the 1948 bill, which led the *Rabinowitz* court to conclude that, in addition to preserving the conformity principle, Congress "rejected the explicit grant of broad discretionary powers to the court clerk and jury commissioner [to look for jurors who were 'honest,' 'intelligent,' and so on]. While jury commissioners exercised this nebulous broad power under the old statute,

39. *Rabinowitz*, 46.
40. Ibid.
41. Ibid., 64.

there is no indication that it was directly conferred by Congress." The practice of seeking such jurors—that is, going beyond "objective" standards such as the ability to read, write, and speak English—had been carried over from the state standards, the court argued, where the statutes used such phrases as "intelligent" or "of sound mind and good character."[42] Thus, the court reasoned, when Congress finally adopted the Judicial Conference's recommendation to abolish the conformity principle in 1957, it conferred a "new civil right" and struck from the federal jury law "all reference to State qualifications, all implicit discretionary powers derived from the State statutes." The exercise of such discretionary authority, the Fifth Circuit concluded, would have to come from Congress, but it had not.[43]

The government's position in the case steered a difficult course between defending the tradition of discretionary jury selection and conceding the illegality of excluding blacks from the jury wheel in Georgia. Congress, the government argued, had intended in 1948 *and* 1957 to establish "minimum" standards for jury service, but "jury commissioners were not compelled to use only that; they could then go on their own experience and their own judgment."[44] That is, in the absence of any scheme to deprive black citizens of their rights, jury commissioners could continue to exercise their own judgment about which jurors were fit for service and which, though formally qualified, were not.

In his dissent, Judge Griffin Bell insisted that the "law permits some care in selection to the end that the more competent citizens are selected," and he complained that the majority had thrown into doubt what would henceforth constitute a "fair jury system"—a question that would have to be settled quickly.[45] In his concurring opinion, Judge Brown agreed that jury selection in the *Rabinowitz* and *Jackson* trials had violated the law, but he maintained that Congress had not intended to abolish discretion, only discrimination. "There is a place," Brown wrote, for "levels of intelligence above the marginal literacy test. . . . [T]he Constitution rescues the judicial structure from the ironic assumption that the law cannot search for or try to get the sort of intellectual preparation for deciding today's complex controversies."[46] And Judge Gewin, joining Bell in dissent, pointed out that the legislative history clearly showed that those who opposed the Civil Rights Act of 1957 from the Left had done so precisely because the statute, in their view, *continued* the practice of discretionary selection—issuing only "one command, which is, that there be no purposeful exclusions based upon race."[47]

42. Ibid. These phrases are taken from the New York State jury statute.

43. Ibid.

44. Ibid., 49.

45. Ibid., 79. Judge Bell was prescient; the question of what constitutes a "fair" jury is still very much in dispute.

46. Ibid., 77.

47. Ibid., 91.

The *Rabinowitz* decision highlighted the role of jury selection in upholding white supremacy in the South, a connection that was well known long before that decision was handed down. In fact, the legislation President Lyndon Johnson sent to Congress in April 1966, which was designed primarily to end racial discrimination in housing, included provisions to end racial discrimination in the selection of juries as well. This was three months before the appeals court made its decision in the *Rabinowitz* and *Jackson* cases.[48] That civil rights bill was rejected by Congress, however, in large part because of disagreement over the sections aimed at discrimination in housing. Title I of the original bill would have required that federal jurors be selected at random from lists of registered voters (or from other lists as required by the Judicial Conference), and it provided a mechanism for challenging verdicts in cases in which racial discrimination in jury selection was suspected—exactly the pattern found in the *Rabinowitz* challenge. But since most of the debate in 1966 was over the housing sections of the civil rights bill, the debate over Title I drew relatively little public attention—although it got some adverse reactions in the federal courts. Senator Sam Ervin Jr. (D-NC), chairman of the subcommittee conducting hearings on Title I, insisted on separating jury reform from the rest of the bill and postponed its consideration until the Ninetieth Congress, and this proposal won the support of a majority of federal judges and chief clerks.[49]

Thus, several different jury reform proposals came before the Senate Subcommittee on Improvements in Judicial Machinery when it held hearings from March through July 1967, just one year after the *Rabinowitz* decision. One of those proposals was S. 383, the administration's bill, which incorporated the provisions of Title I from the failed 1966 civil rights bill; it eventually became the Jury Selection and Service Act of 1968 (JSSA).[50]

These deliberations in 1967 were a direct congressional response to the *Rabinowitz* ruling, and they laid the foundation for the modern regime of jury selection.[51] In some ways, as we will see, this new regime was a natural consequence of the sudden reinvention of the "traditional" American jury system presented as a fait accompli in the *Smith*, *Glasser*, and *Thiel* decisions of the 1940s. In particular, the 1968 act accomplished two reforms aimed at transforming the operation of the jury

48. The administration's civil rights bill was introduced on April 28, 1966; *Rabinowitz* was decided on July 20, 1966.

49. Sen. Sam J. Ervin Jr., "Jury Reform Needs More Thought," *American Bar Association Journal* 53 (1967): 132.

50. Pub. L. No. 9-274, section 101, 82 Stat. 53 (28 U.S.C. §§ 1861–1878).

51. "Congress passed the JSSA in response to Rabinowitz, clearly doing by statute what the Supreme Court had chosen not to do through its constitutional analysis." Nancy Gertner and Judith H. Mizner, *The Law of Juries*, 5th ed. (St. Paul, MN: Thompson/West, 2011), 52.

system in the federal courts and eventually in the states as well (by example, if not by more coercive measures). First, the JSSA established a requirement that each district court submit a report on the jury selection process within its boundaries to the Administrative Office of the United States Courts, under rules to be stipulated by the Judicial Conference; the conference, in turn, would have the authority to adopt rules governing the implementation of plans written under the act.[52] Second, the JSSA declared that it is "the policy of the United States that all litigants in Federal courts entitled to trial by jury shall have the right to grand and petit juries selected at random from a fair cross section of the community." Further, "all citizens shall have the opportunity to be considered for service on grand and petit juries in the district courts of the United States."[53] An "opportunity" is not quite the same thing as a "right," of course, but for the first time, the JSSA placed the rights of the juror and the rights of the defendant on an approximately equal footing.

Because of the *Rabinowitz* decision, and because of the extraordinary events surrounding the civil rights movement, Congress had racial discrimination in mind when it debated jury reform in the summer 1967. In his remarks at the signing ceremony in March 1968, President Johnson made it clear that the purpose of the JSSA was to end the century-old denial of the rights of black Americans. "This measure reinforces the precious legal rights of all of our citizens. . . . It advances the civil rights of those who still reach for their full, and what we believe their proper, place in our society."[54] Yet the testimony during the Senate hearings on the bill made it clear that those who supported the "cross-section" principle had other matters on their minds, as did the *Glasser* and *Thiel* decisions—neither of which had anything to do with race. It quickly became apparent that the intended target of the bill was the key-man system itself and the jury commissioners' discretion, in both federal and state courts, over the management of jury selection, and not just in the South, but everywhere. Beyond these targets was an even more distant and more important one: the traditional understanding of the jury as being properly composed of persons with a special capacity for judgment.

Because the key-man system rests on assumptions that are very old, and because its operation is strikingly different from the modern regime of jury selection, it is important to pause briefly and recall the failings for which the key-man system cannot be held responsible. The exclusion of blacks from juries, like the exclusion of women, was not a by-product of the key-man system; nor was such exclusion the system's secret purpose. The exclusion of blacks from juries was the

52. *Report of the Judicial Conference of the United States*, March 13–14, 1969 (Washington, DC: Administrative Office of the United States Courts, 1969), 11.

53. 28 U.S.C. § 1861.

54. Lyndon Johnson, "Remarks upon Signing the Jury Selection and Service Act of 1968," March 27, 1968, http://www.presidency.ucsb.edu/ws/?pid=28758 (accessed April 21, 2015).

product of deeply embedded social and political customs that would have worked the same damage and had the same result, whatever the law required. And, as we shall see below, the abolition of the key-man system did not end claims of racial discrimination in jury selection. The case of voting rights is an instructive parallel: black citizens had the right to vote, under both federal and state law, since the Civil War Amendments, but they were prevented from registering by the simple tactic of intimidation. It was not registration procedures (such as the poll tax or the literacy test) that excluded blacks from the ballot; it was the power of white officials to adapt any procedure to an unlawful purpose and to back their decisions with highly credible threats of violence. And it was not a change in procedures that stopped these practices; it was a major political movement aimed at transforming the nation's racial consciousness, followed by the direct intervention of the federal government. Women, in contrast, had been statutorily excluded from jury service in many states, despite passage of the Nineteenth Amendment. Until the suffrage amendment, they would have been excluded under any selection method. In states where women did serve on juries, "key women" as well as "key men" were invited to make recommendations.[55]

What *can* be attributed to the key-man system is the slightly "gentrified" quality of the jury pools used in many state and federal courts—a quality revealed, for example, in the research conducted for the American Jury Project in the 1950s. Studying trials in an unnamed federal court in the Midwest, researcher Dale Broeder found that middle-class professionals made up nearly the entire venire in the trials he observed.[56] Otherwise, there is very limited empirical evidence of the demographic characteristics of Americans chosen for jury service, and all of it is from the twentieth century.[57] The direction of that evidence is clear, however: when deliberate efforts were made to enforce nonrandom jury selection—and it is important to remember that these efforts were by no means universal—the result was juries made up disproportionately of men (and later women) from higher occupational or income groups and with higher levels of education. To universalize this pattern was the principal aim of all jury reform efforts prior to 1968—most

55. See Clarence N. Callender, *The Selection of Jurors: A Comparative Study of the Methods of Selection and the Personnel of Juries in Philadelphia and Other Cities* (Philadelphia: University of Pennsylvania Press, 1924), 45. An invitation to the League of Women Voters to suggest names for jury service was one of the grounds for appeal in the *Glasser* case; see chapter 3.

56. Dale W. Broeder, "Voir Dire Examinations: An Empirical Study," *Southern California Law Review* 38 (1964–1965): 503–504.

57. Callender's *Selection of Jurors* is one of the most detailed. Jon Van Dyke's *Jury Selection: Our Uncertain Commitment to Representative Panels* (Cambridge, MA: Ballinger, 1977) contains information on juror demographics from the 1950s that is consistent with the findings of the American Jury Project.

notably, by ending the state practice of exempting so many educated professionals from jury service. Some states and many federal districts attempted to work around these exemptions by using questionnaires and interviews, seeking the best candidates from among those citizens who remained available for service; in those courts, the gentrification of the jury system can be seen most clearly.

In his 1924 study of jury selection procedures, Clarence Callender found that in the county and municipal courts in Philadelphia, where no formal effort was made to seek the "most qualified" individuals, jurors were evenly divided between those with higher- and lower-status occupations. He found a very different pattern for the Federal District of Eastern Pennsylvania, which sat in Philadelphia. There, the federal jury commissioners made a conscious effort to seek those individuals who were most likely to be capable, including the use of recommendations from "qualified individuals." In federal court, half the jurors came from the single highest occupational class (managers, officials, professionals), while only 8.5 percent came from the lowest class.[58]

Callender's research also shows that the use of "recommenders" and "key men" was widespread. This is consistent with what the Judicial Conference found in its surveys of jury practices in federal courts both in the 1940s and in 1960: the use of recommenders was a common method of compiling lists of prospective jurors and was thought to be more reliable than simply using lists of voters or taxpayers. Callender was explicit on this point, noting that neither artisans nor bankers can be judged solely by their professions; thus, it was helpful for someone knowledgeable about the character of an individual to recommend that person for service. And although we can assume, Callender wrote, that jurors from the highest grade of occupations are experienced and intelligent, we cannot assume that they are all "honest and morally competent. Dishonest and profligate bankers are not unknown."[59] The most reliable system, therefore, is one that seeks as much knowledge as possible, before a juror ever reaches the courthouse, about those qualities that are undetectable in the bare demographic data available in city directories, voter rolls, and census records.

At the opposite end of the spectrum was the system used in the municipal and county courts of Philadelphia, where names were chosen at random from various lists, including voter lists and assessors' rolls. This random collection of names did undergo a type of "sorting," but not until the prospective jurors had arrived at court. Callender was certain this was the worst way to choose a jury:

> It is not feasible for the courts to conduct a general inquiry into the fitness of the jurors in the court room and in practice they do not do so. Challenges are designed to rid the sworn jury in a particular case of biased and prejudiced

58. Callender, *Selection of Jurors*, table II, 24.
59. Ibid., 88.

> jurors and for no other purpose. Therefore to rely on excuses and challenges as a means of eliminating unsuitable jurors is both futile and indefensible. To call such jurors in the first place is a waste of the county's money, it is a waste of the time and money of the jurors themselves, it is a waste of the lawyers' time in having to investigate them, it is a waste of the courts' time in having to excuse them and if they still remain on the panel they will contribute nothing to the administration of justice and may indeed seriously interfere with it. Jurors should be investigated before they are chosen.

Callender found that nearly half the jurors called in the city and county courts of Philadelphia were excused.[60]

The pattern Callender found in the federal court in Pennsylvania was not matched precisely in the other jurisdictions studied. However, in all jurisdictions except Philadelphia, "an attempt is made to obtain competent jurors either by personal recommendations, investigations, answers to questionnaires, or by property qualifications."[61] In New York County (Manhattan), for example, juries were at least as gentrified as those in the federal district in Pennsylvania, and in some cases even more so. For petit juries, class A occupations supplied 57.6 percent of jurors, very much like the US District Court in Philadelphia. The second highest occupational class supplied 36.5 percent, and the lowest class accounted for only 1 percent of jurors. This pattern was even more pronounced with respect to special and grand juries, with the highest occupational class supplying 82 percent and 97 percent of jurors, respectively.[62] In the New York system, Callender concluded, there was "an intelligent effort to provide for a careful and selective choice of jurors."[63] But the occupational patterns in Chicago, St. Louis, and Boston were closer to those in the city and county courts in Philadelphia than to the Federal District of Eastern Pennsylvania.

To solve the problem of the incapable juror making it into the courtroom, the American Bar Association (ABA) had recommended in 1938 the use of questionnaires and personal interviews, based on the Cleveland and California models, to sort "qualified" and "unqualified" jurors. As reported in the previous chapter, such questionnaires rejected from one-third (in Cleveland) to two-thirds (in California) of all jurors examined.[64]

60. Ibid., 94. The precise numbers were 43.4 percent in the city courts and 47.3 percent in the county courts. As shown below, the contemporary practice of voir dire approximates very closely the pattern Callender describes in Philadelphia—the effort to remove "unsuitable" jurors takes place in the courtroom.

61. Ibid., 88.

62. Ibid., 55.

63. Ibid., 56.

64. "Report of the Committee on Trial by Jury Including Methods of Selection of Jurors," *Annual Report of the American Bar Association* 63 (1938): 559.

THE JURY SELECTION AND SERVICE ACT OF 1968

Although racial discrimination was the immediate concern of the *Rabinowitz* decision, the 1967 hearings on jury reform targeted discretion itself. All "discriminations" were suspect, not just the ones aimed at racial minorities—to exercise any discretion at all, it seemed, would be to set foot on the slipperiest of slopes. A brief colloquy between Senator Joseph Tydings (D-MD), a member of the Senate Subcommittee on Improvements in Judicial Machinery, and Attorney General Ramsey Clark, testifying on behalf of the bill, suggests the flavor of these other concerns.

Senator Tydings pressed the attorney general on the question of "subjective" standards for jury service. "Do you think," he asked, "that a citizen should be excluded from serving on a jury, if he is so lacking in intelligence, information, probity, or good commonsense as to be unable to render satisfactory jury service?" "I think," Clark replied, "that unless we establish an objective standard . . . we risk discrimination through subjective judgment."[65] Since racial discrimination could hardly be described as the result of "subjective judgment" or "unconscious bias"—to the racist, race is an objective fact and bias is a deliberate choice—then the bill, at least in Clark's estimation, must have had a broader target in mind. It is hard not to draw the conclusion that the target was discretion itself, even when such discretion had no connection to the exclusion of any group from jury service, other than those who had been excluded all along—namely, those unsuited, for reasons of character or intelligence, to the difficult task of judging, or those who could legitimately claim that service would impose on them an "undue hardship."

The focus on discretion raised the possibility that for many reformers, the very idea of a jury chosen for its qualities of character and intelligence was inconsistent with the democratic ideal. Senator Ervin's challenge to this "reform paradigm" would now raise eyebrows at the nation's leading law journals, except as a quaint reminder of the bad old days:

> Perhaps most importantly, no changes should be made in the selection system which will have the effect of lowering the quality of Federal justice. A "jury of peers" does not require representatives of the least intelligent and the least capable of the populace, whatever their race, religion, economic status, national origin, or voting habits. The litigants who seek justice in our courts should not have their rights and their wealth, their lives and freedom placed at the mercy of the least common denominator.[66]

65. *Hearings before the Subcommittee on Improvements in Judicial Machinery of the Committee on the Judiciary*, US Senate, 90th Cong., 1st sess., 1967 (Washington, DC: Government Printing Office, 1967), 46.

66. Ibid., 40.

In his opening testimony, however, the attorney general stressed the importance of the "fair and impartial" jury and identified this as the goal of the administration's bill. He identified the "problem" of the jury with citizens' fear of being unfairly judged, but he set this problem in a context wider than race. "The law does not discriminate in choosing its litigants. It must not discriminate in choosing their peers. Because if it does . . . there comes into the decision process . . . those preferences and prejudices . . . of the select few." And the select few—presumably the key men who recommend names for the jury wheel—cannot hope to represent the many, especially in large cities. If juries are not chosen randomly, the citizen will feel that the system "is selecting its own to judge him."[67]

Clark then identified the principles of what would become the Jury Selection and Service Act. First, the bill announces a "Federal right to serve on a jury" that cannot be denied because of race, color, religion, sex, national origin, or economic status. Second, the voter registration list is identified as the preferable source for juror names, but other methods must be chosen whenever the voter list does not guarantee a "fair cross section of the community."[68] Third, selection from the list should be random. Fourth, the maximum qualifications for service will be the following: that the juror be at least twenty-one years old and a district resident for one year or more; that he be able to read, write, speak, and understand English and be free of "incapacitating mental or physical infirmity"; and that he have no felony convictions on his record. These principles, Clark maintained, will fulfill the command of the Supreme Court in *Smith v. Texas* that the jury should be "a body truly representative of the community."[69]

However, in responding to Senator Tydings's request for a brief restatement of the problem that jury reform was trying to solve, Clark did not, as one might expect, begin with race. Instead, he began with the tendency of the key-man system to distort jury selection away from, for example, blue-collar workers, who might make up 8 percent of the population but only 2 percent of the jury pool. This form of exclusion is fundamentally identical to racial discrimination, he said—ostensibly the main object of the administration's concern.[70] These distortions, Clark

67. Ibid., 41.

68. Although this section clearly had the South in mind, the problem of "unrepresentative" voter lists was not unique to the region. In other parts of the country, jury lists underrepresented a variety of groups, including nonwhites, the poor, the young, and those who had recently moved. It was not intimidation by election officials that caused this underrepresentation but a lack of connection to, or interest in, the political process.

69. Smith v. Texas, 311 U.S. 128 (1940), 130; *Hearings before the Subcommittee on Improvements*, 42. This language is identical to that found in part V, section 152, of the Civil Rights Act of 1957. In this sense, the JSSA does not proclaim but simply reiterates a principle already present in the law, while leaving language in the legislative history of the act that clarifies how the "new" principle should be understood.

70. *Hearings before the Subcommittee on Improvements*, 42.

insisted, were "something that we see almost inherently in the key-man system." The implication is clear: even in the absence of racial discrimination, the effort to search for more than the minimum qualifications required by the bill would unacceptably distort the composition of the jury. "I think that a diversity of background, a freedom [from] prejudice, and some commonsense is what we want in juries. I don't know how . . . we can select from among us those that are the most intelligent or have the most commonsense."[71]

In trying to get the attorney general to acknowledge the distinction between illegal discrimination and the traditional search for capable jurors, Senator Ervin appealed to the understanding that a jury ought to be "drawn from all groups and segments of society"—the Court's meaning in *Smith v. Texas*—and that it should draw from each group "the best in terms of intelligence, integrity, morality, and commonsense." (This was the understanding Judge Otis had offered in response to Justice Murphy's "dictum" in the *Thiel* case. It was also the view of jury selection endorsed by the Judicial Conference.) Like other witnesses who testified in favor of the bill, Clark resolutely denied that it is possible for anyone to choose subjectively without "reflecting preferences and prejudices." However hard the chooser tries, he will inevitably "only represent his own point of view."[72]

Because the bill required only objective standards for jury service (the maximum qualifications identified above), neither judge nor jury commissioner would be able to exclude citizens known to be of dubious character. "They might know the man is a blooming idiot," Ervin protested, or a "notorious keeper of a bawdy house" who has never been convicted of a felony, yet they would have to put his name into the wheel. To this objection Clark had an answer, one that will be of special interest to anyone who has followed the Supreme Court's evolving doctrine on "fair cross-section" or "representative" juries, especially with respect to race: the attorneys will be able to weed out unfit jurors during voir dire by exercising their peremptory challenges or by challenging for cause.[73] Senator Ervin then raised the possibility that the challenge procedure might produce endless and frivolous challenges by defendants claiming bias. "Could a Presbyterian argue that there were not enough Presbyterians in the wheel?" To this objection, too, Clark had an answer that will be of interest to students of contemporary jury trials: "I don't think the court would listen to that sort of

71. Ibid., 45.

72. Ibid., 48–49.

73. Ibid., 51. Since the 1970s, extended voir dire and the use of jury consultants to choose jurors have become common practices at both the state and federal levels, a problem discussed below. Ironically, one consequence of extended voir dire is thought to be the exclusion of blacks from juries. See, for example, Anne Rankin Mahoney, "American Jury Voir Dire and the Ideal of Equal Justice," *Journal of Applied Behavioral Science* 18, 4 (1982): 481–494.

evidence very long. . . . In my judgment this challenge procedure would reduce challenges to jury selection."[74]

Testimony at the subcommittee hearings was evenly divided between defenders and opponents of the key-man system, but as Clark's testimony indicated, the major concern of the bill's supporters was not exclusively, and perhaps not even primarily, race. Dale Broeder, an attorney in private practice and a consultant to the University of Chicago Jury Project, argued that the key-man system leads not to a cross section of the community but rather to "blue-ribbon" juries made up of people with a homogeneous outlook and background.[75] In his observation of 23 jury trials in a midwestern court in the 1950s, and in interviews with 225 jurors, he had encountered only 3 black jurors. Broeder doubted that voting lists would lead to "a broad enough socioeconomic spectrum from which to select Federal jurors"—and not just because some states prevented blacks from registering. The "exclusive use of voting records likewise discriminates against the uneducated and the poor." The jury system, after all, is supposed to give defendants a trial by their peers, yet poor and uneducated defendants are commonly tried by jurors who are neither poor nor uneducated![76] In Broeder's view, the various bills before the subcommittee still gave too much discretion to the judges or to the judicial conferences, especially when it came to professional and hardship exemptions.

Commenting from the vantage point of more than twenty-five years' experience as a private attorney, William L. Marbury from Baltimore found it troubling that the bill would remove all the court's discretion over jury selection. And he quite shrewdly predicted where the discretion would end up: in the hands of the attorneys, who would replace the judge as the prime movers of the voir dire. Marbury found the prospect of extended, lawyer-driven voir dire—now a common and apparently natural part of the courtroom drama—"fantastic. . . . I can't imagine how it would work. In the first place, I don't think jurors ought to be selected

74. *Hearings before the Subcommittee on Improvements*, 52–56.

75. The term "blue-ribbon" jury has been applied to two different types of jury: (1) to the type Broeder had in mind, in which jurors were average or above in terms of their educational and occupational status; and (2) to juries made up of those with certain kinds of professional expertise, impaneled when such expertise was necessary to understand the evidence in a particular case. Only the second kind fits the classic definition of a blue-ribbon jury. This second type of jury was allowed under New York State jury law for courts in New York City. In the 1940s city prosecutors impaneled a blue-ribbon jury to try labor leaders on corruption charges, a practice the New York Supreme Court found constitutionally valid in People v. Fay, 296 N.Y. 510, 68, N.E.2d 453 (1946). However, all juries were supposed to be composed of citizens of "average or above-average" intelligence, character, and so forth. New York State repealed its blue-ribbon jury statute in 1965. Randolph N. Jonakait, *The American Jury System* (New Haven, CT: Yale University Press, 2003), 123. See also "Note: The 'Blue-Ribbon' Jury," *Harvard Law Review* 60 (1946–1947): 613–620.

76. *Hearings before the Subcommittee on Improvements*, 62–67.

by partisan people, who try to get on the jury the people they think are going to vote their way. . . . I don't like the idea of lawyers selecting jurors."[77]

Marbury observed that the problem of jury selection presented two difficulties, neither of which could be resolved completely. The first difficulty was picking a representative jury; the second difficulty was picking an intelligent jury. Just as it would be impossible to guarantee that every identifiable group in the community would be represented on the jury, it would be equally impossible to guarantee that every juror would possess the necessary elements of intelligence, integrity, and common sense. But these goals would be no more achievable under the provisions of the administration's bill than they were under the key-man system, Marbury argued, since voter lists do not accurately reflect the full demographic diversity of a typical federal district. Judges would have to be given some discretion to seek names from beyond the registration lists. And that would also be true with respect to the goal of finding an intelligent jury. "I do not believe," he testified, "that it is possible to obtain [such a result] by any system other than that which gives some discretion to the selectors." Without such discretion, he predicted, there would be an increase in problem jurors:

> One or two questions would make it perfectly apparent that you are dealing with a person whose total lack of information is such that they simply are not going to be able to do the job. Nowadays we sometimes find out about them after they have been on juries. They hang juries, and everybody on the jury says, this man or woman never should have been allowed to serve. They are impossible, they will hang any jury that they are on. . . . I think that some method must be prescribed by which somebody can take the responsibility for eliminating such unfit persons.[78]

The possibility that judges or jury commissions might abuse their traditional discretion would require that protections be built into the statute, and Marbury endorsed two of the bills before the committee to accomplish that goal. Those bills would have given citizens rejected for service the right to appeal, and they would have required the court to approve disqualifications proposed by the commissioners or clerks. But despite the possibility of abuse, Marbury believed:

77. Ibid., 87. The selection of jurors by attorneys in both criminal and civil trials is the subject of the relatively new "science of jury management" and the stock in trade of a small industry of jury consulting firms, discussed below. The Federal Rules of Criminal and Civil Procedure give control of voir dire proceedings to judges in federal courts, but in many districts, judges allow attorneys to suggest and even ask questions. See chapter 5 for further discussion of trial procedures.

78. Ibid., 89.

> There must ultimately be reliance upon the good faith of administrators and the capacity of judicial machinery to control abuse. The only alternative is to abandon the effort to select competent jury panels and to place the entire burden for selecting able juries on lawyers through the voir dire. This approach would be inefficient, time consuming for both courts and litigants, and financially burdensome for parties. . . . These factors would tend to discourage the use of juries and undermine the jury system.[79]

The subcommittee also heard testimony from Harry Kalven Jr. and Hans Zeisel, authors of the recently published *The American Jury*.[80] The central finding of their study—that judge and jury agreed on the verdict in 75 percent of cases—was the basis for the authors' contention that fear of jury incompetence was groundless. "In some basic sense," Kalven concluded, "the jury understands well enough the job it is being asked to do."[81] But under prodding from Senator Tydings, Kalven had to admit that 200 of the federal cases in their study had been tried by juries chosen through the key-man system, and they could not say for certain how many of the juries in their state cases had been chosen by some subjective screening process rather than by random selection from voter lists. Earlier in the hearings, Broeder (a consultant to the same research project that produced *The American Jury*) had testified about the key-man system's tendency to produce "blue-ribbon type juries" as opposed to "representative cross-section" juries, by which he meant juries above average in terms of income, occupation, and education.[82] This was precisely the result that Kalven and Zeisel wished to avoid. "We think," Kalven testified, "that it is very difficult, it turns out, for a variety of reasons, to select the jury for neutral intelligence. That the effort brings along with it some other class bias you would not want directly. You are going to have, as a byproduct of the effort to select an intelligent jury, the introduction of a special set of values which, in a way, must seem arbitrary in terms of the performance of the system."[83]

Zeisel, however, identified one particular "subjective" quality that *would* be captured by random selection from voting lists—namely, the (presumptive) tendency of registered voters to care more than nonvoters about public matters, which Zeisel called a "democratic congruence."[84] But, as Tydings pointed out, a

79. Ibid., 92.

80. Harry Kalven Jr. and Hans Zeisel, *The American Jury* (Chicago: University of Chicago Press, 1966).

81. *Hearings before the Subcommittee on Improvements*, 120.

82. Ibid., 62–72. This was Broeder's claim, based on his own research. Kalven and Zeisel's *American Jury* does not report any findings regarding the socioeconomic characteristics of the jurors in their sample of cases.

83. *Hearings before the Subcommittee on Improvements*, 127.

84. Ibid., 131.

70 percent registration rate was high for a typical congressional district, leaving 30 percent of the potential jury pool unknown and unqualified. "You can't argue," Tydings concluded, that "you should have a cross-section of the community as potential jurors, and then say that the 70 percent of the people who are registered to vote are better qualified to be jurors than the 30 percent [who are not]."[85] In fact, without knowing it, perhaps, Tydings had identified an important source of future litigation: the claim that even the use of lists of voters cannot satisfy the elusive goal of "representative" or "cross-section" juries.[86]

But the most intriguing aspect of these hearings was the appearance—dare we say debut?—of a distinctly postmodern understanding of truth (or "truth"). Kalven, in rejecting the idea of screening jurors for intelligence, had objected to the inevitable by-product of such efforts: "class bias," which he defined as "the introduction of a special set of values" into the jury selection process.[87] Presumably, these would be the values shared by that part of the community not defined as poor, uneducated, or lacking in common sense.

The portrayal of "truth" as a social construct mediated through class structures is a paradigm that has become far more common since the 1960s in academic settings, law journals, and even popular culture.[88] But this general approach to the nature of truth was far less common in 1967, which makes Senator Ervin's perception of it all the more notable. In an essay for the *American Bar Association Journal*, Ervin described the "cross-section" requirement as "philosophically controversial," and he had this to say in conclusion:

> The jury is supposed to decide controverted questions on the basis of facts presented in an environment carefully organized to afford the best opportunity for determining objective "truth," insofar as that is humanly possible. That point of view which places exclusive emphasis on proportional representation—"cross-section of the community" in the words of Title I—necessarily suggests that justice is a function of class. The search for truth is regarded as a partisan operation—there is one truth for the poor and another for the rich.[89]

85. Ibid., 139.

86. This argument has been a staple in the law journals and in court challenges since passage of the Jury Selection and Service Act. For a sample of the debate, see Charles H. Logan and George F. Cole, "Reducing Bias in a Jury Source List by Combining Voters and Drivers," *Judicature* 67 (August 1983): 87–94.

87. *Hearings before the Subcommittee on Improvements*, 127.

88. For a sample, see Ronald J. Allen, "Unexplored Aspects of the Theory of the Right to a Trial by Jury," *Washington University Law Quarterly* 66 (1988): 33–45. In this article, evidence is defined as "whatever influences a jury on propositions material to a case," and knowledge is defined as something that "emerges from community discussion and consensus" (37–38).

89. Ervin, "Jury Reform Needs More Thought," 54.

Ervin feared the result: that we would be "elevating bias to a rule of law and regarding justice as a judicial balance of economics, ethnic origin, and religious and cultural backgrounds."[90]

Ervin posited, as a better model of reform, the recommendations of the Judicial Conference in its 1960 report—that jury reform pursue two goals simultaneously. First, juries should be "representative of the community"; therefore, the "sources from which [names] are selected should include all economic and social groups of the community." Second, "the jury list should also represent as high a degree of intelligence, morality, integrity, and common sense as possible."[91] This implies, if not the key-man system then some version of it, expanded to include more than the usual groups of upstanding folks known to the regulars down at the courthouse.

But it was, in the end, the cross-section requirement that prevailed, and the Jury Selection and Service Act of 1968 required that federal courts choose jurors at random from updated voter registration lists and that each district court submit a plan to the Administrative Office of the United States Courts, detailing how the new law would be implemented. If, in the judgment of the court, the voter registration list was not likely to contain a fair cross section of the local population, it could be supplemented by other lists.[92] Court officials were specifically forbidden to impose any "nonobjective" qualifications on potential jurors—the only way the JSSA differs from the jury provisions of the 1957 Civil Rights Act. Juror questionnaires could ask only for objective information such as age, length of residence in the district, and criminal record. Jury officials were required to "determine solely on the basis of information provided on the juror qualification form and other competent evidence whether a person is unqualified for, or exempt, or to be excused from jury service."[93] There would be no process of interviewing jurors prior to the construction of the jury list, because nothing would be relevant beyond what could be written on the juror questionnaire. In the nearly fifty years that this system has been in place, we have continued to chase the elusive goal of representative juries, supplementing voter registration lists with whatever other lists can supply up-to-date information on names and addresses, thus abandoning the "democratic congruence" that Zeisel was willing, however inconsistently, to admit into the system.[94]

90. Ibid.

91. *Hearings before the Subcommittee on Improvements*, 613, quoting *Jury System in the Federal Courts*, 409.

92. The law even specifies that "the plan for the District of Columbia may require the names of prospective jurors to be selected from the city directory rather than from voter lists." 28 U.S.C. § 1863(b)(2).

93. Ibid., 1863(a).

94. Contemporary jury theory cannot abide restrictions, even when they promote Zeisel's democratic congruence. For example, in 1996 the Oregon legislature enacted a law

Six weeks after passage of the JSSA, the Supreme Court ruled in *Duncan v. Louisiana* that the jury trial guaranteed by the Sixth Amendment is also guaranteed to defendants in state courts, via the due process clause of the Fourteenth Amendment.[95] Seven years later, the Court overturned a felony conviction, in another case from Louisiana, on the grounds that the venire from which the defendant's jury had been chosen was not "representative of the community." The Louisiana Constitution and its jury statute discouraged the service of women, offering them a blanket exemption unless they explicitly asked to be considered.[96] The Court found that this practice could not withstand constitutional scrutiny, in light of the JSSA and *Duncan*. The jury system in both federal and state courts had at last been successfully nationalized, centralized, and reconstructed around the principle of representation.

THE MODERN REGIME OF JURY SELECTION

In hindsight, it is clear that, from the line of cases beginning with *Smith*, *Glasser*, and *Thiel* in the 1940s, up to passage of the Jury Selection and Service Act, the argument about jury reform had been moving along two separate tracks. The oldest track, which the ABA and the Judicial Conference had been following consistently since their creation in the 1870s and 1920s, respectively, had sought to improve the quality of federal juries, first by eliminating the automatic exemptions given to the most educated and experienced members of the community, and then by examining prospective jurors more carefully before their names were placed on the jury list or into the jury wheel. These goals required the federal courts' liberation from state jury selection rules, as well as measures to improve the management of jury selection (e.g., full-time commissioners with full-time salaries). The newer track, first identified by the Supreme Court in *Smith v. Texas*,

requiring that state circuit court jurors serving on criminal trials be registered voters. The law was in effect from 1996 to 1999, but it was criticized on the grounds that it denied jury service to what one law review author refers to as "nonregistered voters." Following a Supreme Court decision (Buckley v. American Constitutional Law Foundation, 525 U.S. 182 [1999]) that had nothing to do with the jury system (it struck down a Colorado law requiring that those gathering signatures for citizen petitions be registered voters), Oregon abandoned the requirement. Arguing for the repeal of the law, the Oregon attorney general insisted that voter registration status should have no bearing on the "qualifications to serve competently or appropriately" on a criminal jury. See Rose Jade, "Voter Registration Status as a Jury Service Employment Test: Oregon's Retracted Endorsement Following *Buckley v. American Constitutional Law Foundation, Inc*.," *Willamette Law Review* 39 (2003): 557–758.

95. Duncan v. Louisiana, 391 U.S. 145 (1968).

96. Taylor v. Louisiana, 419 U.S. 522 (1975).

sought to improve the "representative" quality of juries by forbidding either the exclusion or the automatic exemption of any class of persons, for any reason, with the exception of a few objective criteria.

Reformers rarely acknowledged that these two lines of argument were moving reform in different directions. In one document after another, the goal of a jury pool drawn from a "broad cross-section of the community" was understood to be entirely compatible with the search for jurors who represented "as high a standard of intelligence, character, and integrity as is possible."[97] The first standard can be satisfied by the random selection of jurors from whatever lists are considered comprehensive enough to reflect the cross-section requirement. The second standard can be satisfied only if jury commissioners are free to use some discretion in choosing, from among a wide assortment of citizens, those who are, according to some rational measure, average or above average in their ability to judge evidence, weigh testimony, and render a sensible verdict. On the one hand, the random selection method might produce an especially capable jury, but it is unlikely that it would do so consistently. On the other hand, a discretionary mode of selection could be practiced on lists that were broadly representative of the community—but this would require discretion on the part of jury commissioners, who would need to select individual jurors with the relevant qualities of intelligence, integrity, and common sense, after taking the time and effort to examine them. As the 1960 Judicial Conference report puts it: "while sources from which jurors are selected should include all economic and social groups in the community, there should be a weeding out of unqualified persons."[98] The JSSA settled the matter decisively on the side of broadly representative source lists; then it stipulated that jury commissioners could base their decisions only on objective standards for service—leaving the sorting to take place in court, under the guidance of attorneys.[99]

It is clear why Congress chose this path. Lawmakers believed, given the experience of discriminatory jury selection in the South, that jury commissions would use their discretion to subvert the intention of the law by improperly discriminating

97. This language appears in the Judicial Conference's original 1943 report (Knox Committee Report) and in *The Jury System in the Federal Courts* (1960). It does not appear in any Judicial Conference reports on the jury system after 1960.

98. *Jury System in the Federal Courts*, 40.

99. 28 U.S.C. § 1861 reads: "It is the policy of the United States that all litigants in Federal courts entitled to trial by jury shall have the right to grand and petit juries selected at random from a fair cross section of the community in the district or division wherein the court convenes. It is further the policy of the United States that all citizens shall have the opportunity to be considered for service on grand and petit juries in the district courts of the United States, and shall have an obligation to serve as jurors when summoned for that purpose." Section 1866 provides that "no person or class of persons shall be disqualified, excluded, excused, or exempt from service" except for those disqualifications in section 1865 (the juror is illiterate, a convicted felon, a noncitizen, or mentally or physically impaired).

against blacks, filling the jury list with such a preponderance of whites that black jurors would be vanishingly rare. This had been done in the *Smith* and *Rabinowitz* cases, and there was no reason to believe these were exceptions, especially in the South. But even outside the realm of race and outside the South, jury commissioners had been accused of abusing their legitimate managerial discretion to bar or excuse whole classes of citizens from the venire: day laborers, women, poor people, college students, Asians, and Hispanics, among many others. And even when commissioners did not exclude any "cognizable" groups from the venire, the effort to secure "competent" jurors was itself a form of "discrimination," in the literal sense—that is, the commissioners distinguished between those citizens with and without the requisite qualities. And as supporters of the JSSA pointed out, wasn't the exclusion of the "so-called unqualified" simply another form of "class" or "cultural" bias, enacting "those preferences and prejudices . . . of the select few," as Attorney General Clark put it in his testimony in 1967?

The 1968 reform sought to cut through all these questions once and for all, forbidding all consideration of "nonobjective" characteristics when determining who was qualified for inclusion on the venire. The aim was random selection from lists of registered voters or from other lists, if needed, a matter Congress left to the discretion of each district court.[100] It is now time to examine how the new system works in practice and why there continues to be dissatisfaction, in many different quarters, a half century after its institution.

The composition of grand and petit juries in federal courts is governed by constitutional guarantees, federal statutes, and the supervisory authority of the Supreme Court. The constitutional guarantees are found in Article III, section 2; in the Sixth and Seventh Amendments; and in the equal protection clause of the Fourteenth Amendment. The statutory guarantees are found in chapter 23 of the *United States Code*, sections 1861–1878, which codifies the Jury Selection and Service Act of 1968 and its amendments. The Court's supervisory authority is reflected in its recommendations to Congress for changes in the jury statute or for amendments to the Federal Rules of Civil and Criminal Procedure. But the Court has sometimes exercised its supervisory authority directly while deciding cases—as it did, for example, in *Thiel v. Southern Pacific*, even though there was no state or federal law forbidding the exemption of day laborers, which was at the heart of that case.

100. The Senate report on the JSSA notes: "The defect that calls for congressional action is that the representational goal of jury selection is impaired when the methods used are haphazard or less than adequate to ensure fair selection from a fair sample." But given the unrepresentative quality of voter registration lists, Congress left it for the courts to decide when a voter list is so unrepresentative that it imperils the goal of the jury law. S. Rep. No. 891, 90th Cong., 1st sess. (1968), 10, cited by Gertner and Mizner, *Law of Juries*, 52–53.

The equal protection clause extends the same bar to discrimination found in other areas of the law, such as employment law, to the selection of jurors.[101] Here, the question concerns the criteria by which citizens are excluded from the venire. If a citizen is excluded because of membership in one of several protected groups, the equal protection clause is implicated; if the exclusion is based on other reasons, the equal protection guarantee is not relevant. For example, race is one of the protected categories; therefore, exclusion of African Americans as a group is prohibited. However, if a particular African American individual is excluded on other grounds (e.g., an inability to read English or jury service during the previous year)—and assuming these other grounds are genuine and not pretextual—the equal protection clause does not apply. Usually, an equal protection challenge is available only to a defendant who is a member of the group being excluded, although defendants from outside the excluded group have sometimes been successful in challenging the venire from which their juries were chosen (discussed later).

In the years since the passage of the JSSA, the federal courts (aware of jury commissioners' past misuse of their administrative discretion to accomplish illegal purposes) have established certain standards and burdens of proof to accompany such challenges. If a group is "substantially" underrepresented on the venire, or if the methods for choosing names are not "race neutral" (e.g., if names on the list are identified by race), the court will presume a bias, which shifts the burden of proof from the defendant to the prosecutor. The government then has to prove that a procedure neutral with respect to race (or some other protected category) would have produced substantially the same result. In the era of computer-generated lists, no court will approve a procedure that appears to discriminate against a protected class.

A Sixth Amendment challenge to the jury selection process is much broader. The Sixth Amendment protects the right to trial by an "impartial" jury, which is now understood to mean a jury drawn from a list that represents a "fair cross-section of the community." Such a challenge, rather than focusing on the exclusion of one particular group, focuses on any selection procedure that departs from the standard of random selection or on jury selection results infected by the exclusion of any "distinctive" groups in the community. To mount such a challenge, a defendant need not be a member of any of the groups whose exclusion is alleged.

The burden of proof in a Sixth Amendment challenge is less severe than in an equal protection challenge. Once it has been demonstrated that the construction of the jury lists has excluded some distinctive group, the burden shifts to the government to prove that the challenged procedure advanced a "significant State interest." It is not necessary to demonstrate that jury officials were motivated by

101. I am guided in this section by the very thorough discussion provided by Gertner and Mizner, *Law of Juries*, 34–56.

a desire to discriminate against any particular group; it is necessary only to show that the resulting jury list does not represent a fair cross section of the community. The cross-section requirement, however, applies to the jury list and the venire, not to any particular jury. The Supreme Court has said that a "jury which is selected from a fair cross section is impartial regardless of the mix of individual viewpoints actually represented by the jury."[102] That is, as long as the venire was chosen from a list that did not exclude any cognizable groups, it does not matter which groups are actually represented on any particular jury. This rule also applies to equal protection challenges, since the random selection of 12 individuals from a venire of 300 or more names cannot be expected to reproduce the district's statistical profile.

As Gertner and Mizner put it, an equal protection challenge concerns the "process," whereas a Sixth Amendment challenge concerns the "impact" or result. The equal protection clause "looks to discriminatory *purposes*," while the Sixth Amendment "looks to discriminatory effects." Thus, race-neutral practices are not cognizable under the equal protection clause, even if they have a "disparate impact on the representation of a cognizable class in the jury venire"; such practices would be cognizable under a Sixth Amendment challenge. A Sixth Amendment challenge includes the "intentional exclusion of a distinctive group under a number of circumstances," while an equal protection challenge is concerned only with intentional exclusion motivated by discrimination. "In practice," Gertner and Mizner concede, "these distinctions can be difficult to discern. Administrative convenience may be a pretext for overt discrimination."[103] Or, as was apparently true in the *Thiel* case (despite the Court's skepticism), administrative convenience may be a legitimate goal. The desire to streamline the process by removing from the jury list the names of day laborers, who had always asked for and been granted exemptions in the past, might not be considered discrimination and might therefore be immune to an equal protection challenge. But the absence from the jury list of a "distinctive group," such as day laborers, *would* be actionable under a Sixth Amendment challenge.

These legal developments left the Supreme Court and Congress with a number of questions, and the answers have emerged only gradually, and provisionally, since 1968. Each question has been the source of much litigation and a prodigious outpouring of law journal articles.[104]

102. Lockhart v. McCree, 476 U.S. 162 (1986). Note the reference to "individual viewpoints" in the Court's ruling. The notion that particular "viewpoints" are associated with membership in particular groups is a notable feature of the modern regime of jury selection.

103. Gertner and Mizner, *Law of Juries*, 36. The expectation that administrative arrangements will have a discriminatory purpose comes close to being the prevailing assumption.

104. A Hein Online search for articles with "jury selection" in the title returned 318 hits for the forty-two years between 1968 and 2010. For the forty-two years between 1926 and 1968, the same search yielded only 47 results.

WHICH GROUPS ARE PROTECTED?

The provisional answer is that the courts give special attention to those groups against whom discrimination has been proved in other contexts: blacks, Hispanics, women, and Asians.[105] Exclusion of any of these groups from the venire can trigger either a Sixth Amendment or an equal protection challenge. But under the current understanding of the Sixth Amendment's guarantee of an impartial jury, other groups must be considered in determining whether a venire contains a true cross section of the community, since the four protected groups do not exhaust those found in any particular district. That is, the venire could contain members of all four groups and still be unrepresentative because of its statistically aberrant profile with respect to other categories. The Court has entertained the possibility of a much broader consideration of "inclusiveness" than is suggested by the four protected groups. In principle, if a distinctive group can be counted, it can be, and therefore should be, represented on the jury list, if not the jury itself.

Nor does it matter, in a Sixth Amendment challenge, that the defendant is not a member of the excluded group. In *Peters v. Kiff*[106]—in which a white defendant challenged his conviction by a jury from which blacks had, he claimed, been systematically excluded—Justice Thurgood Marshall argued for the Court:

> [If] any large and identifiable segment of the community is excluded from jury service, the effect is to remove from the jury room qualities of human nature and varieties of human experience, the range of which is unknown and perhaps unknowable. It is not necessary to assume that the excluded group will consistently vote as a class in order to conclude, as we do, that its exclusion deprives the jury of a perspective on human events that may have unsuspected importance in any case that may be presented.[107]

But the Court has not traveled very far down this particular road. It has refused, for example, to describe "attitudes" per se (an important one being opposition to the death penalty) as the basis of a "cognizable group" whose exclusion

105. Gertner and Mizner, *Law of Juries*, 37.

106. Peters v. Kiff, 407 U.S. 493 (1972).

107. Ibid., cited by Gertner and Mizner, *Law of Juries*, 37. In his dissent, joined by Justices Rehnquist and Blackmun, Chief Justice Burger observed that while there "is no longer any question . . . that persons may not be excluded from juries on account of race," it cannot be maintained that the exclusion of black jurors constitutes a "demonstration of prejudice" against a white defendant—in which case the white defendant has no grounds for a reversal of his conviction. Clearly, Burger was looking at the jury from the perspective of the defendant—as the formal theory of the jury had always required—rather than from the perspective of the prospective jurors, whose "right to serve" has become *almost* equal to the defendant's right to an impartial jury.

from the venire constitutes a statutory or constitutional violation.[108] Instead, the Court has stuck to a definition of "distinctive group" based on "some immutable characteristic such as race, gender or ethnic background." Yet this has not stopped the Court from suggesting that the reason for an "inclusive," "cross-section," or "representative" jury is to guarantee that each of the many viewpoints in the community has an equal chance of being represented on the jury—which would also require those representatives to do what Justice Marshall insisted they need not do: "consistently vote as a class." This also leaves open the argument that some viewpoints might actually be incompatible with faithful jury service—for example, the viewpoint that an unjust law should not be enforced and that no one charged with violating such a law should be found guilty; or that, given the nation's sorry history of racial discrimination, no black defendant arrested by a white police officer should be convicted, regardless of the evidence of his guilt. These viewpoints contribute to the modern claim of "jury nullification," a phenomenon considered more fully below.

HOW CAN SIXTH AMENDMENT OR EQUAL PROTECTION VIOLATIONS BE RECOGNIZED?

A Sixth Amendment or equal protection violation is triggered by evidence that a "distinctive" or "cognizable" group has been "systematically" excluded from the venire, resulting in an "unreasonable" disproportion between the group's numbers in the population and its numbers on the venire. In cases involving the exclusion (or automatic exemption) of women and the exclusion of African Americans, the statistical evidence of disproportion has usually been quite easy to establish. In *Taylor v. Louisiana*, evidence showed that women made up 53 percent of the population of St. Tammany Parish but only 10 percent of the jury wheel—the result of Louisiana's constitutional provision automatically exempting (but not excluding) women from jury service. Any woman who wished to be considered for service could file a special petition with the court.[109] In *Duren v. Missouri* (another case in which the state automatically exempted women but did not bar them absolutely), evidence showed that women made up 54 percent of the population of the community but only 15 percent of the venire.[110] In racial discrimination cases, likewise, the demonstration that a venire is not a reasonable cross section

108. See Gertner and Mizner, *Law of Juries*, 38. Those who believe that the death penalty is always wrong can be excluded from capital juries without incurring the danger of reversible error, although this exclusion continues to be a source of litigation.

109. *Taylor*, 525. See Gertner and Mizner, *Law of Juries*, 40. The constitutional provision was La. Const., Art. VII, sec. 41; the statute was La. Code Crim. Proc., Art. 402.

110. Duren v. Missouri, 439 U.S. 357 (1979).

of the district's population is a fairly straightforward proposition.[111] In the decision that set the stage for the JSSA—*Rabinowitz v. United States* in 1966—the appeals court was able to establish that whereas blacks constituted 35 percent of the population in the counties making up the Middle District of Georgia, they constituted only 6 percent of the venire from which the *Rabinowitz* petit jury had been chosen. Such disparities would obviously fail an equal protection challenge, especially given the unconvincing explanation by the clerk of the court that he was "naturally not well acquainted with members of the Negro race." But they would fail a Sixth Amendment challenge as well, even without the lame excuses or any other demonstration of discriminatory intent.

But how obvious does a disparity have to be to trigger a judicial remedy? The judicial standard is contained in what is called the "absolute disparity test."[112] This test compares the cognizable group's percentage of the district's population to its percentage of the venire. For example, if women are 52 percent of the district population but only 10 percent of the venire, there is an absolute disparity of 42 percent. If blacks are 30 percent of the population but only 10 percent of the venire, the absolute disparity is 20 percent. Most courts have held that an absolute disparity of 10 percent is a threshold for judicial intervention, but this is not a

111. Even at the height of the segregationist regime in the South, state officials were pulled by competing incentives. Maintaining segregation meant keeping black citizens off the voter registration lists; maintaining southern numbers in Congress meant ensuring that blacks were counted accurately in the federal census. As already noted, in states where property tax rolls were used along with voter lists, state officials were forced to keep black citizens on the tax list (so they would be obligated to pay taxes) while trying to keep them off the voter list. This made it fairly easy to demonstrate a disparity between the number of blacks in the district and the number on the jury list, since southern jury officials were also careful to record the race of prospective jurors. According to evidence collected by the National Center for State Courts, however, the current regime of jury selection makes it difficult to learn *anything* about the race of prospective jurors, until and unless their names are pulled from the jury wheel and they are summoned to court or asked to fill out a questionnaire. "Few source lists include gender, race or ethnicity in the information provided for the master jury list; that information is collected, if at all, during the qualification stage of the jury selection process or when the juror reports to the courthouse for service. The actual demographic representation of the master jury list is difficult to ascertain due to the inability to reliably determine whether under-representation of cognizable groups on the qualified list or in the jury pool originated with the master jury list or is the result of intermediate steps in the qualification process (e.g., summonses returned undeliverable, nonresponse/failure to appear rates, disqualification, exemption, and excusal rates)." National Center for State Courts, *Juror Manager's Toolbox: Characteristics of an Effective Master Jury List*, http://www.jurytoolbox.org/more/Characteristics%20of%20Effective%20MJL.pdf (accessed April 21, 2015).

112. See Gertner and Mizner, *Law of Juries*, 41–42.

hard-and-fast rule. Further, the rule is applied differently for equal protection and Sixth Amendment challenges. To demonstrate purposeful discrimination against a cognizable group (an equal protection challenge), the presence of strong circumstantial evidence of discrimination is enough—"the starker the disparity, the more likely it did not occur by chance."[113] To mount a Sixth Amendment challenge, it is necessary to demonstrate only that the absolute disparity is connected to the process of jury selection; whether the link is the result of a deliberate effort to discriminate or an accidental by-product of a selection method is immaterial. For example, the motives behind the unconstitutional practices in *Duren* and *Taylor*—exempting women but not disqualifying them—were very different from the ones that prompted the exclusion of blacks. Court administrators were spared the inconvenience of calling a large number of women, most of whom would ask for and be granted hardship exemptions to care for their children. The Court found that this practice, though innocent in its intention, contributed to the exclusion of a cognizable group from the venire and could not stand.[114] But there were no such innocent intentions behind the exclusion of blacks from jury lists.

In the hearings on the JSSA in 1967, the standard to be achieved was described as a "fair selection from a fair sample."[115] But Congress left it to the courts to define when an official voting list was so "unrepresentative" that a "fair sample" could not possibly be obtained from it. In both the House and the Senate, reports on the legislation stated that voter lists should be supplemented whenever there was evidence of "any substantial percentage deviation" between the list and a fair cross section of the community. The Senate report noted that the lists did not have to "perfectly mirror the percentage structure of the community. But any substantial percentage deviations must be corrected by the use of supplemental sources."[116] To date, however, the Court has not clarified what constitutes a "substantial percentage deviation," and perhaps as a result of this uncertainty, many federal jury commissions draw names from as many lists as possible.

WHAT SOURCES MUST JURY OFFICIALS USE IN COMPOSING THE VENIRE?

The jury statute (28 U.S.C. § 1863[b][2]) provides that the names of prospective jurors may be taken from the voter registration list or from a list of those regis-

113. Ibid., 45.

114. Ibid., 45–46. This is undoubtedly a consequence of *Thiel*, which rejected a similar argument about administrative convenience with respect to day laborers; see chapter 3.

115. S. Rep. No. 891, 90th Cong., 1st sess. (1968), at 10, cited in Gertner and Mizner, *Law of Juries*, 53.

116. S. Rep. No. 891, at 17, cited by ibid.

tered who have actually voted in a recent election. A certain number of names—either 1,000 or one-half of 1 percent of the total number of names on the list—is chosen at random and placed into the jury wheel, from which names are then drawn as needed for particular trial dates.

The "randomness" of the selection is qualified only by the requirement of "proportionality" with respect to place—which is designed, according to the statute, to ensure "that each county, parish, or similar political subdivision within the district or division is substantially proportionally represented in the master jury wheel" for the district.[117] This rule is not an innovation of the JSSA; it reflects a much older conception of the "impartial" jury, from a time when it was possible to guess a juror's voting preferences by knowing where he lived. (This is what Jeffersonians believed federal marshals were doing when they summoned jurors for the Sedition Act trials.) Thus, jury statutes have long required that jurors be chosen from lists representing all the district's towns or, in the case of county courts, all the neighborhoods of the county's largest city.[118]

But the question remains: how many citizens eligible for jury service actually live in the various subdivisions of the district, and what are their demographic characteristics? If the current source list does not accurately reflect the population, the venire chosen from it will not "proportionally represent" the various parts of the district, and the law's purpose will be defeated. It is possible, using census records, to get a "second opinion" regarding the source list's "proportionality," and if there is a "significant" deviation, the court may order the original source list—normally, the voter registration list—to be supplemented by other lists.[119] But this is possible only with respect to those characteristics captured by the census.

As Senator Sam Ervin reminded Attorney General Ramsey Clark during hearings on the JSSA in 1968, voter registration lists are notoriously unrepresentative of the population at large, and not only (as in Ervin's home state of North Carolina) because of race. As political scientists have long known, "voters" are a mere subset of "citizens." In some jurisdictions, as much as a third of the eligible electorate does not register to vote. The young, the poor, recent arrivals, the unemployed, and racial minorities often do not register to vote in numbers equal to their presence in the population, even when there is no systematic effort to prevent them from doing so.[120] Voters have at least one quality that might recom-

117. 28 U.S.C.A. § 1863(b)(3), cited by ibid., 48–49.

118. The Judiciary Act of 1789 (1 Stat. 73, section 29) states that jurors "shall be returned as there shall be occasion for them, from such parts of the district from time to time as the court shall direct, so as shall be most favourable to an impartial trial, and so as not to incur an unnecessary expense, or unduly to burthen the citizens of any part of the district with such services."

119. Gertner and Mizner, *Law of Juries*, 49.

120. For the earliest examples of this literature, see Charles E. Merriam and Herbert

mend them for jury service—their public-spirited willingness to take part in their country's political life. But under the current regime of jury selection, what might seem to be a plus is actually a minus. The voter registration lists cannot invariably (if ever) be accepted as a true cross section of the population, and names taken from such lists rarely constitute an "impartial" jury, as that old idea is now newly understood.[121]

The jury statute therefore gives federal district courts the responsibility of determining when other lists are necessary, or appropriate, to "foster the policy and protect the rights secured by sections 1861 and 1862 of this title."[122] For example, Congress amended the statute to allow federal courts in Massachusetts to use municipal census lists (Massachusetts is the only state that still conducts an annual municipal census)—a response to complaints that the voter registration lists failed to adequately capture the commonwealth's nonwhite population. This failure "extended the gap in political participation between the races into the jury arena," and it was hoped that this gap would be closed by using the presumably more complete city and town census lists instead.[123]

F. Gosnell, *Non-Voting, Causes and Methods of Control* (Chicago: University of Chicago Press, 1924); Edward H. Litchfield, *Voting Behavior in a Metropolitan Area* (Ann Arbor: University of Michigan Press, 1941); Paul F. Lazarsfeld, Bernard Berelson, and Hazel Gaudet, *The People's Choice: How the Voter Makes up His Mind in a Presidential Campaign* (New York: Columbia University Press, 1944); Angus Campbell, Gerald Gurin, and Warren E. Miller, *The Voter Decides* (Evanston, IL: Row, Peterson, 1954); Bernard Berelson, Paul Lazarsfeld, and William McPhee, *Voting: A Study of Opinion Formation in a Presidential Campaign* (Chicago: University of Chicago Press, 1954); Angus Campbell, P. Converse, W. E. Miller, and D. Stokes, *The American Voter* (New York: Wiley, 1960).

121. Gertner and Mizner, *Laws of Juries*, 54, make the point in this way: "Congress recognized that the fact that a citizen chose not to register to vote did not necessarily mean it was appropriate to disqualify him or her from jury service. The issue was not that potential juror's individual choice. Rather, it was the right of the defendant to a jury drawn from a fair cross-section of the community; a goal that would be undermined if juries consisted exclusively of those 'who have manifested their civic interest by registering to vote.'" This observation very succinctly captures the dramatic difference between the new and old understandings of an impartial jury.

122. 28 U.S.C.A. § 1863(b)(2). The use of multiple source lists is always an option for jury commissioners, even without a court order.

123. Gertner and Mizner, *Law of Juries*, 32. For a case in which this claim figured, see United States v. Levasseur, 704 F. Supp. 1153, 1164 (D. Mass. 1989). Recent complaints about the accuracy of the municipal census in Massachusetts have called this strategy into question. For some time, in an effort to cut costs, the commonwealth has been mailing census forms to city and town residents, rather than using public employees going door to door. But many residents refuse to return their census forms. See Kathleen Conti, "Everett Struggles to Get a True Population Count," *Boston Globe*, December 30, 2007. Unlike

Taken together, the "proportionality" requirement and the "fair cross section" requirement have generated a blizzard of court challenges from defendants claiming a denial of their right to an "impartial" jury. A brief sampling of these complaints suggests the inherent difficulty with the new standards and the degree to which they have departed from both the modern and the republican understanding of the proper form and function of the jury. Two problems become apparent. First, attainment of the goal of the JSSA—a jury chosen from a venire that represents a fair cross section of the population—is difficult to prove, since the law itself does not precisely define which groups are "cognizable," a task that has been left, by default, to the federal courts. This question is therefore always open to debate and litigation, even if the litigation is ultimately unsuccessful. No defendant has, as yet, complained about the lack of Presbyterians on the jury, to borrow Senator Ervin's fanciful example from 1967. But defendants (and the interest groups that adopt their cases) have raised questions not only about the "exclusion" of definable groups but also about their "underrepresentation" on the venire. Justice William Rehnquist, dissenting in *Duren v. Missouri*, referred to this development as a "constitutional numbers game" that would increase the already onerous burdens on both citizens and court administrators.[124] And in fact, challenges to convictions based on charges of improper jury selection dramatically increased, beginning in the 1970s.[125]

Second, the focus on a "representative" or "cross-section" venire has overshadowed those qualities once thought to be natural components of an "impartial" jury: intelligence, integrity, judgment, fairness, and common sense—qualities easily challenged as mere pretexts for discrimination. Concern about jury selection has shifted from a desire for better jurors to a desire for more representative juries—a concern expressed most importantly in litigation but also in the academic law journals, where the search for the representative jury has begun to resemble the search for the Holy Grail, and where the departure from the republican standard of the impartial jury has been most pronounced.

---

registering to vote, returning the municipal census form is obligatory under state law, and the penalty for "refusal" to do so is a fine of not more than $500 or imprisonment for not more than one year. The penalty for "failure to respond" (a lesser charge) is removal from the voter registration rolls, which means that those citizens who fail to be counted in the municipal census temporarily lose their right to vote, whereas those convicted of refusal become ineligible for jury service because of a felony conviction. Mass. Gen. Laws 56, 4.

124. *Duren*, 375.

125. To be more precise, challenges increased during the first two decades of the postmodern regime, until random selection from numerous lists became the norm in federal and state courts, at which point challenges shifted to the way in which peremptory challenges were used to shape juries in the courtroom itself.

JURY SELECTION AND RACE

The first judicial reference to "representative" or "cross-section" juries occurred in the context of race, in Justice Black's decision in *Smith v. Texas* in 1940.[126] As noted in the previous chapter, that decision introduced something new to the jury debate, in the guise of something old. "It is part of the established tradition in the use of juries as instruments of public justice," Justice Black argued, "that the jury be a body truly representative of the community."[127] But in fact, the traditional notion of the jury was simply that its members must be "fair and impartial," "sober," "honest," "intelligent," or in other ways upstanding, and that they be residents of the "vicinage" or the "district" or the "state." "Representation" was a feature of legislatures but not of juries. It was, of course, a violation of federal law to exclude black citizens from jury service, a ruling first made in *Strauder v. West Virginia* in 1880 and reaffirmed consistently ever since.[128] Thus, Justice Black's remarks on the representative jury were unnecessary to the resolution of Smith's claims against the state of Texas. Nevertheless, it struck a chord and began to appear almost immediately in contexts having nothing to do with race. In 1942 Justice Murphy, in *Glasser v. United States*, described the idea of a "representative jury" (i.e., one that included women) as a view "more in harmony with our basic concepts of a democratic society and a representative government."[129] (This remark was also unnecessary to the case at hand because the *Glasser* jury included women, who were not barred or exempted from jury service in Illinois.) Four years after *Glasser* came the *Thiel* decision (barring automatic hardship exemptions for day laborers), by which time Justice Black's dictum had become one of the essential elements in "the American tradition of trial by jury," which "necessarily contemplates an impartial jury drawn from a cross-section of the community."[130]

Because of the importance of the *Rabinowitz* case to Congress's understanding of the "jury problem" in the 1960s, "representative" juries quickly became associated with juries untainted by racial discrimination, so it is not surprising that many of the hopes raised by the JSSA were the same hopes raised more generally by the civil rights movement and by passage of the Civil Rights Acts of 1957, 1964, and 1968. It was therefore a great disappointment that, in the years after the JSSA's passage, it was common to see, in state and federal courtrooms all over the country, juries as white as those in the South in the bad old days.[131] This time,

126. See the discussion in chapter 3.

127. *Smith*, 130.

128. Strauder v. West Virginia, 100 U.S. 303 (1880).

129. Glasser v. United States, 315 U.S. 60 (1942), 85.

130. *Thiel*, 220.

131. For example, a 2010 study by researchers at the University of Michigan found

the reason was not the exclusion of blacks from the venire by biased or indifferent jury commissioners. It was the removal of blacks during voir dire by the exercise of peremptory challenges and challenges for cause.

The Federal Rules of Criminal Procedure (rule 24[b]) provide that, in criminal trials, defendants may exercise up to ten peremptory challenges and prosecutors may exercise up to six. (In capital cases, both sides have twenty challenges; in misdemeanor cases, both sides have three.) A challenge for cause—for example, that a particular juror cannot be impartial or is incompetent to serve for some other reason—must be entertained by the judge, who may remove the challenged juror or not, at his or her discretion. A peremptory challenge does not require a reason and must be granted, up to the allotted number.

The folklore of the bar has always insisted that a shrewd attorney can "know" which jurors might be favorable to his or her client and which ones might cause trouble. Behavioral clues, clothing, facial expressions, and background information (e.g., a family member who is a police officer) are some of the elements that constitute the old-fashioned core of what has now become a "science" (discussed below). Attorneys and prosecutors argue that it is essential to a fair trial, or to an effective prosecution, that the attorneys conducting the case be allowed some discretion in selecting or rejecting certain jurors. If the judge refuses to remove a prospective juror for cause—and judges are reluctant to do so in all but the most obvious cases—the attorneys use their peremptory challenges instead, hoping to get the "best" possible jury for the particular case. The questions raised by peremptory challenges in the context of race are relatively straightforward ones: Does the deliberate removal of all or most of the African American jurors present in the courtroom constitute an illicit form of discrimination? Does it violate constitutional principles and the intent of the JSSA? But the Supreme Court's answers to these questions have been anything but straightforward.

The use of peremptory challenges to impanel an all-white jury to try a black defendant received the qualified approval of the Supreme Court in 1965. That case, *Swain v. Alabama*,[132] involved circumstances that are quite common in American courtrooms and are not unique to the South, unlike the wholesale exclusion of blacks from the jury pool, the voter rolls, and public life generally. The petitioner, Robert Swain, had been indicted for the capital offense of rape by a

---

that "prosecutors in North Carolina removed qualified African-American jurors at more than twice the rate that they removed all other jurors," and at even higher rates when the defendant was African American. Cassandra Stubbs, "Can the Racial Justice Act Change the Practice of Picking All-White Juries in North Carolina," ACLU Blog of Rights, http://www.aclu.org/blog/capital-punishment/can-racial-justice-act-change-practice-picking-all-white-juries-north (accessed September 10, 2014).

132. Swain v. Alabama, 380 U.S. 202 (1965).

mixed-race grand jury, but he was convicted by a petit jury from which all six eligible Negroes (two turned out to be exempt under state law) had been removed by the prosecution's use of peremptory challenges. Swain was able to demonstrate that blacks were underrepresented on the jury list (26 percent of the population but only 10 to 15 percent of the venire) and that, whereas 80 percent of grand juries had Negro members, no Negro had served on a petit jury in the Talladega County Circuit Court since 1950.[133] Notwithstanding this evidence, the Supreme Court narrowly (five to four) refused to find a constitutional violation—insisting (with qualifications) that the use of peremptory challenges to remove particular jurors in a particular trial was fundamentally different from the wholesale exclusion of blacks (or any other cognizable group) from the jury pool.

Writing for the Court, Justice Byron White first cited the long history of cases, dating to 1880, outlawing the "purposeful or deliberate" discrimination against blacks in constituting the venire. However, such "purposeful discrimination may not be assumed or merely asserted"; it must be proved.[134] Since Negroes had served on grand juries, including the one that had indicted the petitioner, and since "an average of six to seven Negroes" had been on the petit jury venires during the period covered, it was clear, according to White, that in this county at least, "Alabama has not totally excluded a racial group from either grand or petit jury panels."[135]

As in many states prior to the 1968 law, the jury commissioners in Talladega County used a variety of sources in collecting the names of citizens "reputed to be honest, intelligent [men] . . . esteemed for their integrity, good character and sound judgment."[136] Each of the two commissioners, with the assistance of the clerk, was responsible for obtaining the names of those thought to be qualified; these names were taken from "city directories, registration lists, club and church lists, conversations with other persons in the community, both white and colored, and personal and business acquaintances."[137] Unlike the Georgia jury commissioners who would testify in the *Rabinowitz* case that they were "not personally acquainted with any Negroes," the commissioners in Talladega County actually found a reasonable number of black citizens to include on the venire. The percentage of blacks on the jury list was, the Court acknowledged, less than the percentage of blacks in the adult male population of the county (10 to 15 percent versus 26 percent, although in earlier years, blacks had accounted for as much as

133. Ibid., 203–206.

134. Ibid., 205.

135. Ibid. The other cases were Norris v. Alabama, 294 U.S. 587(1935); Hill v. Texas, 316 U.S. 400 (1942); Patton v. Mississippi, 332 U.S. 463 (1947); Hernandez v. Texas, 347 U.S. 475 (1954); and Reece v. Georgia, 350 U.S. 85 (1955).

136. *Swain*, 206, citing Alabama Code, Title 30, §§ 10, 21 (1958).

137. Ibid.

23 percent of the list), but this disparity did not rise to the level of a constitutional violation.[138] Furthermore, no criminal defendant is "constitutionally entitled to demand a proportionate number of his race on the jury which tries him, nor on the venire or jury roll from which petit jurors are drawn."[139] The Constitution requires only that the jury be "impartial" and that no group be systematically excluded, because of race or other characteristics, from the jury list itself. If the exclusion is a product of the exercise of peremptory challenges, there is no violation, even if, as the record conceded, this meant that no blacks had served on petit juries in the county for the past fifteen years.

But why was there no violation? If excluding blacks from the venire violated the equal protection clause, why did it make a difference that blacks had been excluded through the use of peremptory challenges? This is a significant question, because it goes to the heart of the Court's understanding of what it means for a jury to be "impartial."

Justice White began by noting the long history of peremptory challenges, an element of the common-law jury brought over from England to the colonies, along with the challenge for cause, an established tradition long before the adoption of the Constitution and the Bill of Rights. The use of peremptory challenges, or the similar procedure of "striking" names from the jury list (the way challenges were handled in Alabama), had "very old credentials." What could Article III and the Sixth Amendment mean by the phrase "trial by jury" if not the jury the founding generation knew and valued so highly?[140] Furthermore, an important element of peremptory challenges is that they are final and arbitrary ("challenges without cause, without explanation, and without judicial scrutiny"). That is the key to their importance in both civil and criminal cases. "The system, it is said, in and of itself, provides justification for striking any group of otherwise qualified jurors in any given case, whether they be Negroes, Catholics, accountants or those with blue eyes. Based on the history of this system and its actual use and operation in this country, we think there is merit to this position."[141] White then reviewed the long history of legislative and judicial support for this right, up to the adoption of rule 24(b) of the Federal Rules of Criminal Procedure, which provided that in capital cases each side was "entitled to" twenty peremptory challenges.[142] The pattern in the states "paralleled that in the federal system," and the right of challenge was conferred by statute from a very early date. Thus, "by 1870, most, if not all, States had enacted statutes conferring on the prosecution a substantial number of

138. Ibid.

139. Ibid., 208, citing precedents going all the way back to Virginia v. Rives, 100 U.S. 313 (1880).

140. Ibid., 212–214.

141. Ibid., 212.

142. Ibid., 216, n. 15.

peremptory challenges, the number generally being at least half, but often equal to, the number had by the defendant."[143]

Finally, although the peremptory challenge was an English institution imported to the colonies, it had "fallen into disuse" in the United Kingdom, along with the challenge for cause. In contrast, the use of the peremptory challenge was growing more popular in the United States, and White ventured a guess as to why. The reason, "perhaps," is that "juries here are drawn from a greater cross-section of a heterogeneous society." That is, because American jurors are drawn from a broader swath of society than jurors in Britain, where property qualifications were still in place in the 1960s, the vetting of jurors is necessarily more severe.[144] "The voir dire in American trials tends to be extensive and probing, operating as a predicate for the exercise of peremptories, and the process of selecting a jury is protracted. The persistence of peremptories and their extensive use demonstrate the long and widely held belief that peremptory challenge is a necessary part of trial by jury."[145] The peremptory challenge is necessary to inspire confidence in the impartiality of the jurors chosen to hear a case, and for this very reason, it must be "exercised without a reason stated, without inquiry and without being subject to the court's control." Indeed, it might be exercised, White conceded, "for a real or imagined partiality that is less easily designated or demonstrable."[146] Citing *Lewis v. United States*, White agreed that the peremptory challenge might be exercised based on the "sudden impressions and unaccountable prejudices we are apt to conceive upon the bare looks and gestures of another."[147] The peremptory challenge is a way to err on the side of caution in order to inspire the greatest degree of confidence in the impartiality of the jury, a right that pertains to both the defense and the prosecution in criminal cases. It is therefore a fundamental element in the conduct of jury trials in the United States and is nearly as old as the jury itself, and not a "peculiar institution" of the Jim Crow South (although White did not draw this last conclusion).

Yet the fact that no Negroes had served on Talladega County juries for the past fifteen years "presses a broader claim in this Court," White wrote, and "we agree that this claim raises a different issue and it may well require a different

143. Ibid., 216.

144. Until the law was reformed in 1972, eligibility for jury service in Great Britain was restricted by a property qualification established in the early nineteenth century: £10 yearly from real estate or rents, or ownership of property taxed at the rate of at least £20 per year. Although these values had been nullified by property inflation, the law effectively excluded all renters from jury service. House of Commons Debate, March 20, 1962, Hansard vol. 656, cc210–20.

145. *Swain*, 218–219.

146. Ibid., 220.

147. Ibid., citing Lewis v. United States, 146 U.S. 370 (1892), 376.

answer." If it could be shown that the prosecutor had used his peremptory challenges to remove otherwise qualified Negroes from petit juries "in case after case, whatever the circumstances, whatever the crime and whoever the defendant or the victim may be," then there would be "added significance" to a Fourteenth Amendment claim. "If the State has not seen fit to leave a single Negro on any jury in a criminal case, the presumption protecting the prosecutor may well be overcome."[148] But since the record of the case under review "does not with any acceptable degree of clarity, show when, how often, and under what circumstances the prosecutor alone" has been responsible for the removal of Negroes through peremptory challenges (since some black jurors might have been challenged by defendants), the petitioner failed to carry his burden of proof.

Whether intended or not, this indication of what constitutes the burden of proof in such cases—that is, consistent prosecution challenges of Negro jurors in "case after case" over many years—invited future plaintiffs to take greater care in preparing their appeals.[149] However, critics of *Swain* pointed to the immense difficulties in carrying this burden. It was difficult if not impossible to collect data on the number of blacks removed from juries through peremptory challenges because (ironically) many districts outside the South did not keep statistics on the race of either prospective or seated jurors.[150] In the years following the *Swain* decision, many cases made it to the appeals stage and had varying degrees of success, yielding different results in different states and in different federal circuits.[151] Yet it was twenty years before the *Swain* ruling was successfully challenged and overturned in *Batson v. Kentucky* (1985), which was decided by a divided (and differently constituted) Court seventeen years into the era of the postmodern jury.

THE *BATSON* REVOLUTION

Batson had been convicted of second-degree burglary and receipt of stolen goods by an all-white jury achieved as a result of the prosecutor's use of peremptory

148. Ibid., 223–224.

149. Ibid., 226–227.

150. Batson v. Kentucky, 476 U.S. 79 (1986), 93, n. 17.

151. See, for example, People v. Wheeler, 22 Cal. 3d 258 (1978), in which the court found that using peremptory challenges to remove jurors because of "group bias" undermines the impartiality that comes from "the interaction of the diverse beliefs and values the jurors bring from their group experiences"; Commonwealth v. Soares, 377 Mass. 461 (1979), in which the court found that the removal of twelve of thirteen blacks from a jury trying black defendants violated the defendants' right to the "judgment of their peers"; and United States v. Leslie, 783 F.2d 541 (5th Cir. 1986), in which the court found that *Swain* permits the removal of jurors in order to seek "adversary advantage," even when all those challenged are of the same race.

challenges to remove the only four blacks on the venire. The defense had moved to discharge the jury on Sixth Amendment grounds—claiming it was not the "impartial" jury guaranteed by the Bill of Rights—but the trial court had refused to do so, and the Supreme Court of Kentucky declined to reverse Batson's conviction, affirming the traditional authority of both prosecutors and defense attorneys to use peremptory challenges any way they saw fit.

For the Supreme Court, however—or for the *Batson* majority,[152] at any rate—the chief issue raised by Batson's appeal was the heavy "evidentiary burden" of a defendant making an equal protection claim regarding jury selection, even though Batson had not actually made such a claim. In fact, defense counsel had expressly denied any reliance on the Fourteenth Amendment and was not challenging the *Swain* ruling at all. The defense was content to rest its appeal on the Sixth Amendment's "impartial" jury—now defined by post-*Swain* Court rulings and congressional acts (among them the Jury Selection and Service Act of 1968) as a jury chosen from a "fair cross section" of the population.

Nevertheless, Justice Lewis Powell, writing for the Court, began his opinion with an attack on *Swain* and the heavy "evidentiary burden" placed on any defendant launching an equal protection challenge to the composition of his jury. Civil rights activists had pressed ever since the *Swain* ruling for a less burdensome standard, and in *Batson* they finally got one (more or less), even though they received very little help from the defendant. To accomplish this result, Powell shifted the focus away from the pattern of challenges in a judicial district to the challenges exercised at a particular trial, seeking to carve out some space for peremptory challenges in general while narrowing, as much as possible, the space available for the prosecution's removal of black jurors. In a significant footnote, Powell noted that the Court was not commenting on the use of peremptory challenges by defendants; however, as the dissents pointed out, any restrictions on the prosecution's use of peremptory challenges would sooner or later lead to similar restrictions on defense counsel, and this would constitute a profound alteration in the traditional understanding of how an accused can defend his right to an impartial jury.

In making this case, Powell relied on a number of federal court decisions since *Swain* that had clarified the standards for proving a prima facie case of discrimination in the selection of the venire.[153] The accumulated weight of these

152. Although it was decided by the comfortable margin of seven to two, *Batson* generated six separate decisions in addition to the majority decision, which was written by Justice Powell and joined by Justices Brennan, White, Marshall, Blackmun, Stevens, and O'Connor. Justice White wrote a separate concurring opinion, as did Justices Marshall, O'Connor, and Stevens (joined by Brennan). Chief Justice Burger wrote one dissent, joined by Justice Rehnquist, who wrote a separate dissent, joined by Burger.

153. Citing Castaneda v. Partida, 430 U.S. 482 (1977); Washington v. Davis, 426 U.S. 229 (1976); and Alexander v. Louisiana, 405 U.S. 625 (1972).

cases supported the conclusion, which the Court now declared, that a defendant may establish such a case "solely on evidence concerning the prosecutor's exercise of peremptory challenges at the defendant's trial." The defendant must, of course, show that he is a member of a "cognizable racial group" and that the prosecutor used his peremptory challenges to remove members of that group. But the defendant, Powell noted, can also "rely on the fact, as to which there can be no dispute," that the peremptory challenge is a practice that permits discrimination by anyone with a desire to discriminate. That is, because discrimination is a possibility, it will be presumed (at least provisionally) to be a reality, subject to the defendant's demonstration that the facts presented "raise an inference that the prosecutor used that practice to exclude the veniremen from the petit jury on account of their race." Supportive evidence might include the "prosecutor's questions and statements during voir dire" or the existence of a "'pattern' of strikes against black jurors."[154]

Once the defendant made his case, the state would be obliged to provide a nonracial explanation for the removal of black jurors. Conceding that this requirement might impose "a limitation in some cases on the full peremptory character of the historic challenge," Powell insisted that the explanation need not "rise to the level . . . of a challenge for cause." However, the prosecutor could not rebut the accusation of bias by explaining that he had challenged black jurors only because of his assumption that they would be partial to a black defendant. This assumption, Powell claimed, would be the same as the old racist claim that blacks were incapable of serving as jurors; allowing such a claim to stand would make a mockery of the equal protection clause. The prosecutor must therefore be able to "articulate a neutral explanation related to the particular case."[155] But presumably, this would require the prosecutor to assume that a person's race had nothing to do with how he or she responded to a particular prosecution—a presumption that directly contradicts the expectation that there are varieties of experience and outlook that ought to be "represented" on the venire.

Powell noted, but did not concede, the state's contention that the holding in *Batson* would "eviscerate the fair trial values served by the peremptory challenge." As valuable as the challenge has been, Powell rejoined, "the reality of practice . . . shows that the challenge may be . . . used to discriminate against black jurors." Putting a stop to this abuse will enhance "public respect for our criminal justice system" by ensuring that "no citizen is disqualified from jury service because of his race."[156] Justice White, whose ruling in *Swain* was now being partially reversed, wrote a concurring opinion urging that the decision not be applied retroactively (as did Justice Sandra Day O'Connor in her concurrence). But White

154. *Batson*, 96.
155. Ibid., 97.
156. Ibid., 98, 99.

made a significant prediction: "Much litigation will be required to spell out the contours of the Court's equal protection holding today, and the significant effect it will have on the conduct of criminal trials cannot be gainsaid."[157]

Justice Marshall "wholeheartedly" concurred with the decision but would have gone further "in fashioning a remedy adequate to eliminate" discrimination. Marshall was convinced that simply letting defendants object to racially discriminatory challenges would not be enough to end such practices. Prosecutors could easily come up with "facially neutral" explanations for removing black jurors. Would a trial court be able to separate honest responses from pretextual ones? Indeed, prosecutors themselves might be unaware of their own biased motivations—for the time, a somewhat novel theory of how racism works. Marshall stated:

> A prosecutor's own conscious or unconscious racism may lead him easily to the conclusion that a prospective black juror is "sullen," or "distant," a characterization that would not have come to his mind if a white juror had acted identically. A judge's own conscious or unconscious racism may lead him to accept such an explanation as well-supported. . . . Even if all parties approach the Court's mandate with the best of conscious intentions, that mandate requires them to confront and overcome their own racism on all levels—a challenge I doubt all of them can meet.[158]

This "inherent potential" of peremptory challenges to permit racial discrimination "should ideally lead the Court to ban them entirely from the criminal justice system." Marshall was prepared to accept the logical conclusion: if peremptory challenges are taken from the prosecution, they should be denied to the defense as well. And as the Court had already made clear in other decisions, this step would not undermine any constitutional right, since the peremptory challenge was merely "traditional" and not an unqualified constitutional privilege.[159]

The *Batson* decision made the peremptory challenge a central focus of the jurisprudence of the jury system, where it has remained. But this result was inevitable as soon as the "representative" or "cross-section" jury was declared to be the "traditional" American view of the jury system. From colonial times (at least) until the 1940s, the focus had consistently been on the defendant's right to an impartial jury, and one of the most important of the defendant's subsidiary rights was the right to challenge jurors peremptorily. The challenge for cause was meant

157. Ibid., 101–102.

158. Ibid., 106.

159. Ibid., 107–108. The Supreme Court has repeatedly held that while the Constitution does not require federal or state courts to allow the peremptory challenge, it is nevertheless "one of the most important of the rights secured to the accused." *Swain*, 219, citing Pointer v. United States, 151 U.S. 396 (1894), 408.

to remove jurors whose bias, or potential bias, was obvious. But trial outcomes are never determined only by what is obvious, and practitioners have always known this. When twelve citizens are chosen to decide a person's fate or to resolve a conflict between two parties, a thousand factors might come into play that cannot be clearly expressed or described. Thus the reason for the peremptory challenge—the right to challenge without explanation, based on a hunch, a feeling, or even a prejudice—a right that had always been available, though unequally, to defendants and prosecutors alike, in both federal and state courts.

But the advent of the representative, cross-section jury shifted the emphasis of the jury discussion from the parties to the jurors, and from impartiality and competence to representation. It also introduced, gently at first, a novel idea: that jurors have "rights" that approach in dignity the rights of defendants, litigants, and the representatives of the people in whose name criminal trials are conducted. The authors of the Jury Selection and Service Act of 1968 believed that they were declaring a new right to serve on a jury. In fact, they were doing much more: they were changing the understanding of what a jury is for and how it ought to function.

Because Congress was deliberating on jury reform at the height of the civil rights movement, the jury debate in the 1960s tended to conflate two very different forms of "discrimination," and this confusion contributed to a growing hostility to the peremptory challenge. Civil rights legislation was directed at those forms of racial discrimination that underlay the white-supremacy regime, particularly in the South, and required the exclusion of black citizens from all forms of public life.[160] Excluding black Americans from the voting rolls, the jury lists, and public office was one element of a common strategy of subordination, along with the segregation of all aspects of social life. In contrast, the exercise of peremptory challenges—a practice never confined to the South or even to the United States—was a form of "discrimination" that merely took note of the differences between jurors. Does one juror seem more or less likely to favor the prosecution or the defense, or one litigant over another?

This question might naturally be raised in the case of a black juror asked to decide between a black defendant and his white prosecutors (and the white police

160. Jury commissions in some southern states have allegedly continued the practice of removing the names of black citizens from the jury pool, long after passage of the JSSA. See, for example, Paula DiPerna's discussion of the trial of sheriff's deputies in Wrightsville, Georgia, in 1983. Although blacks accounted for 33 percent of the population, they represented only 12.5 percent of the jury pool, even though many more blacks in Georgia had registered to vote since the civil rights movement and legislative reforms of the 1960s. This result was achieved because "jury revisers" (the equivalent of a jury commission) simply removed the names of black voters from the jury list. Paula DiPerna, *Juries on Trial: Faces of American Justice* (New York: Dembner Books/W. W. Norton, 1984).

officers who arrested him),[161] just as it might be raised in the case of female jurors in a rape trial or Catholic jurors (or any juror with strong views on abortion) in the trial of an abortionist. Lawyers look for sympathetic juries, which means spotting possibly unsympathetic jurors and challenging them peremptorily. Would the ability of both prosecution and defense to impanel an impartial jury be compromised if the peremptory challenge were now circumscribed, as the *Batson* ruling seemed to require, or abolished, as Justice Marshall proposed?

This question was the focus of a dissent by Justice Rehnquist, joined by Chief Justice Warren Burger. Pointing out that the majority decision "deals with much more than 'evidentiary [burdens],'" Rehnquist asserted that the decision also "overrules one of the fundamental substantive holdings of *Swain*, namely, that the State may use its peremptory challenges to remove from the jury, on a case-specific basis, prospective jurors of the same race as the defendant." To overrule such a fundamental principle, Rehnquist argued, is "both ill-considered and unjustifiable under established principles of equal protection."[162] *Swain* had presented two "scenarios" involving the dismissal of blacks from a particular jury. The first scenario—in which blacks had been dismissed "in case after case, whatever the circumstances, whatever the crime and whoever the defendant or the victim may be"—might well violate "the guarantees of equal protection." But the second scenario—in which the state used its peremptory challenges "to exclude blacks from a particular jury based on the assumption or belief that they would be more likely to favor a black defendant"—did not, according to the *Swain* majority, violate equal protection principles. In fact, Justice White's opinion in *Swain* was a forthright defense of the traditional understanding of peremptory challenges, which permit "rejection for a real or imagined partiality that is less easily designated or demonstrable."[163] Describing the importance of the peremptory challenge to the task of seating an impartial jury, White's opinion in *Swain* restated the lawyer's traditional understanding:

> For the question a prosecutor or defense counsel must decide is not whether a juror of a particular race or nationality is in fact partial, but whether one from a different group is less likely to be. . . . Hence veniremen are not always judged solely as individuals for the purpose of exercising peremptory challenges. Rather they are challenged in light of the limited knowledge counsel has of them, which may include their group affiliations, in the context of the case to be tried. . . . To subject the prosecutor's challenge in any particular case to the demands and traditional standards of the Equal Protection Clause

161. Distrust of white police officers by black jurors played a significant role in the felony murder trial of O. J. Simpson, as discussed later.

162. *Batson*, 134.

163. Ibid., 135, citing *Swain*, 209–222.

would entail a radical change in the nature and operation of the challenge. The challenge . . . would no longer be peremptory.[164]

In light of the *Swain* majority's forthright defense of the peremptory challenge—a view, Rehnquist pointed out, shared even by the dissenters—the opinion in *Batson* constituted an "unprecedented use of the Equal Protection Clause to restrict the historic scope of the peremptory challenge," which *Swain* had defined as a "necessary part of trial by jury."[165] There is nothing "unequal," Rehnquist concluded, about the use of the peremptory challenge "to strike blacks from the jury in cases involving black defendants, so long as such challenges are also used to exclude whites in cases involving white defendants, Hispanics in cases involving Hispanic defendants . . . and so on." However "stereotypical" and even "hopelessly mistaken" such "seat-of-the-pants instincts" might be, Rehnquist continued, "I do not see—and the Court most certainly has not explained—how their use violates the Equal Protection Clause."[166]

The Supreme Court's effort to tame the peremptory challenge without abolishing it was not the only conundrum generated by the "representative jury" paradigm. If a defendant is entitled to a jury chosen from a fair cross section of the local population, then any practices that cause the jury pool to differ from the demographic profile of the district are suspect, no matter who the defendant is. Yet since the jury selection process always involved a "winnowing," choosing from among the citizenry those judged to be most suitable for service, the stage was now set for an open confrontation between two views of the jury and how it should operate—a confrontation that has continued to trouble the Court's jury decisions, and not merely with respect to race.

JURY SERVICE AND GENDER

Although the concept of the "representative" or "cross-section" jury was first conceived in the context of racial exclusion, there were immediate attempts to apply the principle to other categories: day laborers in *Thiel* and women in *Glasser*. And although the participation of working-class citizens in the jury system ceased to be a major preoccupation in the courts and Congress, the participation of women became an important issue in both the judiciary and the legislature.

The exclusion of women from petit juries was, in the colonial and republican periods, a simple function of the segregation of the public and private worlds by

164. Ibid., quoting *Swain*, 220–222.
165. Ibid., 137, citing *Swain*, 219.
166. Ibid., 138.

gender, with men acting in public and women caring for the home.[167] The decisive challenge to this traditional arrangement came with the push for women's suffrage. When this was attained at the national level in 1919, it created millions of female voters who were suddenly eligible for jury service in states where being an "elector" was the threshold requirement for being a juror. In response, several states promptly rewrote their jury laws to exclude women absolutely. Other states left their statutes untouched but offered automatic exemptions to women who asked for them or exempted women en masse, allowing them to serve only if they requested to do so. It was ostensibly the desire to protect these (and other) arcane arrangements that led Congress, against the advice of the Judicial Conference, to preserve the practice of using state jury qualification rules to choose federal jurors.

Passage of the Civil Rights Act of 1957 overthrew the "conformity principle," thus ending women's disqualification from jury service in the federal courts; henceforth "any citizen of the United States" would be eligible for service, state laws to the contrary notwithstanding.[168] But the 1957 act did not prevent states from offering exemptions to women, who continued to be underrepresented on many state jury lists.[169] Passage of the Jury Selection and Service Act of 1968 set the stage for challenges to these exemptions in two ways: first, by requiring "random selection from a fair cross section of the community in the district or division wherein the court convenes," and second, by proclaiming it to be federal policy that "all citizens shall have the opportunity to be considered for service on grand and petit juries in the district courts of the United States."[170] Exemptions were not directly forbidden by the JSSA, although the clear import of the "fair cross-section" ideal was a jury system in which all "cognizable groups" were included on jury lists in roughly equal proportion to their presence in the district. The jury selection laws of several states were left in something of a legal limbo, with women not fully included but not absolutely excluded either. To complicate matters further, the new federal right to serve as a juror meant that any restriction on such service, including automatic exemptions, might be suspect, either as a violation of the cross-section principle now included in the Sixth Amendment guarantee of an "impartial jury" or under the Fourteenth Amendment's guarantee

167. The arguments for and against jury service by women, and the changing provisions in the states, are summarized by Lucy Fowler, "Gender and Jury Deliberations: The Contributions of Social Science," *William & Mary Journal of Women and the Law* 12, 1 (2005): 2–15; and Joanna L. Grossman, "Women's Jury Service: Right of Citizenship or Privilege of Difference?" *Stanford Law Review* 46, 5 (May 1994): 1115.

168. Pub. L. No. 85-315, § 152.

169. In fact, hearings on the 1957 Civil Rights Act made it clear that Congress's intent was to reform federal jury selection procedures so that federal courts could escape the myriad practices that characterized jury selection in the states.

170. 28 U.S.C. § 1861.

of "equal protection of the laws." Thus, federal courts would be called on to protect not only the rights of defendants but also the rights of prospective jurors, even when those rights might be in conflict.

What had restrained federal courts in the past was the reluctance of federal judges to interfere unduly with the states' administration of their own judicial systems, assuming a basic conformity to federal law. It was not, after all, unusual for states to offer exemptions to whole categories of the population: doctors, firefighters, day laborers, and, since passage of the Nineteenth Amendment, women. Prior to the Civil Rights Act of 1957, even some federal courts had offered such wholesale exemptions. These practices had long been a target of jury reformers, including the Judicial Conference, in part because they were thought to degrade the quality of the available jury pool. But trial court officials argued that some categories of the population so consistently asked to be exempted from jury service that it was easier to issue blanket exemptions than to deal with individual hardship requests, which slowed court proceedings unnecessarily. The willingness of the *Thiel* Court to interfere with such administrative exemptions had earned the rebuke of Justice Frankfurter,[171] and many appellate judges apparently shared his reluctance to second-guess trial courts or state legislatures, at least outside the province of race. In 1961, in fact, a unanimous Supreme Court had refused to question Florida's practice of exempting women unless they asked to serve, finding the practice "reasonable"—even though the defendant in the case, a woman accused of murdering her husband, had been tried and convicted by an all-male jury.[172]

That reluctance to interfere had faded considerably by the 1970s, as the Court became more receptive to arguments for extending the cross-section ideal beyond race and beyond the federal courts. After all, if Congress had stated, in effect, that jury service is a right and that "all citizens have a right to be considered" for jury service, then that right might well be incorporated against the states under the equal protection clause of the Fourteenth Amendment. And in constructing jury pools that represent a cross section of the population, why single out race as the only category worthy of attention? Wouldn't the same principle that forbids the exclusion of blacks from venires and jury panels also forbid the exclusion of women, the

171. See chapter 3 and *Thiel*, 225. Frankfurter made a similar complaint in his concurring opinion in *Ballard v. United States*, as did Justice Burton in his dissent. Burton wrote: "In the absence of a binding statutory or court rule then requiring such inclusion of women, the District Court was compelled to exercise its own discretion in including or excluding them. Without depending on the breadth of the discretion which should be allowed to a District Court under those circumstances, I submit that the reasons for the District Court action strengthen the position that this Court should not now retroactively disapprove the established local federal practice which conformed almost exactly with the established state practice" (329 U.S. 187 [1946], at 203).

172. Hoyt v. Florida, 368 U.S. 57 (1961).

poor, ethnic minorities (e.g., Hispanics and Asians), and other cognizable groups traditionally "marginalized" by jury selection procedures—even when the "exclusion" is actually an "exemption"? Abolishing the discretion of jury commissioners, federalizing (and "rationalizing") the composition of jury lists, and ending the key-man system for choosing venires had been the avowed aims of the authors of the 1968 jury reform. By the mid-1970s, a majority of the Supreme Court was ready to follow where Congress was leading, prompting Justice Rehnquist to issue his warning about a never-ending "constitutional numbers game."[173]

In a 1975 case, *Taylor v. Louisiana*, the Supreme Court ruled (with only Justice Rehnquist dissenting) that Louisiana's jury selection law violated both the Sixth Amendment and the equal protection clause.[174] At the time, the Louisiana Constitution exempted women from jury service, but any woman who wished to serve on a jury could file a letter with the court and request that her name be put on the jury list. Women accounted for 10 percent of the jury wheel, but there were no women on the venire from which Taylor's jury had been chosen, although women constituted 53 percent of the adult citizens in the district, according to the most recent census data.[175] Taylor argued on appeal that this arrangement had denied him the impartial jury guaranteed by the Sixth Amendment.

By 1975, only Louisiana required women to volunteer for jury service; however, a few states continued the practice of automatically granting an exemption to women who requested one.[176] That this arrangement was less than satisfactory is apparent. Whatever women's domestic responsibilities might have been in the not-so-distant past, by the 1970s, a significant percentage of women were in the workforce and could not claim child-care responsibilities. Whatever hardship they suffered from jury service would be no different from the hardship suffered by men. That this less-than-satisfactory arrangement was also a violation of the Sixth and Fourteenth Amendments to the Constitution was not so apparent, however. For example, Louisiana's exemption of women was utterly unlike the criminal exclusion of black citizens from jury and voting lists throughout the South in the heyday of white supremacy. Black citizens were never invited to file letters with the court requesting to be added to jury lists, and their exclusion was not a matter of admin-

173. *Duren*, 370.

174. Taylor v. Louisiana, 419 U.S. 522 (1975). Between the filing of the appeal and the Supreme Court's decision, the Louisiana state legislature amended the state constitution and repealed the jury statute in question. The constitutional provision was Art. VII, § 41; the law was La. Code Crim. Proc. Ann. Art. 402.

175. *Taylor*, 524.

176. Other than Louisiana, Florida and New Hampshire were the last states to abolish the practice of requiring women to volunteer. The states offering automatic exemptions in 1975 were Missouri, Georgia, New York, Rhode Island, and Tennessee. Alabama granted exemptions to women in the event of "good cause shown." By 1979, only Missouri and Tennessee were still granting automatic exemptions. *Duren*, 359–360, nn. 3, 4, 5.

istrative convenience but a form of political oppression. Nor did women live in continual fear of being tried for capital crimes in an atmosphere of mob violence.

Nonetheless, Justice White's decision in *Taylor* repeatedly referred to the "exclusion" of women, explicitly linking Louisiana's practice to the racial exclusion that had long been forbidden by the Court, as well as to the more recent conception of the cross-section jury. "The unmistakable import of this Court's opinions, at least since 1940 [in *Smith v. Texas*] . . . and not repudiated by intervening decisions, is that the selection of a petit jury from a representative cross section of the community is an essential component of the Sixth Amendment right to a jury trial." He also linked his decision to passage of the JSSA in 1968 and noted that act's reliance on the appeals court's decision in *Rabinowitz*—where, as in *Smith*, the issue had been the virtual exclusion of blacks from the jury rolls.[177] And, like many in Congress, Justice White viewed the abolition of the key-man system as a necessary step toward the establishment of juries "chosen from a representative community sample," even though there was no evidence that the key-man system was responsible for either the exclusion of blacks or the exemption of women.[178]

A second element of the *Taylor* decision was the reaffirmation of a principle first established three years earlier in *Peters v. Kiff*: the exclusion of a group from jury service might be challenged on constitutional grounds by a defendant who is not a member of the excluded group.[179] In *Peters*, a white defendant successfully challenged his conviction on the grounds that the venire from which his jury had been chosen excluded blacks.[180] Peters argued that the exclusion of any cognizable group from jury service denies a defendant due process, even if the defendant is not a member of the excluded group. The Supreme Court agreed—although without being able to produce a majority decision. Justice Marshall, joined by Justices Douglas and Stewart, rested his argument on the equal protection clause of the Fourteenth Amendment; Justices White, Brennan, and Powell pointed instead to the clear intent of the JSSA, whose implementation would be speeded if white defendants could challenge the exclusion of blacks from their juries. In dissent, Justices Burger, Blackmun, and Rehnquist insisted that an impartial jury had always meant a jury chosen in a way that did not "systematically" exclude members of the defendant's race, and that no harm could be done to a white defendant by the absence of blacks on his jury.[181]

The *Peters* decision also confirmed the elevation of the rights of jurors to a

177. *Taylor*, 528–529.

178. Ibid., 530, n. 8, citing S. Rep. No. 891, 90th Cong., 1st sess. (1967), 9. Elimination of the key-man system was the "primary focus" of the JSSA, according to Justice White.

179. Peters v. Kiff, 407 U.S. 493 (1972).

180. Peters was convicted of burglary by an all-white jury chosen in Georgia's Middle District, the same district that had produced the *Rabinowitz* decision just six years earlier.

181. *Peters*, 507–513.

position of near parity with the rights of defendants and litigants—a startling idea, but one that had already been stated during the hearings on the JSSA.[182] Whose rights, after all, could a white defendant be protecting when complaining about the absence of blacks on his jury? Past decisions concerning the exclusion of blacks had focused on the harm to black defendants seeking their Sixth Amendment right to a trial by an impartial jury. The Constitution now seemed to be promising that no group would be unfairly "stigmatized" by being excluded from, or even underrepresented on, jury lists, a promise that yoked the jury system to concepts that would prove stubbornly resistant to clarification. How much underrepresentation of a particular group would constitute reversible error? What groups ought to be selected for special attention, aside from blacks, women, Hispanics, and Asians? What would an equal protection standard require, beyond the unmistakable racial context in which the Fourteenth Amendment had been adopted? Furthermore, these questions, first asked in association with construction of the jury pool, would soon be raised (as in *Swain*) about the voir dire and the use of peremptory challenges to shape juries more to the liking of litigants than to appellate courts.

In 1979, four years after the *Taylor* case, a male defendant challenged his murder conviction in Missouri because women were underrepresented on the venire from which his jury had been chosen.[183] Missouri was one of the last states to routinely grant exemptions to women who asked for one.[184] As a result, only a quarter of those on the jury list were women, even though women accounted for slightly more than half the adult population in the district. The week Duren was tried, women were only 14.5 percent of the venire, and of the fifty-three names chosen at random, only five were women. When it was finally impaneled, Duren's jury was all male. This, he claimed, denied him a trial by a jury chosen from a fair cross section of the district's population, in violation of his Sixth Amendment right to an impartial jury.[185]

182. This idea has also gained some traction among legal scholars. See, for example, Jeffrey J. Rachlinski, "Scientific Jury Selection and the Equal Protection Rights of Venire Persons," *Pacific Law Journal* 24 (1993): 1497. Jeffrey Abramson has made a similar argument: that by abolishing peremptory challenges, we would "end those strategies of jury selection that . . . defeat a juror's right to serve" (quoted in Neil J. Kressel and Dorit F. Kressel, *Stack and Sway: The New Science of Jury Consulting* [Boulder, CO: Westview Press, 2002], 214).

183. *Duren*, 357.

184. Missouri also offered exemptions to the elderly; doctors; members of the clergy; schoolteachers; recent jurors; those whose absence from their regular jobs might harm the "public safety, health, welfare or interest"; and anyone whose service would impose an "undue hardship." Ibid., 362, n. 10.

185. In his appeal to the Missouri Supreme Court, Duren also claimed a due process clause violation, which the court rejected. He did not include this claim in his appeal to the Supreme Court, and the *Duren* decision is silent on this question.

In his opinion for the Court, Justice White consistently stressed that the Sixth Amendment's "impartial jury" must now be understood as a jury drawn from a "fair cross section" of the population—that is, a jury list from which no "distinctive" group has been "excluded." Women were clearly a "distinctive group," and with women accounting for only 14.5 percent of the venire, their representation was far from proportional, which meant that the jury had not been chosen from a fair cross section. Nor was there any reasonable doubt about the cause of this disproportion, given the state's practice of granting automatic exemptions to women whenever they asked.

The burden was therefore on the state to explain what "compelling state interest" justified the practice of automatic exemptions. The Court had ruled in *Taylor* that "states remain free to prescribe relevant qualifications for their jurors and to provide reasonable exemptions so long as it may be fairly said that the jury lists or panels are representative of the community." However, a "significant state interest" had to be advanced by such exemptions,[186] and White was unimpressed with Missouri's argument on this score. The state had argued, without presenting any evidence, that the significant underrepresentation of women might have resulted from exemption criteria that were not being challenged, such as exemptions given to schoolteachers, public employees, and persons over age sixty-five.[187] White observed that the "other possible cause of the disproportionate exclusion of women on Jackson County jury venires is, of course, the automatic exemption for women," and the state offered no "substantial justification for this exemption," arguing only that its purpose was to safeguard the duties performed by women at home in the care of their children.[188] But to exempt all women, White concluded, because of the domestic responsibilities of some women was "insufficient justification for their disproportionate exclusion on jury venires." Citing the *Taylor* dictum that the "right to a proper jury cannot be overcome on merely rational grounds," White conceded "that a State may have an important interest in assuring that those . . . responsible for the care of children are available to do so. An exemption appropriately tailored to this interest would, we think, survive a fair-cross-section challenge." But Missouri's current arrangement cast too broad a net, leaving the jury pool unrepresentative of the community. Duren must therefore be tried by a new jury from a properly constructed venire.[189]

Justice Rehnquist's dissent was a masterful presentation of the multiple puzzles generated by the new understanding of the jury system. It identified several

186. *Taylor*, 534.

187. *Duren*, 368.

188. Ibid., 369. It is possible that the actual reason for the exemption was, as in the case of the day laborers in *Thiel*, simple administrative convenience. But clearly, that was an argument the Court would no longer entertain.

189. Ibid., 368, citing *Taylor*, 534.

overlapping difficulties, none of which has been resolved by subsequent decisions. First, Rehnquist pointed to the majority's "half-hearted effort" to pretend that its decision had nothing to do with the equal protection clause—that is, nothing to do with the alleged right of citizens to be equally represented in jury pools, if not on actual juries. As previous decisions had made clear, an equal protection challenge to a jury selection practice requires evidence of intent to discriminate. The absence of such evidence would rebut a prima facie challenge. By contrast, a Sixth Amendment challenge—a defendant's claim that his jury had not been chosen from a fair cross section of the population—requires no such demonstration of intent. The mere fact of disproportion raises a question that the state must answer by showing "adequate justification" for the disproportionate numbers of the group in question. But this relatively clear distinction has been muddied, Rehnquist argued, by the qualifications the Court has added over the years: disproportion cannot be defended "on merely rational grounds" and requires that "a significant state interest be manifestly and primarily advanced" by whatever practice has created the disproportion.[190] Rehnquist was certain that this "hybrid doctrine," developed in *Taylor* and now confirmed in *Duren*, was not required either by the Constitution or by the Court's previous jury rulings.

Second, Rehnquist argued, the blurring of the distinction between equal protection and Sixth Amendment jurisprudence obscures a fundamental but novel conflict "between the equal protection rights of women" to serve on juries and the "Sixth Amendment right of a criminal defendant to be tried by an 'impartial jury.'"[191] Here again is the unintended consequence of the JSSA's language: that the juror's right to be chosen rises to the constitutional importance of the defendant's right to be tried by an impartial jury. The Court's decisions on racial inclusion, dating to *Strauder v. West Virginia* in 1880, had asserted the *defendant's* right to equal protection: that is, his right to a trial before a jury drawn from a venire from which the state has not "expressly excluded every man of his race, because of color alone, however well qualified in other respects."[192] Women, Rehnquist continued, are equal to men in their ability to serve as jurors, as the Court recognized in *Taylor*. So if men and women are "essentially fungible for purposes of jury duty," how does the underrepresentation of either sex violate a defendant's right to trial by an impartial jury?

When asked in oral argument to explain the difference between male and female jurors, counsel for the plaintiff responded that it "is that indefinable something. . . . I think we all understand it when we see it and when we feel it, but it is not that easy to describe; yes, there is a difference."[193] Yet as Rehnquist pointed

190. Ibid., 371.
191. Ibid., 371, n.
192. *Strauder*, 309, quoted by ibid.
193. *Duren*, 371, n., citing Tr. of Oral Arg. 15.

out, the Court appeared to be of two minds on this question. Although each "cognizable group" brings an "indefinable something" to the jury deliberation, it does not appear to be necessary for the actual jury to be composed of a diverse group of people, since in a heterogeneous district, it would not be possible for more than a few groups to be represented:

> "Defendants are not entitled to a jury of any particular composition, . . . but the jury wheels, pools of names, panels, or venires from which juries are drawn must not systematically exclude distinctive groups in the community and thereby fail to be reasonably representative thereof." Thus, a defendant's constitutional right to an impartial jury is protected so long as "that indefinable something" supposedly crucial to impartiality is adequately represented on the jury venire; that the petit jury ultimately struck is composed of one sex is irrelevant. Indeed, under the majority's fair-cross-section analysis, the underrepresentation of women on jury venires in Jackson County, Mo., would entitle petitioner Duren to reversal of his conviction even if the jury chosen in his case had been composed of all women.[194]

Third, Rehnquist feared that the Court had set out on a road with no certain destination. In *Taylor*, the Court had relied on a long string of cases dealing with the absolute exclusion of blacks (*Smith v. Texas*) and women (*Ballard v. New York*). But the facts presented in *Taylor* and *Duren* did not show exclusion at all, only underrepresentation. The venire in *Duren* had been roughly 15 percent female, even though women were about half the eligible population in the district. "If there are indeed 15 percent women on the jury panels in Jackson County, the Court uses the word 'exclusion' contrary to any use of the word with which I am familiar. Women are undoubtedly underrepresented as compared to men . . . but therein lies the difference between this case and *Taylor*."[195] The majority was conflating administrative arrangements of long standing, applied not only to women but also to various professional and occupational groups, with the worst excesses of the white-supremacy regime in the South. And in the process, it was voiding otherwise entirely proper convictions for murder, armed robbery, rape, and other serious crimes. "The lot of a legislator or judge attempting to conform a State's jury selection process to the dictates of today's opinion, and yet recognize what may be very valid state interests in excusing some individuals or classes of individuals from jury service, is surely not a happy one."[196] The likely outcome, Rehnquist predicted, would be that state officials would simply refuse to grant any blanket or automatic exemptions, forcing all such requests to be dealt with on a case-by-case basis in court. To the already burdensome obligation of jury

194. Ibid., 371, n.
195. Ibid., 374.
196. Ibid., 376.

service would now be added the unnecessary time spent by those likely to receive exemptions, "whiling away their time in jury rooms of countless courthouses."[197]

THE POST-*BATSON* COURT

In the years since the *Batson* decision, the Supreme Court has continued to wrestle with the contemporary meaning of the equal protection clause and the Sixth Amendment guarantee of an impartial jury, delivering contradictory rulings that are almost always accompanied by spirited dissents. May a white defendant use peremptory challenges to remove black jurors? Yes, according to *Holland v. Illinois* (1990), but a white defendant can challenge the prosecution's use of peremptory challenges to achieve the same result (*Powers v. Ohio* [1991]). Two years after the *Holland* ruling, the Court reversed itself and found that a white defendant's use of peremptory challenges to remove black jurors violated the rights of the jurors thus removed (*Georgia v. McCollum* [1992]), setting up a direct confrontation, once again, between the rights of defendants and the rights of jurors. To make matters more complex, the Court found no violation when the state of Alabama used peremptory challenges to remove all the male jurors in a paternity case, resulting in an all-female jury (*J.E.B. v. Alabama* [1994]). In 1991 the *Batson* principles were extended to civil trials (*Edmonson v. Leesville Concrete*), opening the other half of the court system to the "constitutional numbers game."[198]

Throughout these rulings, Court majorities have continued to insist that the peremptory challenge, though now under strict scrutiny, is an important and valuable part of the impartial jury guaranteed by the Constitution. The only requirement, in this view, is a clarification of the limits of its use with respect to race, gender, and ethnicity (specifically, Hispanics and Asians). But this effort to police the border between the permissible and the prohibited has continually brought the Court into conflict with the time-honored method of choosing jurors by looking for behavioral "clues": general demeanor, signs of discomfort, nervous tics, even styles of dress and grooming. The peremptory challenge has always been understood to permit this method of culling; indeed, the principal defense of the peremptory challenge is that it allows hunches about juror disposition to be acted on before the jury is sworn. Yet always, below the surface, is the rarely spoken reality: precisely because race is an issue in American life, it can be risky for a prosecutor to try a black defendant before black jurors. Wouldn't it be wiser, then, to replace black jurors with those less likely to harbor suspicions about white prosecutors or white police officers?

197. Ibid., 377.

198. Holland v. Illinois, 493 U.S. 474 (1990); Powers v. Ohio, 499 U.S. 400 (1991); Georgia v. McCollum, 505 U.S. 42 (1992); J. E. B. v. Alabama, 511 U.S. 127 (1994); Edmonson v. Leesville Concrete, 500 U.S. 614 (1991).

Outside the context of race, the search for the best possible jury—that is, the best for a particular client and a particular case—is taken for granted as a normal component of the attorney's job. This is precisely what the prosecutors were doing in *J. E. B. v. Alabama*, acting on the not unreasonable assumption that male and female jurors might constitute two schools of thought on the question of paternity obligations. They did not need to know this absolutely, and perhaps they could not know it, but the availability of peremptory challenges meant that they could play the odds and seat the safest jury. This is how the peremptory challenge has always been used, but the federal courts, the Supreme Court included, have tried to have it both ways: defending the arbitrary quality of the peremptory challenge, while hinting that, where race is concerned, it perpetuates old racist assumptions and efforts to subjugate black Americans to the arbitrary rule of whites.

As more and more cases raised such questions—and as more and more defendants sought yet another path to a new trial—the Court found itself walking an increasingly narrow line. In *Snyder v. Louisiana* (2008) the petitioner claimed that the prosecution had violated his right to a fair trial by removing all five blacks on the venire, two of them on "pretextual" grounds: one juror seemed excessively nervous and had job commitments that might have made him "unwilling" to serve, and a second juror was unsure if she could impose the death penalty.[199] The Court found that the evidence for the first claim was suspect—a white juror with similar work conflicts had not been challenged—and reversed the conviction. (The majority ruling did not consider the death penalty issue.) "The prosecution's proffer of this pretextual explanation naturally gives rise to an inference of discriminatory intent," Justice Samuel Alito wrote for the Court.[200] Justice Clarence Thomas's dissent stressed the deference appellate courts owed to trial courts, insisting that the Supreme Court "will overturn a ruling on the question of discriminatory intent only if it is 'clearly erroneous,'"—a circumstance not present in the case of the "nervous" juror.[201]

In *Johnson v. California* (2005) an all-white jury convicted a black defendant of second-degree murder. The prosecution had removed all three blacks on the venire, and the defendant challenged his conviction on the grounds that the prosecution had discriminated against jurors on account of their race, thus depriving him of a fair trial. But under a California rule, any defendant making such a claim had to show that the preemptory challenges were "more likely than not" to have been

199. The first juror was studying for a teaching certificate and was required to observe classes for a certain number of hours; had the trial lasted longer than five days, this juror, according to his own testimony, would have experienced some professional difficulties. The trial was not expected to be a long one, however. The trial transcript is quoted in Snyder v. Louisiana, 522 U.S. 472 (2008), at 480–482.

200. Ibid., 485.

201. Ibid., 486–490.

discriminatory in intent. This requirement, the state appellate court ruled, was an "undue burden" and could not stand, and it overturned the conviction. The California Supreme Court disagreed, reinstating the conviction, and the US Supreme Court granted certiorari. In a decision with only one dissent (Justice Thomas), the Supreme Court reversed the California Supreme Court, agreeing with the state appellate court's view that the "more likely than not" standard imposed a burden too great for a defendant to meet and was therefore arbitrary. *Batson* had required only that the *party exercising the challenge* be forced to defend it on nonracial grounds; the California rule turned things around, forcing the defendant to bear the burden of proof rather than the prosecutor.[202]

On the same day, just prior to deciding *Johnson*, the Court reversed a murder conviction from a Texas court in which ten of eleven black jurors had been removed peremptorily because, the prosecution argued, they had doubts about the death penalty. The case presented some unusual procedural questions—for instance, the defendant made arguments and offered evidence in his appeal that were never presented at the appellate level in Texas—but the use of peremptory challenges when race might be a factor was the principal issue considered by the Court's majority. The Court found that "happenstance" was unlikely to be the reason for the removal of 91 percent of the available blacks on the venire and that the death penalty explanation was "pretextual." This directly contradicted the decision of the Texas Superior Court, which had found that it was "at least reasonable to conclude" that racial discrimination had *not* been the reason for the challenges. In his dissent, Justice Thomas (joined by Justices Scalia and Rehnquist) stressed the procedural irregularities—the Court was second-guessing a state court based on evidence the state court had never seen and arguments the defendant had never made at the state level. But the heart of Thomas's dissent was the defense of the peremptory challenge as a barrier to suspected but not obvious bias: "The very purpose of peremptory strikes is to allow parties to remove potential jurors whom they suspect, but cannot prove, may exhibit a particular bias"—in this case, a bias against imposition of the death penalty.[203]

In *Campbell v. Louisiana* (1998) the Court agreed that a white defendant charged with killing a white victim could make an equal protection challenge, claiming racial bias in the selection of the jury foreman (i.e., a bias against blacks). In his partial dissent (joined by Justice Scalia), Justice Thomas stated simply: "I fail to understand how the rights of blacks excluded from jury service can be vindicated by letting a white murderer go free."[204]

202. In his dissent, Justice Thomas argued that the states should be allowed to craft their own solutions to difficult policy questions, within the general constraints of the Fourteenth Amendment, and that there was no justification for the federal courts' interference in this particular case. Johnson v. California, 545 U.S. 162 (2005).

203. Miller-El v. Dretke, 545 U.S. 231 (2005), at 292–293.

204. Campbell v. Louisiana, 532 U.S. 392 (1998), at 403.

PAPER CHASE: THE LAW JOURNALS SEARCH FOR THE PERFECT JURY

As extensive as the judicial record is on the question of jury selection, it is dwarfed by the attention paid to the subject in academic law journals. In fact, no aspect of the modern jury has provoked more intense scrutiny in these journals than the "representative" or "cross-section" principle, a concern that can be broken down into several related questions: What does a "representative" jury mean, and how do we know a representative jury when we see one? How can we tell whether a jury venire has been chosen from a "fair cross section" of the local population? If we know what a fair cross section means, how much deviation from that standard should be considered intolerable? When measuring the venire against the population of the district, what are the "cognizable groups" to which special attention should be paid, other than racial minorities and women? Why do these groups deserve special attention, while other groups that are every bit as distinctive as African Americans, women, Hispanics, or Asians go unprotected? And whatever happened to the protection of laborers?

These are new questions, and they reveal how the new understanding of the jury departs from the old. The common-law jury was not "representative" but "impartial." The test for impartiality was that the jurors (1) had no prejudice for or against any of the parties in court and (2) could understand the case well enough to render a sensible verdict. For these purposes, it did not necessarily matter whether they were bankers or plumbers, Catholics or Methodists, old or young—unless these particular facts bore some relevance to the issue being tried.[205] In a lawsuit between a Catholic and a Methodist, for example, it might make a difference what churches the jurors attended. If a bank sought to collect a debt from a plumber, plumbers and bankers might be challenged either for cause or peremptorily. Those practices that stood outside this model—most notoriously, the exclusion of black Americans from both voting lists and the venire and, after the Nineteenth Amendment, the exclusion or exemption of women—were increasingly understood to be departures from the core principles of the common-law jury and not necessary features of it.

205. It might matter, however, whether they were Democrats or Republicans, which is why the 1879 amendments to the federal jury statute required that at least one of the two jury commissioners serving the federal court be from the political party that had not nominated the judge. See Drew L. Kershen, "The Jury Selection Act of 1879: Theory and Practice of Citizen Participation in the Judicial System," *Law Forum* 1980, 3 (1980): 707–767. This principle barely survives in the current jury law. Under 28 U.S.C. §1863(b)(1), only the District of Columbia is authorized to establish a bipartisan jury commission: "The citizen jury commissioner shall not belong to the same political party as the clerk serving with him." Political party affiliation is not among the "cognizable" factors determining whether the jury list represents an adequate cross section of the local population.

But the growing chorus in favor of the "representative jury" directed critics' attention to matters that had not, with the exception of race, been considered important in the past. This new understanding gained its initial credibility because of its association with efforts to end racial segregation in the South. But it acquired its momentum from a more generalized argument about equality that sought to break down all forms of "discrimination," including those once thought to be perfectly appropriate when selecting an impartial jury. Those testifying in support of the Jury Selection and Service Act of 1968 had clearly stated their broader aims: to prevent the subtle infiltration of "class bias" into the judicial system through the use of words such as "judgment," "integrity," or even "intelligence." All too often, as Attorney General Ramsey Clark had testified, these are merely code words for the "preferences and prejudices . . . of the select few."

These views, however, implied a new purpose for the jury. If the jury must be selected from a venire that represents the district demographically, shouldn't the jury reflect the disparate views of the groups in the district? And if this is so, how can we countenance the deliberate or even accidental exclusion of any of these groups? If we are really concerned about viewpoints or perspectives (the "indefinable somethings" referred to in *Duren* and hinted at in Justice Marshall's *Batson* concurrence), aren't we justified in learning how to draw the demographic profile of the district more precisely, making sure that, in the end, the verdict reflects the balance of viewpoints (or biases) in the community? The elimination or exclusion, or even the mere slighting, of any of these "voices" diminishes the utility of the jury trial, denying defendants and litigants their full rights under the Constitution and encouraging public doubts about the integrity of the judicial system.

This view of the jury has also inspired—indeed, it requires—a change in the meaning of "judgment." Writing about the "radical changes" in the jury selection regime in recent decades, Professor Darryl K. Brown notes that these changes raise questions of "whether and how impartiality exists in juries," and he attributes "changes in the jurisprudence of juries" to these "shifts in consensus." Brown does not say whether the changes in the jurisprudence inspired, or were inspired by, these shifts in consensus. But he is certainly correct when he notes that "the model impartial juror is no longer the middle-to-upper class male property owner known among similar citizens as a man of good moral character and moderate temperament. Instead, society recognizes the judgment of such people as one perspective among many, no more or less neutral than any other."[206] In fact, "impartiality" is now impossible outside the context of "diversity." "The contemporary requirement that the jury represent a fair cross section of society premises the concept of impartiality on the jury's diversity. A jury is more likely to fit contemporary notions of neutrality if it includes representatives of all segments and

206. Darryl K. Brown, "The Means and Ends of Representative Juries," *Virginia Journal of Social Policy & Law* 1 (1993–1994): 445.

groups of the community, thereby creating a body that reflects 'the commonsense judgment of a group of laymen.'"[207]

Borrowing from the language of two recent affirmative-action cases, one scholar notes that if diversity is a value that law schools can consider when making admissions decisions, then courts may be warranted in encouraging more diverse juries.[208] In fact, the very effort to find a "color-blind" process for choosing juries is fundamentally misguided, because "color blindness leads society to understand inequality produced by individual and structural bias as the exception rather than the rule."[209] Affirmative action in jury selection would also accomplish what Justice Marshall urged in his concurrence in *Batson*: it would allow jurors to become more aware of their "conscious or unconscious racism." "The participatory language of *Grutter* provides the impetus for courts not only to provide opportunities for more diverse juries but to give meaning to that outreach by encouraging each juror to examine his or her own biases as the jury participates and as the jurors engage in deliberation."[210]

Although a number of dissents and concurring opinions in the growing list of jury selection cases have urged, or looked forward to, the abolition of peremptory challenges, the stubborn survival of these challenges has inspired proposals for various "work-arounds."[211] These suggestions contemplate new methods of jury selection that would deliberately craft racially diverse juries, minimizing the alleged discriminatory impact of peremptory challenges, especially in criminal cases. One such proposal—to randomly strike every nth white individual on the venire to achieve a "balanced" jury—was declared unconstitutional by the Sixth Circuit Court of Appeals in 1998, after it was tried in the Eastern District of Michigan.[212] Other proposals published in the law journals would certainly encounter a similar

207. Ibid., 499, quoting Williams v. Florida, 399 U.S. 76 (1970), 100.

208. Phoebe A. Haddon, "Does *Grutter* Offer Courts an Opportunity to Consider Race in Jury Selection and Decisions Related to Promoting Fairness in the Deliberation Process?" *Temple Political & Civil Rights Law Review* 13 (2004): 547. The decisions in question are Grutter v. Bollinger, 539 U.S. 306, and Gratz v. Bollinger, 539 U.S. 244, both decided in 2003. See also Joshua Wilkenfeld, "Newly Compelling: Reexamining Judicial Construction of Juries in the Aftermath of *Grutter v. Bollinger*," *Columbia Law Review* 104 (2004): 2291.

209. Haddon, "Does *Grutter* Offer Courts an Opportunity," 549.

210. Ibid., 554.

211. Justice Breyer (concurring in Miller-El v. Dretke, 545 U.S. 231 [2005)]), expressed the expectation (or hope) that "a jury system without peremptories is no longer unthinkable" (272).

212. See Andrew J. Lievense, "Note: Fair Representation on Juries in the Eastern District of Michigan: Analyzing Past Efforts and Recommending Future Action," *University of Michigan Journal of Law Reform* 38 (Summer 2005): 941. The case is United States v. Ovalle, 136 F.3d 1092 (6th Cir. 1998).

fate. Using all-black juries to try black defendants,[213] requiring at least three members of the jury to be of the defendant's race,[214] and other "affirmative inclusion" proposals would run afoul of the Court's "equal protection" selection standards. Suggestions to bring back the medieval jury of *de medietate linguae*, which guaranteed that half the jury spoke the defendant's language or belonged to the defendant's "nationality" (used in England in cases involving Christians and Jews), are even less likely to withstand constitutional scrutiny.[215] In fact, a widely discussed proposal by the jury commission for Hennepin County, Minnesota—which would guarantee a minimum of two nonwhite jurors on every grand jury—has never been implemented by the state's courts because of doubts about its constitutionality.[216]

The controlling case, as of this writing, is *United States v. Nelson*,[217] in which federal district court judge David G. Trager impaneled a diverse jury in the trial of Lemrick Nelson, who was charged with violating the civil rights of Yankel Rosenbaum, a Hasidic student murdered in the Crown Heights neighborhood of Brooklyn in 1991.[218] (Nelson had been acquitted of murder in a 1992 trial in state court, although he subsequently admitted his guilt, and he was now being tried on federal civil rights charges.) Judge Trager's plan was to replace a challenged Jewish juror with a Jewish alternate and a challenged black juror with a black alternate, attempting to guarantee that this racially divisive trial would be conducted before a mixed jury. The Second Circuit rejected this effort on the grounds that it violated the equal protection clause. "The circuit court explained that potential jurors' Fourteenth Amendment rights to be free from racially discriminatory state action preclude treating individual jurors differently based on a desire to maintain a certain aggregate jury composition."[219]

213. Harry A. McDougal III, "Note: The Case for Black Juries," *Yale Law Journal* 79 (1970): 548.

214. Sheri L. Johnson, "Black Innocence and the White Jury," *Michigan Law Review* 83 (1985): 1698–1699.

215. See Edward S. Adams and Christian J. Lane, "Constructing a Jury that Is Both Impartial and Representative: Utilizing Cumulative Voting in Jury Selection," *New York University Law Review* 73 (June 1998): 703.

216. Yet the Hennepin County model has received an extraordinary amount of attention in the law journals. A LexisNexis search of "Hennepin County jury selection" turned up eighty-six titles from 1990 to 2010. See Hennepin County v. Perry, 561 N.W.2d 889, 896–897 (Minn. 1997), and Richard M. Re, "Re-justifying the Fair Cross Section Requirement: Equal Representation and Enfranchisement in the American Criminal Jury," *Yale Law Journal* 116, 7 (May 2007): 1568.

217. United States v. Nelson, 277 F.3d 164 (2d Cir. 2002).

218. Wilkenfeld, "Newly Compelling," 2291.

219. Ibid., 2292. Here we see how the Fourteenth Amendment's equal protection clause conflicts with the Sixth Amendment right to a trial by an impartial—that is, cross-section, as it is now understood—jury: how can a cross-section jury be created without considering race and other demographic classifications?

Edward Adams and Christian Lane have proposed an adaptation of the "cumulative voting" model used in corporate shareholder meetings, which is designed to give small shareholders a greater chance to elect at least one or two members to a corporate board of directors. In adapting this model to the selection of petit juries, the aim would likewise be to guarantee minority participation. Under this arrangement, after challenges for cause have been completed, each side would cast votes to either seat or dismiss jurors, the total number of votes equaling the total number of jurors, alternates, and peremptory challenges permitted for the particular trial and court. Litigants could cast multiple votes for or against particularly "desirable" or "undesirable" jurors, making it more likely that minority jurors would end up on the panel, at least in cases with minority defendants.[220]

It is important to note, however, how the authors defend this proposal: "Considering a jury impartial by virtue of a balancing of biases would ease the selection of juries that are both impartial and representative." Or, as another scholar put it, "An impartial jury arises from its partial parts."[221] The claim that impartiality is a "balancing of biases" or that impartiality arises out of competing "partialities" necessitates a transformation of the original understanding of "impartial," which required only that a prospective juror have no link to any of the parties, no fixed predisposition toward either side, and an ability to suspend judgment until after a fair consideration of the evidence. It is quite likely that many in the legal community no longer believe that such a thing is either possible or desirable. The balancing of biases requires, additionally, that each juror hold tightly to whatever predispositions he or she brought into the jury room and not leave those predispositions behind; this is true because all the other jurors will be holding just as tightly to their own competing biases, in no small part because they all have learned, somehow, that this is what they are supposed to do.

Representative juries are good because diversity is good; this much of the postmodern jury regime is clear. But it is not equally clear who or what is to be represented or why, beyond the "cognizable groups" the federal courts have deemed require special scrutiny. These are the groups that state and federal jury commissioners have, in the past, deliberately excluded (blacks, Hispanics, and Asians) or failed to affirmatively include, and those to whom blanket exemptions were offered (women and day laborers). But nothing in the concept of the representative or cross-section jury, and nothing in the new view of what "judgment" means in the context of jury deliberation, places any obvious limits on the number of cognizable groups whose "perspective on human events . . . may have unsuspected importance," especially if the group is "large and identifiable."[222]

220. Adams and Lane, "Constructing a Jury."

221. Ibid., 742–743, citing Brent J. Gurney, "The Case for Abolishing Peremptory Challenges in Criminal Trials," *Harvard Civil Rights–Civil Liberties Law Review* 21 (1986): 257.

222. Justice Marshall, for the Court, in *Peters*, 503–504.

The cognizable group most conspicuous by its absence from those deserving special scrutiny is the poor—an especially ironic omission, given the importance of *Thiel* to the new understanding of the jury system.[223] In *Thiel*, the challenged action was a California state court's blanket hardship exemption for day laborers. But decades after *Thiel*, the Supreme Court has yet to describe the "poor," the "working class," or "blue-collar employees" as a cognizable class deserving of special scrutiny. Yet there are many reasons why the working poor, unemployed welfare recipients, and those whose employment is only intermittent would not be captured in the source lists used to compose the master jury wheel (with the exception of the welfare rolls). The poor are less likely to vote, more likely to move frequently, and more likely to be nondrivers, reducing the chances of their names showing up on state voter registration lists, census records, or motor vehicle registration lists. Many more poor people than rich people are incarcerated felons or recently released ex-convicts with no fixed address. That the poor speak with a single "voice" might be doubted, given the variety of circumstances that lead to poverty. That the group is "large and identifiable," however, is obvious. Yet as long as there is no evidence of a systematic effort to exclude low-income citizens from the master wheel, there is no reversible error—even though, because they do not show up on official lists, their exclusion might be empirically invisible. This anomaly has not gone unnoticed in the law journals.

Writing in 1996, Mitchell S. Zuklie lamented the fact that, despite the withering assaults of "Critical Legal Scholars," the Supreme Court's understanding of a "distinctive group" remains strangely unmoved.[224] This fact, Zuklie believes, has had an unfortunate effect on the "representative" character of the master jury wheel and therefore of the juries seated in federal court, especially with respect to the representation of the poor. As a result, there is more arbitrariness in the exercise of prosecutorial authority, less public confidence in the jury system, and a lost opportunity for the poor to exercise their civic responsibilities.[225] These are important charges, and they deserve discussion before moving on to the consideration of other "large and identifiable" segments of the

223. *Thiel* is discussed more fully in chapter 3. As a result of the *Thiel* ruling, "daily wage earners" may not be systematically excluded from jury service. (The evidence in the *Thiel* case showed that the day laborers were not "excluded" but merely "excused.") Although the Court found that the exclusion of wage earners might imply discrimination, it has never defined wage earners as a "distinctive" or "cognizable" group. The distinctive groups deserving of special attention are defined by race, gender, and ethnicity, not by economic class. See Mitchell S. Zuklie, "Rethinking the Fair Cross-Section Requirement," *California Law Review* 84, 1 (January 1996): 115. See also Gertner and Mizner, *Law of Juries*, 36–39.

224. "Critical Legal Scholars argue that abstract conceptions of merit tend to favor the status quo." Zuklie, "Rethinking the Fair Cross-Section Requirement," 131.

225. Ibid.

population whose law-review advocates are pushing for their inclusion in the "special scrutiny" category.

Zuklie points out, correctly, that the authors of the Jury Selection and Service Act sought to do far more than ban racial discrimination; they wanted to make juries truly representative of the communities from which they were chosen. It was this aim that led to the development of the Supreme Court's "distinctive group" doctrine, which the Court has refused to "precisely define" (e.g., by rejecting jurors opposed to the death penalty as a distinctive group whose exclusion could be challenged).[226] Moreover, the Court has explicitly refused to identify the poor as a distinctive group for purposes of jury selection, rejecting several different "aliases" for the poor: "blue-collar workers," the "urban working class," the "working class," "paupers," "non-working people," "persons with low incomes," the "lower-socio-economic class," and "food stamp recipients." These characteristics have all been presented as markers for the poor, but the Supreme Court has insisted that although it is possible to mark out a category, the persons in that category do not necessarily share "common experiences or beliefs," the threshold test for "distinctiveness."[227]

One reason for the Court's reluctance is that economic status, unlike race, gender, or ethnicity, is not "binary"—that is, one's economic status can change and is relative. One is "poor" or "rich" with reference to those in the immediate vicinity and at a single point in time. Race and gender are, by comparison, innate and absolute characteristics. The Court has also been reluctant to push the "distinctive experiences and viewpoints" argument beyond the field of race, where it made some sense (especially in the past). Black Americans, accounting for roughly 10 percent of the population, have had a singular experience in the United States to be sure—although, as the gains of the civil rights movement have become more commonplace, the experiences of African Americans have become more varied and will continue to do so. Women, at half the population, have never had the same kind of singular experience black Americans have had. The poor, at roughly one-third the population (those who are "ill-clothed, ill-housed, and ill-fed," to borrow FDR's formula), fall somewhere in between.

But the causes of poverty are so varied (compare a debt-ridden college student looking for his first job to a single mother without a high school diploma) that to ascribe "distinctive" views to the poor seems arbitrary. Nevertheless, Zuklie continues to be drawn to the idea that the poor constitute a group that is at least as distinctive in its experiences and outlook as women, whose presence on the jury, he says, "everyone agrees . . . promotes the interests of the trial participants, the community, and the jury itself."[228] Yet if women do not share a common set

226. Lockhart v. McCree, 476 U.S. 162 (1986).

227. See Zuklie's discussion of these various cases in "Rethinking the Fair Cross-Section Requirement," 116–118.

228. Ibid., 128.

of experiences and viewpoints, what "distinctive" contribution do they make to jury deliberations? That question becomes even more pointed when applied to a category as vaguely defined as "people with low incomes."

Beyond the poor, however, are other groups whose protection gets even less notice from the courts but significantly more notice from the law journals: the young, the old, the handicapped, the poorly educated, the overweight, noncitizens, and even felons (whose views on the legal system are no doubt "distinctive").[229] The arguments follow a common pattern: the particular group is said to have a distinctive worldview and a distinctive set of experiences, as well as interests that need to be protected through participation in the judicial system. Their exclusion from the venire, or their peremptory removal from juries, undermines the public's faith in the fairness of the judicial system. For a jury—or a jury venire, at any rate—to be truly representative or a true cross section of the community, the courts should pay special attention to including members of these groups. This is the "constitutional numbers game" Justice Rehnquist worried about, played at an even more frenetic pace. Concern for the proper distribution of demographic categories in the venire has driven out the question that was once at the heart of the selection enterprise: are the twelve jurors chosen to render judgment on a fellow citizen capable of performing that task with the appropriate level of intelligence, honesty, impartiality, and integrity? In the past, that question was always at the

229. On the young, see Carey Hugh Smith, "Sixth Amendment Right to Jury Trial Prohibits Systematic Exclusion of Young People in Jury Selection Process," *Suffolk University Law Review* 18, 4 (Fall 1984): 518: "The exclusion of a class as large and identifiable as young adults deprives the jury of a unique perspective." On the old, see Max B. Rothman, Burton D. Dunlop, and Gretchen M. Hirt, "Jury Selection in an Aging America: The New Discrimination," *Elder's Advisor* 2 (2000–2001): 69. On the handicapped, see Mary A. Lynch, "The Application of Equal Protection to Prospective Jurors with Disabilities: Will *Batson* Cover Disability-Based Strikes?" *Albany Law Review* 57 (1993–1994): 289. On the poorly educated, see H. R. Alker and J. J. Barnard, "Procedural and Social Biases in the Jury Selection Process," *Justice System Journal* 3, 3 (Spring 1978): 220–241: "Poorly educated individuals tend not to register to vote as frequently as better educated people do" and therefore do not show up proportionately on the jury lists then used in the Commonwealth of Massachusetts. Massachusetts has since switched to multiple source lists. On the overweight, see Maggie Elise O'Grady, "A Jury of Your (Skinny) Peers: Weight-Based Peremptory Challenges and the Culture of Fat Bias," *Stanford Journal of Civil Rights & Civil Liberties* 7 (April 2011): 47. On noncitizens, see Amy R. Motomura, "The American Jury: Can Noncitizens Still Be Excluded?" *Stanford Law Review* 64 (2012): 1503: "The demographic portrait of noncitizens and minorities in the United States shows that the citizenship requirement for jury service results in the exclusion of significant numbers of residents in certain regions, and that this exclusion is highly skewed by race and ethnicity. The exclusion and resulting decrease in jury diversity has potentially negative effects on the jury's decisionmaking and its institutional legitimacy." On felons, see Brian C. Kalt, "The Exclusion of Felons from Jury Service," *American University Law Review* 53, 1 (October 2003): 65.

heart of the jury reforms proposed by both the American Bar Association and the Judicial Conference. But that is no longer the case.

THE AMERICAN BAR ASSOCIATION AND THE POSTMODERN JURY

The American Bar Association, almost from the moment of its founding, was devoted to reforming the jury system, issuing major studies and reports dealing partly or mostly with juries in 1885, 1908, 1938, and 1968.[230] The 1968 document was revised in 1978 and again, more substantially, in 1996, taking into consideration "a number of legal, constitutional, and societal issues" that had emerged since the second edition.[231] One example: the Supreme Court has "recently revisited the alleged use of peremptory challenges to strike potential jurors because of their race, an important issue not addressed in prior editions of these standards." The 1996 standards were rewritten to reflect the Court's view that peremptory challenges may not be used "in a racially discriminatory manner."[232] The ABA was also concerned that "the explosive public reaction to recent high-profile jury trials, apparently based on the widespread impression that the process was not fair to the victims, led to the conclusion that the substantive and the apparent fairness of the jury trial process should be addressed." This is an especially ironic pairing of concerns, given that the most recent "explosive . . . high-profile jury trial" was that of O. J. Simpson in 1995, in which the defense used all its peremptory challenges to keep as many black women as possible *on* Simpson's jury.

In 2004 new ABA president Robert J. Grey Jr. asked the association to examine the jury system once again, with an eye to bringing it "into the 21st century."[233]

230. *The Report of the Special Committee Appointed to Consider and Report Whether the Present Delay and Uncertainty in Judicial Administration Can be Lessened, and if so, by What Means* (Philadelphia: Dando Printing & Publishing Co., 1885); "Report of the Special Committee to Suggest Remedies and Formulate Proposed Laws to Prevent Delay and Unnecessary Cost in Litigation," *Annual Report of the American Bar Association* 33 (1908): 542; "Report of the Committee on Trial by Jury Including Methods of Selection of Jurors," *Report of the Section of Judicial Administration, American Bar Association Reports*, 63 (1938): 530; *ABA Standards for Criminal Justice and Trial by Jury* (Washington, DC: American Bar Association, 1968).

231. *ABA Standards for Criminal Justice and Trial by Jury*, 3rd ed. (Washington, DC: American Bar Association, 1996).

232. Ibid., 120.

233. David V. Wilson II, "American Bar Association Principles for Juries and Jury Trials," *Houston Lawyer* 43 (September–October 2005): 48. According to Wilson, the inspiration for the American Jury Project was the realization that jury trials had declined dramatically in both the civil and the criminal courts (49). This matter is taken up in chapter 5.

The result was the American Jury Project, which convened a National Symposium on the American Jury in October 2004. The conclusions of this symposium were incorporated into a set of principles that was adopted unanimously by the ABA House of Delegates (unlike the results of many earlier recommendations).[234]

Principles for Juries and Jury Trials articulates nineteen "principles that define our fundamental aspirations for the management of the jury system," accompanied by a lengthy commentary on each.[235] *Principles* is distinctive for its devotion to the ideal of the "representative jury." Whereas previous ABA reports on the jury system focused on improving the quality of jurors, *Principles* assumes that, beyond the bare minimum statutory qualifications (age, residence, citizenship), every citizen should be considered equally qualified. It follows from this reasoning that courts, rather than searching for the best candidates for jury service (as the ABA had urged them to do for more than a century) should devote their time and attention to the "optimum management" of jurors, making the experience of jury service less burdensome.

Principle 2, for example, asserts that "citizens have the right to participate in jury service and their service should be facilitated." Eligibility for such service "should not be denied or limited on the basis of race, national origin, gender, age, religious belief, income, occupation, disability, sexual orientation, or any other factor that discriminates against a cognizable group in the jurisdiction."[236] What is surprising about this statement is its lack of connection to the actual management of the jury system. Given the requirement that courts use inclusive source lists—even more inclusive than the voting list, if necessary—the only form of "discrimination" that has survived into the modern era is the alleged use of the peremptory challenge in a racially discriminatory manner. There is no evidence that those compiling the jury list have any way of knowing the race of those on the list, much less their sexual orientation. Sorting, if it occurs, now happens only after jurors have been summoned to court and lawyers have the opportunity to exercise their challenges. And while the ABA is on record as opposing "racially discriminatory" peremptory challenges, principle 11-D states that "peremptory challenges should be available to each of the parties."[237]

But the modern focus on the rights of jurors—raising them to a level that is nearly equal to the rights of defendants and parties—has transformed the debate over jury selection in ways that go far beyond the reforms needed to end genuine acts of racial discrimination. The desire to end discrimination against black Americans had morphed, in the wake of the JSSA, into a desire to end all forms

234. Ibid., 48.

235. *Principles for Juries and Jury Trials* (Washington, DC: American Bar Association, 2005).

236. Ibid., 4.

237. Ibid., 14.

of discrimination entirely, including the very necessary discrimination between those who are and those who are not capable of jury service. Whereas in the not-so-distant past, "jury reform" meant questioning members of the venire to weed out the "pudding heads"—or their modern equivalent, the "UFO jurors"—jury reform has now become a seemingly endless quest for the perfectly inclusive jury.[238]

Yet the old problems, pushed to the background, continue to assert themselves nevertheless. It is possible to see in the ABA's 2005 principles evidence of an older set of concerns barely visible beneath the modern surface. For example, *Principles* makes recommendations concerning a number of questions that have vexed jury reformers in the past: (1) How should prospective jurors be examined, and by whom? (2) How should names be collected for the jury wheel? (3) How should voir dire be conducted, and by whom? (4) What is the proper role of the peremptory challenge?

As noted earlier, the pre-1960s movement to reform the modern jury was clear about two principles: (1) the statutory exemption of entire occupations should be ended to improve the quality of those eligible for jury service, and (2) those who are formally eligible for service should be examined in some way to weed out those who are not suitable based on their educational attainment, their demeanor, their apparent intelligence, or their apparent attitude about the trial at hand. Early in the era of the representative jury, this "winnowing"—assuming it was not a pretext for illegal discrimination—was considered entirely compatible with the goal of summoning the venire from a fair cross section of the district. But as the new regime matured, its opposition to discrimination became more single-minded, so that the very distinction between "eligible" and "suitable" became morally suspect.

Having driven out such quaint notions about winnowing, the postmodern jury regime is still faced with the practical difficulty of impaneling juries whose members can be trusted to give impartial as well as sensible consideration to the evidence presented in court. This has always been the central concern of litigators when thinking about jury reform: how to get a fair jury, or even the fairest possible jury, given the individuals available—with "fair" meaning not just unbiased but also capable of understanding what is going on in court. The ABA's *Principles* does not depart from this tradition but merely hides it behind a blizzard of "procedures." "Before voir dire begins," according to principle 11, "the court and parties, through the use of appropriate questionnaires, should be provided with data pertinent to the eligibility of jurors and to matters ordinarily raised in voir dire, including such background information as is provided by prospective jurors in their responses to the questions appended to the notification and summons."[239]

238. See Gregory E. Mize, "On Better Jury Selection: Spotting UFO Jurors before They Enter the Jury Room," *Court Review* 31, 1 (Spring 1999): 10.

239. *Principles for Juries and Jury Trials*, 13.

Sometimes, the ABA recommends, the court should use a special questionnaire "addressing particular issues that may arise" during the trial. Then, after being questioned by the court, the parties should have an opportunity, "under the supervision of the court and subject to reasonable time limits, to question jurors directly, both individually and as a panel."[240] The purpose of this process is to disclose the grounds for challenges for cause and to facilitate the "intelligent exercise of peremptory challenges."[241] The grounds for challenges for cause are the same ones that have always been in force: that a juror has an interest in the case, is connected to one of the parties, is in some other way biased or unqualified, or is "unable or unwilling to hear the subject case fairly and impartially." In ruling on a challenge for cause, the court "should evaluate the juror's demeanor and substantive responses to the questions," just as lawyers have always done when trying to impanel the best jury possible—which is why, under the old regime, much of the winnowing was supposed to take place before the venire was summoned.[242]

Conversely, the claim that peremptory challenges are frequently used as a pretext for racial discrimination has led the ABA to backtrack from this straightforward approach. If a party objects to the peremptory challenge of a juror who is a member of a "cognizable group," then it is enough to demonstrate that the challenged juror is in fact a member of such a group. That demonstration alone, according to principle 11, should establish a "prima facie case of purposeful discrimination," after which the burden shifts to the party making the challenge to show that it was not a mere pretext for discrimination. It then becomes the court's responsibility to evaluate the credibility of such a showing.[243]

Despite these limitations (and the ABA recommendations follow the case law pretty closely), there is no sympathy in the ABA principles for the position endorsed by Justice Marshall—that peremptory challenges should be abolished to forestall even the possibility of discriminatory jury selection. In the "Commentary" section, the ABA authors take note of Marshall's argument but conclude that "this long-standing feature of trial by jury remains necessary," most importantly because the peremptory challenge enables parties to take part in the "construction of the tribunal that is to judge them," avoiding potentially biased jurors even when there is no hard evidence of such bias.[244] To facilitate the proper use of the

240. Ibid.

241. One thing has not changed in the postmodern jury era: as in the earliest ABA reports, there is a visible conflict between the leadership and the members over matters that concern the interests of trial attorneys. Recall that the earliest ABA study of judicial reform recommended abandoning the conformity principle as well as the unanimity requirement in jury verdicts and urged the greater use of directed verdicts. All three proposals were rejected by the membership. See chapter 3.

242. *Principles for Juries and Jury Trials*, 14.

243. Ibid., 15.

244. "Commentary," ibid., 78.

challenge, questioning by the court should take place in a private setting, rather than in open court, and the jurors should be questioned individually, rather than as a group, to encourage honest answers.[245] There should be enough peremptory challenges to "protect the right to 'unpick' the few jurors who don't feel right."[246] This is the classic defense of peremptory challenges, and it is the very argument rejected by Marshall and eventually by Justice Stephen Breyer as well, as being a prime enabler of racism. Finally, instead of suggesting a particular number of peremptory challenges, the ABA recommends the "struck jury system," in which the parties alternately strike names from the jury list, silently, until the required number are left. It bears repeating here that the struck jury was a common method of choosing jurors in the eighteenth century.

Meanwhile, the Judicial Conference of the United States has had little to say about the jury system in recent decades, ending a long tradition of scholarly and professional interest matching that of the ABA. Although the conference issued regular reports on the jury from its founding in 1922 until the 1960s, it dissolved its Committee on the Jury System in 1987. And while it has continued to issue reports on various aspects of the system (e.g., *Jurors' Use of Social Media during Trials and Deliberations* in 2011), there have been no comprehensive studies of the jury since the 1960 *Report on the Jury System in the Federal Courts*. The conference devoted only two pages to the jury in its 1963 report, five pages in 1969, two pages in 1973, and one paragraph in 1987 (the same report that announced the dissolution of the Committee on the Jury System).[247]

THE JURY PROBLEM, REDUX

The modern jury regime is now almost fifty years old, and while it continues to evolve under the pressure of court decisions and acts of Congress, its main fea-

245. Ibid. It is a common belief among practicing attorneys that "box voir dire is simply inadequate at detecting juror bias." Richard Silver and Amanda Whitman, "Preserve the Right to Pick an Unbiased Jury," *Connecticut Law Tribune*, January 31, 2011, 2.

246. "Commentary," in *Principles for Juries and Jury Trials*, citing Myron Moskovitz, "You Can't Tell a Book by Its Title," *Criminal Law Forum* 8 (1997): 138.

247. *Report of the Judicial Conference of the United States*, March 11–12, 1963 (Washington, DC: Administrative Office of the United States Courts, 1963), 49–51; *Report of the Judicial Conference of the United States*, March 13–14, 1969 (Washington, DC: Administrative Office of the United States Courts, 1969), 11–16; *Report of the Judicial Conference of the United States*, September 13–14, 1973 (Washington, DC: Administrative Office of the United States Courts, 1973), 54–57; *Report of the Proceedings of the Judicial Conference of the United States*, September 21, 1987 (Washington, DC: Administrative Office of the United States Courts, 1987), 96.

tures are matters of well-settled jurisprudence.[248] Jury selection in federal courts is governed by federal statutes, and the controlling statute, the Jury Selection and Service Act of 1968, requires that jury lists be constructed in a way that does not "systematically" exclude any of the "cognizable groups" in the judicial district. Several Supreme Court decisions have applied this "cross-section" principle to the states through the due process and equal protection clauses of the Fourteenth Amendment. As a result, many states have been required to clean up their source lists, which means (ironically) that federal courts can once again rely on state lists, as they did in the era of the now discredited "conformity" principle. Typically, the voter registration list is the default source for jurors, but this list may (and sometimes must) be supplemented by other lists if it does not produce a satisfactory cross section of the district. At no stage of the selection process may prospective jurors be screened for "qualitative" measures such as "intelligence," "integrity," or "character." Jurors may, however, be challenged. Challenges for cause are conducted largely as they were in the past, but the use of peremptory challenges is now subject to some important restrictions, and the opportunities for reversible error are legion, especially if the challenged juror is a member of one of the distinctive groups.[249]

This transformation, however, has not stilled complaints about juries; these complaints are as prevalent as they were in the pre-1968 era, and they are remarkably similar in content and tone. As in the past, jurors are described as unserious, reluctant to serve, unable to process complex information, biased for or against the parties, and reluctant to follow the instructions of the judge. Or, like the jurors in *Twelve Angry Men*, they are said to be ruled by their preexisting biases and their superficial impressions, eager to "get things over with" and go home. And just like their Gilded Age forebears, they are charged with being unsympathetic to large corporations and eager to award "outrageous" amounts in civil cases, either because they have been bamboozled by clever attorneys or because they cannot

248. For example, the jury system has been further shaped by the Sentencing Reform Act of 1984 and by several Supreme Court decisions concerning its provisions, a subject taken up in chapter 5.

249. As noted above, many lawyers and legal scholars have attempted to expand the number of groups protected against discrimination, although the Supreme Court has declined to extend this special protection beyond African Americans, women, Hispanics, and day laborers (*Taylor*, *Hernandez*, *Thiel*, and *Strauder*). Gertner and Mizner (*Law of Juries*, 37–38) note that, "conceptually, the Sixth Amendment should cover additional groups beyond those historically protected by the Fourteenth Amendment." The Supreme Court, however, has "implied the opposite," rejecting protected status for those who oppose the death penalty. See Lockhart v. McCree, 476 U.S. 162 (1986). This has not prevented lawyers from filing appeals based on the alleged exclusion of some other identifiable group.

resist the urge to help the unfortunate at the expense of the wealthy.[250] To these traditional complaints has now been added a new one with special relevance for criminal cases: jurors arrive in court with romantic ideas about the legal system gleaned from entertaining but fanciful TV shows and movies, and they expect that every evidentiary question will be definitively answered by the science of forensics. "No DNA, no conviction."[251]

Stephen J. Adler, who is clearly sympathetic to the jury system and aware of its importance, notes the "disappointment" many Americans feel about juries, especially after a number of high-profile failures: the Texaco-Pennzoil takeover case, in which a jury awarded Pennzoil $10.5 billion, including an additional $1 billion (according to one juror) "for each of the Texaco witnesses [the jury] had most despised"; the civil trial of the police officers charged with beating Rodney King, in which the jury found "no excessive force," despite the extensive video evidence; or the Liggett & Myers–Brown & Williamson price discrimination case in Houston, which featured testimony that would have baffled most professional economists and a jury that was clearly predisposed to support the hometown company.[252]

Legal scholar Cass Sunstein, examining punitive-damage jury awards, came to the conclusion that "the legally required decision tasks often seemed to exceed [jurors'] individual and social capacities. . . . The result is a decision process that is unreliable, erratic and unpredictable."[253] Jeffrey Abramson, after noting the emergence and triumph of the "cross-section" jury, concludes that "this very democratization of jury selection has provoked a crisis of confidence in the qual-

250. There continues to be considerable disagreement on the extent of so-called rogue verdicts in civil trials. Taking the state and federal courts together, civil trials are as likely to result in a verdict for the defendant as for the plaintiff, and average monetary awards are in the five-figure range. However, there have undoubtedly been some spectacular exceptions that not only skew the headlines and the public's perception of civil trials but also tempt attorneys looking for a big score. See the highly useful collection Robert E. Litan, ed., *Verdict: Assessing the Civil Jury System* (Washington, DC: Brookings Institution, 1993).

251. See, for example, Linda Deutsch, "TV Distorts Jurors' Expectations: 'No Prints, No DNA, No Conviction,'" Associated Press, January 17, 2006, http://www.concordmonitor.com/article/tv-distorts-jurors-expectations (accessed June 21, 2014); and Michael Mann, "The 'CSI Effect': Better Jurors through Television and Science," *Buffalo Public Interest Law Journal* 24 (2005–2006): 211.

252. Stephen J. Adler, *The Jury: Trial and Error in the American Courtroom* (New York: Times Books/Random House, 1994), 116–144.

253. Cass Sunstein et al., *Punitive Damages: How Jurors Decide* (Chicago: University of Chicago Press, 2002), quoted by ibid., 304. Sunstein also notes that some of the "erratic" quality of jury decisions can be blamed on "lack of effective guidance" by the court.

ity and accuracy of jury verdicts."[254] Verdicts like those in a Texas patent case, in which "unemployed laborers and housewives [who] didn't understand that stuff" (according to the loser's attorney) awarded $35 million to the plaintiffs, have led to calls for restrictions on the types of civil cases that juries may decide. Furthermore, according to Abramson, because of the "search for representative juries," jury selection "bogs down" over intricate questions of racial, ethnic, and gender balance, "creating the impression that justice depends precariously on the race, gender, religion, or even national origin of jurors."[255]

And there is plenty of evidence that many Americans still try to avoid jury service, even at the risk of fines, and even though state legislatures no longer give blanket exemptions to influential professions and occupations. Taking 2007 as a representative year, the National Center for State Courts reported that of the 32 million people summoned for jury service in the state and federal courts, 6 million managed to avoid service, equally divided between those who simply failed to respond to their jury summons and those who requested and received hardship exemptions.[256] But this national "failure to appear" rate of 9.4 percent hides some ugly local variations: rates in big cities often exceed 50 percent.[257] In Los Angeles County in 2010, jury administrators reported that half of the 3 million summonses sent out were simply ignored—not counting those returned by the post office as "undeliverable."[258] In South Florida, two-thirds of those summoned fail to respond—a development that one local judge attributes to the switch from voter registration lists to driver's license records as the prime source for names.[259]

The era of the postmodern jury has also seen an explosion of social science research on jury decision making, inspired by Kalven and Zeisel's landmark 1966 study *The American Jury*. The authors' most famous finding was that judges and juries agreed on verdicts 75 percent of the time. Kalven and Zeisel had less to say about how jurors reach their decisions, largely because they were prevented from carrying out their original research design, which involved surreptitiously record-

254. Jeffrey Abramson, *We the Jury: The Jury System and the Ideal of Democracy* (New York: Basic Books, 1994), 3.

255. Ibid., 3–4.

256. National Center for State Courts, *State-of-the-States Survey of Jury Improvement Efforts* (Williamsburg, VA: NCSC, 2007), http://www.ncscjurystudies.org/~/media/Microsites/Files/CJS/SOS/SOSCompendiumFinal.ashx (accessed April 22, 2015).

257. Paula Hannaford-Agor, "Jury News: Tales of 'Tales' Juries," *Court Manager* 23, 2 (2008): 28, citing statistics from the National Center for State Courts.

258. Richard Guzmán, "Death, Taxes and Jury Duty," *Advocates News*, 2010, http://www.theadvocates.com/news/50PercentofJurySummonsIgnoredinLA.php (accessed June 23, 2014).

259. Georgia East, "Tens of Thousands in South Florida Skip out on Jury Duty," *Sun Sentinel*, April 16, 2011, http://www.articles.sun-sentinel.com/2011-04-16/news/fl-jury-no-shows-20110416_1_jury-duty-potential-jurors-voter (accessed June 23, 2014).

ing jury deliberations—a scheme that led to a congressional investigation and a legislative affirmation of the principle of jury privacy.[260] Blocked from violating the secrecy of jury deliberations, researchers have been forced to come up with alternative means of getting inside the "black box" of jury verdicts, propelled by a variety of motives. Some researchers may be seeking to improve jury decision making (such studies eventually led to increased court acceptance of juror note-taking and juror questions), some are trying to learn how to influence juror decision making, and some are hoping to help attorneys make better use of their peremptory challenges or make more effective arguments in court. The usual research method is to construct mock juries and then conduct "trials" that mimic as nearly as possible the real court proceedings. What this research shows is that the "runaway jury" is largely a myth, but jury performance can be improved by the adoption of some useful and (for the most part) simple reforms.

For example, sensational civil judgments attract lots of press attention, but they are outliers. Several volumes of research on civil jury verdicts in Illinois and California conducted by Mark Peterson and his colleagues at the Rand Institute for Civil Justice, using data from the late 1950s through the 1980s, show that "the median compensatory damage award is much smaller than the mean award, because the occasional very large award inflates the mean."[261] Studies of the same period performed for the American Bar Foundation and the National Center for State Courts show that the median compensatory-damage award in state and federal courts has consistently been low, ranging from just under $30,000 to just under $50,000 in federal and state courts, respectively. Average awards are much higher, of course, but compensatory-damage awards larger than $1 million accounted for less than 6 percent of jury verdicts in California and less than 4 percent in Illinois.[262] Punitive-damage awards were likewise less common than press attention would suggest, and less lucrative as well. Peterson's study found very few punitive-damage awards in California or Illinois, and another research team found fewer than 400 such cases in the entire country between 1965 and 1990.[263] It must be stressed, however, that very high awards, though rare, have an impact on the real world beyond their numbers. For example, there were many fewer awards for medical malpractice than for tort cases in the 1980s, but the medical malpractice awards were higher—and this fact was almost certainly a major cause of the increase in the cost of medical malpractice insurance.

Another common complaint about contemporary jurors—that they fail to understand judicial instructions—is also exaggerated. Robert MacCoun reports

260. See Kalven and Zeisel, *American Jury*, xiv–xv.

261. Robert MacCoun, "Inside the Black Box: What Empirical Research Tells Us about Decisionmaking by Civil Juries," in Litan, *Verdict*, 148.

262. These studies are discussed in ibid., 148–150.

263. Ibid., 149.

that while some studies show that as much as half of the judge's instructions are not well understood by jurors, the same studies show that how the instructions are presented makes a great deal of difference. When instructions are couched in language accessible to laypeople, comprehension goes up; this is why the demand for simpler instructions has been part of the jury reform agenda since the late nineteenth century. The fear of being overturned on appeal often leads judges to direct their instructions to the appellate courts, rather than to the jurors sitting dumbfounded in the box. That is, when judges address jurors as they did during the republican era, juries have a much better understanding of the law.[264]

The complaint that jurors do not pay attention to, or make no serious effort to comprehend, the evidence presented in court gains credibility every time juries render sensational and widely covered "wrong" verdicts (as in the first two trials of the Menendez brothers for murdering their parents). But once again, the jury studies tell a slightly different story. Reflecting on this research and on his own experiences as a defense attorney, Randolph N. Jonakait concluded in 2003 that in the typical trial, "evidence is the prime determinant of a jury's verdict."[265] Therefore, "the best way to improve jury verdicts is to improve the information the jury receives to consider. The better that evidence is, the better the resulting verdicts are likely to be."[266]

Finally, research on jury decision making debunks one of the main arguments in favor of the cross-section or representative jury: that jurors from diverse backgrounds bring different perspectives to the evidence presented in court. This is what might be called the "dark side" of the representative jury paradigm: jurors must come from diverse backgrounds so that all the biases in the community are adequately represented in court. The empirical studies suggest, however, that the demographic characteristics of the jury make very little difference to trial outcomes. MacCoun concludes that, "in general, the demographic characteristics, personality traits, and general attitudes of jurors have weak and unreliable effects on verdicts."[267] This finding was made in the context of civil trials, but there is no reason to think it would not be true of criminal trials as well.

The insights obtained through this research have led to some useful improvements in the way jurors are summoned, accommodated, and instructed in court. More states use the one-day, one-trial summoning procedure, which allows jurors to choose an alternative court date sometime during the next year if the original date is inconvenient, and they are permitted to go home if they are not picked for a jury on their appointed day.[268] The physical conditions of many courthouses

264. Ibid., 152.

265. Jonakait, *American Jury System*, 249.

266. Ibid., 279–280.

267. MacCoun, "Inside the Black Box," 151.

268. Massachusetts was a pioneer, allowing jurors the option of postponing service to a date of their own choosing, up to a year beyond the summons date. The legislature was

have been improved, and jurors are given instructions at the outset that emphasize the nature and importance of what they are about to do. Such improvements have been sought by jury reformers ever since the 1920s.[269] In many courts, jurors are now allowed to take notes, and in some places they share video terminals, where they can follow the exhibits offered in evidence. Judges encourage jurors to ask questions more often than they did in the past; additionally, judges are now free to use the plainest language when answering jurors' questions, charging juries, and commenting on evidence.[270] As a result, contemporary jurors may have a better idea than their early-twentieth-century counterparts about what they are supposed to do.

Jurors are still underpaid, however—another example of how the poor have fallen out of the discussion of the cross-section jury. Federal jurors are currently paid $40 per day for the first ten days of a trial and $50 per day subsequently, which means that the day laborers who figured so prominently in the *Thiel* decision in 1940 would still be justified in asking to be excused, assuming they make the federal minimum wage of $7.25 per hour and work an eight-hour day. This may be one reason—but not the only one—for the high avoidance rate among those called to jury service in some communities. And there are still accusations that employers find ways to penalize workers who attend to their jury responsibilities, even though such retaliation is a violation of federal law.[271]

Yet in the postmodern era, complaints about jurors are presented in an intellectual environment markedly different from that of the past, when it was routine for jury reform proposals to begin with the need for "better jurors," followed by a recognition that jurors should be chosen from a "cross section" of the community.

---

persuaded to make this change when one court, desperately short of jurors, was forced to choose "bystanders" from the line of cars waiting at the stoplight outside the courthouse. Similar reforms have been adopted in Rhode Island, New York, and Colorado. See Karin A. Berris, "Appearance Rates of Potential Jurors Who Confirm, Postpone, or Fail to Respond to the Jury Summons," *Drake Law Review* 59 (2011): 653.

269. For one notable example, see *Jury System in the Federal Courts*, 47–49.

270. An illustrative example comes from a civil trial I observed in federal district court in Boston, Judge William G. Young presiding. After Judge Young admonished the plaintiff's attorney for the second time about her "leading questions," a juror asked to have the term explained. Judge Young replied that "when counsel asks a question in a way that is designed to get the answer she wants, that's a leading question, and she is not allowed to do that."

271. Principle 2(F) of the ABA's *Principles for Juries and Jury Trials* states: "Employers should be prohibited from discharging, laying off, denying advancement opportunities to, or otherwise penalizing employees who miss work because of jury service," and "employers should be prohibited from requiring jurors to use leave or vacation time for the time spent" (5).

Choosing "the best from each sector" is an idea that makes sense in the abstract, but it is largely unenforceable under contemporary jury law, which forbids any attempt to "winnow" the more "intelligent," "prudent," or "upright" characters from the mass of names on the jury list. Indeed, contemporary jury theory undermines the very premise of winnowing—namely, that some citizens are naturally "better" choices for jury service than others. Such "discrimination," as Attorney General Clark said at the time, merely reflects the "preferences and prejudices" of the chooser, who will always be a member of "the few." So powerful is this post-1968 ethos that discussion of the need for "better" jurors has vanished from the professional literature.

But lawyers still want to win cases, so they still attempt to separate the wheat from the chaff during jury selection, despite the formal theory's abhorrence of the very notion of wheat and chaff. This is exactly what attorney William Marbury feared would happen when he testified before the Senate Judiciary Committee in 1967. "I don't like the idea of lawyers selecting jurors," Marbury said then.[272] But that is precisely what has happened. The process of postmodern jury selection is largely driven by attorneys, even when it is supervised by judges. And to do this job more effectively, lawyers have acquired the assistance of a new profession known as "jury consultants"—a practice that has grown since the early 1970s into a $400 million industry.[273]

THE SCIENCE OF JURY CONSULTING

Broadly speaking, jury consulting consists of two separate activities: jury selection and trial preparation. Consultants help attorneys select those jurors who are most likely to be favorable to their cases. (In criminal trials, this almost always means the defense—provided the defendant is wealthy enough to employ consultants; in civil cases, it is not uncommon for both parties to use consultants.) Consultants also help attorneys present their cases in the best way possible by advising on trial strategy, witness preparation, and the presentation of evidence. (As noted above, this has motivated some of the empirical research on jury decision making, and the technical expertise required in the use of mock juries owes much to the jury consultant industry.) Jury selection and trial preparation need not be done by the same consulting firm or at the same trial. Some attorneys hire consultants for help in choosing jurors, others use them for guidance in their presenting cases, and some need assistance with both parts of the trial. But advising on jury

272. *Hearings before the Subcommittee on Improvements*, 87.

273. The estimate is for 2000 and comes from Kressel and Kressel, *Stack and Sway*, 84. See also Franklin Strier and Donna Shestowsky, "Profiling the Profilers: A Study of the Trial Consulting Profession, Its Impact on Trial Justice and What, if Anything, to Do about It," *Wisconsin Law Review* (1999): 441.

selection is probably the one aspect of jury consulting about which the public has heard the most and about which it has the most qualms.

Like the preparation of witnesses and the shaping of trial strategy, the manipulation of jury selection is not a new phenomenon. Lawyers have always understood the importance of selecting a friendly jury, and in the United States the law has cooperated by providing challenges either for cause or peremptorily. In the past, lawyers shared anecdotes and folk wisdom about what kinds of people made the ideal juries for particular kinds of cases. Doctors would obviously be a poor choice for the plaintiff in a medical malpractice suit, while women or men with young daughters would be ideal for prosecuting rapists. People with low incomes (identifiable by their shoes) usually sympathize with the underdog, so the prosecution would not want them deciding the case of a poor man on trial for stealing food. People who have a hard time paying their rent are great jurors if the defendant is a big corporation. And so on.

The problem with this kind of folk wisdom is not that it is wrong but that it is imprecise. Of course women dislike rapists, but most men dislike rapists too. The question is, what kind of women will look at the evidence in precisely the way required by this particular case? Do some women harbor a secret suspicion that "loose" women "invite" rape? Do elderly women and young women have the same views? How about rich women and poor women? Does it matter if the defendant and the juror are of different races? Social scientists have ways of determining the answers to such questions: they do public opinion surveys, sampling the population in the judicial district on a broad range of questions, sometimes supplementing these surveys with focus group interviews designed to probe the connections between the elements of a single set of opinions. They conduct mock trials to try out different arguments and trial strategies. These tools are expensive, of course, so they are normally used only in high-stakes cases such as capital murder trials, trials with significant political implications, or trials in which enormous civil judgments are at stake.

The opportunity to actually use such knowledge, however, is presented by the peremptory challenge. The peremptory challenge has survived because it is useful—not only in the United States but also in other common-law jurisdictions where jury trials continue to be utilized in serious criminal cases. The peremptory challenge has been abolished only in Great Britain and Northern Ireland.[274] There have been many calls for the abolition of the peremptory challenge in the United States over the past few decades, echoing Justice Marshall's suggestion in *Batson*. In 2009 the Supreme Court appeared to strip the challenge of its common-law pedigree,[275] ruling that "states may withhold peremptory challenges 'altogether

274. Criminal Justice Act 1988, section 118(1). Peremptory challenges were abolished in Northern Ireland in 2007 by section 13 of the Justice and Security Act.

275. Rivera v. Illinois, 556 U.S. 148 (2009), 152, quoting Georgia v. McColllum, 505 U.S. 42 (1992), at 57.

without impairing the constitutional guarantee of an impartial jury and a fair trial.'" But the Federal Rules of Civil and Criminal Procedure allow peremptory challenges in civil cases and criminal cases alike, and similar arrangements are common in the states.[276] And so the science of jury consulting has grown apace.

The general consensus is that scientific jury consulting originated in 1972 during the trial of Philip Berrigan, a radical Catholic priest accused of conspiring with several others (the "Harrisburg Seven") to commit various illegal acts aimed at obstructing the prosecution of the Vietnam War (destroying selective service records, for example, but also kidnapping Henry Kissinger). Regarding the charge of destroying draft records, Father Berrigan was, according to his own statements, clearly and defiantly guilty. (The kidnapping charge was a different matter.) For Berrigan and his codefendants to be found not guilty on this charge, the jury would have to "nullify" the prosecution, on the grounds that the defendants' destruction of the records had a noble purpose—namely, opposing American policy in South Vietnam.[277] What kind of juror would be most likely to reach such a conclusion? (And since it takes twelve to convict, only one such juror would be enough.) Would it matter, for example, that the lead defendant was a priest? Would Catholics be more or less sympathetic than non-Catholics to an antiwar priest? The folk wisdom of the bar had nothing to say about clerics who poured blood on draft records. So a group of social scientists sympathetic to Berrigan's cause conducted surveys in Harrisburg, Pennsylvania, where the trial would take place, and came up with a counterintuitive portrait of the ideal juror: a white female Democrat with a dead-end job and no religion. Using this information, the defense was able to pick a jury that hung on all the major charges.[278]

Two years later, a different group of social scientists helped pick the jury that acquitted Joan Little of murdering her jailer, Clarence Alligood. Little, who was black, admitted killing Alligood, a white man, by stabbing him to death with an ice pick. She claimed self-defense against an attempted sexual assault; the state of North Carolina claimed she had lured Alligood with the promise of sex and then killed him so she could escape from jail. Using the results of a public opinion survey, Little's defense team successfully moved for a change of venue from Beaufort County (where racial attitudes among whites were particularly harsh) to Raleigh (where views were more moderate). Additionally, Little's decision to turn herself in may have caused the jury to doubt the state's version of events. What-

276. Each party is entitled to three peremptory challenges in civil cases tried in federal court (28 U.S.C. § 1870). In criminal trials, rule 24 of the Federal Rules of Criminal Procedure allows twenty peremptory challenges for both sides in capital cases, six for the government and ten for the defendant in noncapital felonies, and three each in misdemeanor cases.

277. The phenomenon of jury nullification is discussed separately, below.

278. Kressel and Kressel, *Stack and Sway*, 61–62. Berrigan was convicted only of smuggling letters out of prison.

ever the reasoning, Little's jury (six whites and six blacks) returned a verdict of not guilty after deliberating for an hour and a half.[279]

The same trial consultants that worked on the Little trial helped in several other notorious criminal trials with political overtones: Angela Davis; the Attica, New York, prison riot defendants; and members of Vietnam Veterans Against the War. Other sympathetic consultants helped with jury selection in the trial of American Indian Movement activists from Wounded Knee, South Dakota, and in the prosecution of various members of the Black Panthers. Jury consulting went bipartisan with the Watergate trials of John Mitchell and Maurice Stans. By the 1980s, the new industry was well established, with its own trade association (the American Society of Trial Consultants), conventions, and lots of attention from the press.

Students of the subject speculate that the market for consultants was growing because of an increase in the number of high-stakes trials involving celebrity criminal defendants or corporate defendants in class-action suits. One firm, Trial Behavior Consulting, worked on more than 150 asbestos cases in the 1980s.[280] Success in one trial creates the impression that jury consultants can make a difference, and this encourages clients who can afford it to hire them—and so the cycle continues. By the mid-2000s, consultants were involved in 10,000 cases per year. And even though this represents a small fraction of the total number of jury trials (which constitute less than 3 percent of all criminal and civil cases), the availability of jury consulting changes the strategic context of decision making when parties are headed for court. Jury consultants are now almost always involved in the largest civil suits, and often for both sides. (One lawyer claims it is "almost malpractice" not to use consultants when large judgments are involved.) And it is these high-stakes trials that are most likely to come to the public's attention.[281]

By the time of the O. J. Simpson murder trial in 1995, jury consultants had already acquired a bad reputation (deserved or not) among the public at large and among some students of the jury system, and the Simpson trial only made matters worse. Amitai Etzioni denounced "social-science jury stacking," and jury scholars Stephen Adler and Jeffrey Abramson called for the banning of hired "shadow jurors" in court (Adler) or the imposition of restrictions on their operations (Abramson).[282] These complaints were echoed by Judge Harold Rothwax, commenting on the Simpson verdict specifically: "Jury selection is hostage to peremptory challenges that, with the help of scientific jury experts, can mold a jury in the hope that it will be swayed by emotion and innuendo, not fact."[283]

279. Ibid., 62–63.

280. Ibid., 65–66.

281. Ibid., 74.

282. Ibid., 72–74. See also Adler, *The Jury*, 113–115.

283. Kressel and Kressel, *Stack and Sway*, 73. Jeffrey Abramson has suggested reducing the opportunity to use jury consultants by abolishing peremptory challenges and "ex-

It is precisely this manipulation of jury selection that the public seems to fear the most, even though the opportunities to stack juries are limited, and the knowledge required to "choose wisely" comes at a very high price.[284] For those who can afford it, however, knowing with some precision what to look for in a juror can make a big difference. For example, the focus group experiments conducted by the prosecution in the O. J. Simpson case produced clear evidence that black women doubted the link between violent spousal abuse and murder. "In every relationship, there's always a little trouble," one African American woman on the mock jury declared. These experiments also revealed that black women despised the lead prosecutor, Marcia Clark, and were convinced that Simpson was innocent. Black men were only slightly less likely to believe in Simpson's innocence. On this basis, the prosecution's trial consultant, Donald Vinson, concluded that black women were the worst possible jurors for the prosecution, a conclusion rejected by Clark, for some reason. Meanwhile, the defense team hired jury consultant Jo-Ellan Dimitrius, who conducted an opinion survey as well as focus group experiments and came to exactly the same conclusions as Vinson. The defense team chose to follow her advice, using all twenty of its peremptory challenges to do so. The final Simpson jury had eight African American women; all twelve jurors were Democrats, and nine of them believed that a successful football player was unlikely to commit murder.[285] When the trial was over, Dimitrius was the first person defense attorney Johnnie Cochran publicly thanked.[286]

Jury consultants also help attorneys prepare witnesses, introduce evidence, and tell a "story" that the jury will understand and respond to positively. Sometimes this involves running parallel mock trials to see how citizens with the same general characteristics as the eligible jury population respond to the attorneys'

---

panding" the use of challenges for cause. Ibid., 228–229. Amitai Etzioni has accused jury consultants of selling knowledge about how to "rig" juries. See Amitai Etzioni "Creating an Imbalance," *Trial* 10 (1974): 28. For a discussion of these matters, see V. Hale Starr and Marc McCormick, *Jury Selection* (Aspen Publishers Online, 2009), 5.1.14 ff.

284. Alan Dershowitz, commenting on the defense strategy in the O. J. Simpson trial, said: "Money meant everything in this case." Lorraine Adams and Serge F. Kovaleski, "The Dream Team's Dream Resources," in *Postmortem: The O. J. Simpson Case*, ed. Jeffrey Abramson (New York: Basic Books, 1996), 126. This has led to a spirited discussion in the law reviews about whether jury consultants should fall into the same category as the "court-appointed lawyer"—that is, a "right" to be enforced through the equal protection clause. See, among other examples, Steven C. Serio, "A Process Right Due? Examining Whether a Capital Defendant Has a Due Process Right to a Jury Selection Expert," *American University Law Review* 53 (2003–2004): 1143.

285. See Jeffrey Toobin, *The Run of His Life: The People v. O. J. Simpson* (New York: Touchstone, 1997), 184–207.

286. Adams and Kovaleski, "Dream Team's Dream Resources," 127.

arguments and presentation of evidence.[287] But the effort to persuade the jury with a particular story begins by choosing those jurors most likely to be persuadable. Again, the Simpson trial provides an illustrative example. As soon as the jury consultants had confirmed the importance of race to opinions about Simpson's guilt or innocence, they shaped the "trial story" as a "frame-up" by "racist cops"—before the jury had even been chosen, and before the appearance of an actual cop with a racist reputation, Mark Fuhrman. The jurors were chosen to fit the story, and matching the juror to the story meant focusing on "the values and beliefs that drive people to make certain decisions."[288] The ideal jurors in the Simpson case, in addition to being of a particular race and gender, would have certain "attitudes"—toward police officers, toward white women, toward interracial dating, toward the image of the powerful and successful black male. Those jurors with the right attitudes would be most likely to believe the "story." It is no coincidence that one of the most successful jury consulting firms was founded by a marketing specialist, or that social psychologists are prominent in the industry. The place where the science of psychology meets the science of sales—the rich soil where the advertising industry blossomed—has produced the cognate industry of jury consulting.

In the past, an impartial jury was one whose members had no personal connection to any of the parties and no apparent predisposition for or against any of the parties; they would be able to render a verdict based solely on the evidence, even if they had formed "light impressions" about the case from reading about it in the press.[289] The first two elements can be resolved by the challenge for cause. The third element is more complicated because the solution requires the attorney, or the court, to uncover what a juror might desire to keep hidden or might even be unaware of. This is the reason for the peremptory challenge.

But there is another concern much older than jury consulting that has nothing to do with partiality and everything to do with the jury's ability to deliberate intelligently on the matters before it. Who among the prospective jurors has (or lacks) the character, intelligence, and integrity required to render justice? Who are the "scofflaws" and "UFOs"? Judge Rothwax's complaint about the O. J. Simpson jury—that it was "swayed by emotion and innuendo, not fact"—speaks to this deeper concern. If it is possible for consultants to put together a jury that will not deliberate—because it is already convinced that the prosecution is unjust or that the defendant is guilty, regardless of the evidence entered into the record—then it is because the venire contains a sufficient number of citizens who can be convinced to ignore their duty. Or, to put it more bluntly: it may be possible to buy a

287. On the "story model" of jury decision making, the classic study is Reid Hastie et al., *Inside the Jury* (Cambridge, MA: Harvard University Press, 1983).

288. Kressel and Kressel, *Stack and Sway*, 88.

289. This was Chief Justice Marshall's formula from the Aaron Burr treason trial. See chapter 2.

jury that, rather than seeking to understand the law, simply chooses to nullify the prosecution because the jurors dislike the law in question (drug laws, for example), they do not trust the prosecution (clearly an element in the Simpson case), or they think the prosecutor is "unfair" or a "bitch" (as many of the black women on the Simpson mock juries believed about Marcia Clark).[290] This is the possibility that lies behind the public concern over the Simpson verdict, among many others that were far less famous. And it has led to the introduction of a new idea masquerading as an old one: jury nullification.

FINDING THE LAW, OR NULLIFYING THE LAW?

The contemporary debate over jury nullification shares the same time line as the debate over jury consultants; both phenomena are, at least chronologically, fixtures of the postmodern jury regime, although each bears a resemblance to older practices. Lawyers have always tried to turn jury selection into an art, if not a science, and jurors have often rejected judges' instructions about the evidence and the law. This latter practice is now referred to as "jury nullification," and nullification is invariably cited as one of the "core elements of the common law jury" as it emerged in England, the colonies, and the early republic.[291] One law review article, for example, begins with the blunt assertion that in seventeenth-century England, "it was recognized that a jury had the right to nullify."[292] The author's evidence for this claim is Justice Vaughan's decision in Bushell's Case in 1670, yet that decision very emphatically did not endorse the right of a juror to ignore, or nullify, an act of Parliament—indeed, it is impossible to imagine a moderate royalist like Vaughan even conceiving of such an astounding idea. Vaughan insisted, to the contrary, that the claim of a juror's right to render any judgment about the law was simply "not intelligible."[293] Rather, Vaughan argued that no jury could be punished for returning a verdict that a judge disliked, because no judge could know what facts in the jury's possession had produced the verdict. If jurors reached a conclusion different from the judge's, it had to be because they knew facts that the judge did not; it could not be because of a disagreement about the law, since jurors were too ignorant to have any opinions about the law.

290. Toobin, *Run of His Life*, 192–193.

291. See, for example, the claims made by the Fully Informed Jury Association (founded in 1989) at its website (fija.org). The organization aims to "restore" the jury system so that it will "once again . . . function as our country's founders intended it to function, as people's final check against the government's tendency to encroach upon the rights of its people."

292. Mike Peck, "A Community with No Conscience: The Further Reduction of a Jury's Right to Nullify in *People v. Sanchez*," *Whittier Law Review* 21 (1999–2000): 285.

293. For a discussion of Bushell's Case, see chapter 1.

Another recent article quotes Thomas Jefferson as a supporter of jury nullification, by altering his words in a significant way: "Thomas Jefferson wrote," the article claims, "that juries 'never exercise this power [to nullify] but when they suspect partiality in the judges.'" This is a partial quotation from Jefferson's July 19, 1789, letter to the Abbé Arnoux, explaining to the Frenchman the American understanding and practice of jury trials. But the phrase in brackets (to nullify) appears nowhere in Jefferson's letter, which instead refers to the power "to judge the law as well as the fact."[294]

In the republican era, "judging" or "finding" the law meant "understanding" the law; it did not mean repealing or ignoring the law. And because republican jurors could understand the law (they had, after all, made the law), there was always a chance that their understanding and the judge's understanding would differ. This view is as far from Justice Vaughan as it is from the Fully Informed Jury Association. Citizens are responsible for making the law in the first place; understanding the law is therefore not only the citizen's duty but also a challenge to which most citizens can presumably rise, with a little help from the court, unless they are so ignorant that they should have been kept off the jury in the first place. This is why, during the republican era, judges so often acknowledged the jury's right to judge the law—even while reminding them that the judge was the best authority for determining the law's meaning. Even in seventeenth-century England, subjects insisted that they were fully capable of understanding the law, despite Justice Vaughan's aristocratic doubts. The jurors in the Case of the Seven Bishops, for example, insisted that the king did not, as a matter of English law, have the authority to overturn an act of Parliament, which meant that the bishops' public assertion of this claim could not, as a matter of law, be a criminal libel against the Crown. The bishops' petition had simply stated a fact, one that was known to all students of English constitutional principles.[295] By contrast, "nullification" was what Kentucky and Virginia tried to do to the Sedition Act, what South Carolina sought to do to the "Tariff of Abominations," and what Chief Justice John Marshall did to section 13 of the Judiciary Act of 1801: make them "void," or nullify them.[296]

As noted in chapter 2, the term "jury nullification" did not appear in print until 1911, when it was used to describe Chicago juries' refusal to convict defen-

294. Paula L. Hannaford-Agor and Valerie P. Hans, "Nullification at Work? A Glimpse from the National Center for State Courts Study of Hung Juries," *Chicago-Kent Law Review* 78 (2003): 1256. Jefferson's letter appears in *The Papers of Thomas Jefferson*, ed. Julian P. Boyd et al. (Princeton, NJ: Princeton University Press, 1950), 15:282–283.

295. See chapter 1. The king had, in effect, repealed the act of Parliament denying Catholics the right to practice their religion openly and to participate in the public life of the kingdom.

296. Marshall argued that "a law repugnant to the Constitution is void" by default—that is, it is not necessary for Congress to repeal it. Marbury v. Madison, 5 U.S. 137 (1804), 180.

dants charged with violating the Sunday closing laws.[297] This is clearly what the modern concept of jury nullification has in mind: the refusal to convict even in the face of what the 1911 author refers to as "incontrovertible evidence" of guilt. The jury's power to do this was sometimes equated with lawlessness (as in 1911) and sometimes with a more robust understanding of democracy. For example, a *New Republic* essay from 1929 notes the impossibility of enforcing laws (such as Prohibition) that had lost the moral support of the public. The violators of such laws would rarely be prosecuted, and if they were, they would rarely be convicted by juries—a process the author refers to as "the adjustment of law enforcement to public sentiment."[298]

In this view, the jury stands athwart the law, voiding laws that are generally or locally unpopular and acting as a barrier between the judge and the defendant. Jurors are not exercising a judgment about what the law means; they are simply repealing the law by refusing to convict anyone for breaking it. Often jurors do this because they are members of a community at odds with the authorities, such as when jurors from precincts where there are lots of taverns refuse to enforce the closing laws. Or sometimes jurors nullify because they distrust the authorities more generally, as appears to be the case when black jurors refuse to convict black defendants of certain drug charges.

Abramson has argued that the radical division between the functions of the judge (who is in charge of the law) and the functions of the jury (which is in charge of the facts), established by the *Sparf and Hansen* decision in 1895, is the key to the weakness of the modern jury.[299] He states that, contrary to this view, the "world outside the courtroom does not neatly divide questions of fact from questions of law. When we ask jurors to decide, as a matter of fact, whether the defendant acted with malice, we are asking them to . . . render a judgment."[300] Today, as in the seventeenth century, the law and the facts are mixed "complicately," as Justice Vaughan pointed out. Jurors can be kept from judging the law only by drastically narrowing the scope of jury decision making.

The absence of the phrase "jury nullification" from the debates of the republican era is therefore not a semantic coincidence but a clue to the meaning of the re-

297. The term "jury nullification" first appeared in 1911, but the concern over nullification (to the extent such concern can be gleaned from the contents of law reviews) is a distinctly postmodern development. Jury nullification did not get much attention in the literature before the 1970s. A full-text search of Hein Online, for example, turned up only 40 references to "jury nullification" in the law reviews between 1911 and 1970. The same search found 3,082 references between 1970 and 2010.

298. Robert C. Binkley, "Nullification and the Legal Process," *New Republic*, May 1, 1929, reprinted in *Massachusetts Law Quarterly* 14 (1928–1929): 109.

299. Abramson, *We the Jury*, 90–95.

300. Ibid., 91.

publican jury. The prominence of the phrase in the late twentieth century is a clue, as well, to the meaning of the postmodern jury. The phrase began to appear in the twentieth century because it reflects a contemporary reality: because jurors may say nothing about the law, and because judging the facts means little if the law has already been settled, the only way for a jury to influence the conduct of trials is to say "no" to prosecutions.[301] Jury nullification, which seems to be the exercise of a power, is in fact a sign of weakness, and it reflects a much narrower role for the jury than the older view that jurors could "find" and even "judge" the law.[302]

The jury's "right to say no" is far removed from the partnership in judging in which the republican jury participated. The modern idea assumes, instead, that the court and the jury are not partners but enemies, or at least opponents; that stubborn jurors are not the authors of the law but its passive victims; and that law enforcement is the concern of the authorities but not of the citizens themselves. Once upon a time, this view of the jury—that jurors don't really care about the law—was a criticism, and it emerged in the context of doubts about modern jurors' capacity to understand or to honor their duties. At the time of its appearance in the early twentieth century, "jury nullification" was not a term proudly proclaimed by jurors themselves, unlike older claims about the jury's right to "judge" or "find" the law. "Jury nullification" appeared to be a simple refusal to recognize the authority of the law, a development that fueled the campaign for "better jurors"—a goal once shared by the American Bar Association, the Judicial Conference, and Congress. But modern scholarship has turned a vice into a virtue and, in the process, has exported to the distant past an idea with a modern (or postmodern) meaning: if the jurors don't like the law, they should simply ignore it.

The current preoccupation with jury nullification was launched by the same events that inspired the science of jury consulting: the trials of antiwar activists during the Vietnam War, beginning with the trial of Father Philip Berrigan and the Harrisburg Seven in 1972.[303] At their trial, the defendants demanded the right to

301. Alan W. Scheflin, "Jury Nullification: The Right to Say No," *California Law Review* 45 (1972): 168–227.

302. Jeffrey Abramson argues that while jury nullification "grew out of a general claim that jurors have the right to decide all questions of law necessary to reach a verdict," the "right to nullify is narrow, permitting jurors only the right not to apply the law." Abramson, *We the Jury*, 67.

303. On the Vietnam-era nullification trials, see generally Irwin A. Horowitz and Thomas E. Willging, "Changing Views of Jury Power: The Nullification Debate, 1787–1988," *Law and Human Behavior* 15, 2 (April 1991): 165; United States v. Dougherty, 473 F.2d 1113 (D. C. Circuit, 1972); Alan Scheflin and Jon Van Dyke, "Jury Nullification: The Contours of a Controversy," *Law and Contemporary Problems* 43 (1979–1980): 51; and Steven E. Barkan, "Jury Nullification in Political Trials," *Social Problems* 31 (1983), 28: 1983. On the link between these trials and jury nullification, see Abramson, *We the Jury*, 67–88.

inform jurors of their "right to nullify" the laws in question, but the judge would not allow it. But even without this instruction, the jury hung on all the major charges, giving the new science of jury consulting its first victory.[304]

The second arena in which jury nullification has commonly been proclaimed concerns cases against black or other nonwhite defendants.[305] Some see jury nullification as a "weapon of the weak": when black jurors see young black men facing years in prison for drug crimes or firearms violations, they may choose to acquit, regardless of the evidence, to "send a message" to society.[306] The message might be about police misconduct in a particular case or in general, or it might be a general cry against the way the system seems to be stacked against racial minorities or the poor.[307] This kind of jury nullification, like the refusal to convict antiwar demonstrators, has little or nothing to do with the law itself. The Harrisburg Seven had no objection to laws against trespass or the destruction of property: it was the war in Vietnam they objected to. Likewise, jurors tempted to nullify a drug prosecution might have no objection to laws against the use or sale of cocaine or marijuana; they might simply be refusing to cooperate with a legal system that, in their view, singles out blacks for special treatment through "profiling" or imposes stiffer penalties for the cheap drugs used by poor (and frequently black) addicts (such as crack cocaine) than for the more expensive drugs favored by the wealthy.[308]

304. Kressel and Kressel, *Stack and Sway*, 62. Antiwar demonstrators were not always so successful in court, however. Members of a group calling itself the "DC Nine" were convicted in 1972 for the destruction of property at a Dow Chemical office, where they were protesting the company's manufacture of napalm. They were convicted by a jury and appealed on the grounds that the trial judge had disallowed a "jury nullification instruction." Their appeal was rejected. See Irwin Horowitz, "The Effect of Jury Nullification Instruction on Verdicts and Jury Functioning in Criminal Trials," *Law and Human Behavior* 9, 1 (March 1985): 25. See also United States v. Dougherty, 473 F.2d 1113 (1972).

305. Paul Butler, "Racially Based Jury Nullification: Black Power in the Criminal Justice System," *Yale Law Journal* 105 (1995): 677.

306. Nancy S. Marder, "The Interplay of Race and False Claims of Jury Nullification," *University of Michigan Journal of Legal Reform* 32, 2 (1999): 285.

307. Writing about hung juries in District of Columbia drug cases, Jeffrey Rosen speculates that a frequent cause is African American female jurors, who refuse to send African American youths to prison for what they believe to be nonviolent offenses. See Jeffrey Rosen, "One Angry Woman: Why Are Hung Juries on the Rise?" *New Yorker*, February 24 and March 3, 1997, 54.

308. Butler, "Racially Based Jury Nullification"; Jack B. Weinstein, "The Many Dimensions of Jury Nullification," *Judicature* 81 (1997–1998): 168; Clay S. Conrad, *Jury Nullification: The Evolution of a Doctrine* (Washington, DC: Cato Institute, 1998), 167–179; Nancy S. Marder, "Juries, Drug Laws & Sentencing," *Journal of Gender, Race, & Justice* 6 (2002): 337. See also Arie M. Rubenstein, "Verdicts of Conscience: Nullification and the Modern Jury Trial," *Columbia Law Review* 106 (2006): 959.

Similar arguments have been made about women charged with killing men who allegedly abused them.[309] As in the drug cases, jurors who refuse to convict "battered women" do not object to the homicide statute. They simply do not believe that a battered spouse should be penalized for what amounts to self-defense, even if the crime does not fit the traditional definition of self-defense—that is, the killing did not take place during an attack but was premeditated and committed "in cold blood."[310]

The themes that run through such cases cluster around a set of arguments that pit the jury against the court, the government, and sometimes society itself; or they seem to pit blacks against whites, or at least against white cops and prosecutors. The central idea is opposition: to an "immoral and illegal" war, to racial discrimination, to violence against women, to the misbehavior of "racist" cops. In all these cases, the court is on one side and the defendant is on the other, with the jury interposing itself (or being urged to do so by defense attorneys) between the defendant and a government determined to do wrong. Darryl Brown has identified this form of nullification—which is rooted in a bias either against the prosecution or in favor of the defendant and is impervious to evidence—as the only form that poses a threat to the rule of law.[311]

Nullification in this pure sense is the antithesis of the impartial jury and must therefore be separated from an ordinary acquittal, which stems from the belief (sometimes against strong evidence) that a defendant is not "guilty beyond a reasonable doubt." It also needs to be distinguished from "mistaken" verdicts, resulting from the jury's honest failure to understand the evidence. These are inevitable by-products of the jury system, since in all but the simplest of cases there will be room for disagreement about the meaning of evidence or the reliability of witnesses. (Indeed, bench trials might produce the same imperfect results.) True jury nullification, by contrast, involves a refusal to convict even if the jury has no grounds for a "reasonable" doubt about the defendant's guilt. In this situation, jurors (or, most likely, one or two jurors) are determined to acquit despite the evidence, and this is why some scholars see nullification as a valuable "safety valve" and others see it as a form of anarchy. Nullification, one scholar argues, means that "jurors have the inherent right to set aside the instructions of the judge and

309. On developments in the law of self-defense, see Cynthia K. Gillespie, *Justifiable Homicide: Battered Women, Self Defense, and the Law* (Columbus: Ohio State University Press, 1989); and Robbin S. Ogle and Susan Jacobs, *Self-Defense and Battered Women Who Kill: A New Framework* (New York: Praeger, 2002).

310. Nancy S. Marder, "Gender Dynamics and Jury Deliberations," *Yale Law Journal* 96 (1987): 593.

311. Darryl K. Brown, "Jury Nullification within the Rule of Law," *Minnesota Law Review* 81 (1997): 1149. See also Hannaford-Agor and Hans, "Nullification at Work?" 1249.

to reach a verdict of acquittal based upon their own consciences."[312] Nullification takes place, says another, if a jury acquits "even when the evidence indicates that the defendant has violated the law." It is "the refusal of jurors to convict a defendant despite their belief in the defendant's guilt."[313] "Jury nullification occurs when a jury ignores the law . . . and chooses instead to play by its own rules."[314] Jury nullification takes place when jurors "disregard [the law's] dictates and arrive at unjustified outcomes based on sympathy or prejudice."[315]

Lately, some scholars have portrayed jury nullification as a way to give citizens a greater role in the judicial system, permitting them even "more direct control over the making of laws than the current system allows."[316] Juries, in this view, "provide a second institution through which the people can and should exercise law-making and law-rejecting powers." Citizens "have a right to enact their communal or personal norms in direct contravention of formally enacted laws."[317] But the republican view of the jury's authority was not that it operated in opposition to the court, to the law, to government, or to society in general; nor was it that jurors had a right to enact their "communal" norms in the face of the law. Republican jurors believed—if we can take republican-era debates at their word—that they were engaged in the same kind of activity the judge engaged in: applying the evidence to the law as they understood it. This required that jurors be precisely the kind of citizens the jury statutes have always looked for, until relatively recently: prudent, intelligent, of upstanding character, honest, "good and true."

Does the postmodern rejection of the need for better jurors have anything to do with the increased focus on jury nullification? And does the obvious increase in the attention paid to nullification mean that there is more jury nullification now than in the recent past? To take the second question first, many students of the courts believe that jury nullification has been increasing in recent years.[318] In many cities, prosecutors find it more difficult to secure convictions of minority defendants in districts with large numbers of black or Hispanic jurors—known since

312. Scheflin, "Jury Nullification," 168.

313. Rubenstein, "Verdicts of Conscience," 961–962. However, Rubenstein immediately identifies this phenomenon with "judg[ing] the law," a common confusion.

314. Lawrence W. Crispo, Jill M. Slasky, and Geanene M. Yriarte, "Jury Nullification: Law versus Anarchy," *Loyola of Los Angeles Law Review* 31, 1 (1997): 3.

315. Stephan Landsman, "The Jury's Role in Administering Justice in the United States: Of Mushrooms and Nullifiers: Rules of Evidence and the American Jury," *St. Louis University Public Law Review* 21 (2002): 80.

316. David Pepper, "Nullifying History: Modern-Day Misuse of the Right to Decide the Law," *Case Western Reserve Law Review* 50 (Spring 2000): 600 (paraphrasing an argument with which he is not in sympathy).

317. Ibid., paraphrasing again.

318. See Hannaford-Agor and Hans, "Nullification at Work?" 1249–1253.

the late 1980s as the phenomenon of the "Bronx jury."[319] But several high-profile cases beginning in the 1990s took jury nullification well beyond the Bronx. Lyle and Eric Menendez, on trial for the murder of their parents, mounted a "child abuse defense" that resulted in two hung juries; they were finally convicted in their third trial in 1994. The O. J. Simpson acquittal in 1995 was believed by many Americans (mostly white Americans, to be sure) to be the result of jury nullification. Former Washington, DC, mayor Marion Barry, charged with several major drug offenses, was found guilty of only one minor offense, an outcome attributed to jury nullification. The trials of Susan McDougal and Julie Hiatt Steele for obstructing justice during the independent counsel investigation of President Clinton produced a conviction on only one of several counts (against McDougal); the juries hung on all the other charges against both defendants.[320]

As these examples indicate, when juries hang—when they cannot reach a verdict, often because one or two jurors refuse to join the majority—the result is often blamed on nullification. However, unless jurors consent to post-trial interviews, it is hard to know whether the holdouts objected to the prosecution on principle or whether they were simply unconvinced by the prosecution's evidence. The verdict in O. J. Simpson's murder trial appeared to be a mix of these reasons. On the one hand, Simpson's lead attorney, Johnnie Cochran, made a clear nullification appeal to the jurors in his closing argument, urging them to "do their duty":

> Who then polices the Police? You . . . police the Police. You police them by your verdict. You are the ones to send the message. Nobody else is going to do it in this society. They don't have the courage. Nobody has the courage. They have a bunch of people running around with no courage to do what is right, except individual citizens. You . . . are the ones in war, you are the ones who are on the front line.[321]

On the other hand, sloppy police work might have led some jurors to have reasonable doubts about the chain of evidence, as did the fact that some of the police

319. The phrase has been traced to Tom Wolfe's 1987 novel *Bonfire of the Vanities*, and it was used in a series of *New York Times* and *Wall Street Journal* articles on pro-plaintiff civil verdicts and anti-prosecution criminal verdicts in the late 1980s and early 1990s. See Mary R. Rose and Neil Vidmar, "The Bronx 'Bronx Jury': A Profile of Civil Jury Awards in New York Counties," *Texas Law Review* 80 (2002): 1889. A study for the American Bar Foundation found that there is some empirical support for the idea of the (literal) Bronx jury: Bronx County courts reported a plaintiff victory rate of 72 percent, "with significantly higher awards" than the national average (some California courts also fit the pattern). See MacCoun, "Inside the Black Box," 150.

320. Hannaford-Agor and Hans, "Nullification at Work?" 1251.

321. Christopher C. Schwan, "Student Commentary: Right up to the Line: The Ethics of Advancing Nullification Arguments to the Jury," *Journal of the Legal Profession* 29 (2004–2005): 297.

involved in the investigation had racist views, giving them a motive and an opportunity to plant evidence against a celebrity black defendant.[322]

In other well-known cases, however, jurors have left a clear record of their views. In *United States v. Thomas* a juror told the judge that he disagreed with the drug laws and would never vote to convict, no matter what the evidence.[323] His removal from the jury resulted in an appeal, and the defendant's conviction was overturned. In *California v. Williams* a juror told the judge that he objected to the laws against sex with minors; the judge removed him, although this time the removal did not result in a successful appeal by the defendant.[324] In *Colorado v. Kriho* a juror in a drug trial was removed for failing to reveal a prior drug conviction and her membership in a drug legalization advocacy group. She was the sole "not guilty" vote on the jury, according to her fellow jurors, and the judge declared a mistrial. She was held in contempt of court.[325]

If jury nullification can lead to a hung jury, then one measure of its current prevalence would be the incidence of hung juries. This is difficult to measure, however, since a jury's failure to reach a verdict is technically a mistrial, and some states do not segregate the causes of mistrials, mixing hung juries in with prejudicial error, the death or illness of an attorney, jury tampering, and several other causes. But empirical investigations all reach the same conclusion: hung juries have been increasing since the 1970s. The baseline number is commonly said to be 5.5 percent of jury trials, based on statistics collected by Kalven and Zeisel for *The American Jury*.[326] A study by the National Center for State Courts notes that many jurisdictions are reporting an increase in hung juries, with "up to a quarter of all criminal jury trials . . . routinely resulting in mistrials due to jury deadlock." In the District of Columbia, Manhattan, and Houston, researchers found hung-

322. Alan Dershowitz has made a spirited argument that the O. J. Simpson verdict was the result of "reasonable doubts" caused by the sloppy (and possibly corrupt) police work during the investigation into the murders of Nicole Brown Simpson and Ron Goldman. Alan Dershowitz, *Reasonable Doubts: The Criminal Justice System and the O. J. Simpson Verdict* (New York: Touchstone, 1996). But the best Dershowitz can say on behalf of the verdict is that the jury believed the government was trying to "frame a guilty man" (208–209).

323. United States v. Thomas, 116 F.3d 606 (2d Cir. 1997).

324. California v. Williams, 21 P.3d 1209 (Cal. 2001).

325. Colorado v. Kriho, 996 P.2d 158 (Colo. App. 1, 1999). Relying on the precedent of *United States v. Thomas*, the appeals court overturned her contempt conviction, pointing out that there was only hearsay evidence (the other jurors) of her determination to acquit "regardless of the evidence." These cases are discussed in Paula L. Hannaford-Agor et al., *Are Hung Juries a Problem?* (Williamsburg, VA: National Center for State Courts, 2002), 15–16.

326. Kalven and Zeisel, *American Jury*, table 11, 56. The number is based on the authors' study of 3,576 criminal trials held in a midwestern court in 1955, 1956, and 1958.

jury rates in excess of 10 percent.[327] The problem was even worse in California. A study of courts in California's ten largest counties found that hung-jury rates averaged 12.2 percent between 1971 and 1973. Rates in some counties were even higher: three-year averages of 20.4 percent and 16.2 percent were recorded in San Francisco and Contra Costa Counties, respectively.[328] A second study, done by the California District Attorneys Association, studied hung juries in the early 1990s. This study found the highest rates in Los Angeles, Alameda, and Contra Costa Counties, with three-year averages of 13.6 percent, 11.5 percent, and 18.3 percent, respectively. The Central Valley county of Stanislaus (not included in the 1973 study) reported the highest rate of all: an average hung-jury rate of just under 30 percent over three years.[329]

Now we return to the first question posed above: what does jury nullification have to do with the postmodern jury regime? This is even harder to answer empirically, in part because of the difficulty of penetrating jurors' motivations. If juries increasingly refuse to enforce the law, as some critics have claimed and as the hung-jury rate suggests, is it because they are reaching for a higher and nobler standard, as Cochran asked the Simpson jurors to do? Or is it because they are simply bad jurors, the kind who, in the past, would have been rejected even before the challenge phase of the trial process—the kind who, to borrow Marbury's phrase from 1967, "will hang any jury that they are on"? Again, although the empirical data can tell us that there are more hung juries, they cannot tell us the reason for this pattern, leaving us with mostly anecdotes and the occasional case in which a nullifying juror is candid about his or her motives (such as *United States v. Thomas*).

But beyond anecdotal evidence, there is a fundamental reality to consider: if prosecutors have a limited number of peremptory challenges, and if it takes just one juror to hang a jury, then the quality of the jury pool makes a significant difference to the quality of the judgments rendered in court. Even in the days of the republican jury—at a time when all jurors were propertied white males—lawyers were alert to catch the occasional "pudding head." Yet the postmodern jury selection regime is determined to reject "qualitative" measures of a juror's suitability, rejecting the very idea of the "better" juror and generating an environment in which jury nullification in the purest sense—the stubborn refusal to enforce the law—can thrive.

This brings us back to the thorny and interesting question of the peremptory challenge, which—though it has become heavily encrusted with constitutional and statutory limitations—continues nonetheless. And it is easy to see why: lawyers want to choose jurors, and in the era of the postmodern jury, their opportuni-

327. Hannaford-Agor et al., *Are Hung Juries a Problem?* 1.
328. Ibid., table 1.1, 7.
329. Ibid., table 1.2, 9.

ties to do so have grown, even as the peremptory challenge itself has come under increasing attack.

VOIR DIRE, PEREMPTORY CHALLENGES, AND POSTMODERN JURY SELECTION

The conventional translation of the French *voir dire* is "to speak the truth" (literally, "watch them speak"), and it refers to the critical moment during jury selection when the judge and/or the attorneys ask questions of the prospective jurors and watch as well as listen as they answer. The effectual meaning of the term, therefore, is "watch to see *if* they are speaking the truth." Beyond the obvious questions about a prospective juror's relationship to any of the parties in the case, the questions asked may be designed to elicit more hidden forms of bias. Watching how the members of the venire answer such questions may reveal which ones might be troublesome.[330]

In the United States, attorneys have almost always played a role in voir dire, and at some times and in some places, that role has been a significant one. For many twentieth-century jury reformers, this was a problem: attorneys had too much control over voir dire (especially in state courts), allowing them to *plant* certain biases rather than uncover them. By questioning members of the venire, skilled attorneys could discover which jurors might be persuadable and which ones might be stubborn; at the same time, they could suggest to onlookers how they should understand the case, should they end up on the jury. A vast lawyerly folk wisdom emerged in the nineteenth and twentieth centuries about how to do this, and such information was sometimes codified in "how-to manuals" that explained to new lawyers what to look for and how to spot it. That these practices undermined the true purpose of voir dire—the impaneling of an impartial jury rather than a pliable one—was a common complaint. In 1949, well into the reform era, an anonymous writer for the *Yale Law Journal* had this to say about attorney-conducted voir dire: "Unfortunately, the procedures which at present characterize the examination and challenge of jurymen permit able lawyers to employ the voir dire examination to influence the jury panel, prevent the optimum utilization of challenges for eliminating partial jurymen, obscure, in the eyes of appellate courts, the fundamental issue of impartiality, and waste time and money both at the trial and on appeal."[331] Concluding that

330. Jury selection has been compared to "weeding a garden": that is, it is mostly a process of removing troublesome jurors rather than finding the good ones. See Marvin Zalman and Olga Tsoudis, "Plucking Weeds from the Garden: Lawyers Speak about Voir Dire [parts 1 and 2]," *Wayne Law Review* 51 (2005): 163, 361.

331. "Note: Selection of Jurors by Voir Dire Examination and Challenge," *Yale Law Journal* 58, 4 (March 1949): 640.

these problems occur because "courts allow lawyers wide latitude during the voir dire examination," the author proposes that, to ensure the impaneling of a genuinely impartial jury, "the voir dire examination should be conducted by the court itself," although the attorneys should be allowed to suggest questions to be put to the veniremen by the judge.[332]

It was because of such fears that, from the 1920s on, jury reformers almost always advocated restricting the attorneys' role in voir dire, part of the wider struggle between judges and lawyers for the control of trials. With the adoption of the Federal Rules of Civil Procedure in 1938, judges won a decisive victory in that struggle. The promulgation of the Federal Rules of Criminal Procedure in 1946 gave judges a similar victory with respect to criminal trials. One federal judge observed at the time: "This rule [24(a)] really is a gem. It lets the judge do just as he pleases."[333] This would turn out to be significant, since it meant that the actual practice in federal courts depended on the judges' views of the value of attorney-conducted voir dire, a matter to which I return later.

After 1946, judge-conducted voir dire quickly became the norm in the federal courts, which is exactly what the reformers had hoped for. However, because the extent of attorney participation was left to the discretion of judges, the transition was uneven. A useful benchmark is the 1960 Judicial Conference report,[334] which notes the broad discretion rule 24(a) gives to federal judges in criminal trials: "The court may permit the defendant or his attorney and the attorney for the government to conduct the examination of prospective jurors or may itself conduct the examination."[335] The report then presents the results of a survey of federal district court judges: of the eighty-nine judges who responded, fifty-one (57 percent) reported that they conducted all voir dire examinations themselves, taking full advantage of the leeway allowed by the federal rules. The rest of the respondents allowed attorneys to suggest questions that, if the judge deemed them appropriate, would then be put to prospective jurors. Although this was a limited survey response (there were more than 200 federal district court judges in 1960), the results are consistent with other contemporary accounts of voir dire in the federal courts. Reform had made even more headway by the mid-1980s, when a highly respected

332. Ibid., 643–644.

333. George H. Dession, "The New Federal Rules of Criminal Procedure II," *Yale Law Journal* 56 (January 1947): 226. See also Valerie P. Hans and Alayna Jehle, "Avoid Bald Men and People with Green Socks? Other Ways to Improve the Voir Dire Process in Jury Selection," *Chicago-Kent Law Review* 78 (2003): 1184–1185. The operative rules are 47(a) of the Federal Rules of Civil Procedure and 24(a) of the Federal Rules of Criminal Procedure, governing the examination of jurors. The wording of each rule is essentially the same, and neither has been amended since the rules were first adopted.

334. *Jury System in the Federal Courts*, 1960.

335. Federal Rules of Criminal Procedure, rule 24(a).

trial practice manual reported that only 25 percent of federal judges allowed oral participation by attorneys during voir dire.[336]

Jury scholar Dale W. Broeder provides a glimpse of what this judge-controlled voir dire looked like in the 1950s, based on his study of twenty-three criminal and civil jury trials conducted in an unnamed federal district court in the Midwest in 1955 and 1956:

> The voir dire examinations . . . were more or less perfunctory, stilted affairs, quickly concluded and devoid of the spectacular. The typical voir dire lasted approximately one-half hour and this includes the time spent by the Judge welcoming the veniremen and by the clerk in drawing the names. . . . The Judge then asked the twelve venireman in the box to state their occupations. . . . Following the Judge's question as to occupation came certain other questions from the Judge: Could the veniremen be fair and impartial? Did they have anything so pressing that they could not give their full attention . . . ? Would they follow the law? Did they know any of the parties or their attorneys?[337]

Broeder found this process "grossly ineffective not only in weeding out 'unfavorable' jurors but even in eliciting the data which would have shown particular jurors as very likely to prove 'unfavorable.'" Because the jury list was compiled through use of the key-man system, nearly all the veniremen were "solid, more than usually solid, citizens and while some exceptions appeared, the probability seemed great that if you challenged one venireman you would get another very much like him."[338] Lawyers were given very little background data on which to base a challenge. In civil cases, lawyers were limited to only three challenges in federal court, and publicly challenging a venireman in front of the other jurors might irritate them, proving harmful to the attorney's case. Furthermore, the "judge in question was worshipped by the jurors," so challenging his authority would have been a grave tactical error. As a result, many of the attorneys in the

336. Starr and McCormick, *Jury Selection*, 39–40, cited by Joshua S. Press, "Untruthful Jurors in the Federal Courts: Have We Become Comfortably Numb?" *St. Thomas Law Review* 21 (2008–2009): 257, n. 11.

337. Broeder, "Voir Dire Examinations," 503–504. This research was part of the American Jury Project at the University of Chicago Law School.

338. Ibid., 505. Broeder was one of the jury experts who testified in 1967 in favor of the Jury Selection and Service Act. He argued that the attempt to find "better" jurors inevitably introduced "class bias" into the selection process. The key finding of the American Jury Project—that judges and juries nearly always agreed—was apparently based on juries chosen largely through the "qualitative" screening made possible by the key-man system. Thus, if Broeder were consistent, he would have to conclude that this level of agreement, far from being an argument in favor of juries, was evidence of class bias generating unjust verdicts.

cases Broeder studied looked at voir dire with "disdain," assuming that "one group of twelve was as likely to be as good or bad as another."[339]

Meanwhile, the situation in the states was, and remains, mixed. Attorney-controlled voir dire has always been more common in the state courts than in the federal courts, possibly because trial attorneys and their interest groups have had more influence over state legislatures than over Congress or the Judicial Conference. As federal practice moved in the direction of the 1938 and 1946 procedural reforms, the gap between federal and state practices grew wider—to the great disappointment of reformers, who had hoped the states would freely adopt the federal procedures, whose superiority, they were certain, would be obvious. The 1949 *Yale Law Journal* note cited earlier was at least hopeful: "court-conducted voir dire, though still a minority practice, is becoming increasingly popular. . . . [It would] effectively minimize attempts by counsel to prejudice the jury in the pre-trial stage, since the examination of prospective jurors would be placed in the hands of a neutral third party, the judge."[340]

Nevertheless, a National Center for State Courts survey from 2007 found only nine states where judges conducted the voir dire entirely by themselves; in eighteen states, judges and attorneys shared voir dire equally, and in twenty-three states, lawyers were "predominantly or exclusively" in control of voir dire examinations.[341] If the ending of the conformity principle is a sign of how nationalized the American judicial system had become by the middle of the twentieth century, the survival of such different trial practices in the states is evidence of the tenacity of American federalism.

But a funny thing happened along the way to procedural reform in the federal courts. Almost as soon as judges were firmly in control of voir dire, a movement emerged from inside the legal profession arguing that judge-conducted voir dire was useless at uncovering bias in prospective jurors. That was, in fact, Broeder's conclusion in the study cited above (which was not published until the 1960s), and his research has been supplemented by a small library of studies, all of which suggest, with varying levels of confidence, that lawyers are better than judges at discovering the many hidden biases in the hearts of typical Americans called to jury service. In 1977, for example, a former president of the Association of Trial Lawyers of America made what a Judicial Conference study referred to as a "preposterous" claim: "Trial attorneys are acutely attuned to the nuances of human behavior, which enables them to detect the minutest traces of bias or inability to reach an appropriate decision."[342] Preposterous or not, that claim became

339. Ibid., 505–506, 507.

340. "Note: Selection of Jurors by Voir Dire Examination and Challenge."

341. Gregory E. Mize, Paula Hannaford-Agor, and Nicole L. Waters, *The State of the States Survey of Jury Improvement Efforts: A Compendium Report* (2007), cited by Press, "Untruthful Jurors," 257, n. 11.

342. Gordon Bermant and John Shapard, *The Voir Dire Examination, Juror Challenges, and Adversary Advocacy* (Washington, DC: Federal Judicial Center, 1977), 3.

part of the intellectual foundation of the science of jury consulting and a major argument in favor of giving attorneys more control over voir dire. And although the law reviews remain skeptical about the efficacy of "jury science," lawyers generally accept the notion that the careful questioning of veniremen, backed by surveys, focus group interviews, and other methods of investigation, can provide a slight edge in a difficult case—"a five to ten percent advantage over random selection for criminal cases," according one major review of the evidence.[343] This does not seem to be a significant advantage, given the expense of hiring jury consultants, but it is apparently enough to persuade trial attorneys, who may figure that a small advantage is better than nothing.

Meanwhile, those who argue on behalf of a greater role for attorneys in voir dire insist that the problem of identifying bias has become more difficult—an assertion that, if true, suggests that the contemporary jury pool is more infected by bias than jury pools in the past. "The detection of juror bias," one major study begins, "is a serious challenge in contemporary jury trials."[344] Attorneys must therefore have even more control over the process of jury selection, routinizing the practices associated with "expansive" voir dire. Under expansive voir dire, judges are formally in charge, as always—and in some courtrooms, they are truly in charge—but attorneys do most of the work. An important impetus for this change is the widely believed claim (one of the earliest findings of the social-science jury literature) that jurors are not honest when responding to questions posed in open court, especially when those questions are posed by a judge. "Some jurors, probably the minority, lie purposefully."[345] Jurors are unlikely to confess publicly to racial bias, even if they harbor it—and they almost always do, according to the same research, even though they may not, or perhaps cannot, know that they do. A recent study using mock juries came to the stark conclusion that "jurors were simply unable to diagnose their own biases."[346] Or they may be unlikely to admit their biases to a person in authority, proffering "socially desirable" responses to a judge's questions rather than truthful ones. Questions from "equals" generate more honest responses, according to the social psychology research, especially when the questioning occurs in private and the responses are confidential.[347] For this reason, beginning in the 1970s, members of the trial bar insisted that voir dire should be conducted by lawyers rather than judges, as well as individually and in

343. Reid Hastie, "Is Attorney-Conducted Voir Dire an Effective Procedure for the Selection of Impartial Juries?" *American University Law Review* 40 (Winter 1991): 719.

344. Hans and Jehle, "Avoid Bald Men," 1179.

345. Ibid., 1194.

346. Christopher Robertson et al., "Can Jurors Self-Diagnose Bias? Two Randomized Controlled Trials," Arizona Legal Studies Discussion Paper no. 12-35, 7th Annual Conference on Empirical Legal Studies, February 2014, 2.

347. Hans and Jehle, "Avoid Bald Men," 1197.

private rather than collectively in open court. Litigators had always sought such control; now they could claim the authority of social science to back them up.

Although Supreme Court decisions do not unambiguously endorse attorney-conducted voir dire in all cases, they have consistently focused the trial courts' attention on a defendant's right to probe veniremen more carefully whenever racial, ethnic, or religious bias is suspected. Entering the postmodern era, the controlling doctrine was *Aldridge v. United States*, a 1931 case in which the Court held that although the lower courts have considerable discretion with respect to voir dire, they are subject to "the essential demands of fairness." A failure to ask "any questions which could be deemed to cover the subject" of racial bias is therefore a violation of a black defendant's right to a trial by an impartial jury.[348] This rule was reaffirmed by the Court in a 1973 case, *Ham v. South Carolina*, which reversed the conviction of a black defendant after the trial judge had rejected the defendant's request to pose two questions to the venire intended to dig more deeply for indications of racial bias. Writing for the Court, Justice Rehnquist argued that "the essential fairness required by the Due Process Clause of the Fourteenth Amendment requires that under the facts shown by this record the petitioner be permitted to have the jurors interrogated on the issue of racial bias."[349]

These and other arguments have had their effect, and attorneys have acquired a larger role in questioning jurors about their "implicit biases."[350] The change has been rapid and dramatic, suggesting a sea change in the views of federal judges. By 1998, according to a National Center for State Courts study, some combination of judge and attorney questioning had become the norm in all federal district courts and in forty state courts of general jurisdiction—a significant change from the mid-1980s.[351] A Federal Judicial Center study in 1994 concluded that, "in the

348. Aldridge v. United States, 283 U.S. 308 (1931), 310.

349. Ham v. South Carolina, 409 U.S. 524 (1973), 527. Ironically, Justices Marshall and Douglas, both of whom had voiced their suspicions about the peremptory challenge, thought the Court should have found that the failure to inquire into prejudice against beards was also a constitutional violation (the defendant was bearded). See *Ham*, 529.

350. The emphasis on bias has had another effect: to give reluctant jurors another opportunity to evade their jury obligations by claiming an inability to overcome their prejudices. In 1993 Judge Angelo Guarino, of the Philadelphia Court of Common Pleas, was removed from the bench by the Pennsylvania Supreme Court for disciplining jurors who claimed to be biased as an excuse to avoid jury duty (in Guarino's view). He ordered two jurors to spend an extra day observing trials, and he held a third in contempt. The ACLU filed a lawsuit, charging deprivation of constitutional rights (presumably, the right not to serve). Judge Guarino claimed that his actions grew "out of frustration with what he saw as a growing unwillingness on the part of people to serve as jurors." See *American Bar Association Journal* (March 1993): 40.

351. Hans and Jehle, "Avoid Bald Men," 1184, n. 16, citing David B. Rottman et al., *State Court Organization 1998* (Washington, DC: Department of Justice, 2000), 273–277, table 41.

federal courts, attorney involvement in voir dire has doubled over the past several decades."[352] That study found that 59 percent of federal judges "usually" allowed attorneys to ask questions in civil cases, and 54 percent did so in criminal cases, compared with only 30 percent in 1977—virtually the reverse of the situation reported by the Judicial Conference in 1960.[353] One-third of federal judges in 1998 reported that they asked the initial set of questions but then allowed attorneys to ask a fixed number of preapproved questions. Only 9 percent said they let attorneys do "all or most" of the voir dire on their own, but significantly, no judges reported that they conducted voir dire entirely by themselves, despite the leeway given by the federal rules.[354]

Although there has been no change in the federal rules for civil or criminal voir dire, the actual practice in the federal courts has now reverted to what it was in the era before the reforms of 1938 and 1946. The situation is not uniform; there are still differences between federal and state courts and within the federal system itself. But in general, attorneys now have much more control over the process than they had from the late 1940s through the 1980s. Restricted (i.e., judge-controlled) voir dire has been replaced by expansive voir dire, guided largely by attorneys. Nor is "expansive" simply a euphemism for "longer"—although the time it takes to impanel a jury has increased. Voir dire is also broader and more intrusive than in the past, generating new worries about juror privacy.[355] Rather than the simple yes-or-no questions posed collectively by judges ("Can you be impartial?") and answered publicly by veniremen, voir dire now involves open-ended questions, personal interviews (sometimes conducted privately in chambers), court-administered questionnaires, and jury consultants armed with public opinion surveys. In some state courts, attorneys are even allowed to interview jurors out of the hearing of the judge, who leaves the courtroom until the questioning is completed.[356]

As lawyers have acquired a greater role in voir dire, predictable consequences have followed. For one thing, criminal trials take longer. The median time from

352. Hans and Jehle, "Avoid Bald Men," 1201, citing John Shapard and Molly Johnson, "Memorandum from the Federal Judicial Center, to the Advisory Committee on Civil Rules and Advisory Committee on Criminal Rules," October 4, 1994.

353. Ibid.

354. Ibid., 1184–1185.

355. See, for example, Nancy Novak, "Notes: Jury on Trial: Juror's Constitutional Right to Privacy Falls under Scrutiny of the Courts," *San Diego Justice Journal* 3 (1995): 215: "It is through the process of voir dire that a prospective juror's privacy rights could be infringed if called upon to reveal sensitive, personal information."

356. For example, rule 631 of the Pennsylvania Code states that "voir dire of prospective trial jurors shall be conducted, and the jurors shall be selected, in the presence of a judge, unless the judge's presence is waived by the attorney for the Commonwealth, the defense attorney, and the defendant, with the judge's consent." http://www.pacode.com/secure/data/234/chapter6/s631.html (accessed September 16, 2014).

filing to disposition for criminal cases has grown from 5.9 months in 1992 to 7.3 months in 2013; more extensive voir dire, conducted by attorneys, is certainly part of the reason for slower criminal dispositions. (Median time to completion for civil trials has actually declined over this period, from 9 months in 1992 to 8.5 months in 2013. This may be because of the increased use of summary judgments in the civil courts, an issue addressed in chapter 5.)[357] Critics of the idea of attorney-conducted voir dire always claimed it would prolong jury selection, and it appears they were right. The 1960 Judicial Conference report agreed with this criticism but added another, perhaps more important consideration: that lawyer-dominated voir dire would conflict with the goal of obtaining an impartial jury. That is, in addition to wasting time, attorney-conducted voir dire might have a purpose other than impartiality.

Trial attorneys are often quite candid, admitting that voir dire is not, and perhaps should not be, an effort to impanel an impartial jury. As one lawyer put it, "I do not want an impartial jury. I want a jury that is in my favor from the beginning, and you can quote me on that."[358] Voir dire has become a systematic exercise aimed at choosing the "right jury," to borrow a revealing phrase from a jury consultant's blog.[359] That these are different and perhaps incompatible aims is usually conceded. "There is a conflict between the inherent purpose of voir dire," writes Houston attorney and jury consultant Marni Becker-Avin, "which is to find impartial jurors from a pool representative of the community, and the true yet unstated purpose of every attorney, which is to find jurors predisposed to their position."[360]

Yet this view of voir dire is hardly "unstated." It is stated frequently, candidly, and sometimes defiantly wherever jury consultants advertise their services. Sometimes, it is even stated in the law journals, where courtroom procedures are debated. In fact, the postmodern suspicion of intellectual impartiality has acquired a devoted following. Legal memoirs and accounts of famous cases confess that the aim of jury selection is a jury that is predisposed to the chooser's side, in part because the questioning of jurors can now be done in such a way as to plant in the minds of everyone listening the validity of the "story" the attorney intends to tell.

That this practice must proceed against the "gravitational drag" of *Batson v. Kentucky* is obvious—and a considerable source of tension, if not outright embar-

357. Federal Judicial Center, Federal Court Management Statistics Archive, "Judicial Caseload Profile: 1992–1997" and "Judicial Caseload Profile: 2009–2013," http://www.uscourts.gov/Statistics/FederalCourtManagementStatistics/FederalCourtManagementStatistics_Archive.aspx (accessed July 1, 2014).

358. Quoted in Mark A. Drummond, "Don't Let the Judge Cut You Out," *Litigation News* (Spring 2012), http://www.apps.americanbar.org/litigation/litigationnews/articles-print/050412-practice-points-spring12.html (accessed June 20, 2014).

359. See http://www.therightjury.com/about/html (accessed July 3, 2014).

360. Marni Becker-Avin, "The Real Purpose of Voir Dire," ibid.

rassment.[361] Even in 1985, Justice Marshall's proposal to abolish peremptory challenges struck a chord with a significant segment of the legal profession, especially law school faculties, yet it went largely ignored by practicing attorneys. One attorney explains why: "It is unethical for a defense lawyer to disregard what is known about the influence of race and sex on juror attitudes in order to comply with *Batson v. Kentucky* and its progeny. . . . The task of the lawyer . . . is to outsmart the system—to figure out the demographics of justice and to manipulate it during jury selection by eliminating jurors with the so-called wrong personal characteristics."[362]

But without a generous allotment of peremptory challenges, knowing the "demographics of justice" would be useless, since the sort of "bias" trial lawyers have in mind would not rise to the level of a challenge for cause, at least as that challenge has always been understood. Here, it is useful to recall Chief Justice John Marshall's definition of bias during the jury selection phase of Aaron Burr's treason trial in 1807:

> Light impressions which may fairly be supposed to yield to the testimony that may be offered, which may leave the mind open to a fair consideration of that testimony, constitute no sufficient objection to a juror; but . . . strong and deep impressions which will close the mind against the testimony that may be offered in opposition to them, which will combat that testimony, and resist its force, do constitute a sufficient objection to him.[363]

Yet it is precisely the opportunity to remove a juror with "light impressions" that are unfavorable to the client, in favor of one with fewer impressions or no impressions whatever, that makes the peremptory challenge an indispensable tool during expansive voir dire. This highlights the need to identify jurors with biases who are reluctant to confess them in public or to someone of elevated social status (like a judge) because of their fear of embarrassment.

Yet the call to abolish peremptory challenges continues to haunt the jury debate, exposing the fissures within the theory of postmodern jury selection. To perhaps oversimplify the issue, contemporary jury theory wants to reject the very idea of "selecting" jurors because that idea is tainted by the odor of discrimination. But at the same time, the theory must acknowledge what everyone in court knows very well: that no litigant can get a fair trial unless counsel can reject those jurors who are least inclined to favor the litigant's cause or those jurors who are likely to be so biased, so oblivious to their duties, or so incapable of understanding the evidence that they are unmoved by either the law or the facts. In other words, an impartial jury is one from which the "bad" jurors have been removed (to the extent possible, and based on the available data).

361. The phrase comes from Gregory E. Mize and Paula Hannaford-Agor, "Building a Better Voir Dire Process," *Judges' Journal* 47, 1 (Winter 2008).

362. Hans and Jehle, "Avoid Bald Men," 1191.

363. United States v. Burr, 25 F. Cas. 49, no. 14692g (C.C.D. Va. [1807]).

The tension between these positions—wanting to remove the bad jurors but not wanting to risk discrimination—has produced a somewhat confusing debate. In 2010 federal district court judge Mark W. Bennett proposed that peremptory challenges should be abolished but that attorney-conducted voir dire should be increased—the legal equivalent of squaring a circle.[364] Acknowledging that there is "some tension between increasing lawyer participation in voir dire while stripping lawyers of peremptory challenges," Bennett nevertheless argued that these two reforms "work best in tandem"—a solution he likened to cutting the Gordian knot.[365] Among jury scholars, there is a significant faction in favor of either abolishing or restricting peremptory challenges—sometimes on the grounds that these challenges encourage racial discrimination, and sometimes because they appear to give defense attorneys the opportunity to create hung juries. To take one notable example among many, Jeffrey Abramson's widely read *We the Jury*, published in 1994, argues that now is the time "to fully practice what we preach and to prohibit discriminatory, exclusionary practices from occurring under cover of the peremptory challenge."[366]

There is even a faction within the American Bar Association that has come down, somewhat unexpectedly, on the side of abolition. The ABA's Tort Trial and Insurance Practice Section—a group one would not expect to challenge the litigator's right to choose juries—prepared a report in 2009, *Striking Back against Peremptory Strikes*, urging the ABA to join the campaign to "end the system of peremptory challenges." Success would mean lower litigation costs, less work for judges, and, "most importantly," the creation of a barrier to "possible discrimination."[367] The full ABA greeted this proposal with silence, however, sticking with the position advocated in its *Principles for Juries and Jury Trials* in 2005: a forthright defense of expansive voir dire.[368] In fact, the 2005 document defines what has become the normal practice in federal courts, not as a result of legislative or judicial orders but because of a change in the culture of the federal judiciary. This change is not universal, and it is not uncontroversial; however, the prevailing view among judges in the federal courts (if their views can be deduced from their practice) is that attorneys should be allowed a substantial role in the conduct of

364. Judge Mark W. Bennett, "Unraveling the Gordian Knot of Implicit Bias in Jury Selection: The Problems of Judge-Dominated Voir Dire, the Failed Promise of *Batson*, and Proposed Solutions," *Harvard Law and Policy Review* 4 (2010): 1209.

365. Ibid., 151.

366. Abramson, *We the Jury*, 247.

367. Jameson B. Carroll et al., *Striking Back against Peremptory Strikes,* Tort Trial and Insurance Practice Section, American Bar Association, 2009, http://www.kslaw.com/Library/publication/4–09%20ABA.pdfv (accessed July 8, 2014).

368. For example, principle 11 endorses juror questionnaires, the collection of "appropriate" demographic data, individual questioning, and a "sufficient" number of challenges, among other proposals. *Principles for Juries and Jury Trials*, 13–16.

voir dire, even to the point of dominating it. As long as this is the case, attorneys will fight as hard as they can against any effort to abolish peremptory challenges, and they will no doubt push even harder to acquire more control over voir dire.

UNDERSTANDING THE CONSEQUENCES OF REFORM

It seems highly significant that of all the procedural reforms of the 1930s and 1940s, judge-controlled voir dire is the only one that has failed to thrive, despite a promising start. And since its failure cannot be traced to changes in the laws governing federal trials or to adverse Supreme Court rulings, there must be another explanation. Because this development coincides with the era of postmodern jury selection, we are led to wonder whether there is more than mere coincidence at work.

As we have seen, until passage of the Jury Selection and Service Act of 1968, those who were formally eligible for service could (and in most jurisdictions would) be examined in some way to discover whether they also had the requisite character to serve. Courts were generally in control of this process—and in the federal courts, this control was more firmly established after the procedural reforms of 1938 and 1946. Education and experience mattered, but so did honesty, since there was no guarantee that an educated man was an honest man. Likewise, some otherwise solid citizens might be stubbornly unwilling to let their civic responsibilities interfere with their private business, and it would be important to identify such bad citizens before they took that attitude into the jury room. It was therefore important that the key-man system operate properly, by vetting the "suggesters" and examining those they recommended to discover whether they were truly fit to serve—as opposed to simply meeting the bare minimum statutory qualifications. And before 1968, this vetting had never been held by Congress, the Judicial Conference, or the Supreme Court to be incompatible with the broad goal of finding the "best candidates from each identifiable segment of the population," whether those segments were defined on the basis of occupation, religion, race, or ethnicity. But finding "intelligent," "prudent," and "sensible" jurors is what "jury selection" once meant to those who took the law seriously and were not trying to enforce a regime of white supremacy through the courts.

Looking back on that system from the postreform perspective of 1975, Judge Arthur J. Stanley Jr. noted that "regardless of the sources from which the names [for the jury list] were obtained," the rules required those in charge to "apply subjective tests in deciding who should be retained and who rejected. Such action was encouraged, if not required, by the philosophy expressed" in the Judicial Conference's 1960 report *The Jury System in the Federal Courts*.[369] That report had

369. Hon. Arthur J. Stanley Jr., "Federal Jury Selection and Service before and after 1968," 68 *F.R.D.* (1975): 375.

praised the 1957 Civil Rights Act precisely because its jury provisions would bring into the federal system those "intelligent, qualified citizens, including women and professional people," who would no longer be automatically exempted or excused, as they had been in the states. This would make it possible, according to the conference, to achieve the dual objective of drawing federal jurors "from every economic and social group . . . without regard to race, color, or politics," while also selecting jurors with "as high a degree of intelligence, morality, integrity, and common sense, as can be found."[370] To make this achievement more certain, the conference recommended "putting the [district] court in control of the selection of names, . . . that questionnaires should be used to supply information as to the qualifications of jurors, that where feasible the questionnaires should be supplemented by personal interviews and finally that full-time jury commissioners may be appointed where needed."[371]

That this process was not universally effective, and that it sometimes verged on the buffoonish, must be conceded (such as when some courts in California administered IQ tests).[372] But by far the most common technique for filtering was simply talking to the candidates to get a sense of their abilities. That was the method used, for example, in the federal district court in Connecticut, which was singled out by the Judicial Conference as a model to emulate. The Judicial Conference's 1960 report put it very simply: "In order to get better jurors, the Committee recommends greater care in the compilation of the list of jurors whose names go into the jury wheel or box from which trial jurors are chosen."[373]

This meant that under the old regime, the venire was vetted long before the attorneys got a chance to examine it. Most of the ineligible individuals had been removed, as had those citizens about whom the court had serious doubts. Perhaps their English was not very good; perhaps they did not seem to be particularly attentive or diligent during questioning. Attorneys had limited access to information about the veniremen who survived this vetting, and they could only make educated guesses during a strictly limited voir dire in which the judge (especially after the rule reforms) was clearly in control. They may have been right to believe, as Dale Broeder concluded in the 1950s, that "one group of twelve is as likely to be as good or as bad as another group of twelve." And while lawyers generally sought more leeway and often got it in state courts, they made little headway against federal judges, who had both the inclination and the legal authority to keep tight control over what questions were allowed.

370. Ibid., 378, citing *Jury System in the Federal Courts*, 17.

371. *Jury System in the Federal Courts*, 11.

372. Arthur Vanderbilt, *Minimum Standards of Judicial Administration* (New York: Law Center of New York University, 1949), 183–188.

373. *Jury System in the Federal Courts*, 11.

374. Stanley, "Federal Jury Selection," 380.

But after the 1968 jury act, jury commissions could no longer vet prospective jurors before their names went into the jury wheel. Two years earlier, in fact, in response to the "mortal wound" of the *Rabinowitz* decision, the Judicial Conference had finally voted to endorse the "principle of random selection of the jury venire in a manner that would produce a fair cross section of the community."[374] There would be no more support from the Judicial Conference for the idea of getting the "best jurors from every group." Now, in light of the new law, potential jurors would go on or off the list based solely on their answers to the objective questions contained in the jury summons: Are you of age? Are you a citizen of the United States and a resident of this district for the requisite amount of time? Can you read and understand English? Have you served within the past two years? Do you have a criminal record? Judge Stanley, in his 1975 reflections, conceded that with the demise of the key-man system, the idea that federal jurors should possess a high degree of "intelligence, morality, integrity, and common sense" was now obsolete.[375] Instead, defendants would be guaranteed a jury that had been "fairly selected from a universe comprising a fair cross section of the citizenry of the community, including those with whom he identifies."[376]

Thus did the Jury Selection and Service Act profoundly alter the jury selection regime, although it took some time for the consequences to become visible. If this analysis is correct, we should not be surprised to see the effort to winnow jurors taking place at a different stage of the process, under different circumstances, and with radically different motives. In the past, to note one example, the process of winnowing was not case specific; jurors were ruled fit or unfit for jury service *before* being vetted for a particular trial. Now, by contrast, the first opportunity to separate "suitable" from "unsuitable" jurors takes place as the trial is about to begin, and it is increasingly guided by attorneys who are looking not for "sensible" jurors but for jurors who will be sympathetic to the particular story the attorneys are hoping to sell. No doubt, attorneys always wanted sympathetic jurors; in the past, however, they had a limited opportunity to find them. In the era of the postmodern jury, that opportunity has grown, thanks to expansive voir dire, the strategic use of peremptory challenges, and the widespread acceptance of these practices in both state and federal courts. This is why the peremptory challenge has not been abolished: it is the perfect—indeed, the inevitable—companion to the Jury Selection and Service Act.

375. Ibid.
376. Ibid., 381–382.

5
The Vanishing Jury

> The American jury system is withering away. This is the most profound change in our jurisprudence in the history of the Republic.
>
> —Hon. William G. Young, "An Open Letter to U.S. District Court Judges"

> The death of the trial would be an abandonment of *an aspect of our national character.*
>
> —Robert P. Burns, *The Death of the American Trial*

THE TRIAL IMPLOSION

The contemporary discussion of the jury system is marked—in some circles, at any rate—by a sense of urgency. Many argue that the jury is only a shadow of its former self, and they share Judge William G. Young's fear that the jury is "withering away," as is its important contribution to an independent judiciary rooted in citizen participation.[1] Others maintain that federal courts and Congress have, more or less deliberately, undermined the jury system through decisions and legislation on summary judgment, the testimony of expert witnesses, class-action lawsuits, sentencing requirements, and many other matters. The most visible evidence of this withering is the dramatic decline not just in the percentage of civil and criminal cases settled by juries but also in the absolute number of criminal and civil jury trials in both federal and state courts. The reasons for this decline are complicated, but the fact of the decline is not in doubt.

In 2013, of the nearly 92,000 criminal defendants whose cases were disposed of in federal district courts, only 2.3 percent were tried by juries (2,146 jury trials in all); nine out of ten defendants entered pleas of guilty or nolo contendere (see

1. Hon. William G. Young, "An Open Letter to U.S. District Court Judges," *Federal Lawyer* 30 (July 2003): 31.

Table 1: The Decline of Criminal Trials in the Federal Courts, 1945–2013

		Cases Not Tried		Cases Settled by Trials			
Year	Number of Defendants	Guilty/ Nolo Pleas	Dismissed	All Trials	Bench Trials	Jury Trials	Percentage of Jury Dispositions
1945	42,755	30,817	6,462	6,476	3,413	3,063	7.2
1960	31,984	24,245	2,629	5,110	2,519	2,591	8.1
1970	36,356	24,111	6,608	5,637	1,993	3,644	10.0
1980	36,560	23,111	6,663	6,819	2,134	4,682	12.8
1990	56,519	40,452	8,193	7,874	1,693	6,181	10.9
2000	75,071	63,863	6,992	4,216	1,235	2,981	4.0
2010	98,311	83,707	8,408	3,091	431	2,660	2.7
2013	91,918	81,995	7,418	2,406	260	2,146	2.3

Sources: *Sourcebook of Criminal Justice Statistics Online*, University at Albany, School of Criminal Justice, Hindelang Criminal Justice Research Center, http://www.albany.edu/sourcebook/ind/COURTS.Federal.U.S._District_Courts.Defendants.Disposed.4.html (accessed July 13, 2013). The *Sourcebook* data are taken from Administrative Office of the United States Courts, *Annual Reports of the Director* (Washington, DC: Government Printing Office). Data for 2013 are from the Administrative Office of the United States Courts website, table D-4, http://www.uscourts.gov/statistics-reports/judicial-facts-and-figures-2013 (accessed May 5, 2015).

table 1). Fifty years earlier, with only a third as many defendants, the percentage entering pleas was smaller (75 percent), and 8.1 percent were tried before juries (2,591 trials).[2] That is, with only one-third as many defendants, there were a few hundred more jury trials in 1960 than in 2013. Taking a longer look back makes the point even more dramatically: there were actually fewer jury trials in the federal criminal courts in 2013 than there were in 1945, even though there were more than twice as many cases.[3] Even as recently as 1990, nearly 14 percent of federal criminal cases were settled by trials, most of them before juries rather than judges, and jury trials accounted for nearly 11 percent of all dispositions. Twenty-three years later, juries were deciding just over 2 percent of criminal cases.

In some ways, the decline is even more striking in the case of civil trials. Between 1962 and 2013, federal civil cases going to trial declined both in absolute numbers and as a percentage of cases filed (see table 2). In 1962 there were 5,802 civil trials in the federal system (both bench and jury); by 2013, that number had fallen to 3,186, although this obscures a sharp increase in the middle of the period:

2. *Sourcebook of Criminal Justice Statistics Online*, University at Albany, School of Criminal Justice, Hindelang Criminal Justice Research Center, http://www.albany.edu/sourcebook/ (accessed April 22, 2015). The *Sourcebook* data are taken from Administrative Office of the United States Courts, *Annual Reports of the Director* (Washington, DC: Government Printing Office).

3. Jury figures for 1945 are from *Sourcebook of Criminal Justice Statistics Online*.

Table 2: The Decline of Civil Trials in the Federal Courts, 1962–2013

Year	Number of Terminations	Number of Trials	Percentage Terminated by Trials
1962	50,320	Jury: 2,765	5.5
		Bench: 3,037	6.0
		Total: 5,802	11.5
1972	90,177	Jury: 3,361	3.7
		Bench: 4,807	5.3
		Total: 8,168	9.1
1982	184,835	Jury: 4,771	2.6
		Bench: 6,509	3.5
		Total: 11,280	6.1
1992	230,171	Jury: 4,279	1.9
		Bench: 3,750	1.6
		Total: 8,029	3.5
2002	258,876	Jury: 3,006	1.2
		Bench: 1,563	0.6
		Total: 4,569	1.8
2010	309,361	Jury: 2,251	0.7
		Bench: 1,058	0.3
		Total: 3,309	1.1
2013	202,630	Jury: 2,170	1.1
		Bench: 1,016	0.5
		Total: 3,186	1.5

Sources: For 1962–2002: Marc Galanter, "The Vanishing Trial: An Examination of Trials and Related Matters in Federal and State Courts," *Journal of Empirical Legal Studies* 1, 3 (November 2004): 462, table 1. Data for 2010 and 2013 are from the Administrative Office of the United States Courts website, Judicial Business of the United States Courts, Annual Report, table C4, http://www.uscourts.gov/statistics/table/c-4/statistical-tables-federal-judiciary/2013/06/30 (accessed May 5, 2015).

there were more than 11,000 civil trials in the federal courts in 1982, for example. During this same period, the total number of civil cases grew enormously: by a factor of six between 1962 and 2010, and by a factor of four from 1962 to 2013. This huge increase in the workload of the federal courts explains, in part, the move toward modes of settlement that are less time-consuming than trials.[4]

4. These numbers are taken from American College of Trial Lawyers. *The "Vanishing Trial": The College, the Profession, and the Civil Justice System*, October 2004, 5, http://www.actl.com/AM/Template.cfm?Section=All_Publications&Template=/CM/ContentDisplay.cfm&ContentFileID=57, citing Marc Galanter, "The Vanishing Trial: An Examination of Trials and Related Matters in Federal and State Courts," *Journal of Empirical Legal Studies* 1, 3 (November 2004): 459. Galanter's research and that of Brian Ostrom and his colleagues (reported below) are based on the Vanishing Trials Project, cosponsored

Whatever the causes, the pattern is clear: between 1962 and 2013, civil cases settled by juries declined from 5.5 percent to 1.1 percent of all terminations.[5] But not only are civil juries vanishing in the federal courts; civil trials are vanishing as well. In absolute numbers, there were fewer federal civil trials in 2013 than there were in 1962. Summarizing this trend, Marc Galanter concludes that while "virtually every other indicator of legal activity is rising, trials are declining not only in relation to cases in the courts but to the size of the population and the size of the economy."[6]

In the state courts, where 90 percent of the nation's judicial business takes place, there has been a similar "trial implosion" and the same steep decline in the percentage of cases settled by juries. A Department of Justice study looking at civil trials in state courts from 1992 to 2001 found a 47 percent decline in such trials across all three categories of torts, contracts, and property cases.[7] A study by Brian Ostrom and colleagues published in 2004 found that state civil trials, both bench and jury, declined from 36.1 percent to only 15.8 percent of all dispositions between 1976 and 2002; jury trials declined from 1.8 percent of all dispositions to only 0.6 percent—despite a doubling in the number of filings (see table 3).[8] In both federal and state courts, it seems, the use of juries to settle civil cases has all but disappeared, despite the protections of the Seventh Amendment.[9]

To get a clearer idea of the magnitude of this change, it helps to look back. During the era of the republican jury and well into the modern era, one-fifth to one-third of all civil cases were decided by trials. A study of the St. Louis Circuit Court shows that from 1820 to the 1920s, trials determined the outcome of 25 to 30 percent of all civil cases. The decline of trial dispositions began in the 1920s, sinking to 15 percent and below as early as the 1940s. A separate study of courts in California found that trials in Alameda County dropped from 36 percent of dispositions in 1890 to 16.1 percent in 1970; in San Benito County, trials dropped

---

by the ABA's Civil Justice Initiatives Task Force and the Court Statistics Project at the National Center for State Courts.

5. Galanter, "Vanishing Trial," 462–463, table 1.

6. Ibid. See also Marc Galanter and Angela Frozena, "The Continuing Decline of Civil Trials in American Courts" (presentation at the 2011 Forum for State Appellate Judges).

7. American College of Trial Lawyers, *Vanishing Trial*, citing Thomas H. Cohen and Steven K. Smith, *Civil Trial Cases and Verdicts in Large Counties, 2001* (Washington, DC: Department of Justice, Bureau of Justice Statistics, 2004), 9, table 10.

8. Brian J. Ostrom, Shauna M. Strickland, and Paula L. Hannaford-Agor, "Examining Trial Trends in State Courts: 1976–2002," *Journal of Empirical Legal Studies* 1, 3 (November 2004): 755, appendix B, 776.

9. See Kevin M. Clermont and Theodore Eisenberg, "Litigation Realities," *Cornell Law Review* 88 (2002): 119; Hon. William G. Young, "Vanishing Trials, Vanishing Juries, Vanishing Constitution," *Suffolk University Law Review* 40 (2006–2007): 67.

Table 3: The Decline of Civil Trials in 22 States' Courts, 1976–2002

Year	Number of Dispositions	Number of Trials	Trials as a Percentage of Dispositions
1976	1,464,258	Jury: 26,018	1.8
		Bench: 502,549	34.3
		Total: 528,567	36.1
1981	1,991,291	Jury: 23,555	1.2
		Bench: 626,188	31.4
		Total: 649,743	32.6
1986	2,280,859	Jury: 23,316	1.0
		Bench: 604,333	26.5
		Total: 627,649	27.5
1991	3,015,817	Jury: 23,089	0.8
		Bench: 623,199	20.7
		Total: 646,288	21.4
1996	3,107,930	Jury: 23,649	0.8
		Bench: 616,557	19.8
		Total: 640,206	20.6
2002	3,087,857	Jury: 17,617	0.6
		Bench: 469,547	15.2
		Total: 487,164	15.8

Source: Adapted from Brian J. Ostrom, Shauna M. Strickland, and Paula L. Hannaford-Agor, "Examining Trial Trends in State Courts: 1976–2002," *Journal of Empirical Legal Studies* 1, 3 (November 2004): 776, appendix B. The study treats the District of Columbia and Puerto Rico as states and includes the general jurisdiction courts in the states of Alaska, Arizona, California, Florida, Hawaii, Indiana, Iowa, Kansas, Maine, Maryland, Massachusetts, Michigan, New Jersey, North Carolina, Ohio, Pennsylvania, South Dakota, Texas, Vermont, Virginia, and Washington.

from 25.8 percent in 1890 to 10.7 percent in 1970.[10] This decline has continued. A study of trials in the seventy-five most populous counties found that civil trials declined by 52 percent from 1992 to 2005.[11]

What has happened in the states on the civil side has also happened on the criminal side (see table 4). The Ostrom study found that the trend for criminal trials in state courts over the past few decades resembles that in federal courts: more cases (an increase of 124 percent between 1976 and 2002) but relatively fewer

10. These studies are cited by Galanter, "Vanishing Trial," 465–466. The St. Louis study is by Wayne McIntosh, *The Appeal of the Civil Law: A Political-Economic Analysis of Litigation* (Urbana: University of Illinois Press, 1990), 124, 126–128. The California study is by Lawrence M. Friedman and Robert V. Percival, "A Tale of Two Courts: Litigation in Alameda and San Benito Counties," *Law & Society Review* 10 (1975): 267.

11. Galanter and Frozena, "Continuing Decline of Civil Trials," 10, table 2.

Table 4: The Decline of Criminal Trials in 22 States' Courts, 1976–2002

Year	Number of Dispositions	Number of Trials	Percentage of Dispositions
1976	1,222,972	Jury: 42,049	3.4
		Bench: 61,382	5.0
		Total: 103,881	8.5
1981	1,681,439	Jury: 39,615	2.4
		Bench: 53,328	3.2
		Total: 92,943	5.5
1986	2,031,079	Jury: 39,019	1.9
		Bench: 46,124	2.3
		Total: 85,143	4.2
1991	2,508,408	Jury: 47,518	1.9
		Bench: 56,543	2.3
		Total: 104,061	4.1
1996	2,650,122	Jury: 42,385	1.6
		Bench: 57,938	2.2
		Total: 100,323	3.8
2002	2,780,440	Jury: 35,664	1.3
		Bench: 55,447	2.0
		Total: 91,111	3.3

Sources: Brian J. Ostrom, Shauna M. Strickland, and Paula L. Hannaford-Agor, "Examining Trends in State Courts: 1976–2002," *Journal of Empirical Legal Studies* 1, 3 (November 2004): 755–782. Adapted from Marc Galanter, "The Vanishing Trial: An Examination of Trials and Related Matters in Federal and State Courts," *Journal of Empirical Legal Studies* 1, 3 (November 2004): 513, table 7.

trials, declining from 8.5 percent of dispositions in 1976 to 3.3 percent in 2002.[12] Whereas there were 52 jury trials and 37 bench trials per 1,000 dispositions in 1976, there were only 22 jury trials and 10 bench trials per 1,000 dispositions in 2002. Although trials spiked upward in the 1990s before coming down again, there was a decline in the absolute number of trials as well as in the proportion of cases settled by trials, with fewer jury trials in 2002 than in 1976. Meanwhile, the total number of dispositions increased by 126 percent between 1976 and 2002, while the population of the states included in the survey increased by only 46 percent.[13]

12. Ostrom et al., "Examining Trial Trends in State Courts." State comparisons are difficult because state court systems differ in the way they calculate when a bench trial or a jury trial has "taken place." For example, in Massachusetts the trial is recorded when the jury is sworn; in New Jersey there is no official trial until the verdict is pronounced. See Galanter, " Vanishing Trial," appendix A-25, 564.

13. Ostrom et al., "Examining Trial Trends in State Courts."

In response to urgent appeals from the Judicial Conference, Congress has periodically authorized more judges in the district courts to deal with the growing workload, increasing the number of positions from 307 in 1962 to 665 in 2002.[14] By 2012, the number of Article III judgeships had increased to 677.[15] However, this growth in the number of judgeships (117 percent between 1962 and 2011) has been far outpaced by the growth in the courts' caseloads (336 percent). Consequently, the judicial workload (cases divided by sitting judges) has gone up dramatically, despite the greater number of judges: from 196 cases per judge in 1962 to 443 cases in 2002 and 542 cases in 2011.[16]

It is harder to get a handle on other court resources, such as the number of court reporters and other administrative staff, but there is evidence that these resources have also been beefed up. Galanter reports, for example, that the number of non–Article III personnel in the federal courts increased from 5,602 in 1962 to 25,947 in 1992 (the last year the Administrative Office of the United States Courts kept records of this kind), while expenditures in constant (1996) dollars grew from $246 million in 1962 to over $4.25 billion by 2002.[17] Galanter concludes that "the decline in trials is accompanied by a larger judicial establishment of which judges form a smaller portion."[18] Yet despite the larger establishment, the cases are backed up. In 1997 only 8.3 percent of civil cases were listed as "pending" for three years or more. By 2010, that percentage had almost doubled, to 15.8 percent.[19]

14. Galanter, "Vanishing Trial," 500.

15. Administrative Office of the United States Courts, *2011 Annual Report of the Director: Judicial Business of the United States Courts* (Washington, DC: Government Printing Office, 2012), 16, table 4. The number of authorized judgeships is not the same as the number of judges serving because some positions remain vacant, sometimes for years. According to a report by the Brennan Center, the 2012 judicial vacancy rate (10 percent) was higher than it has been since the early 1990s. Alicia M. Bannon, *Federal Judicial Vacancies: The Trial Courts* (New York: Brennan Center for Justice, New York University School of Law, 2013), 2.

16. Caseload calculations are from Galanter, "Vanishing Trials," 502; Judicial Conference, *Annual Reports*, table X-1A; and *The Judicial Business of the United States Courts, 2011*, Annual Report of the Director, Administrative Office of the United States Courts (Washington, DC: Government Printing Office, 2011), 406. The Federal Magistrates Act of 1968 created a system of judge-magistrates attached to the federal courts, and since 1979, these magistrates have had the authority to try civil cases if both parties consent. These resources have also been augmented in recent decades: there were 82 full-time and 449 part-time magistrates in 1971, increasing to 531 full-time and 39 part-time magistrates in 2012. Galanter, "Vanishing Trial," 474, n. 24 (for 1971); *Judicial Business of United States Courts, 2012*, table 13.

17. Galanter, "Vanishing Trial," 501.

18. Ibid.

19. *Judicial Business of United States Courts, 1997* and *2010*, table C-6.

Thus, a growing cohort of federal judges now spends a decreasing amount of time presiding over trials and more time doing other things. The number of trials per sitting judge (not to be confused with judicial workload, which measures cases) has fallen from thirty-nine in 1962 to sixteen in 2000 to nine in 2012.[20] This means there are many fewer judges with extensive experience running trials, impaneling juries, or instructing jurors on the law.

The pattern is therefore clear, if the reasons are not: more lawsuits and more crime, but fewer trials, and jury trials reduced to a tiny fraction of what they once were, in both federal and state courts. Why?

Answering this question requires some historical perspective. For most our history, the majority of criminal and civil cases were resolved without juries. Most criminal defendants chose to plead guilty rather than go to trial, and this was true even in the republican era.[21] Part of the reason is brutally simple. Although all persons charged with crimes must be presumed innocent until proved guilty, the cases that make it through the indictment stage are those with enough incriminating evidence to make prosecutors confident about their ability to convince a jury of the defendant's guilt. In such cases, defendants are likely to make realistic assessments of their chances of acquittal and conclude that they are not very good. The jury comes into play in those cases that are not so simple, where the charge is difficult to prove "beyond a reasonable doubt." If the defendant risks a trial and loses, the public (and possibly the defendant as well) can take comfort from knowing that the judgment was delivered by the people and not by officials.

Civil cases are a bit more complicated. In a civil case the question is not guilt or innocence but whether one party has wronged another, based on an allegation of certain facts. The jury has always had the authority to judge these factual claims, and by constitutional design, "no fact tried by a jury, shall be otherwise re-examined in any Court of the United States, than according to the rules of

20. Galanter, "Vanishing Trial," 566, table A-26. Data for 2012 are taken from Administrative Office of the United States Courts, *United States District Courts—National Judicial Caseload Profile, 2012*, and *Judicial Business of United States Courts, 2012*, tables C-4 and D-4.

21. The extent of plea bargaining before the nineteenth century is a matter of controversy among legal historians, in part because of the paucity of records. It is also important to distinguish plea bargaining—which can be done by the prosecution, the defense, or both—from a simple decision to plead guilty and "get it over with," a practice that made more sense when noncapital punishment meant whipping or branding rather than a long prison term. Lengthy terms of imprisonment did not become common in the United States until the Jacksonian era. On the history of plea bargaining, see Bruce P. Smith, "Plea Bargaining and the Eclipse of the Jury," *Annual Review Law and Social Science* 1 (2005): 131; John Langbein, "Understanding the Short History of Plea Bargaining," *Law and Social Science Review* 13 (1979): 261; and George Fisher, *Plea Bargaining's Triumph: A History of Plea Bargaining in America* (Stanford, CA: Stanford University Press, 2003).

the common law."[22] Was a contractual obligation fulfilled? Did one party defame another? Did a suitor breach a promise of marriage? These questions involve assertions of fact and are therefore safely within the province of the jury.

But unlike a criminal case, a civil case presents multiple opportunities for the parties to settle their dispute short of a trial in a way that is more or less satisfactory to both sides. Furthermore, the facts to be determined in a civil case are often more complicated than the factual determinations in a criminal case, and litigants may well choose to resolve their dispute in a way that does not rely on amateur jurors who may not understand the litigants' business. Given these uncertainties, many litigants—perhaps doubtful of either the justice of their cause or their ability to explain it to a jury—have been willing (and sometimes eager) to seek a nonjury resolution through summary judgment, a bench trial, or even a settlement, rather than risk an unpredictable outcome. Even Tocqueville, one of the jury's greatest champions, conceded that civil trials might be better for the jurors than for the litigants.[23]

Although juries have never decided more than a minority of civil and criminal cases, their rate of participation in the past was much higher than it has been in recent decades. What explains this relatively recent and dramatic decline?

EXPLAINING THE VANISHING JURY

The decline in the jury's share of dispositions has not taken place in a vacuum. The vanishing jury must be understood in the context of several developments in the law and in the administration of the civil courts that began in the 1930s but did not reach maturity until decades later. In the case of criminal juries, the decline has much to do with the way Congress responded to the sharp increase in violent crime that began in the late 1960s. Collectively, these developments have had a dramatic impact on the American jury system—sometimes on purpose, and sometimes by accident. That is, modern legal reform has displayed either hostility to the jury system or indifference to its fate, and we can now more fully appreciate the consequences of the indifference as well as the hostility.

Any explanation of the vanishing jury must begin with the enormous increase in the workload of the state and federal courts, especially on the civil side, over the past half century. As noted earlier, federal civil case filings grew sixfold between 1962 and 2010, but the nature of these filings changed in response to civil rights legislation and liberalized class-action rules. On the criminal side, the rapid increase in federal crimes (especially newly federalized drug and firearms of-

22. US Constitution, Amendment VII.

23. Alexis de Tocqueville, *Democracy in America*, trans. Harvey C. Mansfield and Delba Winthrop (Chicago: University of Chicago Press, 2000), 262.

fenses) caused criminal cases in the federal courts to nearly double in the 1990s, from just under 55,000 defendants in 1995 to over 98,000 in 2010.[24] State civil cases also grew substantially, although not as dramatically as federal cases, more than doubling between 1976 and 1996.[25]

The Changing Nature of the Business of the Courts

All by itself, this dramatic increase in the workload of the courts would generate strong pressures to dispose of cases without a trial—and especially without a jury trial, which, on average, takes twice as long as a bench trial.[26] But in addition to getting bigger, the judicial caseload has changed in other ways, with a different mix of case types and a larger proportion of complex and time-consuming cases. Galanter's study, cited above, shows that the largest category of civil trials in the early 1960s was torts—where the issue is an allegation that one party has harmed another—traditionally the "bread and butter" of civil litigation. In 1962 more than half of all civil trials, and four-fifths of all civil jury trials, were tort cases. Contract cases were a close second, at one-fifth of all trials, and roughly a quarter of those were decided by juries. By 2002, torts had declined to less than a quarter of all trials and just over a quarter of all civil jury trials; contract cases had declined slightly, to 15.3 percent of all trials, just over half of them before juries.[27]

While contract and tort cases were declining, civil rights cases were replacing them. The number of civil rights cases exploded beginning in the early 1960s, from just over 300 cases in 1962 to more than 50,000 cases in 2010. This trend reflected the heightened "rights consciousness" of the 1960s and 1970s and its embodiment in statutes governing elementary and secondary schools, employment law, the rights of the disabled, the rights of shareholders, and the admissions and athletic policies of colleges and universities (to name a few of the most important examples).[28] In 2002 more than a third of all trials, and 41 percent of jury trials,

24. *Sourcebook of Criminal Justice Statistics Online*.

25. This estimate comes from a study of civil courts of general jurisdiction in twenty-two states (including the District of Columbia) containing 58 percent of the population. See Galanter, "Vanishing Jury," 507, table 4.

26. There is a general consensus that jury trials take longer, but there are dissenters. One study, for example, argues that jury trials *take* longer, but bench trials are on the *docket* longer—that is, there is a longer interval between filing and disposition—because judges may interrupt their consideration of a case to handle other, more pressing business. See, for example, Theodore Eisenberg and Kevin M. Clermont, "Trial by Jury or Judge: Which Is Speedier?" *Judicature* 79, 4 (January–February 1996): 176.

27. Galanter, "Vanishing Trial," 466–467.

28. *Judicial Business of United States Courts, 2010*, table C-2.

involved civil rights claims. "For over 30 years," Galanter concludes, "even as the portion of cases tried has fallen, civil rights has remained the type of case most likely to reach trial."[29] By the 1990s, however, civil rights cases in general, and employment discrimination cases in particular, were also the cases most likely to be disposed of without trials, many of them by summary judgment (more on this below).

The other category of case that has replaced contracts and torts in the federal system is prisoner petitions, a development that reflects not only the heightened emphasis on rights but also the huge increase in the prison population since the 1960s, from 218,830 state and federal prisoners in 1962 to over 1.3 million in 2001 and 1.6 million in 2010.[30] There were just over 3,000 prisoner petitions in 1962, leading to only 96 trials, all of them before judges; there were more than 44,000 petitions in 1992, leading to more than 1,000 trials, about a third of them before juries. The widespread availability, beginning in the 1970s, of pro bono legal counsel for the inmates of state and federal prisons has undoubtedly helped increase the number of these petitions.[31] This huge increase, in fact, led Congress to pass the Prison Litigation Reform Act of 1995, intended to reduce the flow of petitions filling up the courts.[32] The result was a rapid decrease in the number of prisoner filings and an even greater decrease in the number of trials involving prisoner petitions, from a peak of 1,235 trials in 1996 to only 491 trials in 2002, just over half of them in front of juries.[33] By 2010, prisoner petitions were nearly as numerous as they had been in 1992 (roughly 42,000), but only 318 cases were resolved by trial, mostly by juries. Of the cases on which the court took some action, nearly all (97 percent) were disposed of before a trial began.[34]

Taken together, the traditional categories of torts and contracts (including diversity-of-citizenship cases) grew by only 34.5 percent between 1962 and 2002; by contrast, civil rights cases, prisoner petitions, and labor law cases increased by an astonishing 1,818 percent during the same period, constituting 44 percent of

29. Galanter, "Vanishing Trial," 468.

30. Ibid., 468 (for 1962 and 2001); the 2010 figure is from US Department of Justice, Bureau of Justice Statistics, *Prisoners in 2010*, 1, http://www.bjs.gov/content/pub/pdf/p10.pdf (accessed April 22, 2015).

31. The federal Bureau of Justice Statistics reports that by 1989, "nearly 80% of local jail inmates indicated that they were assigned an attorney to represent them for the charges on which they were being held." By 1991, "about three-quarters of State prison inmates and half of Federal prison inmates . . . had a court-appointed lawyer to represent them" while in prison. Bureau of Justice Statistics, *Indigent Defense*, February 1996, 1, http://www.bjs.gov/content/pub/pdf/id.pdf (accessed April 22, 2015).

32. Galanter, "Vanishing Trial," 468, 471.

33. Ibid., 472.

34. *Judicial Business of United States Courts, 2010*, 168, table C-4.

all civil dispositions and nearly half of all civil trials.[35] These increases, combined with increases in the traditional categories of civil litigation, have made it vital to get the courts' business done more quickly.

Rule 23 Class Actions

In 1966 the Supreme Court adopted the recommendations of the Judicial Conference's Advisory Committee on Civil Rules, changing the way classes are certified for the purpose of multiparty litigation. The goal of the amendments was to make class actions easier to file. That had always been the aim of rule 23, but the language of its 1938 version was burdened by what one critic called "a high pitch of abstraction," and reformers insisted that it be rewritten.[36] In particular, the 1966 amendments sought to clarify the circumstances under which a class action would be considered appropriate, both compressing and amending the confusing categories of the 1938 rule, while making it easier to construct a large group of plaintiffs with enough in common to make them a "class" for purposes of the law.

Encouraging class actions was originally intended to make the federal courts more efficient—by bundling many small claims into one—as well as more just—by facilitating suits by plaintiffs whose individual claims might be too small to justify the expense of litigation, especially if the defendant were a large corporation. But the amended rule 23 opened up new possibilities for the class-action strategy, leading to a surge in class actions in the federal courts over the next thirty years. Especially productive was new section (b)(2), which provided that if "the party opposing a class had acted on grounds apparently applying to the whole group, a representative suit should be available to secure for the class any appropriate injunctive or declaratory relief." According to one of its authors, Benjamin Kaplan, this provision was written with civil rights litigation in mind, and class actions alleging violations of civil rights subsequently became an important source of new business for the federal courts, especially as more groups sought to be sheltered under the "civil rights" umbrella.[37] However, when rule 23(b)(2) class actions seek injunctive relief (as is often the case in civil rights cases), they are generally treated as equitable and are therefore outside the Seventh Amendment jury right.[38]

35. See Galanter, "Vanishing Trial," 462, table 1.

36. Benjamin Kaplan, "Continuing the Work of the Civil Committee: 1966 Amendments of the Federal Rules of Civil Procedure (I)," *Harvard Law Review* 81, 2 (December 1967): 377.

37. Ibid., 388–389.

38. On the distinction between equitable and legal relief under rule 23, see Mark A. Perry and Rachel S. Brass, "Rule 23(b)(2) Certification of Employment Class Actions: A Return to First Principles," *NYU Annual Survey of American Law* 65 (2009–2010): 681.

Ultimately, it was the revised section (b)(3) that proved to be the most fertile source of new litigation. This section governs cases in which a class action "promises important advantages of economy of effort and uniformity of result without undue dilution of procedural safeguards for members of the class or for the opposition party." This category is appropriate whenever the court finds (1) that "common questions not only exist but 'predominate' over questions touching only individual members of the class," and (2) that a class action would be "superior" to other methods for disposing of a legal claim. Most importantly, the class can be constructed by making a "reasonable" effort to inform the putative members of the class of their rights under the law; if they choose to do so, individual members can opt out of the suit by filing a notice with the court.[39]

One study of the 1966 amendments argues that their "dominant purpose . . . was to 'enable' litigation by creating effective enforcement mechanisms . . . primarily but not exclusively for civil rights cases, and by facilitating the prosecution of small claims susceptible to group adjudication but otherwise uneconomical to litigate."[40] If this is a true account of what the amendments' authors had in mind, they got what they hoped for, in spades, though not immediately. Until the late 1980s, critics claimed that class-action practice was "slow and halting," and a 1988 *New York Times* editorial pronounced that the class action was "dying" and lamented that "the use of the courts as a vehicle of social change had subsided." But by the 1990s, judges had apparently decided that the class action could be a useful "case management device," aggregating related claims and "minimizing duplicative action."[41] This led to a surge of cases in the 1990s, which in turn led

---

But see also Teamsters v. Terry (494 U.S. 558, 1990), holding that claims for back pay can, under some circumstances, be treated as legal rather than equitable under rule 23 and are therefore within the protection of the Seventh Amendment.

39. Kaplan, "Continuing the Work of the Civil Committee," 388–392. This provision explains the flurry of extremely fine-print legal notices sent to consumers of various products, informing them of their right to participate in a class action with thousands of other consumers. For a sample, see the homepage for the In re Apple In-App Purchase Litigation Settlement, Case No. 5:11-CV-01758-EJD, https://www.itunesinapppurchasesettlement.com/CAClaimForms/AIL/Home.aspx (accessed April 22, 2015).

40. Rule 23(b)(3) states that "the court shall direct to the members of the class the best notice practicable under the circumstances, including individual notice to all members who can be identified through reasonable effort." See Richard A. Epstein, "Class Actions: Aggregation, Amplification and Distortion" (John M. Olin Law & Economics Working Paper no. 182 [2nd series], University of Chicago Law School, April 2003). See also Joel Seligman and Lindsey Hunter, "Rule 23: Class Actions at the Crossroads," *Arizona Law Review* 39 (1997): 407: "Originally adopted by the United States in 1938, Rule 23 represented an attempt to encourage more frequent use of class actions."

41. Seligman and Hunter, "Rule 23," 409.

Congress to limit class actions, first in the area of securities litigation, with the Private Securities Litigation Reform Act of 1995, and then with the Class Action Fairness Act of 2005. The 2005 act sought to end "class action abuse" in the states ("forum shopping," for example) by liberalizing the rules for removing cases from state to federal courts.[42] However, the law had the unintended but predictable result of aggravating the federal case burden.[43]

Class actions in the federal courts have almost certainly helped crowd out trials. Most class actions that are not dismissed are typically settled before trial; therefore, they bring a complex set of cases that occupy the attention of federal judges without generating many trial outcomes. This hypothesis is confirmed by the trial data. Galanter's research shows that trials and class actions are mirror images: as class actions declined in the 1970s and 1980s, the number of trials registered a brief upward spike. As class actions increased from the late 1980s into the 1990s, the number of trials decreased again.[44]

Increasingly Complex Civil Litigation

In addition to being more numerous, federal civil cases have become more complicated and therefore more time-consuming—adding to the pressure to avoid trials, and prolonging many of the trials that do take place. One measure of judicial efficiency is the "time to trial": in 1963 the median time to trial in federal civil cases was sixteen months; by 1997, the time to trial had grown to eighteen months; by 2013, the time to trial was just over two years.[45] The number of longer trials has also increased. Trials lasting more than four days were only 15 percent of all federal civil trials in 1965, but they accounted for 41 percent by 2010.[46] Galanter notes, however, that the number of shorter trials has also grown, making the actual trial time a "relatively insignificant" share of the total.[47] What has grown, in other words, is not the time needed for the trial itself but the run-up and preparation time before the trial begins.

42. The 2005 act may have been inspired by the outcome of product-liability cases tried in Texas state courts. The act gives federal courts jurisdiction over class actions if the amount in controversy is more than $5 million and less than two-thirds of the plaintiffs are residents of the state in which the action was originally filed.

43. See Emergy G. Lee III and Thomas E. Willging, *The Impact of the Class Action Fairness Act of 2005 on the Federal Court* (Washington, DC: Federal Judicial Center, 2008).

44. Galanter, "Vanishing Trials," 485–486.

45. Ibid., 480–481; *Judicial Business of United States Courts, 1997* and *2013*, table C-5.

46. Galanter, "Vanishing Trials," 478; *Judicial Business of United States Courts, 2010*, table T-2.

47. Galanter, "Vanishing Trials," 480, n. 40.

Modern cases take longer from filing to disposition in part because they often involve more defendants, more institutional litigants, more extensive discovery,[48] more documents, more attorneys, larger law firms, and, in some cases, the possibility of enormous payouts to the winners.[49] As John Langbein observes, "Big Cases" breed "Big Law." "With sophisticated counsel on both sides, the paradigm of modern tort litigation consists of discovery to establish the facts, followed by settlement"[50]—or, with increasing frequency, summary judgment from the bench.

More Laws and More Regulations

The courts have more business because Congress and federal administrative agencies have been generating more laws and more regulations than ever before. As Brock Hornby points out, Congress added just under 2,000 pages of new statutes per year in the 1950s; that number increased to over 6,700 pages per year in the 1990s. Meanwhile, the *Federal Register* (which records administrative regulations, proposed new rules, and public notices) grew from roughly 15,000 pages in 1960 to over 81,000 pages in 2010.[51] Since many agency regulations contain ambiguous language, affected parties often "ask federal courts to expound upon what the new law means and the circumstances to which it applies."[52] This means new court cases but not necessarily new trials.

48. Federal discovery, in fact, is sometimes a motive for filing a case, even if the plaintiffs have no intention of following through to the bitter end. A website providing legal information to the business community recently noted that because federal rules require mandatory disclosure, plaintiffs "get some key information early in the case," even if they "don't have any evidence or information supporting their allegations." See "How Moving Your Case to Federal Court Could Benefit Your Business," http://www.sbnonline.com/2012/04/how-moving-your-case-to-federal-court-could-benefit-your-business/ (accessed August 25, 2013).

49. The $247 billion multistate tobacco settlement in 1998 netted the plaintiffs' attorneys between $10 billion and $30 billion. See Barry Meier, "The Spoils of Tobacco Wars; Big Settlement Puts Many Lawyers in the Path of a Windfall," *New York Times*, December 22, 1998, http://www.nytimes.com/articles.html (accessed August 25, 2013).

50. John Langbein, "The Disappearance of Civil Trial," *Yale Law Journal* 122 (2012): 571.

51. D. Brock Hornby, "The Business of the U.S. District Courts," *Green Bag*, 2nd ser., 10, 4 (Summer 2007): 457. *Federal Register* information for 2010 comes from PolitiFact.com, http://www.politifact.com/virginia/statements/2011/jul/01/randy-forbes/rep-forbes-says-federal-registration-containing-re/ (accessed September 18, 2014).

52. Hornby, "Business of U.S. District Courts," 457.

Busier State Courts

The trial implosion in the states closely parallels what has happened in the federal courts, on both the civil and the criminal sides. And as in the federal courts, one explanation is the significant increase in the business of the state courts, multiplying the incentives to avoid trials. The study by Ostrom and colleagues found that from 1976 to 2002, civil dispositions doubled in the twenty-two states studied (from 1.4 million to 3.1 million), while the state populations increased by only 39 percent. Jury trials, meanwhile, declined from 1.8 percent of dispositions to only 0.6 percent.[53] In criminal cases, the pattern was similar: dispositions in the sample states increased by 127 percent—more than three times faster than the population—but jury trials declined by 15 percent and bench trials by 10 percent.[54]

To the extent that states have adopted the Federal Rules of Civil Procedure as their own (and thirty-five states have done so to date), we might expect those rules to have the same impact on trial rates in state courts as they have in federal courts. Galanter points to one important parallel: "for a long time, the great majority of cases of almost every kind . . . have terminated by settlement" in both state and federal courts. He attributes this result to "the exigencies of litigation, which lead parties to trade off the possibility of preferred outcomes for avoidance of the costs and risks of proceeding through trial."[55]

Although a majority of states have adopted the federal rules to greater or lesser degrees, most of the largest states have not. Two-thirds of the nation's population lives in states where the federal rules have not been adopted at all or have been adopted only in part, making it unlikely that procedural reform alone explains why the state courts have become so busy or why so many cases are concluded before a trial can begin.[56] One possibility is that, despite their failure to adopt the federal rules, state courts have imbibed the federal *spirit*, which increasingly involves finding ways to dispose of cases before trial, through settlement or arbitration. And on the criminal side, many states have adopted their own versions of the federal sentencing guidelines, with similar effects on the number of criminal trials.

53. Ostrom et al., "Examining Trial Trends in States Courts," 768.

54. Ibid., 761, 764.

55. Galanter, " Vanishing Trial," 515; see also Thomas J. Stipanowich, "ADR and the 'Vanishing Trial': The Growth and Impact of 'Alternative Dispute Resolution,'" *Journal of Empirical Legal Studies* 1, 3 (November 2004): 843.

56. On the differences between state and federal civil procedure, see John B. Oakley, "A Fresh Look at the Federal Rules in State Courts," *Nevada Law Journal* 3 (Winter 2002–2003): 354. Oakley concludes that "federal procedure is less influential in state courts today than at anytime in the past quarter-century. While the federal model of civil procedure remains substantially influential at the state level, it is no longer true that many state systems of civil procedure replicate the federal model" (355).

Removals from State Court to Federal Court

Civil litigants have become increasingly successful in removing their cases from state court to federal court, adding another (albeit relatively small) burden to the already heavy federal caseload.[57] Parties seek removal for a number of reasons, some of which have not changed for generations. Litigants may fear local prejudice (e.g., a corporate defendant with an out-of-state headquarters) or local pressure on judges who are elected or subject to recall, or they may simply desire the larger jury pool and superior case management resources available in the federal courts.[58] (Conversely, some attorneys contend that the rules and procedures of federal court are more complicated and more expensive to comply with, so they try to keep their cases in state court if at all possible.)

To keep the federal courts from being swamped with small claims, federal law requires the "amount in controversy" in diversity-of-citizenship actions to be in excess of $75,000 (an amount established in 1996). Apparently, this has not significantly slowed the growth of civil cases in the federal courts, since damage claims in tort and product-liability cases can easily exceed this amount, unless the litigants are determined to keep their case local. The Class Action Fairness Act of 2005 loosened both the diversity-of-citizenship and the amount-in-controversy requirements to encourage class actions to be moved from state to federal court.[59] For all these reasons, removals began to increase sharply in the 1980s; since then, they have gone up and down, while generally trending upward. Removals peaked in 2002 at over 55,000, dropped to 30,000 in 2006, and rose to 31,000 in 2010.[60]

The Federalization of Crime

Although the criminal jurisdiction of the federal courts has been expanded at various times—such as federalizing the crimes of kidnapping and armed robbery—

57. Ibid., 455.

58. One scholar notes that there is a "widespread perception among attorneys, litigants, and policymakers that defendants are provided with more favorable forums than plaintiffs in the federal courts. The acceptance of this view is manifested by the growing trend of defendants removing diversity cases from the state to the federal courts." Thomas H. Cohen, "General Civil Jury Trial Litigation in State and Federal Courts: A Statistical Portrait," *Journal of Empirical Legal Studies* 5, 3 (September 2008): 593, 594.

59. See Cameron Fredman, "Plaintiff's Paradise Lost: Diversity of Citizenship and the Amount in Controversy under the Class Action Fairness Act of 2005," *Loyola of Los Angeles Law Review* 39 (2006): 1025.

60. Hornby, "Business of U.S. District Courts," 456. See also *Judicial Business of the United States Courts*, table S-7 (for 1997 and later) and tables S-4 and S-8 (for earlier years).

this pattern has intensified significantly since the 1960s. Using the commerce clause, Congress has federalized a wide range of police-power violations that were once prosecuted in state courts, including garden-variety firearms offenses, drug trafficking, criminal conspiracies (i.e., organized crime), carjacking, money laundering, and even minor offenses such as tampering with odometers. New environmental laws added layers of federal crime, from the serious (polluting interstate waterways) to the relatively trivial (possession of scrimshaw or eagle feathers). Likewise, new categories of federal homicide were added to the *United States Code* (e.g., murder in the context of a racketeering enterprise, or murder of a federal official).[61] Altogether, it is estimated that between the 1960s and the 1990s, Congress added more than 3,000 new crimes to the federal criminal code, and the number continues to grow.[62]

More federal crimes require more federal prosecutions, and more prosecutions require more prosecutors; meanwhile, having more prosecutors makes it easier to bring more federal prosecutions. The number of prosecutors working in US attorneys' offices has steadily increased, from 3,000 in the 1960s to over 8,000 in the 1990s. A large part of this growth can be attributed to the increase in drug and firearms prosecutions, with both categories quadrupling in the 1980s.[63] Overall, criminal filings per sitting judge grew from 58 in 1980 to 84 in 1992. Criminal cases have continued to increase since the 1990s, despite the drop in the violent crime rate beginning in the middle of that decade: 45,000 cases in 1993, 62,000 in 2000, and more than 78,000 cases in 2010. There have been increases in nearly every major crime category, with the exception of homicide and robbery, both of which declined slightly.[64] By 2010, weighted criminal filings per judgeship had reached 130.[65]

The federal criminal caseload is not just larger; like the civil caseload, it now contains a different mix of cases. As a percentage of the caseload, the traditional crimes against persons and property—homicide, robbery, and assault, which are still largely under the jurisdiction of the states—were actually less important in 2010 than they were in 1993. These three offense categories produced (in round numbers) 2,400 cases in the federal courts in 1993 but only 1,700 cases in 2010. In contrast, certain traditional federal crimes, such as immigration offenses,

61. In Administrative Office of the United States Courts, *1950 Annual Report*, table D-2, there are no proceedings listed under "Homicide" (170).

62. Sara Sun Beale, "Federalizing Crime: Assessing the Impact on the Federal Courts," *Annals of the American Academy of Political and Social Science* 543 (January 1996): 44.

63. Ibid., 45.

64. *Judicial Business of the United States Courts* [annual], table D-2. FBI statistics show that the rate of violent crime in the United States declined from a high of 758 per 100,000 in 1991 to 386 per 100,000 in 2012. Federal Bureau of Investigation, *Uniform Crime Statistics*, 1960–2012. http://www.ucrdatatool.gov/ (accessed March 26, 2015).

65. Administrative Office of the United States Courts, *United States District Courts—National Judicial Caseload Profile, 2013*.

have become much more important, growing tenfold between 1993 and 2010. But newly federalized crimes are also a much bigger part of the mix: compared with 1993, there were more federal prosecutions in 2010 for sex crimes, drug offenses, firearms violations, and other crimes that did not even exist in the *United States Code* until the 1970s: violent racketeering, carjacking, terrorism, juvenile offenses, RICO (organized crime) cases, and a separate and rapidly growing category of "regulatory offenses."[66]

In her study of the expanding criminal jurisdiction of the federal courts, Sara Beale notes that the main impact of this increase has been to crowd out civil cases—one of many reasons for the pressure to dispose of federal civil cases more quickly.[67] The problem was highlighted in 1991 when judges in the District of Columbia Circuit publicly criticized the US attorney for bringing routine first-offender drug cases to federal court rather than letting the local superior court handle them. This contributed, the judges argued, to an unhealthy backlog of postponed civil cases. Adding to the problem was that many more defendants being prosecuted in the DC superior court were demanding jury trials; the number of such demands grew by 360 percent in just the four years between 1986 and 1990.[68]

Throughout the federal system, the increase in criminal prosecutions created similar pressures. The Federal Courts Study Committee claimed in 1990 that there was an "impending crisis" in the federal courts: the growing criminal caseload required more time and resources to prosecute criminal cases, leaving fewer resources for civil cases—which were growing even more rapidly than criminal cases.[69] Beale notes an additional problem: the expansion of the federal govern-

66. As its cheeky acronym suggests, the RICO statute (Racketeer Influenced and Corrupt Organization Act [18 U.S.C. §§ 1961–1968]) was intended to make the federal prosecution of traditional Mafia crime families easier. But federal prosecutors have employed this law well beyond organized crime in the traditional sense, such as using it to prosecute state officials whose "criminal enterprise" consists of patronage hiring. For example, federal prosecutors brought successful racketeering charges against the head of the Massachusetts Department of Probation, who was accused of giving jobs to applicants recommended by legislators with control over the department's budget. See Milton J. Valencia, "3 Guilty in Probation Corruption Case," *Boston Globe*, July 24, 2014. On regulatory offenses, see *Judicial Business of the United States Courts* [annual], table D-2.

67. Beale, "Federalizing Crime," 47–48.

68. Ibid., 47.

69. *Report of the Federal Courts Study Committee*, April 2, 1990, 4, 35. See Beale, "Federalizing Crime," 40. Some of this pressure is constitutional—the Sixth Amendment guarantees a defendant's right to a "speedy and public trial"—and the Supreme Court held in 1972 that a delay of one year would be "presumptively prejudicial." Barker v. Wingo, 407 U.S. 514 (1972). In response to this ruling, Congress passed the Speedy Trial Act of 1974, which requires that if a criminal case does not get to trial within seventy days, it must be abandoned and the charges dropped (18 U.S.C. §§ 3161–3162, 3164). There is no similar deadline pressure, either constitutional or legislative, in the case of civil trials.

ment's criminal jurisdiction in the 1980s created not only more federal crimes but also more complex prosecutions, the same pattern seen on the civil side. Whereas the federal courts once handled charges that could be dealt with in a fairly straightforward manner—auto theft, counterfeiting, and forgery, for example—they were now seeing complex drug-distribution and money-laundering offenses involving multiple defendants and multiple charges. Federal criminal trials were also growing longer, from an average of 2.5 days in 1970 to 4.4 days in the early 1990s. Beale concludes that "very long trials have now become commonplace," with the number of criminal trials in the six- to twenty-day range more than doubling by 1996.[70]

Finally, many federal administrative regulations offer prosecutors the option of bringing criminal charges instead of, or in addition to, the civil charges that are the normal consequence of regulatory violations. Although regulatory offenses are a small part of the criminal caseload—only 2.2 percent of cases in 2012—they have been steadily increasing, growing by 43.7 percent between 2001 and 2012.[71]

Sentencing Reform

Part of the new complexity of federal criminal jurisdiction involves congressional efforts to reform the sentencing regime in the federal courts. The Comprehensive Crime Control Act of 1984—a response to increased levels of violent crime and drug trafficking—included the Sentencing Reform Act (Title II), originally proposed by Senator Edward Kennedy in 1975 in response to the separate issue of "sentencing disparities."[72]

Federal judges enjoyed considerable discretion in their sentencing decisions, and judicial discretion was augmented by that of parole officers, who assumed authority over prisoners once their sentences began. It was therefore possible (critics argued) for individuals to be sentenced to, or to serve, very different prison terms for the same crime, depending on where the crime was committed. Congressional liberals had long sought to end these alleged inequities, and congressional conservatives were angered by the perception that some federal judges were letting hardened criminals get away with a "slap on the wrist." This convergence set up the opportunity for a grand bipartisan agreement: Each federal district would be

70. Beale, "Federalizing Crime," 48.

71. *Judicial Business of the United States Courts, 2012* and *2005*, table D-2.

72. On the legislative history of the Sentencing Reform Act, see Kate Stith and Steve Y. Koh, "The Politics of Sentencing Reform: The Legislative History of the Federal Sentencing Guidelines," *Wake Forest Law Review* 28 (1993): 223, and Kate Stith and José Cabranes, *Fear of Judging: Sentencing Guidelines in the Federal Courts* (Chicago: University of Chicago Press, 1998).

Table 5: Impact of Plea Bargaining on Jury Trials in US District Courts, 1945–2014

Year	Number of Defendants	Guilty/Nolo Pleas as Percentage of Defendants	Percentage of Jury Dispositions
1945	43,755	70.4	7.0
1950	38,835	81.7	5.7
1955	40,235	77.4	6.8
1960	31,984	75.8	8.1
1965	33,718	76.9	7.7
1970	36,356	66.3	10.0
1975	49,212	64.7	11.0
1980	36,560	63.2	12.8
1985	47,360	71.4	9.8
1990	56,519	71.6	10.9
1995	54,980	78.4	6.9
2000	75,071	85.1	4.0
2005	86,000	86.1	3.9
2010	98,311	88.9	2.4
2014	86,492	88.8	2.2

Sources: *Sourcebook of Criminal Justice Statistics Online*, University at Albany, School of Criminal Justice, Hindelang Criminal Justice Research Center, http://www.albany.edu/sourcebook/ind/COURTS.Federal.U.S._District_Courts.Defendants.Disposed.4.html (accessed July 13, 2013). The *Sourcebook* data are taken from Administrative Office of the United States Courts, *Annual Reports of the Director* (Washington, DC: Government Printing Office). Data for 2014 are from *The Judicial Business of the United States Courts 2014*, http://www.uscourts.gov (accessed March 27, 2015).

required to use the same sentencing range, based on the nature of the crime and the presence of "aggravating factors"—thus satisfying the liberals. But the sentencing range would include much harsher sentences at the upper end—which is what the conservatives were looking for.

The sentencing guidelines have had an important impact on the number of criminal jury trials. Their most notable consequence was to enable federal prosecutors to threaten draconian sentences in order to extract plea bargains from defendants who might otherwise have chosen to go to trial before either a judge or a jury. The law has received some critical scrutiny from the Supreme Court (discussed in more detail below), which made the sentencing guidelines advisory rather than mandatory.[73] But longer sentences remain a significant possibility, weighing on defendants as they calculate their odds.

There is little doubt about the result: the new guidelines have led to an increase in plea bargaining and a corresponding decrease in the percentage of federal criminal cases disposed of by juries (see table 5). As recently as the 1970s,

73. United States v. Booker, 543 U.S. 220 (2005), discussed in more detail below.

about two-thirds of federal defendants pleaded guilty or nolo contendere, and roughly 10 percent were tried by juries. Beginning in 1985, plea-bargaining rates began a steady climb to their current level of nearly 90 percent of defendants, while jury trials have been reduced to their lowest level in the history of the federal courts: 2.2 percent of dispositions in 2014.

The new sentencing regime has had a second unintended consequence: it has given the federal courts more work to do. Beale's study notes that, in the late 1980s, judges reported spending 25 to 50 percent more time on sentencing than in the past, largely because the sentencing guidelines "require extensive factual findings and legal conclusions in each case and thus increase significantly the time that district judges spend on sentencing."[74] Judges must also spend more time supervising prisoners after conviction, because Title II abolished the traditional probation regime and turned parole decisions over to the federal courts.

More Lawyers

Finally, and perhaps not coincidentally, there has been an enormous increase in the number of licensed attorneys in the United States over the past generation (a growth of 268 percent between 1970 and 2010—more than five times the rate of population growth).[75] If more laws and more regulations can generate more court business, why can't the same be said for more lawyers?

VANISHING TRIALS AND THE REVOLUTION IN THE COURTS

New and different business is only part of the explanation for the vanishing trial. The decline in trials, and the decline in jury trials, is in part the consequence of a deliberate strategy. As discussed in chapter 3, the promulgation of the Federal Rules of Civil Procedure was the result of long-standing dissatisfaction with the complex and cumbersome practices of common-law litigation. Among other important changes, the 1938 rules combined equity and law into a single practice, importing some of the spirit of the equity courts into the handling of common-law cases. Most important, the rules dramatically increased the role of the judge in fact-finding. "The discovery regime of the Federal Rules and the associated practices of judicial case management," writes Langbein, "ostensibly directed at enabling the litigants to prepare for trial, have had the effect of displacing trial in

74. Beale, "Federalizing Crime," 49.

75. American Bar Association, *Total National Lawyer Counts, 1878–2011*, Market Research Department, http://www.americanbar.org/resources_for_lawyers/profession_statistics.html (accessed June 17, 2013).

most cases, causing ever more cases to be resolved in the pretrial process, either by settlement or by pretrial adjudication. Pretrial civil procedure has become non-trial civil procedure."[76] The 1938 reforms had a delayed impact on the business of the federal courts, but looking back on those changes from the vantage point of a half century or more, it is easy to agree with those who describe them as a "revolution" in civil jurisprudence.[77]

For purposes of this discussion, the most important change concerned judges' control over the management of civil cases, especially in the early stages. What had once been a highly formal and even arcane process—circumscribed by rules that kept the judge somewhat above the fray—now became a more informal process in which the judge was expected to gather the attorneys in chambers and come to an amicable agreement about the evidence, the legal issues in play, the witness list, and the facts both parties would agree to before the trial. This informality had been one of the advantages of the equity courts, which did not rely as heavily on the adversarial model that defined the common-law courts.

It is sometimes said, however, that rather than simply being "imported" into the common law, equity "swallowed the common law."[78] This may be a rhetorical exaggeration, but there is no doubt that the new arrangements were attractive precisely because they brought into the civil courts the greater judicial flexibility that made equity practice appealing. The "spirit of equity" would make civil jurisprudence more "efficient," as that word was understood at the height of the Progressive Era: quicker, simpler, less "fussy," and more "businesslike" than the older practices and, above all, under the control of experts. Judges would now have more power to resolve cases before trial, and the spirit of the rules reforms clearly encouraged them to do so. An added advantage, in some quarters, was no opportunity for a jury trial—the absence of juries being a central attraction of equity practice for many critics of the common-law courts. Thus, increasing the chances that cases would be settled before trial was one of the explicit aims of the reformers.

As a consequence, two of the more notable features of the "revolution" in the civil courts have been the expansion of "pretrial adjudication" and the transformation of the judge's role from presiding over trials to managing cases, with much of that case management taking place in the pretrial phase. The evidence of this new role is that 75 to 80 percent of all cases are now disposed of "before trial" or

76. Langbein, "Disappearance of Civil Trial," 526.

77. See, for example, Rex P. Perschbacher and Debra Lynn Bassett, "The Revolution of 1938 and Its Discontents," *Oklahoma Law Review* 61 (2008): 275. Stephen N. Subrin refers specifically to the "revolutionary character of the decision inherent in the Federal Rules to make equity procedure available for all cases." Stephen N. Subrin, "How Equity Conquered Common Law: The Federal Rules of Civil Procedure in Historical Perspective," *University of Pennsylvania Law Review* 135, 4 (April 1987): 913.

78. Subrin, "How Equity Conquered Common Law," 1000.

"during or after pretrial" (the categories used in table C-4 of the Administrative Office's annual reports), leaving a diminishing fraction of cases that actually reach the trial stage (and potentially the jury). By contrast, in 1962 only about 20 percent of cases were disposed of in the pretrial phase.[79] Langbein states, borrowing from Emerson: "Build a better mousetrap . . . and the world will beat a path to your door. The Federal Rules built a better mousetrap: a civil procedure centered in pretrial discovery. Litigants no longer go to trial because they no longer need to."[80]

Lawyers frequently cite an old courthouse proverb: "a bad settlement is better than a good trial." Even before the tidal wave of civil cases broke over the federal courts, many of the parties to civil litigation welcomed a way to get from point A to point B without going through a jury. Juries were said to be unpredictable at best and cantankerous at worst, often (it was claimed) seeking revenge against corporate defendants despite the evidence. Even at their best, jury trials seemed an overly long and expensive way to achieve what might be accomplished more quickly during pretrial negotiations, where sensible attorneys sat down at a table and a judge presided over the discussion. Accordingly, the 1938 rules' most important contribution may have been to increase the judges' authority to prescribe, in greater number, the now familiar pretrial exits from litigation: dismissal for "failure to state a claim upon which relief can be granted" (rule 12[b][6]); settlement, the facilitation of which is the express aim of rule 16(a)(5); and summary judgment (rule 56). Rule 50 dispositions—"judgment as a matter of law in a jury trial"—are not pretrial but they are "preverdict," taking away the jury's opportunity to decide the case.[81] In addition, Congress has provided a new pretrial exit from the courtroom in the form of alternative dispute resolution through various court-affiliated programs run by private contractors working under the authority of the court.[82]

As for the fate of the jury system, the authors of the 1938 reforms were not so much enemies of the jury as they were skeptics. As we saw in chapter 3, reformers shared the traditional doubts about using juries in "complex" cases, and many subscribed to the progressive preference for expert judgment over judgment by

79. Galanter, "Vanishing Trials," 482.

80. Langbein, "Disappearance of Civil Trial," 568.

81. There is an interesting passage in the notes to the 1963 amendment to rule 50: "The practice, after the court has granted a motion for a directed verdict, of requiring the jury to express assent to a verdict they did not reach by their own deliberations serves no useful purpose and may give offense to the members of the jury." "Notes of Advisory Committee on Rules—1963 Amendment, Federal Rules of Civil Procedure, Rule 50," http://www.law.cornell.edu/rules/frcp/rule_50 (accessed August 12, 2013).

82. The Alternative Dispute Resolution Act of 1998 states that each federal district court "shall authorize . . . the use of alternative dispute resolution processes in all civil actions" and "shall devise and implement its own alternative dispute resolution program." 28 U.S.C. § 651(b).

amateurs. If the civil jury system was not the reformers' direct target, it was an institution they had doubts about, and they would not have been unhappy to see it diminished, since its outright abolition faced the insurmountable hurdle of the Seventh Amendment. For the most part, the reformers got what they wished for; what happened to the jury system was, as one analyst put it, "collateral damage."[83]

Today, judges are increasingly willing to dismiss lawsuits under rule 12(b)(6): "failure to state a claim upon which relief can be granted." Either judges are getting fussier about what constitutes a strong case or cases in federal court are getting weaker—or perhaps a combination of both. Given the huge increase in the number of cases, it would not be surprising if many of them turned out to be weak, on closer inspection. But for those who see litigation as a way to achieve social change, this development has been a cause of regret. In fact, the higher rate of dismissals may reflect a somewhat more conservative judiciary compared with the 1960s and 1970s. Writing in the *Journal of Empirical Legal Studies*, for example, one research team concludes that America has entered a "post–civil rights era," citing clear evidence that employment discrimination claims now have a low success rate in the federal courts. A very large number of individual claims were filed during the period of the study (1988–2003), many of them (20 percent) pro se cases; nearly one-fifth of these claims were dismissed, a dismissal rate the authors call "significant."[84] They acknowledge that the "blatant discrimination" that inspired the civil rights acts is largely a thing of the past, and that discrimination has now assumed a more subtle form, even operating "below the level of consciousness" of prospective defendants. But a form of discrimination invisible to everyone but plaintiffs and their attorneys might generate cases so weak that they are either dismissed or settled quickly. It is therefore not surprising that these researchers reported that the most frequent outcome for cases surviving dismissal was early settlement (half of all the closed filings). For those cases that did not settle early, plaintiffs lost summary judgment motions more than half the time; of those that survived summary judgment, half settled before trial. Of the cases that actually went to trial—mostly before juries—plaintiffs lost two out of three times. Thus, only 2 percent of all the employment discrimination cases filed during the fifteen years of the study period ended with a trial outcome favorable to the plaintiffs.[85] This is, coincidentally, not much better than the percentage of criminal defendants acquitted by bench and jury trials in federal court (1.4 percent) during the same period.[86]

83. Langbein, "Disappearance of Civil Trial," 572.

84. Laura Beth Nielsen, Robert L. Nelson, and Ryon Lancaster, "Individual Justice or Collective Legal Mobilization? Employment Discrimination Litigation in the Post Civil Rights United States," *Journal of Empirical Legal Studies* 7 (June 2010): 184.

85. Ibid.

86. Administrative Office of the United States Courts, *Annual Report, 2000*, table D-4. Of 75,071 criminal defendants, 603 were acquitted in bench trials, and 440 were acquitted by juries.

Concerns about the growing dismissal rate in the federal courts have been aggravated by two recent Supreme Court decisions: *Bell Atlantic v. Twombly*,[87] from 2007, and *Ashcroft et al. v. Iqbal*,[88] decided in 2009. Although the details and the subject matter of the two cases were very different—*Twombly* was a routine antitrust case, while *Iqbal* grew out of the post-9/11 war on terror—they both made it more difficult for plaintiffs to prevail in federal court. More precisely, these decisions made it more difficult for plaintiffs to carry a civil action as far as the discovery phase. Because "extended" or "aggressive" discovery is now the sweet spot of many civil actions—another consequence of the modern civil procedure regime—a case that is unlikely to reach discovery is unlikely to be filed in the first place, since discovery, rather than victory, is often the true purpose of the suit. From one perspective, *Twombly* and *Iqbal* appear to be an assault on the American right to one's "day in court." From another perspective, however, they represent "a backlash against flimsy complaints being used as a gateway to lengthy, costly discovery."[89] This appears to be the Supreme Court's perspective as well.

Twombly was a class action in which the plaintiff and the class he represented alleged an antitrust violation by telephone carriers, which were accused of conspiring to keep new service providers from entering their markets. Javaid Iqbal had been arrested after the 9/11 attacks, along with some 700 other Muslims living illegally in the United States on expired visas; he claimed, among other allegations, that he had been singled out for prosecution because of his "race, religion, or national origin." Whether these cases were weak is undoubtedly a matter of opinion; certainly, the stakes were much higher than in the typical weak case from previous generations (the classic "slip and fall" case brought against a store owner, for example). *Twombly* could potentially rearrange the cable television industry; *Iqbal* could result in major changes to counterterrorism policies. But there is evidence in both rulings of the courts' impatience with respect to weak cases that present no facts, relying entirely on "conclusory" statements about what would be actionable if certain facts could be discovered or proved.

Twombly was part of the fallout from the breakup, by court order, of AT&T. Breaking the telephone monopoly led to the creation of six regional phone companies, which soon became four. In 1996 Congress passed the Telecommunications Act, which sought to generate additional competition in an industry that had scarcely seen any since the invention of the telephone. The act proclaimed a policy of encouraging competition by requiring existing regional phone companies to share their cable networks with competing carriers that were new to the business, which now included cable television and Internet service providers. When this new competition failed to emerge in any robust way, a class action was filed

87. Bell Atlantic v. Twombly, 550 U.S. 544 (2007).

88. Ashcroft et al. v. Iqbal, 556 U.S. 662 (2009).

89. Brian D. Wassom, "Rule 12(b)(6) Motions: Not Just for 'Little Green Men' Anymore," *Sidebar* (Winter 2010): 6.

alleging violations of the Sherman Antitrust Act. Specifically, plaintiff Twombly alleged that the regional phone companies had become monopolies, conspiring to block competition. The evidence for this allegation was, essentially, the lack of competition and a remark, quoted out of context, by Richard Notebaert, CEO of Qwest, who said that competing in a neighboring territory "might be a good way to turn a quick dollar but that doesn't make it right."[90]

The district court dismissed the complaint, citing previous rulings that the mere demonstration of "parallel business conduct" does not constitute a violation of the Sherman Act. Relying on other precedents (especially *Conley v. Gibson*, a case from 1957), the Second Circuit reversed, holding that the plaintiff's claims were sufficient to withstand a motion to dismiss. *Conley* had simply reaffirmed the traditional high bar for defendants seeking a dismissal: that there must be "no set of facts" that could validate a plaintiff's claims—a view entirely consistent with the traditional understanding that dismissals, like summary judgment, should be reserved for only the weakest cases. Was Twombly's claim, then, above or below the bar? In a decision written by Justice David Souter (from which only Justices Stevens and Ginsburg dissented), the Court either reset the bar for dismissal a smidgen lower or clarified what the *Conley* ruling meant in its full context, beyond the "no set of facts" formula.

Central to the plaintiffs' claims in *Twombly* was the demonstrable lack of competition in the markets dominated by the successors to AT&T: Bell South, Qwest, SBC, and Verizon. These firms controlled 90 percent of telephone service nationwide, but none of them had demonstrated any desire to compete in territories controlled by their "sister" companies. This, Twombly claimed, was evidence of a "contract, combination in the form of trust or otherwise, or conspiracy, in restraint of trade," thus violating section 1 of the Sherman Act. Twombly could cite no facts in support of this claim, however, relying instead on the obvious lack of competition and the remark, quoted above, by Qwest's CEO. In dismissing the case for "failure to state a claim" (rule 12[b][6]), the district court expressly (and somewhat sarcastically) rejected Twombly's claims about the lack of competition. Although circumstantial evidence "of consciously parallel behavior may have made inroads into the traditional judicial attitude toward conspiracy," this type of "conscious parallelism" has "not yet read conspiracy out of the Sherman Act entirely."[91] The decision then detailed the other, nonconspiratorial reasons why the conduct under question might have made good business sense, citing earlier decisions regarding the tobacco industry: "firms in a concentrated market," recog-

90. *Twombly*, 551. The Court noted that the district court "was entitled to take notice of the full contents of the published articles referenced in the complaint, from which the truncated quotations were drawn." According to Notebaert, entering new markets would "not be a sustainable economic model" because the pricing regime mandated by the 1996 law was "nuts" and the regulatory environment was unstable. See ibid., 569, n. 13.

91. Ibid., 552.

nizing their "shared economic interests and their interdependence with respect to price and output decisions," are not necessarily engaged in illegal conduct; "mere interdependence of basic price decisions is not conspiracy."[92]

On the general question of what a plaintiff must show when entering a plea, the decision sought to clarify earlier precedents without necessarily overturning them. Rule 8 requires "a short and plain statement of the claim showing that the pleader is entitled to relief." Although this excuses the plaintiff from the cumbersome recitation of detailed facts required before the rules reforms, it does not, Souter pointed out, relieve the plaintiff of *any* obligation to plead any facts whatsoever. "Factual allegations must be enough to raise a right to relief above the speculative level," and this requires "more than labels and conclusions, and a formulaic recitation of the elements of a cause."[93] Souter was clear about what would happen if this line were not held: a plaintiff with a "largely groundless claim" might be able to "take up the time of a number of other people, with the right to do so representing an in terrorem increment of the settlement value."[94] This is especially a danger in antitrust cases, Souter reasoned, where "proceeding to . . . discovery can be expensive." Quoting a decision from the 1980s, Souter noted that "the costs of modern federal antitrust litigation and the increasing caseload of the federal courts counsel against sending the parties into discovery when there is no reasonable likelihood that the plaintiffs can construct a claim from the events related in the complaint." It would be idle to insist that judges can prevent this sort of "discovery abuse" later in the proceedings—in their charge to the jury, for example—because "the threat of discovery expense will push cost-conscious defendants to settle even anemic cases" before the judge can intervene effectively. That is, they would constitute the modern version of the "strike suit," an old term describing a lawsuit filed for the express purpose of extorting money from a defendant, even when there is little to no hope of winning.

What of the oft-cited *Conley v. Gibson* precedent? In that decision, Justice Hugo Black had argued that a complaint should not be dismissed "unless it appears beyond doubt that the plaintiff can prove no set of facts in support of his claim which would entitle him to relief." Too much has been made, Souter claimed, of the "no set of facts" language in isolation from its context: such a "focused and literal reading" would enable a "wholly conclusory statement of claim" to survive dismissal "whenever the pleadings left open the possibility that a plaintiff might later establish" some set of facts not yet disclosed. "It seems fair to say that this approach to pleading would dispense with any showing of a 'reasonably founded hope' that a plaintiff would be able to make a case. . . . Mr. Micawber's optimism

92. Ibid., quoting Donald F. Turner, "The Definition of Agreement under the Sherman Act," *Harvard Law Review* 75 (1962): 672.

93. *Twombly*, 545.

94. Ibid., 558.

would be enough."[95] Although in the context of *Conley* the "no set of facts" doctrine made sense, out of context, the standard has led to misunderstanding and "has earned its retirement."[96]

What the plaintiff had left, then, was merely a theory—one that might be true but for which the plaintiff had entered no evidence at all. The lack of competition in the cable business did not even require a conspiracy, Souter concluded, since the telecommunications business had been heavily regulated since its earliest days, and monopoly had long been the norm. "A natural explanation for the noncompetition alleged is that the former Government-sanctioned monopolists were sitting tight, expecting their neighbors to do the same." With no facts to support an alternative explanation, the plaintiffs have "not nudged their claims across the line from conceivable to plausible," and so their complaint must be dismissed.[97]

The *Twombly* ruling generated much commentary, nearly all of it critical, and the decision was generally presented as an antiplaintiff ruling that would protect corporate defendants. But on both sides of the commentary, there was some question whether the ruling would be extended beyond the antitrust context of this particular case—some hoped it would not be, and others doubted it could be. That speculation was laid to rest two years later when *Iqbal* was decided by a more divided Court; this time, Justice Souter was in a minority of four, along with Justices Stevens, Ginsburg, and Breyer.

Javaid Iqbal, after being swept up in the post-9/11 search for visa violators from Muslim countries, was identified as one of 184 "high-profile" detainees who were segregated from other prisoners at the Manhattan Detention Center. There, Iqbal claimed, he and the other prisoners were abused by the staff, placed in twenty-three-hour isolation, and forbidden to gather for prayers. He was subsequently convicted on the visa charges, served his sentence, and was deported to his native Pakistan. From there, with the help of the Center for Constitutional Rights, he sued the personnel of the detention center, as well as attorney general John Ashcroft and FBI director Robert Mueller. Iqbal claimed he had been detained simply because of his race, religion, or national origin, and his First Amendment rights had been violated by forbidding him to participate in religious services with other Muslim prisoners. He also claimed he had been subjected to physical and psychological abuse, for which the attorney general should be held responsible.

95. Ibid., 562.

96. Ibid., 563. The facts in *Conley* were far more sympathetic to the plaintiff than those in *Twombly*. Conley and the other plaintiffs were black railroad workers laid off by the company, apparently with the acquiescence of the union to which they belonged. They were all then replaced by white employees, again with the apparent collusion of the union. The likelihood that the plaintiffs would be able to prove these facts meant that the first bar to a lawsuit had been met.

97. Ibid., 547.

Although Iqbal's case raised several issues (including qualified immunity for public officials), the one of interest here is whether, in light of *Twombly*, a complaint can survive a motion to dismiss, thus keeping it before the court and, potentially, before a jury. The district court denied the defendants' motion to dismiss on qualified immunity grounds, but with the *Twombly* decision so recent, the defendants filed an interlocutory appeal in the Second Circuit, which affirmed the district court's ruling. The Supreme Court, however, found that Iqbal's pleadings, like Twombly's, were insufficient to survive a motion to dismiss, and for essentially the same reason: they did not state sufficient facts to anchor a claim of purposeful and unlawful discrimination.

The essential weakness of Iqbal's claim, of course, was the assertion that nothing could explain the roundup of Muslim visa violators except a deliberate effort to discriminate against them because of their religion, ethnicity, or national origin. But what would one expect, Justice Anthony Kennedy asked, in the wake of an attack by Arab Muslim terrorists, many of them in the country on expired visas, except a law enforcement effort that "would produce a disparate, incidental impact on Arab Muslims, even though the purpose of the policy was to target neither Arabs nor Muslims." Like the phone companies' failure to compete, there was an "obvious alternative explanation" for this law enforcement policy other than the illegal and purposeful discrimination alleged by the plaintiff. Given the circumstances, "discrimination is not a plausible conclusion." Neither Iqbal's arrest nor his special treatment as a "high-interest" detainee could be attributed to purposeful racial or religious discrimination. His complaint suggests only that "the Nation's top law enforcement officers, in the aftermath of a devastating terrorist attack, sought to keep suspected terrorists in the most secure conditions available until [they] could be cleared of terrorist activity." Iqbal would have to allege "more by way of factual content" to nudge his claim "across the line from conceivable to plausible."[98]

Like *Twombly*, reaction to the *Iqbal* ruling focused on its likely impact on the future dismissal rate and therefore the prospect that citizens with grievances would be unable to pursue them in federal court. "The court's conservative majority," the *New York Times* opined, "is increasingly using legal technicalities to keep people from getting a fair hearing"—forgetting that the *Twombly* ruling had been written by the not-very-conservative Justice Souter and that only two justices had dissented.

But of course, it is precisely the point of the pleading and dismissal rules that a plaintiff must have a more substantial reason than "wanting a fair hearing" to tie up the resources of the federal courts. And in any case, getting a fair hearing is not the only reason litigants go to court: in an antitrust case, for example, aggressive discovery might be worth a great deal of money to the plaintiffs, even if they have no hope of winning their case. A civil rights case usually does not hold out the prospect of a lucrative settlement or economically valuable discovery, but

98. *Iqbal*, 682, 683 (citing *Twombly*).

it does offer what some would consider a more significant prize: the opportunity to reshape the law by reshaping the existing interpretation of the law in a way that a legislature never would. The aim of the Center for Constitutional Rights, for example, was clearly to undermine the authorities' ability to carry out broad investigations of the American Muslim community to identify terrorist operatives or terrorists-in-the-making. If efforts to use the courts to implement social and legal change are one cause of the courts' growing workload, then decisions like *Twombly* and *Iqbal* should diminish that workload in the future.

The common impression is that more cases settle than in the past, although the data tell a more complex story.[99] "Settlement" is not a separate category in the tables published in the annual reports of the Administrative Office of the United States Courts. As noted above, the Administrative Office identifies a large category of cases that are terminated "before trial" or "during or after pretrial." In 2010, to use a recent example, these two categories accounted for 217,484 terminations out of a total of 284,126 cases filed. Only 3,356 cases were terminated during or after a trial.[100] Thus, more than three-quarters of the cases filed were disposed of before reaching the trial stage, but it is unclear what percentage was "settled." These two categories include cases dismissed for lack of prosecution, summary judgments, judgments on default, dismissals (both voluntary and "other"), and dispositions resulting from an agreement between the plaintiff and defendant, either privately or through one of the many alternative dispute-resolution mechanisms now available through—and often aggressively marketed by—the court.

Efforts to dig deeper into the data, examining docket sheets for selected courts (which record several types of information for each case), make it clear that the common impression that "90 percent of cases settle" is an exaggeration. A more realistic number is in the range of two-thirds, although settlement rates are higher for some categories of cases (torts, for example) and lower for others (employment discrimination cases); they also vary from one federal district to another. Nor is it clear that settlement rates have changed very much over the past few decades.[101]

But there is little doubt that contemporary judges are far more amenable to

99. Stephan Burbank has warned against an overreliance on the data published by the Administrative Office of the United States Courts, which are collected in response to the needs of the court rather than the needs of researchers. In addition, the accuracy of such data is dependent on the diligence of the many separate collectors. It is not possible, he argues, to get a clear picture of either summary judgments or settlements from the Administrative Office tables. Stephen B. Burbank, "Keeping Our Ambition under Control: The Limits of Data and Inference in Searching for the Causes and Consequences of Vanishing Trials in Federal Court," *Journal of Empirical Legal Studies* 1, 3 (November 2004): 571.

100. Administrative Office of the United States Courts, *2010 Annual Report,* 55, table C-4.

101. For a discussion of the difficulty of calculating settlement rates, see Theodore Eisenberg and Charlotte Lanvers, "What Is the Settlement Rate and Why Should We Care?" *Journal of Empirical Legal Studies* 6, 1 (March 2009): 111; Burbank, "Keeping Our Ambition under Control."

settlement than their predecessors were. Here, for example, is a description of the judge's responsibility written in 1977 by Frederick B. Lacey, a judge in the New Jersey District: "The more efficient the judge and the more talented he is as an administrator the more cases he will settle; the fewer he will have to try; and the more days he will have available for administrative duties, status conferences, trial calls, and the like, all of which in turn will generate more dispositions by settlement."[102] A good judge is one who knows how to reduce the need for trials. Judge Lacey acknowledged that this was not the traditional view, and at the time rule 16 was written, many judges objected to active judicial involvement in promoting settlements, viewing such advocacy as interference with the adversary system. But the rule seems to have inspired a more activist role by judges, authorizing the court to direct parties to appear "for a conference to consider . . . such other matters as may aid in the disposition of the action." This, Lacey pointed out, "sanction[s] the active judicial exploration of settlement." And, in any case, times have changed, and "case loads [have] become increasingly burdensome both in number and complexity of suits."[103]

Clearly, in this understanding of the judge's role, efficient case management is meant to prevent trials unless they are absolutely necessary—that is, the litigants refuse to settle either because they are too stubborn or because the judge has failed in his duties as an efficient case manager. Judge Lacey, for example, argued that a judge should "actively and firmly (but not coercively) seek to settle every case on his docket, that he should 'institutionalize,' if you will, the settlement conference."[104] No more than 5 percent of cases should end in trials; the rest, "if not settled by counsel themselves, should be settled with the judge's active participation."[105] This view makes a good deal of sense, of course, in an overworked court with a huge backload of civil cases and a growing number of criminal cases that must be tried quickly (because of judicial rulings and congressional statutes such as the Speedy Trial Act) and therefore take precedence over civil cases.

As the federal caseload continued to grow, the pressure to dispose of cases more quickly grew apace, and the role of the federal district court judge gradually changed, "evolv[ing] from that of a reticent dispenser of justice merely presiding over trial proceedings to one of an active case manager involved in the formulation and direction of civil litigation."[106] This role has gone far beyond what the

102. Hon. Frederick B. Lacey, *The Judge's Role in the Settlement of Civil Suits*, Education and Training Series (Washington, DC: Federal Judicial Center, 1977).

103. Ibid., 3.

104. One can wonder how far a criminal defendant would have gotten in Judge Lacey's court with an effort to distinguish between "firmly" and "coercively."

105. Lacey, *Judge's Role*, 4. Lacy's 5 percent benchmark was reached sometime in the 1990s. See table 2 in this chapter.

106. W. Whitaker Rayner, "Judicial Authority in the Settlement of Federal Civil Cases," *Washington and Lee Law Review* 42 (1985): 171.

drafters of the original rule intended: "The drafters of the original version of rule 16 believed that settlement negotiations had no place in the pretrial conference. . . . The only purpose of pretrial conferences was to narrow issues for trial."[107] Amendments in 1983 changed this, and rule 16(a)(5) now refers explicitly to settlement as one of the topics to be discussed during the pretrial conference.

Increasingly, settlements are the result of negotiations that take place outside the courtroom, through arbitration by professional mediators attached to the court or other forms of dispute resolution. The state courts first began experimenting with alternative methods of dispute resolution, including pretrial arbitration, mediation, or summary jury trials—a practice in which a "mini-jury" of six chosen from the regular jury pool is presented with each side's case and then asked to reach a nonbinding verdict.[108] All these programs preserved the parties' constitutional right to seek redress in court if the alternatives were unsatisfactory.[109] These programs were explicitly defended as a solution to the growth of "time-consuming and expensive" litigation at the state level, and they date to the early 1970s, when the "litigation explosion" first became a topic of conversation and complaint in and around the courts. Some of these state programs were private, and some were annexed to the courts; some were voluntary and others mandatory, with litigants required to at least try one of the dispute-resolution programs being offered.[110]

Inspired by the success of these state programs, Congress passed the Civil Justice Reform Act of 1990, intending to encourage federal courts to develop their own dispute-resolution programs as a response to "expensive and time-consuming trials."[111] Eight years later, Congress reaffirmed and strengthened this intention with the Alternative Dispute Resolution Act, this time requiring federal courts to "authorize" alternative dispute-resolution (ADR) programs.[112] In 2001 federal courts used ADR programs to settle 24,000 cases.[113] By 2011, all federal districts were using some form of ADR, and a study by the Federal Judicial Center, using data from just forty-nine districts, counted more than 28,000 referrals to ADR, most of them to mediation.[114]

Among the objectives of the 1990 act—introduced and managed by Senator Joseph Biden (D-DE)—were to "improve litigation management, and ensure just,

107. Ibid., 176, n. 32.

108. Note that the members of a summary jury trial are not always told that their verdict is nonbinding until after they have reached it.

109. See "Note: Mandatory Mediation and Summary Jury Trial: Guidelines for Ensuring Fair and Effective Processes," *Harvard Law Review* 103, 5 (March 1990): 1086.

110. Ibid., 1086–1087.

111. 28 U.S.C. §§ 471–482.

112. 28 U.S.C. §§ 651–658. See Stipanowich, "ADR and the 'Vanishing Trial,'" 843.

113. Stipanowich, "ADR and the 'Vanishing Trial,'" 849.

114. Donna Stienstra, *ADR in the Federal District Courts: An Initial Report* (Washington, DC: Federal Judicial Center, 2011), 15.

speedy, and inexpensive resolutions of civil disputes."[115] The bill's supporters believed that making civil justice more efficient and less expensive would enable more citizens to have their claims (especially claims against large corporations) heard by neutral arbiters. The legislation was apparently inspired by a 1989 Harris survey that found significant support among plaintiff and defense counsel, public-interest attorneys, corporate counsel, and federal judges for the proposition that "the high cost of litigation unreasonably impedes the ordinary citizen's access to the courts."[116] During the House debate, one member observed, "This is a good bill that will offer our citizens a reasonable and cost-effective alternative to expensive Federal litigation, while at the same time still guaranteeing their right to have their day in court."[117]

Federal courts are now far more hospitable to alternative dispute resolution than the state courts are. Therefore, whenever cases are removed from the states to the federal system, the opportunities for nontrial resolution increase. What is not clear is whether the availability of court-mandated arbitration has increased the inclination to "make a federal case" out of disputes that otherwise might not have ended up in federal court at all.

There is now greater use of rule 50 (judgment as a matter of law) to take decisions away from juries. Judgment as a matter of law is a motion made during the trial, so it is not a trial-avoidance mechanism but rather a jury-avoidance mechanism. The rule states that "if a party has been fully heard on an issue during a jury trial and the court finds that a reasonable jury would not have a legally sufficient evidentiary basis to find for the party on that issue, the court may (a) resolve the issue against the party; and (b) grant a motion for judgment as a matter of law against the party."[118] Among other elements of this rule, the idea that a jury can and should be "reasonable" stands out as something of an anomaly in the age of the "representative" jury, when characteristics such as "reasonable," "intelligent," and "impartial" have been called into question as pretexts for class bias.

Federal judges are also issuing more summary judgments (rule 56). Efforts to expand summary judgment were controversial in the 1930s because of the threat posed to the Seventh Amendment's jury trial guarantee. Students of the courts point out that the procedure was relatively unused until the 1970s, given the federal bench's traditional reluctance to step too rudely (or perhaps too visibly) on the jury's toes.[119] It almost seems as if the new rules could not work as intended

115. Jeffrey J. Peck, "'Users United': The Civil Justice Reform Act of 1990," *Law and Contemporary Problems* 54, 3 (Summer 1991): 105, citing language from the act.

116. Ibid., 107.

117. *Congressional Record—House*, October 10, 1998, H10457–H10459, "Alternative Dispute Resolution Act of 1998."

118. Federal Rules of Civil Procedure 50(a).

119. For a good discussion of this reluctance, see Arthur R. Miller, "The Pretrial Rush to Judgment: Are the 'Litigation Explosion,' 'Liability Crisis,' and Efficiency Cli-

until a generational shift had occurred in the federal courts. A generation of jurists brought up in the older courtroom milieu had to pass from the scene and be replaced by a fresh class of judges with different attitudes toward (among other things) the relative power of judges and juries.

Rule 56 dispositions were understood, long after the 1938 reforms, to be appropriate only in the most clear-cut cases in which there were no disputes about the facts—that is, nothing for the "triers of fact" to try. Summary judgments were used most often in debt-collection cases, for example, where it was easy to establish the fact of an outstanding debt as well as its amount. A 1902 Supreme Court decision set the century's standard: summary judgment exists, the Court observed, to "preserve the court from frivolous defenses and to defeat attempts to use formal pleading as a means to delay the recovery of just demands."[120] But what is a "frivolous" defense? What is a "just demand"? Here is where the judiciary's commitment to the jury system becomes a critical part of the equation. A useful example is provided by a well-known 1946 appellate decision from the Second Circuit featuring a mini-debate between two distinguished jurists, neither of them famous for their enthusiasm for the civil jury: Jerome Frank and Charles E. Clark (one of the authors of the Federal Rules of Civil Procedure).

Frank's doubts about the jury system were well known; he had written, in his 1930 study *Law and the Modern Mind*, that a "better instrument [than the jury] could scarcely be imagined for achieving uncertainty, capriciousness, lack of uniformity, disregard of former decisions—utter unpredictability."[121] The case in question—*Arnstein v. Porter*[122]—seemed perfectly tailored for summary judgment, given the flimsiness of the plaintiff's accusations. Cole Porter was accused of stealing the lyrics and/or the music for several of his best-known works from an otherwise obscure musician named Ira Arnstein, supposedly by sneaking into Arnstein's room or sending "goons" to shadow him. There was no evidence of copying, and Arnstein had a long history of pro se serial litigation. Porter was the fifth in a series of well-known defendants Arnstein had sued for copyright infringement between 1935 and 1946, including ASCAP, BMI, and Twentieth Century Fox. Accordingly, the district court granted Porter's motion for summary judgment. But the Second Circuit reversed (in part) and remanded in a decision written by Justice Frank and joined by Justice Learned Hand. Justice Clark dissented. The Supreme Court denied certiorari.

If ever a case deserved to be tossed out, this one seemed like a good candi-

chés Eroding Our Day in Court and Jury Trial Commitments?" *New York University Law Review* 78 (2003): 982.

120. Fid. & Deposit Co. v. United States, 187 U.S. 315 (1902), at 320, quoted by ibid., 1018.

121. Jerome Frank, *Law and the Modern Mind* (New York: Brentano's, 1930), 172.

122. Arnstein v. Porter, 154 F.2d 464 (1946).

date. Nevertheless, Justice Frank, the jury skeptic, believed the district court had erred in rejecting Arnstein's demand for a jury trial. The question turned, Frank reasoned, on whether "there is the slightest doubt about the facts," citing existing case law. In this particular case, the facts asserted were (1) the very slight similarity between some of Porter's compositions and Arnstein's (which was enough, Frank said, to be "triable" to a jury), and (2) evidence that Porter could have had access to Arnstein's work (in the form of sheet music and recordings) and therefore could have copied it—once again, a fact allegation that belonged to a jury rather than the court. "Each of these two issues—copying and improper appropriation—is an issue of fact," Frank stated. "If there is a trial, the conclusions on those issues of the trier of the facts—of the judge if he sat without a jury, or of the jury if there was a jury trial—bind this court on appeal, provided the evidence supports those findings, regardless of whether we would ourselves have reached the same conclusions." Even if the plaintiff's claims with respect to the facts strike us, Frank wrote, as they struck the trial court, as "fantastic," the "plaintiff's credibility, even as to those improbabilities, should be left to the jury."[123] A more generous definition of the limits of summary judgment would be, in effect, a slippery slope, leading to judges "usurp[ing] the role of juries"—one aspect of which is to judge the credibility of witnesses by hearing and watching their testimony "in open court." Summary judgment precludes such testimony, with the consequence that a trial by jury becomes a trial by affidavit, and "that procedure . . . would . . . often favor unduly the party with the more ingenious and better paid lawyer. Grave injustice might easily result."[124]

In his dissent, Justice Clark noted that Frank's decision seemed to rest on two premises: a belief that juries can settle plagiarism cases, and a dislike of summary judgment. As to the first belief, Clark was not persuaded that judging the merits of musical compositions was something lay jurors would excel at: it was a job for experts rather than amateurs (a familiar progressive principle). Even though popular music like Porter's was aimed at a popular audience (this had been one of Frank's arguments for letting the jury find the facts), there were technical questions presented by the case that would baffle a lay audience—for example, how likely is it that the same three- or four-note phrase would appear, randomly, in two different compositions? "And I should myself hesitate," Clark concluded, "to utter so clear an invitation to exploitation of slight musical analogies by clever musical tricks in the hope of getting juries hereafter in this circuit to divide the wealth of Tin Pan Alley. This holding seems to me an invitation to the strike suit par excellence."[125] As to the second issue—Frank's dislike of summary judgment—Clark insisted that the summary judgment procedure was a necessary and

123. Ibid., 469.
124. Ibid., 471.
125. Ibid., 479.

proper method of disposing of those cases that do "not deserve a protracted and expensive trial"—Arnstein's suit being typical, in Clark's view, of that genus.[126]

For a long time after the adoption of the Federal Rules of Civil Procedure, the Supreme Court leaned in the direction of Frank's view of summary judgment rather than Clark's: that it should be used sparingly so as to protect the right to a jury trial. Ruling in a 1962 antitrust case (*Poller v. CBS, Inc.*), the Court found that "it is only when witnesses are present and subject to cross-examination that their credibility and the weight to be given their testimony can be appraised. Trial by affidavit is no substitute for trial by jury which so long has been the hallmark of 'even handed justice.'"[127] The four justices dissenting in *Poller* argued what Clark had argued in 1946: that the whole purpose of summary judgment was to avoid unnecessary trials in which there were no genuine issues of fact after all pleadings had been entered and the discovery process had come to an end. The minority pointed out that antitrust cases such as *Poller* presented abundant opportunities for frivolous lawsuits, so in this field, above all others, rule 56 should be given "its full legitimate sweep."[128]

Justice John Marshall Harlan, one of the dissenters, noted that the plaintiff had been given complete access to all the witnesses but had not managed to produce any facts that justified his claims of "conspiratorial" or otherwise improper motives on the part of the defendants. Under these circumstances, the case could not have gone to the jury because no "reasonable" jury would have ruled for the plaintiff, based on the evidence in the record.[129] However, the majority's more latitudinarian view in *Poller*—setting a relatively high threshold for granting motions for summary judgment—continued to be the Court's view into the 1980s. Yet summary judgments began to increase. Certainly, the press of business was one reason. As Judge Richard Posner observed, "The expanding federal caseload has contributed to a drift in many areas of federal litigation toward substituting summary judgment for trial. The drift is understandable, given caseload pressures."[130] From roughly the mid-1970s, the percentage of cases in which one or more motions for summary judgment were granted began to increase, slowly but steadily, from 6 percent in 1975 to 12 percent in 2000—making this rise roughly coincident with the increase in the civil caseload. The percentage of cases terminated by summary judgment rose from 3.7 percent in 1975 to 7.7 percent in 2000.[131]

126. Ibid., 480.

127. Poller v. CBS, Inc., 368 U.S. 464 (1962), at 473. For a discussion of this case in the context of summary judgment, see Miller, "Pretrial Rush to Judgment," 1022–1024.

128. Miller, "Pretrial Rush to Judgment," 1023.

129. Ibid., n. 225.

130. Wallace v. SMC Pneumatics, Inc., 103 F.3d 1394, 1397 (7th Cir. 1997), cited in Miller, "Pretrial Rush to Judgment," 1049.

131. Miller, "Pretrial Rush to Judgment," 1049, citing Joe S. Cecil, Deal P. Miletich, and George Cort, *Trends in Summary Judgment Practice: A Preliminary Analysis* (Wash-

Yet there is more than a "drift" in the direction of summary judgment. There is also a "pull"—that is, summary judgment appears to be more appealing to more judges than it was when the Federal Rules of Civil Procedure were written, while at the same time the pull of the jury right has lost some of its force. One possible reason for this change in perspective is the litigiousness that caused the federal caseload to explode in the first place. When more people want to go to court, and there are more and more lawyers to help them do so—as well as a growing body of laws that proclaim ambiguously defined rights—then we might expect more weak cases and, ultimately, less judicial patience.

The decline of civil juries is thus a phenomenon with many causes, but it is not unique to the United States. The United Kingdom, Canada, Australia, and New Zealand have all sharply reduced the opportunities for jury trials in civil cases. Herbert Kritzer reports that in England, "civil trials had largely disappeared . . . by the 1930s. . . . Those few jury trials that do occur are in cases such as libel and slander, or damage claims related to alleged police misconduct."[132] A 1999 study of English courts found that "less than one percent of civil trials [were] jury trials."[133] In Canada there is a similar pattern of declining civil trials—not just a decline in filings but also a decline in trials as a percentage of filings, "mimicking some of the same pattern as is happening in the United States. As in the United States, there has been an emphasis on judicial facilitation of settlement, and . . . alternative dispute resolution."[134] The civil jury in New Zealand is available in the High (Supreme) Court, at the request of either party, but its use is "so rare that the Department of the Courts no longer even keeps statistics on it."[135] Civil juries are still used in Australia, but in a "decreasing minority of cases."[136]

---

ington, DC: Federal Judicial Center, 2001). There is some dispute about how much influence a "trilogy" of Supreme Court cases in 1986 had on the growth of summary judgment, since there is evidence that summary judgments were increasing before those cases were decided. The cases are Matsushita Electric Industrial Co. v. Zenith Radio Corp., 475 U.S. 574 (1986); Anderson v. Liberty Lobby, Inc., 477 U.S. 242 (1986); and Celotex Corp. v. Catrett, 477 U.S. 317 (1986). Data collected by the Federal Judicial Center and reported in the study by Cecil et al. found that the increase dates from the early 1970s.

132. Herbert M. Kritzer, "Disappearing Trials? A Comparative Perspective," *Journal of Empirical Legal Studies* 1, 3 (November 2004): 738.

133. Sally Lloyd-Bostock and Cheryl Thomas, "Decline of the 'Little Parliament': Juries and Jury Reform in England and Wales," *Law and Contemporary Problems* 62 (Spring 1999): 12.

134. Kritzer, "Disappearing Trials?" 747.

135. Neil Cameron, Susan Potter, and Warren Young, "The New Zealand Jury," *Law and Contemporary Problems* 62 (Spring 1999): 109.

136. Michael Chesterman, "Criminal Trial Juries in Australia: From Penal Colonies to a Federal Democracy," *Law and Contemporary Problems* 62 (Spring 1999): 69, n. 1.

Because the civil jury is protected in the United States by constitutional language beyond the reach of simple legislative majorities, its formal abolition is virtually impossible. Yet the marginalization of the civil jury in modern America is almost as stark as it has been in those regimes where constitutional rights are trumped by the principle of parliamentary supremacy. Even if the reformers of the 1930s did not intend this result, it is hard to believe that many of them would be unhappy that it has finally come to pass.

SENTENCING REFORM AND THE VANISHING CRIMINAL JURY

Reform of the sentencing regime in the federal courts was an idea conceived in the 1960s, but it did not come to fruition until the 1980s, largely because of legislative disagreement over how much sentencing discretion should be left in the hands of federal judges. President Lyndon Johnson had been persuaded that sentencing disparities in the federal courts were causing the public to "lose faith in the criminal justice system," partly because some of those disparities could be blamed on racism, but also because sentencing often seemed arbitrary, with some judges handing down harsh sentences and others erring on the side of leniency for the same offenses. With the exception of those stemming from racial bias, these sentencing disparities were the inevitable consequence of federal judges' long-standing discretion, and reform threatened that tradition. The sticking point was how much sentencing discretion judges would be allowed to retain; some Senate liberals, such as Gary Hart, insisted they should have none.[137]

The initial effort took the form of a commission, chaired by California governor Edmund G. Brown, to study the reform of the criminal code and sentencing at the same time. The Brown Commission's final report, issued in 1971, was concerned largely with criminal code reform (this proved to be a nonstarter), but it also introduced an important idea about sentencing reform: the promulgation of a set of "sentencing guidelines" for federal judges, intended to steer them away from what was routinely referred to as "unwarranted sentencing disparities."

Sentencing reform was given a boost by the 1973 publication of *Criminal Sentences: Law without Order*, a broad attack on sentencing practices by federal judge Marvin E. Frankel.[138] Like President Johnson, Judge Frankel believed that sentencing disparity was at the heart of the public's alleged "loss of faith" in

137. See Stith and Koh, "Politics of Sentencing Reform," 233. For a discussion of the liberal position in the Senate debate, see ibid., 239–242. See also Stith and Carbanes, *Fear of Judging*, 38–77.

138. Hon. Marvin E. Frankel, *Criminal Sentences: Law without Order* (New York: Hill & Wang, 1973).

the courts. Senator Edward Kennedy was particularly moved by this argument; he was soon joined by Senator Strom Thurmond (whose interest was mainly in curbing judicial leniency), and together they pushed for an independent sentencing commission whose members would produce a set of guidelines for use in the federal courts.

After several stops and starts, this plan became the Sentencing Reform Act, Title II of the Comprehensive Crime Control Act of 1984. The actual reform of sentencing practices, however, would be undertaken not by Congress but by an administrative Sentencing Commission, whose members would compose the guidelines. Judges would be required to choose a mandatory sentence from within the narrow range set out in the guidelines, taking into account various "sentencing factors" as well as the particular charges the defendant had been found guilty of. When finally promulgated and approved by Congress, the sentencing guidelines presented judges with a complicated grid (and a 500-page instruction manual), with the offense categories on one axis and the sentencing factors (use of a gun, possession of a large quantity of drugs, extent of the harm suffered by victims, and so forth) on the other.[139] The judge would be "free" to choose a sentence from inside the appropriate box on the grid, factoring in all the offense elements and whatever sentencing factors the judge thought appropriate. Judge Brock Hornby has described the result as "surreal," with judges talking "in algebraic formulae ('base offense level under Guideline 2D1.1(c)(4), enhancement for role in the offense under Guideline 3B1.1')," defendants looking "like deer caught in the headlights," and the extent of the judge's sentencing discretion sometimes reduced to as little as six months.[140]

There is no evidence that anyone involved in this debate—which took place in nearly every session of Congress between 1966 and the bill's passage in 1984—gave any thought to the collateral damage the sentencing guidelines might do to the jury system.[141] But that damage was serious, in two ways. First,

139. Kristina Walter, "Note: *Booker* and Our Brave New World: The Tension among Federal Sentencing Guidelines, Judicial Discretion, and a Defendant's Constitutional Right to Trial by Jury," *Cleveland State Law Review* 53 (2005–2006): 662–663.

140. D. Brock Hornby, "Speaking in Sentences," *Green Bag* 14 (Winter 2011): 149. The sentencing grid, as of 1998, is reproduced as appendix A in Stith and Cabranes, *Fear of Judging*, 179–180. For each offense level (there are forty-three in all) there are six "criminal history categories," and each category can generate a number of "criminal history points."

141. Nancy Gertner, "Circumventing Juries, Undermining Justice: Lessons from Criminal Trials and Sentencing," *Suffolk University Law Review* 32, 3 (1999): 427–428; Rachel E. Barrow, "Recharging the Jury: The Criminal Jury's Constitutional Role in an Era of Mandatory Sentencing," *University of Pennsylvania Law Review* 152, 1 (November 2003): 33. Barrow concludes that "legislators . . . seemed to enact these mandatory sentencing laws believing that their only effect was on judges, not juries. But to describe the effect of mandatory sentencing laws on judges tells only half the story" (37).

by dividing the criminal code into ever more precise sections and subsections, the guidelines gave prosecutors additional opportunities to multiply counts for what was, in essence, a single crime (e.g., a charge of robbery might be enhanced by the additional charge of "brandishing," because the defendant's gun was visible under his T-shirt). And because the sentences were frequently longer than they had been in the past, prosecutors were given a nearly ideal bargaining opportunity, described by Albert Alschuler as a "prosecutor's paradise."[142] Defendants could be charged with several separate counts that added up to very long prison terms, or they could plead guilty in return for fewer charges—in effect, a reduced sentence. A routine bank robbery might involve seventeen different counts, with a particular sentencing range for each; or it could be reduced to seven counts, with considerably less prison time. Second, for those defendants who chose to stand trial, before either a judge or a jury, the sentencing guidelines increased the significance of the "sentencing factors" the judge could take into account should the defendant be convicted—including factors not heard by the jury or even entered as evidence during the trial.

As Judge Nancy Gertner has pointed out, plea bargaining and the incorporation of sentencing factors not proved in court were both traditional elements of federal criminal practice, making the changes wrought by the Sentencing Reform Act more a matter of "degree" than of "kind."[143] In the past, however, that discretion had belonged to judges rather than prosecutors—precisely the problem the sentencing guidelines meant to overcome.[144] For example, in the federal courts, judges could add or subtract from sentences based on nontrial factors such as the defendant's previous record. The late-nineteenth-century birth of the "therapeutic" model of incarceration, a Progressive Era vision of psychological rehabilitation rather than punishment as the purpose of prison time, gave judges even more discretion. The judge became a clinician, applying his particular expertise to the job of giving a convicted defendant the precise punishment that would help him "recover" from the "moral disease" of criminality. As with any therapeutic model, the professional closest to the case would have the greatest chance of finding the appropriate cure—and would need enough leeway to do so efficiently. Similar arrangements could be found in most state courts, although some states continued the republican-era practice of letting the jury determine the sentence.[145]

142. That the practice of mandatory sentencing was a "boon" to prosecutors is discussed by, among many others, Barrow, "Recharging the Jury"; Albert W. Alschuler, "The Failure of Sentencing Guidelines: A Plea for Less Aggregation," *University of Chicago Law Review* 58 (1991): 901; and Gertner, "Circumventing Juries."

143. Gertner, "Circumventing Juries," 422.

144. "From the beginning of the Republic, federal judges were entrusted with wide sentencing discretion." Stith and Cabranes, *Fear of Judging*, 9.

145. As of this writing, there are still five states that give juries the right to determine sentences in criminal trials: Arkansas, Missouri, Oklahoma, Texas, and Virginia. Morris

Gertner writes that, under the old regime, the sentencing discretion of judges was sometimes "stunning."[146] In 1949 the Supreme Court upheld the death penalty for a defendant convicted of first-degree murder by a New York State jury. The jury had recommended a life term, but based on allegations brought up during the sentencing hearing (the defendant displayed a "morbid sexuality," was a "career criminal," and was responsible for a series of unsolved burglaries—"facts" that could not have been admitted in evidence at his trial), the judge ignored the jury's recommendation and imposed the death penalty instead. The Supreme Court found that the introduction of unproved sentencing factors raised no constitutional questions.[147] As recently as 1990, the Court upheld the death penalty in a state homicide case, based on the judge's finding of an "aggravating factor" (that the killing was "especially heinous, cruel, or depraved"), which in turn was based on facts not entered into evidence at the trial.[148]

Nevertheless, "indeterminate sentencing" in the federal courts was not especially controversial until the 1960s, in part because Congress was firmly in charge of writing the laws and determining the range of punishment for each species of federal crime. Furthermore, until the late 1960s, federal criminal prosecutions were rare. The only federal homicide statutes concerned Indian reservations and ships at sea; not even the killing of a federal official was a federal crime until a few years after the assassination of President Kennedy. In 1956 the federal courts reported only one homicide prosecution, but 624 prosecutions for violations of the

Hoffman, "The Case for Jury Sentencing," *Duke Law Journal* 52 (2002–2003): 951, n. 1. Juries never determined sentences in the federal courts; even in the republican era, attaching a sentence to a particular crime was understood to be the job of the legislature. Sentences were straightforward, and "pronouncement of the sentence by a judge was an essentially ministerial task." See Gertner, "Circumventing Juries," 424.

146. Gertner, "Circumventing Juries," 425.

147. Williams v. New York, 337 U.S. 241 (1949). Justice Murphy, in one of two separate dissents (the other was by Justice Rutledge), noted that "the [trial] judge exercised his discretion to deprive a man of his life in reliance on material made available to him in a probation report consisting almost entirely of evidence that would have been inadmissible at the trial. Some, such as allegations of prior crimes, was irrelevant. Much was incompetent as hearsay. All was damaging, and none was subject to scrutiny by the defendant" (253).

148. Walton v. Arizona, 497 U.S. 639 (1990). This was the first decision suggesting that the Court had doubts about the extent to which judges could use sentencing factors beyond what juries had found "beyond a reasonable doubt." Justice White wrote the decision, joined by Chief Justice Rehnquist and Justices O'Connor, Scalia, and Kennedy. But Justice Scalia wrote a separate concurrence, and there were three separate dissents: by Justice Brennan (joined by Justice Marshall), by Justice Blackmun (joined by Justices Brennan, Marshall, and Stevens), and by Justice Stevens, foreshadowing the majority decision he would compose in *Apprendi v. New Jersey* in 2000, discussed below.

migratory bird laws and more than 1,000 prosecutions for juvenile delinquency.[149] Like criminal defendants in the state courts, most federal defendants chose to plead guilty rather than face a trial, without any special encouragement or pressure from prosecutors. From the nineteenth century through the 1960s, judicial controversies in federal court concerned mostly civil trials, except for those few criminal cases that raised constitutional questions (e.g., interfering with enforcement of the Fugitive Slave Act or racial discrimination in jury selection) or that presented juries with the rare opportunity to apply the death penalty when they were reluctant to do so (e.g., *Sparf and Hansen*).

By the time there was a hint of trouble, the new sentencing regime had been in operation for more than a decade. In *Jones v. United States*, decided in 1999, Jones had been convicted of the brand-new federal crime of carjacking, and the sentencing guidelines provided that if the victim of a carjacking suffered "serious bodily injury," the defendant would have to serve additional time in prison.[150] But Jones's indictment had not included a charge of causing bodily harm, serious or otherwise, and the jury had heard no evidence regarding injuries to the victim. At the sentencing hearing, however, the trial judge ruled that, because of the victim's injuries, the sentence would be increased beyond the maximum for carjacking per se. The defendant appealed, and the Supreme Court reversed, stating that the alleged injury was an element of the case that should have been decided by the jury; without such a finding, it could not figure in the sentence. The Court based this decision not on constitutional principles but on the language of the carjacking statute itself. However, the Court provided a warning, in the form of a footnote, that the distinction between an "element" and a mere "sentencing factor" might have to be reconsidered in light of the Constitution's protection of the jury right.[151]

That reconsideration came one year later when the Court decided *Apprendi v. United States*, brought by a defendant convicted of firing shots into the home of an African American family in his New Jersey neighborhood, presumably to frighten the family away.[152] The New Jersey firearms law defined the use of a firearm for "an unlawful purpose" as a second-degree offense, with a sentence of seven to ten years. (New Jersey, like many states, had followed the federal lead and established its own sentencing guidelines for use in state court.) The New Jersey "hate crime" statute extended the term of imprisonment (to a maximum of ten to twenty years) if the firearms offense was motivated by "racial hostility." Accordingly, the state trial judge handed down a maximum sentence of ten years for the firearms

149. Administrative Office of the United States Courts, *Annual Report of the Director, 1956*, 248, table D-2.

150. Jones v. United States, 526 U.S. 227 (1999). On the implications of the Sentencing Reform Act for jury trials, see Hoffman, "Case for Jury Sentencing."

151. *Jones*, 331, n. 11; see also Hoffman, "Case for Jury Sentencing," 976.

152. Apprendi v. United States, 530 U.S. 466 (2000).

violation and an additional two years for the hate-crime "sentencing factor." The defendant appealed his conviction on the grounds that he had been denied a constitutional jury trial. The Supreme Court reversed, in a five-to-four decision written by Justice Stevens and joined by the unusual lineup of Justices Scalia, Souter, Thomas, and Ginsburg. The dissent was written by Justice O'Connor and joined by Justices Kennedy and Breyer and by Chief Justice Rehnquist.[153] Breyer also wrote a separate dissent, joined by Rehnquist, and Scalia and Thomas each wrote separate concurring opinions.

Stevens argued that a defendant's sentence cannot be increased because of the presence of facts not found by the jury, other than the fact of recidivism, which had long been accepted as a justification for increased penalties. The question raised by *Apprendi* "was foreshadowed," Stevens wrote, "by our opinion in *Jones v. United States*," where the Court noted that "under the Due Process Clause of the Fifth Amendment and the notice and jury trial guarantees of the Sixth Amendment, any fact (other than prior conviction) that increases the maximum penalty for a crime must be charged in an indictment, submitted to a jury, and proven beyond a reasonable doubt." *Jones* concerned a federal law, but the "Fourteenth Amendment commands the same answer" in the case of a state law. Quoting Story and Blackstone, Justice Stevens stated that the "historical foundation for our recognition of these principles extends down centuries into the common law," which looked to the jury to "guard against a spirit of oppression and tyranny on the part of rulers" (Story) and required that "the truth of every accusation" should be confirmed by twelve "equals and neighbors" (Blackstone).[154] Stevens insisted that the decision did not raise any constitutional doubts about the authority of judges to issue sentences within certain ranges specified by the legislature. The question was simply whether sentencing enhancement could be based on facts not found by a jury.

O'Connor's dissent shifted the focus from the authority of the jury to the Court's traditional willingness to let legislatures define both punishments and, within reasonable limits, those sentencing factors that need not be proved "beyond a reasonable doubt." She accused the majority of "cast[ing] aside our traditional cautious approach" and embracing "a universal and seemingly bright-line rule limiting the power of Congress and state legislatures to define criminal offenses and the sentences that follow from convictions thereunder." There is no precedent, she argued, in the "200 years since the ratification of the Bill of Rights," for insisting on the rule that the Court "announces today." The Court's decision, O'Connor was certain, would "halt the current debate on sentencing reform in its tracks and . . . invalidate with the stroke of a pen three decades' worth of nationwide reform,

153. In the cases dealing with the sentencing guidelines, Chief Justice Rehnquist did not write a separate dissent. His particular views, to the extent they may have diverged from those of O'Connor et al., are unknown, at least from the Court record.

154. *Apprendi*, 477.

all in the name of a principle with a questionable constitutional pedigree." And she predicted that this line of argument would eventually undermine the very idea of "determinate sentencing" at both the state and federal levels.[155]

And yet this argument seems to miss the point of the majority's ruling, which did not deny the legislature's right to define the punishment for a crime (in this case, intimidation motivated by racial hatred) but only a judge's right to punish someone who had not actually been convicted of that crime. A crime that adds to a sentence is, presumably, another crime—not a "behavioral characteristic" (Stevens's term) such as lack of remorse or being a habitual criminal. In fact, it was the intention of the New Jersey legislature to "criminalize" racial hatred—thus the term "hate crime." But much of the debate over the Court's sentencing decisions has followed Justice O'Connor down this misleading path, attempting to prove what the *Apprendi* majority did not deny—namely, that the legislature might establish sentencing guidelines that limited the discretion of judges.

Justice Breyer's separate dissent (joined by Rehnquist) was in some respects more radical than O'Connor's. Whereas she argued for caution with respect to the prerogatives of the legislature, Breyer posited a rather sharp dichotomy between two visions of government—one with a citizen jury at its center, and the other with a bureaucrat at its center, or the old republican way versus the new way of government by experts. He then came down decisively on the side of the latter.[156] Breyer began by insisting that the "procedural ideal . . . of juries, not judges, determining the . . . facts upon which increased punishment turns" did not fit the circumstances of "the real world of criminal justice." The world has changed, and the law must catch up, whatever the consequences for juries. The real world needs "procedural compromises, particularly in respect to sentencing." Such compromise "precludes" the jury-centric model the majority insisted on, and because that model is "impractical," it is not possible to believe that the Constitution was "intended to embody it." Thus it is that in "modern times, the law has left it to the sentencing judge" to decide which facts will enhance an offender's sentence. Breyer's explanation of this view included such traditional sentencing factors as recidivism, as well as matters the majority decision considered "elements" of a crime, such as the use of a weapon, the amount of money stolen, or the amount of drugs distributed.[157]

155. Ibid., 524–525, 550, 551–552.

156. Before he was appointed to the Supreme Court, Justice Breyer served as a member of the US Sentencing Commission (1985–1989) and was one of the authors of the sentencing guidelines. He is also the author of two books on administrative law, written while he was teaching at the Kennedy School: *Regulation and Its Reform* (Cambridge, MA: Harvard University Press, 1982) and *Breaking the Vicious Circle: Toward Effective Risk Regulation* (Cambridge, MA: Harvard University Press, 1993).

157. *Apprendi*, 555.

According to Breyer, judges, not juries, have traditionally "determined the presence or absence of such sentence-affecting facts in any given case"—and not for a theoretical reason but for a "practical one." It is not "procedural fairness" that is at stake but rather "an administrative need." There are too many "potentially relevant sentencing factors to permit submission of all (or even many) of them to a jury": gun or no gun, hidden gun or brandished gun, lots of drugs or just a little, really bad motives or just ordinarily bad motives, alone or in the company of other criminals, under or not under the influence of alcohol and/or narcotics?[158] Not for the first time, the use of a jury would slow down and complicate the process of judicial decision making. Letting judges make their own decisions about sentencing factors would be one way to speed things up.

There is more than a little irony in this dissent. In his previous life as an administrative law professor, Justice Breyer had been one of the architects of the sentencing guidelines, helping to bring to fruition the most significant reform of the criminal law in a generation. That reform had started out with the aim of reducing the sentencing discretion of federal judges, the "progressive" preference being no discretion at all. Now Breyer was making a spirited defense of that very discretion, on the grounds that it brought expertise to bear on the sentencing decision, saving time and effort and delivering a more rational and efficient result.

But why are there so many factors in the first place—especially if economy of effort is the goal? Why don't prosecutors simply pick those elements of the crime that are most likely to result in conviction and present those to the jury, leaving the judge whatever sentencing discretion the legislature chooses to allow? This was the process in the old days, before the *United States Code* swelled to thirty volumes and before a single burglary could generate a twenty-count indictment. There is one possible answer to this question, and it concerns the other half of the political compromise that made the Sentencing Reform Act possible: the desire to see more criminals sent to prison for longer terms. The sentencing guidelines, by breaking down felonies into many separate compartments with narrow sentencing ranges for each—to limit the discretion of judges—have given prosecutors the opportunity to multiply counts. Multiplying counts means multiplying sentence fragments, maximizing the odds that a prosecutor can persuade a defendant to plead guilty rather than face additional years in prison for each separate count of the indictment. The Sentencing Reform Act took discretion away from judges and gave it to prosecutors. The predictable (but apparently not anticipated) result was the rapid growth of plea bargaining noted at the beginning of this chapter, making the jury's role in the criminal justice system smaller than it has ever been. In 1980, 63.2 percent of defendants in federal court entered guilty or nolo contendere pleas; in 2014, that percentage had shot up to just under 90 percent. In 1980, 12.8 percent of federal defendants had their cases disposed of by jury trials; by 2014,

158. Ibid., 557.

that number had dropped to 2.2 percent—although the more serious the felony, the less likely a defendant is to plead guilty.[159]

Justice Antonin Scalia found Breyer's argument disturbing enough to devote a short concurrence to it, pointing out that Breyer's understanding departed from the tradition of common-law trials in favor of something presumably more efficient and up-to-date. Scalia wrote, "[Breyer] sketches an admirably fair and efficient scheme of criminal justice designed for a society that is prepared to leave criminal justice to the State." But we have juries precisely because the founders chose not to leave criminal justice to the state, "which is why the jury-trial guarantee was one of the least controversial provisions of the Bill of Rights. It has never been efficient; but it has always been free." Breyer's implication that juries in "modern times" are not as efficient as judges at providing "fairness" inspired scorn: how is it fair for a man to be sentenced for a crime (acting out of racial hatred) for which he has not been tried or even indicted? Scalia continued:

> In Justice Breyer's bureaucratic realm of perfect equity . . . the facts that determine the length of a sentence . . . will be determined to exist (on a more-likely-than-not basis) by a single employee of the State. It is certainly arguable (Justice Breyer argues it) that this sacrifice of prior protections is worth it. But it is not arguable that, just because one thinks it is a better system, it must be, or is even more likely to be, the system envisioned by a Constitution that guarantees trial by jury.[160]

The argument laid out in *Apprendi* was affirmed and strengthened in several cases that followed—*Ring v. Arizona* (2002), *Blakely v. Washington* (2004), and *United States v. Booker* (2005) being the most important. As in *Apprendi*, the focus of the majority continued to be the importance of the jury right—not just as a private right possessed by defendants but also as a fundamental element of a republican political order designed to limit the power of the government. The circumstances presented by these cases suggest that, although Gertner was no

159. See table 5 in this chapter. These are the data presented by the Administrative Office of the United States Courts. The data collected by the US Sentencing Commission tell a more alarming story: using slightly different data sets, the commission found that the plea rate in 2003 was 97.1 percent. US Sentencing Commission, *Mode of Conviction in U.S. District Courts for U.S. Sentencing Commission Guideline Cases, Sourcebook of Criminal Justice Statistics* (2003), 439. See Nancy Gertner, "From 'Rites' to 'Rights': The Decline of the Criminal Jury Trial," *Yale Journal of Law and Humanities* 24 (2012): 436. A 2002 study found that, taking state and federal courts together, murder and rape cases are much more likely to go to trial (40 percent and 25 percent of cases, respectively). See Kimberly A. Mottley et al., "The Jury's Role in Administering Justice in the United States: An Overview of the American Criminal Jury," *St. Louis University Public Law Review* 21 (2002): 111.

160. *Apprendi*, 498–499.

doubt correct when she said the Sentencing Reform Act represented a change of "degree" rather than "kind," the distinction was getting harder to spot.

In *Ring v. Arizona* the defendant had been convicted in state court of "felony murder during the course of a robbery." He had been part of a gang that hijacked an armored car and killed the driver. The jury that convicted Ring was not convinced that he was the killer or even that he had played a leading role in the crime, which is why it did not convict him of premeditated murder. The jury recommended a life sentence, even though it could have recommended the death penalty. At the sentencing hearing, however, Ring's partners in crime made claims about him that had not been made during the trial and the truth of which the jury had never considered: that Ring was the leader of the gang, that he had in fact been the shooter, and that he had even "bragged about his marksmanship." If the jury had heard these allegations, and if the state had been prepared to prove them, the jury might well have reached a different sentencing recommendation or even a different verdict. Based on these new and unproved allegations, however, the trial judge set aside the jury's recommendation and sentenced Ring to death, an authority he clearly possessed under a state sentencing law the Supreme Court had upheld twelve years earlier in its *Walton v. Arizona* ruling.[161]

This time, Justice Ruth Bader Ginsburg wrote the decision, reversing the death sentence and applying the *Apprendi* principles to capital cases, overruling *Walton*. Justices Kennedy and Breyer concurred this time—Kennedy insisting that *Apprendi*, though wrongly decided, was now the law of the land, and Breyer basing his concurrence on the Eighth Amendment's prohibition of "cruel and unusual punishment." Justices O'Connor and Rehnquist stuck to their guns, stating that the Court should have overruled *Apprendi* instead of *Walton*.

But the most interesting of the five separate opinions generated by *Ring* was the concurrence written by Justice Scalia, joined by Justice Thomas. Once again, Scalia provided a spirited defense of the jury, noting that "over the past 12 years" there had been an "accelerating propensity of both state and federal legislatures to adopt 'sentencing factors' determined by judges that increase punishment beyond what is authorized by the jury's verdict." To his dismay, he had watched as "a near majority of my colleagues [stated their belief] that this novel practice is perfectly OK." As a result, it was increasingly clear that "our people's traditional belief in the right of trial by jury is in perilous decline."[162]

Scalia's reference here to "our people's traditional belief" must, I think, be understood as a rebuke directed at the legal profession, since the statement references the decline in "belief" rather than the decline in the jury trial itself and makes no claims about public opinion. But sooner or later, judges' and attorneys' disregard for the jury will establish a dangerous pattern: preserving our "vener-

161. Walton v. Arizona, 497 U.S. 639 (1990).
162. Ring v. Arizona, 536 U.S. 584 (2002), at 611–612.

ation" for the jury system will be impossible in a legal order that imposes the death penalty without it. States are free, of course, to let judges impose the death penalty, just as they are free to impose other penalties—provided the "factors" or "elements" supporting the sentence have either been admitted by the defendant or proved to a jury beyond a reasonable doubt.

But why is it important to preserve the jury system in the criminal courts? In *Blakely v. Washington*,[163] decided in 2004, Scalia returned to the theme first touched on in *Apprendi*—that the jury right is "no mere procedural formality" but a core element of the republican government established by the Constitution. It is "a fundamental reservation of power" meant to ensure popular control of the judiciary and, through the judiciary, of government in general. If the authority to issue verdicts were severed from the authority to determine sentences, the jury's power would be crippled. The alternative to the *Apprendi* rule, in other words, is a judicial system in which the jury decides that the defendant "at some point did something wrong, a mere preliminary to a judicial inquisition into the facts of the crime the State actually seeks to punish."[164]

What the dissenters in the *Apprendi*, *Ring*, and *Blakely* cases feared would happen finally did happen in a 2005 case, in which the United States appealed two separate appellate court reversals of sentences handed out to defendants convicted of cocaine distribution, based on the guidelines promulgated by the US Sentencing Commission. The two cases were decided together, in *United States v. Booker*.[165] *Booker* produced two different majority decisions covering different constitutional questions, as well as four dissents involving four different elements of the decision. The Court's first majority (Stevens, Scalia, Souter, Thomas, and Ginsburg, in part) applied the *Apprendi* principle to the two cases and ruled that the facts found by the judges could not be used to increase the sentences because they had not been found by a jury. Justice Breyer, in a separate opinion (joined by Rehnquist, O'Connor, Kennedy, and Ginsburg, in part), found that the appropriate remedy was to rule that the two sections of the Sentencing Reform Act that made the sentencing guidelines mandatory were unconstitutional but severable from the rest of the act, which remained in force. In a separate dissent, Scalia scolded the Court for trying to defend the limitations on judicial discretion by finding unconstitutional the very sections of the law that effectively controlled that discretion. Stevens, joined by O'Connor and Scalia, reminded the Court that *Apprendi* did not require voiding the mandatory nature of the guidelines, so long as each sentencing factor was first proved to the jury. Justices Breyer, Rehnquist, O'Connor, and Kennedy (in part) insisted, as had the first three in the previous cases, that, with respect to sentencing decisions or the factors used by judges to arrive at particular sentences, there was no such thing as a right to a jury trial.

163. Blakely v. Washington, 542 U. S. 296 (2004).
164. Ibid., 306–307.
165. United States v. Booker, 543 U.S. 220 (2005).

The *Booker* case, with its complex mixture of decisions and dissents, made the sentencing guidelines effectively advisory, while leaving the sentencing grid intact. Only time will tell how much judges will depart from the sentencing ranges indicated by that grid. But with respect to the impact of the Sentencing Reform Act on the jury system, the Court's decisions from *Apprendi* through *Booker* leave the plea-bargaining powers of federal prosecutors more or less where they were before.[166] That is, prosecutors can still charge defendants with many separate counts, based on their judgment of which charges can be proved to the jury. The resulting sentences will almost certainly be long enough to dissuade defendants, except in exceptional cases, from rolling the dice if the offered plea bargain promises a much better deal. This means that, in the future, jury trials will resolve even fewer cases than the 2.2 percent recorded in 2014.

DOES THE VANISHING TRIAL MATTER?

Given the many reasons for the vanishing trial—and with it, the vanishing jury—shouldn't we accept its decline as a natural development? Isn't the reluctance to go to trial in civil matters a rational response to the economic facts of life? Why should we worry that there are fewer trials or that juries are deciding such a small fraction of civil and criminal cases, as long as the jury continues to be constitutionally protected?

There is no doubting how most members of the legal community would have answered these questions in the past. Defending the jury has been a constant theme in the literature of the law, as well as in ordinary political debate. In the republican era the jury scarcely needed defending, so deeply ingrained was the idea of the jury as the "lower house" of the judiciary. There were no opponents of jury trials in criminal cases, and the occasional contrarian voice in opposition to civil juries spoke in very circumspect terms. Even in the twentieth century, true contrarians—who objected to jury trials per se—were content to be lonely voices crying in the wilderness (e.g., Jerome Frank in the 1930s).

But the profound changes in the American legal system that began in the 1930s were followed, a generation later, by an equally profound change in the way the legal community understood the jury system and the law itself. The simplest way to characterize this change is to note its solid grounding in earlier changes in the American political system and, in particular, the increasing reliance, since the

166. Justice Scalia writes in his *Blakely* opinion that, "given the sprawling scope of most criminal codes, and the power to affect sentences by making (even nonbinding) sentencing recommendations, there is already no shortage of *in terrorem* tools at prosecutors' disposal" (311). But so far, plea bargaining per se has not been the subject of a serious constitutional challenge.

1930s, on administrative government in preference to the old regime of "courts and parties," in which administrators played a decidedly subordinate role and courts were willing to defer to the judgment of legislatures except in rare cases of constitutional urgency.[167] In this regime, the trial had pride of place in the legal order, and lay juries were both statistically and politically more significant. They invited citizens to participate directly in ruling; they gave assurances that no man could lose life, liberty, or property without the consent of his fellows; and they yoked the government to the public by giving the public the right, and the power, to say no to prosecutions.

The jury, however, is the ultimate form of amateur decision making. It is therefore the bane of all those who value consistency, regularity, professionalism, and expertise—a tribe that has increased mightily since the dawn of the Progressive Era. As America moved in the direction of a more progressive legal culture, it was inevitable that the jury would be devalued. As we saw earlier, it was the progressives and the "legal realists"—exalting expertise, doubting juries' ability to decide complex questions—who fired the first salvos. In the view of an increasingly important faction of the American legal community, the jury was an ancient common-law contrivance that had, like the barrister's wig and the forms of common-law pleading, long outlived its purpose.[168]

Since the 1960s, most graduates of American law schools have been instructed in the traditions of legal realism and progressive jurisprudence. The legal community's doubts about the jury system were deepened by the legal profession's tendency to remember the civil rights movement as a series of lawsuits punctuated by demonstrations. In this version of history, juries were often the villains, along with legislatures dominated by Dixie Democrats bent on defending white supremacy. The heroes of the story were lawyers and judges who resisted popular pressures to defend justice. It helped that popular fiction and occasional real-world jury trials promoted the idea that, rather than a rational forum for democratic deliberation, the jury room was a hothouse of ignorance and prejudice—the natural abode of racists and "angry men." How many law school applications were launched by Atticus Finch and Juror Number 8?

Meanwhile, the American administrative state grew apace. What had begun as a "bold experiment" by New Deal brain trusters was, by the 1960s, the heart of a new American regime in which administrative agencies determined an ever-

167. The "courts and parties" theme comes from Stephen Skowronek, *Building a New American State: The Expansion of National Administrative Capacities, 1877–1920* (New York: Cambridge University Press, 1982).

168. Surveying the literature on juries, Albert W. Dzur concludes that support for the jury among scholars is "wide but shallow." Contemporary scholars are "defensive" about juries, seeing them as the "rough-hewn body within an otherwise smoothly functioning modern courtroom." Albert W. Dzur, *Punishment, Participatory Democracy, and the Jury* (New York: Oxford University Press, 2012), 129–130.

expanding range of benefits (now conceived as "rights") and enforced a wide range of new obligations spawned by the regulatory process. In the authorized version of modern American history, regulatory agencies were better suited to the task of rational decision making than amateur juries, torn in one direction by their biases and in another by their ignorance, or legislatures in thrall to "special interests." In this context, the decline of jury trials—and of deliberative democracy more generally—might be seen as profit rather than loss. But the American political tradition is wedded to the rhetoric of self-government, so outright denunciations of the jury system and celebrations of its apparent demise are still relatively rare. Yet it is not hard to find in the law reviews examples of an important new pattern: damning the jury with faint praise while bidding a fond farewell to an institution that has long outlived its original form and purpose.[169]

So when it became clear that trials were declining and that juries were playing a smaller role in both criminal and civil cases, the counterarguments began immediately—appearing, for example, in the same issue of the *Journal of Empirical Legal Studies* in which Galanter first presented his evidence about vanishing trials. That issue also contains an essay by one of the nation's most prominent legal historians, Professor Lawrence Friedman of Stanford University Law School.[170] The clear purpose of Friedman's essay is to debunk the notion that there is a crisis involving "vanishing trials" by questioning whether trials were *ever* very important. Trials were never as common as "ordinary people" think they were, Friedman points out; "the 'trial' was never the norm, never the modal way of resolving issues and solving problems in the legal system." Friedman then makes a more interesting and significant observation: "insofar as the 'trial' did exist, it served a function that the legal system no longer cares to fulfill, at least not in the traditional way." Friedman describes that function as "didactic or theatrical or educational."[171] He does not elaborate, and his claim that only the "big

169. The perception that the jury is vanishing, and that many in the legal profession welcome that result, has produced some adverse reaction, both among the general public and from lawyers with friendlier views of the jury. The first phenomenon is represented by the Fully Informed Jurors Association, which campaigns for the right to issue "nullification instructions" to juries. The second phenomenon is represented by groups like the American Association for Justice (formerly the American Trial Lawyers Association) and the Save Our Juries website (saveourjuries.com). The AAJ defends the traditional view among trial attorneys that they should have more freedom in the courtroom. Save Our Juries provides a somewhat broader and less lawyer-focused defense of the jury system. Among other services, saveourjuries.com collects and publishes reports on the experiences of jurors.

170. Lawrence M. Friedman, "The Day before Trials Vanished," *Journal of Empirical Legal Studies* 1, 3 (November 2004): 689–703. Friedman's Wikipedia entry states that he is "the most-cited law professor in the field of legal history, with 1,890 citations from 2000–2007." http://www.en.wikipedia.org/wiki/Lawrence_M._Friedman (accessed June 27, 2013).

171. Friedman, "Day before Trials Vanished," 683.

criminal trial is an exception to these general propositions" is more puzzling than suggestive: big criminal trials, such as those of the Menendez brothers or O. J. Simpson, are certainly theatrical, but it is difficult to see how they are educational. Most trials, however, have always been pretty mundane affairs, Friedman notes, especially civil trials, which do not figure vividly in the public's mind. Even in the nineteenth century—allegedly the "golden age" of trials—most civil disputes were settled out of court, although Friedman concedes that many went to trial. As for criminal trials in the nineteenth century, these were usually "quick and dirty, even slapdash," with none of the procedural safeguards in place today, and most defendants—then, as now—pleaded guilty, often in the hope of a more lenient sentence.[172]

If the legal system no longer cares to serve an educational function, one might ask why. Friedman does not ask this question directly, nor does he speculate on what might be lost—to the general public, but more especially to jurors—if this educational function were to disappear. Some people, Friedman concedes, regret the decline of trials, but this is a "scholastic view" and is not the view of most of the judges and attorneys who operate the legal system, who agree with the old saying that "a bad settlement is better than a good trial."[173] Many people in the legal profession, Friedman claims, have come to believe that "a trial is a waste of time and money. And trials are not to be trusted. This is especially true of trials with juries. Juries are strange, unpredictable beasts."[174]

Friedman concedes that the trial was, "in a sense, at the ideological core of the common law," shaping the "whole structure of the law of evidence," which depends on trials and, in particular, on jury trials. That is, the law of evidence evolved with a particular audience in mind—one composed of (presumably) intelligent and "upright" citizens who were impartial and alert but not specialists and not experts in the law. "But the trial was never the working core, the practical core," even of the common law. For most of those who used the courts, even in the past, the trial was too expensive and time-consuming, so that even businesses preferred summary procedures. In any case, what most people experience as "law" in modern times is very different from what people experienced in the past. The law is just as important now, but it is no longer the law developed by trials. What most people experience as law is "administrative law, regulatory law. People are enveloped in a network of rules and practices. It is almost a kind of atmosphere in which they move and breathe." The "law" makes millions of decisions, but only

172. Ibid., 690–691, 692–693.

173. Ibid., 694. If anyone has done a survey of attorneys showing that they are unconcerned about the disappearance of jury trials, I am unaware of it. Friedman's view is definitely not shared by the American Bar Association.

174. Ibid.

the tiniest fraction of these decisions has anything to do with "a trial or adjudication." But the "average person" does not know this.[175]

Does it matter? There is no evidence that Friedman thinks so. Trials, both civil and criminal, involve many questions that are "unanswerable," that is, questions for which there is no rational answer (Friedman's examples are custody disputes or pain and suffering allegations). To settle such difficult questions requires discretion; therefore, discretion must lie somewhere in the legal system. Historically, that discretion was entrusted to juries. No longer. "The vanishing trial is, in many regards, the vanishing jury. Power and discretion have shifted away from the jury and more and more now is in the hands of the judge. To put it another way, the long-term historical development is to shift decision making from amateurs to professionals."[176] In turn, much of this power and discretion has moved from judges to bureaucrats, who are even more expert (i.e., more specialized) than judges. "In the era of the administrative state, most legal questions are firm, fixed, cut and dried."[177] There is little room, and apparently little demand, for the kind of amateur decision making once exercised by juries. There is probably nothing that can be done about this, Friedman concludes. "We can, so to speak, keep the California condor and the whooping crane alive, but we cannot make them as common as pigeons or sparrows."[178] Meanwhile, Friedman believes that the "didactic" or "theatrical" function of trials (and it is interesting that he does not clearly distinguish between them) has now moved to the kind of big trial represented by the O. J. Simpson case and even beyond, from the real world of actual trials to the ersatz realm of "court TV," presided over by characters like Judge Judy.[179]

Another way to diminish the significance of the vanishing trials phenomenon is to argue that trials are not actually "vanishing" but simply "morphing" into dif-

175. Ibid., 697. Professor Robert P. Burns refers to "the trial's cultured despisers—historians, economists, a few judges—[who] have seen its demise as the more or less inevitable atrophying of a primitive vestigial organ unsuited to contemporary society. It may have been appropriate for cruder times, but not for our advanced society." Robert P. Burns, *The Death of the American Trial* (Chicago: University of Chicago Press, 2009), 2. For a particularly vitriolic sample of this pattern, see Michael Lind's diatribe against the jury system in the aftermath of the O. J. Simpson trial, "Jury Dismissed," in *Postmortem: The O. J. Simpson Case*, ed. Jeffrey Abramson (New York: Basic Books, 1996), 155–160. Here is a sample: "The progress of civilization can be measured by the distance between the idea of crime as a matter between the criminal and his victim's relatives . . . and the idea of crime as an offense against the impersonal, constitutional state. The twelve-person jury, which the Vikings bequeathed to Anglo-Saxon England, lies on the barbaric end of the spectrum" (156).

176. Friedman, "Day before Trials Vanished," 698.

177. Ibid., 699.

178. Ibid., 703.

179. Ibid., 701–702.

ferent ways of resolving conflicts and "migrating" into other venues (alternative dispute resolution or court-annexed and even private arbitration and mediation forums).[180] One who has made this argument is Judith Resnik, writing for the same issue of the *Journal of Empirical Legal Studies* that published Galanter's research and Friedman's historical reflections.[181] Resnik proposes her own alternative explanation for the vanishing trials phenomenon: "that while trials have declined in the courts, trials have in fact migrated elsewhere, resulting in a *proliferation* of adjudicatory processes."[182] She blames some of this migration on judges themselves, many of whom have displayed a notable animus against trials, placing the federal judiciary squarely in the "forefront of the anti-adjudication movement." Adjudication has been "eclipsed by the very alternatives that federal judges have promoted."[183] In Resnik's telling, judges are not motivated by a desire to save time and move cases along; rather, many of them think there are actually *too many* trials in the first place and would like to see even fewer rather than more. They would especially like to see fewer of the types of cases responsible for the "litigation explosion," such as class actions, medical malpractice litigation, and the like.[184] Many judges see trials as the result of "failed lawyering" and worry about the cost in time and money if the number of trials increased. Some may even feel some "unease with jury decision-making."[185]

But even as Resnik chides judges for trying to reduce the number of trials in the federal courts, she cannot help wondering whether we might be better off with not just fewer trials but also fewer juries. Juries are not the best decision makers, after all, and agency adjudication (i.e., agency "courts") can be "excellent venues for decision making (including trials)."[186] In any case, we must not get trapped by old concepts, such as the conventional meaning of the word "trial":

> Of course, to the extent that "trials" are defined as fact finding by government-employed judges and government-deployed juries in courtrooms situated in buildings called courthouses provided by the state, then the rate of trials—and the absolute numbers in some courts—have declined. Whether all those criteria ought to be definitional of "trial" is a question requiring a response that, I believe, illuminates an important part of the problem to be

180. This is presumably what Friedman was getting at by his reference to the "trial" rather than to the trial (without the scare quotes).

181. Judith Resnik, "Migrating, Morphing, and Vanishing: The Empirical and Normative Puzzles of Declining Trial Rates in Courts," *Journal of Empirical Legal Studies* 1, 3 (November 2004): 783.

182. Ibid., 785, emphasis in original.

183. Ibid., 789.

184. Ibid., 812.

185. Ibid., 813.

> explored. An alternative definition is that a trial occurs before any neutral third party, anywhere, as long as empowered to impose a judgment that is enforced through the state.[187]

Of course, this is definitely not how Americans have defined a trial, still less a jury trial. A hearing can take place in front of an administrator or an administrative law judge, but most Americans would not confuse this with a jury trial. A jury is not just "any neutral party"; a jury is a group of people assembled to render judgment, a way to secure a popular answer to a legal question—an answer that is likely to have broad popular support. Juries are clearly not efficient. Their value, as Justice Scalia wrote, is that they are free.

As Resnik acknowledges in the same footnote quoted above, the United States may be moving in a "continental" direction, toward "an inquisitional judiciary superintending fact development."[188] She does not seem to be disturbed by this possibility. But there is a world of difference, at least politically, between a system in which government employees render judgments and one in which citizens render judgments. Unlike agency-employed bureaucrats, jurors do not derive their livelihood from their service to the government; they are therefore not under the thumb of public officials, even while they are performing a public function. After serving briefly (as the Anti-Federalist "Federal Farmer" put it) as the "sentinels and guardians of each other," they return to private life.[189] Precisely for this reason, juries anchor public judgment in the judgment of those whom Friedman refers to as "ordinary people," rather than in the judgment of civil servants—or, as most ordinary people would call them, bureaucrats. In the process, the jury trial offers citizens the opportunity to learn the art of judgment in a forum where it matters, and their accumulating judgments, trial by trial and over a long period, give a particular shape to the public order.[190]

No one has ever denied that the jury system comes at a cost, and where that cost has been deemed prohibitive—such as in the types of cases traditionally tried in equity courts—professional judges took charge, avoiding both uneducated jurors and hyperformal legal pleadings without engendering much controversy. But such cases were always understood to be exceptions to an important republican rule, and efforts to expand the exceptions were resisted as threats to republican

186. Ibid., 788.

187. Ibid., 790, n. 15.

188. Ibid.

189. Federal Farmer, Letter IV, in *The Anti-Federalist: Writings of the Opponents of the Constitution,* ed. Herbert J. Storing and Murray Dry (Chicago: University of Chicago Press, 1985), 58–59. See also James Nendza, "The Jury and Republican Government: The Early American Understanding" (unpublished manuscript, 1999).

190. For a fuller defense of the trial as a democratic institution, see Robert P. Burns, *A Theory of the Trial* (Princeton, NJ: Princeton University Press, 1999).

government. And in any case, have we not learned, by the early decades of the twenty-first century, that "expert decision making" involves costs of its own—not just the hollowing out of public liberty but also some spectacularly bad decisions? We have learned, to our sorrow, what the progressives of the early twentieth century could perhaps be forgiven for not knowing, because they had not yet had a chance to see it up close: scientific expertise gave us the National Recovery Administration, the Model Cities Program, thalidomide, and the Edsel. A little populist humility would seem to be called for at last.

FOUR MODERN TRIALS

When republican theorists described the jury as the "lower house of the judiciary," they were highlighting the jury's role as the people's voice in the courts. But the jury was not just an element of the judicial system; it was a fundamental element of the political order within which the judiciary operated. Given the contemporary preoccupation with the quality of decisions, it is important not to lose sight of an obvious point: it also matters who makes the decisions, however well or badly they turn out. In the case of jury trials, the old wisdom still applies: juries give citizens the last word at the moment it matters most. This applies not just to jurors individually. The jury system gives the public collectively what is often the last word on important controversies. In the process, it gives all attentive citizens the opportunity to wonder what judgment they would make if put in a similar position. Modern citizenship, because it necessarily rests on an ever-expanding base reaching hundreds of millions, often seems pretty thin gruel, busily productive of rights but relatively silent about citizens' duties. The military draft is in abeyance; two-fifths of the population pays no taxes; one-third of the public does not bother to vote. Jury duty therefore comes close to being sui generis, which is all the more reason to recognize its importance.

This can be seen more clearly through some examples. The cases I chose for discussion here are not, in themselves, enormously important, and I made no effort to find "typical" cases. What led me to choose these four jury trials is that, in each case, the jury's verdict might be questioned; in fact, these four verdicts were the subject of intense criticism and even ridicule. But the cases have several common features that shed light on the importance of the jury in both civil and criminal trials (there are two of each). First, the public discussion of the "facts" of each case was often wildly off the mark, with media outlets of all kinds stating as fact that which had never been proved in court, much of which was later revealed to be false. In other words, the jury, unlike the general public, is exposed to evidence in a controlled environment where fact claims must be supported by evidence and cross-examination, rather than by what Justice Frankfurter referred to as "atmospheric innuendos." Second, the moral difficulties presented by the four cases go well beyond the questions that dominate the jury debate: they involve not technicalities but prudential questions about right and wrong, about what is reasonable behavior.[191] Third, in each case I am persuaded that the jury made the right decision (although I did not always think so before writing this section), even though those decisions did not come quickly or easily. As noted earlier, the hard cases go to the jury; the easy cases settle or end in plea bargains. And while experts might have made different decisions, the point is precisely that these decisions have a much greater impact and a different meaning when they are made by the people themselves.

Apple Computer, Inc. v. Samsung Electronics Corp.

On April 15, 2011, Apple filed multiple claims of patent infringement against Samsung in the US District Court for the Northern District of California, presenting the precise scenario that critics of civil juries have always feared the most.[192] A random sample of citizens would sit in judgment of a major international corporation, answering more than 700 technical questions of apparently stunning complexity involving seven Apple patents used in its iPhone and iPad products. Apple accused Samsung of copying these features—among them, the "bounce-back" effect, the "tap-to-zoom" feature, various onscreen icons, elements of the finger-activated interface, and the general "ornamental design" of the iPhone and iPad—in twenty-four Samsung devices. In response, Samsung countersued Apple for patent violations of its own, and the jury would have to resolve these charges as well. Here is a sample: "Question #1: For each of the following products, has Apple proven by a preponderance of the evidence that Samsung . . . has infringed Claim 19 of the '381 Patent?" Then came the issue of damages: Apple was demanding $2.75 billion, as well as a ban on the sale of certain Samsung products; Samsung was demanding $422 million.[193] The jury would have to justify its damage award by assigning a particular amount to each of the patent violations, broken down by device. For instance, the jury assigned a damage value of $50,672,869 to just one of Samsung's products, the Droid Charge JX 1025. The verdict form was twenty pages long.[194]

When it was known that a jury would decide the Apple-Samsung dispute ("the patent trial of the century," according to the *Wall Street Journal*), commen-

191. Juries "regularly determine what is reasonable in tort actions and make practical determinations about what constitutes reasonable doubt in criminal cases." Burns, *Death of the American Trial*, 128.

192. Apple Inc. v. Samsung Electronics Co. Ltd. et al., No. 11-1846 (2011).

193. Nick Wingfield, "Jury Awards $1 Billion to Apple in Samsung Patent Case," *New York Times*, August 24, 2012, http://www.nytimes.com/2012/08/25/technology/jury-reaches-decision-in-apple-samsung-patent-trial.html?_r=0 (accessed August 7, 2014).

194. United States District Court, Northern District of California, San Jose Division, Case 5:11-cv-01846-LHK, Amended Verdict Form, Document 1931, August 24, 2012, Question 23, 16.

tators were quick to point out the obvious difficulty of putting such complex questions to a jury of nonexpert citizens. Judge Richard Posner argued at the time (and many times before and since) that patent infringement complaints should be heard by the Patent and Trademark Office, rather than juries. Professor Brian Love of Santa Clara University School of Law predicted that "a lot of the evidence that's presented will be over the head of the jury pool. They'll tend to make more of a decision based on emotion and storytelling." Some of the technology news websites stressed the risks to innovation from allowing amateurs to decide patent cases. Even federal judge Lucy Koh, who would preside at the trial, worried that the jury might be "seriously confused."[195]

That patent disputes are often confusing is unquestionably true, but it is also true that jurors are not the only ones who have a hard time understanding them. Appellate court judges were having similar difficulties, with the twelve regional circuits producing such divergent answers to identical patent questions that Congress passed the Federal Courts Improvement Act of 1982. That act gave the DC Federal Circuit sole responsibility for hearing patent appeals from the district courts, "eliminating inter-circuit conflicts and enhancing uniformity."[196] In those countries where patent appeals are heard by experts rather than jurors, there are similar disagreements about the meaning of the patent laws. This became clear when Apple and Samsung globalized their trade dispute. A district court in Tokyo found for Samsung; in South Korea (Samsung's home), a three-judge panel found both companies guilty of patent infringements. In Germany, courts found that neither company had infringed any patents. In the United Kingdom, the Chancery Division of the Court of Justice declared that, while Samsung's designs were very similar to Apple's, they did not constitute a patent violation.[197]

The media also found *Apple v. Samsung* difficult to decipher. After the verdict in Apple's favor, some media outlets (e.g., the Freakonomics website, but also the *New York Times*) thought the verdict meant that Apple had a "patent on rectangles." (Apple did claim a patent on the distinctive "rectangle with rounded

195. David Kravets, "Who Cheated Whom? Apple v. Samsung Patent Showdown Explained," July 27, 2012, http://www.wired.com/2012/07/apple-v-samsung-explained/ (accessed August 7, 2014). See also Wendy Kaufman, "Jury to Decide Apple's Patent Case against Samsung," NPR, August 22, 2012, http://www.npr.org/2012/08/22/159679099/jury-to-decide-apple-s-patent-case-against-samsung (accessed August 7, 2014).

196. Sanjeev Bajwa, "Apple v. Samsung: Is It Time to Change Our Patent Trial System?" *Pacific McGeorge Global Business & Development Law Journal* 27 (2014): 84. Another motive for the act was the view of some members of Congress that many appellate judges were hostile to the very idea of patents (ibid., 85). Much of the commentary on the jury's verdict in the Apple-Samsung case revealed a similar bias. See Neha Pathak, "How Media Got the Biggest Bite of (the) Apple: A Look at the Media Misperception in the Apple-Samsung Case," *Marquette Intellectual Property Law Review* 18 (2014): 237.

197. Bajwa, "Apple v. Samsung," 95.

corners" shape, but the jury found that Samsung had not violated that patent.) There was confusion over the "pinch-to-zoom" feature on both companies' smart phones, even though Apple held only a "limited ownership" of the pinch feature and was not seeking to defend it at the trial.[198] One website even claimed that Apple was trying to patent "how humans interact with their machines."[199]

But in addition to confusion about Apple's patent claims, many commentators were confused about the relationship between patents and innovation. Calling Apple's eventual victory a defeat for consumers, technology writer Kyle Vanehmert argued that "forcing smartphone developers to come up with a different way of doing things for the sake of coming up with a different way of doing things is outrageously stupid."[200] Jeff John Roberts, writing on the Gigaom technology site, argued that if "patent policy is not effective, it creates monopolies that harm competitors and consumers. In Apple-Samsung, there's a good chance that we're doing the latter, . . . [awarding] Apple sweeping monopolies that may raise prices and stunt the smartphone market."[201]

But of course, staking out a claim to a certain way of doing something—as long as it is genuinely new, which is determined by the Patent and Trademark Office—is precisely the point of patents. They assure inventors a certain fixed period during which they can profit from their inventions without interference. Getting a temporary monopoly on a particular invention is the whole point of the patent laws, because the possibility of making lots of money is the most basic of all "incentives to innovation." In the field of consumer electronics, that particular incentive has created a communications revolution as well as many new fortunes.

The jury chosen to hear *Apple v. Samsung* was, to the surprise of many critics, unusually well educated. But this should not have been a surprise: the trial took place in the heart of Silicon Valley, where the educational level of the jury pool is almost certainly above the national average. Six of the nine jurors (seven men and two women) had bachelor's degrees, and three of the six had postgraduate degrees; two had attended college without graduating. Five of the nine worked for tech companies, including AT&T and Intel, and one juror was a patent holder. At least five of the jurors were over the age of fifty. Ironically, only four jurors owned smart phones. Even a critic of the verdict conceded that this was a "blue ribbon jury based on their experience in the hi-tech industry and their education level."[202]

The jury's task may have been made easier by the defense team's trial strat-

198. Pathak, "How Media Got the Biggest Bite," 246.

199. Ibid., 250.

200. Ibid., citing Kyle Vanhemert, "Apple's Big Verdict: Bad for Usability, but It Won't Stop True Innovation," *Fast Company*, August 27, 2012.

201. "3 Reasons Juries Have No Place in the Patent System," *Cigaom*, August 27, 2012, http://www.gigaom.com/2012/08/27/3-reasons-juries-have-no-place-in-the-patent-system/ (accessed August 7, 2014).

202. Bajwa, "Apple v. Samsung," 90–91; Greg Sandoval, "How Qualified Is the Ap-

egy: Samsung conceded that its products looked a great deal like Apple's and even had some of the same or similar features, but it maintained this copying was not actionable because none of the patents Apple was defending were valid.[203] The features that Apple claimed were distinctive or innovative, Samsung argued, were mere glosses on existing designs and functions (the product of "prior art," to use the legal term) and were unworthy of protection. The US Patent and Trademark Office had therefore erred not once but repeatedly. What many consumers and many in the industry believed—that the iPhone and iPad were interesting and innovative products—was now being attacked as a myth.

The jury apparently saw this argument as an attack on the basic idea of a patent system. The question whether Apple's patents were valid did not, according to postverdict juror interviews, occupy much of the jury's time. (The jury deliberated for twenty-one hours, and Samsung claimed this "brief" deliberation was evidence of juror misconduct.[204]) They spent most of their time identifying which of Apple's patents had been infringed and what damages should be assigned to each of these violations. In all, the jury found that Samsung had infringed six of the seven Apple patents at issue (rejecting the "rectangle with rounded corners" claim). After the trial, jury foreman Velvin Hogan (the patent-holding juror) said the jury had found Apple's defense of innovation persuasive, and the testimony of Samsung executives had showed that the infringement was "absolutely" deliberate. "We didn't want to give carte blanche to a company . . . to infringe someone else's intellectual property," Hogan concluded. However, the jury felt that Apple's

---

ple-Samsung Jury? We Found Out," *CNET*, August 24, 2012, http://www.cnet.com/news/how-qualified-is-the-apple-samsung-jury-we-found-out/ (accessed August 7, 2014). Bajwa notes that Judge Koh "spent a great deal of time screening a large pool of potential jurors by asking various questions regarding their occupation, gadgets owned, knowledge of the legal and patent system, and whether they knew anyone who worked at either company" (91).

203. Michelle Fitzsimmons, "Apple vs. Samsung: 'Designs Substantially Similar,'" *Techradar*, August 6, 2012, http://www.techradar.com/us/news/world-of-tech/apple-vs-samsung-designs-substantially-similiar-1091309 (accessed March 30, 2015). Fitzsimmons reports that "Charles Verhoeven, the Samsung lawyer who spent hours grilling [Apple witness Peter Bressler], presented evidence Samsung claims shows 'prior art' to support the argument Apple was merely designing its devices in an environment where these designs already existed." See also the same author's coverage of Samsung testimony from day 8 of the trial: "Samsung attorney maintains the South Korean company's device designs were the result of a design Zeitgeist and Apple's designs aren't as unique as they claim." Michelle Fitzsimmons, "Samsung's First Witnesses Take the Stand in Apple Patent Trial," *Techradar*, http://www.techradar.com/us/news/world-of-tech/samsung-s-first-witnesses-take-the-stand-in-apple-patent-trial-1092083 (accessed March 30, 2015).

204. Nilay Patel, "Samsung Argues Jury Foreman Was 'Deliberately Dishonest' in Apple Trial," *Verge*, December 6, 2012, http://www.theverge.com/2012/12/6/3737794/apple-vs-samsung-juror-misconduct-allegations-barely-discussed-damages-hearing (accessed August 8, 2014).

demand for $2.75 billion in damages was too high and scaled it back by almost two-thirds.[205]

In a second round of litigation in 2014, Apple scored a less decisive victory. In January, Judge Koh ruled, in a bench trial, that Samsung had violated Apple's patent on the "auto-complete" feature, and a jury would determine the damages in May. That jury also considered Apple's claim that Samsung had violated five patents on ten different devices. Although the jury gave Apple a partial victory, it also determined that Apple had violated one of Samsung's patents. The damage award of $120 million was considerably less than that awarded by the 2012 jury, another victory for Samsung.[206] But the argument for expert decision making in patent cases suffered a blow later that summer when the Patent and Trademark Office, in an ex parte reexamination of Apple's auto-complete patent, decided that it was, after all, the product of "prior art," having been anticipated by two different patents filed earlier.[207]

On August 5, 2014, Apple and Samsung announced in separate news conferences that they would cease their patent litigation—but only outside the United States.[208]

State of Florida v. George Zimmerman

Not since the trial of O. J. Simpson has a criminal case generated as much controversy as the trial of George Zimmerman, charged with second-degree murder in the killing of Trayvon Martin in Sanford, Florida, on February 26, 2012. Every element of the case has been fiercely contested, from the circumstances of the killing to the characters of the victim and the defendant. If the trial proved nothing else, it showed the importance of a public forum where citizens can consider the

205. Dan Levine, "Jury Didn't Want to Let Samsung Off Easy in Apple Trial: Foreman," Reuters, August 25, 2012, http://www.mobile.reuters.com/article/idUSBRE87009U20120825?irpc=932 (accessed August 7, 2014). Several months later Judge Koh reduced the jury's damage award to $4.5 million, on the grounds that the jury impermissibly based the award on Samsung's profits. She also ordered a new trial for infringement claims against two of Samsung's products. See Pathak, "How Media Got the Biggest Bite," 242, n. 9.

206. Martyn Williams, "Jury Finds Samsung Infringed Some Apple Patents, Must Pay $120M in Damages," *MacWorld*, May 2, 2014, http://www.macworld.com/article/2150770/jury-finds-samsung-infringed-some-apple-patents-must-pay-120m-in-damages.html (accessed August 8, 2014).

207. John Ribeiro, "USPTO Rejects Claims of Apple Patent that Figures in Dispute with Samsung," *CIO*, August 7, 2014, http://www.cio.com/article/2463101/uspto-rejects-claims-of-apple-patent-that-figures-in-dispute-with-samsung.html (accessed August 8, 2014).

208. John Ribeiro, "Apple, Samsung Agree to Settle Patent Disputes outside US," *PC World*, August 5, 2014, http://www.pcworld.com/article/2461940/apple-samsung-agree-to-settle-patent-disputes-outside-us.html (accessed August 8, 2014).

facts in an atmosphere that is actually conducive to fact-finding and deliberation, away from the media frenzy, angry demonstrators, and ambitious politicians.

The facts the jury ultimately found, nearly a year and a half after the killing, were essentially the same facts found by the Sanford Police Department in the hours and days after the killing and on which it had based the decision not to file charges. Zimmerman, the captain of the Neighborhood Watch in the gated community of Retreat at Twin Lakes, had reported a "suspicious" character, calling the Sanford PD on his cell phone. This was Trayvon Martin, a black seventeen-year-old who was visiting the neighborhood with his father (although Zimmerman did not know this). There had been a recent increase in break-ins in the community, as well as a shooting, and many of those charged in these crimes had been young black males from outside the complex. Though told by the police there was no need for him to follow the suspect, Zimmerman initially began looking for Martin, whom he had lost sight of; then, changing his mind, he headed back to his car. Zimmerman told the police that Martin suddenly approached him from behind and demanded to know if Zimmerman "had a problem." (Martin's girlfriend, who was on the phone with him at the time, said she heard Martin ask, "Why are you following me?") Whatever other words the two men exchanged is known only by Zimmerman, but a fight ensued. Zimmerman told the police that Martin became angry and attacked him, knocking him to the ground, pummeling his face, and banging his head into the concrete sidewalk. (Zimmerman was heavier than Martin, but Martin was taller.) Unable to restrain Martin, and fearing that he might lose consciousness, Zimmerman pulled a small 9mm pistol from his concealed carry holster and shot Martin once in the chest. Martin died within minutes.

At the trial, the evidence for this version of events came from several different witnesses (Zimmerman did not testify), who reported seeing the two men struggling, with Martin on top. There was also evidence of the wounds to Zimmerman's face and the back of his head, which were fully consistent with his account of the incident. So was the single gunshot wound to Martin, who had been shot "from below," according to forensic testimony. Witnesses testified they had heard someone yelling for help, but there was conflicting testimony about which one it was. (Zimmerman said he yelled for help but no one came.) Nonetheless, the racial "subtext" of the story proved irresistible not only to commentators, civil rights groups, and street demonstrators but also to the governor of Florida. Responding to criticism of the police department's decision not to file charges against Zimmerman, Governor Rick Scott took the case out of the hands of the county prosecutor and appointed a special prosecutor, Angela B. Corey. Three weeks later, Corey held a press conference and announced that she had filed second-degree murder charges against Zimmerman, who was now under arrest.[209]

209. "Gov. Rick Scott Appoints Special Prosecutor for Trayvon Martin Case," *Tampa Bay Times*, March 22, 2012; "George Zimmerman Case Timeline," MyNews13.com, July 13, 2013, http://www.mynews13.com/trayvon-timeline.html (accessed August 11, 2014).

Meanwhile, the racial subtext was becoming a full-blown "narrative" in which a racist gunman had shot an "unarmed child" whose only crime was being black. Zimmerman, in addition to being a racist, was described as a "wannabe cop" with a hero complex, looking for trouble and heedless of the consequences of his actions. Florida's recent (2005) "stand-your-ground" law was said to be partly to blame, since it allegedly encouraged reckless behavior and gave a warrant to killers. Writing in the *New York Times*, columnist Andrew Rosenthal observed, "in this case, Florida's gun laws killed Mr. Martin as surely as Mr. Zimmerman did," because the stand-your-ground law meant "he could shoot with impunity. There was no need to prove his case to the police, let alone a jury."[210] The governor announced a special task force to consider the law's repeal.[211] The police department's failure to charge Zimmerman was attributed to its long acquaintance with him through his Neighborhood Watch activities, but also to his race. Had the victim been white and the shooter black, critics said, the police certainly would have arrested the shooter. Soon after Zimmerman's indictment, Sanford's city manager fired the police chief.

As the trial date got closer, however, much of this racial narrative began to unravel, along with many other aspects of the media's portrayal of events. The FBI, looking into a possible civil rights charge against Zimmerman, announced that its investigation had turned up no evidence that Zimmerman was or had ever been a racist. In fact, Zimmerman had been a vocal participant in a campaign two years earlier to demand an investigation into the beating of a homeless black man by the son of a white Sanford police officer. As it turned out, Zimmerman was not even "white"; his mother was Hispanic, and Zimmerman's father testified that the extended family included not only Hispanics but also African Americans. It also came out that as recently as the December before the shooting, Zimmerman had been mentoring two black high school students.[212]

210. See "Trayvon Martin and the Smoking Gun," *New York Times*, April 2, 2012, http://www.takingnote.blogs.nytimes.com/2012/04/02/trayvon-martin-and-the-smoking-gun/?ref=us (accessed August 12, 2012).

211. In the end, the governor's task force recommended that no changes be made to the stand-your-ground law. Needless to say, the Florida law in question does not authorize armed citizens to "shoot with impunity." It merely states that a person who is otherwise entitled to use or threaten deadly force (where "such force is necessary to prevent imminent death or great bodily harm") does not have a "duty to retreat and has the right to stand his or her ground." In any case, this provision did not apply to the circumstances Zimmerman described—being beaten while pinned to the ground, with no opportunity to retreat—and Zimmerman did not present this defense at his trial. Florida Statute 776.012 (2).

212. Dan Barry et al., "Race, Tragedy and Outrage Collide after a Shot in Florida," *New York Times*, April 1, 2012, http://www.nytimes.com/2012/04/02/us/trayvon.martin-shooting-prompts-a-review-of-ideals.html?pagewanted=all&_r=0 (accessed August 12, 2014).

But for many observers of the trial, including many in the media, the most important element of the case—the only element that mattered—continued to be race. This obsession with race was evidenced by the discomfort in some quarters with Zimmerman's ambiguous "whiteness." Because he was not, after all, the ideal "white guy," the racial narrative became clouded. In her summary of how the *New York Times* covered the story, for example, media reporter Margaret Sullivan noted the tentative way the newspaper described Zimmerman's ethnicity, trying out various terms: "half Hispanic," "half Peruvian," "a self-described Hispanic," and a "white Hispanic." Addressing this confusion, the *Times*' Miami bureau chief Lizette Alvarez, who was responsible for most of the paper's coverage, confessed it had been "a struggle, all along" to describe Zimmerman. "If he were black or if his name was Rodriguez instead of Zimmerman, this would have been a completely different situation."[213] Yet the *New York Times* had no difficulty describing Barack Obama as an "African-American candidate" and "the first black President," even though, like Zimmerman, his mother was of one race and his father of another. Describing Zimmerman simply as "Hispanic," however, would have disrupted the racial narrative in which a "white man" killed an "unarmed black child."

Zimmerman's character did come under question, however, for events having nothing to do with race. He was caught trying to hide more than $100,000 in contributions to his defense fund in order to portray himself as legally "indigent." His wife was charged with abetting this scheme. A relative went public with a sexual abuse allegation against Zimmerman from when he was eight years old and the accuser six. Zimmerman ceased speaking with his attorneys and sought a meeting with Angela Corey, against their advice. They then resigned from the case, expressing public doubts about Zimmerman's mental stability, and he was forced to find a new legal team.[214] Reports in the press revealed that years earlier, a girlfriend had accused Zimmerman of hitting her.[215]

But matters were equally unsettled on the prosecution's side. Information about Trayvon Martin revealed him to be something more complicated than a "child." His cell-phone and Internet activity, for example, demonstrated an interest in martial arts, edgy rap music, and drugs.[216] Prosecutor Corey faced accusations of "unethical behavior" (from Alan Dershowitz) and "agitprop" (from former federal prosecutor Andrew McCarthy). Dershowitz criticized Corey's probable-cause affidavit for leaving out important pieces of evidence that would

213. Margaret Sullivan, "Making Sense of a Sensational Case," *New York Times*, July 14, 2013, SR12.

214. John Schwartz et al., "Tough Decision Looms for Florida Prosecutor," *New York Times*, April 11, 2012, A13.

215. Barry et al., "Race, Tragedy and Outrage."

216. Ibid. Martin's Twitter handle was @no_limit_nigga.

have cast doubt on a second-degree murder charge. "Most affidavits of probable cause are very thin," Dershowitz wrote. "This is so thin that it won't make it past a judge on a second degree murder charge. There's simply nothing in there that would justify second degree murder." He accused Corey of making "a campaign speech" when announcing the indictment and predicted that, in the absence of evidence not in the affidavit, "this case will result in an acquittal."[217]

McCarthy complained of the prosecutor's unprofessional "ambiguity" on the question of the "struggle" between Martin and Zimmerman. If she had information suggesting that Zimmerman had started the fight, McCarthy pointed out, she certainly would have included that evidence in the probable-cause affidavit; the fact that Corey was silent suggested "the additional information would hurt the prosecution's case"—as indeed it did, once it was presented. Corey "probably has a good idea of exactly how the physical altercation started," McCarthy reasoned. "Yet, she knowingly withheld that information," along with the information about Zimmerman's injuries.[218]

Adding to Corey's problems, the original judge, Jessica Recksiedler, was forced to recuse herself after it was revealed that her husband's law partner was doing commentary on the trial for CNN. She was replaced by Judge Kenneth Lester in April 2012, but a Florida appeals court removed him just four months later, after he made public statements about Zimmerman that indicated a bias against the defense. The case was finally tried before a third judge, Debra S. Nelson, of the Eighteenth Circuit Court of Florida.

Given the pretrial media and political circus, the trial was somewhat anticlimactic. (Zimmerman was indicted on April 11, 2012, but jury selection did not begin until more than a year later, on June 10, 2013.) Jury selection was time-consuming, predictably; more than forty of the hundred chosen from the venire were excused based solely on their answers to the juror questionnaire.[219] It took eight days to choose a jury of six plus four alternates, as both the judge and the attorneys interviewed prospective jurors one by one.[220] All six of the jurors finally seated were women; five of them were white, and one was Hispanic. Even the racial makeup of the jury was confusing; the jury was first described as an "all-

217. Dershowitz's comments first appeared on the Mediaite website in an article by Noah Rothman, http://www.mediaite.com/tv/harvard-prof-alan-dershowitz-zimmerman-arrest-affidavit-irresponsible-and-unethical/ (accessed August 10, 2014). For McCarthy's criticism, see Andrew McCarthy, "Martin Case Affidavit," *National Review Online*, April 13, 2012, http://www.nationalreview.com/corner/295997/martin-case-affidavit-andrew-c-mccarthy#more (accessed August 10, 2014).

218. McCarthy, "Martin Case Affidavit."

219. *Tampa Bay Times*, June 12, 2013, 8B.

220. Florida uses a twelve-person jury only in capital cases; all other criminal trials are held with a six-person jury.

white jury," a phrase with particular resonance in the South, especially in cases in which race might be an issue.[221]

The prosecution's case drew heavily on the racial narrative pushed by the public demonstrations that followed the killing. Zimmerman was described as a troublemaker and racial profiler who did not like "people who didn't belong" hanging around his neighborhood. The prosecution's opening statement claimed there was no physical evidence of a fight between Martin and Zimmerman, so Zimmerman could not have feared for his life when he fired the fatal shot. But the prosecution never overcame the burden of proving this theory in light of the physical evidence and the preponderance of witness testimony. Witnesses testified that they had seen Martin on top of Zimmerman, punching him, and the physical evidence of Zimmerman's wounds belied the prosecution's insistence that he had not been hurt. In addition, the prosecution could not provide any evidence of a key component of second-degree murder: that the defendant's "unlawful killing" demonstrated a "depraved mind" or "ill will, hatred, spite, or an evil intent." The hints at racial hatred fell flat when the "racial epithet" Zimmerman had supposedly uttered during his 911 call turned out to be something much more ambiguous: "f***ing punks, these assholes always get away with it."[222] Nor could the prosecution meet the lesser burden of a manslaughter conviction—that Zimmerman had caused Martin's death under circumstances that were not "justifiable or excusable homicide" (i.e., not in self-defense)—since the physical evidence clearly supported Zimmerman's claim that Martin was beating him.[223] After a relatively brief sixteen-hour deliberation, the jury returned a verdict of not guilty on both the second-degree murder charge and the lesser charge of manslaughter.

In an interview after the verdict, "Juror B37"[224] said that in their initial vote, three jurors voted for acquittal, two for conviction on the murder charge, and one for conviction on the manslaughter charge. The jury spent the entire sixteen hours, she said, examining the audio files and other exhibits and rereading the testimony of witnesses; at one point, they asked for clarification about the definition of "manslaughter." Some jurors wanted to find Zimmerman guilty of something, she

221. For example, the *Washington Post* headline announced, "Six White Women to Serve as Jurors for George Zimmerman Trial." However, the story itself reported that only five of the women were white; the "race and ethnicity of the sixth juror was not immediately available." *Washington Post*, June 21, 2013, A3.

222. Patrik Jonnson, "George Zimmerman Trial: Jury Can Consider Lesser Charge of Manslaughter," *Christian Science Monitor*, July 11, 2013.

223. State of Florida v. George Zimmerman, "Instructions Read to Jury by the Honorable Debra S. Nelson, Circuit Judge," in *News-Journal, Daytona-Beach, Florida*, July 12, 2013.

224. The jurors in the *Zimmerman* trial were not sequestered, but the court agreed to shield their identities, and the press agreed not to take their pictures.

claimed, but the law would not allow them to.[225] In a separate statement distancing themselves from the statement of "B37," four other jurors essentially corroborated this part of her statement. They were not fans of George Zimmerman and believed that both he and Trayvon Martin had made tragic mistakes on the night of the killing. But what mattered was the law. "The death of a teenager weighed heavily on our hearts but in the end we did what the law required us to do."[226]

Liebeck v. McDonald's Restaurants

Stella Liebeck's "hot coffee" lawsuit against McDonald's is often referred to as the "poster child for litigation reform." In its telling and retelling, it has become entangled in larger political questions, including the nature of risk, the impact of litigation on the economy, and the proper role of juries in civil cases. And like the other cases in this section, the actual facts of *Liebeck v. McDonald's* manage to be both simple and fiercely contested.

In February 1992 seventy-nine-year-old Stella Liebeck went to a McDonald's restaurant in Albuquerque, New Mexico, in her grandson's car, with her grandson at the wheel. She bought a cup of coffee at the drive-through window. Her grandson then found a place to park in the McDonald's lot, and Mrs. Liebeck placed the container between her legs so that she could remove the lid and add cream and sugar. While removing the lid she spilled the coffee in her lap, where it soaked into her sweatpants and pooled beneath her on the car seat. The skin on her lower abdomen, buttocks, groin, and inner thighs was scalded by coffee that was as hot as 205 degrees when brewed and between 180 and 190 degrees when served. Medical evidence at the trial showed that Liebeck suffered third-degree burns on 6 percent of her body and first- and second-degree burns on another 10 percent, requiring a week in the hospital and multiple skin grafts. In due course, Liebeck sought a private settlement with McDonald's, asking for $10,000 to cover medical costs and another $10,000 in compensatory payments. McDonald's responded with an offer of $800. Liebeck tried twice more to reach a settlement without going to court, but after the third rebuff she found a lawyer and sued. Her lawyer, Reed Morgan, was the perfect choice: he had won a settlement against McDonald's in a similar hot-coffee case in Texas.[227]

225. "Juror: 'No Doubt' Zimmerman Feared for His Life," FoxNews, July 16, 2013, http://www.foxnews.com/us/2013/07/16/juror-no-doubt-zimmerman-feared-for-his-life / (accessed August 10, 2014).

226. "4 Jurors in Zimmerman Trial Distance Themselves from Juror B37," FoxNews, July 17, 2013, http://www.foxnews.com/us/2013/07/17/zimmerman-jurors-request-privacy -in-statement/ (accessed August 10, 2014).

227. Andrea Gerlin, "A Matter of Degree: How a Jury Decided that a Coffee Spill Is Worth $2.9 Million," *Wall Street Journal*, September 1, 1994, 1.

McDonald's executives argued that hot coffee is supposed to be hot, and by keeping the coffee between 180 and 190 degrees, McDonald's was simply following the recommendations of industry groups such as the International Coffee Association, as well as the wishes of consumers. They were supported in this position by other chains that sell coffee, among them Starbucks. However, separate surveys by the attorneys for both the defendant and the plaintiff had found that McDonald's served its coffee 10 to 20 degrees hotter than many other local restaurants did. In the Texas case, Morgan had made the same discovery.[228] In response, McDonald's pointed to the warning on its containers ("Caution: Contents Hot") and argued that if a customer spills coffee on herself, that is her responsibility, not the company's. Many opponents of "unnecessary litigation" agreed, and there was a considerable body of case law to back them up: typically, "hot beverage spills" do not make it to court unless an employee does the spilling. In recent years, twelve courts in the United States had dismissed suits in which the customer was responsible for the spill.[229]

McDonald's admitted, however, that it had received more than 700 complaints about its coffee being dangerously hot in just the past ten years. Executives also testified that they had made financial settlements in some of these "spill and scald" cases, including one for over $500,000. One McDonald's executive conceded that although they were aware their coffee could cause third-degree burns, they chose not to put a larger or more explicit warning on their containers. Liebeck's attorney was allowed to introduce some evidence from the Texas case, including the quality-assurance manager's testimony that he was "aware of this risk . . . and had no plans to turn down the heat." Managers in the Liebeck case agreed: "There are more serious dangers in restaurants," one executive explained.[230]

The most compelling evidence at the trial was undoubtedly the collection of photographs showing the injuries Mrs. Liebeck had suffered and the skin grafts she had endured. In the face of this evidence, the company's defense was to insist that: (1) customers like coffee hot; (2) all restaurants serve it as hot as McDonald's does, or nearly so; and (3) 700 complaints is not very many, considering that McDonald's serves more than a billion cups of coffee each year. What the jury heard was probably something like this: Everybody does it, so why shouldn't we? And in any case, not many people are injured, so it doesn't matter very much. With the pictures of the skin grafts in front of them, the jury may have found this argument both heartless and calculating. One juror later said that although he was initially

228. Ibid.

229. Ted Frank, "Urban Legends and Stella Liebeck and the McDonald's Coffee Case," Overlawyered.com, http://www.overlawyered.com/2005/10/urban-legends-and-stella-liebeck-and-the-McDonald's-coffee-case/ (accessed August 13, 2014).

230. Ibid.

skeptical about a trial over "spilled coffee," McDonald's executives had demonstrated "callous disregard for the safety of the people."[231]

The trial lasted seven days; the jury deliberations took only four hours. The jury assigned most of the responsibility for Liebeck's injuries to McDonald's and 20 percent to her own carelessness, settling on an award of $200,000 for compensatory damages—and $2.7 million in punitive damages! This caused a sensation in the press. McDonald's immediately filed a motion for a new trial and a judgment notwithstanding the verdict; the judge appointed a mediator. A month later he denied the restaurant's post-trial motions but also ruled that the $2.7 million damage award "was excessive, as a matter of law." He said he would grant a new trial on all the issues *unless* Mrs. Liebeck agreed to a total settlement—compensation plus damages—of $640,000. Although both McDonald's and Liebeck made noises about not settling, in the end, they agreed on an amount that was not disclosed. Attorneys familiar with such cases pegged the award at roughly $500,000. One newspaper sent a reporter to test the coffee at the offending McDonald's the day after the verdict, who found it to be a balmy 158 degrees. McDonald's now sells its coffee at lower temperatures and serves it in thick paper containers rather than in Styrofoam cups.[232]

The reaction to the verdict was swift and harsh. In newspaper editorials, on television news panels, and on late-night comedy shows, Stella Liebeck was mocked as a woman who had "hit the jackpot" because of her own carelessness, getting who knew how many hundreds of thousands of dollars for spilling a half-dollar cup of coffee into her own lap. In the rush to judgment, editors displayed some carelessness of their own, getting many of the facts wrong (claiming that Liebeck had been driving when she spilled the coffee or that the $2.7 million had been her idea). The jury was mocked as well, the judge was criticized for allowing the trial to proceed in the first place, Liebeck's lawyers were characterized as ambulance chasers, and the whole event was said to be just one more sad example of America's "absurd" civil litigation system.[233]

The reaction to the *Liebeck* case was no doubt shaped by a spirited debate, already in progress, about the causes and consequences of the litigation explo-

231. Gerlin, "Matter of Degree."

232. See ibid. on the lower temperatures. On the post-trial motions and decisions by the judge, see "The Stella Liebeck McDonald's Hot Coffee Case FAQ," http://www.abnormaluse.com/2011/01/stella-liebeck-mcdonalds-hot-coffee.html (accessed August 12, 2014). In 2009, in an effort to recapture market share from Starbucks, Dunkin' Donuts, and Peets, McDonald's started selling Newman's Own organic coffee in some parts of the country. See William Richards, "The Secret behind McDonald's Coffee," MainSt.com, http://www.mainstreet.com/article/small-business/marketing/secret-behind-mcdonalds-coffee (accessed August 14, 2014).

233. For a sample of this controversy, see Frank, "Urban Legends and Stella Liebeck."

sion—a phrase that is almost always enclosed in quotation marks, as if to suggest there might not really be such a thing. But as demonstrated above, the civil caseload in the federal courts grew by a factor of five between 1962 and 2002, and in the state courts it doubled over roughly the same period. What was really driving the civil litigation debate, however, was not the *amount* but the *type* of litigation crowding the dockets—namely, the type of case once known as a "strike suit," or a "frivolous" lawsuit brought by a shady plaintiff hoping to force a settlement from a wealthy defendant eager to avoid a trial. Under the circumstances created by the modern rules of civil procedure—extended discovery, easier and bigger class actions, court-sponsored mediation, pretrial settlements—the strike suit had metastasized. Hazardous-product litigation, most notably against asbestos manufacturers and tobacco companies, had transferred huge sums of money from corporations to successful litigants and the law firms that represented them. In fact, in the 1990s the debate about "needless litigation" focused more on litigators than jurors. For instance, the Trial Lawyers Association changed its name to the American Association for Justice in 2006, in part because the "plaintiffs' bar" had become the butt of so much criticism—and so many lawyer jokes. But juries were said to be the means by which trial lawyers worked the system as they looked for civil cases they could turn into "jackpots," just as juries had been blamed in the late nineteenth century for "unreasonable" verdicts against the railroads. Consequently, as Speaker of the House Newt Gingrich stumped for the Republican Contract with America, he stressed that the *Liebeck* case was a perfect example of why the country needed clause 9 of the contract: the Common Sense Legal Reform Act, which promised a "losers pay" law and "reasonable limits on punitive damages and reform of product liability laws to stem the endless tide of litigation."[234]

Stella Liebeck's lawsuit had hit a nerve, yet it is not immediately obvious why this case assumed such mythic proportions. One could not have asked for a more appealing plaintiff than the stolid Mrs. Liebeck, whose original request for compensation had been entirely reasonable. The amount of money involved, though hardly trivial, was small compared with the litigation against the tobacco and asbestos companies, even before the judge reduced it substantially. Nor was Liebeck seeking a "jackpot." The jury's $2.7 million award had been its way of "sending a message" to McDonald's. Sending a message was, in fact, exactly what Mrs. Liebeck wanted, in addition to compensation for her medical expenses and suffering. "I was never in it for the money," she said. "I just wanted them to turn down the temperature on their coffee."

234. Republican Contract with America, House of Representatives Archives, web .archive.org/web/19990427174200/http://www.house.gov/house/Contract/CONTRACT .html (accessed August 14, 2014).

Commonwealth of Massachusetts v. Louise Woodward

On the afternoon of February 4, 1997, eight-month-old Matthew Eappen was taken to Children's Hospital in Boston from his home in suburban Newton, after the young woman caring for him, Louise Woodward, made an emergency call about an unresponsive infant. Police officers responding to the scene would later testify that Ms. Woodward claimed she had "dropped" or "popped" the baby onto the floor and that she might have been "a little rough" with him because he would not stop crying. Woodward was arrested for battery of a child. Five days later, Matthew Eappen lapsed into a coma and died. The autopsy and other medical records showed that the baby had suffered a fractured skull, subdural hematoma, fractured wrist (from a month earlier), and retinal hemorrhages consistent with "shaken-baby" syndrome. A month later a grand jury returned an indictment for murder, and Woodward was confined to the state women's prison to await trial.[235]

Massachusetts law defines first-degree murder as "murder committed with deliberately premeditated malice aforethought, or with extreme atrocity or cruelty." Second-degree murder is defined simply as "murder which does not appear to be in the first degree." The statute is also clear that "the degree of murder" is for the jury to decide.[236] The statutes do not define manslaughter, but the common-law understanding, as reflected in the case law, defines involuntary manslaughter as an "unintentional killing occasioned by an act which constitutes such a disregard of the probable harmful consequences to another as to be wanton or reckless; or an unintentional killing resulting from a battery."[237] If a jury believed that Louise Woodward was responsible for Matthew Eappen's death but had exhibited no "malice aforethought" or "extreme atrocity or cruelty," it could convict her of manslaughter, either voluntary or involuntary. The consequences for Woodward would be substantial. A murder conviction required a mandatory life sentence; if convicted of second-degree murder, Woodward would have to serve at least fifteen years before being eligible for parole. The punishment for involuntary manslaughter could be anywhere from one to twenty years in prison.

The district attorney's office, however, believed that Woodward's actions met the "malice" and "atrocity or cruelty" requirements. The prosecution was also concerned that, because of the defendant's age (nineteen), a jury might be tempted by the "compromise verdict" of involuntary manslaughter. For this reason, the prosecution did not originally include manslaughter in the charges against Woodward.[238]

235. Jeff Katrowitz and Matthew Taylor, "Nanny Allegedly Assaulted Newton Infant," *Boston Globe*, February 6, 1997, B1.

236. Massachusetts General Laws, Part IV, Title I, chap. 265, section 13.

237. See http://www.massmurderdefense.com/pages/manslaughter-v.html (accessed August 15, 2014).

238. Unlike most states, Massachusetts does not treat involuntary manslaughter as a "lesser included offense." As a result of Supreme Judicial Court rulings, manslaughter is

But halfway through the trial, the prosecutors changed their strategy, asking Judge Hiller Zobel to include manslaughter in his jury charge. The defense immediately objected, asking the court to limit the charge to murder, mounting what is known as an "all or nothing" (or "noose or loose") defense. The jury would have to find Woodward guilty of murder (first or second degree) or let her go free. Judge Zobel agreed to this request, after getting the defendant's approval.[239]

There was much public speculation during and after the trial about the motives behind this defense strategy, some of it not very flattering. The obvious motive, of course, was the mirror of the state's original decision not to include manslaughter—that is, to avoid the temptation of a "compromise verdict." In interviews conducted after the trial, one of the jury consultants who advised the defense conceded that, based on their research, "if we presented manslaughter to the jury, that was going to be the verdict."[240] By allowing the all-or-nothing defense, Judge Zobel let the defense team avoid the charge it feared the most.

The defense team (though not Louise Woodward) may have had another motive as well. If the jury found that Woodward had not acted with "malice" but that she had killed Matthew "unintentionally" or "accidentally," this might suggest that the agency that employed her, EF Au Pair, had not trained her properly. EF Au Pair (which was paying for Woodward's legal defense, estimated at $750,000) might then be subject to an expensive civil suit brought by Matthew's parents.[241] A murder conviction, by contrast, would have more benign consequences for the company, however bad it might be for the defendant, raising questions about who was really in charge of the defense strategy.

There has also been speculation about why Judge Zobel agreed to the defense's request, in light of the ruling by the Supreme Judicial Court, after the trial was over, that this decision was an "error" on his part, and in light of his ultimate decision to vacate the jury's second-degree murder verdict and convict Woodward of involuntary manslaughter instead.[242] Judge Zobel's manslaughter verdict came

---

treated as a separate charge, and a judge must ordinarily include it in his or her jury charge if the prosecution requests it.

239. William F. Doherty, "Au Pair's Attorneys May Have Conflict, Judge Warns Defendant in Murder Case," *Boston Globe*, June 28, 1997, B3.

240. Neil J. Kressel and Dorit F. Kressel, *Stack and Sway: The New Science of Jury Consulting* (Boulder, CO: Westview Press, 2002), 32.

241. The prosecution actually worried that this conflict could have been the basis for a successful appeal of a guilty verdict on the grounds of "ineffective counsel." Doherty, "Au Pair's Attorneys May Have Conflict," B3. See also Brian MacQuarrie, "Agency Spends Plenty to Defend Au Pair," *Boston Globe*, October 26, 1997, A22.

242. "We have stated repeatedly that, when the evidence permits a finding of a lesser included offense, a judge must, upon request, instruct the jury on the possibility of conviction of the lesser crime." Commonwealth v. Louise Woodward, Supreme Judicial Court, 427 Mass. 659 (1998), at 662, 663.

as a complete shock to lay observers, and it infuriated members of the jury, who felt the judge had betrayed them, first taking away the manslaughter charge and then making them look ridiculous (and himself heroic) by restoring it. His decision on the verdict, however, was well within his authority, and he had used that authority on at least two previous occasions to reduce or vacate murder convictions.[243] Whatever his motives, by permitting the all-or-nothing plea, Judge Zobel allowed the defense to play "chicken" with the jury: "send our client to prison for life for what you know was not really murder, or let her walk." The jury apparently felt this dilemma acutely, and one juror commented after the trial, "there was no way we could face the Eappens or citizens of the Commonwealth and say we thought she did it but we're going to let her go. We were in a no-win situation."[244]

The trial itself presented the jury with the type of medical evidence that lay jurors are often thought to be incapable of understanding. This was a prominent theme in commentary on the case, especially in Great Britain, where the Woodward trial (which was broadcast live on Court TV) was a sensation. The British media, infamous for their lack of restraint, turned Louise Woodward into a national heroine whose freedom was in peril because of America's punitive criminal laws and outdated jury system. A British "human rights" organization, Fair Trials Abroad, compared America unfavorably with Thailand, where "the absence of a jury means that evidence is processed by highly educated Thai judges far more able to grasp the kind of convoluted medical evidence that this well-meaning but ill-schooled American jury was faced with."[245]

But as in the Apple-Samsung trial, the jurors were not the only ones who had trouble making sense of the evidence. Both sides presented medical experts with

243. Both decisions misfired, one of them badly: the first defendant was retried and convicted a second time; the second defendant, whose murder conviction was reduced to manslaughter, committed a second murder thirteen years later and was subsequently sentenced to life in prison. Ellen O'Brien, "Zobel Overturned at Least Two Jury Decisions," *Boston Globe*, November 1, 1997, A9.

244. Daniel Vasquez, "Prosecution Vows Fight to Keep the Verdict," *Boston Globe*, November 3, 1997, A1.

245. Stephen Jakaobi, "Nanny Trial Reveals Flaw in U.S. Legal System," *National Law Journal*, November 17, 1997, quoted by Kressel and Kressel, *Stack and Sway*, 26. Ironically (in light of events described below), Judge Zobel had once addressed this question in an essay for *American Heritage*. Toward the end of his essay, Zobel noted that we "expect average untrained people to absorb evidence for days and weeks on subjects entirely foreign to them without explanation, clarification, or even the opportunity to take notes or ask questions. Thus we imagine that they can understand a judge's 'instructions on the law,' often read to them in a monotone and containing principles that law students take a term to master and whose meaning appellate judges often have palpable difficulty establishing." Hon. Hiller Zobel, "The Jury on Trial," *American Heritage* 46, 4 (July–August 1995), http://www.americanheritage.com/content/jury-trial?page=show (accessed April 29, 2015).

the highest possible credentials and reputations, who proceeded to contradict one another on virtually every element of the case. Was Matthew Eappen's skull fracture of recent origin, or did it occur earlier? And if so, how much earlier? Was the baby violently shaken? Dr. Gerald Feigin, the state medical examiner, performed the autopsy; Dr. Umberto DeGirolami, director of neuropathology at Brigham & Women's Hospital, examined the baby's brain tissue. Both testified for the prosecution that the injury causing the skull fracture had happened within hours of Matthew's admission to the hospital and that there was no evidence of an older injury to the skull.[246] Dr. Feigin said the two-and-a-half-inch fracture in Matthew's skull was caused by his head being "struck against a firm or fixed object" with a level of force equal to a fall from a second-story window onto concrete.[247] Dr. Robert Cleveland, a pediatric radiologist at Boston Children's Hospital, could not tell precisely how old the skull fracture was, but he testified that it "has not been there for a long time because the edges are still sharp."[248] Dr. Joseph R. Madsen, the neurosurgeon who performed emergency brain surgery on Matthew, said the injuries came from "swinging or shaking" the baby's head and then striking it on a "blunt surface." There was a fresh purple bruise surrounding the fracture, indicating a recent event. The cause of death was recorded as blunt-force trauma.[249] Dr. Lois Smith of Children's Hospital testified that, based on her examination of the records, Matthew's eyeballs had been knocked backward into his eye sockets, and "blunt force trauma is the only cause." These injuries were new, she said.[250] Finally, in addition to the head wound, there was evidence of an older fracture of the baby's wrists, possibly three weeks prior to his death.[251]

The medical experts hired by the defense told a very different story.[252] A neuropathologist at Tufts Medical School, Dr. Lester S. Adelman, said there was "evidence of an old lesion" on a CAT scan of the brain.[253] Dr. Jan E. Leestma, a forensic neuropathologist who said he had examined more than 20,000 brains, testified that

246. William F. Doherty, "Doctors: No Sign of Old Brain Injury," *Boston Globe*, September 26, 1997, B7.

247. William F. Doherty, "Doctor Recounts Autopsy of Baby," *Boston Globe*, October 10, 1997, B3.

248. William F. Doherty, "Doctor Says Baby in Au Pair Case Took Blow to the Head," *Boston Globe*, October 9, 1997, A37.

249. Ibid.

250. William F. Doherty, "Eye Doctor Helps Build Case against Au Pair," *Boston Globe*, October 11, 1997, B3.

251. Doherty, "Doctor Says Baby Took Blow to Head."

252. One reason the *Woodward* defense was so expensive was the number of medical consultants hired to advise the defense and testify in court. Expert witnesses were paid fees ranging from $300 to $900 per hour, for as much as twenty-five hours of work. MacQuarrie, "Agency Spends Plenty."

253. Doherty, "Doctors: No Sign of Old Brain Injury."

Matthew's head injuries were old but had begun to bleed again not long before his death. The blood clot tissue, he concluded, was three to four weeks old. What the Boston doctors thought was fresh bleeding was really "rebleeding." Dr. Leetsma thought it was possible that the head injury and the wrist injury—which even the prosecution conceded was an older injury—might have been the result of a single event, consistent with a fall from less than three feet. (On cross-examination he conceded that he had never seen a three-foot fall cause a two-and-a-half-inch skull fracture.)[254] Dr. Alisa D. Gean, a neuroradiologist from San Francisco, testified that the infant suffered from a chronic head injury that had happened long before February 4 and had started to bleed again, building pressure in the brain and causing the baby to lose consciousness. She saw no evidence of the type of neck injuries consistent with shaken-baby syndrome. (The medical examiner, Dr. Feigin, also doubted the shaken-baby diagnosis, saying he could find no evidence of shaking.)[255]

Dr. Laurence Thibault, a professor of bioengineering and neurosurgery at Allegheny University of the Health Sciences, agreed that the baby's injuries could have occurred earlier than February 4 and were consistent with a three-foot fall onto carpet. An expert on shaken-baby syndrome, Dr. Thibault agreed with the other defense experts that there was no evidence of shaking in the Eappen case. He also claimed he had seen cases in which subdural hematomas did not prove fatal immediately, going undiagnosed for weeks until it was too late to treat them.[256]

Meanwhile, the atmosphere around the trial became increasingly toxic. Louise Woodward support groups emerged and staged demonstrations outside the courthouse. The trial became a staple of talk radio and TV newscasts, in addition to its live presence on Court TV. Sometimes the furor seemed to be about everything except what really happened to Matthew Eappen. His parents, Sunhil and Deborah Eappen, both physicians with busy work schedules, were criticized for placing their children in the care of a teenager. Matthew's two-year-old brother had been present when Matthew was rushed to the hospital, and one defense theory, which was eventually dropped, was that the brother might have injured the baby. Readers of major newspapers were invited to participate in a "national conversation" about parenting. Because the trial was televised, English audiences got their fill of American courtroom procedures and customs, which they apparently found appalling. The English had abandoned jury trials for most criminal and nearly all civil cases decades earlier—except, ironically, for first-degree murder.

254. William F. Doherty, "Pathologist Says Old Injuries Led to Death of Newton Infant," *Boston Globe*, October 18, 1997, A1.

255. William F. Doherty, "2d Doctor Says Boy Had Old Injuries," *Boston Globe*, October 2, 1997, B3.

256. William F. Doherty, "3d Defense Witness Testifies that Baby's Injuries Were Old," *Boston Globe*, October 22, 1997, B4.

Had Louise Woodward been tried in England for the murder of a child under her care, she would have been entitled to a jury trial.[257]

For critics of the jury system, and especially those who focused on the problems associated with nonexperts looking at complex scientific evidence, the testimony at the *Woodward* trial was an object lesson. Many observers were convinced the jury would never be able to make sense of what they were hearing. Roger Witkin, a Boston attorney, said the jurors "really can't follow the medical evidence because of the complexity of it. The intricacies of what they're talking about, the jury doesn't get it at all."[258] Attorney Barry Scheck, a member of the defense team, claimed that the four alternate jurors were more educated than the deciding jury and that this piece of "bad luck" led to the guilty verdict (all sixteen jurors sat through the trial, and the jury of twelve was picked just before deliberations). "By the luck of the draw we lost those individuals. . . . I think that the scientific evidence was not as important . . . in their deliberations as it should have been. The evidence before the jury is very clear that this was an old injury."[259]

But of course, it was not very clear that the injury was old—and that is precisely the point. If it had been clear, the experts would not have presented such opposing theories about what the evidence meant, and the prosecution would not have staked everything on a first-degree murder charge. It was *because* the expert testimony was so contradictory that the jury faced such a difficult decision: the problem was not *understanding* the complex testimony but trying to decide between competing experts who could not agree, among themselves, what the evidence meant. Ironically, there is evidence from the *Woodward* case for the proposition offered decades ago by the authors of *The American Jury*: that judges and juries agree most of the time about how cases should be decided. As the jury consultants discovered, when test jurors looked at the evidence, they quickly moved in the direction of a verdict of involuntary manslaughter—exactly why the defense sought to take that option off the table. The actual jurors were inclined in that direction as well, which is why they found the choice presented by the judge—murder or nothing—so painful. "Potentially, manslaughter may have been the verdict," one juror said after the trial was over.[260] Convinced that Louise Woodward was in some way responsible for Matthew Eappen's fatal injuries, they could not turn her loose. But they were deeply troubled by the idea of a life sentence or even the minimum fifteen years

257. The United Kingdom has abolished jury trials for most criminal offenses, but it continues to use juries for serious (so-called indictable) offenses, which include first-degree murder. See Lloyd-Bostock and Thomas, "Decline of the 'Little Parliament,'" 15–16.

258. John Ellement, "Medical Jargon May Escape Jurors," *Boston Globe*, October 21, 1997, B3.

259. Barry Scheck, appearing on Court TV, quoted in Kressel and Kressel, *Stack and Sway*, 29.

260. "Several Jurors Speak Out," *Boston Globe*, November 5, 1997, A16.

mandated by a second-degree murder conviction. One anonymous juror said this to the *Boston Globe* after Judge Zobel vacated the verdict:

> I don't think any of us thought she tried to murder him, but the basis was: "Would a reasonable person have known that such actions would have caused harm to a baby?" And we felt a reasonable 18-year-old would know that hitting a baby's head against a wall would cause harm. . . . Nobody wants to [convict] a kid. It wasn't easy deciding this verdict. Nobody liked doing it. But we weren't asked whether we liked it.261

"They only had two choices: murder or murder," said the father of one juror. Another father, speaking for his daughter, said that "it was the toughest decision she has made in her 24 years." Another juror said that although the two sides had presented "conflicting evidence," the jury "understood the medical testimony very well . . . and felt the prosecution had proven its case."[262]

Vacating the jury's verdict was only the first surprise; later that afternoon, in a hearing to determine Louise Woodward's sentence for involuntary manslaughter, Judge Zobel announced that it would be time served (279 days), and he released her from prison. The second-degree murder verdict had caused a storm of criticism and abuse directed against the jurors, the trial court, and the district attorney's office. Now the outrage was directed at the judge, and some of it came from the jury. Juror Edward Welch, who did not object to Zobel's reduction of the verdict to involuntary manslaughter, said he felt like he was "having a heart attack" when he heard that Woodward would serve no prison time. "I'm flabbergasted," he said. "I'm appalled. This is unbelievable. This is a complete injustice to that child's life, and this is not a reasonable sentence."[263]

CONCLUSION

In a typical year, 30 million Americans will be summoned for jury duty in the state and federal courts, and of these, roughly 1.5 million will be impaneled for just over 150,000 trials.[264] Although jury verdicts have declined, both as a fraction of dispositions and in absolute numbers, there are still a lot of jury trials in the

261. Anne E. Kornblut and Ellen O'Brien, "Juror: Charges Left No Choice," *Boston Globe*, November 2, 1997, A1.

262. Ibid.

263. Joe Ryan and Anne E. Kornblut, "Juror 'Appalled' at Sentence," *Boston Globe*, November 11, 1997, B1.

264. These statistics are from 2007 and are taken from National Center for State Courts, *State-of-the-States Survey of Jury Improvement Efforts* (Williamsburg, VA: NCSC, 2007).

United States: 30 percent of Americans reported in 2004 that they had served as a trial juror at least once.[265] As a consequence, the American public is leavened (for the moment, at least) with a body of experience in the art of judgment, and as the cases discussed above demonstrate, this experience is often gained under very trying circumstances. Nevertheless, although not everyone who is summoned to court looks forward to serving, most of those who have served report that doing so gave them genuine satisfaction, and it is an experience they look forward to repeating.[266] When called to a difficult task, they rose to the occasion. That's the good news. The bad news, according to critics of the jury system, is that this experience comes at an appalling cost in money, time, uncertainty, and questionable verdicts. Is the jury system worth all the trouble? And should we really be troubled that the jury is vanishing?

It is no doubt true, as the critics point out, that contemporary jurors often fail to rise to the occasion. We have seen some of the reasons for these accusations: huge punitive-damage awards in civil cases; "outrageous" verdicts in homicide cases, often with racial overtones; jurors who insist on nullifying statutes they disagree with; citizens who cannot even be bothered to reply to a jury summons; and the growing problem of hung juries. Those who look with indifference at the prospect of juries vanishing entirely would cite these facts as evidence on their side of the ledger.

Unlike the costs imposed by the jury system, its benefits are difficult to measure with any degree of precision. But we would certainly have reason to lament the loss of the leavening the jury system brings to American democracy. There is abundant evidence that jury service does precisely what Tocqueville believed it would do: it teaches the importance of civic engagement, combating the "rust" of individualism that democracy has introduced into the modern state. Even regular voters are likely to extend their political participation *beyond* voting once they have served on a jury, and nonvoting jurors are more likely to vote in the future.

265. "Jury Service: Is Fulfilling Your Civic Duty a Trial?" *Harris Interactive*, July 2004, http://www.americanbar.org/content/dam/aba/migrated/2011_build/american_jury/harris_poll_report.authcheckdam.pdf (accessed August 30, 2014). In the 1990s, surveys found that 45 percent of Americans aged eighteen and older reported serving as a juror. Shari Seidman Diamond, "What Jurors Think: Expectations and Reactions of Citizens Who Serve as Jurors," in *Verdict: Assessing the Civil Jury System*, ed. Robert Litan (Washington, DC: Brookings Institution, 1993), 282–305.

266. "In a survey by Janet T. Munsterman and her colleagues of 8,468 jurors in sixteen federal and state courts, a substantial majority of respondents reported having favorable attitudes toward jury duty after serving." Diamond, "What Jurors Think," 285. According to Diamond, studies show that one-third to two-fifths of those summoned ask to be excused when they receive their notices, but their views of jury service change in a positive direction after they have served (285–286).

Additionally, those citizens with positive memories of jury service become more generally engaged in public affairs, reading more newspapers, watching more TV news, and even attending public talks on political matters.[267] Jury service also makes citizens more appreciative of the legal system, and those who have served are more likely to describe the system as "fair."[268] That so many Americans have experienced a form of civic participation that is both more demanding and more edifying than voting is something for which we should be grateful—especially as so much of public life in America is descending to the level of Instagram and Twitter and to depths not yet imagined.

But jury trials do not just educate citizens; they also make citizens powerful. Jurors can stop criminal prosecutions by insisting on the distinction between wanton killing and self-defense, just as English jurors did under the Angevin kings. They can change the behavior of corporations, redefine the idea of negligence, temper justice with mercy. They establish the outer boundaries of the American system of "litigotiation," in which the threat of a jury trial is always in the background, pushing parties to either moderate their claims or settle them out of court.[269] They signal what the local community thinks about particular crimes or particular claims in civil court—especially in those states where juries also determine criminal sentences. And juries guarantee that, no matter how centralized political affairs become in other respects, the rendering of verdicts will remain as decentralized as possible, countering the century-long trend toward decisions by scientific or political elites and the drift toward "bureaucratic modes of social ordering."[270] After all, the only genuine civic life is a decentralized one; it is therefore not a stretch to say that the jury system makes a genuine civic life possible at a time when so many other aspects of public life are pushing in exactly the opposite direction.

In any case, bad juries, like bad judges and bad lawyers, are a minority; most juries manage to resolve cases in ways that give rise to no hint of scandal or outrage. Jurors are as likely to find for defendants as for plaintiffs in civil cases, and truly outrageous punitive-damage awards are rare, though not so rare as to put them beyond the temptation of hungry lawyers. Most criminal trials are determined on the basis of evidence, rather than emotion, and this is true regardless of the demographic makeup of the jury panel or the race or ethnicity of the defen-

267. See, for example, John Gastil et al., *The Jury and Democracy: How Jury Deliberation Promotes Civic Engagement and Political Participation* (New York: Oxford University Press, 2010), especially chap. 6.

268. John Gastil, Hiroshi Fukurai, Kent Anderson, and Mark Nolan, "Seeing Is Believing: The Impact of Jury Service on Attitudes toward Legal Institutions and the Implications for International Jury Reform," *Court Review* 48 (2012): 124.

269. Marc Galanter, "The Regulatory Function of the Jury," in Litan, *Verdict*, 61 ff.

270. Burns, *Death of the American Trial*, 119, 128.

dant.[271] We cannot know, of course, whether jury verdicts are "correct"; as Robert MacCoun has observed, "if we knew the right verdict, we wouldn't need a jury."[272] Each of the four cases described above might have been decided differently by a different and equally reasonable jury, by a judge, or by the readers of this book. But the vast majority of jury verdicts are well within the respectable range.

Furthermore, the cases above show that jurors often make better decisions than the judges and attorneys managing our courts and better than the reporters, TV pundits, and bystanders (including public officials) peering through the courtroom doors. Jurors understood the *Zimmerman* case better than the media did; in fact, they understood it better than the governor of Florida and the attorney general of the United States. Jurors in the *Woodward* trial knew what the correct verdict was even before the judge did, and they would have pronounced it if he had allowed them to do so. The jurors who decided the Apple-Samsung patent case reached the same conclusions as the experts at the US Patent Office, and at least some foreign tribunals came to the same conclusions when the companies took their patent disputes overseas. The McDonald's "hot-coffee" jurors were angered by corporate executives' refusal to take customer safety seriously and punished them accordingly—after which the company did what it should have done long before.

When the jury system works the way it is meant to, the reasons are pretty clear. First, jurors are people who take their jobs seriously—meaning that they are sensible, even if not highly educated, and they respect the serious task they have been called on to perform. Second, jurors are helped rather than hindered by their experiences in court when they are guided, and not bullied, by the judge; when they are allowed to concentrate on the evidence while ignoring the chatter surrounding notorious cases, in a courtroom setting that is congenial to their deliberations; and when they are informed of the evidence by attorneys who are competent at their own jobs.[273] As much as we value deliberation in the abstract, there are very few public venues where serious deliberation by citizens is actually possible; the jury room is one of them. In fact, the jury room might be the only one.

But if juries can collectively leaven public judgment, they can also be degraded by public confusion, and some of that confusion is inspired by the legal system itself and by the wider political culture it is part of. I believe that the new

271. Randolph N. Jonakait, "Juries Decide on the Evidence, Not on Biases," *Insights on Law & Society* 5, 2 (Winter 2005): 17.

272. Robert MacCoun, "Inside the Black Box: What Empirical Research Tells Us about Decisionmaking by Civil Juries," in Litan, *Verdict*, 167.

273. Robert P. Burns has argued that it is the particular "structure of the trial" that makes deliberation possible. The trial is a "forum that privileges 'facts' rather than the 'mechanical application of legal rules.'" Burns, *Death of the American Trial*, 117.

regime of jury selection, going well beyond what would have been necessary to combat racial discrimination, was inspired by and has helped promote a new postmodern understanding of judgment in which truth is seen as nothing more than a compromise among private biases determined by race, ethnicity, gender, and class. In the process, the new regime has inevitably changed our understanding of how the jury system should operate and what jurors are supposed to do. The logic is inescapable. If deliberation is *not* a cognitive process that some people are better at than others, if it is only an opportunity for the expression of competing biases, then the only thing one needs to know about a prospective juror is which demographic group he or she belongs to. In this view, jurors are asked not to think but only to react to the effective presentation of cues. Those who have learned to understand the jurors' "attitudes and beliefs" (and this does not necessarily require the services of professional jury consultants) will know how to plant ideas in the jurors' minds and how to appeal to what they already believe. The jurors' existing biases can then be used to draw them (or at least one or two of them) in the desired direction. This, of course, requires an "extended" voir dire over which attorneys have a significant degree of control.

This is not just an alternative understanding of jury deliberation; it is the necessary consequence of the belief that there is no such thing as truth, that there are only competing biases—another reason for having a jury list that is "representative" of the wider population, to ensure the representation in the courtroom of the broadest spectrum of bias. This is not, I should emphasize, how the typical jury actually behaves—and it would be difficult to find anyone in the legal system who would state the postmodern view as baldly as I have here. As many jury scholars have pointed out, despite some sensational exceptions, jury verdicts are driven largely by the nature of the evidence presented in court (and by the skill of the attorneys who present it) and by the way the judge explains the law—not by preexisting biases. And as many courtroom practitioners have noted, there is deep regard for the jury system among many of those who practice the law and who are convinced that most jurors are capable of rendering sensible judgments based on a clear presentation of the facts and a clear explanation of the law. But from the point of view of contemporary jury theory—and that includes contemporary jury law—evidence-based decision making is an anomaly, not an expectation.

But more is involved here than just a change in the jury selection laws. The performance of jurors is inevitably shaped by the larger intellectual culture in which jurors have grown up. We live, it is said, in a "nonjudgmental" society. We do not "impose our values" on others (even though that is precisely what we do every time we pass a law that we expect everyone to obey equally). We do not deny the validity of other persons' "narratives." And so on. These ideas have become familiar not only on college campuses but also in high schools and grade schools and in the popular culture more generally. It was only a matter of time before this postmodern paradigm had an effect on the legal order. To the extent that this is a post-1960s phenomenon, there are few people employed in the judiciary, and few who are called to serve on juries, who have not grown up in its shadow. Soon there will be none.

Reflecting on her own experience with jury service, Yale professor Norma Thompson argues that many Americans have simply lost the capacity for "prudential judgment."[274] Thompson was the jury foreperson in a murder trial in New Haven, one of four Yale professors on a jury composed almost entirely of people in white-collar occupations. These were precisely the educated and experienced professionals the old jury reformers hoped to put back in the jury box. Still, after six days, three jurors refused to vote for conviction, and the jury hung. One of the holdouts was a scientist who, Thompson believed, was unable to interpret the evidence; he insisted that proof in a criminal trial must rise to the level of proof in a scientific experiment, even though most of his fellow jurors had found no room for reasonable doubt. Another holdout asked for evidence the prosecution had never presented, and a third could not explain her "reasonable doubts" but held on to them anyway. "The jury," Tocqueville wrote, "teaches each man not to recoil before responsibility for his own acts—a virile disposition without which there is no political virtue."[275] If the four cases described above show the jury at its best, the New Haven jury shows how political virtue has eroded in our time.

What to do? This book has described a debate about the jury system that, from the republican era until roughly the 1940s, focused almost entirely on the quality of the citizens summoned and the authority they could rightfully exercise. Did they have the qualities of character and judgment suitable for the grave responsibility of judgment? What jury selection procedures would guarantee that juries were not only impartial but also capable? How far did the jury right extend? That debate took a detour in the 1960s, partly in response to the unfolding civil rights movement, but also because of broader doubts about whether the impartial judgment of "twelve good men and true" was not just a code for class bias. We have been living with, and sometimes complaining about, the results of that paradigm shift without fully confronting its source: the claim that juries should be "representative" of the community from which they are chosen and that they must be chosen from lists that have not been screened for any of the qualities necessary for judgment. Instead, jury scholars—even those who are fully sympathetic to the jury system—have focused on the consequences of the postmodern perspective and not (for the most part) the perspective itself.

For example, Stephen J. Adler proposes the elimination of peremptory challenges but suggests no reforms that would winnow the bad jurors from the good at an earlier stage in the process of jury selection. Relishing the prospect that such

274. Norma Thompson, *Unreasonable Doubt: Circumstantial Evidence and an Ordinary Murder in New Haven* (Columbia: University of Missouri Press, 2006), 49–105, 158–168.

275. Tocqueville, *Democracy in America*, 262.

a reform would destroy "the huge market for jury consultants," Adler also anticipates that the "formerly spurned would finally get their due: the chance to exercise true power in a democracy."[276] He then wonders how it will be possible "for a conscientious jury, whatever its makeup, to understand its task and perform it well."[277] But that word, "conscientious," is smuggled quietly into the sentence with no indication of where it came from or why it is there. Not all citizens are conscientious. Not all those who are "spurned" should be empowered. These facts are known to anyone who spends any time out in public—on the highway, at the ballpark, at the shopping mall, or wherever one can glimpse a random sample of humanity going about its business. It we want conscientious jurors, we are going to have to look for them. To be sure, good jurors might be *anyone*, but they cannot be *everyone*.[278]

Jeffrey Abramson, author of *We the Jury*—published in the wake of the notorious Rodney King verdicts—has also urged the abolition of peremptory challenges, believing them to be the last mechanism for practicing racial and ethnic discrimination in jury selection. "The time has come," he writes, "to fully practice what we preach and to prohibit discriminatory, exclusionary practices from occurring under cover of the peremptory challenge."[279] But Abramson is one of the rare jury scholars to acknowledge that a line has been crossed, from the ancient "deliberative" ideal of the jury to a new "representative" ideal, and that the new ideal is a mixed blessing. His comments deserve to be quoted at length:

> The deliberative ideal was a demanding one, seeking to inspire jurors to put aside narrow group allegiances in favor of spying common ground. It was a model of democracy that believes that face-to-face meetings matter, that voting is secondary to debate and discussion, that power should ultimately go to the persuasive, that collective wisdom results from gathering people in conversation from different walks of life, that unanimity is practicable and desirable, and that there is a justice shared across the demographic divides of race, religion, gender, and national origin. The new and competing ideal is a group-representation model, one that seeks to redesign the jury so that it basically fits the pluralist paradigm of democracy and interest group politics. This model is openly skeptical about whether deliberation inside the jury room matters; it insists, in the name of realism, that there is no one justice to

276. Stephen J. Adler, *The Jury: Trial and Error in the American Courtroom* (New York: Times Books/Random House, 1994), 224.

277. Ibid., 225.

278. I have discussed this problem in Dennis Hale, "The Natural History of Citizenship," in *Friends and Citizens: Essays in Honor of Wilson Carey McWilliams*, ed. Dennis Bathory and Nancy Schwartz (New York: Rowman & Littlefield, 2000), 151–170.

279. Jeffrey Abramson, *We the Jury: The Jury System and the Ideal of Democracy* (New York: Basic Books, 1994), 247.

> share, that juries are not above the political fray but are a microcosm of the biases and prejudices, the bartering and brokering among group interests that dominate democratic deal making in general. According to this point of view, the key to jury verdicts becomes whom the jurors are, not what the evidence shows. . . . [T]he highest aspiration we can have for jury democracy [under this view] is to represent the perspectives of groups in some fair way, to balance the biases of jurors and therefore achieve an overall impartial verdict.[280]

This new paradigm, though it acknowledges the reality of group prejudice in America, "goes too far," Abramson concedes, "when it discards the deliberative ideal entirely and turns instead to theories of proportional representation and the divisive notion that jurors are there to be allegiant advocates for their own kind."[281] But that turn toward "proportional representation" is precisely the paradigm enacted by the Jury Selection and Service Act of 1968, and it will remain until that law is changed.

Improving the performance of the jury system will require what it has always required: better jurors. This is not simply a matter of how juries are selected. It matters a great deal what happens to jurors from the moment they arrive at the courthouse to the moment they retire to deliberate their verdict. I have already noted the many improvements made in the way jurors experience their service: one-day, one-trial summoning; permission to take notes and ask questions; and so forth. All these reforms have had a positive effect on how jurors experience their service and on how effectively they perform it.[282] They have become common in the federal courts, but not universal. Their continued spread should be encouraged in both the federal and state courts.

As always, however, the most important step is the selection of those who will be called to the courthouse. The modern theory of jury selection is "random selection from a jury list that represents a cross-section of the population."[283] No *qualitative* filters may be applied to jury lists at any step in the process. Yet this is not how juries are selected *in fact*: there are filters all along the way that remove some people and let others through. But these filters are hidden, sometimes even from those who employ them. At the outset, a huge number of potential jurors recuse themselves by failing to respond when summoned, and there is little serious effort in most jurisdictions to round them up and get them to court—almost as if

280. Ibid., 245.

281. Ibid.

282. On jury reforms generally, see Randolph N. Jonakait, *The American Jury System* (New Haven, CT: Yale University Press, 2003) 279 ff.; Paula DiPerna, *Juries on Trial: Faces of American Justice* (New York: Dembner Books/W. W. Norton, 1984), 217 ff.; and Adler, *The Jury*, 218 ff.

283. 28 U.S.C. § 1861.

a quiet decision has been made that those who refuse to respond would probably not make very good jurors anyway. In some large cities, half the citizens called fit this description. Of those who do respond, many are rejected during voir dire, either because they reveal some experience or opinion dangerous to one of the parties or because they do not appear to be capable of handling the task at hand. The first is a case-specific objection; the second is not. Those who seem incapable of handling a *particular* trial would probably have difficulty with any trial. The voir dire has many purposes, but one of them is surely to spot such jurors—what the republican era referred to as "pudding heads" and what are now called "UFO jurors" or "nullifiers."[284] Some of these can be removed through challenges for cause; others must be weeded out by the expenditure of each side's limited peremptory challenges, and this is one reason such challenges have managed to survive the almost universal hostility directed at them by legal reformers. In the end, *the jury list must be culled*. In the past, this was done openly; in the present, it is done covertly. But it is done, nonetheless. We might as well admit that we do not really believe in choosing juries from a random sample of the entire adult population, and preach what we practice.

This would be less a reform than a concession to reality. After all, is there any other area of life in which we insist that everyone is equally capable of performing a difficult task at a satisfactory level? We do not make that claim about first-grade teachers, firefighters, plumbers, brain surgeons, or baseball players. Why should we make it about jurors? And note the important consequence of the claim: if everyone can do it, it must not be very hard to do; and if it isn't very hard, it's probably not very important. If we insisted that everyone is capable of teaching first grade, we would be doing a grave disservice to those people who actually *can* teach first grade, maligning both them and their profession. In the same way, we trivialize the jury by insisting that its task is so simple that there is no one who can't do it. Jury service is not brain surgery, of course; it might even be easier, in some cases, than teaching first grade. But the point to be stressed is that jury service is a skill that, like every other skill, is unevenly distributed throughout the population. If we want jury service to mean something—if we want *juries* to mean something—we cannot pretend that everyone is equally capable of being a good juror.

In any case, since the system has already developed a number of "work-arounds" to honor the law in the breach, why not just change the law? The obvious objection is that this would drag us back to the bad old days when jury selection discriminated against blacks, women, Hispanics, and the poor. It is often said that the Jury Selection and Service Act "democratized" the jury system (this is Abramson's view, to cite just one of many examples); any change would there-

284. An attorney with a notably weak case might well prefer to *keep* such jurors rather than more sensible ones. This might explain some of the controversial jury verdicts that have diminished the jury's reputation.

fore work in an antidemocratic direction. But as I hope the preceding discussion has demonstrated, the exclusion of women or discrimination against disfavored minorities had nothing to do with the process of selecting jurors for the qualities of integrity and judgment. The jury system was already "democratic." That is, the understanding of the "good juror" was not that he (and later she) was from the upper class or a member of an elite social group. The ideal juror was simply an ordinary, sensible citizen from any walk of life who displayed the qualities of judgment required for jury service. Nor is there any reason why the search for capable jurors should discriminate against any demographic slice of the community, since, as the Judicial Conference insisted until the 1960s, there are capable and less capable citizens in every group in the community, and it is the proper job of a jury selection system to go out and find them.

It bears repeating what the Judicial Conference stated in its 1960 report: "In order to get better jurors, the Committee recommends *greater care in the compilation of the list of jurors whose names go into the jury wheel or box from which trial jurors are chosen*."[285] The current law, however, states that the court "shall determine solely on the basis of information provided on the juror qualification form and other competent evidence" whether a person is "not qualified" for service on a federal jury.[286] These statutory qualifications refer to objective criteria only: age, citizenship, residency, literacy (in English), lack of a criminal record, and lack of any mental or physical "infirmity" that would make the person incapable of rendering "satisfactory jury service."[287] This last requirement is not precisely objective, since it requires a judgment about the likelihood of "satisfactory" service and how "satisfactory" should be understood. It therefore opens the door to a broader understanding of "satisfactory" that could look beyond the narrow meaning of "infirmity." (Nor should every physical "infirmity" be an automatic bar to serving.) Why not open that door a little wider, adopting statutory language specifically authorizing the court to look for jurors who appear to be "capable" of the tasks before them? Would this really require a *radical* change from our actual current practice?

Consider, in this context, the long (sometimes very long) juror questionnaires that have become a feature of so many trials, especially those with notably high stakes. These questionnaires, approved and administered by the court, seek all sorts of information, most of it relevant to challenges for cause and the strategic use of peremptory challenges, and unlike the juror questionnaires from previous generations, they are mostly case specific. Attorneys for both sides contribute

285. *The Jury System in the Federal Courts: Report of the Judicial Conference Committee on the Operation of the Jury System*, ed. Shackelford Miller Jr. (St. Paul, MN: West Publishing Co., 1960), 11, emphasis added.

286. 28 U.S.C. § 1865(a). The requirement to use only the jury form and "other competent evidence" was apparently meant to prevent a return to the key-man system—which might return anyway, since it has never been ruled unconstitutional.

287. 28 U.S.C. § 1865(b)(4).

questions, approved by the court, and the court "may conduct its own examination" of prospective jurors.[288] Yet the questionnaires often go beyond the strategic, looking for information that is relevant to the general issue of "satisfactory" service. The questionnaire in the O. J. Simpson criminal trial, for example, asked 302 questions and was more than 100 pages long. In addition to basic demographic information (age, sex, race) and case-specific questions ("Do you personally know anyone who works for the Los Angeles district attorney's office?"), the form sought answers to more general questions about the respondent's suitability: "Does your job involve management or supervisory duties?" (21). "What is the last level of education you completed?" (31). "Have you ever served on a jury before?" (62). "Have you read about a juror's experience on a particular case in a newspaper or magazine? If yes, what do you recall and what was your impression of his-her experience?" (106).[289]

For the 2007 murder trial of Moe Gibbs in North Dakota—a far less notorious case than Simpson's—the trial court administered a thirty-four-page questionnaire that sought information about job experience, education, supervisory responsibilities, reading habits, and the ability to "judge character."[290] The questionnaire in the trial of the al-Qaeda terrorist Zacarias Moussaoui posed 159 questions—not only predictable questions about attitudes toward Islam but also information about the respondent's educational, occupational, and legal background.[291] Before the *Apple v. Samsung* jury was impaneled, Judge Lucy Koh "spent a good deal of time screening a large pool of jurors" before voir dire even began.[292]

The amount of this pre–voir dire screening can sometimes be extraordinary. In the federal murder trial of Dzhokhar Tsarnaev for the terrorist bombing of the Boston Marathon, the US District Court in Boston started with a list of 35,000 qualified jurors from the court's Eastern Division, supplied by the state jury commissioner. (In Massachusetts, names are taken from voter registration lists and the annual city and town census, and the federal court uses the state list.) From this list, 1,373 names were chosen at random and summoned to the courthouse during the first week of January 2015. The summoned jurors were given a twenty-eight-page questionnaire, with questions supplied by the defense, the prosecution, and the court.[293] Judge George O'Toole then screened the responses, dismissing all

288. Federal Rules of Criminal Procedure 24(a)(1).

289. *People v. O. J. Simpson*, Juror Questionnaire, Deliberations' Library of Sample Juror Questionnaires, http://www.jurylaw.typepad.com/deliberations/sample_juror_questionnair.html (accessed March 31, 2015).

290. *State v. Moe Gibbs*, Juror Questionnaire, ibid.

291. *United States v. Zacarias Moussaoui*, Juror Questionnaire, ibid.

292. Bajwa, "Apple v. Samsung," 90–91.

293. *United States v. Dzhokhar Tsarnaev*, Juror Questionnaire, Case 1:13-cr-10200-GAO Document 1178, http://www.scribd.com/doc/259151331/Tsarneav-Trial-Juror-Questionnaire-pdf (accessed April 22, 2015).

but 600 names; these individuals were called back later that month for oral questioning by Judge O'Toole, in the presence of counsel. (It took six days to question just eighty-one potential jurors, a task reporters described as "culling" the list.)[294] What the judge was looking for, the *Boston Globe* reported, was "roughly 70 suitable jurors," after which he would let the lawyers and prosecutors exercise their peremptory challenges.[295] Thus, only 5 percent of the original 1,373 were left to experience the traditional sorting that takes place during voir dire. Jury selection remains a *selective* process, one in which many are called but relatively few are found "suitable"—whatever the law pretends. We know why lawyers ask so many questions: they are looking for friendly jurors free of bias. But the court is looking for what courts have always looked for: twelve jurors who are "good and true."

For much of its history, the Judicial Conference of the United States paid close attention to the problem of jury selection. This has not been true for quite some time. The conference abolished its Committee on the Jury System in 1987, and since then, its annual reports and long-range planning documents have had almost nothing to say about juries.[296] So here is a practical suggestion: the Judicial Conference should reestablish its Committee on the Jury System and consider the difficulties posed by the need to winnow jury lists in search of those citizens who are most suitable for jury service. This is what we used to do in most courts; it is what we try to do now, surreptitiously, sometimes through the use of lengthy questionnaires but much more routinely through the use of peremptory challenges.

But that leaves another, equally difficult problem. As juries resolve fewer and fewer cases in both the criminal and civil courts, the question of who serves on juries moves steadily in the direction of making no difference at all. As trials shrink in importance, the jury shrinks as well. The problem of the vanishing trial might also benefit from some Judicial Conference scrutiny. But solving this problem will require more than adding or subtracting from the jury law. It will require a revision of the state and federal criminal statutes that give prosecutors enormous discretion to charge defendants with multiple counts, amassing so many penal-

294. Martin J. Valencia and Patricia Wen, "Dzhokhar Tsarnaev Case Jury Is Slow to Form," *Boston Globe*, January 24, 2015.

295. Patricia Wen and Martin J. Valencia, "Lawyers Hunt Too-Eager Tsarnaev Jurors," *Boston Globe*, January 26, 2015.

296. An example of how the Judicial Conference approaches the jury system is a recommendation from its most recently published report (dated September 16, 2014). To help district court personnel comply with the requirements of the Jury Selection and Service Act, "the Administrative Office will provide specially programmed Census Bureau information that shows racial, ethnic, and sex data and percentages for the citizen population by county for every federal jury division in your district." *Report of the Proceedings of the Judicial Conference of the United States*, September 16, 2014, Jury Form A012, (b), part IV, http://www.uscourts.gov/FederalCourts/JudicialConference/Proceedings/Proceedings.aspx?doc=/uscourts/FederalCourts/judconf/proceedings/2014–09.pdf (accessed May 4, 2015).

ties that defendants are pressured to plead guilty in return for the possibility of a shorter sentence. More complicated still are the incentives (not limited to the Federal Rules of Civil Procedure) that have led to the massive increase in civil litigation in state and federal courts, putting greater pressure on litigants to resolve their disputes in ways other than trials before either judges *or* juries.

The jury is vanishing. Trials are vanishing. It is reasonably clear why; what is not clear is whether there is any support for reversing a trend that is now two generations old, the product of policies supported by both political parties, both houses of Congress, the leadership of the American bar, the faculties of almost every law school, and the editors of nearly every law journal. If this book has managed to sow a few doubts about the wisdom of this trend, I will consider my work a success.

Bibliography

ARTICLES, BOOKS, AND OTHER DOCUMENTS

ABA Standards for Criminal Justice and Trial by Jury. Washington, DC: American Bar Association, 1968.

ABA Standards for Criminal Justice and Trial by Jury. 3rd ed. Washington, DC: American Bar Association, 1996.

Abramson, Jeffrey. *We the Jury: The Jury System and the Ideal of Democracy.* New York: Basic Books, 1994.

———, ed. *Postmortem: The O. J. Simpson Case*. New York: Basic Books, 1996.

An Act Declaring the Rights and Liberties of the Subject and Settling the Succession of the Crown (The English Bill of Rights), 1689. http://avalon.law.yale.edu/17th_century/england.asp (accessed January 9, 2014).

Adams, Edward S., and Christian J. Lane. "Constructing a Jury that Is Both Impartial and Representative: Utilizing Cumulative Voting in Jury Selection." *New York University Law Review* 73 (June 1998): 703–764.

Adams, John. *Diaries of John Adams*. Massachusetts Historical Society. http://www.masshist.org/digitaladams/archive/diary (accessed February 9, 2014).

Adams, Lorraine, and Serge F. Kovaleski. "The Dream Team's Dream Resources." In *Postmortem: The O. J. Simpson Case,* ed. Jeffrey Abramson, 126–131. New York: Basic Books, 1996.

Adams, Willi Paul. *The First American Constitutions: Republican Ideology and the Making of the State Constitutions in the Revolutionary Era*. Raleigh: University of North Carolina Press, 1980.

Adler, Stephen J. *The Jury: Trial and Error in the American Courtroom*. New York: Times Books/Random House, 1994.

Administrative Office of the United States Courts. *Annual Reports of the Director.* Washington, DC: Government Printing Office.

Alker, H. R., and J. J. Barnard. "Procedural and Social Biases in the Jury Selection Process." *Justice System Journal* 3, 3 (Spring 1978): 220–241.

Allen, Ronald J. "Unexplored Aspects of the Theory of the Right to a Trial by Jury." *Washington University Law Quarterly* 66 (1988): 33–45.

Alschuler, Albert W. "The Failure of Sentencing Guidelines: A Plea for Less Aggregation." *University of Chicago Law Review* 58 (1991): 901–952.

———. "Our Faltering Jury." In *Postmortem: The O. J. Simpson Case*, ed. Jeffrey Abramson, 135–144. New York: Basic Books, 1996.

Alschuler, Albert W., and Andrew G. Deiss. "A Brief History of the Criminal Jury in the United States." *University of Chicago Law Review* 61 (1994): 867–928.

Alternative Dispute Resolution Act of 1998. Congressional Record—House, October 10, 1998, H10457-H10459.

Amar, Akhil Reed. *The Bill of Rights: Creation and Reconstruction*. New Haven, CT: Yale University Press, 1998.

American Bar Association. "Report of the Section of Judicial Administration." *Annual Report of the American Bar Association* 63 (1938).

———. *Total National Lawyer Counts, 1878–2011*. Market Research Department. http://www.americanbar.org/resources_for_lawyers/profession_statistics.html (accessed June 17, 2013).

American College of Trial Lawyers. *The "Vanishing Trial": The College, the Profession, and the Civil Justice System*. October 2004. http://www.actl.com/AM/Template.cfm?Section=All_Publications&Template=/CM/ContentDisplay.cfm&ContentFileID=57.

"Attack U.S. Jury System." *New York Times*, March 4, 1949, 22.

Bajwa, Sanjeev. "Apple v. Samsung: Is It Time to Change Our Patent Trial System?" *Pacific McGeorge Global Business & Development Law Journal* 27 (2014): 77–106.

Bannon, Alicia M. *Federal Judicial Vacancies: The Trial Courts*. New York: Brennan Center for Justice, New York University School of Law, 2013.

Barkan, Steven E. "Jury Nullification in Political Trials." *Social Problems* 31 (1983): 28–44.

Barrow, Rachel E. "Recharging the Jury: The Criminal Jury's Constitutional Role in an Era of Mandatory Sentencing." *University of Pennsylvania Law Review* 152, 1 (November 2003): 33–128.

Barry, Dan, et al. "Race, Tragedy and Outrage Collide after a Shot in Florida." *New York Times*, April 1, 2012. http://www.nytimes.com/2012/04/02/us/trayvon.martin-shooting-prompts-a-review-of-ideals.html?pagewanted=all&_r=0) (accessed August 12, 2014).

Beale, Sara Sun. "Federalizing Crime: Assessing the Impact on the Federal Courts." *Annals of the American Academy of Political and Social Science* 543 (January 1996): 39–51.

Becker-Avin, Marni. "The Real Purpose of Voir Dire." http://www.therightjury.com/about/html (accessed July 3, 2014).

Bennett, Judge Mark W. "Unraveling the Gordian Knot of Implicit Bias in Jury Selection: The Problems of Judge-Dominated Voir Dire, the Failed Promise of *Batson*, and Proposed Solutions." *Harvard Law and Policy Review* 4 (2010): 1207–1230.

Bentham, Jeremy. *Principles of Judicial Procedure* (1837).

Berelson, Bernard, Paul Lazarsfeld, and William McPhee. *Voting: A Study of Opinion Formation in a Presidential Campaign*. Chicago: University of Chicago Press, 1954.

Bermant, Gordon, and John Shapard. *The Voir Dire Examination, Juror Challenges, and Adversary Advocacy*. Washington, DC: Federal Judicial Center, 1977.

Berns, Walter. "Freedom of the Press and the Alien and Sedition Laws: A Reappraisal." *Supreme Court Review* (1970): 109–159.

Berris, Karin A. "Appearance Rates of Potential Jurors Who Confirm, Postpone, or Fail to Respond to the Jury Summons." *Drake Law Review* 59 (2011): 649–688.

Binkley, Robert C. "Nullification and the Legal Process." *New Republic,* May 1, 1929. Reprinted in *Massachusetts Law Quarterly* 14 (1928–1929): 109–110.

Blackstone, William. *The Commentaries of Sir William Blackstone, Knight, on the Laws and Constitution of England*. New York: American Bar Association, 2009.

Blume, William Wirt. "Jury Selection Analyzed: Proposed Revision of Federal System." *Michigan Law Review* 42 (1943–1944): 831–862.

Boston, Charles. "Some Practical Remedies for Existing Defects in the Administration of Justice." *University of Pennsylvania Law Review* 61 (1912): 1–32.

A Brief Narrative of the Case and Trial of John Peter Zenger (1735). http://www.nycourts.gov/history/legal-history-new-york/legal-history-eras-01/History_Tryal-John-Peter-Zenger.pdf (accessed April 30, 2015).

Broeder, Dale W. "Voir Dire Examinations: An Empirical Study." *Southern California Law Review* 38 (1964–1965): 503–528.

Brown, Darryl K. "Jury Nullification within the Rule of Law." *Minnesota Law Review* 81 (1997): 1149–1200.

———. "The Means and Ends of Representative Juries." *Virginia Journal of Social Policy & Law* 1 (1993–1994): 445–474.

Browning, Andrew. *English Historical Documents 1660–1714*. New York: Oxford University Press, 1953.

Budd, Martin L. "The Legal System of 1691." *Harvard Law Review* 80 (1967): 1752–1772.

Burbank, Stephen B. "Keeping Our Ambition under Control: The Limits of Data and Inference in Searching for the Causes and Consequences of Vanishing Trials in Federal Court." *Journal of Empirical Legal Studies* 1, 3 (November 2004): 571–590.

Bureau of the Census. *Historical Statistics of the United States: Colonial Times to 1957*. Washington, DC: Bureau of the Census, 1960.

Bureau of Justice Statistics. *Indigent Defense*. Washington, DC, 1996.

———. *Prisoners in 2010*. Washington, DC, 2010.

Burns, Robert P. *The Death of the American Trial*. Chicago: University of Chicago Press, 2009.

———. *A Theory of the Trial*. Princeton, NJ: Princeton University Press, 1999.

Butler, Paul. "Racially Based Jury Nullification: Black Power in the Criminal Justice System." *Yale Law Journal* 105 (1995): 677–726.

Callender, Clarence N. *The Selection of Jurors: A Comparative Study of the Methods of Selection and the Personnel of Juries in Philadelphia and Other Cities*. Philadelphia: University of Pennsylvania Press, 1924.

Cameron, Neil, Susan Potter, and Warren Young. "The New Zealand Jury." *Law and Contemporary Problems* 62 (Spring 1999): 103–139.

Campbell, Angus, P. Converse, W. E. Miller, and D. Stokes. *The American Voter.* New York: Wiley, 1960.

Campbell, Angus, Gerald Gurin, and Warren E. Miller. *The Voter Decides*. Evanston, IL: Row, Peterson, 1954.

Carroll, Jameson B., et al. *Striking Back against Peremptory Strikes*. Tort Trial and Insurance Practice Section, American Bar Association, 2009. http://www.kslaw.com/Library/publication/4–09%20ABA.pdfv.

Carter, Dan T. *Scottsboro: A Tragedy of the American South*. Baton Rouge: Louisiana State University Press, 2007.

"Case of the Imprisonment of Edward Bushell for Alleged Misconduct as a Juryman." 22 Charles II A.D. 1670 [Vaughan's Reports, 135]. http://www.constitution.org/trials/bushell/bushell.htm (accessed April 30, 2015).

Cecil, Joe S., Deal P. Miletich, and George Cort. *Trends in Summary Judgment Practice: A Preliminary Analysis*. Washington, DC: Federal Judicial Center, 2001.

"Challenge to Jury in Red Trial Ended." *New York Times*, March 2, 1949, 17.

The Charter of Massachusetts Bay: 1629. http://avalon.law.yale.edu/17th_century/mass03.asp (accessed January 10, 2014).

Chesterman, Michael. "Criminal Trial Juries in Australia: From Penal Colonies to a Federal Democracy." *Law and Contemporary Problems* 62 (Spring 1999): 69–102.

Chitwood, Oliver Perry. *Justice in Colonial Virginia*. Baltimore: Johns Hopkins Press, 1905.

Choate, Joseph H. "Trial by Jury." Annual address to the American Bar Association, Philadelphia, 1898.

Chroust, Anton-Herman. "The Legal Profession in Colonial America." *Notre Dame Lawyer* 34, 1 (1957–1958): 44–64.

Clark, Charles E., and Harry Shulman. "Jury Trial in Civil Cases—A Study in Judicial Administration." *Yale Law Journal* 43 (1934): 867–885.

Clermont, Kevin M., and Theodore Eisenberg. "Litigation Realities." *Cornell Law Review* 88 (2002): 119–154.

Cockburn, J. S., and Thomas A. Green. *Twelve Good Men and True: The Criminal Trial Jury in England, 1200–1800*. Princeton, NJ: Princeton University Press, 1988.

Cohen, Thomas H. "General Civil Jury Trial Litigation in State and Federal Courts: A Statistical Portrait." *Journal of Empirical Legal Studies* 5, 3 (September 2008): 593–618.

Cohen, Thomas H., and Steven K. Smith. *Civil Trial Cases and Verdicts in Large Counties, 2001*. Washington, DC: Department of Justice, Bureau of Justice Statistics, 2004.

"Comment: The Changing Role of the Jury in the Nineteenth Century." *Yale Law Journal* 74 (1964): 170–192.

"Comment: A Constitutional Renvoir: Unanimous Verdicts in State Criminal Trials." *Fordham Law Review* 41 (1972): 115–139.

Conrad, Clay S. *Jury Nullification: The Evolution of a Doctrine*. Washington, DC: Cato Institute, 1998.

Conti, Kathleen. "Everett Struggles to Get a True Population Count." *Boston Globe*, December 30, 2007.

Crispo, Lawrence W., Jill M. Slasky, and Geanene M. Yriarte. "Jury Nullification: Law versus Anarchy." *Loyola of Los Angeles Law Review* 31, 1 (1997): 1–62.

Croly, Herbert D. *The Promise of American Life*. New York: Macmillan, 1914.

Dershowitz, Alan. *Reasonable Doubt: The Criminal Justice System and the O. J. Simpson Verdict*. New York: Touchstone, 1996.

Dession, George H. "The New Federal Rules of Criminal Procedure II." *Yale Law Journal* 56 (January 1947): 197–257.

Deutsch, Linda. "TV Distorts Jurors' Expectations: 'No Prints, No DNA, No Conviction.'"

Associated Press, January 17, 2006. http:///www.concordmonitor.com/article/tv-distorts-jurors-expectations (accessed June 21, 2014).

Diamond, Shari Seidman. "What Jurors Think: Expectations and Reactions of Citizens Who Serve as Jurors." In *Verdict: Assessing the Civil Jury System*, ed. Robert Litan, 282–305. Washington, DC: Brookings Institution, 1993.

Dillon, John F. *The Laws and Jurisprudence of England and America: Being a Series of Lectures Delivered before Yale University.* Boston: Little, Brown, 1894.

DiPerna, Paula. *Juries on Trial: Faces of American Justice*. New York: Dembner Books/W. W. Norton, 1984.

Doherty, William F. "Au Pair's Attorneys May Have Conflict, Judge Warns Defendant in Murder Case." *Boston Globe*, June 28, 1997, B3.

———. "Doctor Recounts Autopsy of Baby." *Boston Globe*, October 10, 1997, B3.

———. "Doctor Says Baby in Au Pair Case Took Blow to the Head." *Boston Globe*, October 9, 1997, A37.

———. "Doctors: No Sign of Old Brain Injury." *Boston Globe*, September 26, 1997, B7.

———. "Eye Doctor Helps Build Case against Au Pair." *Boston Globe*, October 11, 1997, B3.

———. "Pathologist Says Old Injuries Led to Death of Newton Infant." *Boston Globe*, October 18, 1997, A1.

———. "2d Doctor Says Boy Had Old Injuries." *Boston Globe*, October 2, 1997, B3.

———. "3d Defense Witness Testifies that Baby's Injuries Were Old." *Boston Globe*, October 22, 1997, B4.

Douglas, D. C., ed. *English Historical Documents*, vol. 2. New York: Oxford University Press, 1981.

Drummond, Mark A. "Don't Let the Judge Cut You Out." *Litigation News* (Spring 2012). http://www.apps.americanbar.org/litigation/litigationnews/articles-print/050412-practice-points-spring12.html (accessed June 30, 2014).

Du Bois, Grant P., Jr. "Desirability of Blue Ribbon Juries." *Hastings Law Journal* 13 (1961–1962): 479–489.

Dzur, Albert W. *Punishment, Participatory Democracy, and the Jury*. New York: Oxford University Press, 2012.

East, Georgia. "Tens of Thousands in South Florida Skip out on Jury Duty." *Sun Sentinel*, April 16, 2011. http://www.articles.sun-sentinel.com/2011-04-16/news/fl-jury-no-shows-2011-04-16_1_jury-duty-potential-jurors-voter (accessed June 23, 2014).

"Eighth Annual Report of the Special Committee to Suggest Remedies and Formulate Proposed Laws to Prevent Delay and Unnecessary Cost in Litigation." *American Bar Association Journal* 1 (1915): 375–382.

Eisenberg, Theodore, and Kevin M. Clermont. "Trial by Jury or Judge: Which Is Speedier?" *Judicature* 79, 4 (January–February 1996): 176.

Eisenberg, Theodore, and Charlotte Lanvers. "What Is the Settlement Rate and Why Should We Care?" *Journal of Empirical Legal Studies* 6, 1 (March 2009): 111–146.

Elkins, Stanley, and Eric McKitrick. *The Age of Federalism: The Early American Republic, 1788–1800*. New York: Oxford University Press, 1993.

Ellement, John. "Medical Jargon May Escape Jurors." *Boston Globe*, October 21, 1997, B3.

Elliot, Jonathan. *The Debates in the Several State Conventions on the Adoption of the Federal Constitution*, vol. 2. New York: B. Franklin, 1968.

Epstein, Richard A. "Class Actions: Aggregation, Amplification and Distortion." John M. Olin Law & Economics Working Paper no. 182 (2nd series), University of Chicago Law School, April 2003.

Ervin, Sen. Sam J., Jr. "Jury Reform Needs More Thought." *American Bar Association Journal* 53 (1967): 132–135.

Etzioni, Amitai. "Creating an Imbalance." *Trial* 10 (1974): 28–30.

Faulkner, Robert K. "John Marshall and the Burr Trial." *Journal of American History* 53, 2 (September 1966): 247–258.

———. *The Jurisprudence of John Marshall*. Princeton, NJ: Princeton University Press, 1968.

Federal Bureau of Investigation. *Uniform Crime Statistics*, 1960–2012. http://www.ucrdatatool.gov/ (accessed March 26, 2015).

Federal Judicial Center, Federal Court Management Statistics Archive. "Judicial Caseload Profile: 1992–1997" and "Judicial Caseload Profile: 2009–2013." http://www.uscourts.gov/Statistics/FederalCourtManagementStatistics/FederalCourtManagementStatistics_Archive.aspx (accessed July 1, 2014).

Ferling, John. *Adams v. Jefferson: The Tumultuous Election of 1800*. New York: Oxford University Press, 2004.

Fischer, David Hackett. *Albion's Seed: Four British Folkways in America*. New York: Oxford University Press, 1989.

Fish, Peter Graham. *The Politics of Federal Judicial Administration*. Princeton, NJ: Princeton University Press, 1973.

Fisher, George. *Plea Bargaining's Triumph: A History of Plea Bargaining in America*. Stanford, CA: Stanford University Press, 2003.

Fitzsimmons, Michelle. "Apple vs. Samsung: 'Designs Substantially Similar.'" *Techradar*, August 6, 2012. http://www.techradar.com/us/news/world-of-tech/apple-vs-samsung-designs-substantially-similiar-1091309 (accessed March 30, 2015).

———. "Samsung's First Witnesses Take the Stand in Apple Patent Trial." *Techradar*, August 2012. http://www.techradar.com/us/news/world-of-tech/samsung-s-first-witnesses-take-the-stand-in-apple-patent-trial-1092083 (accessed March 30, 2015).

Flaherty, Daniel H. "Criminal Practice in Provincial Massachusetts." In *Law in Colonial Massachusetts, 1630–1800*, ed. Daniel R. Coquillette, 191–243. Boston: Colonial Society of Massachusetts, 1984.

Forman, James, Jr. "Juries and Race in the Nineteenth Century." *Yale Law Journal* 113 (2004): 895–938.

"4 Jurors in Zimmerman Trial Distance Themselves from Juror B37." FoxNews, July 17, 2013. http://www.foxnews.com/us/2013/07/17/zimmerman-jurors-request-privacy-in-statement/ (accessed August 10, 2014).

Fowler, Lucy. "Gender and Jury Deliberations: The Contributions of Social Science." *William & Mary Journal of Women and the Law* 12, 1 (2005): 1–48.

Frank, Jerome. *Law and the Modern Mind*. New York: Brentano's, 1930.

Frank, Ted. "Urban Legends and Stella Liebeck and the McDonald's Coffee Case." Overlawyered.com. http://www.overlawyered.com/2005/10/urban-legends-and-stella-liebeck-and-the-McDonald's-coffee-case/ (accessed August 13, 2014).

Frankel, Hon. Marvin E. *Criminal Sentences: Law without Order*. New York: Hill & Wang, 1973.

Frankfurter, Felix, and James Landis. "The Business of the Supreme Court of the United

States—A Study in the Federal Judicial System—VI: The Conference of Senior Circuit Judges." *Harvard Law Review* 40 (1926–1927): 431–468.

Fredman, Cameron. "Plaintiff's Paradise Lost: Diversity of Citizenship and the Amount in Controversy under the Class Action Fairness Act of 2005." *Loyola of Los Angeles Law Review* 39 (2006): 1025–1066.

Friedman, Lawrence M. "The Day before Trials Vanished." *Journal of Empirical Legal Studies* 1, 3 (November 2004): 689–703.

———. *A History of American Law.* New York: Simon & Schuster, 1973.

Friedman, Lawrence M., and Robert V. Percival. "A Tale of Two Courts: Litigation in Alameda and San Benito Counties." *Law & Society Review* 10 (1975): 267–302.

Galanter, Marc. "The Regulatory Function of the Jury." In *Verdict: Assessing the Civil Jury System,* ed. Robert Litan, 61–102. Washington, DC: Brookings Institution, 1993.

———. "The Vanishing Trial: An Examination of Trials and Related Matters in Federal and State Courts." *Journal of Empirical Legal Studies* 1, 3 (November 2004): 459–570.

Galanter, Marc, and Angela Frozena. "The Continuing Decline of Civil Trials in American Courts." Presentation at the 2011 Forum for State Appellate Court Judges.

Gastil, John, et al. *The Jury and Democracy: How Jury Deliberation Promotes Civic Engagement and Political Participation.* New York: Oxford University Press, 2010.

Gastil, John, Hiroshi Fukurai, Kent Anderson, and Mark Nolan. "Seeing Is Believing: The Impact of Jury Service on Attitudes toward Legal Institutions and the Implications for International Jury Reform." *Court Review* 48 (2012): 124–130.

"George Zimmerman Case Timeline." MyNews13.com, July 13, 2013. http://www.mynews13.com/trayvon-timeline.html (accessed August 11, 2014).

Gerlin, Andrea. "A Matter of Degree: How a Jury Decided that a Coffee Spill Is Worth $2.9 Million." *Wall Street Journal*, September 1, 1994, 1.

Gertner, Nancy. "Circumventing Juries, Undermining Justice: Lessons from Criminal Trials and Sentencing." *Suffolk University Law Review* 32, 3 (1999): 419–440.

———. "From 'Rites' to 'Rights': The Decline of the Criminal Jury Trial." *Yale Journal of Law and Humanities* 24 (2012): 433–438.

Gertner, Nancy, and Judith H. Mizner. *The Law of Juries*. 5th ed. St. Paul, MN: Thompson/West, 2011.

Gillespie, Cynthia K. *Justifiable Homicide: Battered Women, Self Defense, and the Law.* Columbus: Ohio State University Press, 1989.

Glaeser, Edward L., and Andrei Shleifer. "Legal Origins." *Quarterly Journal of Economics* 117, 4 (November 2002): 1193–1229.

Goebel, Julius, Jr., and T. Raymond Naughton. *Law Enforcement in Colonial New York: A Study in Criminal Procedure: 1664–1776*. New York: Commonwealth Fund, 1944.

Goodman, James. *Stories of Scottsboro*. New York: Pantheon, 1994.

Gordon, Robert W. "The American Codification Movement." *Vanderbilt Law Review* 36 (1983): 431–458.

"Gov. Rick Scott Appoints Special Prosecutor for Trayvon Martin Case." *Tampa Bay Times*, March 22, 2012.

Green, Leon. *Judge and Jury*. Kansas City, MO: Vernon Law Book Co., 1930.

Green, Thomas A. "The Jury and the English Law of Homicide, 1200–1600." *Michigan Law Review* 74, 3 (January 1976): 413–499.

———. "The Jury, Seditious Libel, and the Criminal Law." In *Juries, Libel, & Justice: The*

Role of English Juries in Seventeenth- and Eighteenth-Century Trials for Libel and Slander, ed. R. H. Helmholtz and Thomas A. Green, 37–91. Los Angeles: University of California, 1984.

———. "A Retrospective on the Criminal Trial Jury, 1200–1800." In *Twelve Good Men and True: The Criminal Trial Jury in England, 1200–1800*, ed. J. S. Cockburn and Thomas A. Green, 358–400. Princeton, NJ: Princeton University Press, 1988.

———. *Verdict According to Conscience: Perspectives on the English Criminal Trial Jury, 1200–1800*. Chicago: University of Chicago Press, 1985.

Greenberg, Douglas. "The Effectiveness of Law Enforcement in Eighteenth-Century New York." *American Journal of Legal History* 19, 3 (1975): 173–207.

Groot, Roger D. "The Jury of Presentment before 1215." *American Journal of Legal History* 26, 1 (January 1982): 1–24.

Grossman, Joanna L. "Women's Jury Service: Right of Citizenship or Privilege of Difference?" *Stanford Law Review* 46, 5 (May 1994): 1115–1160.

Grutman, Roy, and Bill Thomas. *Lawyers and Thieves*. New York: Simon & Schuster, 1990.

Guinther, John. *The Jury in America*. New York: Facts on File, 1988.

Gurney, Brent J. "The Case for Abolishing Peremptory Challenges in Criminal Trials." *Harvard Civil Rights–Civil Liberties Law Review* 21 (1986): 227–284.

Guzmán, Richard. "Death, Taxes and Jury Duty." *Advocates News*, 2010. http://www.theadvocates.com/news/50PercentofJurySummonsIgnoredinLA.php (accessed June 23, 2014).

Haddon, Phoebe A. "Does *Grutter* Offer Courts an Opportunity to Consider Race in Jury Selection and Decisions Related to Promoting Fairness in the Deliberation Process?" *Temple Political & Civil Rights Law Review* 13 (2004): 547–566.

Hale, Dennis. "All Rise." *Boston College Magazine* (Summer 2005): 26–33.

———. "The Evolution of the Property Tax: A Study of the Relation between Public Finance and Political Theory." *Journal of Politics* 47, 2 (June 1985): 387–388.

———. "The Natural History of Citizenship." In *Friends and Citizens: Essays in Honor of Wilson Carey McWilliams*, ed. Dennis Bathory and Nancy Schwartz, 151–170. New York: Rowman & Littlefield, 2000.

Hall, Jerome. *Theft, Law and Society*. Indianapolis: Bobbs-Merrill, 1952.

Hamilton, Alexander, John Jay, and James Madison. *The Federalist*, ed. Robert Scigliano. New York: Modern Library, 2000.

Hammond, Scott J., Kevin R. Hardwick, and Howard L. Lubert, eds. *Classics of American Political and Constitutional Thought*, vol. 1. Indianapolis: Hackett, 2007.

Hannaford-Agor, Paula. "Jury News: Tales of 'Tales' Juries." *Court Manager* 23, 2 (2008).

Hannaford-Agor, Paula, et al. *Are Hung Juries a Problem?* Williamsburg, VA: National Center for State Courts, 2002.

Hannaford-Agor, Paula, and Valerie P. Hans. "Nullification at Work? A Glimpse from the National Center for State Courts Study of Hung Juries." *Chicago-Kent Law Review* 78 (2003): 1249–1280.

Hans, Valerie P., and Alayna Jehle. "Avoid Bald Men and People with Green Socks? Other Ways to Improve the Voir Dire Process in Jury Selection." *Chicago-Kent Law Review* 78 (2003): 1179–1202.

Hastie, Reid. "Is Attorney-Conducted Voir Dire an Effective Procedure for the Selection of Impartial Juries?" *American University Law Review* 40 (Winter 1991): 703–726.

Hastie, Reid, et al. *Inside the Jury*. Cambridge, MA: Harvard University Press, 1983.

Hearings before the Subcommittee on Courts, Civil Liberties, and the Administration of Justice of the Committee on the Judiciary. House of Representatives, 95th Congress, 2nd session, on Judicial Housekeeping, May 4, 1978. Washington, DC: Government Printing Office, 1978.

Hearings before the Subcommittee on Improvements in Judicial Machinery of the Committee on the Judiciary. US Senate, 90th Cong., 1st sess., 1967. Washington, DC: Government Printing Office, 1967.

Hendrickson, Kim Kosman. "Progressives Try the Jury." Unpublished manuscript, 2005.

Hershkowitz, Leo, and Milton M. Klein, eds. *Courts and Law in Early New York: Selected Essays*. Port Washington, NY: Kennikat Press, 1978.

Hickey, William J. "Improvement of the Jury System in Federal Courts." *Georgetown Law Journal* 35 (1946–1947): 500–516.

Hirsch, Hugo. *A Practical Treatise on Juries, Their Powers, Duties, and Uses, in All Actions and Proceedings, Both Civil and Criminal, under the Common Law, and under the Statutes of the United States and of the State of New York*. New York: George S. Diossy, 1879.

History of the Congress Exhibiting a Classification of the Proceedings of the Senate and House of Representatives from March 4, 1789 to March, 1793 (1843). Reproduced in Bernard Schwartz, *The Bill of Rights: A Documentary History*, vol. 2. New York: Chelsea House Printers, 1971.

Hobson, Charles F. "The Aaron Burr Treason Trial." In *Federal Trials and Great Debates in United States History*. http://www.fjc.gov/history/docs/burrtrial.pdf (accessed January 15, 2014).

Hoffman, Morris B. "The Case for Jury Sentencing." *Duke Law Journal* 52 (2002–2003): 951–1010.

Holmes, Oliver Wendell, Jr. "The Path of the Law." *Harvard Law Review* 10 (1897): 457–478.

Hornby, D. Brock. "The Business of the U.S. District Courts." *Green Bag*, 2nd ser., 10, 4 (Summer 2007): 453–468.

———. "Speaking in Sentences." *Green Bag* 14 (Winter 2011): 147–161.

Horowitz, Irwin A. "The Effect of Jury Nullification Instruction on Verdicts and Jury Functioning in Criminal Trials." *Law and Human Behavior* 9, 1 (March 1985): 25–36.

Horowitz, Irwin A., and Thomas E. Willging. "Changing Views of Jury Power: The Nullification Debate, 1787–1988." *Law and Human Behavior* 15, 2 (April 1991): 165–182.

House of Commons Debate, March 20, 1962. Hansard vol. 656, cc210–20.

Hurnard, Naomi D. "The Jury of Presentment and the Assize of Clarendon." *English Historical Review* 56, 223 (July 1941): 374–410.

Hyams, Paul R. "Trial by Ordeal: The Key to Proof in the Early Common Law." In *On the Laws and Customs of England: Essays in Honor of Samuel Thorne*, ed. Morris S. Arnold et al., 90–126. Chapel Hill: University of North Carolina Press, 1981.

Improvement of the Jury System in Federal Courts. Hearings before the Committee on the Judiciary, House of Representatives, 79th Congress, 1st Session, on H.R. 3379, H.R. 3380, H.R. 3381, June 12 and 13, 1945. Washington, DC: Government Printing Office, 1945.

Jade, Rose. "Voter Registration Status as a Jury Service Employment Test: Oregon's Retracted Endorsement Following *Buckley v. American Constitutional Law Foundation, Inc*." *Willamette Law Review* 39 (2003): 557–758.

Jefferson, Thomas. *The Papers of Thomas Jefferson*, ed. Julian P. Boyd et al. Princeton, NJ: Princeton University Press, 1950.

———. *The Works of Thomas Jefferson*, ed. Paul Leicester Ford. New York: G. P. Putnam's Sons, 1904.

Johnson, Herbert Alan, ed. *John Marshall Papers*, vol. 1. Chapel Hill: University of North Carolina Press, 1974.

Johnson, Lyndon B. "Remarks upon Signing the Jury Selection and Service Act of 1968." March 27, 1968. In *Public Papers of the Presidents of the United States: Lyndon B. Johnson*, book 1. Washington, DC: Office of the Federal Registrar, 1970.

Johnson, Sheri L. "Black Innocence and the White Jury." *Michigan Law Review* 83 (1985): 1611–1708.

Jonakait, Randolph N. *The American Jury System*. New Haven, CT: Yale University Press, 2003.

———. "Juries Decide on the Evidence, Not on Biases." *Insights on Law & Society* 5, 2 (Winter 2005): 17–18.

Jonnson, Patrik. "George Zimmerman Trial: Jury Can Consider Lesser Charge of Manslaughter." *Christian Science Monitor*, July 11, 2013.

Journal of the Constitutional Convention of the Commonwealth of Massachusetts, Begun and Held in Boston, on the Fourth Day of May, 1853. Boston: White & Potter, 1853.

The Judicial Business of the United States Courts, 2011. Annual Report of the Director, Administrative Office of the United States Courts. Washington, DC: Government Printing Office, 2011.

Judicial Conference of the United States. *Operation of the Jury System in the Federal Courts*. St. Paul, MN: West Publishing Co., 1958.

Judicial Conference of the United States, Committee on the Operation of the Jury System. *Annual Reports*, 1953–1960.

Judicial Conference of the United States, Committee on Selection of Jurors. *Report to the Judicial Conference of Senior Circuit Judges of the Committee on Selection of Jurors*. 1943.

Judiciary Act of 1789, 1 Stat. 73 (1789).

"Juror: 'No Doubt' Zimmerman Feared for His Life." FoxNews, July 16, 2013. http://www.foxnews.com/us/2013/07/16/juror-no-doubt-zimmerman-feared-for-his-life/ (accessed August 10, 2014).

"Jury Service: Is Fulfilling Your Civic Duty a Trial?" *Harris Interactive*, July 2004.http://www.americanbar.org/content/dam/aba/migrated/2011_build/american_jury/harris_poll_report.authcheckdam.pdf (accessed August 30, 2014).

The Jury System in the Federal Courts: Report of the Judicial Conference Committee on the Operation of the Jury System, ed. Shackelford Miller Jr. St. Paul, MN: West Publishing Co., 1960.

J. W. G. "Juries as Judges of the Law." *Journal of the American Institute of Criminal Law and Criminology* 2, 2 (July 1911): 183–185.

Kalt, Brian C. "The Exclusion of Felons from Jury Service." *American University Law Review* 53, 1 (October 2003): 65–190.

Kalven, Harry, Jr., and Hans Zeisel. *The American Jury*. Chicago: University of Chicago Press, 1966.

Kaplan, Benjamin. "Continuing the Work of the Civil Committee: 1966 Amendments of the Federal Rules of Civil Procedure (I)." *Harvard Law Review* 81, 2 (December 1967): 356–416.

Katrowitz, Jeff, and Matthew Taylor. "Nanny Allegedly Assaulted Newton Infant." *Boston Globe*, February 6, 1997, B1.

Kaufman, Wendy. "Jury to Decide Apple's Patent Case against Samsung." NPR, August 22, 2012. http://www.npr.org/2012/08/22/159679099/jury-to-decide-apple-s-patent-case-against-samsung (accessed August 7, 2014).

Kerr, Margaret H., Richard D. Forsyth, and Michael J. Plyey. "Cold Water and Hot Iron: Trial by Ordeal in England." *Journal of Interdisciplinary History* 22, 4 (Spring 1992): 573–595.

Kershen, Drew L. "The Jury Selection Act of 1879: Theory and Practice of Citizen Participation in the Judicial System." *Law Forum* 1980, 3 (1980): 707–767.

———. "Vicinage." *Oklahoma Law Review* 29, 4 (Fall 1976): 801–860.

Knox, Hon. John C. "Selection of Federal Jurors." *Journal of the American Judicial Society* 31 (1947): 9–15.

Kornblut, Anne E., and Ellen O'Brien. "Juror: Charges Left No Choice." *Boston Globe*, November 2, 1997, A1.

Kravets, David. "Who Cheated Whom? Apple v. Samsung Patent Showdown Explained," July 27, 2012. http://www.wired.com/2012/07/apple-v-samsung-explained/ (accessed August 7, 2014).

Kressel, Neil J., and Dorit F. Kressel. *Stack and Sway: The New Science of Jury Consulting*. Boulder, CO: Westview Press, 2002.

Kritzer, Herbert M. "Disappearing Trials? A Comparative Perspective." *Journal of Empirical Legal Studies* 1, 3 (November 2004): 735–754.

Lacy, Hon. Frederick B. *The Judge's Role in the Settlement of Civil Suits*. Education and Training Series. Washington, DC: Federal Judicial Center, 1977.

Landsman, Stephan. "The History and Objectives of the Civil Jury System." In *Verdict: Judging the Civil Jury System*, ed. Robert Litan, 22–60. Washington, DC: Brookings Institution, 1993.

———. "The Jury's Role in Administering Justice in the United States: Of Mushrooms and Nullifiers: Rules of Evidence and the American Jury." *St. Louis University Public Law Review* 21 (2002): 65–84.

Langbein, John. "The Criminal Trial before the Lawyers." *University of Chicago Law Review* 45 (1978): 263–316.

———. "The Disappearance of Civil Trial." *Yale Law Journal* 122 (2012): 522–573.

———. "Understanding the Short History of Plea Bargaining." *Law and Social Science Review* 13 (1979): 261–272.

Latta, Kristin Knudsen. "The Role of Non-Lawyers on Administrative Tribunals." *Alaska Law Review* 31 (2014): 37–86.

Lawson, P. G. "Lawless Juries? The Composition and Behavior of Hertfordshire Juries, 1573–1624." In *Twelve Good Men and True: The Criminal Trial Jury in England, 1200–1800*, ed. J. S. Cockburn and Thomas A. Green, 117–157. Princeton, NJ: Princeton University Press, 1988.

Lazarsfeld, Paul F., Bernard Berelson, and Hazel Gaudet. *The People's Choice: How the Voter Makes up His Mind in a Presidential Campaign*. New York: Columbia University Press, 1944.

Lee, Emergy G., III, and Thomas E. Willging. *The Impact of the Class Action Fairness Act of 2005 on the Federal Court*. Washington, DC: Federal Judicial Center, 2008.

"Legislative History of the 1948 Judicial Code as It Relates to the Process of Selection of Federal Jurors." Appendix A in *Rabinowitz v. United States*, 366 F.2d 34 (1966).

Lerner, Ralph. "The Supreme Court as Republican Schoolmasters." *Supreme Court Review* (1967): 127–180.

Lerner, Renee Lettow. "The Rise of Directed Verdict: Jury Power in Civil Cases before the Federal Rules of 1938." *George Washington Law Review* 81 (2013): 448–525.

Levine, Dan. "Jury Didn't Want to Let Samsung Off Easy in Apple Trial: Foreman." Reuters, August 25, 2012. http://www.mobile.reuters.com/article/idUSBRE87009U20120825?irpc=932 (accessed August 7, 2014).

Levine, James. *Juries and Politics*. Pacific Grove, CA: Brooks/Cole, 1992.

Levy, Leonard. *Constitutional Opinions: Aspects of the Bill of Rights*. New York: Oxford University Press, 1986.

The Liberties of the Massachusets Collonie in New England (1641). https://history.hanover.edu/texts/masslib.html (accessed April 30, 2014).

Lievense, Andrew J. "Note: Fair Representation on Juries in the Eastern District of Michigan: Analyzing Past Efforts and Recommending Future Action." *University of Michigan Journal of Law Reform* 38 (Summer 2005): 941–978.

Lincoln, Abraham. *Speeches and Writings 1859–1865*. New York: Literary Classics of the United States/Viking Press, 1989.

Lind, Michael. "Jury Dismissed." In *Postmortem: The O. J. Simpson Case*, ed. Jeffrey Abramson, 155–159. New York: Basic Books, 1996.

Lippmann, Walter. *Public Opinion*. New York: Harcourt, Brace, 1922.

Litan, Robert E., ed. *Verdict: Assessing the Civil Jury System*. Washington, DC: Brookings Institution, 1993.

Litchfield, Edward H. *Voting Behavior in a Metropolitan Area*. Ann Arbor: University of Michigan Press, 1941.

Lloyd-Bostock, Sally, and Cheryl Thomas. "Decline of the 'Little Parliament': Juries and Jury Reform in England and Wales." *Law and Contemporary Problems* 62 (Spring 1999): 7–40.

Logan, Charles H., and George F. Cole. "Reducing Bias in a Jury Source List by Combining Voters and Drivers." *Judicature* 67 (August 1983): 87–94.

Lynch, Mary A. "The Application of Equal Protection to Prospective Jurors with Disabilities: Will *Batson* Cover Disability-Based Strikes?" *Albany Law Review* 57 (1993–1994): 289–364.

Macaulay, Thomas Babbington. *The History of England from the Accession of James II*, vol. 3. New York: Cambridge University Press, 2008.

MacCoun, Robert. "Inside the Black Box: What Empirical Research Tells Us about Decisionmaking by Civil Juries." In *Verdict: Assessing the Civil Jury System*, ed. Robert Litan, 137–180. Washington, DC: Brookings Institution, 1993.

Mack, William. *Cyclopedia of Law and Procedure*. Vol. 24. New York: American Law Book Company, 1907.

Macnair, Roger D. "Vicinage and the Antecedents of the Jury." *Law and History Review* 17, 3 (Autumn 1999): 537–590.

MacQuarrie, Brian. "Agency Spends Plenty to Defend Au Pair." *Boston Globe*, October 26, 1997, A22.

Madison, James. *Notes of Debates in the Federal Constitution of 1787*. New York: W. W. Norton, 1987.

Mahoney, Anne Rankin. "American Jury Voir Dire and the Ideal of Equal Justice." *Journal of Applied Behavioral Science* 18, 4 (1982): 481–494.

Mann, Horace. *Lectures on Education*. Boston: Ide & Dutton, 1855.

Mann, Michael. "The 'CSI Effect': Better Jurors through Television and Science." *Buffalo Public Interest Law Journal* 24 (2005–2006): 211–238.

Marcus, Maeva, and James R. Perry, eds. *Documentary History of the Supreme Court of the United States, 1789–1800*. 8 vols. New York: Columbia University Press, 1985–2007.

Marder, Nancy S. "Gender Dynamics and Jury Deliberations." *Yale Law Journal* 96 (1987): 593–612.

———. "The Interplay of Race and False Claims of Jury Nullification." *University of Michigan Journal of Law Reform* 32, 2 (1999): 285–322.

———. "Juries, Drug Laws & Sentencing." *Journal of Gender, Race, & Justice* 6 (2002): 337–380.

Marshall, John. "Report of the Minority on the Virginia Resolutions." January 22, 1799. In *Classics of American Political and Constitutional Thought*, vol. 1, ed. Scott J. Hammond, Kevin R. Hardwick, and Howard L. Lubert, 669–673. Indianapolis: Hackett, 2007.

McDougal, Harry A., III. "Note: The Case for Black Juries." *Yale Law Journal* 79 (1970): 531–550.

McIntosh, Wayne. *The Appeal of the Civil Law: A Political-Economic Analysis of Litigation*. Urbana: University of Illinois Press, 1990.

McKirdy, Charles R. "Massachusetts Lawyers on the Eve of the American Revolution: The State of the Profession." In *Law in Colonial Massachusetts: 1630–1800*, ed. Daniel Coquillette, 313–358. Boston: Colonial Society of Massachusetts, 1984.

McLane, Bernard William. "Juror Attitudes toward Local Disorder: The Evidence of the 1328 Lincolnshire Trailbaston Proceedings." In *Twelve Good Men and True: The Criminal Trial Jury in England, 1200–1800*, ed. J. S. Cockburn and Thomas A. Green, 36–64. Princeton, NJ: Princeton University Press, 1988.

McLynn, Frank. *Crime and Punishment in Eighteenth Century England*. New York: Routledge, 1989.

McWilliams, Wilson Carey. "Democracy and Mystery: On Civic Education in America." In *Redeeming Democracy in America*, ed. Patrick J. Deneen and Susan J. McWilliams, 211–220. Lawrence: University Press of Kansas, 2011.

McWilliams, Wilson Carey, and Dennis Hale. "The Constitutional Convention and the Founding Principles." In *Principles of Constitutional Order: The Ratification Debates*, ed. Robert L. Utley Jr. and Patricia B. Gray, 11–32. Lanham, MD: University Press of America, 1989.

Meier, Barry. "The Spoils of Tobacco Wars; Big Settlement Puts Many Lawyers in the Path of a Windfall." *New York Times*, December 22, 1998. http://www.nytimes.com/articles.html (accessed August 25, 2013).

Meier, Pauline. *Ratification: The People Debate the Constitution: 1787–1788*. New York: Simon & Schuster, 2010.

Merriam, Charles E., and Herbert F. Gosnell. *Non-Voting, Causes and Methods of Control*. Chicago: University of Chicago Press, 1924.

Milkis, Sidney M., and Jerome M. Mileur. *Progressivism and the New Democracy*. Amherst: University of Massachusetts Press, 1999.

Miller, Arthur R. "The Pretrial Rush to Judgment: Are the 'Litigation Explosion,' 'Liability Crisis,' and Efficiency Clichés Eroding Our Day in Court and Jury Trial Commitments?" *New York University Law Review* 78 (2003): 982–1134.

Miller, F. Thornton. *Juries and Judges versus the Law: Virginia's Provincial Legal Perspective, 1783–1828*. Charlottesville: University of Virginia Press, 1994.

Miller, John Chester. *The Wolf by the Ears: Thomas Jefferson and Slavery*. New York: Free Press, 1977.

Miller, Perry. *The Life of the Mind in America, from the Revolution to the Civil War*. Cambridge, MA: Harvard University Press, 1965.

Miller, Samuel F. "The System of Trial by Jury." *American Law Review* 21 (November–December 1887): 859–868.

Mirsky, Jeanette, and Allan Nevins. *The World of Eli Whitney*. New York: Macmillan, 1952.

Mize, Gregory E. "On Better Jury Selection: Spotting UFO Jurors before They Enter the Jury Room." *Court Review* 36, 1 (Spring 1999): 10–15.

Mize, Gregory E., and Paula Hannaford-Agor. "Building a Better Voir Dire Process." *Judges' Journal* 47, 1 (Winter 2008): 4–9.

Mize, Gregory E., Paula Hannaford-Agor, and Nicole L. Waters. *The State of the States Survey of Jury Improvement Efforts: A Compendium Report* (2007). http://www.ncsc-jurystudies.org/.

Morris, Thomas D. *Southern Slavery and the Law: 1619–1860*. Chapel Hill: University of North Carolina Press, 1996.

Moskovitz, Myron. "You Can't Tell a Book by Its Title." *Criminal Law Forum* 8 (1997): 138.

Motomura, Amy R. "The American Jury: Can Noncitizens Still Be Excluded?" *Stanford Law Review* 64 (2012): 1503–1550.

Mottley, Kimberly A., et al. "The Jury's Role in Administering Justice in the United States: An Overview of the American Criminal Jury." *St. Louis University Public Law Review* 21 (2002): 99–122.

Munson, C. La Rue. "Selecting the Jury." *Yale Law Journal* 4 (1894–1895): 173–189.

Murrin, John M. "Magistrates, Sinners, and a Precarious Liberty: Trial by Jury in Seventeenth-Century New England." In *Saints and Revolutionaries: Essays in Early American History*, ed. David Hall, John M. Murrin, and Thad W. Tate, 152–206. New York: Norton, 1984.

National Center for State Courts. *Juror Manager's Toolbox: Characteristics of an Effective Master Jury List*. http://www.jurytoolbox.org/more/Characteristics%20of%20Effective%20MJL.pdf (accessed April 21, 2015).

———. *State-of-the-States Survey of Jury Improvement Efforts*. Williamsburg, VA: NCSC, 2007.

Nelson, Harold L. "Seditious Libel in Colonial America." *American Journal of Legal History* 3, 2 (April 1959): 160–172.

Nelson, William E. "The Law Finding Power of Colonial American Juries." *Ohio State Law Journal* 71, 5 (2010): 1003–1030.

Nendza, James. "The Jury and Republican Government: The Early American Understanding." Unpublished manuscript, 1999.

Nielsen, Laura Beth, Robert L. Nelson, and Ryon Lancaster. "Individual Justice or Collective Legal Mobilization? Employment Discrimination Litigation in the Post Civil Rights United States." *Journal of Empirical Legal Studies* 7 (June 2010): 175–201.

"Note: The 'Blue-Ribbon' Jury." *Harvard Law Review* 60 (1946–1947): 613–620.
"Note: Mandatory Mediation and Summary Jury Trial: Guidelines for Ensuring Fair and Effective Processes." *Harvard Law Review* 103, 5 (March 1990): 1086–1104.
"Note: Selection of Jurors by Voir Dire Examination and Challenge." *Yale Law Journal* 58, 4 (March 1949): 638–644.
Notes of Advisory Committee on Rules—1963 Amendment, Federal Rules of Civil Procedure, Rule 50. http://www.law.cornell.edu/rules/frcp/rule_50 (accessed August 12, 2013).
Novak, Nancy. "Notes: Jury on Trial: Juror's Constitutional Right to Privacy Falls under Scrutiny of the Courts." *San Diego Justice Journal* 3 (1995): 215–248.
Oakley, John B. "A Fresh Look at the Federal Rules in State Courts." *Nevada Law Journal* 3 (Winter 2002–2003): 354.
O'Brien, Ellen. "Zobel Overturned at Least Two Jury Decisions." *Boston Globe*, November 1, 1997, A9.
Ogle, Robbin S., and Susan Jacobs. *Self-Defense and Battered Women Who Kill: A New Framework*. New York: Praeger, 2002.
O'Grady, Maggie Elise. "A Jury of Your Skinny Peers: Weight-Based Peremptory Challenges and the Culture of Fat Bias." *Stanford Journal of Civil Rights & Civil Liberties* 7 (April 2011): 47–82.
Ostrom, Brian J., Shauna M. Strickland, and Paula L. Hannaford-Agor. "Examining Trial Trends in State Courts: 1976–2002." *Journal of Empirical Legal Studies* 1, 3 (November 2004): 755–782.
Otis, Hon. Merrill E. "Selecting Federal Court Jurors." Address delivered before the Section of Judicial Administration, American Bar Association. *American Bar Association Journal* 29 (January 1943): 19–21.
Parrish, Jenni. "The Booth Cases: Final Step to the Civil War." *Willamette Law Review* 29 (1993): 237–278.
Patel, Nilay. "Samsung Argues Jury Foreman Was 'Deliberately Dishonest' in Apple Trial." *Verge*, December 6, 2012. http://www.theverge.com/2012/12/6/3737794/apple-vs-samsung-juror-misconduct-allegations-barely-discussed-damages-hearing (accessed August 8, 2014).
Pathak, Neha. "How Media Got the Biggest Bite of (the) Apple: A Look at the Media Misperception in the Apple-Samsung Case." *Marquette Intellectual Property Law Review* 18 (2014): 237–260.
Peck, Jeffrey J. "'Users United': The Civil Justice Reform Act of 1990." *Law and Contemporary Problems* 54, 3 (Summer 1991): 105–118.
Peck, Mike. "A Community with No Conscience: The Further Reduction of a Jury's Right to Nullify in *People v. Sanchez*." *Whittier Law Review* 21 (1999–2000): 285–314.
People v. O. J. Simpson, Juror Questionnaire. Deliberations' Library of Sample Juror Questionnaires. http://www.jurylaw.typepad.com/deliberations/sample_juror_questionnair.html (accessed March 31, 2015).
Pepper, David. "Nullifying History: Modern-Day Misuse of the Right to Decide the Law." *Case Western Reserve Law Review* 50 (Spring 2000): 599–643.
Perry, Mark A., and Rachel S. Brass. "Rule 23(b)(2) Certification of Employment Class Actions: A Return to First Principles." *NYU Annual Survey of American Law* 65 (2009–2010): 681.
Perschbacher, Rex P., and Debra Lynn Bassett. "The Revolution of 1938 and Its Discontents." *Oklahoma Law Review* 61 (2008): 275–298.

Potter, Henry D. *Laws of the State of North Carolina, Including the Titles of Such Statutes and Parts of Statutes of Great Britain as Are in Force in Said State*, vol. 1. Raleigh, NC, 1821.

Pound, Roscoe. "The Causes of Popular Dissatisfaction with the Administration of Justice." 29th Conference, pt. 1. *Annual Report of the American Bar Association* (1906): 395–417.

———. *The Formative Era in American Law.* Boston: Little, Brown, 1938.

Powell, Edward. "Jury Trial at Gaol Delivery in the Late Middle Ages: The Midland Circuit, 1400–1429." In *Twelve Good Men and True: The Criminal Trial Jury in England, 1200–1800*, ed. J. S. Cockburn and Thomas Green, 78–116. Princeton, NJ: Princeton University Press, 1988.

Press, Joshua S. "Untruthful Jurors in the Federal Courts: Have We Become Comfortably Numb?" *St. Thomas Law Review* 21 (2008–2009): 253–280.

Principles for Juries and Jury Trials. Washington, DC: American Bar Association, 2005.

Proffatt, John. *A Treatise on Trial by Jury: Including Questions of Law and Fact*. San Francisco: Sumner, Whitney, 1880.

Quincy, Josiah, Jr., ed. *Reports of Cases Argued and Adjudged in the Superior Court of Judicature of the Province of Massachusetts Bay, between 1761 and 1772*. Boston: Little, Brown, 1865.

Rabinowitz, Victor. *Unrepentant Leftist: A Lawyer's Memoir.* Urbana: University of Illinois Press, 1996.

Rachlinski, Jeffrey J. "Scientific Jury Selection and the Equal Protection Rights of Venire Persons." *Pacific Law Journal* 24 (1993): 1497–1566.

Rakove, Jack N. *Original Meaning: Politics and Ideas in the Making of the Constitution*. New York: Vintage Books, 1997.

Rankin, Hugh F. "Criminal Trial Proceedings in the General Court of Colonial Virginia." *Virginia Magazine of History and Biography* 72, 1 (January 1964): 50–74.

———. "The General Court of Colonial Virginia: Its Jurisdiction and Personnel." *Virginia Magazine of History and Biography* 70, 2 (April 1962): 142–153.

Rayner, W. Whitaker. "Judicial Authority in the Settlement of Federal Civil Cases." *Washington and Lee Law Review* 42 (1985): 171–192.

Re, Richard M. "Re-justifying the Fair Cross Section Requirement: Equal Representation and Enfranchisement in the American Criminal Jury." *Yale Law Journal* 116, 7 (May 2007): 1568–1614.

Records of the Court of Assistants of the Colony of the Massachusetts Bay, 1630–1692, vol. 1, ed., John F. Cronin. Boston: County of Suffolk, 1901.

Records of the Court of Assistants of the Colony of the Massachusetts Bay, 1630–1692, vol. 2. Boston: County of Suffolk, 1904.

"Report of the Committee on Trial by Jury Including Methods of Selection of Jurors." *Report of the Section of Judicial Administration, American Bar Association Reports* 63 (1938): 530.

"Report of the Committee on Uniform Judicial Procedure." In *36th Annual Report of the American Bar Association*. Baltimore: Lord Baltimore Press, 1913.

Report of the Judicial Conference of the United States, March 11–12, 1963. Washington, DC: Administrative Office of the United States Courts, 1963.

Report of the Judicial Conference of the United States, March 13–14, 1969. Washington, DC: Administrative Office of the United States Courts, 1969.

Report of the Judicial Conference of the United States, September 13–14, 1973. Washington, DC: Administrative Office of the United States Courts, 1973.

Report of the Proceedings of the Judicial Conference of the United States, September 21, 1987. Washington, DC: Administrative Office of the United States Courts, 1987.

The Report of the Special Committee Appointed to Consider and Report Whether the Present Delay and Uncertainty in Judicial Administration Can Be Lessened, and if so, by What Means. Philadelphia: Dando Printing & Publishing Co., 1885.

"Report of the Special Committee to Suggest Remedies and Formulate Proposed Laws to Prevent Delay and Unnecessary Cost in Litigation." *Annual Report of the American Bar Association* 33 (1908): 542.

Report to the Judicial Conference of Senior Circuit Judges of the Committee on Selection of Jurors. Washington, DC: Judicial Conference of the United States, 1943.

Resnik, Judith. "Migrating, Morphing, and Vanishing: The Empirical and Normative Puzzles of Declining Trial Rates in Courts." *Journal of Empirical Legal Studies* 1, 3 (November 2004): 783–842.

Ribeiro, John. "Apple, Samsung Agree to Settle Patent Disputes outside US." *PC World*, August 5, 2014. http://www.pcworld.com/article/2461940/apple-samsung-agree-to-settle-patent-disputes-outside-us.html (accessed August 8, 2014).

———. "USPTO Rejects Claims of Apple Patent that Figures in Dispute with Samsung." *CIO*, August 7, 2014. http://www.cio.com/article/2463101/uspto-rejects-claims-of-apple-patent-that-figures-in-dispute-with-samsung.html (accessed August 8, 2014).

Richards, William. "The Secret behind McDonald's Coffee." MainSt.com. http://www.mainstreet.com/article/small-business/marketing/secret-behind-mcdonalds-coffee (accessed August 14, 2014).

Robertson, Christopher, et al. "Can Jurors Self-Diagnose Bias? Two Randomized Controlled Trials." Arizona Legal Studies Discussion Paper no. 12-35. 7th Annual Conference on Empirical Legal Studies, February 2014.

Rose, Mary R., and Neil Vidmar. "The Bronx 'Bronx Jury': A Profile of Civil Jury Awards in New York Counties." *Texas Law Review* 80 (2002): 1889–1898.

Rosen, Jeffrey. "One Angry Woman: Why Are Hung Juries on the Rise?" *New Yorker*, February 24 and March 3, 1997, 54–64.

Rothman, Max B., Burton D. Dunlop, and Gretchen M. Hirt. "Jury Selection in an Aging America: The New Discrimination." *Elder's Advisor* 2 (2000–2001): 69–80.

Rottman, David B., et al. *State Court Organization 1998*. Washington, DC: Department of Justice, 2000.

Rubenstein, Arie M. "Verdicts of Conscience: Nullification and the Modern Jury Trial." *Columbia Law Review* 106 (2006): 959–993.

Ryan, Joe, and Anne E. Kornblut. "Juror 'Appalled' at Sentence." *Boston Globe*, November 11, 1997, B1.

Sandoval, Greg. "How Qualified Is the Apple-Samsung Jury? We Found Out." *CNET*, August 24, 2012. http://www.cnet.com/news/how-qualified-is-the-apple-samsung-jury-we-found-out/ (accessed August 7, 2014).

Scheflin, Alan W. "Jury Nullification: The Right to Say No." *Southern California Law Review* 45 (1972): 168–227.

Scheflin, Alan, and Jon Van Dyke. "Jury Nullification: The Contours of a Controversy." *Law and Contemporary Problems* 43 (1979–1980): 51–115.

Schwan, Christopher C. "Student Commentary: Right up to the Line: The Ethics of Advancing Nullification Arguments to the Jury." *Journal of the Legal Profession* 29 (2004–2005): 293–303.

Schwartz, Bernard. *The Bill of Rights: A Documentary History*. 2 vols. New York: Chelsea House, 1971.

Schwartz, John, et al. "Tough Decision Looms for Florida Prosecutor." *New York Times*, April 11, 2012, A13.

Scott, Arthur. *Criminal Law in Colonial Virginia*. Chicago: University of Chicago Press, 1930.

Scott, William L. "Should Trial by Jury in Civil Cases Be Abolished?" *American Law Review* 20 (1886): 661–679.

Seligman, Joel, and Lindsey Hunter. "Rule 23: Class Actions at the Crossroads." *Arizona Law Review* 39 (1997): 407–412.

Serio, Steven C. "A Process Right Due? Examining Whether a Capital Defendant Has a Due Process Right to a Jury Selection Expert." *American University Law Review* 53 (2003–2004): 1143–1186.

"Several Jurors Speak Out." *Boston Globe*, November 5, 1997, A16.

Shapard, John, and Molly Johnson. "Memorandum from the Federal Judicial Center, to the Advisory Committee on Civil Rules and Advisory Committee on Criminal Rules." October 4, 1994.

Shiras, Oliver P. "The Jury System." *Yale Law Journal* 1, 2 (December 1891): 45–51.

Silver, Richard, and Amanda Whitman. "Preserve the Right to Pick an Unbiased Jury." *Connecticut Law Tribune*, January 31, 2011, 1–2.

Skowronek, Stephen. *Building a New American State: The Expansion of National Administrative Capacities, 1877–1920*. New York: Cambridge University Press, 1982.

Smith, Bruce P. "Plea Bargaining and the Eclipse of the Jury." *Annual Review Law and Social Science* 1 (2005): 131–149.

Smith, Carey Hugh. "Sixth Amendment Right to Jury Trial Prohibits Systematic Exclusion of Young People in Jury Selection Process." *Suffolk University Law Review* 18, 4 (Fall 1984): 512–519.

Smith, J. Allen. *The Spirit of American Government*. New York: Macmillan, 1907.

Smith, James Morton. *Freedom's Fetters: The Alien and Sedition Laws and American Civil Liberties*. Ithaca, NY: Cornell University Press, 1956.

Smith, Joseph H., ed. *Colonial Justice in Western Massachusetts (1639–1702): The Pynchon Court Record*. Cambridge, MA: Harvard University Press, 1961.

Sourcebook of Criminal Justice Statistics Online. University at Albany, School of Criminal Justice, Hindelang Criminal Justice Research Center. http://www.albany.edu/sourcebook/ (accessed April 30, 2015).

Spooner, Lysander. *An Essay on the Trial by Jury*. Boston: B. Marsh, 1852.

———. *The Unconstitutionality of Slavery*. Boston: B. Marsh, 1860.

Standards for Criminal Justice and Trial by Jury. 3rd ed. Washington, DC: American Bar Association, 1996.

Stanley, Hon. Arthur J., Jr. "Federal Jury Selection and Service before and after 1968." *F. R. D.* 66 (1975): 375–382.

Starr, V. Hale, and Marc McCormick. *Jury Selection*. 3rd ed. New York: Aspen Law and Business, 2001; Aspen Publishers Online, 2009.

"*State of Florida v. George Zimmerman*: Instructions Read to Jury by the Honorable Debra S. Nelson, Circuit Judge." *Daytona Beach News-Journal*, July 12, 2013.

State v. Moe Gibbs, Juror Questionnaire. Deliberations' Library of Sample Juror Questionnaires. http://www.jurylaw.typepad.com/deliberations/sample_juror_questionnair.html (accessed March 31, 2015).

"The Stella Liebeck McDonald's Hot Coffee Case FAQ." http://www.abnormaluse.com/2011/01/stella-liebeck-mcdonalds-hot-coffee.html (accessed August 12, 2014).

Stephens, J. E. R. "The Growth of Trial by Jury in England." *Harvard Law Review* 10, 3 (October 26, 1896): 150–160.

Stern, Simon. "Note: Between Local Knowledge and National Politics: Debating Rationales for Jury Nullification after Bushell's Case." *Yale Law Journal* 111 (2002): 1815–1860.

Stewart, Estelle May, and Jessie Chester Bowen. *History of Wages in the United States from Colonial Times to 1928*. Washington, DC: Bureau of Labor Statistics, 1934.

Stienstra, Donna. *ADR in the Federal District Courts: An Initial Report*. Washington, DC: Federal Judicial Center, 2011.

Stipanowich, Thomas J. "ADR and the 'Vanishing Trial': The Growth and Impact of 'Alternative Dispute Resolution.'" *Journal of Empirical Legal Studies* 1, 3 (November 2004): 843–912.

Stith, Kate, and José Cabranes. *Fear of Judging: Sentencing Guidelines in the Federal Courts*. Chicago: University of Chicago Press, 1998.

Stith, Kate, and Steve Y. Koh. "The Politics of Sentencing Reform: The Legislative History of the Federal Sentencing Guidelines." *Wake Forest Law Review* 28 (1993): 223–290.

Stoebuck, William B. "Reception of English Common Law in the American Colonies." *William and Mary Law Review* 10, 2 (1968): 393–426.

Storing, Herbert J. *The Complete Anti-Federalist*. Chicago: University of Chicago Press, 1981.

———. *What the Anti-Federalists Were For: The Political Thought of the Opponents of the Constitution*. Chicago: University of Chicago Press, 1981.

Strier, Franklin, and Donna Shestowsky. "Profiling the Profilers: A Study of the Trial Consulting Profession, Its Impact on Trial Justice and What, if Anything, to Do about It." *Wisconsin Law Review* (1999): 441–500.

Stubbs, Cassandra. "Can the Racial Justice Act Change the Practice of Picking All-White Juries in North Carolina." ACLU Blog of Rights. http://www.aclu.org/blog/capital-punishment/can-racial-justice-act-change-practice-picking-all-white-juries-north (accessed September 10, 2014).

Subrin, Stephen N. "How Equity Conquered Common Law: The Federal Rules of Civil Procedure in Historical Perspective." *University of Pennsylvania Law Review* 135, 4 (April 1987): 909–1002.

Sullivan, Margaret. "Making Sense of a Sensational Case." *New York Times*, July 14, 2013, SR12.

Sunderland, Edson R. "Directing a Verdict for the Party Having the Burden of Proof." *Michigan Law Review* 11 (1912–1913): 198–209.

———. *History of the American Bar Association and Its Work*. Ann Arbor: University of Michigan Press, 1953.

———. "The Inefficiency of the American Jury." *Michigan Law Review* 13 (1914): 302–316.

Sunstein, Cass, et al. *Punitive Damages: How Jurors Decide*. Chicago: University of Chicago Press, 2002.

Swift, Zephaniah. *The Public Statute Laws of the State of Connecticut, as Revised and Enacted by the General Assembly, in May 1821*. Hartford, CT, 1821.

Taft, William Howard. "The Administration of the Criminal Law." *Yale Law Journal* 15, 1 (1905–1906): 1–17.

Thayer, James B. "'Law and Fact' in Jury Trials." *Harvard Law Review* 4, 4 (1890–1891): 147–175.

Thompson, Norma. *Unreasonable Doubt: Circumstantial Evidence and an Ordinary Murder in New Haven*. Columbia: University of Missouri Press, 2006.

"3 Reasons Juries Have No Place in the Patent System." *Cigaom*, August 27, 2012. http://www.gigaom.com/2012/08/27/3-reasons-juries-have-no-place-in-the-patent-system/ (accessed August 7, 2014).

Tocqueville, Alexis de. *Democracy in America*, trans. Harvey C. Mansfield and Delba Winthrop. Chicago: University of Chicago Press, 2000.

Toobin, Jeffrey. *The Run of His Life: The People v. O. J. Simpson*. New York: Touchstone, 1997.

Towers, Joseph. *Observations on the Rights and Duty of Juries in Trials for Libels*. Dublin: Moncrieffe, Jenkin, White, 1785.

"Trayvon Martin and the Smoking Gun." *New York Times*, April 2, 2012. http://www.takingnote.blogs.nytimes.com/2012/04/02/trayvon-martin-and-the-smoking-gun/?ref=us (accessed August 12, 2012).

"The Trial of Mr. John Peter Zenger." 17 How. St. Tr. 675 (1735).

"Trial of the Seven Bishops for Publishing a Libel." 12 How. St. Tr. 183 (1688).

Truxillo, Douglas. "Maritime Defendants Now Have a Right to Jury Trial in Louisiana State Court." http://www.corporate.findlaw.com/law-library/maritime-defendants-now-have-right-to-jury-trial-in-louisiana.html (accessed January 30, 2014).

Turner, Ralph V. "The Origins of the Medieval English Jury: Frankish, English, or Scandinavian?" *Journal of British Studies* 7, 2 (May 1968): 1–10.

"The Twenty Dollars Clause." *Harvard Law Review* 118, 5 (March 2005): 1665–1686.

United States Congress, House. *A Bill to Establish an Uniform Mode of Drawing Jurors by Lot, in All the Courts of the United States*. Washington, DC, 1804.

United States District Court, Northern District of California, San Jose Division. Case 5:11-cv-01846-LHK, Amended Verdict Form, Document 1931, August 24, 2012.

United States v. Dzhokhar Tsarnaev, Juror Questionnaire, Case 1:13-cr-10200-GAO Document 1178. http://www.scribd.com/doc/259151331/Tsarneav-Trial-Juror-Questionnaire-pdf (accessed April 22, 2015).

United States v. Zacarias Moussaoui, Juror Questionnaire. Deliberations' Library of Sample Juror Questionnaires. http://www.jurylaw.typepad.com/deliberations/sample_juror_questionnaire.html (accessed March 31, 2015).

Valencia, Milton J. "3 Guilty in Probation Corruption Case." *Boston Globe*, July 24, 2014.

Valencia, Milton J., and Patricia Wen. "Dzhokhar Tsarnaev Case Jury Is Slow to Form." *Boston Globe*, January 24, 2015.

Vanderbilt, Arthur. *Minimum Standards of Judicial Administration*. New York: Law Center of New York University, 1949.

Van Dyke, Jon. *Jury Selection: Our Uncertain Commitment to Representative Panels*. Cambridge, MA: Ballinger, 1977.

Vanhemert, Kyle. "Apple's Big Verdict: Bad for Usability, but It Won't Stop True Innovation." *Fast Company*, August 27, 2012. http://www.fastcodesign.com/1670642

/apples-big-verdict-bad-for-usability-but-it-wont-stop-true-innovation (accessed April 30, 2015).

Vasquez, Daniel. "Prosecution Vows Fight to Keep the Verdict." *Boston Globe*, November 3, 1997, A1.

Vidmar, Neil, and Valerie P. Hans. *American Juries*. Amherst, NY: Prometheus Books, 2007.

Walker, Robert. "Security, Freedom of Speech and Criminal Justice in the Age of Pitt, Burke, and Fox." Bentham Club Address at UCL Faculty of Laws, March 2008. http://www.ucl.ac.uk/laws/alumni/presidents/docs/walker_08.pdf (accessed February 2, 2014).

Walter, Kristina. "Note: *Booker* and Our Brave New World: The Tension among Federal Sentencing Guidelines, Judicial Discretion, and a Defendant's Constitutional Right to Trial by Jury." *Cleveland State Law Review* 53 (2005–2006): 657–688.

Wassom, Brian D. "Rule 12(b)(6) Motions: Not Just for 'Little Green Men' Anymore." *Sidebar* (Winter 2010): 6.

Weinstein, Jack B. "The Many Dimensions of Jury Nullification." *Judicature* 81 (1997–1998): 168–171.

Wells, Marguerite M. *A Portrait of the League of Women Voters at the Age of Eighteen*. Washington, DC: National League of Women Voters, 1938.

Wen, Patricia, and Milton J. Valencia. "Lawyers Hunt Too-Eager Tsarnaev Jurors." *Boston Globe*, January 26, 2015.

Wilkenfeld, Joshua. "Newly Compelling: Reexamining Judicial Construction of Juries in the Aftermath of *Grutter v. Bollinger*." *Columbia Law Review* 104 (2004): 2291–2327.

Williams, Martyn. "Jury Finds Samsung Infringed Some Apple Patents, Must Pay $120M in Damages." *MacWorld*, May 2, 2014. http://www.macworld.com/article/2150770/jury-finds-samsung-infringed-some-apple-patents-must-pay-120m-in-damages.html (accessed August 8, 2014).

Williams, Sandra Boyd. "The Indiana Supreme Court and the Struggle against Slavery." *Indiana Law Review* 30 (1997): 305–318.

Williamson, Chilton. *American Suffrage from Property to Democracy, 1760–1860*. Princeton, NJ: Princeton University Press, 1960.

Willis, Paul G. "Juries and Judicial Review." *Western Political Quarterly* 3 (1950): 66–70.

Willoughby, W. F. *Principles of Judicial Administration*. Washington, DC: Brookings Institution, 1929.

Wilson, David V., II. "American Bar Association Principles for Juries and Jury Trials." *Houston Lawyer* 43 (September–October 2005). http://www.thehoustonlawyer.com/aa_sep05/page48.htm#area.

Wilson, James. *Lectures on Law*. 1791.

Wilson, Woodrow. *Congressional Government*. Boston: Houghton, Mifflin, 1885.

———. "The Study of Administration." *Political Science Quarterly* 2, 2 (June 1887): 197–222.

Wingfield, Nick. "Jury Awards $1 Billion to Apple in Samsung Patent Case." *New York Times*, August 24, 2012. http://www.nytimes.com/2012/08/25/technology/jury-reaches-decision-in-apple-samsung-patent-trial.html?_r=0 (accessed August 7, 2014).

"Woman and the Law." *American Bar Association Journal* 26 (1940): 157.

Young, Hon. William G. "An Open Letter to U.S. District Court Judges." *Federal Lawyer* 30 (July 2003): 30–31.

———. "Vanishing Trials, Vanishing Juries, Vanishing Constitution." *Suffolk University Law Review* 40 (2006–2007): 67–94.

Zagarri, Rosemarie. "Suffrage and Representation." In *A Companion to the American Revolution*, ed. Jack Greene and J. R. Pole, 661–667. Malden, MA: Blackwell, 2000.

Zalman, Marvin, and Olga Tsoudis. "Plucking Weeds from the Garden: Lawyers Speak about Voir Dire." *Wayne Law Review* 51 (2005): 163–448.

Zobel, Hon. Hiller. "The Jury on Trial." *American Heritage* 46, 4 (July–August 1995). http://www.americanheritage.com/content/jury-trial?page=show.

Zuklie, Mitchell S. "Rethinking the Fair Cross-Section Requirement." *California Law Review* 84, 1 (January 1996): 101–150.

SELECTED COURT CASES

Aldridge v. United States, 283 U.S. 308 (1931).

Alexander v. Louisiana, 405 U.S. 625 (1972).

American Publishing Co. v. Fisher, 166 U.S. 465 (1897).

Anderson v. Liberty Lobby, Inc., 477 U.S. 242 (1986).

Apple Inc v. Samsung Electronics Co Ltd et al., No. 11-CV-01846-LHK, November 21, 2013.

Apprendi v. United States, 530 U.S. 466 (2000).

Arnstein v. Porter, 154 F.2d 464 (1946).

Baker v. Frobisher, August Term 2 Geo. 3 (1765).

Ballard v. United States, 329 U.S. 187 (1946).

Baltimore & Carolina Line v. Redman, 295 U.S. 654 (1935).

Baltimore & Ohio Railroad Co. v. Goodman, 275 U.S. 66 (1927).

Barker v. Wingo, 407 U.S. 514 (1972).

Batson v. Kentucky, 476 U.S. 79 (1986).

Bell Atlantic v. Twombly, 550 U.S. 554 (2007).

Blakely v. Washington, 542 U.S. 296 (2004).

Campbell v. Louisiana, 532 U.S. 392 (1998).

Castaneda v. Partida, 430 U.S. 482 (1977).

Celotex Corp. v. Catrett, 477 U.S. 317 (1986).

Colorado v. Kriho, 996 P.2d 158 (Colo. App. 1, 1999).

Commonwealth v. Louise Woodward, Supreme Judicial Court, 427 Mass. 659 (1998).

Commonwealth v. Soares, 377 Mass. 461 (1979).

Duncan v. Louisiana, 391 U.S. 145 (1968).

Duren v. Missouri, 439 U.S. 357 (1979).

Edmonson v. Leesville Concrete, 500 U.S. 614 (1991).

Fay v. New York, 322 U.S. 261 (1947).

Fid. & Deposit Co. v. United States, 187 U.S. 315 (1902).

Georgia v. McCollum, 505 U.S. 42 (1992).

Glasser v. United States, 315 U.S. 60 (1942).

Gratz v. Bollinger, 539 U.S. 244 (2003).

Grutter v. Bollinger, 539 U.S. 306 (2003).

Ham v. South Carolina, 409 U.S. 524 (1973).

Hennepin County v. Perry, 561 N.W.2d 889, 896–897 (Minn. 1997).

Hernandez v. Texas, 347 U.S. 475 (1954).
Hill v. Texas, 316 U.S. 400 (1942).
Holland v. Illinois, 493 U.S. 474 (1990).
Hoyt v. Florida, 368 U.S. 57 (1961).
Jackson v. Foye, August Term 2 Geo. 3 (1765).
Jackson et al. v. United States, 366 F.2d 34 (1966).
J.E.B. v. Alabama, 511 U.S. 127 (1994).
Johnson v. California, 545 U.S. 162 (2005).
Lewis v. United States, 146 U.S. 370 (1892).
Lockhart v. McCree, 476 U.S. 162 (1986).
Marbury v. Madison, 5 U.S. 137 (1804).
Matsushita Electric Industrial Co. v. Zenith Radio Corp., 475 U.S. 574 (1986).
McNabb v. U.S., 318 U.S. 332 (1943).
Miller-El v. Dretke, 545 U.S. 231 (2005).
Moore v. New York, 333 U.S. 565 (1948).
Norris v. Alabama, 294 U.S. 587 (1935).
Parsons v. Bedford, 28 U.S. 433 (1830).
Patton v. Mississippi, 332 U.S. 463 (1947).
Patton v. United States, 281 U.S. 276 (1930).
People v. Croswell, 3 Johns. Cas. 337 (1804).
People v. Fay, 296 N.Y. 510, 68, N.E.2d 453 (1946).
People v. Wheeler, 22 Cal. 3d 258 (1978).
People v. Williams, 25 Cal. 4th 441, 106 Cal. Rptr. 2d 295, 21 P. 3d 1209 (Cal. 2001).
Peters v. Kiff, 407 U.S. 493 (1972).
Poller v. Columbia Broadcasting System, Inc., 388 U.S. 464 (1962).
Powers v. Ohio, 499 U.S. 400 (1991).
R v. Shipley, 4 Dougl. 73, 99 E.R. 774 (1784).
Rabinowitz v. United States, 366 F.2d 34 (1996).
Reece v. Georgia, 350 U.S. 85 (1955).
Rex v. Dean of St. Asaph, 21 St Tr 847 (1784).
Ring v. Arizona, 536 U.S. 584 (2002).
Rivera v. Illinois, 556 U.S. 148 (2009).
Smith v. Texas, 311 U.S. 128 (1940).
Strauder v. West Virginia, 100 U.S. 303 (1880).
Swain v. Alabama, 380 U.S. 202 (1965).
Taylor v. Louisiana, 419 U.S. 522 (1975).
Thiel v. Southern Pacific Railway Co., 328 U.S. 217 (1946).
United States v. Booker, 543 U.S. 220 (2005).
United States v. Burr, 25 F. Cas. 49, no. 14,692g (C.C.D. Va. [1807]).
United States v. Callender, 25 F. Cas. 239, no. 14,709 (1800).
United States v. Dougherty, 473 F.2d, 1113 (D.C. Cir. 1972).
United States v. Leslie, 783 F.2d 541 (5th Cir. 1986).
United States. v. Levasseur, 704 F. Supp. 1153, 1164 (D. Mass. 1989).
United States v. Morris, 1 Curt. 23 (1851).
United States v. Ovalle, 136 F.3d 1092 (6th Cir. 1998).
United States v. Thomas, 116 F.3d 606 (2d Cir. 1997).
United States v. Wonson, 28 F. Cir. 745 (C.C.D. Mass. 1812).

Virginia v. Rives, 100 U.S. 313 (1880).
Wallace II v. SMC Pneumatics, Inc., 103 F.3d 1394 (7th Cir. 1997).
Walton v. Arizona, 497 U.S. 639 (1990).
Washington v. Davis, 426 U.S. 229 (1976).
Williams v. Florida, 399 U.S. 76 (1970).
Williams v. New York, 337 U.S. 241 (1949).

Index

www.ingramcontent.com/pod-product-compliance
Lightning Source LLC
Chambersburg PA
CBHW030932050926
50963CB00055BA/314/J
9780700622009